Grantees of Arms
Named in Docquets and Patents
Volume 2 (K to Z)
1687 – 1898
Alphabetically arranged by
The Late Joseph Foster Hon. M.A. Oxon.
Edited by
W. Harry Rylands F.S.A

First Published in 1917
A facsimile copy produced and privately printed by
The Armorial Register Limited 2017

First Published in 2017
by
The Armorial Register Limited
All rights reserved

ISBN: 978-0-9957246-1-7

British Library Cataloguing-in-Publication Data
A catalogue record of this book is available on request from the British Library

THE

Publications

OF

The Harleian Society.

ESTABLISHED A.D. MDCCCLXIX.

VIRTVE ET FIDE

THE GLORY OF CHILDREN ARE THEIR FATHERS

Volume LXVIII.

FOR THE YEAR MDCCCCXVII.

Grantees of Arms

NAMED IN

DOCQUETS AND PATENTS

BETWEEN THE YEARS

1687 AND 1898,

PRESERVED IN

VARIOUS MANUSCRIPTS,

COLLECTED AND

ALPHABETICALLY ARRANGED BY

The Late JOSEPH FOSTER, Hon. M.A. Oxon.,

AND CONTAINED IN THE ADDITIONAL

MS. No. 37,149, IN THE BRITISH MUSEUM.

EDITED BY

W. Harry Rylands, F.S.A.

LONDON.

1917.

LONDON:

PRINTED BY ROWORTH AND COMPANY LIMITED,

NEWTON STREET, W.C. 2.

Preface.

THIS Volume contains the remainder of Additional Manuscript No. 37,149, commenced in Vol. II, Part I (Harl. Soc., Vol. LXVII), of the Grantees of Arms, completing Foster's Alphabetical Lists. The two volumes being now printed, it may be useful to add a few notes on them.

In looking up a Patent, it will be well also to refer to the second Vol. of Edmondson's Heraldry, in which a section following the Alphabet of Arms is headed : "To which is added, by way of Appendix, A Collection of New Arms, Crests, Mottoes, &c., which have been granted at the Heralds' Office since the year 1770." The book bears the date 1780. This includes some of the Grants made by Stephen Martin Leake, Sir Charles Townley, Thomas Browne, Ralph Bigland and Isaac Heard. Also Berry's Encyclopædia Heraldica, Burke's Armory, a Calendar of Printed Grants of Arms, published by my brother, Mr. J. Paul Rylands, F.S.A., in the Historic Society of Lancashire and Cheshire, Vol. LII, 1901, and Shropshire Grants of Arms, published by the Rev. W. G. D. Fletcher, M.A., F.S.A., in the Transactions of the Shropshire Archæological and Natural History Society in 1909, and lastly for references to MSS. in the British Museum, "Grants and Certificates of Arms," by Mr. Arthur J. Jewers, F.S.A., communicated to the Genealogist, beginning in Vol. XIII, 1897, of the New Series, and completed in Vol. XXIX, 1913, may also be referred to.

Two references by Foster in the first volume (Harl. Soc., Vol. LXVI) may be mentioned. The letters "V. O. G." refer to a collection called Vincent Old Grants. The words "Le Neve's MS." constantly occur. This MS. was offered for sale by Mr. E. Menken, among other books from the library of the late Joseph Foster, in November, 1905. In the catalogue, under No. 213, it occurs as follows :—"Heraldic Manuscript—Shirley (Sir Thomas). A Collection of Grants of Arms by sundry Kings of Arms and their Lieutenants, inside the cover of which Peter le Neve, Norroy, has written :—'Formerly Sir Thomas Shirley's book, of Wistandson in Sussex,

Kt., see Sir Thomas Shirley's hand, page 269. Memorand. This book I have Xtened by the name of "Shirley," P. le Neve, Norroy', a neatly written old MS. of 516 pp. showing nearly 1,500 Coats of Arms, excellently Tricked and with 11 pp. of Index. . . . old hf. binding, with bookplates of Wm. Constable, F.R.S., and Joseph Foster, with MS. insertions.'"

This manuscript is often quoted by Peter le Neve, under the title it was christened by him, in his Book of Knights, published by the Harleian Society. Another MS. volume also referred to by Le Neve was Morgan's Book of Grants, and it is perhaps the one that occurs in Messrs. Ellis & Elvey's Sale Catalogue, No. 73, under No 426: "Morgan (Sylvanus) Pattents of Armes [about 1640]. Folio, The Original Manuscript of an unpublished collection of nearly two hundred grants, with the greater part of the coats-of-arms richly emblazoned in gold and colours, half calf. The chief portion of this valuable compilation is in the autograph of Sylvanus Morgan, the author of the 'Sphere of Gentry.'"

The list, called "Miscellanea, College of Arms," 1637 to 1637, printed on pages ix to xiii, has been added because it gives a number of notes and references to the Grant Books Vols. I, II and III, not always included in Foster's Alphabetical List, printed in Vol. I (Harl. Soc., Vol. LXVI) of Grantees of Arms. It may be mentioned that in looking for a Patent dated towards the end of the seventeenth century it will be well to look in both the printed volumes, as Foster has not strictly adhered to the dates fixed by him for the division of the two manuscripts.

Our thanks are due to him for having collected all these valuable references, but it is much to be regretted that when he compiled the list contained in his Volume of Grants made between the years 1687 and 1898 (really 1900) that he paid so much attention to the later Grants beginning about the year 1847. It would have been more useful if he had been careful to collect all the dates of the earlier and more interesting Patents, as the dating of them is, of course, very difficult. There are no Harleian and other manuscripts to refer to, as was the case in Vol. I.

It is quite clear that his list is a series of abstracts from the index to the Grant Books, and that he did not examine the copies of the Patents contained in the volumes.

I feel sorry that at first I relied on Foster's List of the Grant Books, given in Vol. II, Part 2, page 7; it soon became evident, however, that the only way to get with any safety out of this maze of over two hundred years of dates and figures was to tabulate all the information contained in the Manuscript under the volumes, years, and pages. This I have done, giving all the year-dates of the Patents mentioned by Foster, as well as those gleaned from printed books. It did not quite clear up all the difficulties, although it proved what I had already suspected, that necessary delays and alterations had caused the Grants in some volumes not to be entered in strict chronological order. This, as well as the difference between the Old Style and New Style, added to the uncertainty. The dates of the Patents given by Foster are probably correct, as also those given in the printed copies, but it will be noticed that they do not always agree with the volume-date.

From this tabular list it was possible to give a date to many of the Patents; it must, however, be clearly understood that in Vol II the years in square brackets immediately before the numbers of the volumes cannot always be taken with certainty as the date of any Patent. It is the year-date that fits in with the number of volume and page, given in Foster's List.

It must also be pointed out that, although, as I have said, the dates inserted by myself in square brackets are not necessarily exactly the date of the Patent, many of them are, and those that are not, I think, cannot be far wrong, and some of them may be checked by the year in which some honour was given.

Whatever may be the errors in the condensed form of the tabulated list of the contents of the volumes, it seems useful to print it as a kind of Hand List. It will be found on pages xxxvii to xl (List B) in the present Volume. Fortunately, I had by me another List (List A, pp. xxxv and xxxvi), and it will be noticed that some of the dates differ from those given in List B. Differences occur at the beginning or end of some of the volumes, and only in one instance is this difference more than one year. It is the end of Volume XVIII, List B has 1795 instead of 1793 in List A, and, in this instance, 1793 would suit the entry for Sir Charles Whitworth, K.B., and it may be that the Grant of Supporters was entered, like others, out of place. In some of the other cases the same explanation may hold good, and in others the date may be that of another kind of document, bearing on, but not absolutely, a Grant. Foster only copied references to Patents. It will be noticed, also, that each Volume of Grants contains entries covering two or more years, so it is not surprising that I have been unable to state in List B the exact page on which one year ends and the next begins. This, with all the other difficulties, could only be settled by an examination of the whole series of the original books, and this is naturally impossible.

All additions to the original text are placed in square brackets.

I have worked through these volumes with one object, and I can only hope that, however imperfectly the work has been done, they may before long form the foundation of an Armory of Authorised Arms.

Perhaps, after what I have written above, it will be unnecessary for me to apologise for the long, but unavoidably long, list of Additions and Corrections. It will be found to contain a number of references to the printed copies of Grants, and I very gratefully acknowledge the kind assistance I have received, in this as well as in other matters connected with the book, from friends and correspondents.

To the Rev. W. G. Dimock Fletcher, who has spared no pains or trouble to add to the correctness and interest of the volumes; to the Chairman, Sir George J. Armytage, Bart., F.S.A.; Mr. William F. Carter; Mr. J. Paul Rylands, F.S.A.; Mr. F. C. Beazley, F.S.A.; the Secretary, Mr. W. Bruce Bannerman, F.S.A.; Mr. Francis A. Foster, of Edgartown, Massachusetts; Mr. S. A. Grundy-Newman; Mr. Herbert C. Andrews; and Mr. Vere L. Oliver; I would offer my best thanks for all the help they have so kindly and freely given.

I must also add that the printers, Messrs. Roworth & Co., have always continued to give me the same consideration and advice.

W. HARRY RYLANDS.

ERRATUM.—List A.

Page xxxv, *for* Vol. VI, 15 Oct. 1711, ends 7 Aug. 1700, *read* Vol. VI, 15 Oct. 1711, ends 7 Aug. 1720.

"MISCELLANEA, COLLEGE OF ARMS."

"REFERENCES TO GRANT BOOKS, 1, 2, 3, 1637 TO 1687. ALL THESE GRANTS ARE INCLUDED IN THE EARLIER ALPHABETICAL LIST."

[This List occurs on folios 162 to 171 of Add. MS. No. 37,149, printed in the present volume of Grantees of Arms. The following List contains the entries from Foster's "Miscellanea," as above, from the Grant Books, Vols. I, II, III, which are *not* included in the earlier Alphabetical List or contain any differences from or additions to the information given in that List. In some instances the name is crossed through though the reference remains.]

ALLEN, Thomas and Edward, of London and co. Northampton. Quarterly with HEDDE, 1620, Vol. II, fol. 578.

AMYAS, ..., of Hingham, co. Norf., 1684, Vol. III, fol. 234.

ANDERSON, Henry, of Newcastle-upon-Tyne, co. Northumberland, 1547, Vol. I, fol. 336.

ANDROS, ... [crossed through], of co. Oxf. Match with KIRTON, ..., Vol. II, fol. 523.

ASHEHURST, [crossed through], of co. Lanc. Arms. Match with DELALYND, ..., Vol. I, fol. 352 [sic].

ASHTON, Christopher, of Croston, co. Lanc., 1548, Vol. I, fol. 332 [sic].

ASTON, [crossed through], Knt. Match with COLEIRE, ..., Vol. II, fol. 686.

ATHEROLD, [crossed through], of Burch, Suff., ..., Vol. II, fol. 594b.

ATHILLE, [crossed through], of Colne, ... Arms. Match, Vol. II, fol. 639b.

BARNET, alias HODDESDON, of co. Hertf., 1452, Vol. II, fol. 643 [sic].

BARRET, General, [crossed through], of London. Seal, Vol. III, fol. 261.

BELIALD, Thomas (1 s. of John, of P[ater] N[oster] Row). Adm. 16 May 1623, Vol I, fol. 429.

BELLEMAIN [see Bellman], John, 1552, Vol. I, fol. 27.

BERTIE (VENABLES), Montague, Lord NORREYS, 1687, Vol. III, fol. 333.

BLAGROVE, Thomas, of Wilts., 1567, Vol. I, fol. 43 [sic].

BOLL, alias BOLLYS, Robert, or Richard, of co. Linc. Quarterly Arms, Crest, 1560, Vol. I, fol. 272.

BOURCHIER, Anthony, of Bederley, co. Glouc., 1584, Vol. II, fol. 483b.

BRAGE, [crossed through], of Stratford. (Match, VESEY, of Essex), Vol. II, fol. 591b.

BRATTELL, [crossed through], Knt., Tower of London. Seal with Arms, Vol. III, fol. 237.

BRETHERTON, [crossed through], of Hay, co. Lanc. Seal with quartering, Vol. III, fol. 315.

BRIGHOUSE, Martyn, of Colley, co. Linc., 1590, Vol. II, fol. 481.

BRODNAX, [crossed through], Goldsmith, of London. Seal with Arms and Crest, ..., Vol. III, fol. 103.

BURNETT, Thomas, of Wood Dalling, co. Norf., &c., 1640, Grants II, fol. 612.

BURTON, Humphrey, date given 1682.

CASTILLION, 1562, Grants I, fol. 33, II, fol. 652.

CHAPMAN, [crossed through], of London. Seal, Arms and Crest, Grants III, fol. 318b.

LE NEVE, William, York Herald, of London, 1627, Grants I, fol. 26.

LEONARD, [crossed through], of Suffolk. Arms? Match, Grants II, fol. 598.
  [See Lewknor, below.]

LEVESON, John, of Wolverhampton. Match, 1561, Grants II, fol. 686 (COLEIRE).

LEWKNOR, [crossed through], Knt. Match, Arms, Grants II, fol. 598. [This
  is connected by a line with Leonard above.]

LEYS, see HEYS, of Rattingdon, co. Essex, Grants II, fol. 652.

LITTLETON, alias LODGE, Margaret. Match, Arms, 1556, Grants I, fol. 372ª.

LOADES, Henry, Chamberlain, of London, Crest, 1687, Grants III, fol. 323.

LOCK, ... A Seal, Grants III, fol. 261.

LOWNDES, John, of Overton, co. Chester, 1612, Grants II, fol. 583.

LYONS, John, of London, 1550, Grants II, fol. 462.

MAMPAS, ... Match, Vol. I, fol. 199ᵇ.

MANTELL, [crossed through], of co. Kent. Arms, Vol. II, fol. 604ᵇ.

MARIANUS, Sir Angelus, of Cremona, 1537, Vol. I, fol. 21.

MARONNE, of Rouen, in Normandy, 1550, Vol. I, fol. 117.

MASTER, Richard, "D. Med.," of Oxf., 1568, Vol. I, fol. 91.

MOFFETT, [crossed through], Deputy Alderman, of London. Seal with Arms,
  Vol. III, fol. 269.

MOORE, Nicholas, of the Inner Temple, London, and Burghfield, Berks., 1569,
  Vol. I, fol. 236.

MORGAN, see TURBERVILE, of Llanvair, co. Monmouth. Arms and Crest, Vol. II,
  fol. 617ª.

MORRES, ... Match with BUTTS. Arms, Vol. II, fol. 597ᵇ [crossed through,
  see Butts].

MURRAY, Anne, Viscountess BAYNING, of Bayning, Berks., 1674, Vol. III, fol. 6.
  [See Bayning.]

NORREYS, Lord (VENABLES-BERTIE). Name and Arms of Venables in addition
  to Bertie, [Roy. Lic., 10 Nov.] 1687. Vol. III, fol. 333.

OSBORNE, Viscount LATIMER [15 Aug. 1673]. Supporters, 1673, Vol. III, fol. 40.

PAGE [crossed through]. Match, Vol. II, fol. 508.

PALMER, Thomas, of Northampton, not a Grant, 1682, Vol. II, fol. 682.

PARKER, John, of Rayton, co. Sussex, with quartering, 1559, Vol. I, fol. 188.

PARRY, Henry (by CAMDEN), of Wormebridge and Old Court, co. Hereford,
  Vol. II, fol. 588.

PAULET, Mary, nat. dau. of SCROPE, Earl of SUNDERLAND. Arms and Supporters,
  wed. Mary, of Winchester, Vol. III, fol. 119ᵇ. [See Scrope.]

PAYNE, ..., of Hutton, [co.   ], Vol. II, fol. 686, see DODINGTON alias
  DORRINGTON. Match with (COLEIRE). [See Collier.]

PECKE, ..., Haberdasher, of London. Seal with Arms and Crest, Vol. III,
  fol. 103.

PELLICANS, ..., of Pellicans, parish of Wateringbury, co. Kent, Vol. I, fol. 393ᵇ.

PETERBOROUGH, Kenneth WHITE, Bishop of, 1686, Vol. III, fol. 293. [Thomas
  White was Bishop of Peterborough from 1685 to 1691, when he was
  deprived. (See White.) White Kennet was Bishop, 1718 to 1728.]

PHILLIPS, see HARPHAM, Alice, wife of Thomas Phillips, of co. Lincoln. Match,
  1627, Vol. I, fol. 379.

PIGOTT, ..., of co. Norf., Impaled Arms, Vol. II, fol. 597ᵇ.

PLEYDELL, [crossed through], of St. Andrew, Holborn, Vol. III, fol. 127.

POORE, ..., of St. Olave's, Jewry, London, Vol. III, fol. 97 [date 1680
  crossed through].

PRESTON, ... Arms and Pedigree, Vol. II, fol. 604ᵇ.

PRICE [see Prise], Thomas, of Brecon, 1632, Vol. II, fol. 617ª.

PRIOTTE [see Pryotte], John, born in New (the North of) England, 1547 or 1560,
  Vol. I, fol. 109.

QUEROÙALLE, Julia, Duchess of PORTSMOUTH. Supporters, 1674, Vol. III,
  fol. 44. [See Portsmouth, Louise de Querouaille, cr. Duchess of Portsmouth, 19 Aug. 1673.]

RAYMOND, Baron of Abbot's Langley. Match, Vol. I, fol. 225ᵃ. [Robert Raymond was *cr.* 15 Jan. 1731, Lord Raymond, Baron of Abbot's Langley, co. Hertford.]
RENOLD, [crossed through], of Olton, Vol. II, fol. 594ᵇ.
REVILE DE OGSTONE, ..., of co. Derby. Match, Vol. II, fol. 686.
ROOKES, ... Match, Vol. I, fol. 352ᵇ.
RUSHBURGH, John and Richard, of Aylesham and Baldoke, co. Norf., 1558, Vol. II, fol. 546.
RUSSELL, (TINDALL, Jane), Gent. of the Privy Chamber, Vol. I, fol. 230. [*See* Tindall.]
SANDS (SONDS), George, Earl of FEVERSHAM. Quartering, 1677, Vol. III, fol. 53 (11 quarterings).
SCOBELL, John, of Plymouth, co. Devon, 1629, Vol. II, fol. 683.
SCRAS, Tuppyn, of Bletchington, co. Sussex, 1616, Vol. I, fol. 281.
SEEBOURN [*see* Sebone], Richard, of Sutton, co. Hereford, 1556, Vol. I, fol. 186.
SHELDON, William, of Ardern, co. Warw., 1475, Vol. II, fol. 541.
SHERLEY [*see* Shirley], Robert, Goldsmith, of London, 1609, Vol. II, fols. 479 and 532.
SKILLICORNE, ..., of Presthall, co. Lanc. Match [*see* Jadwine], Vol. I, fol. 358.
SMYTH, ..., of Gray's Inn. Seal, Arms and Crest, Vol. III, fol. 318.
ST. GEORGE, ..., King of Arms, Vol. III, fol. 290 ; Garter Seal, fol. 305.
SWYNBORNE, John, of Chopwell [co. Durham ?], and Nathertou, co. Northumberland, 1551, Vol. II, fol. 553.
TAYLOR, Thomas, of Battersea, London, and Haseldon Grange, Rodmarton, co. Glouc., 1600, Vol. II, fol. 632.
THORNICROFT, John, of Thornicroft, co. Chester, Oct. 1687, Vol. III, fol. 327 ; Declaration, Vol. IV, fol. 139.
TROWTE, Alan, of co. Norf., 1376. Vol. II, fol. 619.
TUKE, ..., of co. Kent, Vol. II, fol. 444.
TUNSTALL, ... Arms. Match with COLEIRE, Vol. II, fol. 686.
TURBERVILE, ..., of co. Glamorgan, Vol. II, fol. 617ᵃ.
TURCK, ... Match with COLEIRE, Vol. II, fol. 686.
TURNER, ..., of co. Kent, Vol. I, fol. 393.
TYTLEY, ..., of co. Chester, Vol. I, fol. 352.
VENABLES, ... Additional Name and Arms of Venables, Vol. II, fol. 686. Match with COLEIRE, Arms.
VERE, ..., of Henley, co. Suff. Match, Vol. II, fol. 594ᵇ.
VERNON [George ?], Knt. [23 Dec. 1627], of London. Seal, with Arms, Vol. III, fol. 269.
VESY, ..., of Hintlesham, co. Suff. Pedigrees, Vol. II, fol. 594ᵇ.
VIOLETT, ..., of Lynn, co. Norf., Vol. II, fol. 598.
WELLMOTT, ..., of Newent, co. Glouc., Vol. I, fol. 234. [*See* Wilmot, Edward.]
WENLOCK, ... Pedigree and Arms, Vol. II, fol. 604ᵇ.
WESSELL, Weblin ?, of London. [*See* Webley.] Seal with Arms, Vol. III, fol. 261.
WEST, Reynold, of Sudbury, co. Suff., and Burstwick, co. York, 1446, Vol. II, fol. 639.
WHITE, Kenneth, Bishop of Peterborough, 1686, Vol. III, fol. 293. [? In 1685, Thomas White was made Bishop of Peterborough and was deprived 1 Feb. 169⁹⁰. White KENNET became Bishop in 1718. *See* White, Thomas, Bishop of Peterborough.]
WOODCOCK, ..., of London. Arms, Match with COLEIRE, Vol. II, fol. 686.
WOODGATE, ..., of co. Kent, Vol. II, fol. 578.
WRIGHT, Sir Benjamin, Bart. [15 Feb. 166⁹⁰], of Cranham Hall, co. Essex, 1687, Vol. III, fol. 306 [d. 1706].
YELVERTON, Henry, Lord GREY. Supporters and Quarterings, 1680, Vol. III, fol. 117. [*See* Grey.]

(xiv)

ADDITIONS AND CORRECTIONS, GRANTEES OF ARMS, Vol. I.

(Continued from Vol. I, p. xx.)

PAGE
vii Abbot, *see* Allott, *read* Allett.
viii *For* Cherourice *read* Cherouriee.
xi *Dele* Marshall, *see* Locksmith.
xv *Dele For* Allett *read* Abbott, John, *and insert* on p. 1.
„ Bonnatree, *for* Vol. V, p. 27, *read* Vol. V, p. 270.
„ *Add* p. 32 *before Add* Branthwaite *and before Add* Bretarge.
„ *For* p. 37 *before* Bubb *read* p. 38.
xvi *For* De Cuslin *read* De Moline, *and add* Guillim, p. 433.
„ Giustiniani, *for* fol. 102^{b} *read* 52^{b}.
„ Leveson, *after* gouted *add* s.
„ *Before* Saffin *add* p. 221.
„ Tyson, *after* (? or) *add* MS. Rawl., B. 100, fol. 3.

[Acres, Capt. George, s. of Robert Acres, of Accers Hall, co. Lanc., 16 Mar. 1576, by Ulster K. of Arms. Hist. Soc. Lanc. and Chesh., XXXIII, p. 257.]
[Allenson, John, of Norwood, co. Middx., by Sir John Borough, Garter K. of Arms, 18 Jan. 163$\frac{3}{4}$. Misc. G. et H., 5th S., II, p. 173.]
Altham, James, of London, 1559, *add* [Crisp, Fragm. Geneal., V, p. 57].
[Andrewes, Launcelot, Bishop of Winchester, 1618. Muskett, Suff. Manorial Fams, III, 37.]
[Arbroath, Burgh of, 12 Jan. 1900. Geneal. Mag., IV, p. 109.]
Archer, Henry, of Theydon Gernon, *add* [Misc. G. et H., 5th S., II, p. 101].
Ashby, *add* [George].
Ashe als Esse, *add* [Misc. G. et H., 5th S., I, p. 12, ? granted by Sir W. Dethick, p. 13.]
Atslow, Edward, of London, *after* Lobenham of Brikelsworth, co. Norfolk, *add* [John Levenham of Bricklesworth, co. Northampton, *see* Genealogist, New S., XXI, p. 62].
Avery, William, *add* [Misc. G. et H., I, p. 230].
Aylett, John, 1 April, 1646, *add* [Genealogist, New S., XXVIII, p. 35].
[Backhouse, Thomas, of Whitrig, co. Cumberland, by Gilbert Dethick, 26 Feb. 15$\frac{7}{8}\frac{9}{0}$. Harl. Soc., LVI, p. 160.]
Backhouse, Nicholas, *add* [Harl. Soc., LVII, pp. 57, 58].
Baker, George (same coat), *add* [Harl. Soc., LVI, p. 60].
Baker, Thomas Swaney, 14 Oct. 1649, *add* [Genealogist, New S., XXII, p. 112; Shropshire Arch. Soc. Trans., 3rd S., VI, p. xvj].
Baker, William, of New Windsor, *add* [Harl. Soc., LVII, p. 61].
Baldwin, Richard, *add* [Genealogist, New S., XXII, p. 155].
Ball [Balle], William, 1572, *add* [Crisp, Fragm. Geneal., XIII, p. 2].
Banester, Laurence, of Easington, co. York, *add* [in Latin. Hist. Soc. Lanc. and Chesh., LXIII, p. 179].
Barbery and Surgery, *add* [Young's Annals of the Barber Surgeons, p. 432].
Barber Chirurgeons, *add* [12 June 1569, Young's Annals of the Barber Surgeons, p. 437].
Barker, James, *after* Proc. Soc. Antiq., &c., *add* [3 Nov. 1562].
Barker, Rowland, of Wollerton, *add* [Crisp, Fragm. Geneal., XIII, p. 8].
Barnes, Richard, Bishop of Durham, *add* [in Latin. Hist. Soc. Lanc. and Chesh., LXIII, p. 180].

Barret, Leonard, *after* Collectanea *add* [Vol. j].

[Barrymore, 28 Feb. 162⅘.   Crisp, Fragm. Geneal., X, p. 84.]

Bartellot, Walter, *add* [Misc. G. et H., 2nd S., II, p. 296].

[Bayliff, John, of St. Clement Danes, London, 5th son of William Bayliff, 28 Sept. 22 James I [1624].   Genealogist, New S., XXVIII, p. 152.]

Baylye, Thomas, of Coventry, *add* [Harl. Soc., LXII, pp. 107, 157].

Beckwith, Hamon, *for* Malolaan, *read* Malolacn.

Bee, John, *after* quartering Bowyer *add* [Bee, Bowyer and Swettenham].

[Bennett, Thomas, 13 Dec. 1631.   Hist. Soc. Lanc. and Chesh., XXXVIII, p. 37.]

Best, John, Bishop of Carlisle, *add* [1st grant by Lawrence Dalton, Norroy K. of Arms, 5 March 1560, Argent, on a chevron Sable, three pheons (fers de fleches) of the first, in chief two doves proper, beaked and membered Gules, and in the point (base) a book of the second garnished Or ; 2nd grant, by Sir Gilbert Dethick, Garter K. of Arms, 10 Feb., 3 Eliz. : [1561] Or, on a chevron Sable, three pheons, (fers de fleches) between three books Gules, on a chief Gules, a St. Esprit issuing from a cloud (no tincture but no doubt to be represented as a dove)].

Bingley, Richard, *add* of *before* Blythe.

[Binning, Sir William, of Wallyford (Midlothian), 1676.   Misc. G. et H., 5th S., I, pp. 205, 320 ; Lyon Register, No. 314, dated (1672-7) ; Nisbet's Her., I, plate 12.]

[Birkenhead, Borough of, co. Chester, 28 Aug. 1878.   Hist. Soc. Lanc. and Chesh., XLII, p. 13.]

Birkhead, John, *add* of *before* Croutou.

Blaikway, Anne, *add* [Shropshire Arch. Soc. Trans., 4th S., III, p. xix].

Bolton, John, of Bolton Hall, reference to M. G. et Her., *read* p. 103 *not* 163.

Bolton, Thomas, of Woodbridge, *add* [Genealogist, New S., XXII, p. 144].

Bonrchier, Thomas and James, *add* [Bouchier, Bourchier, Boucher.   *See* Genealogist, New S., XXVIII, p. 75].

Bowerman, *after* James *add* of.

Bowes, Elizabeth, *for* Harbowe *read* Harlowe.

Boyle, Stephen, of Kentish Town, *add* [Misc. G. et H., I, p. 285].

Braham, Sir Richard, *add* [Harl. Soc., LVII, p. 81].

Branthwaite, Richard (p. 33), *insert* on p. 31 *after* Bramhall.

Brathwayte, Thomas, *add* [Harl. Soc., VIII, p. 276].

Braybrooke, Robert, *add* [Misc. G. et H., 4th S., V, p. 267].

Braybrooke, James, *add* [Harl. Soc., LVII, p. 82].

Bretarghe, William (p. 33), *insert* on p. 32 *after* Breres.

Broad, Henry, *add* [Crisp, Fragm. Geneal., V, p. 7].

Brock, Robert, of Chester, *add* [Hist. Soc. Lanc. and Chesh., LXII, p. 182].

Brock, William, of the Inner Temple, London, *add* [Exemplification of Arms and Grant of Crest.   Hist. Soc. Lanc. and Chesh., LXII, p. 124].

Brodbent, John, *add* [Misc. G. et H., New S., III, p. 49].

Bronde, Benjamin (top of p. 35), *for* [?] *read* (?).

Browne, John, of Brenchley, *for* 126^b *read* 126.

Browne, Richard, son of Thomas, of Upton, co. Chester, *add* [Hist. Soc. Lanc. and Chesh., LII, p. 126].

Buck (Thomas and John), *add* [Genealogist, III, p. 238].

Buckler, Sir Walter, *add* [Misc. G. et H., 2nd S., II, p. 204].

[Bulkeley, Thomas, of Bickerton, co. Chester.   Bulkeley and Bickerton quarterly, certified by R. St. George, Norroy K. of Arms, 1613.   Hist. Soc. Lanc. and Chesh., LXII, p. 124.]

[Bulkeley, Robert, of Chester, certified by W. Dugdale, Norroy, 1663.   Hist. Soc. Lanc. and Chesh., LXII, p. 124.]

Bunbury, Henry (of Bunbury) [of Stanney], co. Chester [*add* Quarterly Arms, Bunbury, Stanney, Aldersey and Bamvile.   Hist. Soc. Lanc. and Chesh., LXII, p. 123].

Burnaby, Richard, *add* [Hill, Hist. of Market Harborough, p. 333].

[Burnam, quartering to William Tupholme, of Boston, co. Linc., by William Hervye, Clar. K. of Arms, 26 Oct. 1562. Misc. G. et H., 4th S., I, p. 41.]

Burton, Robert, Sir, is wrong, add [Shropshire Arch. Soc. Trans., 3rd S., IX, p. 384].

Bury St. Edmunds, after Antiq. add [71].

Butler, John, of Kirkland, add [Hist. Soc. Lanc. and Chesb., LXVII, p. 156].

Butler, Thomas, of Bewsey, add [Hist. Soc. Lanc. and Chesh., LXVII, p. 155].

Butler, Margaret, Lady North, add [Misc. G. et H., 3rd S., II, p. 193].

Caldicott, Mathias, add [son of Clement, son of William, of Melbourne, co. Camb.], and add at the end [Misc. G. et H., 5th S., II, p. 55].

[Cambell, Thomas, Citizen and Alderman of London, 20 Sept. 1600. Genealogist, New S., XXI, p. 187].

Cambridge, Regius Professors of, add [Her. Exhib., 69 ; Geneal. Mag., II, p. 125].

Cambridge University, after Exhib. add 67.

Cambridge, Town of, add [Genealogist, III, p. 234].

Cambridge, [Colleges, Genealogist, III, pp. 231-233 ; Her. Exhib., 66 and 69].

Carlos, Col. William, add [son of John Carlos, of Bromwall, parish of Brewood (Broomhall in Brewood), co. Staff. Misc. G. et H., 5th S., II, p. 81].

Castillion, add [Harl. Soc., LVII, p. 92].

[Cerjat, of Moudon, in Switzerland, Grant by Sigismund, Emperor of Germany and King of Hungary, 9 Oct. 1415. Genealogist, New S., XVIII, frontispiece].

[Chadwick, James, of the Inner Temple, London, s. of John Chadwick, of Helye Hall, co. Lanc. Exemplification by W. Segar, Norroy, 1630. Hist. Soc. Lanc. and Chesb, LXII, p. 121.]

[Chedley, Thomas and Roland his brother. Grant and Confirmation of Arms by Sir John Borough, Norroy K. of Arms, as representatives of an ancient family of that name in co. Chester, 4 Dec. 1630, in Latin.]

Choke, Richard, add [Harl. Soc., LVII, p. 106].

Cholmondeley, Robert, Visct. [Cholmondeley], add [Hist. Soc. Lanc. and Chesh., LX, p. 168, plate of Arms, LXI, p. 215.]

Cholmeley, Sir Hugh, add [5 Dec., 1st Edw. VI (1547). Hist. Soc. Lanc. and Chesh., LX, p. 162].

Clarke, Edward, add [Harl. Soc., LVII, p. 108].

Codrington, John, of Codrington, add [see Misc. G. et H., 4th S., V, pp. 265 and 266].

Collens, Jane, [read Collyns], and add [Crisp, Fragm. Geneal., XIII, p. 15].

Collett, for Crispe's read Crisp's.

Collins, John, of Betterton, add [Harl. Soc., LVII, p. 110].

Cooke, John, s. of George, by Ryley, Norroy K. of Arms [Gynn quarterly. Crisp, Fragm. Geneal., XIII, p. 1].

Cookes, Sir Tho⁸, Bart., after Clar. add [? confirmed] Sir William, for High Slip. read ? High Sheriff, after fol. 216 add [217 ?].

Cosyn, John, add [Misc. G. et H., 5th S., II, p. 256].

Criketot, after Clervowe add [Clanvowe].

Cuerton, John, dwelling at Bilbao, add [Hist. Soc. Lanc. and Chesb., LXII, p. 183].

Curteys, Griffin, add [Harl. Soc., LVII, p. 111].

Cutler, Robert, add [Crisp, Fragm. Geneal., X, p. 80].

Dancastle, add [Harl. Soc., LVII, p. 112].

Dawe, William, add [20 June] before 1588 and [Misc. et G. H., 2nd S., II, p. 255].

Day, William, B.D., Provost of Eton, add [Harl. Soc., LVII, p. 113].

[De Bordeaux, Arnold, 28 Mar. 1444. Geneal. Mag., III, p. 502.]

De Granato should be placed after Degge.

[Douglas, John, of Scotland, 17 Feb. 1675, by Lyon K. of Arms. Genealogist, V, p. 203.]

Draper, Henry, of Colebrook, add [Misc. G. et H., 3rd S., IV, p. 169].

Draper, Thomas, of Stroud Green, add [Harl. Soc., LVII, p. 118].

Ducke, Nicholas, add [Misc. G. et H., New S., I, 317, and Wells Cathedral, Jewers, p. 44].

Dudley, John, *add* [of Hackney, co. Middx., and Misc. G. et H., 2nd S., V, p. 54].
Dugdale, William, *after* Antiquaries *add* [73], *and after* Hamper's Life *add* [pp. 519 and 520].
Dylke. *See* Dilke.
Dymock, Francis, *read* Dymoke, Francis, *and after* 1589 *add* [17 June 1581, *see* Genealogist, New S., XXI, p. 186].
Egerton, John, of Egerton and Oulton, *add* [Patent of a Crest, 7 Aug. 1580, in Latin. Hist. Soc. Lanc. and Chesh., LXIII, p. 185].
Elken, Richard, of London, *add* [Misc. G. et H., 5th S., II, p. 26].
Essington, *add* [Misc. G. et H., 4th S., II, p. 2].
Evelyn, *add after* Antiq. [67].
Fairborne, Sir Palmes, *after* Knt. *add* [13 April 1675].
Fisher, John, of co. Huntingdon, *add* [Misc. G. et H., 4th S., V, p. 269].
Fletewood, Thomas, of London, Auditor, &c., *add* [Crisp, Fragm. Geneal, X, p. 79].
Freemen in the Suburbs, Corporation of. *See* London.
Fulwer, James and John, *should be placed on* p. 96 *after* Fuller, *and add* [to John, Ralph and James, to whom a Crest was granted in 1560. *See* Misc. G. et H., 4th S., IV, p. 67].
[Gall, Robert, of London, s. and h. of Robert Gall, of Weneston, co. Suff., by Robert Cooke, Clarenceux K. of Arms, 7 June 1576. Crisp, Fragm. Geneal. IV, p. 18.]
Gans, William [of Holland], *add* [Her. Exhibition, 72].
Gidley, Bartholomew, *add* [Crisp, Notes, XI, p. 119].
[Gleave, ... of High Leigh, co. Chester, attested by William Flower, Norroy K. of Arms, and Robert Cooke, Chester Herald, 1566. Hist. Soc. Lanc. and Chesh., LXII, p. 135.]
Grafton, Richard (son of Ralph, out of Cheshire), *add* [dwelling in the Canary Islands (in Latin). Hist. Soc. Lanc. and Chesh., LXIII, p. 186].
[Graham, Henry, of Breckness, in Orkney, Scotland, Lyon office, 9 Dec. 1676. Misc. G. et H., 5th S., I, p. 1.]
Gray, Sir Richard, *after* (*see* Anne Grey), *add* [Payton]).
Grey, Lord, *read* Gray de Ruthin (Yelverton).
Gurney, John, *add* [Crisp, Fragm. Geneal., XIII, p. 6].
Gygges, p. 100, *add* [Genealogist, New S., XI, p. 191].
Hall, Joseph, S. T. D., Bp. of Exeter, *add* [Crisp, Fragm. Geneal., X, p. 78].
Halsteed, Laurence, of Sonning, *add* [Harl. Soc., LVII, p. 136].
Hanke, *add* [Hankey] *and at end add* [Hist. Soc. Lanc. and Chesh., LXIII, p. 188].
Hans, or Hansby, *for* Berverley *read* Beverley.
Harbottle, John, *for* Sussex *read* [Suffolk].
Harvey, George, *add* [Crisp, Notes, I, p. 58].
Hastings, William, *add* [Misc. G. et H., I, 322].
Heynes, Nicholas, *add* [Harl. Soc., LVII, p. 144].
Haber, Raynold, *add* [16 May 12th Eliz. 1569, Genealogist, New S., XXVII, p. 222].
Heblethwayte, *add* [Misc. G. et H., 3rd S., II, p. 17].
Hedges als Lacy, III [? IV, *see* Harl. Soc., VIII, Le Neve's Knights, p. 415. Misc. G. et H., 5th S., II, p. 84].
Henn als Hene, *add* [Harl. Soc., LVII, p. 145].
Herbert, Edward, *add* [Misc. G. et H., 2nd S., II, p. 169].
Herbert (Henry), of Cherbury, *not* Caerbury.
Hereford, City of, *add* [Geneal. Mag., IV, p. 57].
Herrys, Arthur, of Crixsey, *for* 19 Nov. *read* 29 Nov.
Hill, Alice, Jane and Elizabeth, *after* John Barker *add* [James Barker], *and the same addition* (p. 125) Hill, Sir Rowland ; *for* 2nd S., XVII, *read* XVI.
[Hill, James (from Suffolk). Exemplification by Sir William Segar, Garter K. of Arms, 2 Sept. 1618. Harl. Soc., LVII, p. 146.]
[Hill, Rowland, 20 Oct. 1534. *See* Crisp, Frag. Geneal., XIII, p. 10.]
Hoby, Edward, *add* [Harl. Soc., LVII, p. 149].

Hoby, Peregrine. *add* [Harl. Soc., LVII, p. 150].

Hollynshed, Hugh, *for* Bonocus *read* ? Bouacous, *and add* [Exemplification of Arms, and grant of Crest, 1 July 1560. Hist. Soc. Lanc. and Chesb., LXII, p. 135].

Hooper or Howper. John, *for* Grants L *read* Grants I.

Hooper, John, of New Sarum, *add* [Misc. G. et H., 4th S., III, p. 65].

[Horton, ..., attested by William Flower, Norroy K. of Arms, and Robert Cooke, Chester Herald (1566), exhibited 1663, by Ralph Horton, of Coole, co. Chester. Hist. Soc. Lanc. and Chesh., LXII, p. 127.]

[Houghton, Richard, of Park Hall, co. Lanc., by R. St. George, Norroy K. of Arms, 2 Nov. 1606. Misc. G. et H., 3rd S., I, p. 193.]

Hovell, Allan, 1562, *add* [Misc. G. et H., 5th S., II, pp. 1 and 122.]

Hulton, Adam, of the Parke, *add* [Family of Hulton, of Hulton, co. Lanc., p. 20, and Hist. Soc. Lanc. and Chesh., LXVIII, p. 110].

Humfrey, William, of London, *add* [Misc. G. et H., 4th S., I, p. 1].

Hunston, William, of Walpole, *add* [Misc. G. et H., 4th S., V, p. 1].

Huys, Thomas, *add* [of Kenmerton] co. Glouc. [by William Hervy, Clarenceux K. of Arms, 28 July 1558. Misc. G. et H., 4th S., II, p. 145].

Jackson, *add* [Richard, of Killingwold, co. York. Confirmed 16 June 1613.].

Jemmett, Philip, *add* [Crisp, Fragm. Geneal., XIII, p. 3].

Jenkinson, Sir Robert, of London, *add* [Jenkenson, Sir Robert, of Walcott, in "Oxford-sheyer." Crisp, Notes, II, p. 47].

[Jennings quartering. *See* Lingard-Monk. Genealogist, V, p. 144.]

Jevon, Daniel and Thomas, *add* [Salopian Shreds and Patches, VIII, p. 36; F. W. Hackwood's Sedgley Researches, 1898, p. 117].

Kemble, George, *add* [Harl. Soc., LVII, p. 164].

Kempe, William, *add* [6 Dec. 1662. Crisp, Fragm. Geneal., X, p. 82].

Kendall, John, *add* [Genealogist, New S., XXII, p. 61; Misc. G. et H., 4th S., V, p. 121].

Kevall, George, *add* [Crisp, Fragm. Geneal., XIII, p. 12.]

Kidermister, *read* KIDERMISTER.

Kingeston, John de, *add* [Genealogist, New S., XVIII, p. 35; Geneal. Mag., III, p. 261].

Knight, Robert, *add* [Misc. G. et H., 5th S., I, p. 287].

Knowles, Richard, *after* 8 Nov. *add* [6] *and add* [Crisp, Fragm. Geneal., VII, p. 10].

Lane, Thomas, *for* Gent. Mag. *read* Geneal. Mag.

Lany, John, *for* Cratfold *read* Cratfield, *and add* [Crisp, Fragm. Geneal., XIII, p. 13].

Lee, Sir Robert, of Quarrendon, *add* [Her. and Geneal., III, pp. 117-118, and Misc. G. et H., 2nd S., I, p. 102, give the date 1513].

Legh, Sir Piers, *after* East Cheshire, II, 303, *add* [Hist. Soc. Lanc. and Chesh., LX, p. 166, Shield of 8 Quarterings and Crest, LXII, p. 138].

Legh, Sir Piers, *at end after* 1665 *add* [Crisp, Fragm. Geneal., X, p. 72; Geneal. Mag., I, p. 17].

Leversage. *See also* Liversage.

[Liversage, Lyversage, or Leversage, William, of Wheelock, co. Chester, by William Flower, Norroy K. of Arms, grant of Crest, 24 Sept. 1580. Hist. Soc. Lanc. and Chesh., LXIII, 189, Lyversage quartering Wheelock.]

[London, Armes of the New Corporation of Freemen in the Suburbs about London, by Sir John Borough, Garter K. of Arms, between Dec. 1633 and Oct. 1643. Geneal. Mag., IV, p. 187.]

[Londonderry, City of, 1 June 1623. Geneal. Mag., II, 256, IV, 58.]

[Maddison, Edward, of Formaby, co. Linc., s. of Edward Madison, Esq., s. of Sir Edward Madison, Knt., 13 May 1587, by Robert Cooke, Clarenceux K. of Arms. Crisp, Visit. Eng. and Wales, facsimile, p. 149.]

[Mariet, Thomas, of Remenham, Berks., 16 June 1586, by Robert Cooke, Clarenceux K. of Arms. Harl. Soc., LVII, p. 177.]

[Masons' Company, London, 1472, Conder, Hole Craft, p. 84 and plate, frontis-piece.]
[Massey, of Denfield, co. Chester, attested by William Flower, Norroy K. of Arms (1566) and allowed by Richard St. George, Norroy, 1613. Hist. Soc. Lanc. and Chesh., LXII, p. 128.]
[Massey, John, of Coddington, co. Chester, confirmation by Richard St. George, Norroy K. of Arms, 1613? Hist. Soc. Lanc. and Chesh., LXII, p. 125.]
Mathew, Dame Mary, add [Crisp, Fragm. Geneal., V, p. 56].
Merick, Gelly, [of Basarden, Wales], 1583, add [Misc. G. et H., 5th S., II, p. 130].
Mildmay, Sir Walter, Knt., of Essex, after the reference to Misc. G. et H., II, p. 261, add [p. 192].
Minshull, Richard, add [Misc. G. et H., II, p. 182].
Moigne, after 2 Nov. add [22].
Moore, Thomas, of Wigenhall, add [Crisp, Fragm. Geneal., XIII, p. 4.]
Monte-acuto, add [Geneal. Mag. III, p. 296].
More, John, a Cheshire man, add [Hist. Soc. Lanc. and Chesh., LXIII, p. 190].
[Moreton, of Moreton, co. Chester, attested by Robert Glover, Somerset Herald, 1580, and allowed by Richard St. George, Norroy. K. of Arms, 1613. Hist. Soc. Lanc. and Chesh., LXII, p. 129].
Morewood, for Alpeton read Alfreton.
[Morgan, John, of Morganshays, co. Devon, 20 Dec. 1528, by Wryothesley, Garter K. of Arms, and Thomas Benolt, Clarenceux. Geneal., New S., XXIV, pp. 138-139.]
Mowbray, Thomas de, add [MS. Ashm. 804, II, fol. 16ᵇ], and for Gents. Mag. read Geneal. Mag.].
Norreys, Thomas, of Orford, add [Grant of a Crest, 10 Nov. 1581. Hist. Soc. Lanc. and Chesh., XLIII, p. 193].
North, John, of Cubley, add [Crisp, Fragm. Geneal., I, p. 32].
Northe, Lady Margaret. See Butler.
Northey, references to the Genealogist, read p. 172.
Northland, Thomas, add [Crisp, Fragm. Geneal., X, p. 75].
Nonell, Andrew, 10 Feb. 1582, add [Genealogist, New S., XXII, p. 111].
Nuthall, John, of Cattenhall, co. Chester, 13 June 1581, 23 Eliz., add [Quartering Griffin and Horton, (in Latin) Grant of Crest. Hist. Soc. Lanc. and Chesh., LXIII, p. 194].
Oldfield, Philip, of Bradwall, add [Hist. Soc. Lanc. and Chesh., LXII, p. 121. Arms exemplified and Grant of Crest, 7 Feb. 165⅚, by William Flower, Norroy K. of Arms, p. 130. Somerford Crest, allowed by Richard St. George, Norroy 1613, p. 130; another copy, LXIII, p. 197].
Oliver, Sir Benjamin, add [Facsimile, Misc. G. et H., 4th S., III, p. 193, gives the date 1 Sept. 1672].
Overbury, Thomas, add [1592, by Robert Cooke, Clar. ?].
Owen, Edward, 8 Dec. 1582, add [Genealogist, New S., XXII, p. 155; Powys-Land Club, VI, p. 39].
Palmer Richard, add [Harl. Soc., LVII, p. 190].
Paltock, Edward, add [Crisp, Fragm. Geneal., IV, p. 79].
Parkes, Richard, add [F. W. Hackwood's Sedgley Researches, 1898, p. 30].
Paulet. See Winchester [?].
[Perrott, Robert, of the City of Oxford. Arms confirmed by Sir Gilbert Dethick, Garter K. of Arms, 4 Jan., 3 Edw. VI, 1550. Misc. G. et H., 3rd S., III, p. 1.]
Pierson, Thomas (of the Receipts a Teller, &c.) [Patent to, in Latin, Hist. Soc. Lanc. and Chesh. LXIII, p. 195.]
[Pott, of Pott, co. Chester, attested by Henry St. George, Richmond Herald of Arms, 1634. Hist. Soc. Lanc. and Chesh., LXII, p. 134.]
Povey, John, one of the Clerks, &c., add [Grant of Crest. Hist. Soc. Lanc. and Chesh., LXIII, p. 198].

Power, Francis, *add* [Misc. G. et H., 4th S., III, pp. 98, 241].

Power, John, *add* [Misc. G. et H., 4th S., III, p. 273].

Powle, Thomas, of London, *add* [Crisp, Fragm. Geneal., XIII, p. 6].

Pratt, Ralph, *for* Crispe's *read* Crisp's.

Prince, Richard, 2 Nov. 1584, *add* [*see* Genealogist, New S., XXII, p. 154].

Prujean, Francis, *add* [Crisp, Fragm. Geneal., V, p. 57].

Quarles, John, *add* [Harl. Soc., LVII, p. 201].

Rawe or Raux, George, of Skipton, *add* [Crisp, Fragm. Geneal., XIII, p. 10].

Reddish, Alexander, of Reddish, *add* [Grant of a Crest, and to the descendants of his grandfather, John Redich, of Redich. Hist. Soc. Lanc. and Chesh., LXIII, p. 202].

Rocke, Richard, 6 Mar. 1603, *add* [*see* Genealogist, New S., XXII, p. 155].

Rogers, Robert, *add* [Crisp, Fragm. Geneal., XIII, p. 5].

Rowe, William, *add* [Scout-Master-General, s. of John Rowe], of Pontefract, *add* [Crisp, Fragm. Geneal., XIII, p. 14].

Royal Fishing Company, *add* [Crisp, Fragm. Geneal., XIII, p. 20].

Ryder, Anthony, *add* [Harl. Soc. LVII, p. 205].

St. Aubyn, *after* iv, 1, *add* [facsimile].

Sames, *add* [Sammes].

Shadwell, Thomas, *after* iii, 106, *add* [Crisp, Notes, V, p. 23].

Sheldon, Daniel, *add* [Crisp, Notes, I, p. 101].

Sheldon, Gilbert, *add* [Crisp, Notes, I, p. 101].

Scofeld [Schofield], Cuthbert, *add* [Grant of a Crest. Hist. Soc. Lanc. and Chesh., LXIII, p. 202].

Sitsilt, *after* Beaufort *add* [Beauport].

Smallman, Thomas, 10 Oct. 1589, *add* [Shropsh. Arch. Soc. Trans., 4th S., II, vii].

Smith, Thomas, of Campden, *after* 1540 *add* [1544].

Smith, Thomas, s. and h. of Sir Laurence Smith, of Hough, co. Chester, s. of Sir Thomas Smith, *add* [Exemplification of Arms to Sir Laurence Smith and Thomas, his eldest son, and to the descendants of the first named Sir Thomas Smith, given at London, in Latin. Hist. Soc. Lanc. and Chesh., LXIII, p. 203].

Smithes, George, *after* of the Court of *add* [?].

[Somerford, of Somerford. Crest allowed by Richard St. George, Norroy K. of Arms, 1613, to Philip Oldfield, of Somerford, co. Chester. Hist. Soc. Lanc. and Chesh., LXII, p. 130.]

South, Sir Francis, *add* [Misc. G. et H., 5th S., I, p. 239].

South, William, of Amesbury, Wilts., by Gilbert Dethick, 1575. Misc. G. et H., 5th S., I, p. 239].

Sponer [Spooner], Thomas, *after* Worc. *add* [29 Nov.].

[Stanley, Sir Rowland, of Hooton, co. Chester, attested by William Flower, Norroy K. of Arms, and Robt. Glover, Somerset Herald. Shield of 9 Quarterings, 22 Aug. 1580. Hist. Soc. Lanc. and Chesh., LXII, p. 136.]

Staunton, John, *add* [Crisp, Fragm. Geneal., V, p. 62].

Swettenham, Laurence, of Somerford, *add* [Hist. Soc. Lanc. and Chesh., LXIII, p. 205].

[Swettenham, ..., of Swettenham, co. Chester. Crest confirmed to Swettenham, of Somerford, co. Chester, by William Flower, Norroy K. of Arms. Arms allowed by Rich. St. George, Norroy K. of Arms, 1613. Hist. Soc. Lanc. and Chesh., LXII, p. 129.]

Swettenham, Laurence, of Somerford, co. Chester, *add* [Exemplification of Arms and Grant of Crest, by Sir Gilbert Dethick Garter K. of Arms, Robert Cooke, Clarenceux, and William Flower, Norroy, 9 Feb. 1568 (156$\frac{8}{9}$). Hist. Soc. Lanc. and Chesh., LXII, p. 133.]

Tallow Chandlers' Company, 1546, *add* [Heraldic Exhibition, Edinburgh, plate 5].

Thornicroft, Edward and John, brothers, *after* Norr. *add* III, 327, *and before* Grants IV, fol. 139, *add* [declaration].

[Thornycroft, Edward, of Thornycroft, co. Chester. Exemplification of Arms and Crest by William Ryley, Norroy K. of Arms, 10 Sept. 1651. Hist. Soc. Lanc. and Chesh., LXII, p. 142.]

Tilson, read Tilston, Ralph, of Huxleigh [Huxley], add [Grant of a Crest. Hist. Soc. Lanc. and Chesh., LXIII, p. 206.].

Townsend, Sir Robert, add [Harl. Soc., LXII, p. 183.]

[Trevor, Mark, Visct. Dungannon. Supporters by R. St. George, Ulster K. of Arms, 20 Sept. 1662. Misc. G. et H., 2nd S., IV, p. 89.]

Tristram, Matthew, 29 Aug. 1467, add [Proc. Soc. of Antiq., XVI, p. 341].

Trumbull, William, add [Harl. Soc., LVII, p. 220].

Tupholme, William, add [Misc. G. et H., 4th S., I, p. 41].

Turton, William, add [Harl. Soc., LXII, p. 184.]

Upholders', Craft and Fellowship of, add [Crisp, Fragm. Geneal., XIII, p. 20].

[Valerisi, Aloisius (a Patrician), Ambassador of Venice, 19 Sept. 1624, on his being knighted by the King (James I).]

[Venables, Robert, of Antrobus, co. Chester, now of Chester, attested by W. Flower, Norroy, 1566 and 1580. Hist. Soc. Lanc. and Chesh., LXII, p. 122.]

Venables, Sir Thomas, add [Exemplification and Augmentation. Hist. Soc. Lanc. and Chesh., LX, p. 164. Plate of Arms, LXI, p. 215.].

Vermuyden, Sir Cornelius, add [of Hatfield, co. York, son of Giles Vermuyten, of St. Martin's Dyke, Zealand, of an honorary addition to his Arms] by Sir John Borough [Norroy, 10 July 1629].

Vernon, John, out of Cheshire, add [Patent to, given at London, in Latin. Hist. Soc. Lanc. and Chesh., LXIII, p. 208.].

[Villiers, Major John, of Ireland, from co. Staff. Certificate, 17 Sept. 1647, by W. Roberts, Ulster K. of Arms. Misc. G. et H., 4th S., II, p. 327.]

Warburton, Piers, of Northwich, co. Chester, add [Exemplification in French. Dutton, quartering Warburton and Warburton. Hist. Soc. Lanc. and Chesh., LXIII, p. 210.].

Wedgwood, John [? 1566, ? 9th, or 1576, 19th, Q. Eliz. See Genealogist, XXII, p. 62].

Weld, John, of London, Haberdasher, 28 Jan. 1559, add [Misc. G. et H., 5th S., II, p. 171].

Weldische, William, add [Misc. G. et H., 5th S., I, p. 245].

Westbye, John, add [Hist. Soc. Lanc. and Chesh., LXVIII, p. 196.]

Westbye, John, after late add [?], and after Dalton add [Norroy K. of Arms].

Westfaling, Herbert, add [Crisp, Fragm. Geneal., X, p. 76].

[Wever, of Poole, co. Chester, attested by William Flower, Norroy K. of Arms, and Robert Cooke. Charter Herald (1566). Hist. Soc. Lanc. and Chesh., LXII, p. 128.]

[Weynman, Richard, of Witney, co. Oxf., by Thomas Wriothesley, Garter, 20 Sept. 1509. Misc. G. et H., 5th S., I, p. 287.]

Wharton, Thomas, Lord Wharton, add [23 April 1553. Genealogist, New S., VIII, pp. 127-128.].

[Whichcote, Charles, of Mobberley, co. Chester, attested by Hen. St. George, Richmond Herald of Arms, 1633. Hist. Soc. Lanc. and Chesh., LXII, p. 132.]

Whyte, Thomas, of Fytleford, add [Misc. G. et H., 5th S., II, p. 60].

Wiche or Wyche, Thomas, enter under Wyche, add [Quarterly Arms, Wyche and Brett. Grant of Crest, by William Flower, Norroy K. of Arms, 28 June 1587. Hist. Soc. Lanc. and Chesh., LXIII, p. 214. Brette pedigree, p. 216.].

Wicksteed, John, of Wicksteed, co. Chester, add [Exemplification of Arms and] before Crest, and add at end [Hist. Soc. Lanc. and Chesh., LXII, p. 127].

Wilbraham, Thomas, of Woodhay, co. Chester, add [Grant of Crest, in Latin. Hist. Soc. Lanc. and Chesh., LXIII, p. 212].

[Wilcoxon, of Sproston, co. Chester, attested by Richard St. George, Norroy K. of Arms, 1613. Hist. Soc. Lanc. and Chesh., LXII, p. 131.]

Wilde, John, of Kettleworth, add [Nettleworth], and see Wyld, William.

Wilkinson *alias* Harlyn, *add* [Misc. G. et H., 2nd S., II, p. 200 ; Crisp, Fragm. Geneal., X, p. 77].

Wilkinson, William, of Dorrington ; *for* Sus. *read* Susannah.

Willmott, George, of Letcombe Regis, *add* [Harl. Soc., LVII, p. 230].

Wiseman, Richard, *add* [Medical Times and Gazette, 6 Oct. 1872 ; West London Medical Journal, July 1912].

Wright, Richard, Serg^t at Arms [of Bickley, Cheshire], *add* [Hist. Soc. Lanc. and Chesh., LXIII, p. 213].

Wodeson, Elizabeth, [20 Nov.] 1573.   [*See* Misc. G. et H., 2nd S., I, p. 141.]

Wyche, Thomas, of Davenham, co. Chester, *add* [Hist. Soc. Lanc. and Chesh., LXII, p. 140].

Wynchecombe, John, *add* [Harl. Soc., LVII, p. 233].

Wyrley, Roger de, *after* Berry ; *add* [Wyrley, True use of Arms], *and after* Bell, *add* [1853, p. 24].

Yallop, Sir Robert, *for* Yaldwin *read* Yallop.

Young, Lionel, *add* [Young and Hawking quarterly, 8 May 1558, by Cooke, Clarenceux. Crisp, Fragm. Geneal., XIII, p. 18.].

ADDITIONS AND CORRECTIONS, Vol. II,

Parts I and II.

(Continued from Vol. II, Part I, p. iv.)

Abbot, of Sudbury, *after* 1774-77 *add* [1777].

Abbot, Henry Alexis, *after* 1802-4 *add* [1804].

Abdy, *after* 1848-1851, *add* [1849].

A'Beckett, W. A. Callendar (3rd entry), *after* 1891 *add* [1895].

Abercrombie, Lieut.-Gen. Sir John, *after* 1815-17 *add* [1815].

Abercrombie, Sir Ralph, *after* 1797-180 . . *add* [1797].

Abercrombie [General], Sir Robert, *for* 179 . . *read* [1798].

Abercrombie, Baroness, *after* 1800-2 *add* [1801].

Aberdein to Harvey, *for* 17 . . . *read* [1791].

Abingdon, Countess, *for* 17 . . . *read* [1728].

Abney, *after* 1823-24 *add* [1823].

Accrington, co. Lanc., *after* 1897 *add* [1879].

Acland (Palmer after Fuller), *for* 185 . . *read* [1853].

Acland (Fuller), *for* Vol. LIX *read* Vol. XLIX.

Acton, John, *for* 17 . . *read* [1759].

Acton, Edward William, *after* 1813 *add* [1814].

Acton after Dalberg [1833] *and for* 183 . . *read* [1834].

Adam, John William, *after* 1799 *add* [1801].

Adam James, *after* 1810 *add* [1811].

[Adam, Right Hon. William, Baron of the Exchequer, of Blairadam, 1815. Misc. G. et H., 5th S., I, p. 42].

Adams to Anson [1773 ?], *after* 1804 *add* [1806], *and after* Sambrooke *add* [1806].

Adams, William, M.P., *for* 183 . . *read* [1832], *and after* 1832-3 *add* [1832].

Adams, now Rawson, *after* 1824 *add* [1825].

Adams, late Cuffe, *after* 1843 *add* [1842].

Adams, William Cokayne, *after* 1869 *add* [1868].

Adams, George, *for* 18 . . *read* [1868].

[Adams, Very Rev. Samuel, Dean of Cashel, Confirmation 16 Sept. 1854 (Ulster Office). Misc. G. et H., 5th S., I, p. 41].

Adcock to Hall, *after* 1835 *add* 1836.

Addington, Henry, *after* Sidmouth *add* [12 Jan. 1805], *and for* [1805] *read* [1804].
Addison, Edward, *after* 1786 *add* [1788].
Addison, Samuel, *for* Eccleshill *read* Eccleshall, *and after* 1837 *add* [1838].
A'Deane, late Tucker, *after* 1827 *add* [1824].
Alavoine, *after* fol. 424 *add* [1753].
Albert, Sophia Nancy, *for* Courtail *read* COURTAIL.
Aldridge, John, *after* 1820 *add* 1821.
Aldworth to Neville, *after* 1792 *add* [1797].
Allan, Robert Henry, *after* 1830 *add* [1831], *and for* XXXVII *read* XXXVIII.
Allan after Havelock, *after* 1880 *add* [1882].
Allanson to Winn, *add* [Roy. Lic., 20 Feb. 1777], *and after* Bart. *add* [14 Sept. 1776], *after* York *read* [1777].
Allenby-MONTGOMERY, *after* 1893 *add* [1894].
Allgood, Lancelot, *after* 1750 *add* [1752?].
Alliston, Frederick Pratt, *for* 187 . . *read* [1897].
Allsop, Henry, *read* Allsopp.
Alt, Henry, *after* 1749 *add* [1747].
Amherst after Tyssen, *for* 188 . . *read* [1867].
Anderson, James, *after* 1789 *add* [1788].
Andrews, Biggs, *for* 183 . . *read* [1840].
Angell, late Brown, *after* 1800 *add* [1801].
Antonie after Lee, *for* 182 . . *read* [1817].
Antrim, Earl of, *for* McDonald *read* MacDONNELL [Roy. Lic., 27 June 1836], *and after* 1835 *add* [1836].
Arcedukne *read* Arcedeckne.
Archer-Burton, *after* 1834 *add* [1835].
Armistead, Rev. John, *after* 1799 *add* [1797].
Ashby, late Lathom, *read* Latham, *for* 180 . . *read* [15 July 1807].
Ashby, late Bernard, *after* M. H. A. *read* [Nicholas Herman Ashby].
Asgill, *after* Bart. *add* [16 April 1761] *and before* Vol. XXXII *add* [1820] [1761 is Vol X].
Ashbourne, Baron, *for* Gilson *read* Gibson.
Ashenhurst, *for* co. Derby *read* co. Stafford.
[Aspinwall, of Hale, co. Lanc., quartering to Blackburne, 1803. *See* Blackburne, John, F.R.S.]
Assheton-Smith, *for* Carmarthen *read* Carnarvon.
Aston to Pudsey, Thomas Peach, *read* 2nd line (and [1847] Vol. XLVIII, fol. 269, John).
Atkins *before* Bowyer, *for* LXI *read* XLI.
Atkins-Roberts, *before* fol. 58 *add* [1883].
[Auden, Rev. Thomas, M.A., F.S.A., Vicar of Condover, Shropshire, and Prebendary of Lichfield, and to the descendants of his father William Auden, of Rowley Regis, co. Stafford, 10 Nov. 1905].
Baker, Richard, of Westbrook, *for* 17 . . . *read* [1840].
Ball-Hughes, Edward, *for* 329 *read* 239.
Dykes-Ballantyne-Dykes, *for* 17 . . . *read* [1800].
Baltimore, Baron, *for* Calvert *read* CALVERT, ? this entry. *See* Calvert in Vol. I.
Banks, Rev. Frederick [grant 1850] *for* 185 . . *read* [1852].
Barker, late Cragg, *for* 17 . . . *read* [1833].
Barker after Darling, *dele* [?] *after* fol. 68.
Barlow, Sir George H., *add* [1806] *before* Vol. XXIV, fol. 45.
Barnard, Gilbert Vane, Baron, *after* 27 Sept. *add* [?].
Barrett, Susannah, *read* dau. [of Henry], of London, Merchant, and wife of Sir Justinian Isham, Bart. Edmondson and Berry [give] azure, &c., as printed *for* or *read* proper.
Barretto, *after* 1813 *add* [1812].
Bartlett, William, *add* [1882, fol.] *before* 326.
Baskerville before Mynors, *after* 1818 *add* [1817 ?].

Baskerville, Col. Thomas, *for* Evenglode *read* Evenlode.
Bass, *for* Sir M. I. *read* Sir M. T.
Bassett, late Davie, *for* Beninharbor *read* Berry Narbor.
Bateman, late Buckley, *read* Buckby [Rev. John].
[Beck, Peter Arthur, of Trelydan Hall, co. Montgomery, 18 . . .].
Bedford to Edwards, *add* [*see* Edwards].
Bedford, John, *for* Oughtsbridge *read* Oughtibridge.
Bellairs, [or Bellaers, Abel Walford], *after* 1782 *add* Vol. XV, fol. 26.
Bensley, William, *for* X, p. 32, *read* X, p. 82.
Berkeley before Calcott, *for* 182 . . *read* [1826].
Best, Sarah, *after the date add* [Vol. XLI, fol. 21].
Beswicke-Royds, *for* 186 . . *read* [1820] ; *and for* (? LVII, fol. 155) *read*
    ([1869] ? LVII, fol. 155) ; *delete the comma after* Clement.
Bethell, late Codrington, Christopher, ? *for* late *read* before ; Roy. Lic., 17 Nov. 1797.
Bethell, late Codrington, *add* [? William John, Roy. Lic., 12 Mar. 1798].
Bettesworth before [to Bettesworth-]Trevanion, *for* John F. Purnel *read* John
    T. Purnell.
Bewicke-Capley, R. C. A., *read* Copley.
Bewicke-Capley, late Anderson, *read* Copley ; *for* Calverley Berwicke *read*
    Calverley Bewicke.
Biandos, *add* [1873] *before* Vol. LVIII.
Bickerton, *after* XXIII *add* [? 1815, Vol. XXIX].
Birch, Samuel, *before* Vol. XX *add* [1800].
Birkenhead, Borough of, *add* [Hist. Soc. Lanc. and Chesh., XLII, p. 13].
Birt (and Stayner, his wife), *after* 1844 *add* [1843].
Bischoffsheim, *for* 185 . . *read* [1860 ?].
Biscoe, Anne, *after* 1829 *add* [1830].
Bishop, James, *for* 181 . . *read* [1810].
Bisse, *for* 182 . . *read* [1831].
Black, *after* 1819 *add* [1809].
Blackburn, John, F.R.S., *read* Blackburne ; *for* Greeve *read* Green [Green and
    Aspinwall quarterings granted] ; *for* 18 . . *read* [11 May 1803] ; *and add*
    [Genealogist, XXXIV, p. 87].
Blackman, George, *before* 1803 *add* [16 May], *and add* [Genealogist, New S.,
    XXII, fol. 156].
Blair, *place a full point after* design (designation).
Blicke, Sir Charles, Knt., *after* 1809 *add* [1811].
Blomfield, late Mason, *after* Norf. *add* [1836].
Blomfield, Elizabeth, *after* 1797 *add* [1798].
Blunt, Robert, *after* 1850 *add* [1853 ?].
Boase, Henry, *for* 180 . . *read* [1810].
Bolton, Capt., *for* 184 . . *read* [1851].
[Booker, Frank William, of Nottingham. Grant of Arms, 1906. (*See* Phillimore's
    County Pedigrees of Nottinghamshire, p. 123).]
Booker, Thomas William, *for* Gansrew *read* Janarew ; *for* Velindia *read* Velindra ;
    add the date [18 Aug. 1855] ; *and add at the end* [On 18 Sept. 1855, License
    to use the Arms of Blakemore and Booker quarterly].
Boord, *for* Sir J. W. *read* Sir T. W.
Borthwick before Gilchrist, *after* Arms *add* [1806].
Borwick, *in both delete the* ? *after* fol. 141.
Boswall, *delete the* ? *before* 1847.
Bottomley, *for* 184 . . *read* [1851].
Bourne, Ralph, *after* 1815 *add* [1816].
Boustead, *for* 184 . . *read* [1850].
Bovey, *after* Camb. *add* [1712].
Bowdon, Richard Catlow, *after* 1840 *add* [1842].
Bowdon-Butler, *before* Vol. XLV *add* [1841].
Bowman, formerly Coates, *add* [Charles].

Boycott, *after* 1844 *add* [1843].
[Brace, Frauk Addison, of Doverbridge Hall, co. Derby. Confirmation about 1896.]
Bracebridge, *for* Ansley *read* Anstey.
Bradford, Baron, *for* Bridgman *read* Bridgeman.
[Bradbrooke, Dr. W . . . ., of Bletchley, Bucks., to the descendants of his grand-father, 1912].
Bradney, Ellen, *for* Pem *read* Penn.
Bradney, J. A., *for* Llanfiliangel *read* Llanfihangel.
[Braham, Sir Richard, of New Windsor, Berks., by Sir Edward Walker, Garter K. of Arms. 10 June 1646. Harl. Soc., LVII, p. 81.]
Braikenridge, *for* 182 . . *read* [1830].
Brawston, *for* 17 . . . *read* [1801].
Braybrooke, Baron [1788], Aldworth to Neville [? 1762], Berks., [1797] Vol. XX, fol. 47.
Braybrooke, Baron, Neville, *for* 179 . . *read* [1797] Vol. XX, fol. 50.
Brettel-Vaughan, *for* Braiufield *read* Bromfield.
Brettingham, *for* 17 . . *read* [1801].
Brewin, *add* [Ambrose].
Brickdale, John, *after* 1765 *add* [1766] *and after* Bromley *add* [1768].
Britton, *after* Vol. LXIX *add* [1896] *and after* 195 *insert* [19 June 1897].
Brock after Clutton, *after* 1809 *add* [1810].
Brock, Maj.-Gen., *after* 1813 *add* [1812 ?].
Brockholes, *after* 1782 ? *add* [1783].
Brograve, *after* 1830 *add* [1831].
Bromilow, David, *for* Bittesworth *read* Bitteswell.
Bromley after Davenport, Rev. Walter, *for* Ullerton *read* Ellaston.
Brooke, Rev. John, *after* George *add* [1788].
Brooke, (Sir) Thomas [Bart. 1899], *and for* 187 . . *read* [1871].
Brookes before Kemp, *for* 188 . . *read* [1839].
Brookfield, *after* 1872 *add* [1877] *and for* Berry's *read* Burke's.
Brooksbanke, William Lyon, *for* Berry's *read* Burke's.
Browell, *after* 1830 *add* [1831].
Brown, late Candler, *after* 1804 *add* [1803].
Brown (late Robinson), *for* 180 . . *read* [1810].
Brown to Trotter, *after* 1869 *add* [1868].
Browne, Thomas, of London, *after* 1724 *add* [172⅝].
Browne, late Eaton, Rev. Richard, *after* 1845 *add* [1844 ?].
Browne before Wylde, Ralph, *before* 1788 *add* [26 Mar.] *and* [Misc. G. et H., 2nd S., IV, p. 180].
Browne before Mill, *for* Cariaçon *read* Cariacou.
Browne, William James, *after* Australia *add* [1858].
Brownsword, *after* 1747 *add* [1748] *and after* and *add* [174⅜ ?].
Bryan, ..., co. Camb., *for* 172 . . *read* [1730].
Brydges, Samuel Egerton, *after* [24 Dec.] *before* 1814 *and after* *add* [1815] ; *at end add* [Chandos Peerage Case, 1834, Appx., p. xxvii].
Buckley, Edmund, *after* 1863 *add* [1864].
Buckley, formerly Peck, *after* 1863 *add* [1864].
Bulkeley after Warren, *for* Beaumoris *read* Beaumaris.
Bulkeley after Williams, *after* 1827] *add* [1826 ?].
Buller-Manningham, *for* Dilborne *read* Dilhorn.
Bullock, late Watson, *for* 180 . . *read* [1810].
Bulmer, *for* 180 . . *read* [1824].
Bunny, now Hartopp, [1778, Vol. XIV ?] and Hurlock, his wife, of Freeby, co. Leic. (? Newark), [Hartopp and Cradock quarterly, and Hurlock on an Escutcheon of Pretence, 1796] Vol. XIX, fol. 249.
Burchardt-Ashton, F., *for* 285-311 *read* ? 285 and 311.
Burnett, Sir Robert, *for* 180 . . *read* [1811].
Burridge, Robert, *after* 1700 *add* [1701].

Burridge, William, *for* 17 .. *read* [1801].
Burrows, Henry William, *for* Berry's *read* Burke's.
Burton, Bartholomew, *after* 1696 *add* [1697].
Burton (Sir Richard), *for* 182 .. *read* [1810].
Burton, Archer, *after* 1834 *add* [1835].
Burton, Mrs. Catherine Sophia, *for* Longnor *read* Longner.
Butcher to Pemberton, *after* Nottingham *add* [1842].
Butterworth to Freeman, *for* 182 .. *read* [1831].
Byrom, late Fox, *after* 1870 *add* [1871].
Calcott after Berkeley, *for* 181 .. *read* [1826].
Caldwell, ..., of Linley Wood, *for* 183 .. *read* [1840].
Calvert, Lieut.-Gen., *after* 1815 *add* [1816].
Cameron, Col., *after* 1815 *add* [1816].
Campbell, Marchioness Grey, *for* 174 .. *read* [1753 ?].
Campbell, Sir John, *for* 174 .. *read* [1753].
Campbell, Sir Archibald, *for* 182 .. *read* [1831].
Campion to Coates, *for* 178 .. *read* [1790].
Cann after Skoulding, *after* 1866 *add* [1867].
[Cape of Good Hope, Colony of, 29 May 1876. Geneal. Mag., IV, p. 185.]
[Cape Town, City of, 29 Dec. 1899. Geneal. Mag., IV, p. 156.]
Carew, George Henry, *after* 1810 *add* [1811].
Carew after Hallowell, *read* [1828], Sir Benjamin, K.C.B. [1815], of co. Surrey,
   [1828] Vol. XXXVII, fol. 176; [G.C.B., 6 June 1831]. Supporters,
   [1831, Vol. XXXVIII ?] fol. 239.
Carleton, late Metcalfe, *for* 178 .. *read* [1791].
Carlyon (*see* Britton), *after* LXIX *add* [1896] *and after* 195 and *insert*
   [19 June] 1897.
Carter, John Robert, *read* (s. of John, Superintendent of Sandhurst).
Carteret, Baron, *after* 171½] *add* [1715].
Cartwright, late Cobb, *after* 1865 *add* [1866].
Caton, John, *after* Bastwick *add* [Woodbastwick].
Cecil, Baron, Countess of Exeter, *for* 179 .. *read* [5 April 1794]; ? *delete* Baron;
   and add [*See* Shropshire Arch. Trans., 4th Ser., IV, p. 381].
Cecil, Mary, *for* 180 .. *read* [1810].
Chafy, William W., *after* 1868 *add* [1869].
Chambers, John, *for* 187 .. *read* [1869].
Chapman, William, of Skegness, *add* [Misc. G. et H., 4th S., II, p. 196].
Chapman to Yapp, *after* fol. 183 *add* [1839].
Chappel, *for* 184 .. *read* [1844 or 1845].
Charlton, late Lechmere, Nicholas, *after* 1st Feb. *add* [? 3rd Feb.]
Charters. *See* Garvis [not entered].
Chatteris, William, *after* 1826 *add* [1831], of Brasenose Coll. [in] 1826 ?.
Chauncey after Snell, *after* 1783 *add* [1781].
Checkland, *add* [George, and Millicent, dau. of John Taylor].
Chetham before Strode, *after* 1808 *add* [1811].
Childe, late Baldwin, William, *read* of Kinlet, Shropsh.
Chiswell, formerly Muilman, *after* 1772 or 3 *add* [1772].
Cholmley, late Strickland, *after* 1865 *add* 1858 [Vol. LV ? for 1865].
Cholmondeley to Owen, *for* Condone Park *read* Condover Park.
Christy, William Miller, *after* 1855 *add* [1854].
Church after Pearce, *at the end read* [1846] fol. 178.
Churchward (Dimond-), *for* 189 .. *read* [1859].
Clarges after Hare, *after* co. Glouc. *add* [1843].
Clark (*see* Bellairs), *add* [Susanna Walford, late wife of John Clark, of London
   (her descendants). Walford quartering, 9 Mar. 1782 (*see* Genealogist, New S.
   XXII, p. 157).].
Clark, Henry, *after* 1857 *add* [1858].
Clark, quartered by David Milligan, *after* 1775 *add* [1774].

Clarke, David Ross, for 185 .. read [1860].

[Clarke, William, of Cork, Ireland, by Ulster K. of Arms, 4 June 1804. Misc. G. et H., 4th S., V, p. 65.]

Clay, Charles, for 185 .. read [1860 ?].

Clifton, now Burton, after co. Linc. add [1821].

Clifton, widow of Tabor, for 185 .. read [1852 or 1853].

Clifton, late Markham, after 1869 add [1870 ?].

Clifton-Hastings-Campbell, after 1896 add [1895 ?].

Climenson, for 185 .. read [1860 ?].

Clinton-Pelham, Major-Gen., for [1815] read [1813] and after Supporters add [1814].

Clydesdale, for 180 .. read [1810].

Coape to Coape Arnold, after LXX add [1898 ; ? 1867, Vol. LVI].

Cock, John, D.D., after 1796 add [1795].

Cockburn after Kidney, for Gamley read Gumley.

Cockburn after Ker, M.A., of Norton-in-Hales and Bellaport, Shropsh. [1833], Vol. XXXIX, fol. 298. [See Cokburne.]

Coham, William H. B., after 1845 add [1844 ?].

Coldwell to Thicknesse, add [Francis Henry], for 18 .. read [1859] and [see Burke's Landed Gentry].

Cole, now Tudor, before fol. 316 insert [1799].

Coleman to Proctor, for Monmouth read Montgomery.

Coles, James, for 183 .. read [1840].

Collins to Bury, for 17 ... read [1800].

Collins-Trelawney [1838 ?] and after 1839 add [1838].

Colvin, after London add [1818].

Colyear-Dawkins, add [Crisp, Fragm. Geneal., XIII, p. 23].

Combe, late Maddison, after 1850 read [1849].

Corner, after London add [1850].

Coningsby, Vicountess, after 1716* add [1717].

Conyngham to Denison, for 184 .. read [1849] and after Supporters add [1850].

Cooke, William, after 1812 add [1814].

Corbet, late D'Avenant, for 178 .. read 1786, and after Vol. XV. add [XVI ?].

Cosserat, Bernard, after 1729 add [17 $\frac{29}{30}$].

Cotton, add Combermere after Baron, after Supporters for 18 .. read [1830].

Courtenay (see Jackson), for 177 .. read [1780].

Cradock-Hartop (late Bunny), for Harlock read Hurlock and add Bart. after Edmund.

Craggs [before Eliot, Roy. Lic. dat. 15 April 1789], and before Vol. XVII add [1789].

Cradock, late Grove, before 1849 add [Roy. Lic., 22 May].

[Crawfurd, George, of Thornwood, co. Lanark, 9 April 1864 (Scotch grant).]

Crawley (-Boevey), for 179 .. read [1789].

Croker, of co. Oxf., add [1775] before Vol. XXX.

Cropper, Edward, after 1872* add [1873].

Cropper after Thornburgh, after 1874 add [1876].

Cross, John, of Hollybank. [The Grant was made to John Cross, of Staple Inn, co. Middx., and to the descendants of his father, William Cross, of Holly Bank, Pontesbury, Shropsh., dated 15 May 1865.]

[Crowe. See Marlowe.]

Cumming, George, after 1840 add [1843 ?].

Cunliffe-Offley, for 182 .. read [1830 ?].

Currey, Robert, for LXVII read XLVII.

Curtis, Richard Arthur F., for 182 .. read [1830].

Cust, Baron Brownlow, before fol. 295 add [1777].

Cutts, John, after 1692 add [1690].

De Costa, read Da Costa, Leonor, for 172 .. read 172$\frac{3}{4}$.

Dalgety, for 186 .. read [1870].

Dalton to Norcliffe, [Aug. 1807], *and after* York *add* [1808].
Daniel, C. Tyssen-Amherst, *after* and *insert* [1867].
Darby, of Sunniside, *after* 1835 *add* [1836].
D'Arcy, *for* 172 .. *read* [172$\frac{6}{7}$].
Darley, late Wilks, *after* and *add* [1807].
Darlington, *for* [1722] *read* [6 April 1722] *and after* Supporters *add* [172$\frac{2}{3}$].
Darnell, *after* [21 Dec. 1832] *add* [1833].
Dartinequinave, *after* 1720 *add* [1710], Vol. VI is 1720.
Darwin, late Rhodes, *for* 184 .. *read* [1850].
Dashwood, Sir Henry W., *before* fol. 174 *add* [1884].
[Daval, quartering to Burr, 13 June 1821. Misc. G. et H., New S., III, pp. 156 and 157.]
Davenport-Bromley, *for* Baggington, co. Derby, *read* Bagginton, co. Warw.
Davenport-Handley, *add* [Genealogist, VII, p. 23].
[Davis, quartering to Burr, 13 June 1821. Misc. G. et H., New S., III, pp. 156 and 157.]
Davison, John, B.D., *for* 180 .. *read* [1819].
Daw, *after* 1781 *add* [1783].
Dawkins, James, *after* 173$\frac{3}{4}$ *add* [1734].
Dawson, Betty Anne, *for* 177 .. *read* [1780].
Dawson before Lambton, *after* 1815 *add* [1814].
Dawson, Baker, *for* 183 .. *read* [1840].
Dawson, Christopher H., *before* fol. 162 *add* [1867 ?].
De Coussmaker, *for* [1798] *read* [1779].
De Eresby, *delete the* ? *after* 1829.
De Killi Kelby, *the* [?] *refers to the reference to* Kelby.
Derwent, Baron, *after* 1882* *add* [1881].
Derwentwater, Earl of, *read* fol. 212 or [1697] 232.
Des Bouverie, *after* 1695 *add* [1694 ?].
Devas, of Newgate Street, *after* 1812 *add* [1811].
De Windt, *for* 184 .. *read* [1851].
Dimsdale, Baron Thomas Robert, *after* 1829 *add* [1830].
Dinevor, Baroness [1782] (Rice), *and for* [1782] *read* [1784].
Dipple, *after* Vol. IV *add* [VIII ?], Vol. IV is 1688 to 1700.
Dixon-Nuttall, *for* 185 .. *read* [1860].
Dobede, *for* 1830 *read* [1836].
Dobree, William, *after* 1726 *add* [1718 ?].
Dominick, Andrew, *for* co. Hertf. *read* Hampsh. *and add* [Crisp, Fragm. Geneal., V, p. 59].
Douglas, late Mackenzie, *after* 1831 *add* [1833].
Downes (*see* Jackson), *for* 182 .. *read* [1830].
Drake (*see* White-Beighton), *for* 182 .. *read* [1830].
Drax (Erle-), *after* 1828 *add* [1829].
Drinkwater, Sir William Leece, Knt., *after* Isle of Man *add* [24 April].
Ducie (Moreton, late Reynolds), *after* 1771] *read* [1772] *and before* fol. 63 *read* [1771].
Dudley, Lord, *read* [Ferdinando Dudley] (Lea).
Dugdale, Sir John, *after* 1698 *add* [?].
Dugdale, William, *after* 1698 *add* [1699].
Duncan, Admiral Adam, *read* Supporters [1798] *before* Vol. XX.
Duncan (Beveridge-) [1798 ?], James.
Dunell, *before* fol. 305 *add* [1812].
Duppa, late Lloyd, *for* Wistanston *read* Wistanstow.
Dykes-Ballantine-Dykes, *after* 1799 *add* [1800].
Dymoke after Wells, *after* 1866 *add* [1867].
Eamer, Sir John, *after* 1808 *add* [1809].
Earle, ..., of Lacells, *for* 1 ... *read* [1730].
Earle, Hardman, *read* Sir Hardman.

Eastwood, George, *after* 1747 *add* [1748].

Edgcumbe, *for* [Earl of Mount Edgcumbe, 31 Aug. 1789] *read* [Baron Edgcumbe, of Mount Edgcumbe, 20 April 1742].

Edwardes (Hope-), *after* S. F. *add* [St. Leger Frederick] *and for* 186 . . *read* [1871].

Edwards after Williams, *for* 182 . . *read* [1819].

Edwards, of Ruthen, *for* 185 . . *read* [1849].

Edwards, Thomas, *after* 1832 *add* [1833].

Edwards, Richard, *for* Frimbley *read* Trimpley.

Ellenborough, *after* 1889 ? *add* [1890].

Elliott, John Lettsom, *for* 184 . . *read* [1850].

Ellis, of Sunning Hill, *for* 180 . . *read* [1810].

Ellis, Baron Howard de Walden, *delete the* ? *after* [1810] *and add* Misc. G. et H., New S., I, p. 187.

Ellis after Joyner, *for* 1813 *read* 1817.

Embleton-Fox, of Northoppe, *after* 1860 *add* [1862].

Emerson to Amcotts, *for* 183 . . *read* [1854].

England, Sir Richard, *delete* ? *after* [1843].

Esmead, *add* [? MICHELL-ESMEAD *after* MOORE].

Estcourt after Sotheron, *after* 1853 *add* 1855.

Estlen, *for* 180 . . *read* [1810].

Evans, Evan, *after* 1861 *add* [1864].

Evans, Edward, *after* 1864* *add* [1866] *and* [Powys-Land Club, IX, p. 426].

Evershed, *after* 1696 *add* [189$\frac{9}{7}$?].

Every, [Sir Henry], *after* Somerset *add* 1804 or 1805.

Farley after Turner, *after* 1827 *read* [1828 ?].

Farmer, Joseph (Harley), not quarterly. [Arms for Harley, to Caroline, dau. of Edward Harley, wife of Joseph Farmer.]

Farmer-(Haywood), *after* 1871 *read* [1872].

Farquharson, of Scotland, *for* XXXIV *read* XXIV.

Faudel-Phillipps, (Sir) George, *for* Pond *read* Park.

Fawsitt, late Wetherell, *for* 182 . . *read* [1831].

Fawsitt after Ferguson, *after* 1866 *add* [1867 ?].

Fazakerley, late Gillibrand, *for* 182 . . *read* [1830].

Fellowes to Benyon, *after* 1854 *add* [1855].

Fenwick before Stuart, *for* 180 . . *read* [1816 ?].

Ferrers, Henry F. (formerly Croxon), *for* Pentraheylin *read* Pentreheylin.

Fetherstonhaugh, late Smallwood, *after* 1797] *read* [1798 ?].

Feversham, Lord, *delete the comma after* Baron.

Field, Jane Ann Elizabeth, *after* 1815 *add* [1816].

Fielder, *for* 182 . . *read* [1830].

Fisher, John, *for* Foremonk *read* Foremark ?.

Fisher, John, Bishop of Salisbury, *after* 1812 *add* [1811].

Fisher, Joseph, *after* 1730 *add* [1720].

Fisher, of Laxfield, *for* 180 . . *read* [1810].

Fitz-Patrick, *for* OSSORRY *read* OSSORY.

Fleetwood after Hesketh, *after* co. Lanc. *add* [1831].

Fletcher, Thomas, *for* Besley *read* Betley.

Fletcher, John, *after* 173½ *add* [1732 ?].

Fletcher-Twemlow, *for* Pilmaston *read* Pitmaston.

Fletcher, Thomas William, of Handsworth. [*The entry should read*, of Dudley, co. Worc., and to the descendants of his father, Thomas Fletcher, of Handsworth, co. Staff., 29 May 1835, Vol. XLI, fol. 26.]

Floyd, *for* 180 . . *read* [1810].

Foljambe. *See* Hawkesbury.

Forrester after Weld, *read* Forester *and for* Dosthill *read* Dothill *and* Willey, Shropsh., *not* co. Warw.

Foster, George, *after* 1703 *add* [170$\frac{2}{3}$].

Foster to Baird, *delete the ? after* 233.
Foster, Ebenezer, *after* 1851 *add* [1849].
Foster, William (s. of Thomas), of Boston, New England [now resident in London; and to the descendants of the said Thomas], *for* Hinde *read* Hurd, [*see* Hurd], *and for* 178 .. *read* [7 April 1783].
Fowler to Leeves, *for* 180 .. *read* [1810].
Fownes to Somerville, *for* 182 .. *read* [1831].
Fox after Embleton, *after* 1860 *read* [1862].
Fox after Embleton, William, *after* 1874 *read* [1877].
France, late Hayhurst, *after* 1796 *add* [1795].
France-Hayhurst, Col. Charles, *after* 1869 *add* [1870 ?].
Frean, *for* 186 .. *read* [1870].
Freind, Rev. William Maximilian, *after* 1800 *add* [1802].
Freman, late Button, *for* 182 .. *read* [1831].
Friend, of Magdalen Coll., Oxf., *after* 1813 *add* [1814].
Frost, Sir Thomas Gibbons; Francis Aylmer and Robert, of Lime Grove, Chester, *for* 186 .. *read* [1871].
Fructuozo, *for* 182 .. *read* [1830].
Fuller-Meyrick, Augustus ?, *after* 1825 *read* [1826].
Gamon, (Sir) Richard, *after* 1795 *add* [1794].
Gardiner after Smythe, *after* 1798 *add* [1797].
Gardner, Cecil, *for* 184 .. *read* [1850].
Gardner, late Panting, Robert, *to read* of Leighton, Wellington, Shropsh.
Garthwaite, Edward, *add* [Crisp, Fragm. Geneal., II, p. 21].
Gascoigne after Oliver, *for* 180 .. *read* [1810].
Gaskell, of Chalfont St. Peter, *for* 180 .. *read* [1822].
Gaulis, *after* 1793 *add* [1794 ?].
Geary, Francis, *for* 178 .. *read* [18 Nov. 1782. *See* Shropsh. Arch. Trans., 3rd S., IX, p. 354].
Gee to Gibb, of London, *for* 184 .. *read* [1850].
Gibbons, Rev. Bery John, *to read* Rev. Benjamin, of Poollands, Hartlebury, co. Worc. (M.A., Wadham Coll., Oxford), [15 June 1871].
[Gillibrand, late Hawarden, Thomas, of Appleton and Liverpool, co. Lanc., Surname and Arms only. Roy. Lic., 17 May 1779. Genealogist, XXXIII, p. 233.]
Gillibrand to Fazakerley, Henry Hawarden *add* [Name and Arms of Fazakerley only. Roy. Lic., 6 May 1814, Arms of Fazakerley and Gillibrand quarterly. Genealogist, XXXIII, p. 236].
Girdlestone, *add* [Rev. John]; *after* Camb. *add* [and of Walpole, co. Norf.]; *for* 180 .. *read* [1809].
Girdlestone, Samuel, *add* [Q.C., of the Middle Temple, London, and to the descendants of his grandfather, Zurishaddi Girdlestone, date of Grant 1840 ? *See* General Notes on the Girdlestone Family, p. 54].
Gitton, Thomas, *to read* of Bridgnorth, Clee St. Margaret and Norton, Shropsh.
Glenesk, Baron, *after* 1896 *read* [1895].
Goodrich, Sir Henry, *add* [Misc. G. et H., 2nd S., II, p. 248].
Goodson, (Thomas ?), *after* 1852 *read* [1854].
[Gore, quartering, *see* Underwood, 15 Mar. 1831].
Gough, Viscount, *after* 1849] *add* [1850].
Grant, Charles, *for* 182 .. *read* [1830].
Granville, George, *before* fol. 211 *add* [171$\frac{4}{5}$].
Granville, late Dewes, *after* 1826 *add* [1827].
Gratwick after Kinleside, *after* 1823 *add* [1822].
Grave, Rev. William Cecil, *for* Quickerwood *read* Quickswood.
Gray, late Hunter, *for* 184 .. *read* [1851].
Gray, of Brafferton, *for* 185 .. *read* [1868 ?].
[Green, of Childwall, co. Lanc., quartering to Blackburne. *See* Blackburne, John, F.R.S.]
Gregory after Welby, *before* fol. 178 *add* [1861].

Gregory, Capt. William, *for* 186 . . *read* [1870].
Grevis before James, *for* [1817] *read* [1818].
Griffiths, ..., of Broomhall, Shropsh., *not* Broomhead.
Grimshaw after Atkinson, *after* 1877 *add* [1878].
Grindall, *after* allusion) *add* [1817].
Grosvenor, Erle-Drax, *delete* [? Vol. XXVII].
Grout, Joseph, *for* Buckeridge *read* Puckeridge.
Guest, Lord Ivor, *delete the* ? *after* [1838].
Guise, Lieut.-Gen. Sir John W., *after* 1863 *add* [1862].
Gurteen, *for* 185 . . *read* [1860 ?].
Guy, Thomas, Executors of. [Grant of Arms, Crest, Supporters and Motto to Guy's Hospital (?), by John Anstis, Garter K. of Arms, 24 May 1725, with permission to set these Arms, Crest and Motto on the Monument of the late Thomas Guy.]
Gwydir, Baron, *delete the* ? *before* [1796].
Haffenden (Wilson-), *after* 1872 *add* [1871].
Hale, Thomas Jacob John, *delete the* ? *after* [1827].
Hamlet [Thomas], *after* 1816] *add* [1815].
Hammett, Richard, *after* 1790 *add* [1791].
Hammond, Baron [5th Mar. 1874], *and delete* [5 March] *after* Supporters.
Hanbury after Bateman, *for* fol. 53 *read* fol. 58 *and delete* [? Vol. XLII].
Hancock to Liebenrood [14 Jan. 1865], *and before* Vol. LV *add* [1865].
Hanson, William Henry, *for* 182 . . *read* [1831].
Hardy, Edward, *for* 184 . . *read* [1850].
Harley, late Bickersteth, *delete the* ? *after* [1853].
Harris, Joseph, *to read of* Westcotes, St. Mary, Leicester.
Harris, Alfred, of Oxton Hall, *after* 1878 *add* [1877].
Harris, Alfred, *read* (Descendants of Samuel Harris ; London, 1878).
Harrison, *for* William Bealy *read* William Bealey.
Harrison, William Bealy, *after* 1899 *add* [1897].
Harrop after Hulton [8 Dec. 1866], *and after* Lanc. *delete* 8 Dec. *and read* [1866], Vol. LVI, fol. 158.
Harthill *should be* Hartill.
Harvey, John Springett, *after* 1802 *add* [1803].
[Harwarden, Thomas, of Appleton and Liverpool, co. Lanc. Surname and Arms of Gillibrand only. Roy Lic., 17 May 1779. Genealogist, XXXIII, p. 233.]
Hasell, Edward, *after* 1699 *add* [1698].
Hasledine, William, Mayor of Shrewsbury [1836], *and for* 183 . . *read* [1838].
Hatfield, late Harter, *for* 180 . . *read* [1816].
Hayne, John (s. of John), *for* (XX, fol. 300 ?) *read* ([1799] Vol. XX, fol. 300 ?).
Heathcote, Sir Gilbert, *after* 1709 *add* [1708].
Heathcote after Unwin, *for* Sheephall *read* Shephall.
Heathcote-Hacker, *delete the* ? *after* [1819].
[Heber-Percy, Algernon, to Alice Charlotte Mary, wife of, and only child of Frederick Lockwood, decd. Arms for Lockwood, 14 Feb. 1908.]
Herrick after Perry, *for* co. Linc. *read* co. Leic.
[Herries, Robert, of Rotterdam, from Scotland, 19 Dec. 1747. Lyon Register. Misc. G. et H., 4th S., IV, p. 301.]
Hervey, page 180, line 1, *for* 180 . . *read* [1810].
Hickman, Sir Alfred, *for* Goldtham *read* Goldthorn.
Hill, Baron Berwicke, *read* Berwick.
Hill, Edward Smith, *delete the* ? *after* [1863].
Hill after Clegg, *delete the* ? *after* 1875 ; *add* [Grant of the Arms of Hill and Clegg quarterly, and Crest for Clegg, 17 April 1875], *and for* 157, the page in the Genealogist, *read* 156.
Hill, late Lowe, *for* Court Hill *read* Court of Hill.
Hillersden, late Grove, *for* [?] *after* S. *read* [Surrey].
Hillyar, Rear-Adm., *for* 183 . . *read* [1840].

Hinckes, *for* H. J. *read* H. T., *and for* Ralph I. *read* Ralph T.

Hind, John (s. of Jacob), *delete the whole entry and see* Hurd.

Hindlip, Baron, *for* [Alsopp] *read* Allsopp.

Hippisley, Bart., *delete the ? after* [1797].

Hirons, late Brewerton, *delete the ? after* [1827].

Hoadly, Benjamin, D.D., *after* 1715 *add* [171⁴⁄₆].

Hodgetts, John, of Prestwood, in the parish of Swinford Regis, co. Staff. (High Sheriff of the said county, 1765), [and to the descendants of his late father, John Hodgetts, of Shute End, in the parish aforesaid, co. Staff.], *for* 26 Oct. *read* 6 Oct. *and add* [Mis. G. et H., 5th S., II, p. 259].

Hoggins, Sarah, *after* Shropsh. *read* [Arms to her and], *at the end add* [Shropsh. Arch. Trans., 4th S., IV, p. 381].

Holbrow, John, *after* King's Stanley *read* [son of William Holbrow, of Uley, and grandson of John Holbrow, of Kingscote, all in co. Glouc. (*delete* Kingscite). Grant to him and the descendants of his grandfather, 8 Feb. 1787 (Copy of Grant, Phillimore's Family of Holbrow, p. 7.)].

Holden, *for* E. J. *read* E. T., *and for* Glenaly *read* Glenelg.

Holles, Baron Pelham, *for* [14 May 1762] *read* [17 Nov. 1768] ; *for* 17 . . *read* [1768] *and delete* [? X].

Hollinshead after Brock, *for* [180 . .] *read* [1802 ?] *and before* fol. 359 *insert* [1804].

Holmes, John, of Bombay C. S., *delete the ? after* [1831].

[Homer, John Twigg, of Sedgeley, co. Staff., J.P., and to the descendants of his grandfather, Charles Kemp Homer, deceased, 27 Feb. 1912. *See* Burke's Landed Gentry, 1914.]

Homfray to Addenbrooke, *delete the ? after* [1795].

Hood, Baroness, *delete the ? after* [1796].

Hope, Lieut.-Gen. [Hon.] Sir John, *delete the ? after* [1810].

Hope, Lieut.-Gen. [Hon.] Sir Alexander, *delete the ? after* [1814].

Hope, ..., of Netley, *add* [Thomas Henry].

Hope-Edwardes, *delete the ? after* [1871].

Hornby, Rev. Hugh, *delete the ? after* [1846].

Hornyold, late Gandolfi, *delete the ? after* [1859].

Horton, Anne, *after* 1725 *add* [172⁶⁄₇] *and delete* [? 333].

Houblon, Sir John, Knt., *delete the ? after* [1819].

Howe, Baroness, *delete the ? after* [1799].

Huggett, late Towle, *delete the ? after* [1851].

Hughes, late Whitelock, *for* Hoddesden *read* Hoddesdon, *and delete the ? after* [1795].

Hughes, Rev. Hugh, *for* [1829 ?] *read* [1830].

Hulse, ..., *delete the ? after* [1803].

Hungerford, late Walker, *for* [1788] *read* [1789].

Hunt to Andrews, *delete the ? after* [1822].

Hunt after Dalby, *delete the ? after* [1848].

[Hunt, ..., of Borecatton, Shropsh. (1772), Vol. XII, fol. 152.]

Hunter, William Henry, *delete the ? after* [1851].

Hunter to Gray, *delete the ? after* [1851].

Hurd, John, *delete the ? after* [1783].

Hurd, John (s. of Jacob), of Boston, New England, *add* [and to the descendants of the said Jacob, deceased] ; *for* [1783] *read* [7 April 1783] *and add* (*see also* Foster, William).

Hurst, John, *after* 171⁵⁄₆ *add* [1715].

Ibbetson, formerly Selwyn, *delete* [? Sir John Thomas] *and add at the end* [*See* Selwyn].

Ingram [5th Viscount Irvine [*succ.* 18 May 1714]], *after* Supporters *add* [1713 ?].

[Innes, Robert, of Edinburgh, 12 June 1693, Lyon Office. Misc. G. et H., New S., II, p. 395.]

Insole, James Harvey, *delete the ? after* [1872].

Inwen, Thomas, *after* 173⅔ *add* [1730].
Irving, Miss J. E., *after* 1892 *add* [1893 ?].
Israel to Ellis, *delete the ? after* [1865].
Jackson, formerly Galley, *delete the ? after* [1821].
Jalfou, Isaac, *delete the ? after* [1839].
James, Sir William, *delete the ? after* [1869].
Jamieson after Young, *delete the ? after* [1848].
Jarrett, James, *after* 1696 *add* [1697].
Jefferson after Dunnington, *delete the ? after* [1841].
Jenkins, Sir Richard, G.C.B., *for* 183 .. *read* [25 Oct. 1838] *and after* Supporters *add* [27 Oct. 1838].
[Jenkins (Wolseley-), Col. Charles Bradford Harries. Grant of Arms for Wolseley, 1894, on taking that name.]
Jenkinson, Sir Paul, *for* [1687] *read* [1688].
Jenyns to Bloomfield, *delete the ? after* [1871].
Jervis after Parker, *for* Swynford *read* Swynfen.
Jervoise, of Herriard, *delete the ? after* [1792].
John to Freke, *delete the ? after* [1835].
Johnson, Elizabeth. Edmondson gives the date 1741.
Johnson, late Clanchy,   } *for* Benleighfield *read* Burleigh Fields, parish of
Johnson, late Lillingston, }   Loughborough, co. Leic.
Joliff, late Milner, *delete the ? after* [1807].
Jones, late Tyrwhitt, *read* [Thomas] *and after* fol. 213 *add* [Eliza Walwyn Jones, widow of Sir Thomas Tyrwhitt, 1841].
Jones, of Poulston Fawley, *for* co. Hertf. *read* [Hampsh. ?] *and delete the ? after* [1807].
Jones, Thomas, of Sunderland, *delete the ? after* [1814].
Jones, Thomas, of Gresford, *delete the ? after* [1809].
Jones to Chambers, *delete the ? after* [1813].
Jones to Atcherley, *add* [David Francis, of Marton, 1834].
Jones to Tyrwhitt (foot of p. 207), *delete this entry. See above.*
Jones to Norbury, *delete the ? after* [1841].

Part 2.

Keeling, *read* [Frederick John] *and add before* 1886 [16 Oct.].
[Keeling, Arms quarterly to the Rev. William Fletcher, 21 Jan. 1836. Crisp, Notes, V, p. 14.]
Kettle, *read* [Sir Rupert Alfred], *and add before* 1881 [11 Mar.] *and* [Midland Antiquary, I, pp. 77-79].
Kynaston, late Owen, *add* [the Sheriffs of Montgomeryshire, p. 317], *and for* Powys-Land Club, XL, p. 42, *read* X, p. 422.
Landor, Walter, of Rugeley, 1687, *add* [Misc. G. et H., 4th S., V, p. 49].
Latham to Ashby, *add* [Mary Elizabeth, of Querly Hall], *and for* 1807 *read* [15 July 1807].
Lechmere to Charlton, *add* [Genealogist, New S., XXII, p. 155].
[Leigh to Mallory, Rev. George Leigh, now Mallory, Rector of Mobberley, co. Chester, Roy. Lic., 8 Dec. 1832. Arms and Surname of Mallory, 11 April 1833. Genealogist, New S., XXXII, p. 116.]
[Leigh-Mallory, 6 Oct. 1914, Rev. Herbert Leigh-Mallory, of The Manor House, Mobberley, Cheshire. Genealogist, New S, XXXII, p. 117; Leigh and Mallory quarterly. Exemplification, 14 April 1915, p. 119.]
Leyland, John, *add* [Lanc. and Chesh. Hist. and Geneal. Notes, ed. Josiah Rose, III, p. 34].
Lillingston, late Spooner, *for* Elendon *read* Elmdon.
[Lloyd, Charlotte. *See* Robarts, James Thomas.]
Lloyd to Duppa, *for* Winstanton *read* [The Grove, Winstantow].

[Lockwood, Alice Charlotte Mary, dau. of Frederick Vernon Lockwood and wife of Algernon Heber-Percy, 14 Feb. 1908.]

Longueville, Thomas, *for* Pengllan *read* Penyllan.

Lorimer, John, *for* New S., IV, *read* New S., II.

[Loughborough, Borough of, co. Leic., 10 April 1889, Vol. LXV, fol. . . . .]

Maddocks to Ashby, *add* [George Ashby, of Naseby Wooleys], of co. Northampton [and of Greenfields, Crosshill aud Westbury], Shropsh.

[Mallory, Rev. George, formerly Leigh, Rector of Mobberley, co. Chester, Roy. Lic., 18 Dec. 1832, Surname and Arms of Mallory, and Julia his wife, only child and heir of the Rev. John Holdsworth Mallory, 11 April 1833. Genealogist, New S., XXXII, p. 116.]

Mason, John, *add* [Crisp, Fragm. Geneal., V, p. 60].

Langton-Massingberd, Mrs. Emily, *for* co. Leic. *read* co. Linc.

Masters (John Smalman), *for* Chelton *read* Chetton.

Maurice to Corbet, *add* [Edward], of Petton.

Mill, George G., *in both entries for* Cariacou *read* Cariacou.

Mitton with Halston, *read* Mitton [William, of Halston], Shropsh.

Nicholls to Brodhurst, *add* [of Drayton Lodge], Shropsh.

Norcop after Radford, *for* Belton Hall *read* Betton Hall.

Owen, E. W. C. R., *add* [Supporters, G. C. B., 16 Jan. 1846. Powys-Land Club, X, p. 417].

Pairer after Russell, *for* Hammerwick *read* Hammerwich.

Palgrave, late Cohen, *add* [Genealogist, III, p. 285].

Passingham, Jonathan, *add after* Wales [quarterly with Lloyd].

Passingham, Jonathan, *add* Misc. G. et H., 4th S., III, p. 327.

Peel, late Ethelstin, *read* Ethelston.

Pelham *after* Thursby, (? Sussex), an error, Cound is in Shropsh.

Peploe, Ven. Samuel, *add* [Copy of Grant in G. B. Morgan's Browne Family, p. 32].

[Perkins, Martha, wife of Sir William Farmer, 24 Jan. 1885. Crisp, Notes, X, p. 106.]

Perry-Herrick, *for* [? Herrick to] *read* [William Herrick to]

Pigott-Corbet *should read* [PIGOTT to CORBET, Rev. John Dryden (1865), Vol. LV, fol. 328, PIGOTT to CORBET, Rev. George William (1890, Vol. LXV, fol. 309].

Plymley to Corbett, *add* [Ven. Joseph], M.A., [Archdeacon] of Shropsh.

Powel, late Kynaston, *for* Wortham *read* Worthen.

Pudsey, *in both entries for* Tysall *read* Trysale.

Radford-Norcop, *for* Belton Hall *read* Betton Hall.

Ratton, Sr Jaques, for 9 Dec. *read* 19 Dec.

Robarts after Lloyd, *read* Roberts after Lloyd, Thomas, *and add* [of Langley Farm, Stanton Lacy, Shropsh.].

Rogers, Samuel, *for* TRESAKER *read* TRESAHER.

Russell-Pavier, *for* Hammerwick *read* Hammerwich.

p. 323, *add* [Sandars, Ellen Barbara, wife of the Rev. John Buddicom. Arms, 1897, Vol. LXIX, fol. 274. *See* Buddicom.]

[Sandford, ..., of Up Rossall, Shropsh. Match with Brickdale, [1766] Vol. XI, fol. 166.]

Sandiford, *read* Sandford, of Shropsh.

Scott, Mrs., *add* [Louisa G.], *for* Belton Strange House, Chad., *read* Betton Strange House, Parish of St. Chad.

Sheppard to Hall, William, *add* [of Chatwell, Middleton and Hopton Wafers], Shropsh.

Sherston, Peter, *add* [Misc. G. et H., 4th S., I, p. 121].

Shropshire County Council, *add* [Shropshire Arch. Trans., 2nd S., XII, p. 45].

Slaney after Kenyon, William, *add* [of Hatton Grange and Walford Manor], Shropsh.

Smith, of Appleby (foot of p. 338). *for* Beewood *read* Brewood, co. Staff.

Smith (top of p. 340), Richard, *for* Berry Hill *read* Brierley Hill.

Smyth to Owen, Nicholas Owen, of Condover. *See* Owen.

Stanier, Mary, *add* [(Wilkinson), widow [of Francis Stanier], of Madeley Manor, &c. [and to the descendants of her husband, 2 July 1858, Vol. LII, fol. 370. Fol. 372 is an exemplification of her petition of the Arms of Broade and Stainier quarterly, to her son Francis, then a minor, and his descendants].

Stone, Arthur, *add* [Misc. G. et H., 4th S., III, p. 230].

Sweetapple, Sir John, *add* [Misc. G. et H., 2nd S., I, p. 133].

Tennant (late Vidler), *for* Shottesdon *read* Stottesdon.

Tyrwhitt, late Jones, *add* [Eliza] widow, &c.

[Tytler, of Woodhouselie, Midlothian, Scotland, 1768, 1803, 1824, 1864. Misc. G. et H., 5th S., II, pp. 253-256.]

Vaughan to Halford, *add* [Henry, *cr.* a Bart. 27 Sept. 1809, son of James Vaughan, M.D., Roy. Lic., 26 Aug. 1809].

Veel, late Jones, *for* Alum, Oxf., *read* Alumni Oxonienses.

[Walwyn. *See* Jones, late Tyrwhitt.]

Warburton after Egerton, *add* [Rowland Eyles] *and* [Roy. Lic., 10 Aug. 1813].

Waring, late Scott, *add* [John, M.P.].

Wartnaby, *add* [William].

Warrington to Carew, *add* [George Henry, of Pentrepant], Shropsh. ; *and* [Arms to issue by wife Carew].

Watkins to Griffith, *add* [John and William] (minors).

Watt, *add* [James] F.R.S.

Weld before Forester [*not* Forrester. Cecil, M.P., of Rose Hall, Dothill and Willey], Shropsh.

Wight-Boycott, *add* [Cathcart Boycott (*not* C.B.). Roy. Lic., 18 Feb. 1886].

Willis-Bund, *add* [John William, Roy. Lic., 1864].

Wolsley-Jenkins, *add* [Colonel Charles Bradford Harries had a Grant for Wolseley on taking that name in 1894].

Worsley to Pennyman, *add* [James White, Roy. Lic., 28 April 1873].

Wright, Francis, *for* Langan *read* Langar.

Wynn (*read* Wynne), late Fletcher, *add* [Rev. Lloyd].

Yates after Park, *add* [Edmund Waldegrave, Roy. Lic., 8 Dec. 1857].

LIST A.

DATES OF THE FIRST AND LAST PATENTS ENTERED IN THE GRANT BOOKS FROM VOL. IV TO VOL. LXXI.

IV	begins	6	April	1688,	ends	20 May	1700.
V	,,	7	Feb.	1699,	,,	22 Oct.	1711.
VI	,,	15	Oct.	1711,	,,	7 Aug.	1700.
VII	,,	20	June	1720,	,,	4 July	1728.
VIII	,,	3	Feb.	1727,	,,	19 Nov.	1740.
IX	,,	8	Dec.	1740,	,,	17 Dec.	1754.
X	,,	11	Jan.	1755,	,,	4 Nov.	1763.
XI	,,	15	Dec.	1763,	,,	15 Dec.	1769.
XII	,,	18	Dec.	1769,	,,	2 June	1774.
XIII	,,	18	Aug.	1774,	,,	23 June	1777.
XIV	,,	23	Oct.	1777,	,,	12 Dec.	1781.
XV	,,	16	Jan.	1782,	,,	31 May	1784.
XVI	,,	31	Jan.	1785,	,,	7 June	1788.
XVII	,,	26	April	1788,	,,	19 Oct.	1790.

XVIII	begins	24	Feb.	1792,	ends	1 Oct.	1793.
XIX	,,	24	Jan.	1795,	,,	18 Dec.	1797.
XX	,,	12	July	1797,	,,	8 Mar.	1800.
XXI	,,	29	Mar.	1800,	,,	21 June	1802.
XXII	,,	27	Oct.	1802,	,,	11 June	1804.
XXIII	,,	6	May	1804,	,,	16 Sept.	1806.
XXIV	,,	19	June	1804,	,,	25 July	1807.
XXV	,,	16	Sept.	1808,	,,	20 June	1810.
XXVI	,,	20	June	1810,	,,	15 May	1812.
XXVII	,,	11	May	1812,	,,	22 Sept.	1813.
XXVIII	,,	23	Nov.	1813,	,,	14 Oct.	1815.
XXIX	,,	1	June	1815,	,,	12 Aug.	1817.
XXX	,,	19	Aug.	1816,	,,	14 April	1817.
XXXI	,,	1	May	1818,	,,	15 Nov.	1819.
XXXII	,,	5	Jau.	1820,	,,	28 May	1821.
XXXIII	,,	13	Aug.	1821,	,,	25 Feb.	1823.
XXXIV	,,	25	Feb.	1823,	,,	24 Aug.	1824.
XXXV	,,	17	Aug.	1824,	,,	3 April	1826.
XXXVI	,,	11	Mar.	1826,	,,	20 Dec.	1827.
XXXVII	,,	31	Dec.	1827,	,,	25 Sept.	1829.
XXXVIII	,,	4	Aug.	1829,	,,	14 Jan.	1832.
XXXIX	,,	27	Jan.	1832,	,,	28 Sept.	1833.
XL	,,	13	Sept.	1833,	,,	16 May	1835.
XLI	,,	19	May	1835,	,,	21 Nov.	1836.
XLII	,,	6	Sept.	1836,	,,	16 April	1838.
XLIII	,,	30	April	1838,	,,	23 May	1839.
XLIV	,,	17	May	1839,	,,	21 Sept.	1840.
XLV	,,	17	Sept.	1840,	,,	1 Mar.	1842.
XLVI	,,	7	Feb.	1842,	,,	24 Nov.	1843.
XLVII	,,	31	Oct.	1843,	,,	18 Aug.	1845.
XLVIII	,,	30	June	1845,	,,	30 Mar.	1848.
XLIX	,,	21	Feb.	1848,	,,	30 May	1851.
L	,,	6	June	1851,	,,	6 Feb.	1854.
LI	,,	10	Feb.	1854,	,,	23 Oct.	1855.
LII	,,	4	April	1856,	,,	2 Sept.	1858.
LIII	,,	21	Aug.	1858,	,,	12 July	1860.
LIV	,,	17	July	1860,	,,	25 Jan.	1863.
LV	,,	15	Jan.	1863,	,,	25 Aug.	1865.
LVI	,,	25	Aug.	1865,	,,	28 April	1868.
LVII	,,	28	April	1868,	,,	10 May	1871.
LVIII	,,	18	May	1871,	,,	22 June	1874.
LIX	,,	22	June	1874,	,,	4 June	1877.
LX	,,	8	June	1877,	,,	8 April	1880.
LXI	,,	27	April	1880,	,,	6 April	1883.
LXII	,,	8	Nov.	1882,	,,	29 Dec.	1884.
LXIII	,,	29	Dec.	1884,	,,	9 April	1887.
LXIV	,,	2	Mar.	1887,	,,	22 Feb.	1889.
LXV	,,	22	Feb.	1889,	,,	12 Nov.	1890.
LXVI	,,	24	Nov.	1890,	,,	30 June	1892.
LXVII	,,	4	July	1892,	,,	21 Mar.	1894.
LXVIII	,,	27	Mar.	1894,	,,	16 Dec.	1895.
LXIX	,,	20	Dec.	1895,	,,	31 Aug.	1897.
LXX	,,	30	Aug.	1897,	,,	24 Mar.	1899.
LXXI	,,	13	April	1899,	,,	14 Sept.	1900.

LIST B.

ATTEMPTED ARRANGEMENT OF THE YEARS AND PAGES OF THE GRANT BOOKS.

Vol. IV.

1688, fols. 5 to 27.
$168\frac{8}{9}$,,   30.
1689 ,,   33 to 55.
1690 ,,   59 to 71.
$169\frac{0}{1}$,,   73 and 74.
1691 ,,   77 to 100.
$169\frac{1}{2}$,,   103.
1692 ,,   106 to 125.
$169\frac{2}{3}$,,   130 to 137.
1693 ,,   127 to 150.
$169\frac{3}{4}$,,   153 to 156.
1694 ,,   158 to 176 ?
$169\frac{4}{5}$,,   178 to 187.
1695 ,,   190 to 206.
1696 ,,   212 to 215.
$169\frac{6}{7}$,,   218 to 222.
1697 ,,   225 to 242.
1698 ,,   244 to 278.
1699 ,,   283 ? to 326.
$\frac{1699}{1700}$,,   328 to 337.
1700 ,,   340 to end ?

Vol. V.

$\frac{1699}{1700}$, fols. 2.
1700 ,,   3 to 42.
$170\frac{0}{1}$,,   21 to 30.
1701 ,,   37 to 54.
$170\frac{1}{2}$,,   56 to 71 ?
1702 ,,   75 to 85.
$170\frac{2}{3}$,,   89 to 122.
1703 ,,   126 to 132.
$170\frac{3}{4}$,,   135 to 148.
1704 ,,   151 to 168.
1705
1706 ,,   171 to 197.
1707 ,,   205 to 281.
$170\frac{7}{8}$,,   285.
1708 ,,   287 to 325.
$170\frac{8}{9}$,,   332 to 336.
1709 ,,   339 to 395.
1710 ,,   399 to 409.
$171\frac{10}{11}$,,   412.
1711 ,,   415 to 457.

Vol. VI.

1711, fols. 1 to 9.
$171\frac{1}{2}$,,   13 to 32.
1712 ,,   36 ? to 80.
$171\frac{2}{3}$,,   85.
1713 ,,   90 ? to 118.

Vol. VI (*continued*)—

$171\frac{3}{4}$, fols. 122 to 141.
1714 ,,   145 to 175.
$171\frac{4}{5}$,,   179 to 211.
1715 ,,   201 to 218.
$171\frac{5}{6}$,,   222 to . . .
1716 ,,   230 to 286.
1717 ,,   290 to 348.
$171\frac{7}{8}$,,   354 and 362.
1718 ,,   365 ? to 384.
1719
1720 ,,   391 to 448.

Vol. VII.

1720, fols. 1 to 48.
$172\frac{0}{1}$,,   52, 69, 79.
1721 ,,   55 to 73 ?
$172\frac{1}{2}$,,   75 ?
1722 ,,   84 to 146.
$172\frac{2}{3}$,,   150 to 176.
1723 ,,   186 to 220.
$172\frac{3}{4}$,,   229 to 264.
1724 ,,   271 ? 273 ?
$172\frac{4}{5}$,,   261 ?
1725 ,,   274 to 496.
$172\frac{5}{6}$,,   437, 451, 481, 501, 506.
1726 ,,   510 to 523, and 586.
$172\frac{6}{7}$,,   527, and 539 to 544, and
1727 ,,   547 ? to 561.   [581.
$172\frac{7}{8}$,,   567 to 573.
1728 ,,   577 to 588.

Vol. VIII.

1727, fols. 2, 16, 21, 24 ?
1728 ,,   6 to 20.
$172\frac{8}{9}$,,   23 and 47.
1729 ,,   26 to 56.
$172\frac{29}{30}$,,   31, 54 to 73^b ?
1730 ,,   65, 67^b, 75^b to 106.
$173\frac{0}{1}$,,   93, 93^b, 102^b ?
1731 ,,   109 to 115^b.
$173\frac{1}{2}$,, 117^b, 118, 120^b, 122, 139^b,
1732 ,,   130 to 159^b.   [161, 162.
$173\frac{2}{3}$,,   163.
1733 ,,   165 to 181.
$173\frac{3}{4}$,, 183^b.
1734 ,,   182 to 190.
1735 ,,   191 to 195^b.
1736 ,,   197 to 205.
$173\frac{6}{7}$,, 207^b.
1737 ,, 209^b to 226^b.

Vol. VIII (*continued*)—
$1737\frac{7}{8}$, fols. 228ᵇ to 232.
1738 „ 234 to 250.
1739 „ 251 to 260.
$1739\frac{39}{40}$ „ 263 to 266?
1740 „ 271 to 283.

Vol. IX.
1740, fols. 1 to 8.
$1740\frac{0}{1}$ „ 13 to 17?
1741 „ 19 to 41.
$1741\frac{1}{2}$ „ 45, 47.
1742 „ 50 to 79.
$1742\frac{2}{3}$ „ 81.
1743 „ 84 to 114?
1744 „ 119? to 125.
$1744\frac{4}{5}$ „ 123, 126.
1745 „ 145 to 155.
1746 „ 161? to 194.
1747 „ 197 to 215.
$1747\frac{7}{8}$ „ 220.
1748 „ 223 to 299.
$1748\frac{8}{9}$ „ 302.
1749 „ 316 to 346.
1750 „ 308?, 351 to 383.
1751 „ 387 to 393.
1752 „ 401? to 428.
1753 „ 432 to 483?
1754 „ 486? to 511.

Vol. X.
1755, fols. 2 to 45.
1756 „ 49 to 74.
1757 „ 82 to 120.
1758 „ 129 to 165.
1759 „ 168 to 208.
1760 „ 215 to 266.
1761 „ 268 to 405.
1762 „ 412 to 450.
1763 „ 460 to 483?
1764 „ 485?

Vol XI.
1764, fols. 3 to 45.
1765 „ 49 to 126.
1766 „ 130 to 190.
1767 „ 194 to 260.
1768 „ 264 to 350.
1769 „ 354 to 374.

Vol. XII.
1770, fols. 3 to 43.
1771 „ 46 to 111.
1772 „ 114 to 218.
1773 „ 220 to 282.
1774 „ 284 to 300.

Vol. XIII.
1774, fols. 2 to 59.
1775 „ 61 to 156.

Vol. XIII (*continued*)—
1776, fols. 159? to 251.
1777 „ 255 to 309.

Vol. XIV.
1777, fols. 3 to 10?
1778 „ 14? to 61.
1779 „ 80 to 195?
1780 „ 200? to 280?
1781 „ 290 to 361.

Vol. XV.
1782, fols. 1 to 125?
1783 „ 127 to 239?
1784 „ 247 to 383.
1785 „ 389.

Vol. XVI.
1785, fols. 3 to 97?
1786 „ 103 to 203?
1787 „ 209 to 315?
1788 „ 319 to 413.

Vol. XVII.
1788, fols. 3 to 121?
1789 „ 127 to 185.
1790 „ 189? to 282.
1791 „ 290 to 448.

Vol. XVIII.
1792, fols. 1 to 143.
1793 „ 147? to 287.
1794 „ 288 to 419?
1795 „ 422? to 440.

Vol. XIX.
1795, fols. 3 to 178.
1796 „ 189? to 324.
1797 „ 345? to 465?

Vol. XX.
1797, fols. 2 to 115?
1798 „ 117? to 275.
1799 „ 283 to 402.
1800 „ 411 to 453.

Vol. XXI.
1800, fols. 3 to 114?
1801 „ 125 to 286.·
1802 „ 291? to 459.

Vol. XXII.
1802, fols. 3 to 36?
1803 „ 44 to 318?
1804 „ 320? to 455?

Vol. XXIII.
1804, fols. 2 to 119.
1805 „ 125 to 272?
1806 „ 274 to 432.

Vol. XXIV.
  1806, fols. 3 to 121 ?
  1807 „   125 ? to 315.
  1808 „   317 to 465.

Vol. XXV.
  1808, fols. 2 to 65 ?
 ·1809 „   69 to 295 ?
  1810 „   304 to 451.

Vol. XXVI.
  1810, fols. 1 to 156.
  1811 „   165 to 445.

Vol. XXVII.
  1811, fols. 1 to 101.
  1812 „   106 ? to 306.
  1813 „   327 ? to 456.

Vol. XXVIII.
  1814, fols. 1 to 251 ?
  1815 „   255 to 445.

Vol. XXIX.
  1815, fols. 1 to 232 ?
  1816 „   239 ? to 461.

Vol. XXX.
  1816, fols. 3 to 72.
  1817 „   81 to 310.
  1818 „   318 to 340.

Vol. XXXI.
  1818, fols. 1 to 150.
  1819 „   152 ? to 399.

Vol. XXXII.
  1820, fols. 1 to 247 ?
  1821 „   263 to 397 ?

Vol. XXXIII.
  1821, fols. 1 to 106.
  1822 „   110 ? to 342.
  1823 „   333 ? to 398.

Vol. XXXIV.
  1823, fols. 5 to 226 ?
  1824 „   245 ? to 401.

Vol. XXXV.
  1824, fols. 3 to 65 ?
  1825 „   71 ? to 315 ?
  1826 „   320 to 403.

Vol. XXXVI.
  1826, fols. 3 to 176.
  1827 „   180 to 406.

Vol. XXXVII.
  1828, fols. 3 to 229 ?
  1829 „   241 ? to 417.

Vol. XXXVIII.
  1829, fols. 2 to 26 (42 ?).
  1830 „   37 to 179.
  1831 „   181 to 370.

Vol. XXXIX.
  1832, fols. 1 to 166.
  1833 „   174 to 392.

Vol. XL.
  1833, fols. 1 to 86.
  1834 „   91 ? to 299, and 319.
  1835 „   301 to 393.

Vol. XLI.
  1835, fols. 1 to 174 ?
  1836 „   176 to 414.

Vol. XLII.
  1836, fols. 3 to 46.
  1837 „   50 ? to 265.
  1838 „   269 ? to 340.

Vol. XLIII.
  1838, fols. 2 to 335.
  1839 „   344 ? to 445.

Vol. XLIV.
  1839, fols. 8 to 184.
  1840 „   188 ? to 403.

Vol. XLV.
  1840, fols. 3 to 51.
  1841 „   53 to 335 ?
  1842 „   343 ? to 393.

Vol. XLVI.
  1842, fols. 1 to 247.
  1843 „   253 to 403.

Vol. XLVII.
  1843, fols. 2 to 192 ?
  1844 „   198 ? to 331.
  1845 „   341 ? to 440.

Vol. XLVIII.
  1845, fols. 5 to 98 ?
  1846 „   103 to 224.
  1847 „   240 to 393 ?
  1848 „   403 to 468 ?

Vol. XLIX.
  1848, fols. 3 to 90 ?
  1849 „   92 ? to 264.

Vol. XLIX (*continued*)—
1850, fols. 281 ? to 411 ?
1851 „ 418 to 493.

Vol. L.
1851, fols. 1 to 92 ?
1852 „ 104 to 259 ?
1853 „ 271 to 428.
1854 „ 435 ? to end.

Vol. LI.
1854, fols. 1 to 186 ?
1855 „ 192 to 422.
1856 „ 424 to 464.

Vol. LII.
1856, fols. 3 to 170.
1857 „ 172 to 330.
1858 „ 334 to 389.

Vol. LIII.
1858, fols. 2 to 54.
1859 „ 56 ? to 278 ?
1860 „ 282 ? to 368.

Vol. LIV.
1860, fols. 1 to 85 ?
1861 „ 90 ? to 232.
1862 „ 234 to 423.

Vol. LV.
1863, fols. 1 to 144 ?
1864 „ 148 ? to 270.
1865 „ 276 to 356.

Vol. LVI.
1865, fols. 1 to 63 ?
1866 „ 65 ? to 158 ?
1867 „ 162 ? to 324.
1868 „ 327 ? to 364.

Vol. LVII.
1868, fols. 1 to 125.
1869 „ 127 to 210.
1870 „ 212 to 300.
1871 „ 302 to 339.

Vol. LVIII.
1871, fols. 1 to 84.
1872 „ 92 to 190.
1873 „ 193 to 290 ?
1874 „ 296 ? to 355.

Vol. LIX.
1874, fols. 1 to 69.
1875 „ 71 to 171.
1876 „ 173 to 300.
1877 „ 302 to 363.

Vol. LX.
1877, fols. 1 to 74.
1878 „ 76 to 207.
1879 „ 209 to 330.
1880 „ 332 to 385.

Vol. LXI.
1880, fols. 1 to 98.
1881 „ 100 to 251.
1882 „ 253 to 393.

Vol. LXII.
1882, fols. 1 to 31.
1883 „ 33 to 170.
1884 „ 172 to 337.

Vol. LXIII.
1884, fol. 1.
1885, fols. 3 to 165.
1886 „ 167 to 319.
1887 „ 320 to 355.

Vol. LXIV.
1887, fols. 1 to 134.
1888 „ 136 to 323.

Vol. LXV.
1889, fols. 1 to 168.
1890 „ 170 to 353.

Vol. LXVI.
1890, fols. 1 to 29.
1891 „ 31 to 241.
1892 „ 243 to 318.
1893 „ 320 to 338.

Vol. LXVII.
1892, fols. 1 to 106.
1893 „ 109 to 283.
1894 „ 285 to 306.

Vol. LXVIII.
1894, fols. 1 to 140.
1895 „ 142 to 363.

Vol. LXIX.
1895, fols. 1 to 13 ?
1896 „ 15 to 199
1897 „ 203 to 325

Vol. LXX.
1897, fols. 3 to 78.
1898 „ 80 to 318.
1899 „ 320 to 340.

Vol. LXXI.
Early 1899 to late 1900.

A fairly Complete and Unique Alphabetical List

OF

Personal Grants of Arms

ON RECORD AT THE

College of Arms, 1687—1898.

With reference to the Grant Books at the Heralds' College, printed books and MSS. in British Museum, incorporated by J. F.

AS CONTAINED IN ADDITIONAL MS. 37,149.

By J. FOSTER, Hon. M.A., Oxon, 1898.

(Refer also to Brit. Museum Add. MSS. 14,830 and 14,831, and Add. MS. 35,336, by Townley, Bluemantle, since incorporated 1898.)

---

* Indicates special limitations to relatives of the Grantees other than descendants.

K

KARR after RAMSAY, ..., of Hatchford Cobham, Surrey, and Kippilaw, co. Roxburgh, Scotland, late Gov. of Bombay. Quarterly Arms, [1795] Vol. XIX, fol. 5.

,, after SETON, ..., of co. Surrey and Scotland. Quarterly Arms, [1799] Vol. XX, fol. 340.

,, after SETON, ..., of co. Surrey and Scotland. Quarterly Arms, [1815] Vol. XXVIII, fol. 372.

KATER, Edward, of Mexborough, co. York, [1837] Vol. XLII, fol. 69.

KAY, Sir William, 2nd Bart., of Adelphi Terrace, London, [1808] Vol. XXIV, fol. 321. [Grandnephew of the 1st Bart., Sir Brook WATSON, Bart., 5 Dec. 1803, succeeded by remainder.]

,, James Openshaw, of Bedhampton, Hampsh., [1840] Vol. XLV, fol. 49.

KAY-SHUTTLEWORTH, James Phillips, Bart., Sec. to Committee of the Privy Council, of Gawthorp Hall, co. Lanc. [s. of Robert Kay], of Brookshaw, Bury, co. Lanc., [1842] Vol. XLV, fols. 368 and 393. [Surname and Arms of Shuttleworth, 14 Feb. 1842; Bart. 1850.]

KAY, John Robinson, of Bury and Rawtenstall, co. Lanc., [1855] Vol. LI, fol. 380.

,, Thomas, of Moorfields, Stockport, co. Chester, 1895, Vol. LXVIII, fol. 194.

,, Samuel, of Davenport, Stockport, co. Chester, 1895, Vol. LXVIII, fol. 194.

KAY-KAY, Elizabeth, dau. and sole heiress of Josiah, and wife of Sir John THORNYCROFT, Bart., of Milcombe [co. Oxf.], March 170⅞ [?], Vol. V, fols. 158 and 202.

KAYE after LISTER, ... (reputed s. of LISTER-KAYE, Bart.), of Denby Grange, co. York. Quarterly Arms, [1806] Vol. XXIII, fol. 334.

KAYE, ..., of Dalton Hall, Kirkheaton, co. York, [1843] Vol. XLVII, fol. 106.

KEALY, J. R., of Ashley House, Alverstoke, Hampsh., 1891, Vol. LXVI, fol. 231.

KEANE, Baron [Lieut.-Gen. Sir John], of Ireland. Augmentation, [1840] Vol. XLIV, fol. 371.

KEANE, Baron [Lieut.-Gen. Sir John], of Ireland. G.C.B. [12 Aug. 1839]. Supporters [cr. Baron Keane, 23 Dec. 1839], [1840] Vol. XLIV, fol. 378.

KEARNANE (wife of NOWELL), Maria T., of London. Crest to brother, [1806] Vol. XXIII, fol. 309.

KEARSEY (formerly THOMAS), ..., of Burstow Hall, co. Surrey, [1867] Vol. LVI, fol. 238.

KEATES, ..., of Greenfields Hall, co. Flint, Wales, [1862] Vol. LIV, fol. 318.

KEATING, Lieut.-Gen. Sir Henry Sheehy, K.C.B. [21 Dec. 1836], [1840] Vol. XLV, fol. 34.

„ Rev. William (s. of William), of 26, Palace Court, Bayswater, London, 1898, Vol. LXX, fol. 206.

KEATS, Rear-Adm. Sir Richard Goodwin, K.B. [15 Oct. 1808], of Bideford and King's Nympton, co. Devon, [1810] Vol. XXV, fol. 344. Supporters, [1810] Vol. XXV, fol. 347.

KEBLE, Maj.-Gen., E.I.C.S., of Tunbridge, co. Kent, and London, [1818] Vol. XXX, fol. 411.

KECK after POWYS, The Hon. Henry Lyttleton (s. of 2nd Baron LILFORD), of Stoughton Grange, co. Leic., 1861, Vol. LIV, fol. 102.

KECK, formerly JAMES, Anthony, 1737, by assumption.

KEELING, Frederick J., of Colchester, 1886,* Vol. LXIII, fol. 295.

KEENE, Sir Benjamin, K.B. [23 Sept. 1754]. Supporters, [1754] Vol. IX, fol. 506.

KEET, John, s. of Edward, of Canterbury, co. Kent, 1745, Vol. IX, fol. 150. (Berry.)

KEIGHLEY, ..., wid. of Capt., of co. Warw., [1838] Vol. XLIII, fol. 199.

KEIGHLEY-PEACH, ... of Iddicote, co. Warw., [1838] Vol. XLIII, fol. 219.

KEIR-GRANT, Maj.-Gen., K.H. [K.C.H. 1821], of Rossie, co. Fife, Scotland, [1822] Vol. XXXIII, fol. 158.

KEITH, Sir Robert Murray, K.B. [29 Feb. 1772], of Scotland. Supporters, 2 June 1772, Vol. XII, fol. 165 (see Misc. G. et H., 2nd S., III, p. 88, plate).

KELCEY. See FINN and FOORD.

KELHAM, late LANGDALE, ..., of Bush Hill and Edmonton, co. Middx., and London. (Match), [1811] Vol. XXVI, fol. 442.

KELK, ..., of Bentley Priory, Harrow, co. Middx., [1859] Vol. LIII, fol. 186.

KELLETT to LONG, ..., of Dunston and Swainthorpe, co. Norf. Quarterly Arms, [1797] Vol. XX, fol. 4.

KELLY, William Henry, of Porchester Terrace, London, [1861] Vol. LIV, fol. 142. (Berry's Suppl.)

KELSALL to PECKHAM-PHIPPS, ... (Spr.), of Little Green Compton, co. Sussex, [1837] Vol. XLII, fol. 215.

KELSO to HAMILTON, ..., Madras C.S., of Topsham, co. Devon, and Huller-hurst, co. Ayr, Scotland. Quarterly Arms, [1811] Vol. XXVII, fol. 87.

KELVIN, Baron, [THOMSON], of Scotland. Supporters only ?, 1892, Vol. LXVI, fol. 332.

KEMBALL, C. G., of Cranley Gardens, London, 1888,* Vol. LXIV, fol. 152.

KEMBLE, ..., of Kentish Town, co. Middx., [1792] Vol. XVIII, fol. 109.

KEMEYS-TYNTE after JOHNSON, ..., of co. Surrey and Wales. Quarterly Arms, [1785] Vol. XVI, fol. 97.

KEMP, Thomas, of Lewes and Pangdean, co. Sussex, 1771, Vol. XII, fol. 91.

KEMP after BROOKES, George Brookyers, of Hendon, co. Middx., [1839] Vol. XLIV, fol. 162.

„ after KITCHEN, Frederick William, of Hendon, co. Middx., and Margate, co. Kent, 1868, Vol. LVII, fol. 29.

KEMPT, Maj.-Gen. Sir James, G.C.B. [22 June 1815], of Fortwilliam, Scotland. Supporters, [1816] Vol. XXIX, fol. 341.

KEMSLEY, J. C., of Rolvenden, co. Kent, 1894, Vol. LXVIII, fol. 77.

KENDALL, ..., of Laurigg, Bramfield, co. Cumberland. (Match), [17$\frac{39}{40}$] Vol. VIII, fol. 271.

„ . . . ., of Dan-y-paic, Brecon, Wales. (See DARLING.) (Match), [1813 ?] Vol. XXVII, fol. 322.

KENDALL to MITCHELSON, James, of Pickering, co. York, [1860] Vol. LIV, fol. 79.

„ to LUMB, Percy, of Wakefield, co. York. [1870] Vol. LVII. fol. 264.

KENNARD, Robert William, of Theobalds. co. Hertf., [1845] Vol. XLVIII. fol. 68.

KENNAWAY, ... , Bart., of Exeter and Kingsbridge, co. Devon, [1791] Vol. XVII, fol. 322.

KENNEDY before LAURIE, ..., of Jamaica and London. Quarterly Arms, [1802] Vol. XXI, fol. 425.

„ [Richard Hartley], Alderman of London, late Phys. Genl. and President Bombay Med. Board, [1855] Vol. LI, fol. 219.

KENNEDY to HUME, John, of East Melbourne, Victoria, [1877] Vol. LIX, fol. 348.

KENNET to DAWSON, ..., of co. Lanc. and York, [1807] Vol. XXIV, fol. 133.

KENNETT, BARRINGTON-, V. H. B., of The Manor House, Dorchester, co. Dorset, and London, 1885, Vol. LXIII, fols. 10, 19 and 29.

KENNION, ..., of Finsbury Square, London, [1809] Vol. XXV, fol. 118.

KENRICH to KYFFIN, Elizabeth (Spr.), of Belmont, co. Denbigh, Wales, [1842] Vol. XLVI, fol. 91.

KENSINGTON, ..., of London, [1787] Vol. XVI. fol. 245.

„ [Borough of, London, 23 May 1901. (Geneal. Mag., V, p. 313.)]

KENSIT, Thomas Glover, of Bedford Row and Skinners' Hall, Dowgate, London, H. Reg. 6, [1842] Vol. XLVI, fol. 45.

KENT to GREEN, ..., of Poulton Lancelyn, co. Chester, [1793] Vol. XVIII, fol. 164.

„ to GREEN, ..., of co. Chester, [1828] Vol. XXXVII, fol. 47.

KENYON, Lord [Baron of Gredington, 1788], of co. Flint, Wales. Supporters, [1788] Vol. XVII, fol. 27.

KENYON, late BEDFORD, ..., of Highfield-within-Pemberton, Wigan, co. Lanc., [1824] Vol. XXXIV, fol. 308.

KENYON-SLANEY, ..., of Hatton Grange, and Walford Manor, Shropsh., [1862] Vol. LIV, fol. 300.

KENYON, J. W., of Copley House, Kirkburton, co. York, 1891,* Vol. LXVI, fol. 51.

KEPPEL, Lieut.-Gen. Sir William, K.B. [1 Feb. 1813], of co. Suff. Arms, Groom of H.M. Bedchamber, [1812] Vol. XXVII, fols. 279 and 292.

„ [Viscount. 1782, Adm. The Hon Augustus Keppel]. Supporters, [1782] Vol. XV, fol. 39.

KER-BELLENDEN, late GAWLER. John, of co. Surrey and Scotland. (See Duke of ROXBURGH.) [1804] Vol. XXIII, fol. 96.

KER-COCKBURNE, ..., M.A., of co. Derby, [1833] Vol. XXXIX, fol. 298.

KER-SEYMOUR after CLAY, Harry E., of Hanford, co. Dorset, Sec. to Embassy, Paris, 1865, Vol. LV, fol. 276.

KERR to McDONNELL, ... [1836]. (4th Earl of ANTRIM), of Ireland and Scotland, [1836] Vol. XLI, fol. 345.

„ to McDONNELL, ... [1855, Mark, 5th Earl], [1855] Vol. LI. fol. 347.

KERR, Robert M., of Chester Terrace, Regent's Park, London, 1891, Vol. LXVI, fol. 57.

KERR-PEARSE, Rev. B. K. W., of Ascot Rectory, Berks., 1891, Vol. LXVI, fol. 188. See 1889, Vol. LXV, fol. 110.

KERRICH-WALKER, Henry Walker, of Newker House, co. Durham, and Stelling Hall, co. Northumberland, 1877, Vol. LIX, fol. 308. (Berry's Suppl.)

KERRISON, Sir Roger, Knt., of Brooke, co. Norf., lord of several Norfolk manors, 12 Aug. 1806, Vol. XXIV, fol. 12.

„ Lieut.-Col. Edward, of Barsham and Bungay, co. Suff. (Match), 11 June 1810, Vol. XXVI, fol. 19.

„ Lieut.-Gen. Sir Edward, Bart. [K.C.B., 1840], of co. Suff. and Norf. Augmentation and Supporters, [1841] Vol. XLV, fols. 205 and 216.

KERSCHNER to CROSSLEY, ..., of co. Kent, [1880] Vol. LX, fol. 385.

KERSEY, Robert, of Hunt Lodge, Lee, co. Kent, 1879, Vol. LX, fol. 267. (Berry's Suppl.)

KERSHAW, William, of Warley House and Savile, co. York, [1836] Vol. XLI, fol. 218.

KERSHAW-LUMB, Richard, of Silcotes Green, Halifax, co. York, [1836] Vol. XLI, fol. 220.

KERSHAW. E. W., of Hanover Square, London, 1892,* Vol. LXVI, fol. 260.

„ Richard, D.D. (see KIRSHAW), 1724.

KETLAND, ..., of Birmingham, co. Warw., [1796] Vol. XIX, fol. 276.

KETT, Elizabeth, relict of Thomas Kett, of London, and dau. of NEWNHAM, of co. Norf. ?, 11 April 1718, Vol. VI, fol. 378.

„ William, of Kelsale, co. Suff., 1756, Vol. X, fol. 61. (Berry.)

KETT-THOMPSON, ..., of Witchingham Hall, Seething Hall, and Brooke House, co. Norf., [1872] Vol. LVIII, fol. 144.

KETTLE, Sir Rupert A., of Meridale, Wolverhampton, co. Staff., and Glan-y-don, Towyn, Wales (decd.), 1881, Vol. LXI, fol. 140. (Berry's Suppl.)

KETTLEWELL, Henry William (s. of Samuel), of ? co. Somerset, and Trinity Coll., Camb. EYRES quarterly, 1878, Vol. LX, fols. 155 and 157. (Berry's Suppl.)

„ W. W., of Harptree Court, East Harptree, co. Somerset, 1888, Vol. LXIV, fol. 154.

KEVILL, James, B.D., of Wigmore Hall, co. Hereford, and Trevenson, co. Cornw., [1820] Vol. XXXII, fol. 71.

KEVILL-DAVIES, Edward Hamand, of Croft Castle, co. Hereford, [1838] Vol. XLIII, fol. 143.

„ -DAVIES, William Trevelyan, of Croft Castle, co. Hereford, [1844] Vol. XLVII, fol. 259.

KEVINGTON, alias KEDINGTON, Henry, of co. Suff., 28 July 1709, Vol. V, fol. 380.

KEY, alias KAY, Josiah, of Melcomb, co. Oxf., 1688, Vol. IV, fol. 21. (Berry.)

„ alias KAY, Elizabeth, of Melcomb, co. Oxf., [1704] Vol. V, fol. 157.

„ alias KAY, Elizabeth, of Melcomb, co. Oxf., [1707 ?] Vol. V, fol. 202.

KEY, John, Bart., of Newport, Shropsh., and London, 181 . ., Vol. XXVI, fol. 96.

„ Elizabeth (widow), dau. of Garrett, of Weston-under-Lizzard, co. Staff., and Hampstead, co. Middx., [1810] Vol. XXVI, fol. 100.

„ Alexander (s. of John), of co. Dumfries and London, 181 . ., Vol. XXX, fol. 141.

KEYES, Roger, J. B., s. of Gen. Sir Charles [Patton] Keyes, [G.C.B., 30 May 1891] 18 . ., Vol. LXXI, fol. . . . . .

KEYSALL, John, of London, [1782] Vol. XV, fol. 88.

KIDD, John, M.D., of Christ Ch., Oxf. (died 17 Sept. 1851), [1826] Vol XXXVI, fol. 62.

„ Lieut.-Col. William Archibald, of co. Armagh, by Sir B. BURKE, Ulster ; with remainder to the descendants of his great-grandfather, Benjamin, of Millmount Keady, co. Armagh, Ireland, 16 Oct. 1891. (Misc. G. et H., 2nd S., V, p. 331.)

KIDNEY, David, of Market Harborough, co. Leic., and London, 1765, Vol. XI, fol. 57. (Berry.)

KIDNEY-COCKBURN, Sir James, Bart., of Scotland, co. Leic., and Northampton, [1828] Vol. XXXVII, fol. 69.

KILBURNE, William, M.A. of Magdalen Coll., Camb., of Saffron Walden, co. Essex, by Henry, Earl of BINDON, Deputy Earl Marshal, 10 Feb. 170$\frac{8}{9}$; Stowe MS. 714, fol. 74.

KILDERBEE, Spencer Horsly, of Ipswich, co. Suff., [1811] Vol. XXVI, fol. 354.

KILDERBEE to DE HORSEY, S. H., of Glembam, Frimley St. Martin, and Bury, co. Suff., [1832] Vol. XXXIX, fol. 91.

KILLAM after NEWSOME, ..., of Stainforth and Barnby-upon-Don, co. York, [1871] Vol. LVIII, fol. 30.

KILLAM (late MATTHEWS), Thomas Killam (Pembroke Coll., Oxf.), of Stainforth and St. George's Villas, Doncaster, co. York, 1880, Vol. LX, fol. 369.

KILPIN, E. F., of Haughley, Rondesbock, Cape of Good Hope, 1893, Vol. LXVII, fol. 245.

KILVINGTON, John, s. of Edward, of Thirsk and York, co. York, [1761 ?] Vol. X, fol. 408.

KINCAID-LENNOX after BATEMAN-HANBURY, ..., of co. Stirling, Scotland, [1862] Vol. LIV, fol. 234.

KING, Richard, of Exeter, co. Devon, 1691, [1692 ?] Vol. IV, fol. 110. (Match), [1698] Vol. IV, fol. 263.

   "   Daniel, nephew of Sir William PRICHARD, Lord Mayor of London, of Eltham, co. Kent, 14 June 1707, Vol. V, fol. 208. (Misc. G. et H., New S., I, p. 350.)

   "   Baron [1725], Lord Chancellor, of Oakham, co. Surrey, [1725] Vol. VII, fol. 420.

   "   John, of Thorpe, co. Essex, 14 Mar. 172⁷/₈, Vol. VII, fol. 567.

   "   . . . . (see GREEN), of Apethorp, co. Northampton, [1768] Vol. XI, fol. 338.

   "   . . . . (see HARVEY), of Trowbridge, Wilts. Quarterly Arms, [1783] Vol. XV, fol. 197.

   "   . . . ., of Worthing and Hinfield, co. Sussex (see also next entry), [1796] Vol. XIX, fol. 211.

KING- (BIGLAND, wife of), ..., of Bristol (see preceding entry), [1796] Vol. XIX, fol. 211.

KING (HALL, wife of), ..., of London. (? See HALL DARE.) Arms for wife and descendants, [1815] Vol. XXIX, fols. 132 and 133.

   "   and BEAN, his wife, of Watford, co. Hertf., [1826] Vol. XXXV, fol. 351.

KING after MEADE, John, of Taunton, North Petherton, and Lyngall, co. Somerset, 1830, Vol. XXXVIII, fol. 138.

KING, Thomas William, Rouge Dragon Pursuivant of Arms, of London, [1835] Vol. XLI, fol. 103 ; Extension of limitations, [1840] Vol. XLIV, fol. 315.

KING, late SIMPKINSON, Rev. James, M.A., of Slanton Park, co. Hereford, [1837] Vol. XLII, fol. 114.

KING, William Read, of Sergeant's Inn, London, and Tulse Hill, co. Surrey, [1838] Vol. XLIII, fol. 322.

   "   . . . ., of Broomfield, co. Essex, [1839] Vol. XLIV, fol. 88.

   "   . . . ., of Southampton, Hampsh., [1846] Vol. XLVIII, fol. 137.

   "   1. Henry John (-CHURCH), of Albury and Manor of Acton, co. Surrey ; 2. William James, Lieut.-Col., died s.p., of co. Surrey. ; 3. Richard Thomas, Lieut.-Col. Artillery, died s.p., [1849] Vol. XLIX, fols. 107 and 112.

   "   John Thomas, of Highbury Crescent and Muswell Hill, London, [1855] Vol. LI, fol. 213.

KING-NOEL, [William, 1st] Earl of LOVELACE, of co. Surrey, [1860] Vol. LIV, fol. 58.

KING-NOEL to MILBANKE, [Ralph Gordon] [1861], 2nd s. of William, [1st] Earl of LOVELACE, of Halnaby, co. York, and Seaham, co. Durham, [1861] Vol. LIV, fol. 98.

KING-NOEL, Hon. L. F., of Horsley Towers and East Horsley, co. Surrey, 1895, Vol. LXVIII, fol. 304.

KING, Robert, of Ferm House, Upper Clapton, co. Middx., [1865] Vol. LV, fol. 314.

   "   George, M.P., of Waratah, in Sydney, New South Wales, and Howrie, Queensland, [1873] Vol. LVIII, fol. 237.

   "   Richard, of Goldhurst Terrace, London, 1895,* Vol. LXVIII, fol. 324.

KING-WYNDHAM, Richard, by Roy. Lic. [no reference].

KINGFORD, Robert, of co. Cornw., 1691, Vol. IV, fol. 94.

KINGSLEY, ..., of co. Chester, [1772] Vol. XII, fol. 147.

KINGSMILL, late BRICE, Edward, of Hampsh., 1787, Vol. XVI, fol. 313.
   „   late BRICE, Sir Robert, of Hampsh., 1800, Vol. XXI, fol. 93.
   „   late STEPHENS, Rev. John, of Sidmanton, Hampsh., and Chewton Mendip, co. Somerset, 1806, Vol. XXIII, fol. 311.
KINGSMILL after WOODHAM, John, of Sidmanton, Hampsh., and Lincoln's Inn, London, 1824, Vol. XXXIV, fol. 394.
KINGSMILL, late WOODHAM, John, of Hampsh., 1826, Vol. XXXV, fol. 335.
KINGSTON, John, M.P., of Oakhill Park, co. Hertf., [1805] Vol. XXIII, fol. 128.
KINGTON, ..., of Charlton, co. Somerset, and Nottery, Wilts., [1793] Vol. XVIII, fol. 174.
KINLESIDE, William, M.A., Rector of Angmering, co. Sussex, [1822] Vol. XXXIII, fol. 131.
KINLESIDE-GRATWICKE, Capt., of co. Sussex, [1822] Vol. XXXIII, fol. 132.
KINLESIDE, ..., wife of GRATWICKE (see ARCHDALL), of co. Sussex, [1863] Vol. LV, fol. 44.
KINLOSS, Baroness, of Scotland, 1893, Vol. LXVII, fol. 145.
KINNAIRD, Baron, of Scotland. Quartering, [1806] Vol. XXIII, fol. 357.
KINNEAR, Baron [Alexander Smith]. Supporters, 1897, Vol. LXIX, fol. 269.
KINNERSLEY, ..., of Newcastle, co. Staff. Improved descent, [1812] Vol. XXVII, fol. 185.
KIRBY, Thomas, of Lutterworth, co. Leic., 23 Aug. 1729, Vol. VIII, fol. 56.
   „   John, B.A., Vicar of Mayfield, co. Sussex, 30 April 1811, Vol. XXVI, fol. 230.
   „   Richard Charles, C.B., Acct.-Genl. to Army, of London, [1859] Vol. LIII, fol. 87.
KIRBY to BAGNALL WILD, ... (B.A., Camb.), of Costock, co. Nottingham, and of the Inner Temple, London, [1868] Vol. LVII, fol. 88.
KIRBY, Sir Alfred, of Deptford, co. Kent, Sheriff of London, 1887, Vol. LXIII, fol. 344.
KIRK, William Kilvington, of Stockton-on-Tees, co. Durham, 1881,* Vol. LXI, fol. 162. (Berry's Suppl.)
KIRKLAND, Sir John, Knt., of Clympy Carnwal, co. Lanark, Scotland, [1838] Vol. XLIII, fol. 237.
KIRKMAN, ... (Spr.), of Manchester, co. Lanc., 1818-19, Vol. XXX, fol. . . . .
KIRSHAW, Richard, D.D., of Ripley, co. York, 9 Mar. 172¾, Vol. VII, fol. 243.
KIRSOPP, late GIBSON, ..., of co. Northumberland, [1823?] Vol. XXXIV, fol. 220.
KIRTON, William Ferdinand, of the Indian C.S. (s. of William Ferdinand), of Duke Street, St. James's, London, 1898, Vol. LXX, fol. 270.
KITCHENER, Francis Elliot, of Oulton Old Hall in Stone, co. Staff., s. of William Cripps, and to uncles Thomas, Henry Horatio and Philip Elliott Kitchener, 1899, Vol. VII [LXX], fol. 326.
KITCHIN, F. W., 1868. See KEMP.
KITCHINER, ..., of London (See W. C. GRAVE.) [1773] Vol. XII, fol. 228.
KITCHING, A. E., of Ayton Firs, Great Ayton, co. York, 1887,* Vol. LXIV, fol. 28.
KITSON, Sir James, of Gledhow Hall, co. York, 1886, Vol. LXIII, fol. 272. (Berry's Suppl.)
KNAPP, John Matthew (s. of Matthew Grenville Samuell), of Little Linford Hall, Newport Pagnell, Bucks., 1897, Vol. LXIX, fol. 227.
KNAPTON, late BRINE, Augustus L., M.A., Oxf., of Boldre, Hampsh., [1860] Vol. LIV, fol. 46. (Crisp, IV, 16.)
KNATCHBULL-HUGESSON [1849], [Sir Edward, 9th] Bart., of co. Kent, [1849] Vol. XLIX, fols. 212 and 214.
KNIGHT, John, of London, Rec.-Gen. of Customs, 7 Nov. or 24 Dec. 1710, Vol. V, fol. 408.
KNIGHT, late MAY, formerly BROADNAX, Thomas, of Chawton, Hampsh., 14 May 1738, Vol. VIII, fol. 241^b.

KNIGHT, late DAVIES, Jane, of Marylebone, London, to take the Name and Arms of Knight, under the will of Robert Knight, late Earl of CATHERLOUGH, 23 May 1772, Vol. XII, fol. 142 (*see* exemplification of Arms, Misc. G. et H., 2nd S., I, p. 173).

„ late DAVIES, Robert and H. R., of Wootton Wawen, co. Warw., nat. sons of Knight, Earl of CATHERLOUGH, [1791] Vol. XVII, fol. 448.

KNIGHT to BRUCE, ..., of Wales, [1805] Vol. XXIII, fol. 241.

KNIGHT, late AUSTEN, Edward, of Chawton, Hampsh., and co. Kent, 1812, Vol. XXVII, fol. 181. (Berry.)

KNIGHT after LEAKE, ... (minor), of Holt, co. Norf. Quarterly Arms, [1815] Vol. XXVIII, fol. 314.

KNIGHT-PRYCE after BRUCE, ..., of co. Devon, and co. Glamorgan, Wales, [1837] Vol. XLII, fol. 185.

„ -BRUCE, ... of co. Devon, [1837] Vol. XLII, fol. 190.

KNIGHT to GREGSON, Henry, of co. Northumberland, [1842] Vol. XLVI, fol. 145.

KNIGHT after ROUSE-BOUGHTON, Andrew, of Downton Castle, co. Hereford, and Downton Hall, Shropsh., 1857, Vol. LII, fol. 172 [272?] [*see* Burke].

KNIGHT, Henry Edmund [Alderm. of London] (afterwards Lord Mayor), of St. Albans, co. Hertf., and London, and to descendants of his father, John William Davison, 1874, Vol. LIX, fol. 59 [*see* Burke].

KNIGHTON [William], M.D., of [Hanover Square, co. Middx., and his sister, Thomasine, wife of John Wills STEPHENS, of Beerferris, co. Devon], [2 Nov. 1812] Vol. XXVII, fol. 135. [Crisp, Fragm. Geneal., XIII, p. 24.]

„ (Sir) William, Bart. [1813?], of London, [1813] Vol. XXVII, fol. 347.

KNILL, Sir Stuart, Bart., Lord Mayor of London, of Blackheath, co. Kent, 1892, Vol. LXVII, fol. 95.

KNOLLYS, late WELLDALE, ..., of Fernhill, Winkfield, Berks., [1794] Vol. XVIII, fol. 335.

KNOTT, late NEWBERRY, Thomas Stockland, of co. Dorset, [1780] Vol. XIV, fol. 247.

KNOTT to HOTHAM-WILLIAM, of Wimbledon, co. Surrey, and Bognor, co. Sussex, [1799] Vol. XX, fol. 379.

KNOWLES, ..., of Hunslet, nr. Leeds, co. York, and Stratford Grove, West Ham, co. Essex, [1845] Vol. XLVIII, fol. 45.

„ A., of Swinton Old Hall, Eccles, co. Lanc., 1889,* Vol. LXV, fol. 128.

„ R. M., of Colston Basset, Bingham, co. Nottingham, 1890,* Vol. LXV, fol. 317.

KNOWSLEY, ..., of North Burton, co. York. (*See* TURTON.) [1817] Vol. XXX, fol. 198.

KNUTSFORD, Baron, of co. Surrey. Supporters, 1888, Vol. LXIV, fol. 187.

KOLLE to HORTON, ..., of co. Surrey, [1869] Vol. LVII, fol. 186.

KUPER, Vice-Adm. Sir Augustus Leopold, G.C.B. [1869]. Arms, [1869] Vol. LVII, fol. 188; Supporters, fol. 190.

KYD, Alexander, of Graz, Styria, Austria, 1889, Vol. LXV, fol. 41.

KYFFIN, late LENTHALL, William Kyffin, of Besselsleigh, Berks.; Belmont, co. Denbigh; and Maynan, co. Carnarvon, Wales, [1871] Vol. LVIII, fol. 58.

„ late KENRICH, Elizabeth (Spr.), of Belmont, co. Denbigh, Wales, 1843, [1842] Vol. XLVI, fol. 91.

KYNASTON to POWELL, ..., of Shrewsbury and Worthen, Shropsh. (Match), [1797] Vol. XIX, fol. 351.

KYNASTON, late OWEN, Rev. Walter Charles Edward, M.A., of Hardwicke Hall, Ellesmere, Shropsh., 2 June 1868, Vol. LVII, fol. 13 (*see* Powys-Land Club, XL, p. 22).

KYNNERSLEY after SNEYD, Thomas, of Sutton Hall, co. Derby; Loxley Park, Bishtons, and Belmont, co. Staff. Quarterly Arms, 1815, Vol. XXIX, fol. 3.

KYNNERSLEY-KYNNERSLEY, Thomas, of Leighton Hall, Shropsh., 1887, Vol. LXIV, fol. 104.
KYRLE before MONEY, [Col.] James, of Ham House, Hereford, [26 April 1809] Vol. XXV, fol. 197.
„ before MONEY, Rev. William, of Pitsford, co. Northampton ; Much Marcle, co. Hereford ; and Whetham, Wilts., [1843] Vol. XLVI, fol. 371.

L

LABOUCHERE [Henry], Baron TAUNTON [18 Aug. 1859], of co. Somerset, [1859] Vol. LIII, fols. 208 and 210.
LACE, ..., of Ingthorpe Grange, Marton, co. York, [1836] Vol. XLI, fol. 326.
LACHATRE, Duc de, French Ambassador at St. James's, London. Crest of Augmentation, [1816] Vol. XXIX, fol. 410.
LACK, ..., of Chelsea, co. Middx., [1808] Vol. XXV, fol. 16.
LACON, Sir Edmund, Knt. and Bart., of Great Yarmouth, co. Norf., and Otley, co. York, [1819] Vol. XXXI, fols. 268, 273, and 339.
LACON, late ATKINSON, Walter Lacon, of Linley and Newport, Shropsh., [1829] Vol. XXXVII, fol. 344.
LACY, ..., of Salkeld Lodge, co. Cumberland, and Newcastle-upon-Tyne, co. Northumberland, [1802] Vol. XXI, fol. 309.
LAERY, Robert, of Willis Street, Wellington, New Zealand, 1895, Vol. LXVIII, fol. 198.
LAFONE, Alfred, M.P., of Hanworth Park, co. Middx., 1885,* Vol. LXIII, fol. 53.
LA FONTAINE, ..., Chief Justice, of Montreal, [1855 ?] Vol. LI, fol. 184.
LAFOREY, John (s. of John), afterwards a Baronet, of Plymouth, co. Devon, 1789, Vol. XVII, fol. 160.
LAHORE, See of, India, 1878, Vol. LX, fol. 96.
LAING to OLDHAM, ..., of Hatherleigh, co. Devon ; Caynham, Shropsh. ; and Haydon, co. Somerset, [1830] Vol. XXXVIII, fol. 118.
„ to WOLRYCHE-WHITMORE, ..., M.A., of Dudmaston, Shropsh., and The Mythe, co. Glouc., [1864] Vol. LV, fol. 270.
LAING, Sir James Thornhill, of Sunderland, co. Durham, 1885, Vol. LXIII, fol. 23.
LAINSON, John, of Euston Square, Alderman and Sheriff of London, 1835, [1838] Vol. XLII, fol. 290.
LAKE, Rear-Adm. Sir John, 7 April 1713, Stowe MS. 716.
LAMB. See MELBOURNE.
LAMB, late COCK, ..., of Golden Square, London. Quarterly Arms, [1798] Vol. XX, fol. 129.
„ late BURGES, Sir James Burges, Bart., of co. Sussex, [1821] Vol. XXXIII, fol. 55 ; Knight Marshal of H.M's Household, canton, [1825] Vol. XXXV, fol. 154.
LAMB, John, D.D., Rector of Charwalton and Chipping Norton, co. Northampton, and of Sandford, Worcop, co. Westmorland, [1824 ?] Vol. XXXIV, fol. 230.
„ Sir Peniston, Bart., Baron MELBOURNE [8 June 1770], of Brocket Hall, co. Hertf., 9 Mar. 1774, Vol. XII, fol. 289. (Berry.)
„ Sir Fred. James, G.C.B. [1827], Envoy at Madrid [afterwards Viscount Melbourne], [1828] Vol. XXXVII, fol. 24.
„ John L., of Burley Hurst, Mobberley, co. Chester, 1885,* Vol. LXIII, fol. 161.
LAMBE, Patrick, of Stoke Poges, Bucks., to Lady (Jane) CROSS and the issue of her father, Patrick Lambe, 14 April 1736, Vol. VIII, fol. 197 ?.
LAMBERT, Daniel, of St. Olave, Hart Street, London, and Banstead, co. Surrey, 30 Sept. 1737, Vol. VIII, fol. 220. (Berry.)
LAMBERT to FENWICK, Thomas, s. of Robert, of co. Lanc., 180 . ., Vol. XXI, fol. 241.

LAMBERT, Sir Henry John, Bart., of Mount Ida, co. Norf., [1816] Vol. XXIX, fol. 259 ; Lord of the Manor of Stockwell, co. Surrey, [1830] Vol. XXXVIII, fol. 50.

„ James, ... ? see [1862] Vol. LIV, fol. 294.

„ Lieut.-Gen. Sir John, G.C.B. [19 July 1838]. Supporters, [1838] Vol. XLIII, fol. 150.

„ . . . ., of Gosfield, co. Essex, and Greenhurst, Capel, co. Surrey, [1862] Vol. LIV, fol. 294.

LAMBORN, Richard, J.P., of Greenwich, co. Kent, Bucks. and co. Oxford, [1720] Vol. VI, fol. 433.

LAMBTON after DAWSON, John, of Biddick Waterville, co. Durham, [1801] Vol. XXI, fol. 212.

LAMEGO, ..., of London. Match with BARUH-LOUSADA, [1777] Vol. XIII, fol. 255.

LAMINGTON, Baron [Alexander Douglas Cochrane], of Scotland. Supporters, 1880, Vol. LXI, fol. 29.

LAMPLUGH, late BROUGHAM, Peter, of Cumberland, [1783] Vol. XV, fol. 148.

LAMPLUGH, ..., of Lamplugh, co. Cumberland. Match with IRTON, [1783] Vol. XV, fol. 148.

LAMPLUGH-RAPER, John, of Lamplugh, co. Cumberland, and Lotherton, &c., co. York, 1825, Vol. XXXV, fols. 165 and [1826] 337.

LAMPLUGH, Charles E., of Cornhill, London, and Chalêt des Rosiers, Mentone, 1886, Vol. LXIII, fol. 223.

„ Rev. David, of co. York, formerly of co. Kent, 1883, Vol. LXII, fol. 96. (Berry's Suppl.)

LAMPSON, ..., of Rowfant, co. Sussex, [1863] Vol. LV, fol. 34.

LANCASHIRE, John, of Budge Row, London, and Manchester, 8 March 1729, Vol. VIII, fol. 31.

LANCASTER-LUCAS, ..., of Wateringbury Place, co. Kent, [1849] Vol. XLIX, fol. 173.

LANCASTER, Jane Elizabeth, only dau. of John, and wife of Bentley SHAW, 1874, Vol. LIX, fol. 21.

„ Edward Snow (s. of James), of Durnford House, East Stonehouse, co. Devon, 1897, Vol. LXIX, fol. 205.

„ William John (s. of John), of Putney Hill, co. Surrey, and Snettisham, co. Norf., 18 . . ., Vol. LXXI, fol. . . . .

LANDELL, ..., of St. John's, Southwark, co. Surrey, [1832] Vol. XXXIX, fol. 123.

LANE, Obadiah, of Longton and Lane End, co. Staff., 11 Feb. 170$\frac{3}{4}$, Vol. V, fol. 138 ; Add. MS. 14,831, fol. 38.

„ [George FOX-LANE], Baron BINGLEY [13 May 1762]. Supporters, [1762] Vol. X, fol. 414.

LANE to LUTWYCHE, William, of 1st Troop of Horse Guards, 9 Sept. 1776, Vol. XIII, fol. 229.

LANE, ..., of Broadborne Place, co. Kent, and Southover, Lewes, co. Sussex, [1803] Vol. XXII, fol. 146.

„ . . . ., of Arundel and Slindon, co. Sussex, [1812] Vol. XXVII, fol. 145.

„ . . . ., of Greenhill, Ettingshall, Womborne, co. Staff., and Farindon, co. Surrey, [1825] Vol. XXXV, fol. 124.

LANE after LUCAS, ..., of Brighton, co. Sussex, [1856] Vol. LI, fol. 448.

LANE, C. P., of Moundsley Hall, King's Norton, co. Worc., 1891, Vol. LXVI, fol. 118.

LANE-MULLINS, J. T., of Killounton, Sydney, New South Wales, [1892] Vol. LXVII, fol. 18.

LANGDALE to KELHAM, ..., of New Ormond Street, London, and Bush Hill, Edmonton, co. Middx., [1811] Vol. XXVI, fol. 442.

LANGDALE, ..., of New Ormond Street, London, [1816] Vol. XXIX, fol. 447.

LANGDALE (formerly STOURTON), Hon. Charles, of Houghton, co. York, 1815, Vol. XXVIII, fol. 255.

LANGDALE, Baron [1836] (BICKERSTETH), of Langdale, co. Westmorland. Arms, [1836] Vol. XLI, fol. 212 ; Supporters, Vol. XLI, fol. 214.

LANGFORD-NIBBS, ... (see [1757] Vol. X, fol. 88). See Rev. MANDEVILL.

LANGFORD to SAINSBURY, ..., of London, and Caius Coll., Camb., [1800] Vol. XXI, fol. 16.

LANGFORD, ..., Post-Capt., R.N., son of [William, D.D.], Canon of Windsor, [1824 ?] Vol. XXXV, fol. 69.

LANGFORD to POOLL, ..., of Frome, Tunsbury, and Road, co. Somerset, [1871] Vol. LVIII, fol. 12.

LANGHAM to CARTER, ..., of co. Norfolk, [1813] Vol. XXVII, fol. 430.

LANGHAM, Johann Gottlieb Julius, of Hertford Coll., Oxf., 1897, Vol. LXIX, fol. 253.

LANGLEY, late DAWNAY, Hon. Marmaduke, of Wykeham Abbey, co. York, 1824, Vol. XXXIV, fol. 338.

LANGLEY. (See Crisp, Visit. of England and Wales, II, p. 101.)

LANGMAN, John Lawrence (s. of Joseph), of Stanhope Terrace, Hyde Park, London, 1897, Vol. LXX, fol. 38.

LANGMEAD, ..., of Plymouth, co. Devon, [1787] Vol. XVI, fol. 253.

LANGMORE, W. B., M.R.C.S., of Upper Norwood, London, 1882,* Vol. LXI, fol. 259. (Berry's Suppl.)

LANGSLOW, Capt., Bengal Army, of Hutton House, Strand-on-the-Green, co. Middx. ; Ludlow and Halesworth, Shropsh. ; and Clifton, co. Glouc., [1826] Vol. XXXVI, fol. 95.

LANGSTAFF, Joseph, E.I.C.S., of Newcastle-upon-Tyne, co. Northumberland, and Mickleton, co. York, Surgeon, Fort William, Bengal, [1840] Vol. XLIV, fol. 256.

LANGSTON (see HOPE), ..., of Cavendish Square, London, [1811] Vol. XXVI, fol. 351.

LANGTON, late GORE, William, of Newton Park, co. Somerset, [1783] Vol. XV, fol. 205.

LANGTON to MASSINGBERD, Peregrine, of co. Linc. Escutcheon of Pretence for wife, [1803] Vol. XXII, fol. 248.

LANGTON-MASSINGBERD, Mrs. Emily, of Gunby Park, co. Linc., (died 28 May 1897) 1888, Vol. LXIV, fol. 128 [138 ?].

LANSDELL, John, of Chamberhouse, Berks., and Halstead, co. Kent, 13 Aug. 1720, Vol. VII, fol. 13.

LANSDOWNE, Baron [1712], (GRANVILLE), [171½] Vol. VI, fol. 32 ; Supporters, [171¾] Vol. VI, fol. 211.

LARK, ..., of Upper Bedford Place, London, [1815] Vol. XXIX, fol. 6.

LARKEN (A. Staunton), [Richmond Herald of Arms, and ?] Rev. E. R., of Burton Rectory, co. Linc., 1884,* Vol. LXII, fol. 324.

LARKIN, John Delrow, of Aldenham, co. Hertf., 1891,* Vol. LXVI, fol. 67.

LAROCHE, ..., Post-Capt., R.N., of Totnes, co. Devon, [1803] Vol. XXII, fol. 220.

LARPENT after DE HOCHPIED, ..., of co. Surrey, [1819] Vol. XXXI, fols. 333 and 336.

LASCELLES, ..., Baron HAREWOOD [1790], of co. York. Supporters, [1790] Vol. XIX [XVII ?], fol. 285.

LA SERRE, ..., of Hackney, co. Middx., and London, [1845] Vol. XLVIII, fol. 38.

LATHAM, John, M.D., of Bradwall, Gawsworth, co. Chester, and Bedford Row, London, [1806] Vol. XXIV, fol. 115. (Berry.)

LATHAM to ASHBY, ..., of co. Leic., [1807] Vol. XXIV, fol. 222.

LAURIE after KENNEDY, ..., of London. Quarterly Arms, [1802] Vol. XXI, fol. 425.

LAURIE, John, Maj., Bombay C.S., of London, and Hadley, co. Middx., [1839] Vol. XLIV, fol. 133.

LAURIE (late FECTOR), ..., of Maxwelton, Scotland (and co. Kent), [1848] Vol. XLIX, fol. 53.

LAURIE, formerly BAYLEY, Rev. Sir J. R. L. E., Bart., of London, and Scotland, 1887, Vol. LXIV, fol. 9.

LANTOUR, ..., of Devonshire Place, London, [1803] Vol. XXII, fol. 149.

LAVIE, ..., of Putney, co. Surrey, and Orthesin, Provence, France. Sir Thomas, his younger brother. Crest altered, [1820] Vol. XXXII, fol. 92.

LAVINGTON (Ralph PAYNE), Baron [1795], grant to William PAYNE, his brother of half blood [who assumed the Surname and Arms of GALLWEY, 1814; Bart., 1812], [1813] Vol. XXVII, fol. 454.

LAW, ..., Baron ELLENBOROUGH, of London. Arms extended to descendants of the first Peer, 22 Mar. 1890, Vol. LXV, fol. 227.

LAW after DRINKWATER, John, of the Isle of Man, 1879, Vol. LX, fol. 269. (Berry's Suppl.)

LAWES, Sir J. B., Bart., of Rothamsted, co. Hertf., 1882, LXI, fol. 275.

„ H. T., BENNET, wife of, of London. Arms to wife and descendants, 1812, Vol. XXVII, fol. 198.

LAWFORD, John ?, Capt., R.N., of Portsmouth, Hampsh., [1803] Vol. XXII, fol. 212.

LAWLEY, ..., Bart., of Clanwell, co. Staff. Match, [1816] Vol. XXX, fol. 19.

LAWLEY to THOMPSON, ..., Bart., of Shropsh., [1820] Vol. XXXII, fol. 170.

LAWLEY [Robert], Baron WENLOCK [1831], of Shropsh., [1839] Vol. XLIV, fol. 25.

LAWLOR-HUDDLESTON, D. A. S., of Sawston Hall, co. Camb., 1891, Vol. LXVI, fol. 176.

LAWRELL, James, of Berkeley Street, London, 10 Oct. 1775, Vol. XIII, fol. 132.

LAWRELL to BEBB, ..., of Berks. and co. Surrey, [1850] Vol. XLIX, fol. 338.

LAWRENCE before TOWNSEND, ..., of Alderton, Shurdington, and Steanbridge, co. Glouc. Quarterly Arms, [1806] Vol. XXIII, fol. 375.

LAWRENCE, late MORRIS (L., wife of), Walter, of Sevenhampton, co. Glouc., [1815] Vol. XXIX, fol. 146 ; [1824-26] Vol. XXXV, fol. . . . .

LAWRENCE, Sir William, Knt. [1887], Alderman of London [1855] (see Barts.), 1848 [1849], Vol. XLIX, fol. 195.

„ (Sir) Alexander Hutchinson, Beng. C.S., [1858] Vol. LII, fol. 376.

„ . . . . (or a Peer), of co. Cornw., to descendants with Baronetcy, [of] 1858 [1859], Vol. LIII, fol. 200. [? Sir Alexander Hutchinson, Bart., 10 Aug. 1858.]

„ Sir John Laird Mair, Bart., G.C.B. [1857], of co. Cornw. Supporters [afterwards Baron Lawrence], 1858 [1859], Vol. LIII, fol. 198.

„ Sir William, Bart. [1867], Serg.-Surg. to His Majesty, of Cirencester, co. Glouc., and London, [1867] Vol. LVI, fol. 197.

LAWRENCE to VILLIERS (reputed son of Villiers), of Croft, co. York, [1876] Vol. LIX, fol. 256.

LAWRENCE, Mary (wife of William MORRIS, [and] d. of Walter [Lawrence], of Sevenhampton), by Mary, dau. of Thomas HAYWARD. Escutcheon of Pretence, Lawrence and HAYWARD quarterly, [1824-6] Vol. XXXV, fol. . . . .

„ Joseph (s. of Philip), Sheriff of London, 18 . . ., Vol. LXXI, fol. . . . .

LAWSON to MAIRE, Thomas, of Lartington, co. York, 1772, Vol. XII, fol. 143.

LAWSON, late CORMAC, of Scotland, London, and co. Kent, [1802] Vol. XXI, fol. 294.

„ late WYBERGH, Thomas (minor), of Linton, co. York, and Brayton, co. Cumberland, 1804, Vol. XXIII [XXII ?], fol. 428.

„ late WYBERGH, William, of Linton, co. York ; Brayton, co. Cumberland ; and Clifton Hall, co. Westmorland, 1814, Vol. XXVIII, fol. 376 [176 ?].

„ late WRIGHT, William, Bart., of Brough Hall, co. York, 1834, Vol. XL, fol. 145.

LAWSON-SMITH, E. M., of Longhurst, Bothal, co. Northumberland, 1881, Vol. LXI, fol. 146. (Berry's Suppl.)

LAX, John, of Eryholme, co. York, 23 Nov. 1775, Vol. XIII, fol. 156.

LAX, now MAYNARD, Sarah, widow of John, of co. York. Crest to male descendants, [1785] Vol. XVI, fol. 7.

LAY, Horatio Nelson, Insp.-Gen. of Customs, China, [1862] Vol. LIV, fol. 342.

LAYARD, Daniel Peter, s. of Peter, of Woodhurst, co. Huntingdon, and Mount-flaquin, Guienne. Quarterly Arms, 1779, Vol. XIV, fol. 179.

LAYLAND-BARRATT, Francis, of 68, Cadogan Square, London, impaling Arms of Frances, dau. of Thomas [Longland], of Stone House, Wallasey, co. Chester, 1898, Vol. LXX, fol. 208.

LEA, William, Physician, of Kingsnorton, The Grange, &c., Shropsh., Sheriff, co. Worc., 12 Nov. 1740, Vol. VIII, fol. 279. (See Her. and Geneal., V, p. 214.)

„ Baron DUDLEY, Ferdinando, of Shropshire. Supporters ?, 19 Nov. 1740, Vol. VIII, fol. 283.

„ . . . ., of Astley Hall and Kidderminster, co. Worc., [1844] Vol. XLVII, fol. 294.

„ Sir Thomas, Bart., of The Larches, Kidderminster, co. Worc., 1892,* Vol. LXVII, fol. 43.

LEADBITTER after GIBSON, Thomas, of Newcastle-upon-Tyne and Low Warden, co. Northumberland, 1875, Vol. LIX, fol. 88.

LEADBITTER-SMITH, John, of Bird Hall, Durham, and Nether Warden, co. Northumberland, [1843] Vol. XLVI, fols. 285 and 295.

LEADER, John Williamson, M.A., of Buntingford, co. Hertf., 1876, Vol. LIX, fol. 282. (MS., Her. Coll., 19 D. 14, fols. 261-263.)

„ Robert, of Moor End, Sheffield, and Moor End, co. Essex, s. of Robert, s. of Daniel, 1876, Vol. LIX, fol. 286.

LEAF, ..., of Park Hill, Streatham, co. Surrey, [1838] Vol. XLIII, fol. 319.

LEAINE, ... Match with ROGERS, [1772] Vol. XII, fol. 168.

LEAKE, Rear-Adm. Sir John, Knt., of co. Essex and Sussex, 6 or [16] April 1713, Vol. VI, fol. 95.

„ (MARTIN-), Stephen, F.R.S., of co. Essex and Sussex (afterwards Garter King of Arms), 19 Feb. 172½, Vol. VII, fol. 75. (Berry.)

LEAKE before KNIGHT, ... (minor), of Holt, co. Norf. Quarterly Arms, [1815] Vol. XXVIII, fol. 314.

LEAKE, Sir Luke Samuel, Knt., of Perth, Western Australia, Speaker of the Leg. Assembly, 1877, Vol. LIX, fol. 319, (Burke's Suppl.)

„ George Walpole, Q.C., and Crown Solr., of Western Australia, brother of Sir Luke, 1877, Vol. LIX, fol. 319. (Berry's Suppl.)

LEAMINGTON, Borough of, co. Warw., 1876, Vol. LIX, fol. 276.

LEANDER, ... (see WYNDHAM), 1813, Vol. XXVII, fol. 242 [342 ?].

LEAPER to NEWTON, ..., of Micleover and Norton, co. Derby, [1789] Vol. XVII, fol. 181.

LEAR-CHOLWICH, ..., of co. Somerset and Devon, [1835] Vol. XLI, fol. 130.

LEARMOUTH, ..., of Brunswick Square, London. Match. (See ANNAND.) [1813] Vol. XXVII, fol. 422.

LEATHAM (? William Henry), of Hemsworth, co. York, [1854] Vol. LI, fol. 132.

LEATHER, ..., of Leventhorpe Hall, co. York, and Middleton Hall, Belford, co. Northumberland, [1859] Vol. LIII, fols. 120 and 121. (Berry's Suppl.)

„ . . . ., of Liverpool, co. Lanc., [1863] Vol. LV, fol. 20.

LEATHER-CULLEY, A. H., of Fonberry Tower, Chatton, co. Northumberland, 1896, Vol. LXIX, fol. 174.

LEATHES, formerly MUSSENDEN, Carteret, of Herringfleet, co. Suff., [1783] Vol. XV, fol. 167.

LEAVES, Henry, of Kennington, &c., co. Surrey, 1 Aug. 1741, Vol. IX, fol. 34.

LE BLANC, Thomas, s. of Simon, of Charterhouse Square, London, and Rouen, Normandy, 1753, Vol. IX, fol. 464. (Berry.)

LECHMERE to CHARLTON, Nicholas, of Ludford, co. Hereford, [1 Feb. 1785] Vol. XV, fol. 389.

Lee, John, of Lyon's Inn, London, s. of John, of Ottery St. Mary, co. Devon, to descendants of his father, 10 April 1729,* Vol. VIII, fol. 26 ; Add. MS. 4,831, fol. 123.

Lee, late Fiott, John, LL.D., of Doctors' Commons ; Colworth House, co. Bedf. ; and Totteridge, co. Hertf., [1817] Vol. XXX, fol. 145.

Lee, Matthew, of Elford, co. Devon, 1759, Vol. X, fol. 168. (Berry.)

„ late Philipps, William, of St. Mary Bootham, co. York, and Binfield, Berks., [1761] Vol. X, fol. 367.

„ late Ayton, Richard, of Lombard Street, London. R. C. Lee-Bevan? [1773] Vol. XII, fol. 239.

Lee-(Warner), late Woodward, Daniel Henry, of co. Norf., [1806] Vol. XXIII, fol. 274.

Lee-Warner, ..., of Little Walsingham, co. Norf., 5 March 1806, Vol. XXIII, fol. 278.

„ -Warner (late Bagge), "1. William, 2. Edward," of Quebec House ; 3. Arthur ; 4. Thomas, sons of Charles Elsden Bagge, M.D., [1814] Vol. XXVIII, fol. 124.

Lee, ..., of Ilfracombe, co. Devon, [1818 ?] Vol. XXXI, fol. 167.

Lee to Harvey, ..., Maj. in Army, of Scotland, the reputed dau. of Rai. Harvey, his wife, [1820] Vol. XXXII, fol. 235.

Lee, late Hanning, ..., of Orleigh Court, co. Devon, and Dillington House, co. Somerset, [1820] Vol. XXXV, fol. 187.

Lee, Wright, of Flixton House, Flixton, co. Lanc., [1833] Vol. XXXIX, fol. 233.

Lee after ? Thornton, Richard Napoleon, of the Middle Temple, London, 1865, Vol. LVI, fol. 1.

Lee, G. A. de Lisle-, Bluemantle Pursuivant, Coll. of Arms, London, 1893,* Vol. LXVII, fol. 123. (Crisp, II, p. 63.)

„ Lennox Bertram (s. of Sir Joseph Cockney Lee), of Rossendale, co. Lanc., 1897, Vol. LXIX, fol. 327.

Leece, Elizabeth and Mary (sisters), of St. Anne, Soho, London, [1799] Vol. XX, fol. 334.

Leech, ..., of Kensington Garden Square, London, 1868, Vol. LVII, fol. 47.

Leeds, Duke of. Crest of Godolphin, [1785] Vol. XVI, fol. 71.

„ George William (Bart.), of Croxton Park, co. Camb., permission to continue the name of Leeds, [1812] Vol. XXVII, fol. 115.

Leek, ... (see Hayley), of London, [1701] Vol. V, fol. 51.

Leeming, Major John Fishwick, of Whalley Range, co. Lanc., 1895,* Vol. LXVIII, fol. 233. Alteration in Coat, [1897] Vol. LXX, fol. 62.

„ Richard, of Greaves House and Lentworth Hall, co. Lanc., 1881, Vol. LXI, fol. 152. (Berry's Suppl.)

Lees, Thomas and John, sons of Jonathan, of London and Manchester, [1753] Vol. IX, fol. 452.

Lees to Carill-Worsley, John, of Platt, Manchester, co. Lanc., 1775, Vol. XIII, fol. 61.

Lees, ... (wife of Du Velluz), of Platt, Manchester, [1775] Vol. XIII, fol. 112.

„ John Frederick, of Werneth, nr. Oldham, co. Lanc., [1836] Vol. XLI, fol. 198. (Berry's Suppl.)

„ James, of Green Bank and Mount Pleasant, Oldham, co. Lanc., 1864, Vol. LV, fol. 256.

„ Edward B., of Thurlan Castle, co. Lanc. (decd.), 1887, Vol. LXIV, fol. 126.

„ John, of Clarksfield, Oldham, co. Lanc., 1885, Vol. LXIII, fol. 67. (Crisp, IV, p. 147.)

Lees-Milne, J. H., of Park House, Oldham. co. Lanc., 1890,* Vol. LXVI, fol. 23. (Crisp, IV, p. 157.)

Leese, ..., of Glenfield, Dunham, co. Chester, [1868] Vol. LVII, fol. 82.

Leete, William John, Lieut., 2nd Batt. Northampton Regt., of 38, Eaton Terrace, London, 1897, Vol. LXX, fol. 26.

LEEVES, William, of Tortington and Rowdall, co. Sussex, and Washington, and to the descendants of William, his grandfather, 5 or 25 July 1738, Vol. VIII, fol. 243ᵇ (see Misc. G. et II., 2nd S., I, p. 53).

LEEVES, late FOWLER, William, of Tortington, Walberton, and Chichester, co. Sussex, 1839, Vol. XXV [XLIII ?], fol. 445.

LEE-WARNER. *See above.*

LEFEVRE to SMITH, Thomas, of Hadley, co. Middx., and France, 8 May 1728, Vol. VII, fol. 577.

LEFEVRE after SHAW, Charles, of Lincoln's Inn, London, [1789] Vol. XVII, fols. 151 and 153.

LEFEVRE, John, of Old Ford, co. Middx., and wife, Helena SELMAN, 7 July 1789, Vol. XVII, fols. 151 and 153.

LE FLEMING after HUGHES, ..., of co. Westmorland, [1862] Vol. LIV, fol. 258.

LEGG, Rev. William, of Hawkinge Rectory, Folkestone, co. Kent, 1897, Vol. LXIX, fol. 209.

LEGGATT, Maj., Madras C.S., [1861] Vol. LIV, fol. 196.

LEGGE [Mary], Baroness STAWELL [1760]. Supporters, [1760]* Vol. X, fol. 246.

LEGH after ROWLLS, Elizabeth Rowlls, widow, of Kingston-upon-Thames, co. Surrey, [1781] Vol. XIV, fol. 352.

LEGH, late CROSSE, Richard, of Adlington Hall, co. Chester, and Shaw Hill, Crosse Hall, and Chorley, co. Lanc., [1806] Vol. XXIV, fol. 32. (*See* Lanc. Pedigrees.) Match, Crest, [1806] Vol. XXIV, fol. 34.

  „ late CROSSE, Thomas, of Adlington House, co. Chester. (*See* Foster's Lanc. Pedigrees.) [1823] Vol. XXXIV, fol. 108.

LEGH, 1. Thomas, 2. William, 3. Peter, 4. Maria, 5. Margaret, 6. Emma, 7. Mary, *see* Burke's Armory (nat. children of Col. Thomas Peter Legh, of Lyme, co. Chester, Haydock Lodge and Bradley, co. Lanc.). (In escucheon as an augmentation first granted to Sir Piers Legh, A° 1575, of Bradley and Lyme.) 30 Aug. 1806, Vol. XXIV, fols. 57 to 69. [*See* Genealogist, V, p. 142.]

  „ Arthur Masterton ROBERTSON-, of Adlington Hall, Prestbury, co. Chester, and his wife Caroline Mary Florence, dau. of F. H. COTTON, of Mayfield, Ashbourne, co. Derby, 1897, Vol. LXX, fol. 15.

LE GREW to HESSE, ..., of London, [1794] Vol. XVIII, fol. 371.

LEHEUP, Peter, and brothers Isaac and Michael, of Steeple Morden, co. Camb. ; Gunthorpe, co. Norf. ; Hersett, co. Suff. ; and St. Lo, Normandy, [13 Sept. 1744] Vol. IX, fol. 134 [?]. [Misc. G. et II., 4th S., II, p. 114.]

LEHOOK, Samuel, s. of John, of Canterbury, co. Kent, and London, [1745 ?] Vol. IX, fol. 128.

LEICESTER quartering BYRNE, Baron DE TABLEY, of co. Chester, [1826] Vol. XXXVI, fol. 57. Supporters, [1826] Vol. XXXVI, fol. 87.

LEICESTER to WARREN, ..., of co. Chester, [1832] Vol. XXXIX, fol. 82.

LE HUNT after BAINBRIGGE, Peter, of Derby, 1832, Vol. XXXIX, fol. 199 [139 ?].

LEIGH, ..., of Blakeland, co. Staff. (*See* BROOKE.) [1785] Vol. XVI, fol. 41.

LEIGH to TRAFFORD, ..., of Over Darwen, co. Lanc., and the Inner Temple, London, [1791] Vol. XVII, fol. 438.

LEIGH, late HANBURY, Capel, of Pontpool House and Gnoll Castle, Wales, 1797, Vol. XIX, fol. 430.

LEIGH, Lord [? 6th Viscount], Thomas Charles TRACY, of Rathcoole, Dublin, Ireland, 1789, Vol. XVII, fol. 183.

LEIGH, late TRACY, Henry, last Viscount, of Ireland, 1793, Vol. XVIII, fol. 170.

  „ late TRACY, Thomas Charles (minor), of Toddington House, co. Glouc., 1806, Vol. XXIII, fol. 359.

  „ late SMITH, ..., of Combhay, co. Somerset, and Stoneleigh, co. Warw., [1802] Vol. XXI, fol. 385.

LEIGH, William (*see* the Landed Gentry), of Oak Hill, nr. Liverpool, co. Lanc., and London, 6 Mar. 1811, Vol. XXVI, fol. 186.

LEIGH to HARE, ..., Bart., of Ivor, Bucks., and Stow Hall and Stow Bardolf, co. Norf., [1814] Vol. XXVIII, fol. 5.

LEIGH, Robert Holt, M.P., of Whitley and Wigan, co. Lanc., [1815] Vol. XXVIII, fol. 286.

„ Roger (s. of Sir Robert HOLT, Bart.), of Hindley Hall, co. Lanc., [1869] Vol. LVII, fol. 162.

„ Roger, of Barham Court, co. Kent, [1869] Vol. LVII, fol. 162. (Burke.)

LEIGH (BOUGHTON) after WARD, John, of Guilsborough, co. Northampton, and Brownsover Hall, co. Warw., [1832] Vol. XXXIX, fols. 63 and 67.

LEIGH to MALLORY [1833], Rev. George, M.A., of Mobberley, co. Chester, [1833?] Vol. XXXIX, fol. 292. [See Geneal., New S., XXXII, p. 116.]

LEIGH after AUSTEN, James Edward, of Berks., [1836] Vol. XLII, fol. 42.

LEIGH to HANBURY-TRACY, ..., of co. Glouc., [1839] Vol. XLIII, fol. 349.

LEIGH after PEMBERTON, Thomas, Q.C., of Bispham and Hindley Halls, co. Lanc., Atty.-Genl. to the Prince of Wales, [1843] Vol. XLVI, fol. 276.

LEIGH (PEMBERTON-), Baron KINGSDOWNE [28 Aug. 1858, Right Hon.], Thomas, of co. Kent. Supporters, [1858] Vol. LII, fol. 389.

LEIGH, late YATES, ... (minor), of co. Lanc. Arms of Leigh, [1850] Vol. XLIX, fol. 387.

LEIGH, Richard, of Standish Gate, Wigan, co. Lanc., only s. of Ralph, 1874, Vol. LIX, fol. 3.

„ . . . ., J.P. (s. of William), of Grange, co. Chester, and Upton, co. Lanc., [1843-1845] Vol. XLVII, fol. . . . .

„ [Borough of, co. Lanc., 23 Dec. 1899 ; Geneal. Mag., III, p. 523.]

LEIGHTON, ..., of Watlesborough, Shropsh. (See OWEN, formerly SMYTH.) [1790] Vol. XVII, fol. 205.

„ Maj.-Gen. Sir David, K.C.B. [1837], [1837] Vol. XLII, fol. 240.

LEIGHTON, Sir Frederick, Bart., of London (afterwards Lord Leighton), 1886,* Vol. LXIII, fol. 167.

LEITH to HAY, ..., of Leith Hall, Aberdeen, Scotland, and Raunes, [1789 ?] Vol. XVII, fol. 187.

LEITH, Maj.-Gen. Sir James, K.B. [1813], of Scotland. Augmentation, [1812] Vol. XXVII, fol. 248 ; Supporters, Vol. XXVII, fol. 254 [1813 ? 354].

LEMAN, late ORGILL, M.A., Naunton Thomas, of Brampton and Worlingham, co. Suff., 1808, Vol. XXIV, fol. 372.

LE MARCHAND, Michael Joseph, Bengal C.S., [1839] Vol. XLIV, fol. 101.

LE MARCHANT, William and Eleazar, of Hampsh., and Guernsey, 1689, Vol. IV, fol. 39.

LE MARCHANT after THOMAS, ..., of Sea View, Isle of Wight, and La Haye, du Puits, Guernsey, [1865] Vol. LV, fol. 304.

LE MESSURIER, John, s. of John, grandfather Thomas, Gov. of Alderney, and St. Peter's Port, Guernsey, [1780] Vol. XIV, fol. 233.

LEMON, William, Bart. [1774], of Carclew and Truro, co. Cornw., [1802 ?] Vol. XXII, fol. 24.

LE MOINE, ..., of Westminster and London. (Match), [1783] Vol. XV, fol. 230.

LEMPSTER [LEOMINSTER], Baron [1692, Sir William Fermor, 2nd Bart.], of co. Hereford [Easton Neston, co. Northampton]. Supporters, 16 . . ., Vol. IV, fol. 15 [?].

LE NEVE, William, York Herald of Arms, London. Confirmed by W. SEGAR, 5 May 1627, Vol. I, fol. 26.

„ Edward, Water-Bayliffe of the City of London, 7 July 1726, Vol. VII, fol. 523 ; Add. MS. 14,831, fol. 71.

LENG, John, nominated Bp. of Norwich, co. Norf., 7 Oct. 1723, Vol. VII, fol. 220.

LENNARD after BARRETT (late THOMAS), ..., of Bellhouse, co. Essex. Quarterly Arms, [1801 ?] Vol. XXI, fol. 200.

LENNARD, late CATOR [1861], John Farnaby, Bart., of Wickham Court, co. Kent, [1861] Vol. LIV, fol. 226.

LENNOX (KINCAID) after BATEMAN-HANBURY, ..., of Scotland, [1862] Vol. LIV, fol. 234.

LENNOX, ..., GORDON AND RICHMOND, Duke of, [? cr. Duke of Gordon, 13 Jan. 1876] of Scotland. Quarterly Arms, Gordon and Lennox, [1876] Vol. LIX, fol. 244.

LENTHALL to KYFFIN, ..., of Berks. and co. Denbigh, Wales, [1871] Vol. LVIII, fol. 58.

LEPPINGTON, ..., of Louth, co. Linc., and London, [1854] Vol. LI, fol. 38.

LERMITTE, J. H., of Knighton, Finchley, co. Middx., and Marine Parade, Brighton, co. Sussex, 1882, Vol. LXII, fol. 23. (Berry's Suppl.)

LERNOULT, ..., of Stratford-le-Bow, co. Middx. (Match), (see CLARKE), [1788] Vol. XVII, fol. 45.

LERNOULT, late VAUX, ..., of Bushey, co. Hertf. (London). Match, [1795] Vol. XIX, fol. 93.

LESCHALLAS, ... See PIGÉ. (Berry's Suppl.)

LESCHER, Joseph Samuel Boyles, of South Weald, co. Essex ; and his cousin, William Joseph, of Upton, co. Essex, grandsons of Laurence, of Kertzfeld, Alsace, [25 April 1837],* Vol. XLII, fol. 95.

LESINGHAM to SHELDON, ..., of Abberton, and Upton-on-Severn, co. Worc., [1828] Vol. XXXVII, fol. 119.

LESLIE, late ANSTRUTHER, William, of London, and Scotland, 14 Nov. 1799, Vol. XX, fol. 396.

 „ late DUFF, ... (relict of Duff), of co. Hereford, [1802] Vol. XXI, fol. 388.

 „ late GWYTHER, ... [? 1817], Countess of ROTHES, of Scotland, [1817] Vol. XXX, fol. 206.

LESLIE after WALDEGRAVE, [Hon. George] Waldegrave, and Countess of ROTHES, of co. Hertf. and Surrey, [1861] Vol. LIV, fol. 230.

LESLIE, late HAWORTH, Martin Leslie [1865], of co. Surrey, [1865] Vol. LV, fol. 282.

LESLIE to SLINGSBY, Thomas, of Scriven Park and Lofthouse Hill, co. York, [1869] Vol. LVII, fol. 156.

LESTER, Sir John, Knt. [1802], of Poole, co. Dorset, [1802] Vol. XXI, fol. 447.

LESTER, late GARLAND, Lester, of Poole, co. Dorset, [1805] Vol. XXIII, fol. 136.

 „ late GARLAND, ..., of co. Dorset, [1853] Vol. L, fol. 426.

 „ late GARLAND, ..., of co. Dorset, [1854?] Vol. LI, fol. 186.

LE STRANGE after STYLEMAN, ... [1839], of Hunstanton Hall and Snettisham, co. Norf., [1839] Vol. XLIV, fol. 69.

LETCHWORTH, Edward, of Enfield, co. Middx., 1890,* Vol. LXV, fol. 248.

LETHBRIDGE, ..., of Westaway and Kirkley, co. Devon, and Sandhill Park, co. Somerset, [1804] Vol. XXIII, fol. 86.

 „ Sir E. ROPER-, of The Lodge, Lynsted, co. Kent [Knt. 1885, K.C.I.E. 1890], 1890, Vol. LXV, fol. 295.

LETT-COLEMAN, Susannah, wife of Thomas, of Lambeth, Surrey. Escutcheon of pretence, Thomas Lett and wife Sarah, 4 Feb. or 4 July 1795, Vol. XIX, fol. 3 (see Berry's Suppl.).

LETTEREWE-BANKES, Mrs. Eleanor Starkie, of Winstanley House, Wigan, co. Lanc., 1882, Vol. LXI, fol. 288.

LETTSOM, ..., of London, [1802 ?] Vol. XXI, fol. 289.

LEVERSON, ..., of London, [1874] Vol. LVIII, fol. 315.

LEVESON GOWER, ... (see GOWER), of co. Lanc. Supporters, [1818] Vol. XXXI, fol. 141.

LEVESON-GOWER to EGERTON, ..., [1833] Vol. XXXIX, fol. 361.

LEVESON-GOWER, ..., [1841] Vol. XLV, fol. 176.

 „ -GOWER, Duke of SUTHERLAND, [K.G., 11 Mar. 1841]. Supporters, [1841] Vol. XLV, fol. 180.

 „ -GOWER, ..., to bear CROMARTIE Supporters, [1862] Vol. LIV, fol. 241.

LEVETT, Rev. Richard, of Milford, Baswick, co. Staff., 1823, Vol. XXXIV [XXXIII ?], fol. 366.
„ John, of Wichnor Park and Packington Hall, co. Staff., [1835] Vol. XLI, fol. 55.
LEVETT-PRINSEP, Thomas, of Wichnor Park, co. Staff., and Croxall, co. Derby, [1835] Vol. XLI, fol. 61.
LEVI, ..., of London, [1823] Vol. XXXIII, fol. 377.
LEVI to RICKMAN, ..., of Hookland Park, co. Sussex, [1823 ?] Vol. XXXIV, fol. 226.
„ to WALEY, ..., of Stockwell, co. Surrey, [1834] Vol. XL, fol. 251.
LEVIEN, Joachim, wife of, of Low Layton, co. Essex. Escutcheon of pretence, [1796] Vol. XIX, fol. 219.
LEVIN, Nathaniel William, of Cleveland Square, Hyde Park, London, late M. of Leg. Council of New Zealand, 1877, Vol. LIX, fol. 337. (Burke's Suppl.)
LEVINZ, Sir Creswell, Knt. [1678], of London, Serg.-at-Law, [1699] Vol. IV, fol. 303.
LEVY, ..., of Walthamstow, co. Essex, and London, [1813] Vol. XXVII, fol. 436.
„ Rev. Thomas Bayley, M.A., Oxf., of co. Westmorland, and Rev. George, B.A., of co. Westmorland, and Bolton-le-Moors, co. Lanc., [1846] Vol. XLVIII, fol. 143.
„ . . . ., of Porchester Gate, London, and Jamaica, [1872] Vol. LVIII, fol. 162.
„ Joseph Moses, of Lancaster Gate, London, and Ramsgate, co. Kent (father of Sir Edward Levy LAWSON, Bart.), 1876, Vol. LIX, fol. 238.
„ Benn Wolfe, merchant, of Pembridge Square, London, 1898, Vol. LXX, fol. 292.
LEWIN, Richard, Sheriff of Kent, 8 June, 1746, Vol. VII [IX ?], fol. 447 [?].
„ . . . ., of March, Isle of Ely, co. Camb., [1847] Vol. XLVIII, fol. 267.
LEWIS, ..., of Plymouth, co. Devon, and Wales, [1782] Vol. XV, fol. 18.
LEWIS to VILLIERS, ..., of Ledburn Green, Bucks., [1791] Vol. XVII, fol. 328.
„ to OWEN, ..., of Five Fields Row, London, and Wales, [1798] Vol. XX, fol. 267.
LEWIS, ..., of St. Pierre, co. Monmouth, [1799] Vol. XX, fol. 334.
LEWIS to WILKINSON, ..., of Castlehead, co. Lanc. (nat. children of John Wilkinson), [1808] Vol. XXV, fols. 18 to 22.
LEWIS, William (surname formerly DAVID), of Brunswick Square, London, and Wales, [1810] Vol. XXVI, fol. 156.
„ Lewis, of co. Cardigan, Wales, [1815] Vol. XXIX, fol. 119.
„ Israel, M.A., of Foxcote, Long Ashton, and Whitchurch, co. Somerset, Llansawell and Llancruwys, co. Carmarthen, Wales, [1825] Vol. XXXV, fols. 209 and 210.
LEWIS after HAMPTON (formerly JONES), ..., of Wales, [1832] Vol. XXXIX, fols. 76 and 79.
LEWIS, Right Hon. Sir Thomas Frankland, Bart. [1846], P.C., M.P., of Harpton Court, co. Radnor, Wales, [1846] Vol. XLVIII, fol. 155.
LEWIS-BARNED, Israel, of Gloucester Terrace, Regent's Park, London, 1858, Vol. LII, fol. 383 (see Burke).
LEWIS, Sir C. E., Bart. (M.P., Londonderry). died 1893 s.p., 1887, Vol. LXIV, fol. 5.
„ James, of Draw, Aberdare, and Pwll-Ivor, Llanfigan, Brecon, Wales, 1892,* Vol. LXVI, fol. 271.
„ Sir William Thomas, of the Mardy, Aberdare, co. Glamorgan, Wales, 1884, Vol. LXII, fol. 268.
LEWTHWAITHE, Rev. George, of Broadgate, Millom, co. Cumberland, Rector of Adel, co. York; and brothers William and John, and sister Alice, wife of Rev. Richard ARMITSTEAD, [1816] Vol. XXIX, fol. 352.

LEY, late GREAVES, ..., of Derby, and co. Staff., [1820] Vol. XXXII, fol. 207.

LEY, F., of The Manor House, Barrow-upon-Trent, co. Nottingham, and Epper-stone Manor, nr. Nottingham, 1888,* Vol. LXIV, fol. 269.

LEYBORNE before POPHAM [Brig.-Gen. William Leyborne?], of Littlecot, Wilts., [Gov. of the?] Isle of Granada, &c. Quarterly Arms, [1804] Vol. XXIII, fols. 107 and 109.

LEYBOURNE, ..., of London and Barbados, [1809] Vol. XXV, fol. 200.

LEYLAND, late BULLIN, of co. Chester and Lanc.; Richard, [1827] Vol. XXXVI, fol. 285; Christopher, [1844] Vol. XLVII, fol. 265. BULLEN quartering to Mrs. NAYLOR, [1856] Vol. LI, fol. 420.

„ late NAYLOR, Thomas, of Hartford Hill, co. Chester, [1849] Vol. XLIX, fol. 254.

LEYLAND, John, of Hindley, Wigan, co. Lanc. (s. of John), 19 Dec. 1863, Vol. LV, fol. 136 (see Genealogist, V, p. 184).

LEYLAND (late NAYLOR), C. J., of Haggerston Castle, co. Northumberland, and Kidlandlee and Filey, co. York, 1894, Vol. LXVIII, fol. 1.

LEYSON to STALLARD-PENOYRE, ..., of Wales, and co. Somerset, [1834] Vol. XL, fol. 270.

LIAS, ..., of Middleton Square, London, [1851] Vol. XLIX, fol. 484.

LIBERTY, Arthur Lasenby (s. of A. L.), of The Lee, Great Missenden, Bucks., 1898, Vol. LXX, fol. 304.

LICHAGARAY to BERTIE, ..., of co. Essex, [1823] Vol. XXXIV, fol. 39.

LICHAGARAY, ..., reputed son, DOWNAM to BERTIE, [1823] Vol. XXXIV, fol. 158.

„ dau. BERTIE, wife of CODWISE, now BERTIE, [1832] Vol. XXXIX, fol. 115.

LIDDELL, ..., Baron RAVENSWORTH [1747]. Supporters, [1748] Vol. IX, fol. 260.

„ . . . ., of Newcastle-upon-Tyne, co. Northumberland, [1845?] Vol. XLVIII, fol. 101.

LIDDELL-GRAINGER, H., of Middleton Hall, Belford, co. Northumberland, 1893, Vol. LXVII, fol. 193.

LIDGBIRD, John, Sheriff, of Plumstead, co. Kent, and Rougham, co. Suff., 15 Dec. 1740, Vol. IX, fol. 3. (Berry.)

LIEBENROOD, late ZEIGENBEIN, ..., of Purley, Berks., [1795] Vol. XIX, fol. 13.

„ late HANCOCK, John, Capt., R.N., of Berks. and co. Kent, 1865, Vol. LV, fol. 288. (Berry's Suppl.)

LIGONIER, Sir John, K.B. [1743], of London, and Languedoc, France, [1743] Vol. IX, fol. 99; Supporters, IX, fol. 102; Add. MS. 14,831, fol. 144.

LILFORD, Baron [1797], (POWYS). Supporters, [1797] Vol. XX, fol. 64.

LILL to DE BURGH, ..., of co. Middx. and Ireland. Escutcheon of pretence, [1800] Vol. XXI, fol. 52.

LILLEY, Joseph Edward, of Wealdstone, co. Middx., 18 . . ., Vol. LXXI, fol. . . . .

LILLINGSTONE, late SPOONER, Abraham and Elizabeth, of Elendon, co. Warw., and Ferriby Grange, co. York. Escutcheon of pretence, [1797] Vol. XX, fol. 14.

LILLINGSTONE to JOHNSON, George William, of co. Derby, Essex, and Leic. and Worcester Coll., Oxf., [1859] Vol. LIII, fol. 138.

LINCOLN, ..., of Catton, co. Norf. (see FREEMAN). Match, [1782] Vol. XV, fol. 55.

[LIND, George Martin, of Croydon, co. Surrey, 1903, Vol. LXX . . ., fol. . . . .]

LINDLEY, late SLEIGH, John, of Skegby, co. Nottingham, 1773, Vol. XII, fol. 225; [1782] Vol. XV, fol. 85.

„ late WILKINSON, ..., of Skegby, co. Nottingham, and Blackwell, co. Derby, [1782] Vol. XV, fol. 121.

LINDLEY, Sir Nathaniel [Knt., 1875], a Justice of the Court of Common Pleas, of East Carleton, co. Norf., [1875] Vol. LIX, fol. 126. (Berry's Suppl.)

LINDO, ..., of Devonshire Square, London, [1819?] Vol. XXXI, fol. 177.

LINDOW, late RAWLINSON, Henry, of Lancaster, [1792] Vol. XVIII, fol. 61.

LINDOW, Samuel, of Ingwell, St. Bees and Cleator, co. Cumberland, [1861] Vol. LIV, fol. 124.

LINDOW to BURNS-LINDOW, Jonas, of Ingwell and Hazel Holme, Kinniside, co. Cumberland [of Irton Hall, co. Cumberland (*see* Burke)], [1871] Vol. LVII, fol. 324.

LINDSAY, [Rear-Adm. ?] St. John, K.B. [1770], Capt., R.N. Supporters, [1772] Vol. XII, fol. 150.

   ,, ... *See* WEIR.

LINDSAY after LLOYD, ... [1858], of co. Northampton, and Scotland, afterwards Baron WANTAGE, [1858] Vol. LIII, fol. 44.

LINDSAY, Colin, of Deer Park, co. Devon. Quarterly Arms, 1891, Vol. LXVI, fol. 140.

LINGARD, Richard Boughey Monk, of Mill Gate, Northenden and Cheadle, Moseley, co. Chester ; Heaton Norris, co. Lanc. ; and Cooga, co. Clare, Ireland, 5 Jan. 1871, Vol. LVII, fols. 302 and 306.

LINGARD-MONK, Richard Boughey Monk, of Broome House, Manchester, co. Lanc., and Heaton Norris, Millgate, Northenden, co. Chester, 3 Nov. 1875, Vol. LIX, fol. 160 (*see* Genealogist, V, p. 144, and Berry's Suppl.).

   ,, -MONK, Richard Boughey Monk, of Manchester, s. of Roger Rowson Lingard, of Millgate, par. of Northenden, decd., &c. Arms and Crest of Lingard, with remainder to the descendants of his uncles Thomas and Alexander, both dead, 5 Jan. 1871, Genealogist, V, pp. 142 and 144.

LINGARD, BOUGHEY and JENINGS Quarterings and ROWSON, 16 Jan. 1871, Genealogist, V, p. 144.

   ,, ... Arms and Crest of MONK to Richard Boughey Monk Lingard Monk, 3 Nov. 1875.

LINGWOOD, Robert Maulkin, of Brome, co. Suff., and Christ's Coll., Camb., [1835] Vol. XL, fol. 309.

LINTOT, Thomas, of Walhurst, co. Sussex, Nov. 1723, Vol. VII, fol. 434 [?].

LINZEE, Susannah (dau. of Edward, of Portsmouth), Baroness HOOD [27 Mar. 1795], [1795] Vol. XIX, fol. . . . .

LIPPINCOTT after CANN, Henry, nat. s. of Cann-Lippincott, Bart., of co. Glouc., [1831] Vol. XXXVIII, fol. 248.

LIPPINCOTT, Henry, of Stoke Bishop, co. Glouc. Crest of CANN and escutcheon of pretence, 1776, Vol. XIII, fol. 170.

LIPPITT, Alfred Joseph George, of 11, King's Bench Walk, Temple, London, 27 Mar. 1897, Vol. LXIX, fol. 275.

LIPSCOMB, William, of Barnard Castle, co. Durham, and Winchester, Hampsh., M.A., Christ's Coll., Oxf., and Rector of Welbury, co. York, [1824] Vol. XXXIV, fol. 336.

LISBURNE, Viscount, John (VAUGHAN). Supporters, 1695, Vol. IV, fol. 201.

   ,, Earl of, consent for his brother to bear supporters of that title, [1792] Vol. XVIII, fol. 104.

LISLE, late TAYLOR, Edward Hales, of Blashford, par. of Ellingham, Hampsh., s. and h. of Christopher Taylor, D.D., of Selbourne, and Mary Lisle, his wife, 1 Oct. 1822, Vol. XXXIII, fol. 334 (*see* Genealogist, VII, p. 270.)

   ,, late MOISES, of Barndale House, Alnwick, and Acton House, Felton, co. Northumberland, [1860] Vol. LIV, fol. 36.

LISLE, William Beresford, of Alnwick, co. Northumberland, 1882, Vol. LXI, fol. 355. (Berry's Suppl.)

DE LISLE, Thomas March Phillipps [for Arms] (*see* Burke).

LISTER to NEVILE, John Pate, of Mears Ashby, co. Northampton ; Holbech and Chevet, co. York, [1782] Vol. XV, fol. 109.

LISTER, late STOVIN, George, of Titley, Crowle and Girsby, co. Linc., [1783] Vol. XV, fol. 215.

LISTER, Baron RIBBLESDALE [26 Oct. 1797, Thomas Lister]. Supporters and escutcheon of pretence, [1797] Vol. XX, fol. 77.

LISTER before KAYE, John (reputed father, L. Kaye, Bart.), of Denby Grange, co. York. Quarterly Coat, [1806] Vol. XXIII, fol. 334.

LISTER to MARSDEN, of Gargrave, co. York, and Hornby Castle, co. Lanc., [1827] Vol. XXXVI, fol. 264.

LISTER, Sir Joseph, Bart., of London, 1884,* Vol. LXII, fol. 184; Supporters (Baron Lister), 1897, Vol. LXIX, fol. 267.

LISTON, Sir Robert, G.C.B. [21 Oct. 1816], Turkish Amb. Extra. and Plenip. Supporters, 1817, Vol. XXX, fol. 434 [134 ?].

LITT, William Peatt, of Liverpool, [1806] Vol. XXIII, fol. 291.

LITTLE, late WOODCOCK, ..., of Newbold Pacey and Coventry, co. Warw., [1834] Vol. XL, fol. 96.

  ,, (late HOWMAN), George A. Knightley, of Newbold Pacey, co. Warw., 1879, Vol. LX, fol. 293.

  ,, Henry Clince, of Fair Oak House, Forest of Bowland, co. Lanc., s. of Robert Parker Little, of Belmont House, Melksham, and St. Chadfield, Wilts., 1878, Vol. LX, fol. 197.

LITTLE to PARKER, Henry Clince, of Yarmouth, Isle of Wight, 1879, Vol. LX, fol. 216.

LITTLEJOHN, Alexander, of Pembroke Gardens, London, and Invercharron, co. Ross, Scotland, 1890,* Vol. LXV, fol. 240. (Berry's Suppl.)

  ,, Rev. William D., B.A., of Sydenham, co. Oxford; Stoke Damerell, co. Devon; and co. Aberdeen, Scotland, [1872] Vol. LVIII, fol. 154 (see Berry's Suppl.).

LITTLEDALE, ..., of Whitehaven, co. Cumberland, [1840] Vol. XLIV, fol. 387. (Crisp, I, p. 238.)

LITTLEGROOM, Nicholas, late FRANKLIN, of Dean's Place and Hall's Place, Berks. Quarterly Arms, [1806] Vol. XXIV, fol. 55.

LITTLEHALES, ..., of Wembley, co. Middx., and Moulsey, co. Surrey, [1802] Vol. XXI, fol. 416.

LITTLEHALES to BAKER [17 Jan. 1817], Bart., of Wembley, co. Middx., and Ranston, co. Dorset, [1817] Vol. XXX, fol. 101.

LITTLER, Maj.-Gen. Sir John Hunt, Indian Army, [1820] Vol. XXXII, fol. 238. Additional Crest, [1847] Vol. XLVIII, fol. 334; G.C.B. [31 Jan. 1848]; Supporters, [1848] Vol. XLIX, fol. 56.

LITTLETON, late WALHOUSE, ..., of Hatherton and Teddesley Hay, co. Staff., [1811] Vol. XXVII, fol. 68. (Wife WELLESLEY, nat. dau., [1812] fol. 261.)

LIVERPOOL, Charles JENKINSON, Earl of. Augmentation and Arms, 24 Mar. 1797, Vol. XIX, fol. 391. (Palatine Note Book, ed. by J. E. Bailey, II, p. 162, and Crisp [Notes], II, p. 48.)

LIVERPOOL, Town of, co. Lanc. Confirmed 28 Mar. 1797. Supporters granted next day (see Richard Brooke's Hist. of Liverpool, pp. 180-184). [See Hist. Soc. of Lanc. and Cheshire, XLII, p. 9.]

  ,, [co. Lanc., Bishopric of, 17 July 1882, Hist. Soc. Lanc. and Cheshire, XLII, p. 11.]

LLANDAFF, Viscount (MATTHEWS), of London, 1896, Vol. LXIX, fol. 90.

LLANGATTOCK, Baron (ROLLS), of co. Monmouth, 1892, Vol. LXXVII, fol. 91.

LLANOVER, Baron [1859], (HALL). Supporters, [1859] Vol. LIII, fol. 177.

LLEWELLIN, William, of Hall Grange, Abergavenny, Wales, 1895,* Vol. LXVIII, fol. 318.

LLOYD, ..., of Cynfell, co. Merioneth, Wales, 1784. (Berry's Appx.)

LLOYD to TOPP, Richard, of Shrewsbury, Shropsh., [1778] Vol. XIV, fol. 44.

LLOYD, Frances, late wife of BAMFORD-HESKETH, of Wales (heiress of Gwyrch Castle), 1810, Vol. XXV, fol. 382.

LLOYD, late ELLIS, ..., of Wales. (Match), [1815] Vol. XXVIII, fol. 326.

LLOYD, ..., M.P., of Lancing, co. Sussex, [1831] Vol. XXXVIII, fol. 292.

  ,, [Charlotte, dau. of Martin Allen Lloyd, decd. and wife of Thomas Robarts, of London, 12 June 1821. Misc. G. et H., 4th S., V, pp. 46 and 47.]

LLOYD after CARR, Lieut.-Col., Militia, of Lancing, co. Sussex, [1855] Vol. LI, fol. 261.

LLOYD, ..., Baron MOSTYN [1831], of co. Flint, Wales. [Surname and] Arms [of Mostyn] and Additional Crest, [1832] Vol. XXXIX, fol. 50. Supporters, Vol. XXXIX, fol. 52.

LLOYD-MOSTYN, Edward, son of Baron Mostyn, of co. Flint, Wales, [1832] Vol. XXXIX, fol. 55.

LLOYD to PHILIPPS, John, of Dale Castle, Wales, [1833] Vol. XXXIX, fol. 224.

„ to PHILIPPS, Col. James, [1833] Vol. XXXIX, fol. 226.

LLOYD-ANSTRUTHER, ..., of co. Suffolk, [1837] Vol. XLII, fol. 146.

LLOYD to DUPPA, ..., of Cheney Longville and Winstanston, Shropsh., [1837] Vol. XLII, fol. 251.

LLOYD, Sir William, Knt. [1838], Major [E.I.C.S.], of Bryneston. co. Denbigh, Wales (s. of Richard Middleton Massie Lloyd), [1838] Vol. XLIII, fol. 269.

„ . . . ., of Chester, late B.C.S., [1843] Vol. XLVII, fol. 26.

„ Capt. . . . ., of Chester, Capt., Indian Army, and officiating Surveyor-General, India, [1846] Vol. XLVIII, fol. 188.

LLOYD after DAVIS, ..., of co. Cardigan, Wales, and the Inner Temple, London, [1848] Vol. XLVIII, fol. 440.

LLOYD-ROBERTS, ... (Roberts Arms illegit.), of Langley Farm, Stanton Lacy, Shropsh., [1854] Vol. LI, fol. 45.

LLOYD, Capt. (Mil.) John, of Bank House, Church Stretton, Shropsh., [1855] Vol. LI, fol. 345.

LLOYD to YARBURGH, George John, of Heslington Hall and Lingcroft Lodge, co. York, [1857 ?] Vol. LII, fol. 185.

LLOYD, Sir Martin O. M. [Sir Thomas Davies Lloyd ?], Bart. [21 Jan. 1863, of Bronwydd, co. Cardigan], of Wales. [? Arms, 1862] Vol. LIV, fol. 346.

LLOYD-GRAEME, Yarburgh Graeme, of co. York, [1867] Vol. LVI, fol. 254.

LLOYD, late HINDE, Jacob Youde William, of co. Essex, and Clochfaen, co. Montgomery, 26 Dec. 1868, Vol. LVII, fol. 100 (see Powys-Land Club, XL, p. 13).

LLOYD, Joseph Skipp, M.A., of St. John's Coll., Oxf., and Inner Temple, London ; of Flaxley Gr[ange], Fl[axley] Abinghall, co. Glouc., Adj. to Hon. Corps Gent.-at-Arms, [1869] Vol. LVII, fol. 194.

„ George William, of Stockton Hall, co. York, 1895,* Vol. LXVIII, fol. 245.

„ Thomas Edward J., of Aberdeen, and co. Carmarthen, Wales, Bar.-at-Law, of Lincoln's Inn, London, 1881, Vol. LXI, fol. 191. (Berry's Suppl.)

LLOYD-VERNEY, Lieut.-Col. G. H., of Clochfaen, Llanweig, co. Montgomery, 1888, Vol. LXIV, fol. 200.

LLOYD, Henry (s. of Richard Harman Lloyd), of Pitsford Hall, co. Northampton, 1899, Vol. LXX, fol. 334.

„ Samuel Jones, of co. Northampton, and Wales, [1835] Vol. XL, fol 366 ; Baron OVERSTONE [1850]. Supporters, [1850] Vol. XLIX, fol. 288.

LLOYD before LINDSAY (afterwards Baron WANTAGE [1885]), of co. Northampton, and Scotland, [1858] Vol. LIII, fol. 44.

LOCH, Baron [18 July 1895, Loch], of London. Supporters, [1896] Vol. LXIX, fol. 49.

LOCK, Thomas, Rouge Dragon, Pursuivant, Heralds' College, London, and Warnford, Hampsh. (afterwards Clarenceux), 1767, Vol. XI, fol. 216.

„ John, of Mildenhall and Rowton, co. Suff., 8 Dec. 1770, Vol. XII, fol. 39. (Berry.)

LOCKE, Joseph, F.R.S., of Honiton, co. Devon, and Rothwell Haigh R., co. York, [1847 ?] Vol. XLVIII, fols. 252 and 253.

LOCKER, Frederick, of Chesham Street, Chelsea, 1883,* Vol. LXII, fol. 37.

LOCKER-LAMPSON, F., of Chesham Street, Chelsea, 1885, Vol. LXIII, fol. 109 (see Berry's Suppl.).

LOCKETT, R. R., of Sefton Park, Liverpool, 1893,* Vol. LXVII, fol. 251. (Crisp, 11, p. 108.)

LOCKHART, ..., of Scotland and Calcutta. (Ochterlony, wife). Lockhart arms to descendants, [1803] Vol. XXII, fol. 291.

„ Wastie, of Great Haseley House, co. Oxf. Wastie Arms, [1832] Vol. XXXIX, fol. 51.

LOCKLEY, J. H., of Rockleaze, Westbury-on-Trym, co. Glouc., 1890, Vol. LXV, fol. 194.

LOCKTON, John (s. of John), of Almack Road, Hackney, London, 1897, Vol. LXIX, fol. 207.

LOCKWOOD to WOOD (Wood, Bart.), of Dews Hall, co. Essex ; Gatton Park, co. Surrey, and Hare Park, co. Camb. ; [1838] Vol. XLIII, fol. 34.

LOCKWOOD, ..., B.A., of London and co. Leic., [1845] Vol. XLVII, fol. 427.

„ Sir Frank [Knt., 1894], Q.C., of London, 1893,* Vol. LXVII, fol. 169.

LOCKYER, Sir Edmund Leopold, of Plymouth, Wembury, and Luppit, co. Devon, [1804] Vol. XXIII, fol. 20.

LOCOCK, ... [? Sir Charles, Bart., 1857], M.D., of Northampton, [London], and Holmewood Speldhurst, co. Kent, [1856 ?] Vol. LII, fol. 180.

LODDER, Capt. William Philip James, of Hampsh., [1851] Vol. L, fol. 56.

LODER, Sir Robert, Bart., of co. Northampton and Sussex, 1887,* Vol. LXIV, fol. 38.

LODGE to WILCOCKS, ..., of Lodyplace, Hurley, Berks. ; Reigate, co. Surrey ; and London, [1798] Vol. XX, fol. 187.

LODGE, Edmund, Norroy King of Arms, of London. (See FIELD.) [1822] Vol. XXXIII, fol. 240.

„ Adam (s. of John), of Walburne, co. York, and Carnarvon, Wales, [1837]* Vol. XLII, fol. 99.

LODGE-ELLERTON, John, of Walburne, co. York, and Wales, [1838] Vol. XLIII, fol. 72.

LOFFT, Henry Capell, J.P., of Glemham House, Troston Hall, and Stanton, co. Suff., 1 April 1864, Vol. LV, fol. 156. (Genealogist, I, p. 277.)

LOFFT-MOSELEY, Henry Capell, of Glemham House, Troston Hall, and Stanton, co. Suff. Exemplification of quartering, 20 April 1864, Vol. LV, fol. 162. (Genealogist, I, p. 277.)

LOFT to WALLIS, ..., of Healing and Grimsby, co. Linc., [1838] Vol. XLII, fol. 271.

LOGAN to HORNE, ..., of Berwick, [1850] Vol. XLIX, fol. 305.

LOGGINS to COLE, ..., of co. Devon, Glamorgan, Northampton, Oxford and Worc. (Match), [1803] Vol. XXII, fol. 137.

LOMAX, Richard, of Croft Head and Town Head, Rochdale, co. Lanc., [1860] Vol. LIII, fol. 336.

LOMBE, Edward, of [Weston, co.] Norf., Sheriff, and of Bylaugh Hall, co. Norf., 10 (or 11) Feb. $\frac{1633}{1700}$, Vol. V, fol. 2. (Crisp, Notes, I, p. 104.)

LOMBE, late HASE, John, of Bylaugh Hall, co. Norf. Quartering, 1750, Vol. IX, fol. 367 (? 1762).

„ late BEEVOR, Edward (self and son Edward), [1817] Vol. XXX, fol. 225 ; Edward, s. of Edward, 184 . ., Vol. XLVIII, fol. 380 ; Charles, 185 . ., Vol. L, fol. 139.

„ late EVANS, Henry, [1861] Vol. LIV, fol. 83 ; [1862] fol. 336.

LONDON, ..., of Leighton Buzzard, co. Bedf., [1808] Vol. XXIV, fol. 445 (no grant).

LONE, John, of Linton and Cambridge, 1695, Vol. IV, fol. 190.

LONG, David, Sheriff, of co. Devon, 14 July 1707, Vol. V, fol. 247.

„ Edward, of Aldermaston House, Berks. ; Tredudwell, St. Blaze, co. Cornw. ; Saxmundham, co. Suff. ; and the Island of Jamaica, 1797, Vol. XIX, fol. 423 ; 1795 [in pencil].

LONG, now NORTH, Dudley, of Glemham Hall and Saxmundham, co. Suff., [1797] Vol. XIX, fol. 440.

LONG, late KELLETT, Robert, of Dunstan and Swainsthorpe, co. Norf., [1797] Vol. XX, fol. 4.

Long, Edward, Charles and Samuel, of Saxmundham, co. Suff., and Carshalton, co. Surrey, 1800 [1801 ?], Vol. XXII, fol. 247.

„ Sir Charles, G.C.B. [1820], Paym.-Gen. to H.M. Forces. Supporters, 1820, Vol. XXXII, fol. 377 [?].

Long before Wellesley, afterwards Pole-Tylney-(Tylney-Long, wife of nephew of Baron Wellesley). Quarterly Arms, [1812] Vol. XXVII, fol. 178.

Long after Jones, Daniel, of Whaddon and South Wraxall, Wilts., [1814] Vol. XXVIII, fol. 66.

Long to Sugden, William James, of Weston, nr. Bath, co. Somerset, and Ringley, co. Lanc., [1834] Vol. XL, fol. 266.

Long, ..., of Threadneedle Street, and Kingsland, London, [1849] Vol. XLIX, fol. 104.

Long-Sutton, Alma, 1897, Vol. LXIX, fol. 229 ; Beatrice Jane, fol. 233 ; Cecilia, fol. 235 ; Magdalene, fol. 237 ; Emma Julia (see Mackenzie-Sutton), fol. 231 ; daughters of the Rev. Henry Churchman Long, late of Newton Flotman, co. Norf. Taking the name and Arms of Sutton by direction of their aunt Julia, wife of Peter Wells, of London, and widow of Samuel James Sutton, of Ditchingham, co. Norf.

Longcroft, Charles Beare Coroun, of Hall Place, Havant, Hampsh., [1849] Vol. XLIX, fol. 97.

Longden, now Gregory, ..., of co. Linc., and Nottingham, 1860, Vol. LIV, fol. 56.

Longley, Charles Thomas, D.D., Bp. of Ripon. Arms for See only, permission to impale, [1836] Vol. XLI, fol. 397.

Longman, William C., of Abbess Grange, Leckford, Hampsh., [1859] Vol. LIII, fol. 242.

„ . . . ., of Broadwater, co. Sussex, [1869] Vol. LVII, fol. 145.

„ William Holmes, of Highgate, co. Middx., 1878, Vol. LX, fol. 159.

Longmore, ..., of Clifton Wood, Clifton, Tewkesbury, co. Glouc., [1823] Vol. XXXIII, fol. 398.

Longmore to Skinner, ..., of Great Baddow, co. Essex, Wood Norton and Swanton Novers, co. Norf., [19 Oct. 1825] Vol. XXXV, fol. 339.

Longmore, Sir Thomas, K.C.B. [? C.B., Knt., 30 July 1886], of Woolstone, Southampton, Hampsh., 1888, Vol. LXIV, fols. 150 and 95 [195 ?].

Longstaff, Dr. George D., of Wandsworth, co. Surrey, 1881, Vol. LXI, fol. 245. Crisp, VI, p. 70. (Berry's Suppl.)

Longueville, Thomas, of Penyllan, Oswestry, Shropsh., 1889, Vol. LXV, fol. 13.

Longworth, Thomas J., of Walworth House, Cheltenham, co. Glouc., 1889, fol. 103.

Lonsdale, Baron, of co. Cumberland (see Granville), 1786, Vol. XVI, fol. 103.

„ Viscount, John, of co. Cumberland. Supporters, 1698, Vol. IV, fol. 254 ; Earl, Supporters, [1784] Vol. XV, fol. 317.

„ John (afterwards Bishop of Lichfield), of co. Staff., and Darfield and Chapelthorpe, co. York, [1811] Vol. XXVI, fol. 244.

Lonsdale to Heywood-Lonsdale, A. P., of co. Lanc., York, and Wales, 1877, Vol. LX, fol. 74. (Berry's Suppl.)

Lopes, Manasseh Masseh, of Clapham, co. Surrey (Bart., died s.p.), [1782] Vol. XV, fol. 14.

Lopes, late Franco, Sir Ralph, Bart., of co. Devon, [1831] Vol. XXXVIII, fol. 240.

Loraine-Broke, Sir J., Bart., of co. Bedf., 1888, Vol. XIV [? LXIV], fol. 240.

Lord, now Owen, ..., of Wales, and Lincoln's Inn, London, [1809] Vol. XXV, fol. 255.

Lord, ..., of Tooting, co. Surrey, [1822] Vol. XXXIII, fol. 167.

„ Sir Riley [Knt., 1900, Mayor of Newcastle-upon-Tyne], of Gosforth, co. Northumberland, [1900], Vol. LXXI, fol. . . . .

[LORIMER, John, M.D., Inspector of Hospitals and Physician H.E.I.Co., 1794. (Misc. G. et II., New S., IV, p. 421.)]

LORING, Rear-Adm. Sir John William, K.C.B. [July 1840, Sir John Wentworth Loring], [1840] Vol. XLIV, fol. 329.

LOSCOMBE, Joseph, of Stowey, co. Somerset, and Luscombe, co. Devon, 1762, Vol. X, fol. 412. (Berry.)

LOTEN, John Gideon, of St. James's, Westminster, originally of Flanders, 1765, Vol. XI, fol. 106. (Edmondson's Armory and Berry.)

LOTT, Valentine. (See HARRISON.) [1821] Vol. XXXII, fol. 301.

LOUGHBOROUGH, Baron (WEDDERBURN), [14 June 1780]. Supporters, [1780] Vol. XIV, fol. 225.

„ Baron (ST. CLAIR-ERSKINE) and Earl of ROSSLYN. Quarterly Arms, [1805] Vol. XXIII, fol. 171 ; Supporters, [1805] Vol. XXIII, fol. 174.

LOUIS [Thomas], Capt. [R.N.], of Chelston, co. Devon, formerly of Paris, [1802] Vol. XXI, fol. 339. ? Supporters, [1806] Vol. XXIII, fol. 422. (Knt. Comr. St. Ferdinand and Merit) of Cadewell [?], [afterwards Adm. Sir Thomas] Bart. [1806, d. 1807].

„ . . . ., of Colyton, co. Devon, [1838] Vol. XLIII, fol. 300.

LOUSADA, Emanuel Baruh, of London, and Jamaica. (See DE CARDONELL.) 28 Jan. 1777, Vol. XIII, fol. 255.

LOVAINE, Baron [28 Jan. 1784] (Percy). Supporters, [1786] Vol. XVI, fol. 173.

LOVEDAY, Feenes, of Berks., and Williamscote and Caversham, co. Oxf., [1844] Vol. XLVII, fol. 257.

LOVEDEN, late TOWNSEND, Edward, of Burscot and Weston House, Berks., [17 July or] 1 Aug. 1772, Vol. XII, fol. 208. (Berry.)

„ late PRYSE, Pryse, M.P., of Weston House, Berks., and Gogorddan, co. Cardigan, Wales. (See PRYSE.) [1849] Vol. XLIX, fol. 184 ; [1863] Vol. LV, fol. 90.

LOVELAND, late OLDERSHAW, John P[ryse ?], of London, 1861, Vol. LIV, fol. 138.

LOVELL. See PUGH. (Berry's Suppl.)

LOVIBOND after IMPEY, ..., Archd. of Berks. and Glouc., 1872, Vol. LVIII, fol. 156.

LOWBRIDGE, ... (See BRIGHT.)

LOWDELL, ..., M.D., of Lewes, co. Sussex, and Great Bookham, co. Surrey. LANGRIDGE quartering, [1825] Vol. XXXV, fol. 106.

LOWDHAM after ALLSOPP, Lewis, of co. Nottingham, [1825] Vol. XXXV, fol. 160.

LOWE, John, of Westminster, an Under-Chamberlain of the Court of Exchequer, 25 May 1694, Vol. IV, fol. 170 ; Add. MS. 14,831, fol. 166.

„ Thomas, of Daisybank and Hordes, co. Chester, 3 Oct. 1738, Vol. VIII, fol. 250 ; Add. MS. 14,830, fol. 35.

LOWE, late DRURY, William, of co. Derby, 1791, Vol. XVII, fol. 334.

LOWE, ..., of Worley, Shropsh., and Claverton, co. Somerset, [1804] Vol. XXII, fol. 330.

„ . . . . (see JELF), of Birmingham, [1809] Vol. XXV, fol. 180.

LOWE, late HOLDEN, William, of co. Derby and Nottingham, 1849, Vol. L [XLIX], fol. 356 [156 ?].

LOWE to HILL, ..., of Shropsh. and co. Worc., [1866] Vol. LVI, fol. 75.

LOWNDES, William, of Overton, Bucks. [? co. Chester], and Winsloe [Bucks.], Sec. to Treasury, and Chairman of the Committee of Ways and Means, Q. Anne and Geo. I, 16 . . ., Vol. II, fol. 583. Confirmation, 28 April 1704, Vol. V, fol. 153. (Berry's Appx. and Burke.)

LOWNDES after SELBY, Francis and Nathaniel, brothers (sons of Richard), of Whaddon Hall and Wavendon, Bucks. Quarterly Arms, [1813] Vol. XXVII, fol. 438.

LOWNDES to GARTH, ..., of co. Oxf. and Surrey, [1837] Vol. XLII, fol. 86.

LOWNDES, late GORST, E. C. L., of co. Derby and Somerset, [1841] Vol. XLV, fol. 59 ; [1853] Vol. L, fol. 350.

„ late CLAYTON, G. A., of co. Essex and Lanc., [1842] Vol. XLV, fol. 325.

LOWNDES-STONE-NORTON, Robert Thomas, of Brightwell Park, co. Oxf., [1872] Vol. LVIII, fol. 177.

LOWTEN, late WAINWRIGHT, ..., of Dunham and Manley, co. Chester, and the Inner Temple, London. (Match), 2 Aug. 1814, Vol. XXVIII, fol. 137.

„ late ROBINSON, ..., of Manley, Frodsham, co. Chester, and Liverpool, co. Lanc., [1830] Vol. XXXVIII, fol. 120.

LOWTHER, Baron LONSDALE, [Baron and] Viscount [1696] Vol. IV, fol. 254 [?] ; [Baron and] Earl Supporters, [1784] Vol. XV, fol. 317 ; [Earl] Supporters, [1807] Vol. XXI, fol. 375 [? XXIV, fol. 275] [see Peerages].

LOWTHORPE, Hannah, dau. of James and widow of Thomas Scott ANDERSON, 1891, Vol. LXVI, fol. 33.

LOXTON, Samuel, of Ferndell, Cannock, co. Staff., 1883, Vol. LXII, fol. 116. (Berry's Suppl.)

LUBBOCK, Thomas, of Norwich, co. Norf., s. of Richard, who mar. Elizabeth PALGRAVE, co-heir, 8 June 1730, Vol. VIII, fol. 75ʰ. (See Palgrave Memorials, p. 183.)

„ Lamas N. (descended from MAYES, of Norwich, 1717), [1806] Vol. XXIII, fol. 306.

ROCKLIFF-LURÉ, William, of Liverpool (Burke.) (See LUNN.) 1862, Vol. LVII [LIV ?], fol. 256.

LUCAS, Joseph, of Foxhunt Manor, Waldron, co. Sussex, 1898, Vol. LXX, fol. 125.

„ John Seymour, R.A., of Woodchurch Road, Hampstead, London, 18 . . ., Vol. LXXI, fol. . . . .

„ Richard, of Oaklands House, West Lavington, co. Sussex (s. of William), 1898, Vol. LXX, fol. 88.

LUCAS to CALCRAFT, of Ancaster, co. Linc., and Ingress, co. Kent. Match, [1786] Vol. XVI, fol. 197 ; Match, [1792] Vol. XVIII, fol. 39.

LUCAS, late NAYLOR, of London, and Twickenham, co. Middx., [1829] Vol. XXXVIII, fol. 17.

LUCAS, Matthias Prime, Alderman and Lord Mayor of London, of Wateringbury, co. Kent, [1833] Vol. XXXIX, fol. 202.

LUCAS before RENNIE, ..., of Wateringbury, co. Kent, [1833] Vol. XXXIX, fols. 271 and 273.

LUCAS after LANCASTER, ..., of Wateringbury, co. Kent, [1849] Vol. XLIX, fol. 173.

LUCAS, ..., of Hasland and Chesterfield, co. Derby, [1838] Vol. XLII, fol. 328.

LUCAS-SHADWELL, late STENT, William Drew, of Fittleworth and Hastings, co. Sussex, [1844 ?] Vol. XLVII, fol. 283.

LUCAS, ..., of Hitchin, co. Hertf., and Llangattock House, co. Monmouth, [1847] Vol. XLVIII, fol. 286.

LUCAS-LANE, ..., of Brighton, co. Sussex, [1856] Vol. LI, fol. 448.

LUCAS, ..., of Lower Grove House, Roehampton, and Clapham Common, co. Surrey ; Lowestoft, co. Suff. ; and Folkestone, co. Kent, [1861] Vol. LIV, fol. 168.

LUCY, late HAMMOND, Rev. John, of Charlecote, co. Warw., [1787] Vol. XVI, fol. 229.

LUCY, William, Mayor [of] Birmingham, [1850] Vol. XLIX, fol. 385.

LUDFORD after NEWDIGATE (formerly BRACEBRIDGE), John, D.C.L., of co. Middx., and Ansley Hall, co. Warw., 1808, Vol. XXIV, fol. 454. (Berry's Appx.)

LUDFORD (NEWDIGATE-), ..., of Chetwode, co. Staff., and Warw., [1826] Vol. XXXVI, fol. 73.

LUDGATER, James, of Eltham, co. Kent, [1840] Vol. XLIV, fol. 353.

LUDLAM, Sir George, Knt., of London, Chamberlain of the City of London, s. of
    Thomas Ludlam, Mayor, of co. Leic., to descendants of his father, 3 Feb.
    172⁶₉, Vol. VII, fol. 539 ; Add. MS. 14,831, fol. 32 (*see* Berry).
LUDLOW, Maj.-Gen. the Hon. Sir George James, K.B. [1804], of Wilts., s. of Peter,
    Earl of Ludlow. Supporters, [1805] Vol. XXIII, fol. 187.
  „   Baron [Lopes]. Supporters, 1897, Vol. LXX, fol. 40.
LUDLOW-BRUGES, ..., of Wilts., [1835] Vol. XL, fol. 368.
LUDLOW-HEWITT, ..., of co. Glouc., and Ireland, [1857] Vol. LII, fol. 263.
  „   Edwin, of Wimbledon, co. Surrey, 1890, Vol. LXV, fol. 250.
  „   John Malcolm Forbes, C.B., 18 . . ., Vol. LXXI, fol. . . . .
LUGARD, Lieut.-Gen. Sir Edward, G.C.B. [1867], [1859] Vol. LIII, fol. 73.
    Supporters, [1867] Vol. LVI, fol. 236.
LUKIN to WINDHAM, Rear-Adm. (William), s. of George William, Dean of Wells,
    of Braintree, co. Essex, and Felbrigg Hall, co. Norf., 1823 [1824 ?]
    Vol. XXXIV, fol. 372.
LUKIS, Capt. (Mil.), of Grange Parish, St. Peter Port, Guernsey, 1806, Vol. XXIV,
    fol. 164 [? 104]. (Burke.)
LUMB after KERSHAW, Richard, of Silcotes, co. York, [1836] Vol. XLI, fol. 220.
LUMB, formerly KENDALL, Peacy, of co. York, [1870] Vol. LVII, fol. 264.
LUMB, ..., of Brigham Hall, co. Cumberland, [1861] Vol. LIV, fol. 166.
LUMLEY to SAVILE, the Hon. and Rev. John, s. of Earl of SCARBOROUGH, of
    Rufford, co. Nottingham, 1807, Vol. XXIV, fol. 273.
LUMLEY, Maj.-Gen. Sir James Rutherford, K.C.B. [1844], Adj.-Gen. Bengal
    Army, [1845] Vol. XLVIII, fol. 95.
  „   Lieut.-Gen. [the Hon.] Sir William, G.C.B. [1831], of co. Nottingham.
    Supporters, [1832] Vol. XXXIX, fol. 144.
LUMLEY-SAVILE, John, Earl of SCARBOROUGH, 1836, Vol. XLII, fol. 17.
LUMLEY to SAVILE, Henry, of Rufford Abbey, co. Nottingham (nat. s.), [1856]
    Vol. LII, fol. 137.
LUMLEY, Sir John Savile, K.C.B. [1878, G.C.B., 1885], of Rufford Abbey, co.
    Nottingham (Baron), 1887, Vol. LXIV, fol. 40 ; Supporters, [1888] fol. 299.
LUMLEY-SAVILE, John Savile, 2nd Baron Savile, of co. Nottingham. Savile Arms
    exemplified, 1898, Vol. LXX, fol. 131.
LUND, Thomas, of Loveley Hall, (Mayor) Blackburn, co. Lanc., [1863 ?] Vol. LV,
    fol. 138.
  „   Edward, F.R.C.S., of Whalley Range, Manchester, 1894, Vol. LXVII,
    fol. 287.
  „   James, of Malsie Hall, co. York, 1890,* Vol. LXV, fol. 291.
LUNN, ..., of Kingston-upon-Hull, co. York, [1861] Vol. LIV, fol. 214.
LUNN to ROCKLIFFE, William, of Kingston-upon-Hull and Asenby, co. York,
    [1870] Vol. LVII, fol. 256.
LUSCOMBE, ..., (*see* LOSCOMBE), of co. Devon, [1762] Vol. X, fol. 412.
  „   . . . . (*see* HAWKER), of Combe Royal, co. Devon, [1813] Vol. XXVII,
    fol. 347.
  „   John Henry, of Havelock House, Lewisham, co. Kent, [1864] Vol. LV,
    fol. 174.
LUSHINGTON, Stephen (s. of Rev. Henry, D.D., decd.), of Southill Park, Berks.,
    and Sittingbourne, co. Kent, 1791, Vol. XVII, fol. 340.
  „   Maj.-Gen. Sir James Law, G.C.B. [1838], of co. Kent. Supporters, [1838]
    Vol. XLIII, fol. 181.
LUSHINGTON after WILDMAN, of Norton Court, co. Kent, [1870] Vol. LVII,
    fol. 234.
LUSK, Sir Andrew, Lord Mayor of London (s. of John), of Colney Park,
    St. Albans, co. Hertf., and Barr, co. Ayrshire, Scotland, 1874, Vol. LIX,
    fol. 36.
LUTLEY after BARNEBY, of co. Hereford, [1823] Vol. XXXIV, fol. 142.
LUTMAN, Samuel, of Langley, co. Sussex, and Bentley, Hampsh., 1 April 1738,
    Vol. VIII, fol. 239. (Berry.)

LUTON, Borough of, co. Bedf., 1876, Vol. LIX, fol. 247.
LUTTMAN-JOHNSON, Rev. Henry W. R., late MICHELL, M.A., Fellow, Trinity
 Coll., Oxf., and of co. Sussex, [1832] Vol. XXXIX, fol. 31.
LUTTRELL, now OLMIUS [? after Luttrell, 3 April 1787], of New Hall, co. Essex
 (Earl of CARHAMPTON), [1787] Vol. XVI, fol. 275.
LUTWYCHE, late LANE, William, of Shropsh., 9 Sep. 1776, Vol. XIII, fol. 229.
LUXFORD, John Odiame, of Higham, co. Sussex, 1880, Vol. LX, fol. 379.
LUXMOORE-BROOKE, C., of Ashbrooke Hall, Church Minshull, co. Chester, 1887,
 Vol. LXIV, fol. 64.   BROOKE discontinued, [1887] fol. 94.
LYDE, Lyonel, Bart. [1772], of co. Somerset, [1778] Vol. XIV, fol. 33.
LYDE, late POOLE, Lieut.-Gen., of Shirehampton, co. Glouc., and Ayot St. Lawrence,
 co. Hertf., [1792] Vol. XVIII, fol. 91.
 „ late AMES, Lionel, of Shirehampton, co. Glouc., and Ayot St. Lawrence,
  co. Hertf. (Match), [1806] Vol. XXIII, fol. 348.
 „ after AMES, Lionel N. F., of co. Hertf. and Norf. (HOGG, Escutcheon of
  pretence), 1874, Vol. LVIII, fol. 349.
LYDIARD, Elizabeth, widow, of co. Surrey, [widow of ?] Charles, Capt., R.N., decd.,
 [1829] Vol. XXXVII, fol. 326.   (Berry's Suppl.)
LYELL, Sir . . . ., Knt., of Kinnorde, co. Forfar, Scotland, [1864] Vol. LV,
 fol. 196.
LYGON, late PYNDAR, William, Baron BEAUCHAMP, [of Powyk, co. Worc., 26 Feb.
 1806].   Arms and Supporters, [1806] Vol. XXIII, fol. 332.
LYGON to PYNDAR, John Reginald, s. of William [1st Baron Beauchamp], [1813]
 Vol. XXVII, fol. 439.
LYMINGTON, Viscount [1720, Wallop].   Supporters, [1723] Vol. VII, fol. 199.
LYNCH, Sir William, K.B. [1771], 12 July 1771.   Supporters, Vol. XII, fol. 84
 (see Misc. G. et H., New S., IV, p. 360).
LYNCH before DE KILLIKELLY, Bryan Paul, of Bilbao, Spain, [1781 ?] Vol. XIV,
 fol. 282.
LYNCH-STAUNTON, ..., of Leigh Park, Hampsh., and co. Galway, Ireland,
 [1859] Vol. LIII, fols. 267 and 268.
LYNCH, James Birnley, s. of Samuel, of Weston Wood, Newport, Shropsh., Vol. I
 or LXXI, fol. . . . . .
LYNE, late HARFORD, ..., of co. Somerset and Surrey, [1820], Vol. XXXII,
 fol. 121 ; [1826] Vol. XXXVI, fol. 176.
LYNE-STEPHENS, Charles, of Liskeard, co. Cornw., and Weymouth, co. Dorset,
 1826, Vol. XXXVII [XXXVI ?], fols. 81 and 83 [XXXVII, 81, 83,
 is 1828].
LYNES, ..., of Corley, co. Warw., and Kirkby Mallory, co. Leic., [1827] Vol.
 XXXVI, fol. 218 ; wife, [1827] fol. 289.
LYNN, ..., and HALL, his wife, of Woodbridge, co. Suff., [1815], Vol. XXVIII,
 fol. 341.
LYNN, late JOHNSON, [Major] George Francis, of Norton, co. Durham, 23 April
 1796, Vol. XIX, fol. 251.   (Genealogist, I, p. 116.)
LYNNE, late JOHNSON, Walter, of Bucks. and co. Linc., Norf., and Northampton,
 [1831] Vol. XXXVIII, fol. 281.
LYON, Joseph, of Ashfield, Neston, co. Chester, [1820] Vol. XXXII, fol. 96.
LYON-WINDER, John (Trinity Coll., Oxf.), of co. Montgomery, [1820] Vol. XXXII,
 fol. 98 ; Ellen H. Lyon-Winder, [1859] Vol. LIII, fol. 173 ; UVEDALE-
 CORBETT-WINDER-, [1869] Vol. LVII, fol. 147.
LYON, ..., of Enfield, co. Middx., and Kendal, co. Westmorland, [1825] Vol.
 XXXV, fol. 172.
 „ Rev. Ralph, D.D., of Hexham, co. Northumberland, and Sherborne, co.
  Dorset, [1843] Vol. XLVII, fol. 113.
 „ Lieut.-Gen. Sir James, K.B. [K.C.B., 1815] (see Burke) [granted 1815].
 „ . . . ., of Goring, co. Sussex, [1825] Vol. XXXV, fol. 172 ; [1826-7] Vol.
  XXXVI, fol. . . . . ; [1839-40], Vol. XLIV, fol. . . . . ; [1842-3] Vol.
  XLVI, fol. . . . .

Lyons, Sir Edmoud, Knt., K.C.H. [1835], and Bart. [1840], Minister Plenipotentiary to Greece, Capt., R.N., of Lyons, Isle of Antigua, and St. Austin, Hampsh., [1841] Vol. XLV, fol. 150. Augmentation, [1843] Vol. XLVI, fol. 360. G.C.B. [1844] Supporters, [1844] Vol. XLVII, fol. 233.

Lysley, William John, of Warnfield and Ripponden, co. York, and the Island of Dominica, [1832]* Vol. XXXIX, fol. 95.

Lysons, Gen. Sir Daniel, G.C.B. [1886], of co. Glouc. Supporters, 1888, Vol. LXIV, fol. 171.

Lyttelton, [Lieut.-Gen. The Hon.] Sir Richard, K.B. [1753]. Supporters, [1753] Vol. IX, fol. 474.

„ . . . . Match with Ayscough, [1772] Vol. XII, fol. 189.

Lyttleton, Baron [1756]. Supporters, [1756] Vol. X, fol. 70.

„ Baron [1794], of Frankley. Supporters, [1794] Vol. XVIII, fol. 388.

Lyttleton-Annesley, Lieut.-Gen. Arthur Lyttleton, of Templemore, Weybridge, co. Surrey, 1884, LXII, fol. 332.

Lytton after Bulwer, ..., of co. Hertf., [1811] Vol. XXVI, fol. 371 ; [1843] Vol. XLVII, fol. 61.

Lytton, Edward Robert, Baron Lytton. Supporters, [Viscount Knebworth and Earl of Lytton, 28 April 1880] Vol. LX, fol. 336.

Lyveden, Baron [1859], (Smith) of co. Northampton. Supporters, [1859] Vol. LIII, fol. 190.

„ [Baron], Smith to Vernon [1859], of co. Northampton, [1859] Vol. LIII, fol. 192.

M

Macarthur, Maj.-Gen. Sir Edward, K.C.B. [1862], Gov., Victorian Colony, [1862] Vol. LIV, fol. 334.

„ A., of 79, Holland Park, London, and Merstham, co. Surrey, 1891, Vol. LXVI, fol. 213.

Macartney, Sir George, K.B. [1772], of Ireland. Supporters, [1772] Vol. XII, fol. 196.

Macaulay, Baron [1857], of co. Leic. Arms and Supporters, [1857] Vol. LII, fols. 273 and 275.

Macbean to Bell, Frederick, of co. Devon and York, [1852] Vol. L, fol. 121.

MacCleverty, Capt. R. M., [1806] Vol. XXIV, fol. 48.

MacCormac, Sir William [Knt., 7 Dec. 1881], President, Roy. Coll. Surgeons, 1897, Vol. LXX, fol. 7.

McCreagh, Col. [Michael], C.B., K.C.H., for widow Frances Elizabeth, who mar. with W. J. Wright-Armstrong, [1868] Vol. LVI, fol. 339.

McCreagh-Thornhill, Maj., of Eccleston Square, London, 1882, Vol. LXI, fol. 291. (Berry's Suppl.)

McCumming to Beaumont, ..., of co. York, [1857 ?] Vol. LII, fol. 219.

McCutchan, Ivie (f[ormerly ?] Ivie), of Roseneath and Beckenham, co. Kent, 1877, Vol. LX, fol. 32.

Macdonald to Bosvile, Godfrey, s. of Baron [Macdonald, of] Slate [co. Antrim], of co. York, [11 April 1814] Vol. XXVIII, fol. 82. Quarterly Arms, fol. 85. Lieut.-Col. (in Portuguese infantry) Macdonald after Bosvile, [1824] Vol. XXXV, fol. . . . . . Maj.-Gen. and Baron Macdonald, [1824] Vol. XXXV, fol. 11. Macdonald to Bosvile, [1833] Vol. XXXIX, fol. 228.

Macdonald, Lieut.-Col. (Sir) John, of Dalhousie, co. Perth, Scotland, [1829] Vol. XXXVII, fols. 297 and 299.

„ Gen. Sir John, G.C.B. [17 Sept. 1847], Adjutant-General of the Forces. Supporters, [1849] Vol. XLIX, fol. 156.

MacDonnell (Countess of Antrim), late Phelps [Edmund Phelps, her 2nd husband, 1817], of Ireland. Quarterly Arms, [1817] Vol. XXX, fol. 215.

MacDonnell, late Kerr, [1836, 4th] Earl of Antrim, of Ireland, [1836] Vol. XLI, fol. 345 ; [1855, 5th Earl] Vol. LI, fol. 347.

Mace before Gigger, James, of Reading, Berks., and co. Dorset, 25 March, 1803, Vol. XXII, fol. 95.

Macfie to Shaw, John (minor), of America Square, London, nephew of Shaw, Bart., [1807] Vol. XXIV, fol. 279.

MacGarell before Hogg [8 Feb. 1877], Sir James, Bart., K.C.B. [1874]. Supporters, Baron Magheramorne, [5 July 1887] Vol. LXIV, fol. 74. 1877, Vol. LIX, fol. 232 [? 332].

McGeachy, widow of Mayor [of] Clifton, co. Glouc., and Windsor, Nova Scotia, [1843] Vol. XLVI, fol. 318.

McGillwray, Lieut.-Col., of Bhein Gael, Isle of Mull, Scotland, and St. Antoine, 160m, Montreal, [1823] Vol. XXXIV, fol. 68.

MacGregor, Lieut.-Col., Bart., C.B., R.N. Augmentation, Macgregor, of co. Perth, [1823] Vol. XXXIV, fol. 71.

Machin, ..., of Gateford Hall, Worksop, co. Nottingham, [1827] Vol. XXXVI, fol. 260.

McInnes to Nicholson, Lieut., Ind. Life Guards, [1822] Vol. XXXIII, fol. 162.

MacIver, C. W., of Liverpool and Calderstone, co. Lanc., 1884,* Vol. LXII, fol. 307.

Mack, ..., of Plumstead, co. Norf. (See Tilyard.) [1772 ?] Vol. XII, fol. 114.

Mackarness, ..., of Elstree House, Bath, co. Somerset, [1869] Vol. LVII, fol. 208.

Mackay, late Prevost, James, of London and Geneva, 27 Sept. 1775, Vol. XIII, fol. 125.

Mackenzie to Mackenzie-Ashton-, ..., of co. Chester and Kent, [1879] Vol. LX, fol. 324. (Berry's Suppl.)

Mackenzie, W. D., of Fawley Court, Henley-on-Thames, co. Oxf. ; Scotland ; and co. Northampton, 1881,* Vol. LXI, fol. 148. (Berry's Suppl.)

„ Baron, with Barony of Seaforth, [1797] Vol. XX, fol. 115.

Mackenzie before Fraser, Maj.-Gen. Alexander, M.P., [30 Dec. 1803] Vol. XXII, fol. 365 [265 ?]. [Misc. G. et H., 4th S., 11, p. 301 ; III, p. 235]

Mackenzie after Stuart-Wortley, [Baron Wharncliffe, 12 July 1826], of Wortley Hall, co. York, and Belmont Castle, co. Perth. Quarterly Arms and Supporters, [1826] Vol. XXXVI, fols. 37 and 41.

Mackenzie to Douglas, [31 Oct. 1831], Bart., [30 Sept. 1831] [1833] Vol. XL, fol. 21.

Mackenzie (Mackenzie-Stuart-Wharncliffe-), 3rd Baron Wharncliffe, 1880.

Mackenzie-Sutton, Emma Julia, 1897, Vol. LXIX, fol. 231.

Mackerell, John, of Norwich, co. Norf., 10 April 1718, Vol. VI, fol. 371 ;
• (2 seals, fol. 365).

Mackereth to Freeman, Rev. John, of co. York, [1788 ?] Vol. XVI, fol. 327.

Mackeson, ..., of Hythe, co. Kent, [1871] Vol. LVIII, fol. 74.

Mackie, Robert Bownas, of Wakefield, co. York, and his brother, Col. Edward Alexander, [1865]* Vol. LVI, fol. 7. (Berry's Suppl.)

Mackinnon to Campbell, ..., of Scotland, [1806] Vol. XXIII, fol. 430.

Mackintosh after Fraser, ..., of Scotland, [1865 ?] Vol. LVI, fol. 63.

Macklin to Wilson, ..., of Derby, and Bath, co. Somerset, [1784] Vol. XV, fol. 325.

Macklin, ..., of Cambridge, [1785] Vol. XVI, fol. 33.

Mackreth after Williams, Henry, of Ewhurst, Hampsh., 5 Jan. 1820, Vol. XXXII, fol. 1.

Mackworth-Dolben, William Harcourt Johan, 1835 (Burke).

Maclaverty to East, ..., of co. Glouc., [1879] Vol. LX, fol. 320.

Macleod to Hume, ..., of Harris, co. Inverness, Scotland, and Charlestown, South Carolina, and Madras, [1802] Vol. XXI, fol. 383.

MACLEOD, Maj.-Gen. Sir Donald, K.C.B. [1838], 18 . . ., Vol. XLIV [? 1838, XLIII], fol. 170.

MACLEOD to ANNESLEY (s. of Maj.-Gen. Sir Donald [? K.C.B.]), of Shropsh., [1844] Vol. XLVII, fol. 281.

MACLURE, John William (Bart.), s. of John, of Whalley Range, Manchester, 1898, Vol. LXX, fol. 98.

MACMAHON to CREE, Capt. (Mil.), of Thornhill, co. Dorset, and Cullenswood, co. Dublin, Ireland, [1815] Vol. XXIX, fol. 55.

„ Gen. Sir Thomas, Bart. [1859], G.C.B., of Ireland. Baronetcy Supporters, [1859] Vol. LIII, fols. 214 and 220.

MACMANUS, Lieut.-Col. Alexander, of Mount Davis, co. Antrim, by Betham, Ulster, 23 Oct. 1810. (Misc. G. et H., New S., I, p. 167.)

MACNAGHTEN after WORKMAN, ..., Knt., of Upper Clogher, co. Antrim, and Matinnin, co. Armagh, Ireland. Quarterly Arms, [1810] Vol. XXV, fol. 308.

MACNAGHTEN, Baron [1887]. Supporters, [1888] Vol. LXIV, fol. 230.

McNEILL, Baron COLONSAY [1867]. Supporters, [1867] Vol. LVI, fol. 286.

McNICOL to NAIRNE, ..., of Quebec, [1834] Vol. XL, fol. 94.

MACNISH to PORTER, ..., of Troquhair and Borgue, co. Kirkcudbright, Scotland, [1804] Vol. XXIII, fol. 70.

McPHERSON-GRANT, ... (Spr.), of Scotland, [1854] Vol. LI, fol. 100.

MacRAE-GILSTRAP, John, of Northgate, Newark-on-Trent, co. Nottingham, 1897, Vol. LXIX, fol. 223.

MADDISON, late RAWLING, George, of Durham, Watergate and Birtley, and Newcastle-upon-Tyne, co. Northumberland, 16 . . ., Vol. II, fol. 608. (Match), [1811] Vol. XXVII, fol. 37.

MADDISON to COMBE, ..., of co. Somerset, [1849] Vol. XLIX, fol. 244.

MADDOCKS, John, of Maple Hill, Bradford, co. York (s. of Thomas), 18 . . ., Vol. LXXI, fol. . . . .

MADDOCKS to ASHBY, ..., of co. Northampton and Shropsh., [1857] Vol. LII, fol. 252.

MADDY, Edwin, LL.D., of co. Glouc., 30 April 1838, Vol. XLIII, fol. 2.

MADOCKS, ..., of London and Wales, [1803] Vol. XXII, fol. 216.

MADRAS, University of, India, [15 Sept.] 1898, Vol. LXX, fol. 253. [Geneal. Mag., IV, p. 234.]

MADRYLL before CHLERE, ..., of co. Camb. and Essex, [1808] Vol. XXIV, fols. 434 and 436.

MAGHERAMORNE, Baron (see McGARELL HOGG). Supporters, 1887, Vol. LXIV, fol. 74.

MAGÈRE (see DE LA MAGÈRE). (Match), [1760] Vol. X, fol. 250.

MAGNALL, same as MANGNALL, Thomas, of co. Linc.; St. Peter's, Cornhill, London; and Prestwich, co. Lanc., 1765, Vol. XI, fol. 61. (Berry.)

MAGNAY, William, of London, Lord Mayor elect, [1821] Vol. XXXIII, fol. 59.

MAGUTH, Rev. G. S., of Norsey Manor, Great Burstead, co. Essex, 1885, Vol. LXIII, fol. 159.

MAIDA, Count of, Lieut.-Gen. Sir John STUART, K.B. [1806, G.C.B. 1815]. Augmentation, [1810] Vol. XXV, fol. 423.

MAIDMAN, Richard, of Portsea, Hampsh., 1765, Vol. XI, fol. 93. (Berry.)

MAIN, Rev. Thomas John, M.A., Chaplain, R.N., of Portsmouth, Hampsh. (s. of Thomas), 1880, Vol. LX, fol. 364. (Berry's Suppl.)

MAINE, John, of Bucks., 1765, Vol. XI, fol. 89.

MAINE to COGHILL, John. Quarterly Arms, [1779] Vol. XIV, fol. 171.

MAINWARING, ..., of Over Peover, co. Chester. (See TUFNELL.) [1708] Vol. V, fols. 287 and 292.

MAINWARING, late WETENHALL, Thomas, of co. Chester, [1797] Vol. XIX, fol. 404.

„ late PARKER, ..., of Kermincham, co. Chester, and London, [1809] Vol. XXV, fol. 133.

MAINWARING-ELLERKER-ONSLOW, James H., of Woodbridge House, Guildford, co. Surrey, and Risby, co. York, [1843] Vol. XLVII, fols. 48 and 54.

MAINWARING after MILMAN, Charles E. F., and sisters, of the Old Palace, Richmond, co. Surrey, and Staindrop, co. Durham, 1874, Vol. LIX, fols. 9 and 11.

„ after MASSY, Hon. W. F. B., of the Old Palace, Richmond, co. Surrey, and Staindrop, co. Durham, 1874, Vol. LIX, fol. 12.

MAIR, Arthur, of St. Martin's-in-the-Fields, co. Middx., and Kincardine O'Neil, co. Aberdeen, Scotland, 7 Nov. 1774, Vol. XIII, fol. 26.

MAIRE, late LAWSON, Thomas, of co. York, 1772, Vol. XII, fol. 143.

MAIRIS, ..., of Wallingford, Berks., Marston Potterne, Great Cheverell, and Bishop Lavington, Wilts., [1830] Vol. XXXVIII, fol. 75; [1835] Vol. XLI, fol. 126.

MAITLAND, Lieut.-Gen. [The Rt. Hon.] Sir Thomas, G.C.B. [1815], of Hampsh., Gov. of Malta [1813], (2nd s. of James, [7th] Earl of LAUDERDALE). Supporters, [1815] Vol. XXIX, fol. 87.

„ Maj.-Gen. Sir Peregrine, K.C.B. [1815], of Shrub's Hill, near Lyndhurst, Hampsh., 1818, Vol. XXX [? XXVIII, 1815], fol. 369.

MAJOR, Sir John, Bart., of Worlingworth Hall, co. Essex, 1765,° Vol. XI, fol. 102. (Berry.)

MAJOR to HENNIKER, Sir John, Bart. Quarterly Arms, 1765, Vol. XI, fol. 103.

MAJOR, late HENNIKER, [2nd Baron Henniker, 1792], of Thornton Hall, co. Suff., [1792] Vol. XVIII, fol. 97.

MAJOR after HENNIKER [1822], of co. Essex and Suff., [3rd] Baron Henniker, [1822] Vol. XXXIII, fol. 236.

MAJOR, Anne, commonly called WRIGHT (nat. dau. of Wright), wife of Robert ANDERSON, of Mottram Hall, co. Chester, [1812] Vol. XXVII, fol. 224.

MAKDOUGALL-BRISBANE, Lieut.-Gen. Sir Thomas, K.C.B., of Makerstown, co. Roxburgh, Scotland, [1826] Vol. XXXVI, fol. 83.

MAKEPEACE, William, of the Middle Temple, London, and to the descendants of his father, William, of co. Warw., decd., 4 May 1724, Vol. VII, fol. 271; Add. MS. 14,830, fol. 96. (Berry.)

MAKINS, Charles, of London, 7 Feb. 1872, Vol. LVIII, fol. 80 (see Misc. G. et H., New S., II, p. 34).

MALCOLM, Maj.-Gen. Sir John, G.C.B. [Nov. 1819]. Supporters, [1822] Vol. XXXIII, fol. 320 [1819, Vol. XXXI, fol. 320].

„ Sir Pulteney, K.C.B., G.C.M.G. [1832]. Supporters, [1833] Vol. XXXIX, fol. 218.

MALCOLMSON, ..., of London, and Cluny Cottage, Forres, and Muchrach, Cromdale, Scotland, [1859] Vol. LIII, fol. 265.

MALE, Richard, of Pontypridd, Llanwonno, co. Glamorgan, 1882, Vol. LXI, fol. 269. (Berry's Suppl.)

MALET, [Rt. Hon.] Sir Edward Baldwin [G.C.M.G., 1885], G.C.B. [Feb 1886]. Supporters, 1885, Vol. LXIII, fol. 132.

MALLARD, Mary, widow of Robert, of London and Essex, dau. of Thomas JACKSON. Escutcheon of pretence, [1793] Vol. XVIII, fol. 266.

MALLARD, late GOFF, ..., of London, and Plaistow, co. Essex, [1794] Vol. XVIII, fol. 325.

MALLET-DE-CARTERET, Seigneur, of Jersey, [1859] Vol. LIII, fol. 155.

MALLINSON, John, of Manchester and Arkholm, co. Lanc. (s. of Richard), 1879, Vol. LX, fol. 297. (Berry's Suppl.)

MALLORY, late LEIGH, Rev. George, Rector of Mobberley, co. Chester, [11 April 1833] Vol. XXXIX, fol. 392. [See Genealogist, New S., XXXII, p. 116, and 14 April 1915, p. 119.]

MALMSBURY, Baron (HARRIS, K.B.). [? Augmentation and] Supporters, [21 Oct. 1788] Vol. XVII, fol. 135.

MALTBY, Thomas, of London, and Maltby and Northallerton, co. York, [1799-1800] Vol. XX, fol. 408.

,,   Edward, D.D., of Norwich, Preacher of Lincoln's Inn, London, to descendants of his father George, of Norwich, 9 July 1829, Vol. XXXVII, fol. 352. (Misc. G. et H., 2nd S., I, p. 81.) (Berry's Suppl.)

MALTON, Baron of [1728] (WATSON-WENTWORTH). Supporters, [1728] Vol. VIII, fol. 7ᵇ.

MALTRAVERS, Baron [1841] (HOWARD). Supporters, [1841] Vol. XLV, fol. 329.

MAMMATT to WYNTER, ... (Spr.), of London, [1803] Vol. XXII, fol. 78.

MANBEY, late TIDEY, ..., of Stratford Grove, West Ham, co. Essex, and Bethnal Green, co. Middx., [1821] Vol. XXXII, fol. 263; [1821] 294.

MANBY to COLEGRAVE, ..., of co. Essex and Norf., [1819] Vol. XXXI, fol. 152; [1868] Vol. LVII, fol. 37.

MANCHESTER, Borough of, co. Lanc.   Arms, 1 Mar. 1842, Vol. XLVI, fol. 1.

MANCHESTER AND SALFORD BANKING COMPANY, 1875, Vol. LIX, fol. 71.

MANDEVILLE, John, D.D., Dean of Peterborough, s. of George, of Worksop, co. Nottingham, and to his descendants, 9 Oct. 1722, Vol. VII, fol. 114. (See Misc. G. et H., 2nd S., IV, p. 91.)

MANFIELD, Sir [Philip], M.P., of [Redlands, Cliftonville], Northampton.   [Knt., 18 July 1894], 1895, Vol. LXVIII, fol. 146.

MANGLES, ..., of Wapping, London, and Hurley, Berks., [1801] Vol. XXI, fol. 235.

MANGNALL (see MAGNALL), Thomas, of Manchester and London, 1765, Vol. XI, fol. 61.

MANISTY, James, B.D., of Edlingham, co. Northumberland, [1824] Vol. XXXV, fol. 48.

MANN, Sir Horace, Bart., K.B. [1768], (5th Earl of CORNWALLIS). Supporters, 1768, Vol. XI, fol. 288.

MANN, late CORNWALLIS, ... (s. of the [Hon. James Cornwallis] Bp. of Lichfield and Coventry), [1814] Vol. XXVIII, fol. 70; [1823] Vol. XXXIV, fol. 168; [1844] Vol. XLVII, fol. 253.

MANN, Frances and Edith, daughters of Thomas Alfred, of Round Green, nr. Barnsley, co. York, 18 . . ., Vol. LXXI, fol. . . . . .

,,   Ann, widow of John Mann, of Boldshay Hall, co. York, [1880] Vol. LXI, fol. 41.

MANNERS, William, of Hanby Hall and The Grange, co. Linc., [1793 ?] Vol. XVIII, fol. 151.

,,   Baron [20 April 1807], ([The Rt. Hon. Sir Thomas Manners-] SUTTON, Knt.), of Foston, co. Linc.   Supporters, [1807] Vol. XXIV, fol. 183.

MANNERS to TOLLEMACHE [Louisa], Countess of DYSART [wife of John Manners], and her sons [and dau.], [1821] Vol. XXXII, fols. 275, 277 and 279. Sir William TALMASH, of co. Linc. and Leic. [Talmash only, 1821], [1821] Vol. XXXII, fol. 287.

MANNERS-SUTTON, Sir Charles, G.C.B. [1833], Speaker.   Supporters, [1833] Vol. XL, fol. 9.   Supporters, [Baron Bottesford and] cr. Viscount CANTERBURY [10 Mar. 1835], [1835] Vol. XL, fol. 378.

MANNERS, Lord John James Robert (now [7th] Duke of RUTLAND), G.C.B. [1880]. Supporters, 1882, Vol. LXI, fol. 374.

MANNINGHAM-BULLER, ..., of Dilhorne Hall, co. Staff., [1866] Vol. LVI, fol. 71.

MANNOCK, formerly COMYNS, William Valentyne, of co. Suff., [1799] Vol. XX, fol. 400.

MANNOCK, late POWER, Patrick, of Gifford's Hall, co. Suff., and Island of Teneriffe, [1830] Vol. XXXVIII, fol. 130.

MANSEL, Baron [1712, Sir Thomas Mansell, 4th Bart.].   Supporters, [1712] Vol. VI, fol. 59.

MANSEL to PHILIPPS, Richard, of Coedgaing, co. Carmarthen, Wales, grandfather of the 10th Bart., 1793, Vol. XVIII, fol. 159.

MANSEL, late PHILIPPS, Courteney, of Coedgaing, co. Carmarthen, Wales, father of the 10th Bart., [1871] Vol. LVIII, fol. 4.

„ late VILLIERS, William Augustus Henry [1802], (2nd s. of the 4th Earl of Jersey) (died unmar.), [1802] Vol. XXI, fol. 372.

MANSELL, Col. Robert Henry, of The Broad Towers, Caerleon, co. Monmouth, 1898, Vol. LXX, fol. 276.

MANSER, William, of Penryn, co. Cornw., and Hoddesdon, Broxbourne, co. Hertf., [1873] Vol. LVIII, fol. 262.

MANSERGH, James (2nd s. of John), of Rhayader, co. Radnor, Wales, 18 . . ., Vol. LXXI, fol. . . . .

MANSFIELD, Baron [1756] (MURRAY), of Scotland. Supporters, [1756] Vol. X, fol. 67.

„ Borough of (? co. Leic.) [co. Nottingham], [1786] Vol. XVI, fol. 115.

„ Lieut.-Gen. Sir William Rose, G.C.B. [1870], G.C.S.I. [1866], [afterwards] Baron SANDHURST [1871], [1870] Vol. LVII, fol. 266 ; Supporters, fol. 268.

MANSHIP, John, of Compton, co. Surrey, and London, 26 July 1724, Vol. IX [? VII], fol. 73 [fol. 273 ?].

MANT, Rev. Richard [D.D.], of Hampsh., and East Horsley, co. Surrey, Rector of St. Botolph Without, Bishopsgate, London (Irish Bishop), 29 Mar. 1820, Vol. XXXII, fol. 20. (Crisp, I, p. 193, [and Notes] III, 49.)

MANVERS to RIGGS MILLER, ..., of Swalcliffe House, nr. Banbury, co. Oxf., and Balleasey, co. Clare, Ireland, [1826] Vol. XXXVI, fol. 71.

MAPLE, Sir John Blundell, Bart., of co. Camb. and Hertf., 1893, Vol. LXVII, fol. 179.

MAPPIN, John Newton, of Beckland and Sheffield, co. York, July 1857, Vol. LII, fol. 233.

„ Sir Frederick Thorpe, Bart., of Thornbury, Sheffield, co. York, 1886,³ Vol. LXIII, fol. 276 [or 270].

MARCH, ..., of Waresley Park, co. Huntingdon, and London, [1792] Vol. XVIII, fol. 7. Match, widow of HARVEY, [1797] Vol. XX, fol. 35.

MARCH before PHILLIPPS, Thomas, of More Critchill, co. Dorset, and Garendon, co. Leic. Quarterly Arms, 1777 [1796], Vol. XIX, fol. 311.

MARCH to WEELEY, ..., of Weeley Hall, co. Essex, [1796] Vol. XIX, fol. 317.

MARCH, ..., of Gosport, Hampsh., [1804] Vol. XXII, fol. 408.

MARCHANT, ..., of Freshford, co. Somerset, and Manamarie, co. Stanley, South Australia, [1864] Vol. LV, fol. 236.

MARESCOE, ..., of Lisle [Court, Hampsh. ?]. Match with JOYE, [1738] Vol. VIII, fol. 246.

MARGARY, Joshua J., LL., of Kensington, London, [1852] Vol. L, fol. 218.

MARGERISON, John Lister, of Bradford and Leeds, co. York, [1855] Vol. LI, fol. 383.

MARJORIBANKS to ROBERTSON, [David Marjoribanks, and] Mariana, [Sarah, his wife], of Ladykirk, co. Berwick, Scotland, [2 Sept. 1834] Vol. XL, fol. 264.

MARJORIBANKS, [Baron, David Robertson]. Supporters, [12 June 1873] Vol. LVIII, fol. 230.

MARK, John, of Greystoke, Didsbury, co. Lanc., 1893, Vol. LXVII, fol. 267.

MARKER, late SMITH, Rev. George T., decd., of Exmouth and Aylesbeare, co. Devon, Vicar of Uffculme, co. Devon, [1855] Vol. LI, fol. 272.

MARKHAM to SALISBURY, Richard Anthony, of Chapel Allerton Hall, co. York, [1785] Vol. XVI, fol. 89.

„ to CLIFTON, Robert Henry, of Clifton Hall, co. Nottingham, [1870 ?] Vol. LVII, fol. 296.

MARKLAND to ENTWISLE, John, of Leeds, co. York, [1787] Vol. XVI, fol. 289.

MARKS, Harry Hananel, M.P., of Callis Court, St. Peter's, Thanet, co. Kent, 1897, Vol. LXX, fol. 44.

MARKWICK to EVERSFIELD, ..., of Catsfield, co. Sussex, [1807] Vol. XXIV, fol. 246.

MARLBOROUGH, [George, 5th] Duke of. [Surname of Churchill after Spencer, and] Quarterly Arms. SPENCER before CHURCHILL [26 May 1817]. Supporters, [1817] Vol. XXX, fol. 286.

MARLING, Sir Samuel Stephens, Bart., of co. Glouc. and Monmouth, 1882, Vol. LXI, fol. 277.

MARLOW, ..., of Shirley Milbrooke, Hampsh., [1784] Vol. XV, fol. 289.

MARLOW, late VAUGHAN, Capt., R.A., of Gosport, Hampsh., [1784], Vol. XV, fol. 319.

MARLOWE, late CROWE, Marlowe Sidney, of co. Heref., [of St. Benet, Gracechurch Street, London, to bear the Arms of Marlowe]. 13 April 1776, Vol. XIII, fol. 179. (Crisp, Fragm. Geneal., II, p. 56.)

MARPLES, George Jobson, Bar.-at-Law, of (Brinckliffe Tower) Eccleshall, co. York, 1884,* Vol. LXII, fol. 222.

MARRABLE, ..., Sec. to Board of Green Cloth, St. James' Palace, [1832] Vol. XXXIX, fol. 16.

„   . . . ., of Canterbury, co. Kent.   Arms to be borne by others, [1835] Vol. XL, fol. 347.

MARRIOTT after SMITH, William Marriot (minor), of Sydling St. Nicholas, co. Dorset, and Horsmonden, co. Kent. Quarterly Arms, [1811] Vol. XXVI, fol. 223.

MARRIOTT-DODINGTON, ..., of co. Somerset, [1853] Vol. L, fol. 377.

MARRIOTT, Major H. C., of Avonbank, co. Worc., 1892,* Vol. LXVI, fol. 287.

MARROW, W. J., of Cavers, Bournemouth, Hampsh., 1895, Vol. LXVIII, fol. 184.

MARRYAT, Joseph Henry, Post-Capt., R.N., C.B.   Additional Crest, 1827, Vol. XXXVI, fols. 385 and 387.

MARSDEN, James, of Manchester, co. Lanc., and Chelmorton, co. Derby, 10 Dec. 1733, Vol. VIII, fol. 176^b.

„   . . . ., of Westminster, First Sec. to the Board of Admiralty, [1804] Vol. XXIII, fol. 14.

MARSDEN, late LISTER, of co. Lanc. and York, [1827] Vol. XXXVI, fol. 264.

MARSDEN, Rev. J. H., B.D., of co. Essex, 1892,* Vol. LXVII, fol. 12.

MARSH, ... (a testatrix), of Britwell House, Bucks., [1862] Vol. LIV, fol. 324.

„   Lieut.-Col. John William, Solicitor, East India Board, 1886, Vol. LXIII, fol. 301.

MARSHALL-HACKER, ..., of Oxf., [1819] Vol. XXXI, fol. 380 ; [1827] Vol. XXXVI, fol. 254.

MARSHALL, Charles and James, of Cranbrooke, co. Kent, 3 Jan. 1821, Vol. XXXII, fol. 197.

„   John, of Ardwick, Manchester, co. Lanc., 15 June 1822, Vol. XXXIII, fol. 244.

„   Sarah, widow of John, arms impaled, dau. and co-h. of James EARNSHAW and his descendants, 2 Aug. 1833, Vol. XXXIX, fol. 341.

„   John William Phillips, R.N., C.B., of Rochester, co. Kent, Knight of St. George of Russia, Knight of Sword of Sweden, 10 Feb. 1829, Vol. XXXVII, fol. 249.

MARSHALL, late COLE, ..., of co. York, [1829] Vol. XXXVII, fol. 251.

MARSHALL to HATFIELD, William, of co. York, [1833] Vol. XL, fol. 52 ; Christiana, sister of William, [1844] Vol. XLVII, fol. 242.

MARSHALL, George, of Broadwater and Catteshill, Godalming, co. Surrey, 14 Dec. 1850, Vol. XLIX, fol. 403.

„   Col. Hubert, Mil. Sec., Government at Madras, 5 Sept. 1863, Vol. LV, fol. 94.

„   George William, [afterwards] Rouge Croix [Pursuivant and York Herald of Arms], of Ward End House, Aston, co. Warw., and Middle Temple, London, to his descendants and the descendants of his uncle, William Marshall, 2 April 1867, Vol. LVI, fol. 193 (see Misc. G. et H., II, p. 65).

MARSHALL, M. Bell, of The Uplands, Strood [co. Glouc.]; Thomas P. D., of
South Shore, Blackpool, co. Lanc.; Roger R., of Eccleshill, co. York,
1895,* Vol. LXVIII, fol. 218. (Crisp, IV, p. 119.)

  ,,   Thomas Bingham, of Sussex Street, London, 1895,* Vol. LXVIII, fol. 237.

  ,,   Elizabeth, dau. of Francis, of Lambeth, co. Surrey, widow of Walter
BURROWS, of the same (see Miscel. Marescalliana, Vol. II, p. 102),
12 July 1785, Vol. XVI, fol. . . . . .

  ,,   Julian, 3rd. s. of John, M.P., of Leeds, co. York, 18 . . ., Vol. LXXI,
fol. . . . .

MARSHAM, Baron ROMNEY [1716]. Supporters, [1716] Vol. VI, fol. 263.

MARSHAM (JONES-), Adm. Henry Shovell, R.N., of co. Kent, and Ireland, died s.p.,
[1857 ?] Vol. LII, fol. 290.

MARSHAM-TOWNSHEND, Hon. Robert, of co. Kent and London, 1893, Vol. LXVII,
fol. 147.

MARSHE, Blandine and Mary, daus. and exors. of John, of Dunstable and Leighton
Buzzard, co. Bedf., decd., 18 Nov. 1700, Vol. V, fol. 36 ; Harl. MS. 6834,
fols. 87 to 96.

MARSLAND, . . . :, of Holly Vale, Cheadle, Moseley and Stockport, co. Chester,
[1824] Vol. XXXV, fol. 24.

MARSTON to VAUSE, ..., of Belgrave, co. Leic., [1794] Vol. XVIII, fol. 381.

MARTELLI to HOLLOWAY, of London, [1828] Vol. XXXVII, fol. 227.

MARTEN, His Honour Sir Alfred George, Knt., Judge, of Prince of Wales Terrace,
London, 1896,* Vol. LXIX, fols. 134 and 121.

MARTIN-LEAKE, Rear-Adm. Sir Stephen, Knt., of Beddington, co. Surrey ; Mile
End Old Town, co. Middx. ; and Thorpe Hall, co. Essex ; 19 Dec. 1721,
Vol. VII, fol. 75 (see Guillim, p. 421).

MARTIN, Matthew, M.P., of Wivenhoe, co. Essex, Capt., H.E.I.C.S., 18 Sept. 1722,
Vol. VII, fol. 104. [Augmentation, see Burke.]

  ,, ..., (see WHISH), of Ely, co. Camb. Match, 1776, Vol. XIII, fol. 243.

MARTIN to FAIRFAX, Denny, [1782] Vol. XV, fol 83.

MARTIN, late PHELPS, of Withy Bush, co. Pembroke. Crest to male descendants,
[1788] Vol. XVII, fol. 13.

MARTIN, ..., of Great Lockinge, Berks., and co. Antrim, Ireland, [1791], Vol.
XVII, fol. 364.

MARTIN to ATKINS, Edwin, of Priory and Kingston Lisle, Berks., and Clapham,
co. Surrey, 31 Mar. 1792, Vol. XVIII, fol. 15.

MARTIN, ..., of St. Kitts, [1810] Vol. XXVI, fol. 123.

  ,,   Thomas, of Ham Court and Poole House, Overbury, co. Worc. ; Ivy Hall
Court, Sneed Park, co. Glouc. ; and Eastwick Park, co. Surrey, [1811]
Vol. XXVI, fol. 267.

  ,,   (widow), dau. of PITNEY, of Trowbridge, co. Wilts., [1814] Vol. XXVIII,
fol. 95.

  ,,   Francis, Bluemantle Pursuivant of Arms, London, of co. Camb., and
Pattentown Kirk Andrews, co. Cumberland. MARTIN and PENCE
quarterly, [1817] Vol. XXX, fol. 111.

MARTIN after WYKEHAM FIENNES, ..., of Chalcombe Priory, co. Northampton,
and Leeds Castle, co. Kent, 1821, Vol. XXXIII, fol. 65. (Berry and
Burke.)

MARTIN-WYKEHAM to CORNWALLIS, ..., [1859] Vol. LIII, fol. 255.

MARTIN, Adm. Sir George, G.C.B. [1821] (s. of Capt. William, R.N., of
"Hemingstone"), [1822] Vol. XXXIII, fol. 308 ; Supporters, fol. 312.

  ,, ..., Post-Capt., R.N., of The Wilderness, Reigate, co. Surrey, [1835] Vol.
XLI, fols. 152 and [1836] fol. 380.

  ,, ..., of Great Ness and Ness Strange, Shropsh., Manchester and Bombay,
maternally descended from the Duchess of ATHOLL, [1838] Vol. XLIII,
fol. 18.

  ,, ..., and RICHARDS, his wife, of Anstey Pastures, co. Leic., [1845 ?] Vol.
XLVIII, fols. 26 and 27.

MARTIN [Sir James], Knt. [5 May 1869]. First Minister and Attorney-General, N. S. Wales, of Clarens District, Darlinghurst, Sydney, N. S. Wales, [1869] Vol. LVII, fol. 139.

„ E. Pritchard, of Dowlais, co. Glamorgan, Wales, 1894, Vol. LXVIII, fol. 33.

„ John, of Darley Hall and Worsborough, Darfield, co. York, 1880,* Vol. LXI, fol. 41.

„ J. A. Napier, of West Leigh, Havant, Hampsh., 1888,* Vol. LXIV, fol. 219.

MARTINEZ, ..., of London, [1838] Vol. XLIII, fol. 135.

MARTINEZ after ARMSTRONG, William Joseph, of London, [1838] Vol. XLIII, fol. 201.

MARTINEZ, Danson R. J., of Cambridge Terrace, Hyde Park, London, 1895, Vol. LXVIII, fol. 154.

MARTINS, ..., Gent. Usher, St. James' Palace, [1833] Vol. XXXIX, fol. 267.

MARTYN-LINNINGTON, R. L., of Thornton Heath, co. Surrey, 1892, Vol. LXVII, fol. 65.

MARTYR to COBHAM, ... (minor), of Berks. and co. Kent, [1812] Vol. XXVII, fol. 283.

MARWOOD, late METCALFE, William, of Little Busby, co. York, [1809] Vol. XXV, fol. 212.

MARWOOD-ELTON, Rev. Alfred, of Widworthy Court, co. Devon, 1885, Vol. LXIII, fol. 27.

MARYBOROUGH, Baron [1821] [William WELLESLEY-POLE], of Queen's County, Ireland. Supporters, [1821] Vol. XXXIII, fol. 15.

[MARYLEBONE, Borough of, co. London, 17 Aug. 1901 (Geneal Mag., V, p. 444).]

MASEMORE, ... (See ASTON.) [1794] Vol. XVIII, fol. 363.

MASERES, Peter Abraham, of St. James's, Westminster, 12 June 1736, Vol. VIII, fol. 202 ; Ped. 3, D. 14, and Magdalen DUPRATT, his wife. Add. MS. 14,831, fol. 33.

MASEY (HEARD), ..., of Wrenton, co. Somerset, 1761 [1762]. Vol. X, fol. 445. Quarterly to HEARD (see HEARD), [1774] Vol. XIII, fol. 33.

MASHAM, Baron [1712, Sir Samuel Masham, 4th Bart.]. Supporters, [1712] Vol. VI, fol. 36.

„ [Baron][15 July 1891] ([CUNLIFFE-] LISTER), of co. York. Supporters, [1891] Vol. LXVI, fol. 208 ; Quartering, [1894] Vol. LXVIII, fol. 104.

MASHITER, ..., of Cottons and Romford, co. Essex, and J.P., Liberty of the Tower, [1812 ?] Vol. XXVII, fol. 314.

MASON [Thomas A., of Gawthrop and Dent, co. York, and Reigate, co. Surrey, Vol. LXXXIV, fol. 176.]

„ John, of Greenwich, J.P., and to the descendants of John, his father, 4 July 1739, Vol. VIII, fol. 255 (see Misc. G. et H., 2nd S., I, p. 295, and Berry).

MASON to VILLIERS, George Viscount, of Ireland, 21 Oct. 1771, Vol. XII, fol. 107.

„ to POMEROY, of London, and co. Glouc., [1789] Vol. XVII, fol. 185 ; [1797] Vol. XX, fol. 59.

„ to BLOMEFIELD, George (Maj. in the Army), of Necton and Swaffham, co. Norf., [1836] Vol. XLII, fol. 5.

MASON, ..., of Eynsham Hall, co. Oxf., and Pomeron and San Domingos, Portugal, [1866] Vol. LVI, fol. 115.

MASON after HUMFREY, Robert H. B., of co. Norf., 1879, Vol. LX, fol. 258. (Burke.)

MASON, Thomas [Bartlet], of the Inner Temple, London, Student-at-Law, and his younger brother ; (sons of Nathaniel, of Stratford-on-Avon, co. Warw. ?), 6 Mar. 172⅚, Vol. VIII, fol. 23 or 32.

„ Bartlett, of Stratford-upon-Avon, co. Warw., Attorney-at-Law. Ped. 3, D. 14, fol. 97, and Add. MS. 14,831, fol. 52.

„ . . . ., of co. Glouc., [1797] Vol. XX, fol. 59.

MASSEY after OLIVER, Richard M., of Melton Lodge, Melton Mowbray, co. Leic., [1846 ?] Vol. XLVIII, fol. 217.

MASSEY-MAINWARING, William Frederick Barton, of co. Durham and Surrey, 1874, Vol. LIX, fol. 12.

MASSEY-STANLEY now ERRINGTON, ..., Bart., of co. Chester and Hampsh., [1877] Vol. LX, fol. 22.

MASSICKS, Thomas, of The Oaks, Millom, co. Cumberland, 1875, Vol. LIX, fol. 151. (Berry's Suppl.)

MASSINGBERD, late LANGTON, Peregrine, of co. Linc. Escutcheon of pretence, [1803] Vol. XXII, fol. 248.

MASSINGBERD-MUNDY, of South Ormesby, co. Linc., and Burton, co. Leic., [1863] Vol. LV, fol. 40.

LANGTON-MASSINGBERD, Mrs. Emily, of Gunby Park, co. Leic. (*See* LANGTON.) 1888, Vol. LXIV, fol. 128 [138 ?].

MASSY-DAWSON, ..., of co. Linc., and Ireland, [1827] Vol. XXXVI, fols. 279 and 283.

MASTERMAN, Henry (s. of Henry), of Wheelhall, E. Riding, co. York, [1752 ?] Vol IX, fol. 397.

MASTERMAN, late BARLOW, of co. York and Hampsh., [1823] Vol. XXXIV, fol. 45.

  „ late PATTON, John, of Stokesley, co. York, [1788] Vol. XVI, fol. 326.

  „ late [?] SYKES, Sir Mark, of co. York, [1796] Vol. XIX, fol. 287.

MASTERMAN before SYKES [? 1795], Sir Mark [3rd Bart.], of co. York, [1796 ?] Vol. XIX, fol. 327.

MASTER-WHITAKER, Rev. A., of Holme, co. Lanc., 1890, Vol. LXV, fol. 198.

MASTERS (John Smalman), M.A., Jesus Coll., co. Oxf., of Ewdon, par. of Chelton, Shropsh., and Greenwich, co. Kent [and to the descendants of his father, William], [21 Mar. 1834] Vol. XL, fol. 103 ; alteration, [18 Sept. 1834] Vol. XL, fol. 259. [Genealogist, New S., XXVIII, p. 80.]

MASTERS (SMITH-), late COWBURN, Rev. Allen, of co. Kent, [1862] Vol. LIV, fol. 308.

MATCHAM, George, of Fiddleford, co. Dorset, and Bishopsbourne, co. Kent, [1818] Vol. XXX, fol. 369.

MATCHETT to GORDON, ..., of Pulham, co. Norf., Madeira, and Jersey, [1837] Vol. XLII, fol. 249.

MATEOS, Anthony, of Gibraltar, [1862] Vol. LIV, fol. 316.

MATHER, Thomas, s. of Thomas, of Toxteth Park, Liverpool, and Glyn Abbot, co. Flint, Wales, [1847 ?] Vol. XLVIII, fol. 264.

  „ William, M.P., of Broughton, co. Lanc., 1886, Vol. LXIII, fol. 243.

MATHEW (and NAYLOR), H. E., of co. Cornwall, and Shrub's Hill and Clanville Lodge, Hampsh., [1819] Vol. XXXI, fol. 293.

MATHEW to BERTIE, Bromlow Bertie, of Shrub's Hill and Clanville Lodge, Hampsh., [1819] Vol. XXXI, fol. 296.

MATHEW, John [Francis ?], M.P., of co. Hereford [Tipperary ?], (Viscount [Baron] LLANDAFF), [12 Oct. 1783], [1784] Vol. XV, fol. 329.

MATHEWS to COOKE. of Berks. and co. Suff., [1850] Vol. XLIX, fol. 301.

MATHISON, Rev. William Collings, M.A., Fellow of Trin. Coll., Camb., [1868] Vol. LVII, fol. 23.

MATSELL, John, of Great Yarmouth, husband of Elizabeth, the sister of Charles ABBOTT. (*See* ABBOTT.) [1810] Vol. XXVI, fol. 92.

MATTHEWS to KILLAM, Rev. Thomas Killam, of co. York, [1880] Vol. LX, fol. 369.

MATTERSON, Mrs., of Drayton, Curry Rivel, co. Somerset, 1891, Vol. LXVI, fol. 122.

MAUDE now ROXBY, Rev. . . . ., LL.B., of Clapham Rise, co. Surrey, Vicar of St. Olave, Jewry, and Rector of St. Martin's, Ironmonger Lane, London, [1837 ?] Vol. XLII, fols. 103 and 105.

MAUNDRELL, Rev. Herbert, of Sands, Calne, Wilts., 1875, Vol. LIX, fol. 145.

MAULE, ..., Baron PANMURE [10 Sept. 1831], of Scotland.   Supporters, [1831] Vol. XXXVIII, fol. 370.

MAULEVERER, late GOWAN, William, of co. York, [1834] Vol. XL, fol. 143.

DE MAULEY, Baron [10 July 1838] (PONSONBY), of Canford, co. Dorset, [1838] Vol. XLIII, fol. 127.

MAURICE to CORBET, ..., of Petton, Shropsh., [1783] Vol. XV, fol. 146.

„   to CORBET, ..., of Wales, [1820] Vol. XXXII, fol. 217.

MAUVILLAIN, Peter, of Morden, co. Surrey, 27 April 1743, Vol. IX, fol. 89.

MAWBEY, Joseph, High Sheriff, of Kennington, co. Surrey, and to the posterity of his father, John, of Ravenston, co. Leic., 15 Sept. 1757, Vol. X, fol. 108 (*see* Misc. G. et H., New S., III, p. 447). (Edmondson's Armory and Berry.)

MAWHOOD, Col. Charles, certified at College of Arms, May 1779 (*see* Burke and Berry).

MAWSON, Charles, Chester Herald of Arms, of London, s. of Thomas, of Great Wigston, co. Leic., Capt. of Horse to Lord LOUGHBOROUGH, 1692, Vol. IV, fols. 123 and 125.

MAXTED (*see* CANTIS), ..., of the Isle of Thanet, co. Kent.   (Match), [1769] Vol. XI, fol. 366.

MAXWELL, now BROWN, ..., of London, [1786] Vol. XVI, fol. 203.

MAXWELL, late CHARLETON, ..., of Birds Town, Ireland, [1790] Vol. XVII, fol. 189.

MAXWELL to GOODWIN, ..., of co. Chester, and Wales.   Escutcheon of pretence, [1815] Vol. XXVIII, fol. 370.

MAXWELL, ..., of Parson's Green, Fulham, co. Middx., [1819] Vol. XXXI, fol. 157.

MAWDSLEY, James Platt, of Falkner Square, Liverpool, co. Lanc., 1876, Vol. LIX, fol. 242.   (Berry's Suppl.)

MAY, late BRODNAX to KNIGHT, Thomas, of co. Sussex, [1738] Vol. VIII, fol. 241.

MAY, Lieut.-Col. Sir John, K.C.B. [1815], K.T., and S. of Portugal, [23 Mar. 1816] Vol. XXIX, fol. 377.   [*See* Crisp, Fragm. Geneal., XIII, p. 16.]

„   . . . . (Spr.), of Bath, and Jamaica, [1838] Vol. XLIII, fol. 187.

„   William, of The Knowles, Brenchley, co. Kent (? of the Bank of England), 1881, Vol. LXI, fol. 160.   (Berry's Suppl.)

MAYBRICK, James, of Liverpool, 1881,* Vol. LXI, fol. 189.

MAYDWELL, late SMITH, Lieut. Henry Lawrence, of Whittlesea, Isle of Ely, co. Camb., [1841] Vol. XLV, fol. 229.

MAYER, John Baptista, Merchant, of London, and Augsburg, in default to Peter MEYER, s. of Peter, lately decd., 29 Oct. 1740, Vol. VIII, fol. 275 ; Add. MS. 14,831, fol. 42.

„   . . . ., of London.   Quartering with WICKHAM, [1785] Vol. XVI, fol. 45.

MAYNARD, late HESILRIGE, Thomas, of co. Leic. (nephew of Bart.), 28 Mar. 1770,* Vol. XII, fol. 15.

MAYNARD, Viscount [1775] (5th Bart.).   Supporters, [1775] Vol. XIII, fol. 145.

MAYNARD, late LAX, Sarah (widow of John Lax), of co. York.   Crest to male descendants, 1784, [1785 ?] Vol. XVI, fol. 7.   [Geneal. Mag., IV, p. 243.]

MAYNARD, ... (*see* NOURSE), of Pentonville, London, [1811] Vol. XXVII, fol. 11.

MAYOR to BROWN, ..., of co. Lanc., [1841] Vol. XLV, fol. 299.

MAYOR, Rev. Charles, of Rugby, co. Warw.   (Burke) [no date].

MAZE, Peter, Sheriff, of Bristol, co. Glouc., [1840] Vol. XLIV, fol. 323.

MAZE after BLACKBURNE, William Ireland, of Spring Hill, Boughton, co. Chester, and Prestwich, par. of Eccles, co. Lanc., 1855, Vol. LI, fol. 401 ; [1869] Vol. LVII, fol. 204.

MEACKHAM after BERKIN, Rev. William, of Wales, [1803] Vol. XXII, fol. 108.

MEADE, ..., of North Petherton, Lyngall, and Taunton, co. Somerset, [1811] Vol. XXVI, fol. 331.

MEADE-KING, ..., of co. Somerset, [1830] Vol. XXXVIII, fol. 138.

MEADE-WALDO, E. W., of Stonewall, Cheddingstones, co. Kent, 1896,* Vol. LXIX, fol. 96.

MEADS, Thomas (Naval Capt.), of St. Andrew, Holborn, London, 24 Oct. 1720, Vol. VII, fol. 20; Add. MS. 14,830, fol. 37.

MEAKIN, Rev. James, M.A., of Hinstock and Drayton, Shropsh., [1798] Vol. XX, fol. 273.

MECHI, Alderman Sir Joseph John, of London, and Tiptree Hall, Tollesbury, co. Essex, [1856] Vol. LII. fol. 57.

MEDHURST, Rev. (Charles), M.A., Vicar of Ledsham, Otterden Place, co. Kent, of Ledstone Hall and Kippax Hall, co. York, [1843] Vol. XLVII, fol. 12.

MEDHURST to WHELER, Rev. Charles, M.A., of co. York, [1843] Vol. XLVII, fol. 14.

MEDLAND, Richard, of co. Cornw., and Launceston, co. Devon, Mayor of Bath, co. Somerset, 17 May 1730, Vol. VIII, fol. 106. (Berry.)

MEDLYCOTT, late HYLL, ..., of Cottingham, co. Northampton, 24 Dec. 1801, Vol. XXI, fol. 275.

MEDLYCOTT, formerly HUTCHINGS, ... [1 Jan. 1765], Bart., [3 Oct. 1808], of co. Dorset and Somerset, [1809] Vol. XXV, fols. 163 and 166.

MEDOWS to PIERREPONT, ..., of Thoresby Park, co. Nottingham, [1788] Vol. XVII, fol. 31.

MEDOWS, Maj.-Gen. Sir William, K.B. [1792]. Supporters, [1792] Vol. XVIII, fol. 139.

MEDOWS, late NORIE, ..., of Conholt Park, Chute, Wilts., [1864 ?] Vol. LV, fol. 246.

MEDWIN, Frank Medwin Gardner, s. of Joseph GARDNER, of Folkestone, co. Kent, 1898, Vol. LXX, fols. 239 and 271.

MEE, Rev. John, M.A., of Hampsh., Incumb. of St. Jude, Southwark, and Dean of Grahamstown, S. Africa, [1865] Vol. LVI, fol. 51.

MEEKE to MEYER, William, of Wighill and Baildon Park, co. York, [1770] Vol. XII, fol. 20.

MEEKE, now TAYLOR, ..., of Broome, co. Staff., and co. York, [1840] Vol. XLIV, fol. 369.

MEEKING, C., of Richings Park, Bucks., 1888,* Vol. LXIV, fol. 293.

MEGGOT, George, s. of Sir George, of St. Olave's, co. Surrey, M.P. (see Elwe's Pedigree), [1712] Vol. VI, fol. 39. Certif. for Thomas COOPER, [1693] Vol. IV, fol. 148.

MEIGH, Job, of Ash Hall, Stoke-on-Trent, and Hanley, co. Staff., 1840, Vol. XLIV, fol. 272.

MEILAN, ..., of London, and Berne, Switzerland, [1802] Vol. XXI, fol. 342.

MEIN, ... (3 brothers), of co. Sussex; (1) Surgeon in the Army, (2) Lieut.-Col., (3) Lieut.-Col, C.B., [1817] Vol. XXX, fols. 115 and 117.

MEISSNER, ..., of Tottenham Place, Clifton, Bristol, co. Glouc., [1873], Vol. LVIII, fol. 224.

MELBOURNE, Lord, Baron of Kilmore [8 June 1770] (LAMB). Arms and Supporters, 1774, Vol. XII, fol. 289.

MELBOURNE UNIVERSITY. 15 Jan. 1863 [? Vol. LV, fol. 1].

MELCOMBE, Baron [1761] (DODINGTON). Change of Crest and Supporters, [1761] Vol. X, fol. 289.

MELLER, John, of the Middle Temple, London, and Little Longton, co. Derby, 3 July or 30 June 1707, Vol. V, fol. 230; Stowe MS. 714, fol. 130.

MELLIAR after FOSTER, Andrew, of co. Somerset, [1840] Vol. XLV, fol. 11.

MELLISH, ..., of St. Paul, Shadwell, London, [1798] Vol. XX, fol. 235.

MELLON, Harriet, dau. of Matthew, wife of Thomas COUTTS, Banker, [1823] Vol. XXXIV, fol. 26.

MELLOR to BRADLEY, ..., M.D., reputed son of James, of co. York and London, [1833] Vol. XXXIX, fol. 346.

MELLOR, John William, of Culmhead, Pitminster, co. Somerset, 1894,* Vol. LXVIII, fol. 10 (see Crisp, III, p. 85).

„ John, of the Middle Temple, London, Bar.-at-Law, s. and h. of John, late of City of London, and sometime of Little Longston, par. of Bakewell, co. Derby, 3 July 1707 (Stowe MS. 714, fol. 130ᵇ), and grandson of John of the same, 30 June 1707. MELLER in Add. MS. 14,830, fol. 38, to descendants of his father.

„ Walter Clifford (s. of Walter), of 12, Hyde Park Place, London, 1899, Vol. LXX, fol. 336.

MELVELLE to MILBANKE, William, of Thorpe Perrow, co. York, [1792] Vol. XVIII, fol. 59.

MELVILLE, Viscount [24 Dec. 1802]. Supporters, [1803] Vol. XXII, fol. 87.

MENDEL, Samuel, of Manley Hall, Withington, co. Lanc., [1865] Vol. LV, fol. 308.

MENDES, ... See MENDIZ.

„ . . . ., of Margaret Street, Cavendish Square, London, and Calcutta, [1820] Vol. XXXII, fol. 82.

MENDIP, Baron [13 Aug. 1794] (ELLIS), of co. Somerset, and Ireland. Supporters, [1795 ?] Vol. XVIII, fol. 422.

„ Baron [1802] and [Viscount] CLIFDEN, AGAR to ELLIS, of co. Somerset, and Ireland, [1804] Vol. XXII, fol. 367.

MENDIZ, Anthony, of London, Merchant, 1st s. of Fernando, Doctor in Physic, by his wife, Rachel MARQUEZ, of Portugal, 2 May 1732, Vol. VIII, fol. 146 ; Add. MS., 14,830, fol. 39. (See DA COSTA.)

MENDS, Capt., R.N., of Bagshot, co. Surrey, and Wales, [1803] Vol. XXII, fol. 101.

MERCER-HENDERSON, Lieut.-Gen. (See HENDERSON.) [1853-1854] Vol. L, fol. 405.

MEREDITH, ..., of Berrington Court, co. Worc., [1824] Vol. XXXIV, fol. 254.

„ Edward Phillipps, of Glenely, South Australia, 1878, Vol. LX, fol. 151. (Berry's Suppl.)

MERIVALE, Rev. Charles, B.D., Dean of Ely (and his brother, John Lewis Merivale, Regr. Court of Canterbury), 1887,* Vol. LXIV, fol. 7.

MERRIMAN, Samuel, M.D., of Rodbourne Cheney, Wilts., to descendants of grandfather, Nathaniel, of Marlborough, Wilts., 21 Dec. 1833, Vol. XL, fol. 48.

„ John, of Kensington Square, London, 1834 (see Berry's Suppl.).

MERRY, ..., of Gower Street, London, [1827] Vol. XXXVI, fol. 194.

MERRYE, Capt. John, of Whitby, co. York ; Hatton Garden, London ; and Barton, co. Derby, s. of Robert, formerly of Yarmouth, co. Norf., afterwards of London, Merchant, 2 June 1720, Vol. VI, fol. 420 ; Add. MS. 14,831, fol. 242.

MERTTINS, Sir George, Knt., and Alderman of Bridge Ward, London, and of Frankfort, April, or 20 July 1713, Vol. VI, fol. 110 ; Add. MS. 14,830, fol. 40.

MERYWEATHER, Capt. William Stephen, of Brighton, co. Sussex, and Kempsey, co. Worc., [1830] Vol. XXXVIII, fol. 173.

MERYWEATHER to TURNER, William Stephens T. Mellish, of Trinity Coll., Camb., and Lincoln's Inn, London, and two brothers, [? 1830, Vol. XXXVIII] fols. 175, 177 and 179.

MESHAM, Capt. Arthur, B.A., of co. Flint and Denbigh, Wales, [1874] Vol. LVIII, fol. 342.

MESSENGER, Michael James, of Fountains Abbey, co. York, [1764] Vol. XI, fol. 25.

MESSURIER. (See LE MESURIER.) [1780], Vol. XIV, fol. 233.

METCALFE to BARTON, Henry, of London, [1795] Vol. XIX, fol. 141.
   „ to CARLETON, ..., of co. Westmorland, [1791] Vol. XVII, fol. 410.
     (Berry's Suppl.)
   „ to MORE, Thomas Peter, of Glanford Briggs, co. Linc., and Bamborough,
     co. York, [1797] Vol. XIX, fol. 452.
   „ to MORE, John, M.D., [1810] Vol. XXV, fol. 301.
METCALFE, Thomas Theophilus, M.P., of Chilton, Bucks. (afterwards a Baronet),
     [1802 ?] Vol. XXII, fol. 27.
   „ Sir Charles [Theophilus], Bart., G.C.B. [1835], of Chilton, Bucks. Sup-
     porters, [1835] Vol. XLII [? XL], fol. 304 ; Supporters, Baronetcy, [1850]
     Vol. XLIX, fol. 303.
METCALFE to MARWOOD, William, of Little Busby, co. York (d. 26 Aug. 1818),
     [1809] Vol. XXV, fol. 212.
METCALFE, John, M.D., of Glanford Briggs and Bamborough, co. York, s. of
     Frederick Morehouse Metcalfe, of Inglethorpe House, co. Norf., 1810,*
     Vol. XXV, fol. 304. (Berry's Suppl.)
METHOLD to EDEN, ..., of co. Durham, [1844] Vol. XLVII, fol. 224.
METHUEN, Sir Paul, K.B. [1725], of Wilts. Supporters, [1725] Vol. VII, fol. 413.
   „ Paul, of Corsham, Wilts., to bear the Arms on an imperial eagle, 11 May
     1775, Vol. XIII, fol. 98.
   „ Baron, of Corsham, Wilts. Supporters, [1838] Vol. XLIII, fol. 103.
   „ . . . ., 1886, Vol. LXIII, fol. 291.
MEWS, John, of London, and Hartwell, Hartfield, co. Sussex, 1891, Vol. LXVI,
     fol. 31.
MEYER, Sir Peter, Knt., of London, Hamburg and Holstein, 30 June 1716, Vol.
     VI, fol. 253 ; Add. MS. 14,831, fol. 42.
   „ . . . . (see MAYER, John Baptista), 29 Oct. 1740, Vol. VIII, fol. 275.
MEYER, late MEEKE, William, of co. York, [1770] Vol. XII, fol. 20.
MEYER to THOMPSON, ..., of Kirk Hamerton and Baildon, co. York. (Match),
     [1794] Vol. XVIII, fol. 337.
MEYER, ..., of London, [1814] Vol. XXVIII, fol. 90.
MEYMOTT [John Gilbert], of the parish of Christ Church, co. Surrey, and to the
     descendants of Rev. Samuel Meymott, Rector of North Chapel, co. Sussex,
     born 11 Feb. 1691, 1835, Vol. XLI, fol. 100. (Burke.)
MEYNELL-INGRAM, Hugo C., of Temple Newsam, co. York, and Hoar Cross, co.
     Staff., [1842 ?] Vol. XLV, fol. 335.
MEYRICK, ..., of London, [1788] Vol. XVI, fol. 345.
MEYRICK, late CHARLTON, Bart., of Shropsh., [1858 ?] Vol. LIII, fol. 50.
MEYRICK after FULLER, of co. Sussex, [1826] Vol. XXXV, fol. 403.
   „ after TAPPS-GERVIS [16 Mar. 1876], Bart., of Hampsh., co. Surrey, and
     Anglesey, [1876] Vol. LIX, fol. 208.
MEYRICK, WILLIAM-, Rev. John, of Wales, [1877] Vol. LX, fol. 12. (Berry's Suppl.)
MEYSEY-WIGLEY-GRESWOLDE, Edmund, of co. Warw. and Worc. (died s. p. 1833),
     [1829] Vol. XXXVIII, fol. 13.
MICHAEL, William Henry, Q.C., of 54, Cromwell Gardens, London, 1880, Vol.
     LXI, fol. 71. (Berry's Suppl.)
MICHAELSON, ..., of the Isle of Barrow, co. Lanc. (See HUSE.) Quartering,
     [1815] Vol. XXIX, fol. 91.
MICHAELSON to YEATES, ..., of Kirkland, Kendal, co. Westmorland, and
     St. John's Coll., Camb., [1837] Vol. XLII, fol. 131.
MICHELL, ..., of Slade, co. Devon. (See HEARD.) [1762] Vol. X, fol. 445.
MICHELL to LUTTMAN-JOHNSON, Henry W. R. (M.A., Oxf.), of co. Middx. and
     Sussex, [1832] Vol. XXXIX, fol. 31.
MICHELL-ESMEAD after MOORE, ..., of Wilts., and the Inner Temple, London,
     [1844 ?] Vol. XLVII, fol. 315.
MICHELL, John, of Forcett Hall, Gilling, co. York, and Glassel and Elsick, co.
     Kincardine, Scotland, [1848] Vol. XLVIII, fol. 431.
   „ Edward, of Michell Hall, Truro, co. Cornw., 1886,* Vol. LXIII, fol. 219.

MICHELL, John and Robert, sons of John, M.D., of Lostwithiel, co. Cornw., 18 . . ., Vol. LXXI, fol. . . . .

MICHIE, John, Esq., of York Buildings, par. of St. Martin's, co. Middx., Sec. to Adm. Pocock and late Agent for victualling H.M.'s Squadron in the East Indies, by J. C. Hooke, Lyon King of Arms, 25 May 1761 ; Stowe MS. 677, fol. 30.

MICKLETHWAITE after PECKHAM, ..., of Beeston, co. Norf., and Iridge Place, co. Sussex, Sir S. B. Peckham Micklethwaite, Bart., 1824 [Vol. XXXV], [1838] Vol. XLIII, fol. 95.

MIDDLEDITCH, ..., of Broad Street, London, and Wisbech, co. Camb. Arms impaled, [1792] Vol. XVIII, fol. 85.

MIDDLEMARCH, John, of co. Dorset, and Thorley, Hampsh., 15 Feb. 174⅔, .Vol. IX, fol. 81.

MIDDLETON, Baron [1 Jan. 1712] (WILLOUGHBY [2nd Bart.]).   Supporters, [171½ ?] Vol. VI, fol. 28.

MIDDLETON to MONCK, ... [Sir Charles Miles Lambert Middleton, 6th Bart.], of Belsay Castle, co. Northumberland, and Caenly, co. Linc., [1799] Vol. XX, fol. 289.

MIDDLETON, Sir William, Bart., M.P., of Crowfield and Shrubland Halls, co. Suff., [1804] Vol. XXII, fol. 437.

„ Adm. Sir Charles, Bart., Baron BARHAM [1 May 1805].   Arms and Supporters, [1805] Vol. XXIII, fol. 157.

„ Earl of B. [?].   Supporters to [Diana] Baroness BARHAM, [1816] Vol. XXIX, fol. 381.

„ . . . ., wife of BILKE, [1814] Vol. XXVIII, fols. 41 to 43.

„ Miss (Spʳ), [1814], Vol. XXVIII, fols. 45 and 46.

„ [Thomas Fanshawe], D.D., Bp. of Calcutta, of Kedlestone, co. Derby, [1814] Vol. XXVIII, fol. 103.

„ . . . ., of Newport Pagnell, Bucks., and Weybridge, co. Surrey, [1818] Vol. XXXI, fol. 38.

MIDDLETON, formerly CARVER, Marmaduc, of Leam., co. Derby, and co. York, 1792 [is Vol. XVIII], [1822] Vol. XXXIII, fol. 220.

MIDDLETON to ATHORPE, John, of co. Derby and York, [1822] Vol. XXXIII, fol. 222.

MIDDLETON, George, of The Grove, Norwich, co. Norf., [1856?] Vol. LI, fol. 435.

MIDDLETON after BROKE, ..., Bart., of co. Suff., [1860] Vol. LIV, fol. 3.

MIDFORD, now AYNSLEY, ..., of co. Northumberland.   Crest to male descendants, [1793] Vol. XVIII, fol. 224.

MIDGLEY, ..., of Beverley, co. York. (See DENISON, formerly BECKETT.) (Match), 9 June 1709, Vol. XXX [1816], fol. 9.

„ Robert, of Leeds, co. York, and his second cousins, Jonathan, of Brearley, and Samuel, of Alwoodby, Leeds, co. York, 9 [? 29] June 1709, Vol. V, fol. 366 ; Stowe MS. 714, fol. 77 [?].

MIDLETON, ..., of "Twittenham," co. Middx. (See HARWOOD.) (Match), [1722] Vol. VII, fol. 84.

MIEHL, William, of Sackville Street, London.   Quartering, 1888, Vol. LXIV, fol. 320.

MIGNOT, David, M.D., of Kensington Crescent, London.   (Burke.) [no date.]

MIHELL, John, of Chatham, co. Kent, 7 June 1725, Vol. VII, fol. 457.

MILBANK, Sir F. A., Bart., of Well, co. York, and Hart, co. Durham, 1882,* Vol. LXI, fol. 271.

MILBANKE, late MELVELLE, William, of Thorpe Perrow, co. York, [1792] Vol. XVIII, fol. 59.

MILBANKE to NOEL [1815], Sir Ralph, Bart., M.P., of Halnaby, co. York ; Seaham, co. Durham ; Willesboro, co. Leic. ; and Nettlested, co. Suff., [1815] Vol. XXIX, fol. 1.

MILBANKE-HUSKISSON [1866], Sir John Ralph, Bart., of co. Sussex, [1866] Vol. LVI, fol. 93.

MILBANKE, late KING, William, of co. York (2nd s. of Earl LOVELACE), [1861] Vol. LIV, fol. 98.

MILBORNE-SWINNERTON, late PILKINGTON, ..., of co. York, [1856] Vol. LII, fol. 78 ; [1859] Vol. LIII, fol. 94.

MILBOURNE to THISTLETHWAYTE-PELHAM, ..., of Southwick, Hampsh., and South Newton and Winterslow, Wilts. Quarterly Arms, [1811] Vol. XXVI, fol. 340.

MILDMAY, late [? after] ST. JOHN [8 Dec. 1790], Sir Henry P., Bart., of Marks Hall, co. Essex, and Dogmersfield and Shawford, Hampsh., [1790] Vol. XVII, fol. 274.

MILDMAY, Gerald A. Shaw-Lefevre-St. John, of Taplins, Hampsh. (2nd s. of Sir Henry), 18 . . ., Vol. LXXI, fol. . . . .

MILES, ... (see HEYWARD), of St. Andrew, co. Berkeley, South Carolina. (Match), [1768] Vol. XI, fol. 326.

MILES, Samuel (s. of Samuel), both of Leicester, [1801] Vol. XXI, fol. 232.

,, Lieut.-Col. Edward, C.B. Augmentation, [1816] Vol. XXX, fol. 67.

,, William, of Windsor, Berks., Assist.-Surg., 2nd Life Guards, [1831] Vol. XXXVIII, fol. 265.

,, ..., of Leigh Court, Abbots Leigh, co. Somerset, [1859] Vol. LIII, fol. 102.

MILFORD, Baron [21 Sept. 1847] [Bulkeley-Philipps, Bart.], of Wales [? surname of PHILIPPS in place of GRANT, 10 Feb. 1824] [1824], Vol. XXXIV, fol. 260 ?. Supporters, [1847 ?] Vol. XLVIII, fol. 391.

MILL, George G. [? David], of Bath, co. Somerset, and Carriacon, W. Indies, [16 July 1803] Vol. XXII, fol. 294. [Crisp, Fragm. Geneal., V, p. 60.]

MILL after BROWNE, George G. [?], of Carriacon, W. Indies, [1803] Vol. XXII, fol. 298.

,, after BARKER, Rev. John, M.A., of Hampsh., 1835, Vol. XLI, fol. 1.

MILLAIS, Sir John Everett, Bart., of London, 1885,* Vol. LXIII, fol. 77.

MILLARD, Dr. W. J. K., of co. Hereford, and Brighton, co. Sussex, now of Rockleaze, Stoke Bishop, Bristol, 1882,* Vol. LXII, fol. 21.

MILLCAR, Thomas, of Edgarley, Wickley Road, Victoria, New South Wales, 1891, Vol. LXVI, fol. 170.

MILLER, Pancefoot, of London, merchant, Jan. 172⅔, Vol. VII, fol. 150 ; Add. MS. 14,831, fol. 138.

,, (THOMPSON), Elizabeth, 24 Mar. 172¾, Vol. VII, fol. 259 ; Add. MS. 14,830, fol. 20.

,, John, of Dunstable (Sheriff), co. Bedf., and Berks., 1765, Vol. XI, fol. 110. (Berry.)

MILLER to CODRINGTON, James, of Dodington, co. Glouc., nat. s. of Sir William Codrington, of Dodington, [1792] Vol. XVIII, fol. 33.

MILLER, Thomas, of Whitehaven, co. Cumberland, and Mayor of Preston, co. Lanc., 29 Aug. 1821, Vol. XXXII, fol. 347. (Berry.)

,, Thomas, of Winckley Square, Preston, co. Lanc., 1848 [1851], Vol. XLIX, fol. 493.

MILLER after CHRISTY, Samuel, M.P., of Bucks., co. Essex, and Scotland, 1862, Vol. LIV, fol. 324. (See also [1854] Vol. LI, fol. 162.)

MILLER, Wakefield Christie, of Bromfield, co. Essex, 1890, Vol. LXV, fol. 200.

,, ... See RIGGS.

MILLER, Elizabeth, d. and h. of Thomas Miller, of Rye, co. Sussex, and relict of Ralph THOMPSON, 6 April 1734, Vol. VIII, fol. 182.

MILLES, Jeremiah, s. of Jeremiah, grandfather Isaac, D.D., Dean of Exeter, of Dulo, co. Cornw. ; High Clere, Hampsh., and Cocktield, co. Suff., [1780] Vol. XIV, fol. 286.

MILLES, late WATSON, [Roy. Lic., 27 Dec. 1820] 2nd [4th ?] Lord SONDES, of co. Kent and Norf., [1821 ?] Vol. XXXII, fol. 257.

MILLET, Lieut., R.N. (See DAVY.) (Match), [1818] Vol. XXX, fol. 351.

MILLIGAN, David, of London. Quartering CLARK, 1774, Vol. XIII, fol. 52.

MILLINGTON, ..., of London (see BRICKWOOD). (Match) [1782], Vol. XV, fols. 5 and 6.

„ of Crowley House, Greenwich, co. Kent, [1822] Vol. XXXIII, fol. 286.

MILLS, ..., Banker, of Lexden Park, Colchester, co. Essex, 4 Jan. 1800, Vol. XX, fol. 411. (Berry.)

„ Capt., E.I.C.S., [1815] Vol. XXIX, fol. 122.

MILLS to HOLT, William ?, of co. Chester and Lanc., [1841] Vol. XLV, fol. 174.

MILLS [Sir Charles], Bart. [17 Nov. 1868], of Hillingdon Court, co. Middx., and Bisterne, Hampsh., [1868] Vol. LVII, fol. 56.

„ Joseph, of The Beeches, Kingswinford, co. Worc., 1881,* Vol. LXI, fol. 111. (Berry's Suppl.)

MILMAN, ..., of London, and East Ogwell and Levaton, co. Devon, Physician to H.M. Household, [1800] Vol. XXI, fol. 87.

MILNE, Vice-Adm. Sir David, K.C.B. [1816], of Scotland. Augmentation, [1817] Vol. XXX, fol. 163. G.C.B. [1840]. Supporters, [1840] Vol. XLIV, fol. 350.

„ Adm. Sir Alexander, Bart., G.C.B. [1871], of Scotland, Bart. [1876]. Supporters, [1871] Vol. LVIII, fol. 44 ; [1876] Vol. LIX, fol. 298.

MILNE after STOTT, James, of Brownwardle, Burnedge, Castleton, Rochdale, co. Lanc., [1843] Vol. XLVII, fol. 49.

„ . . . ., of Burnedge, Rochdale, co. Lanc. Quarterly Arms, [1854] Vol. LI, fol. 72.

„ . . . ., of Prestwich-in-the-Wood, co. Lanc., [1867] Vol. LVI, fol. 234.

MILNE (late SMITH), Samuel Milne, of Calverley House, Leeds, and Cliff House and Gordon Bank, Halifax, co. York, 1878, Vol. LX, fol. 99. (Berry's Suppl.)

MILNER, William, Alderm., of Leeds, co. York (afterwards a Baronet), 14 Feb. 17$\frac{1}{1}$°, Vol. V, fol. 412.

MILNER, late COTTAM, Charles, of Aylesford, co. Kent, 24 May 1788, Vol. XVI, fol. 407. (Crisp's Fragm. Geneal., V, p. 67.)

MILNER to JOLLIFF, Capt., Mil. (nat. s. of Joliff), of Nun Monkton, co. York, [1807] Vol. XXIV, fol. 198.

MILNER-GILSON-CULLUM, George Gery, of Hardwick House, co. Suff., 2nd s. of Thomas MILNER-GIBSON, 1879, Vol. LX, fol. 230 ; Milner-Gibson-Cullum, [1879] Vol. LX, fol. 241. (Crisp, I, pp. 151 and 171.)

MILNER, William Mordaunt, Bart., June 1772. Crest, [? 171$\frac{0}{1}$] Vol. V, fol. 412. (See Edmondson's Armory.)

MILNER, Sir Alfred, K.C.B., of Duke Street, St. James's, Westminster, 1897, Vol. LXIX, fol. 247.

MILNES, Pemberton, of Chesterfield, co. Derby, and Wakefield, co. York, 13 Mar. 1776, Vol. XIII, fol. 177.

„ . . . ., of Newark-on-Trent, co. Nottingham. Escutcheon of pretence, [1785] Vol. XVI, fols. 63 and 64.

„ William, of Aldecar Park and Dunstan, co. Derby, and Colston Basset, co. Nottingham. Escutcheon of pretence, [1795] Vol. XIX, fol. 85.

„ . . . ., of Dunstan Hall, co. Derby, [1816] Vol. XXIX, fol. 308.

MILNES after SMITH (Rev. William Smith), of Dunstan Hall, co. Derby, 1831, Vol. XXXVIII, fol. 269.

„ after SMITH, William B., of Dunstan Hall, co. Derby, 1873, Vol. LVIII, fol. 271 (see PEGGE-BURNELL).

MILNES, now RICH, James, of Thornes House, co. York, and Bull House, died s. p. Escutcheon of pretence, [1802] Vol. XXI, fol. 456 [see Burke].

MILNES, William, of Stubbin Edge Hall and The Butts, both in Ashover, co. Derby, [1852] Vol. L, fol. 254.

MILNES to WALTHALL, ..., of Alton Manor and Darley Dale, co. Derby, and Trinity Coll., Oxf., [1853] Vol. L, fol. 340.

MILNES, ..., Baron HOUGHTON [20 Aug. 1863, Richard Monckton Milnes],
of co. York. Supporters, [1866] Vol. LVI [? Vol. LV, 1863], fol. 120.
MILSOM, Dr. R. H., of Finchley Road, London, 1888, Vol. LXIV, fol. 271.
MILWARD, Robert (s. of William), of Woodthorpe, co. Derby, and St. Sepulchre's,
London, [1748] Vol. IX, fol. 247.
MILWARD, late SAYER, ..., of Hastings, co. Sussex, and The Charterhouse,
London, [1836] Vol. XLI, fol. 266.
MILWARD, ..., of The Manor House, Lechlade ; The Priory, Broadmarston ;
and Wincote, co. Glouc., [1839] Vol. XLIII, fol. 373.
MILWARD, late PARKINSON, ..., of Hexgrave Park, Thurgarton Priory, and
Leyfield, co. Nottingham, [1844] Vol. XLVII, fol. 296.
MILWARD after SAYER, ..., of London, and East Horndon, co. Essex, 1856,
Vol. LII, fol. 96.
MILWARD, Rev. William Carlisle, of Polloxhill, co. Bedf., and London, Rector of
St. Leonard's, Wallingford, Berks., 1873 [1874], Vol. LVIII, fol. 319.
MINE ADVENTURERS OF ENGLAND, Earl Marshal's Warrant, 1704 (see Harl MS.
6834, fol. 109).
MINET, Hughes [of Fulham, co. Middx.] ; Dover, co. Kent, [s. of the Rev. John
Minet, M.A., late Rector of] Eythorne and Lower Hardres, co. Kent,
14 Oct. 1799, Vol. XX, fol. 372.   Cat. Her. Exhib., p. 74. (Crisp, I,
p. 269 [and Notes], iii, p. 88.)
MINTO, Capt. of Mil., of Water Valley, par. of Trelawney, co. Cornw., and
Jamaica, [1815] Vol. XXVIII, fol. 332.
MINTON, ..., of Stoke, co. Staff., 1829 [1830], Vol. XXXVIII, fol. 125.
MIRTLE, William, s. of Thomas, of Calcutta, and Edinburgh, 1768, Vol. XI,
fol. 350.
MISA, ..., (of Crutched Friars, London) and Jerez de la Frontera, Spain,
[1866] Vol. LVI, fol. 113.
MISSENY [?], Thomas, of Portsmouth and Stubbington, Hampsh., 27 Nov. 1728,
Vol. VIII, fol. 18.
MITCHELL, Sir Andrew, K.B. [1765], of Thainstown, co. Aberdeen, Scotland.
Supporters, [1766] Vol. XI, fol. 146. (Berry's Suppl.)
   „   Vice-Adm., [Sir Andrew, K.B., 1800]. Arms and Supporters, [1800] Vol.
XXI, fol. 7.
   „   . . . . [?], Hook. (Match), [1810] Vol. XXVI, fol. 5.
   „   . . . ., of London ; Medlock Bank, nr. Manchester, co. Lanc.; Riga, Russia,
and Gottenberg, in Sweden, [1810] Vol. XXVI, fol. 148.
   „   . . . ., of Enderby Hall and Smeeton Westerby, co. Leic., [1839 ?], Vol.
XLIII, fol. 338.
   „   . . . ., of Clapham and Camberwell, co. Surrey, [1852] Vol. L, fol. 187.
   „   . . . ., of Sheffield, co. York, [1862] Vol. LIV, fol. 246.
MITCHELL-WITHERS, ..., of Sheffield, co. York, [1862] Vol. LIV, fol. 248.
MITCHELL, ..., of Bolton Hall, Doncaster, co. York, [1872] Vol. LVIII,
fol. 188.
   „   James William (s. of Joseph Theophilus), Lieut., 42nd Foot, of Audley,
Sidmouth, co. Devon, died Lyon clerk-depute, 1898. Quartering SYKES,
1878, Vol. LX, fol. 125. (Berry's Suppl.)
   „   Charles, of Jesmond Towers, Newcastle-upon-Tyne, co. Northumberland,
1888, Vol. LXIV, fol. 140.
   „   F. J., of The Grange, Llanfechfahower, co. Monmouth, 1894, Vol. LXVII,
fol. 300.
   „   Sir Henry, of Parkfield House, Manningham, co. York, 1890, Vol. LXV,
fol. 277.
   „   H. D. Parry, of co. Warw., 1889, Vol. LXV, fol. 106.
MITCHELSON, late KENDALL, James, of Pickering, co. York, [1860] Vol. LIV,
fol. 79.
MITFORD, Sir John, Knt., Baron REDESDALE [15 Feb. 1802], of co. Glouc. and
Northumberland. Supporters, [1802] Vol. XXI, fol. 297.

MITFORD after FREEMAN, ... [28 Jan. 1809], Baron REDESDALE, of co. Glouc. and Northumberland. Quarterly Arms, Augmentation to Supporters, [1809] Vol. XXV, fols. 112 and 115.

MITFORD to OSBALDESTON, Bertram, of co. Northumberland, and Hunmanby, co. York (died s.p. 1842), [1836] Vol. XLI, fol. 204.

MITTON with HALSTON, ..., of Shropshire. (See OWEN, formerly SMYTHE.) [1790] Vol. XVII, fol. 205.

MITTON to EADON, ..., of Snaith and Selby, co. York, [1835-1836] Vol. XLI, fol. 176.

MOCATTA, ..., of London, [1819] Vol. XXXI, fol. 182.

MOGG, Rev. John Rees, of Farington Gurney, co. Somerset, 1805 [1806], Vol. XXIII, fol. 299.

MOGG after REES, William, of Cholwell House, co. Somerset, and Brufton, co. Glamorgan, [1841] Vol. XLV, fol. 101. (Berry's Suppl.)

MOINE. See LE MOINE.

MOISES, alias MOYSES, alias MOYSER, Rev. Hugh, of Newcastle-upon-Tyne, co. Northumberland ; Keyworth, co. Nottingham ; Oswestry, Shropsh. ; and St. Peter Coll., Camb., [1766] Vol. XI, fol. 138.

MOISES to LISLE, ..., of co. Northumberland, [1860] Vol. LIV, fol. 36.

MOKE, George E., of Cromwell Houses, South Kensington, London, 1884, Vol. LXII, fol. 272.

MOLESWORTH-ST. AUBYN, Rev. H[ender], M.A., of Clowance and Pencarrow, co. Cornw., [1839] Vol. XLIV, fol. 182 ; [1843] Vol. XLVII, fol. 82. (Crisp, IV, p. 1.)

MOLINEUX before MONTGOMERIE, George, Capt., Norfolk Mil. Quartering, [1782] Vol. XV, fol. 32.

  „   (CRISP) before MONTGOMERIE, George, of Garboldisham, co. Norf. Quarterly Arms, [1813] Vol. XXVII, fol. 392.

MOLINEUX, late HOCKENHALL, William, of Lymme, co. Chester, and Hawkley Hall, Pemberton, co. Lanc., 20 June 1806, Vol. XXIII, fol. 372. (Crisp, I, p. 117 [and Notes], II, p. 116.)

MOLYNEUX after HOWARD [1812 ? Henry Thomas, brother of the 12th Duke of NORFOLK]. Quarterly Arms, [1811] Vol. XXVII, fol. 66 ; [1816] Vol. XXIX, fol. 305 ; 1825, Vol. XXXV, fol. 118. [See the next.]

MOLYNEUX-HOWARD, Lord [1817 ? Henry Thomas, brother of the 12th Duke of NORFOLK]. Exemplification [1816] Vol. XXIX, fol. 305. Supporters, [1818] Vol. XXXI, fol. 1.

MOLYNEUX SEEL, late UNSWORTH, ..., of Maghull, Liverpool and Newhall-within-Westerby, co. Lanc. Quarterly Arms, [1815] Vol. XXVIII, fol. 429 ; [1816] Vol. XXIX, fol. 315 ; [1845] Vol. XLVIII, fol. 15.

MONCK, late MIDDLETON, Sir Charles, Bart., of co. Linc. and Northumberland, 1799, Vol. XX, fol. 289.

MONCKTON, ..., of Hanover Square, London, [1788] Vol. XVI, fol. 375.

MONCKTON to ARUNDELL, ..., Viscount GALWAY. Arms of Arundell with Supporters, [1770] Vol. XII, fol. 8.

  „   to ARUNDELL, ..., Viscount GALWAY. Quarterly Arms, [1826] Vol. XXXV, fol. 371. (R. C. Fam., III, p. 165.)

MONCREIFF, Baron [1874], of Scotland. Supporters, [1873 ?] Vol. LVIII, fol. 294.

MONEY before KYRLE, (Sir) James, of co. Hereford, 1809, Vol. XXV, fol. 197.

MONEY, Col. John Ernle, of Horn House, co. Hereford, [1836] Vol. XLI, fol. 355.

MONEY-KYRLE, Rev. William, of Horn House, co. Hereford, and Whetham, Wilts. (Potsford, co. Northampton), 1844 [1843], Vol. XLVI, fol. 371.

MONEY, Rev. William (and the other descendants of the late William Taylor Money), B.C.S., of Walthamstow, co. Essex, K. H. Consul-General at Venice and Milan, [1843] Vol. XLVI, fol. 401.

MONEY-COUTTS, Mrs., of Stodham Park, Hampsh., 1880, Vol. [LXI], fol. 65.

  „   -COUTTS, F. B. T., of Ancotes, Weybridge, co. Surrey, 1880, Vol. LXI, fol. 67.

MONGREDIEU, ..., of Liverpool and France (father emigrated from France), [1844] Vol. XLVII, fol. 262.

MONINS, ..., of Canterbury, co. Kent. Escutcheon of pretence, [1791] Vol. XVII, fol. 396.

MONK, William, Citizen and Draper, of London, 10 Feb. 17$\frac{11}{12}$, Vol. VI, fol. 13 ; Add. MS. 14,831, fol. 54.

MONK after LINGARD, R. B. M., of co. Chester and Lanc., 1871, Vol. LVII, fols. 311 and 313 ; 1875, Vol. LIX, fol. 160. (Berry's Suppl.)

LINGARD-MONK, Richard Boughey Monk, of Manchester, s. of Roger Rowson Lingard Monk, of Mill Gate, par. of Northenden, decd. Arms and Crest of Lingard, with remainder to the descendants of his uncles Thomas and Alexander, both decd., 5 Jan. 1871. (Geneal., V, pp. 142 and 144 ; Berry's Suppl.)

  „ -MONK, ... Arms and Crest of Monk, 3 Nov. 1875.

  „ -MONK, BOUGHEY and JENNINGS quarterings and ROWSON, 16 Jan. 1871. (Geneal., V, p. 144.)

MONK-BRETTON, Baron (DODSON), of co. Sussex. Arms, 1884, Vol. LXII, fol. 317. Supporters, 1884, Vol. LXII, fol. 319.

MONKHOUSE, ..., of Moulse, Coombe Place, Patcham, and New Shoreham, co. Sussex, [1829-1830] Vol. XXXVIII, fol. 34.

MONKHOUSE-TILLSTONE, ..., of Moulse, Coombe Place, Patcham, and New Shoreham, co. Sussex, [1829-1830] Vol. XXXVIII, fol. 39.

MONKLAND, ..., of Bath, co. Somerset, [1795] Vol. XIX, fol. 71.

MONKSWELL, ..., Baron [1885] (COLLIER), of London. Arms, [1885] Vol. LXIII, fol. 138. Supporters, fol. 144.

MONSELL, ..., Baron EMLY [1874?], of Ireland. Supporters, [1874] Vol. LVIII, fol. 296.

MONSON, Sir John, K.B. [1725]. Supporters, [1725] Vol. VII, fol. 415. Baron Monson [1728]. Supporters, Vol. IX, fol. 267 [is 1748] [? Vol. VIII, fols. 26 and 27].

MONTAGUE [Charles], Baron HALIFAX [13 Dec. 170?, of Halifax, co. York], [with special remainder to his nephew, of] Horton, co. Northampton. Supporters, and addition to Crest, [1700] Vol. V, fol. 27.

MONTAGU, Sir Edward [Hussey ?], K.B. [1753]. Supporters [afterwards Earl BEAULIEU] [1753], Vol. IX, fol. 467.

  „ [Lieut.-Gen.] Sir Charles, K.B. [1771]. Supporters, [1771] Vol. XII, fol. 69.

  „ Adm. Sir George, G.C.B. [1815]. Supporters, [1815] Vol. XXIX, fol. 21.

MONTAGU, late ROBINSON, Matthew, of Charlton, co. Kent, and Denton, co. Northumberland, 1 July 1776, Vol. XIII, fol. 197. (Quartering, MONTHERMER, 13 Feb. 1777, fol. 265.)

  „ late WILKINSON, ..., widow W. [of Wilkinson ?], [1798] Vol. XX, fol. 202.

MONTAGU to WROUGHTON, Lieut.-Col., of Wilcote House, Wilts., [1826] Vol. XXXV, fol. 369.

MONTAGU, late FOUNTAYNE-WILSON, Andrew, of Melton Hill, co. York, and Papplewick, co. Nottingham, [1826] Vol. XXXV, fol. 375.

  „ late DERBISHIRE, ..., of London and Montreal, [1841] Vol. XLV, fol. 125.

MONTAGU-POLLOCK, ..., Bart. [26 Mar. 1872], of co. Suff. and Surrey, [1873] Vol. LVIII, fol. 248.

MONTAGU, Baron, of Hampsh. Arms, 1888, Vol. LXIV, fol. 226 ; Supporters, fol. 228.

MONTAGU-STUART-WORTLEY, Hon. F. D., of co. York, 2nd s. of Baron WHARNCLIFFE, 1881, Vol. LXI, fol. 201.

SAMUEL-MONTAGU, Sir M., Bart., of London, 1894, Vol. LXVIII, fol. 49.

MONTAGUE, Rev. Horatio. (See Burke.) [No date given.]

MONTEATH, Lieut.-Col. Thomas, C.B., B.C.S., of Scotland, [1841] Vol. XLV, fol. 161.

MONTEATH-DOUGLAS, ..., of Scotland, [1851] Vol. XLIX, fol. 442.

MONTEFIORE, Moses, of Tinley Lodge, nr. Tonbridge, [1818] Vol. XXXI, fol. 142. Alteration and Augmentation, Crest, [1831] Vol. XXXVIII, fol. 257.

„ Sir Moses, of East Cliff Lodge, Ramsgate, co. Kent. Additional Crest and Supporters, [1841] Vol. XLV, fol. 282.

„ Rev. Thomas Law, M.A., of Trinity Coll., Camb. (see BRICE), Rector of Catherston Lewston, co. Dorset, [1854] Vol. LI, fol. 43 [see Burke].

„ Sir F. A., Bart., of Sussex. Supporters. (See GOLDSMID.) 1887, Vol. LXIV, fol. 1.

MONTFORT, Baron [9 May 1741] (BROMLEY). Supporters, change of Arms and Crest, [1741] Vol. IX, fol. 23.

MONTGOMERIE after MOLINEUX, ..., of co. Norf., Capt. Norf. Militia, [1782] Vol. XV, fol. 32.

„ after CRISP-MOLINEUX, ..., of London, and Garboldisham, co. Norf. Quarterly Arms, [1813] Vol. XXVII, fol. 392.

MONTGOMERY, [? Henry Herbert, Earl of] Great [?] E[arl of] Pembroke, [1791] Vol. XVII, fol. 376.

„ Rev. George Augustus, B.A., Oriel Coll., Oxf., of Wilts., [1821] Vol. XXXIII, fol. 30.

„ Allenby H. C. Hynman, of Gainsgate Hall, Long Sutton, co. Linc., 1894 [1893], Vol. LXVII, fol. 227.

„ S. Hynman (Montgomery, formerly ALLENBY), of co. Linc., 1894, Vol. LXVII, fol. 298.

MONYPENNY after GYBBON, ..., of co. Kent, [1837] Vol. XLII, fol. 144.

MOODY, ..., of Porchester, Hampsh.; Kingsdon, co. Somerset; and Whiteparish, Wilts., 1802, Vol. XXI, fol. 450.

„ Henry Riddell, of Aspley, co. Bedf., and Chartham, co. Kent, 1829 [1828], Vol. XXXVII, fol. 149.

MOON [Sir Francis Graham, Bart., 1855], Lord Mayor of London [1854-55], [1855] Vol. LI, fol. 253.

„ Sir R., Bart. [1887], of Copsewood Grange, Coventry, co. Warw., [1887] Vol. LXIV, fol. 44.

MOORE. See GWYN.

„ . . . ., of Little Appleby, co. Leic. WILDE quartering to TOWNLEY. York Herald of Arms, [1743] Vol. IX, fol. 87.

„ [Vice-Adm.] Sir John, Bart., K.B. [1770] (died 2 Feb. 1779), grandson of Henry, 3rd Earl of Drogheda. Supporters, [1771] Vol. XII, fol. 66.

„ Maj.-Gen. Sir John, K.B. [1804] (died at Corunna, 1809). Supporters, [1804] Vol. XXIII, fols. 89 and 91.

„ . . . ., of St. Michael, Barbados, [1784] Vol. XV, fol. 367.

„ . . . ., of London, and Skelton, co. Cumberland, [1786] Vol. XVI, fol. 155.

MOORE-(MOOR), ..., of Islington, rightly MOORHOUSE. (See MOORHOUSE.) [1790] Vol. XVII, fol. 227.

MOORE, ..., of Brockwell, Halifax and Sowerby, co. York, [1804] Vol. XXIII, fol. 68.

„ . . . ., of Kentish Town, London, and Keyham, co. Leic., [1815] Vol. XXIX, fol. 206.

MOOR, John Frewen (minor), of Swabey, co. Linc.; Sapcote, co. Leic.; Rugby, co. Warw.; and Lilbourne, co. Northampton, [1816] Vol. XXX, fol. 51.

MOORE to STEVENS, ..., of the Middle Temple, London, and Cross, Great Torrington, Smythacoat and Winscot, co. Devon. (Match.) [1817] Vol. XXX, fol. 223.

MOORE-STEVENS, ..., Archdeacon of Exeter, of Otterton, Great Torrington, Smythacot and Winscot, co. Devon, [1832] Vol. XXXIX, fol. 146.

Moor, Henry Isaac, Capt., R.N., E.I.C.S., of Greenwich and Otterham, Upchurch, co. Kent, Lord of the Manor, [1820] Vol. XXXII, fol. 163.
Moore-Halsey, ..., of Ivinhoe, Bucks., and Great Gaddesden, co. Hertf., [1820] Vol. XXXII, fol. 229.
Moore, William, of Grimeshill-in-Middleton, Kirkby Lonsdale, co. Westmorland, [1834] Vol. XL, fol. 181.
  „   Vice-Adm. Sir Graham, G.C.B. [1836], G.C.M.G. Supporters, [1836] Vol. XLI, fol. 299.
  „   . . . ., of Aigburth, co. Lanc., [1841] Vol. XLV, fol. 128.
Moore-Michell-Esmead, ..., of Wilts., [1844 ?] Vol. XLVII, fol. 315.
Moore-Brabazon, ..., M.A., St. John's Coll., Camb., of co. Hertf., [1845] Vol. XLVII, fol. 420 ; [1868] Vol. LVII, fol. 3.
Moore, ..., of Hilden, Tonbridge, co. Kent, [1845] Vol. XLVIII, fols. 42 and 43.
  „   . . . ., of Blandford, co. Dorset, [1846] Vol. XLVIII, fol. 203.
  „   William Cameron, of Bamford, co. Derby, and Manchester, co. Lanc., [1853] Vol. L, fol. 348.
  „   George, of White Hall, Allhallows, Meals Gate, Bolton, co. Cumberland, [1860] Vol. LIII, fol. 282.
Moore after Foljambe, F. J. S., of co. Nottingham and York, 1876, Vol. LIX, fol. 232 ; 1879, Vol. LX, fol. 213.
Moore, William Williams Thomas, of Wales, 1878, Vol. LX, fol. 103.
  „   John Leach Mitchell, M.A., s. of John, of Hapton and Thetford, co. Norf., 1879, Vol. LX, fol. 243.
  „   Anne (wife of Sir James Graham, Bart.), only dau. of the Rev. Thomas Moore, of Kirkstall, co. York, heir of brother Thomas, [1808-1810] Vol. XXV, fol. . . . .
  „   Mary (wife of Richardson Harrison), dau. and h. of Rev. Richard Moore, of Helston, co. Cornw., [1809] Vol. XXV, fol. 175.
  „   Charles, of Coogee, Sydney, New South Wales, an Irish grant.
  „   William Parkin, of Whitehall, co. Cumberland, 18 . . ., Vol. LXXI, fol. . . . . (See [1860] Vol. LIII, fol. 282.)
Moorhouse, William James, of Islington, London, s. of Joseph, of London, Banker, [1790] Vol. XVII, fol. 227.
Moorsom, Vice-Adm. Sir Robert, K.C.B. [1815], of Whitby, co. York, [1815] Vol. XXVIII, fol. 345.
Morant to Gale, Edward G., of Hampsh., [1796 ?] Vol. XIX, fol. 189.
Mordaunt, [Major-Gen.] Sir John, K.B. [1749]. Supporters, [1749] Vol. IX, fol. 325.
More late Metcalfe, Thomas Peter, of co. Linc. and York, died s.p., 1797, Vol. XIX, fol. 452.
Moreau, David, [? of] Guilford, to grandfather Philip, certified May 1779. (Berry.) [1754] Vol. IX, fol. 499.
Moresby, Rear-Adm. Sir Fairfax, K.C.B. [1855], of Stow House, Lichfield, co. Staff., [1856] Vol. LII, fol. 113.
Moreton, late Reynolds [1771], Baron Ducie. (See also Moreton below.) Match. Supporters, [1771] Vol. XII, fol. 63.
Moreton, John, of Wyboston [? co. Bedf.], and Tadhouses and Moseley Court, Bushbury, co. Staff., 1875, Vol. LIX, fol. 116.
Moreton, Mathew Ducie, Baron Ducie [9 June 1720], of Ingleton, co. Staff. Supporters, [1720] Vol. VI, fol. 426.
Morewood, ..., of London ; Alfreton, co. Derby ; and Oaks, Bradfield, co. York. Match with Danvers, Butler, &c., [1797] Vol. XIX, fol. 373.
Morewood, late Casey, Rev. Henry, of Ladbroke, co. Warw. ; Alfreton, co. Derby ; and Oaks, Bradfield, co. York, 1793, Vol. XVIII, fol. 157.
Morewood after Casy, Rev. Henry, of Ladbroke, co. Warw. ; Alfreton, co. Derby ; Mindern Hall, co. Suff. ; and Appleton, co. Norf., [1793] Vol. XVIII, fol. 191.

MOREWOOD after PALMER, William, of Ladbroke, co. Warw., and Alfreton, co. Derby, [1826] Vol. XXXV, fol. 373.

MORGAN, Sir William, K.B. [1725].   Supporters, [1727] Vol. VII, fol. 547.

„   . . . ., of Tredegar, co. Monmouth.   (*See* PARRY.)   [1787] Vol. XVI, fols. 300 and 305.

MORGAN, late GOULD, Charles, of Ruperra, co. Monmouth, 1792, Vol. XVIII, fol. 141.   Supporters, Baron TREDEGAR [16 April 1859], [1859] Vol. LIII, fol. 130.

MORGAN, Arabella (Sp^r), of Dowrich, co. Devon, and Higham, co. Somerset. Arms to self and descendants of her sister Mary CLAYFIELD.   (*See* Landed Gentry, p. 848.)   [1801] Vol. XXI, fol. 143.

MORGAN to CROFT, ..., of co. Somerset, [1822 ?] Vol. XXXIII, fol. 356. [1823 ?] Vol. XXXIV, fol. 210.

MORGAN, of St. Mary Cray, co. Kent, [1823] Vol. XXXIV, fol. 204.

„   . . . ., Nelson Smith, M.R.C.S., of Henfield and Street, co. Sussex, [1843] Vol. XLVII, fol. 63.

MORGAN to STRATFORD, ..., of Swindon, co. Glouc., and Lugwardine, co. Hereford, [1844] Vol. XLVII, fol. 211.

MORGAN-PAYLER, (Rev.) Frederick, M.A., of Patrixborne and Heden, co. Kent (Rector of Wolley, co. Worc.), 1854, Vol. LI, fol. 151.

MORGAN, John (s. of John), of Tenby, co. Pembroke, Wales, and Barnet, co. Hertf., [1860] Vol. LIII, fol. 311.

„   Howard Spear, of Tregfynydd, Llanfolteg, co. Carmarthen, Wales, [1872] Vol. LVIII, fol. 115.   (Berry's Suppl.)

„   Sir G. O., P.C., of London and Brymbo Hall, Brymbo, Wales, 1892,* Vol. LXVII, fol. 31. ·

MORGAN-STRATFORD, Rev. H., of St. Athan Rectory, Cowbridge, co. Glamorgan, Wales, 1888, Vol. LXIV, fol. 148.

MORIER, Sir Robert, Envoy at Dresden, [1821 ?] Vol. XXXII, fol. 261.

MORIN, Tirel, of London and Caen, and to his grandfather John.   Quartering, [1779] Vol. XIV, fol. 108.

„   . . . ., of Aylesbury, Bucks., [1787] Vol. XVI, fol. 311.

MORKILL, John William, of Ansthorpe, co. York, 1897, Vol. LXIX, fol. 243. (Crisp, V, p. 50.)

MORLAND after BERNARD, ..., M.P., of Nether Winchendon, Bucks., [1811] Vol. XXVI, fol. 271.

MORLAND, ..., of Court Lodge, in Lamberhurst, co. Kent.   (*See* SMITH MARRIOTT.)   [1811] Vol. XXVI, fol. 224.

„   . . . ., wife of BERNARD.   Match and quartering, LEVING, [1788] Vol. XVII, fol. 119.

MORLEY, Francis, of Hollington, co. Derby, 30 Oct. 1700, Vol. V, fol. 19; Add. MS. 14,831, fol. 196.

„   John, of Halstead, co. Essex, 17 Dec. 1722, Vol. VII, fol. 141.

„   John, of Hackney, London, s. of Samuel, of Sneinton, co. Nottingham, and to his descendants, [1846] Vol. XLVIII, fol. 115.

„   Elizabeth Martha, wife of Henry HIGGINS, of Moreton Jeffries, &c., co. Hereford, 1874, Vol. LIX, fol. 18.

MORPHETT, ..., M. L. Council, Adelaide, South Australia, [1858] Vol. LIII, fol. 14.

MORRELL, Mrs., of 14, Edith Grove, 95, Chelsea, 1885, Vol. LXIII, fol. 128.

MORRICE, ... (*see* CHURCH), of Brecon, Wales, a testatrix, [1869] Vol. LVII, fol. 158.

MORRIS, Robert, of Barnewood and Sheephouse, co. Glouc., 12 Feb. 1795, Vol. XIX, fol. 17.   (Berry's Suppl.)

„   . . . ., of Bishops Castle, Shropsh., and Wales, [1806] Vol. XXIII, fol. 324.

„   Rear-Adm. Sir James Nicoll, K.C.B. [1815], of Great Marlow, Bucks., and co. Pembroke, Wales, with medals, and without medals to John Williams Morris, Col., E.I.C.S., [1815] Vol. XXVIII, fol. 400.

MORRIS to LAWRENCE, Walter, of Gloucester and Sevenhampton, co. Glouc., [1815] Vol. XXIX, fol. 146; his mother Mary (see Lawrence, [1824-1826] Vol. XXXV), [? next entry].

MORRIS, ..., of co. Carmarthen, Wales, [1826] Vol. XXXV, fol. 397.

  „ . . . ., of London, and Woodford Hall. co. Essex, [1843] Vol. XLVI, fol. 298.

  „ Evan, of Putney and the Inner Temple, London (s. of Evan, of Aberystwith, co. Cardigan, Wales), [12 June 1843] Vol. XLVI, fol. 337.

  „ . . . .. of Peckham, co. Surrey, and Woolwich Common, co. Kent, [1851-1852] Vol. L, fol. 137.

  „ . . . ., of Elmsdale, Tettenhall, Mayor of Wolverhampton, co. Staff., [1867] Vol. LVI, fol. 296.

  „ James, of Duke Street, St. James', London, 1891,* Vol. LXVI, fol. 190.

  „ Thomas Henry, of The Lodge, Halifax, co. York, 1883,* Vol. LXII, fol. 98. (Berry's Suppl.)

  „ Baron, of London and Ireland. Supporters, 1892, Vol. LXVI, fol. 255.

  „ Capt. Richard, 10 April 1677. [No reference.]

MORRISON, ..., of The Mint, London, Deputy Master and Worker, [1809] Vol. XXV, fol. 147.

MORSE [Hannah. dau. of William], of Gosport, Hampsh. (see MARLOW, formerly VAUGHAN), [and mother of Benjamin Vaughan, afterwards Marlowe, Marlow Arms only], [1784] Vol. XV, fol. 319.

  „ . . . ., of London and Jamaica. (See GRIFFITHS.) [1810] Vol. XXVI, fol. 108.

  „ John [Elizabeth Hall, wife of] of Mount Ida, co. Norf. (See HALL, Elizabeth, dau. of Gen. Thomas Hall.) (Match.) [Hall Arms only], [1815] Vol. XXIX, fol. 214.

MORSE-BOYCOTT, John Hall, of Sprowston Hall, Norwich, and Mount Ida, co. Norf., 1844 [1843], Vol. XLVII, fols. 152 and 175 (see Burke).

MORSE, Charles, of the Inner Temple, London, and Sprowston, co. Norf., [1862] Vol. LIV, fol. 332.

MORSHEAD, William, of Cartuther, co. Cornw., s. of William, and to his descendants, 11 Mar. 174⅘, Vol. IX, fols. 123 and 126. (Maclean's Trigg Manor, L, p. 81.)

MORSHEAD, late TREMELLYN-HUSSEY, ..., of Lavethan, co. Cornw., [1830] Vol. XXXVIII, fol. 132.

MORSON, Richard, Citizen and Goldsmith of London, s. of Le Strange Morson, of Norwich, co. Norf., 19 or 17 Feb. 172¾, Vol. VII, fol. 229; Add. MS. 14,830, fol. 148. (Berry.)

MORTIMER, John, of Cheshunt, co. Hertf., 14 June 1688, Vol. IV, fol. 8.

  „ (Harley), Earl of OXFORD [and Earl Mortimer, 23 May 1711]. Supporters, [1711] Vol. VI, fol. 9.

MORTLOCK, Thomas, of Abington Hall, co. Camb. (High Sheriff), 1840, and Sir John Cheetham Mortlock, Commissioner of Excise, his brother, 1840. (Burke.)

MORTON, [Sir John, 2nd] Bart., of co. Staff., and St. Andewes, Milborne, co. Dorset. (Match), [169¾] Vol. IV, fol. 154.

MORTON-HERBERT, ..., of the Isle of Nevis. Arms of Herbert, [1822] Vol. XXXIII, fol. 208.

MOSELEY after LOFTT, Henry Capel, of Glemham House, Glemham, and Troston Hall, Troston, co. Suff., [1864] Vol. LV, fol. 162.

MOSER, Richard, of Tulse Hill, s. of Richard, of Penge, co. Surrey, [1863] Vol. LV, fol. 126.

MOSES, now GOLDSMID, ... of London, [1824] Vol. XXXIV, fol. 346.

MOSES, ..., of Bombay, [1865] Vol. LV, fol. 292.

MOSLEY, Hannah, wife of Edward, of Newcastle-upon-Tyne, co. Northumberland (dau. of Cample ASTON), [1764] Vol. XI, fol. 11.

  „ . . . ., (Bart.) of Ancoats, co. Lanc. Quarterly Arms, [1807] Vol. XXIV, fol. 228.

Moss to Scott (widow). Arms for widow and Crest for son, of Bankfel House, Moreton-in-the-Marsh, and Stow-on-the-Wold, co. Glouc., [1838 ?] Vol. XLIII, fol. 335.

Moss, Samuel, Capt. of Artillery, of Kingston, Jamaica, [1845] Vol. XLVIII, fol. 87.

Moss to Edwards-Moss, ..., of Otterspool, and Roby Hall, co. Lanc., [1851] Vol. XLIX, fols. 454 and 466.

„ Mark, ..., of Rosebank, Melbourne, Victoria, 1891, Vol. LXVI, fol. 194.

Mossop, ..., of St. Leonard's and Heathfield, co. Sussex, and co. Kent, [1869] Vol. LVII, fol. 184.

Mostyn, Baron [10 Sept. 1831] (Lloyd), of co. Flint, Wales. Arms and additional Crest, [1832] Vol. XXXIX, fol. 50. Supporters, fol. 52.

Mostyn after Lloyd, ... [9 May 1831], for son, [1832] Vol. XXXIX, fol. 55.

Motion, A. R., of Faulkbourne, co. Essex, 1892,* Vol. LXVI, fol. 267.

Motley, Thomas, of Beckenham, co. Kent, and William, of Abingdon, Berks., and co. Kent, brothers, 12 June 1732, Vol. VIII, fol. 150[b].

Mott, ... (see Piddock), of co. Staff. (Match.) [1730] Vol. VIII, fol. 73[b].

„ W. H., of Gunnersbury, Acton, co. Middx., 1881, Vol. LXI, fol. 221.

Mott, formerly Vertue, Thomas (see Burke [no date]).

Motteux, Peter, grandfather John, of London, and Rouen, Normandy, [1749 ?] Vol. IX, fol. 312.

Moubray to Hussey, Adm., K.C.B., of co. Huntingdon, and Scotland. Augmentation, [1832] Vol. XXXIX, fol. 101. Supporters, [1835 ?] Vol. XLI, fol. 156.

Moulton to [? after] Barrett, Edward Barrett, of New York, and Cinnamon Hill, Island of Jamaica, and his brother Samuel, [1797] Vol. XX, fol. 110.

Moulton, Edward (wife Barrett), of Wakefield, Island of Jamaica, [1815] Vol. XXIX, fol. 25.

Mounsey to Cranmer, ..., of co. Essex. Quartering, [1814] Vol. XXVIII, fol. 189.

Mounsey, William, Post-Capt., R.N., C.B., of Tarn Lodge, and Castle Carrock, co. Cumberland (Heysham, 1871). Arms and distinction, [1825] Vol. XXXV, fol. 200.

„ J. G., of Castle Street, Carlisle, co. Cumberland, 1883,* Vol. LXII, fol. 71. (Berry's Suppl.)

Mountain, ..., B.D., Bp. of Quebec, of Reedham Hall and Thwaite Hall, co. Norf., [1793] Vol. XVIII, fol. 250.

Mountford to Newte, ..., of London, [1806] Vol. XXIV, fol. 25.

Mountford, Frederick Batting, s. of John, of Charlton, Berks., London, and Henley-on-Thames, co. Oxf., 1878, Vol. LX, fol. 135. (Berry's Suppl.)

Mountstephen, Baron [Sir George Stephen, Bart.], of co. Hertf. (Arms, Lyon Office). Supporters, 1891, Vol. LXVI, fol. 182.

Mountstuart, Lord (Stuart). Supporters, [1776] Vol. XIII, fol. 221.

„ Crichton-Stuart, son of. (Match), [1817] Vol. XXX, fol. 169.

Mount Temple, Baron [25 May 1880, Cowper Temple] (extinct). Supporters, 1880, Vol. LXI, fol. 51.

Mowbray, Baron (Stourton). Supporters, 1878, Vol. LX, fol. 131.

„ George Isaac, of Mortimer, Bucks. ; Ford, co. Durham ; and Yapton Place, co. Sussex, 1821, Vol. XXXII, fol. 327.

Mowbray, late Cornish, John Robert, of Yapton Place, co. Sussex ; Sutton Coldfield, co. Warw. ; Christ Church, Oxf. ; and the Inner Temple, London, 1847, Vol. XLVIII, fol. 385.

Mower, ..., of Woodseats, co. Derby. (Milnes and Smith.) (See Thorold of Welham in Landed Gentry.) [1815] Vol. XXIX, fols. 38 and 58.

Moxon, ..., of Kingston-upon-Hull and Pontefract, co. York, [1806] Vol. XXIII, fol. 435.

MOYER, Sir Samuel, Bart., and another, of co. Essex, fined for Lord Mayor, 5 July 1707, Vol. V, fol. 234.

MOYSE before BELWARD, ..., of co. Suff., and Gonville and Caius Coll., Camb., [1813] Vol. XXVII, fol. 337.

MOYSER, late WHYTE, ..., of London, and Beckington Cottage, co. Devon, [1815] Vol. XXIX, fol. 27.

MOYSES (see MOISES), Hugh, [1766] Vol. XI, fol. 138.

MOYSEY, Abel (St. John's Coll., Oxf.) ; Hinton, co. Somerset ; and Warington and Cold Ashby, co. Northampton, 1765, Vol. XI, fol. 77.

MOZLEY, ..., of Liverpool and Beaconsfield, Woolton, co. Lanc., [1861] Vol. LIV, fol. 212.

MUGGERIDGE, Henry, Alderman of London, of Streatham, Banstead and Chipstead, co. Surrey, [1853] Vol. L, fol. 380.

MUILMAN, Richard (Frank ?), of Debden Hall and Little Yeldham, co. Essex, London and Amsterdam, 8 Nov. 1772, Vol. XII, fol. 216.   (Berry.)

MUILMAN to TRENCH-CHISWELL, Richard, of Debden Hall and Little Yeldham, co. Essex, 10 Dec. 1773, Vol. XII, fol. 218.

MUIRHEAD (GROSETT-) after STEWART, Robert Dalrymple, of Beedisholm, co. Lanark, Scotland, [1863] Vol. LV, fol. 86.

MULCASTER, Capt., R.E., of Greenford, co. Middx., [1803] Vol. XXII, fol. 180.

MULGRAVE, Baron [3 Sept. 1767] (Constantine PHIPPS) [of co. York], [1767] Vol. XI, fol. 240.

MULLENS, ..., wife of EYLES, of Brierley House, East Meon, Hampsh. Escutcheon of pretence, [1817] Vol. XXX, fol. 291.

MUNDY after MASSINGBERD, ..., of co. Leic. and Linc., [1863] Vol. LV, fol. 40.

MUNKHOUSE, Ann-Maria (Spr.), of co. Westmorland and York.   Crest to Dr. Munkhouse's issue, Richard, Vicar of Wakefield, [1810] Vol. XXV, fols. 402 and 403.

MUNKHOUSE after GORMAN, Edward Sexton, of Winton, co. Westmorland, [1810] Vol. XXV, fol. 421.

MUNRO, Sir Hector, K.B. [1779], of Novar, Scotland.   Supporters, [1779] Vol. XIV, fol. 155 ; Arms and Supporters to descendants ? [1783] Vol. XV, fol. 219.

   „   Maj.-Gen. Sir Thomas, K.C.B. [1819], of Scotland, Gov., Fort St. George, Madras [Bart., 6 Aug. 1825], [1822] Vol. XXXIII, fol. 374.

MUNT, ..., of Cheshunt, co. Hertf., and Kingston, Island of Jamaica, [1832 ?] Vol. XXXIX, fol. 170.

MUNTZ, G. F., of Umberslade Hall, Tamworth, co. Staff., 1895,* Vol. LXVIII, fol. 216.

MUNYARD, Joseph, of Camden Town, London, [1828] Vol. XXXVII, fol. 127.

MURCHISON, ..., of Westminster, [1786] Vol. XVI, fol. 111.

MURE after STRANGE, ..., of Three Mills Distillery, West Ham, co. Essex, [1868] Vol. LVI, fol. 346.

MURHALL before GRIFFITH, Thomas, of Whitchurch, Shropsh., and Wrexham, Wales.   Crest for Murhall, [1813] Vol. XXVII, fols. 331 and 333.

MURRAY, Baron MANSFIELD [8 Nov. 1756].   Supporters, [1756] Vol. X, fol. 67.

MURRAY, late FOXLOW, Lieut.-Gen. William, of co. Derby and York, [1782] Vol. XV, fol. 41.

MURRAY, formerly YOUNG, ..., of Scotland, nat. s. of Lord ELIBANK, [1787 ?] Vol. XVI, fol. 207.

MURRAY to AYNSLEY, Lord Charles, of co. Northumberland, 24 June 1796, [1793] Vol. XVIII, fol. 226.   (Berry's Add.)

MURRAY [Henrietta Laura Pulteney, wife of Sir James Murray, Bart.], Baroness of BATH [26 July 1792], (Scotland), [1794] Vol. XVIII, fol. 373.

MURRAY to ALLAN, ..., of co. Cornw., [1800] Vol. XXI, fol. 37.

MURRAY, Maj.-Gen. Sir George, K.B. [1813], Lieut.-Gov., Edinb. Castle. Supporters, [1814] Vol. XXVIII, fol. 64.

MURRAY, late COTTIN, Adolphus, of Ardeleybury, co. Hertf. (*see* Murray of Clermonte, in Baronets, Murray of Ochtertyre), 1834, Vol. XL, fol. 299.

MURRAY, George Moore, of Mexico, and Douglas, Isle of Man, [1841] Vol. XLV, fol. 237.

MURRAY after STEWART, ..., of Broughton, co. Wigtown, and Calley House, co. Kirkcudbright, Scotland, [1846] Vol. XLVIII, fol. 134.

„ after STEWART, ..., late STEWART MURRAY, "of Broughton," [1855] Vol. LI, fol. 369.

MURRAY-GOSTLING, Col. Charles Edward, of Whitton Park, Twickenham, co. Middx., 1875. (Burke.)

MUSGRAVE, 1. George, of Nettlecomb, co. Somerset ; 2. William, and 3. Richard, and to the descendants of John, their great-grandfather. Exemplified, 1690, Vol. IV, fol. 66.

„ William, M.D., of Oxford, F.R.S., 3rd s. of Richard, of Nettlecombe, co. Somerset, 1 Aug. 1720, Vol. VI, fol. 448.

MUSGRAVE, late WALKER, George (s. of George, M.P.), of co. Kent, and . . . . . ., nat. son and dau. of Musgrave, of Borden, co. Kent, [1816] Vol. XXIX, fols. 288 and 290.

MUSGRAVE after SOGAR, John, of Sandford House, and Bramley, Leeds, co. York, [1863] Vol. LV, fol. 30 ; [1875] Vol. LIX, fol. 167.

„ after WYKEHAM, ..., of Swalcliffe, and Chimsor, co. Oxf., and Barnaby, co. Glouc., [1876] Vol. LIX, fol. 268.

MUSGROVE, Sir John (s. of John), Lord Mayor of London, of Speldhurst, co. Kent, [1851] Vol. L, fol. 33.

MUSGROVE-MUSGROVE, John, of Head Gate, Colchester, co. Essex, 1882, Vol. LXI, fol. 265. (Berry's Suppl.)

MUSSABINI, ..., (naturalized), of West Derby, and Consul at Liverpool, [1856] Vol. LII, fol. 7.

MUSTARD, Daniel, of Mistley, co. Essex, 1883, Vol. LXII, fol. 83. (Berry's Suppl.)

MUSTERS, late CHAWORTH, ..., formerly Musters, of co. Nottingham, [1824] Vol. XXXIV, fol. 362.

MUSTERS to CHAWORTH, ..., of co. Nottingham, [1806] Vol. XXIII, fol. 343. SHERWIN quartering, [1828-1829] Vol. XXXVII, fol. . . . .

MYATT, William James, Solicitor, of Abchurch Lane, London, 1896, Vol. LXIX, fol. 191.

MYDDLETON, late BIDDULPH, ..., of Crofton Hall, co. Worc., and Chirk Castle, co. Denbigh, Wales, [1804] Vol. XXIII, fol. 8.

MYERS, Lieut.-Gen. [Sir] William, of Monkstown, Ireland [Bart., 21 June 1804]. [1806], Vol. XXIII, fol. 343.

MYERS after WASKETT, Sir Francis [Knt., 1824], of Monkstown and Marlesfield, co. Dublin, Ireland, 1818, Vol. XXX, fol. 365.

„ Capt. W. J., of Porter's Park, co. Hertf., 1892,* Vol. LXVII, fol. 6.

MYERS-BESWICK, W. B., of Gristhorpe, Filey, co. York, 1896, Vol. LXIX, fol. 94.

MYLCHREEST, Thomas George, of Thorner, nr. Leeds, co. York, 18 . . [?] Vol. LXXI or IX [? LXXIX].

MYLLES, late SPEED, John, of Eling and Ashley, Hampsh., [1780] Vol. XIV, fol. 221.

[MYLNE, William John Horne, 29 June 1891. (X, Right to bear Arms, 1900.)]

MYNORS, late RICKARDS, Peter, of co. Hereford, and Evenjobb [co. Radnor], [1787] Vol. XVI, fol. 305.

MYNORS after BASKERVILLE (formerly RICKARDS), T. B., of Poulto House, Wilts. ; Treago, co. Hereford ; and Aberedw Court, co. Radnor, Wales, [1817] Vol. XXX, fol. 301.

MYNORS-BASKERVILLE, T. B., of Poulto House, Wilts., and Treago, co. Hereford. POWELL quartering, [1837] Vol. XLII, fol. 77.

MYRES, ..., of Preston, co. Lanc., [1867] Vol. LVI, fol. 225.

MYSTER, John, of Hornton, co. Oxf., and Epsom, co. Surrey, 17 May 1725, Vol. VII, fol. 303.

MYTTON to THORNYCROFT, ..., of Thornycroft and Eccleston, co. Chester, [1831] Vol. XXXVIII, fol. 343.

MYTTON, late WENLOCK, ... (Spr.), (nat. dau.), of Cleobury North, Shropsh., [1865] Vol. LVI, fol. 44.

N

NAGLE, Lieut.-Col. James, late Madras S.C., [1819] Vol. XXXI, fol. 209.

NAINBY-LUXMOORE, W. C., of Thorganby Hall, co. Linc., 1885, Vol. LXIII, fols. 61 to 93.

NAIRN, late AVELING, William, of co. Sussex. Nairn and Aveling quarterly, [1834] Vol. XL, fol. 239.

NAIRNE, late McNICHOLL, of Quebec, [1834] Vol. XL, fol. 94.

NAISH, James, of St. Andrew's, Holborn, London, 28 Mar. 1721, Vol. VII, fol. 55 ; Add. MS. 14,830, fol. 130.

NAPER to DUTTON [1748], James Lenox, Baron SHERBORNE [20 May 1784], [1784] Vol. XV, fol. 283.

NAPIER [Lieut.-Gen. Sir Robert Cornelis, Baron Napier] of Magdala [17 July 1868], G.C.B. [1868]. Arms, [1868] Vol. LVII, fol. 62 ; Supporters, fol. 64.

„ . . . ., of Montagu Place, Russell Square, London, [1870] Vol. LVII, fol. 272.

NAPIER-CLAVERING, Rev. J. W., of Axwell Park, co. Durham, 1894, Vol. LXVII, fol. 306.

NASH after ROSTON, ... (Spr.), of Park Hill House, Bristol, and Newent, co. Glouc., [1831] Vol. XXXVIII, fol. 214.

NASH, James, M.D., of Worcester, 1841, Vol. XLV, fol. 172.

NASH-WOODHAM to BELDAM-JOHNS, ..., of co. Camb. and Hertf., [1867] Vol. LVI, fol. 232.

NASH, ..., of Chesham, Bucks., [1872] Vol. LVIII, fol. 170.

„ . . . ., of Old Broad Street, London, [1874] Vol. LVIII, fol. 317.

NAYLER, George, York Herald, Blanc Coursier Herald, of London, wife WILLIAMS, nat. dau. of Sir John GUISE, Bart., [1808] Vol. XXV, fols. 54 and 56 ; Sir George, Garter King of Arms, Heralds' Coll., London. Quartering, [1822] Vol. XXXIII, fol. 199.

NAYLOR to LUCAS, ..., of co. Middx., [1829] Vol. XXXVIII, fol. 17.

„ to LEYLAND, Thomas, of co. Chester and Lanc., 1894 [? figures misplaced], [1849] Vol. XLIX, fol. 254.

NAYLOR, John, of Hooton Hall, co. Chester, and Leighton Hall, co. Montgomery, [1850] Vol. XLIX, fol. 359. BULLIN quarterly, his mother, [1855 ?] Vol. LI, fol. 420.

NAYLOR-LEYLAND, H. S. (Bart.), of London, 1895, Vol. LXVIII, fol. 267.

NAYLOR, Harriet Ann. (See BERTIE-MATHEW.) [1819] Vol. XXXI, fol. 293.

NEAL, John, of Christ Church, co. Surrey, High Sheriff, 14 Feb. 172⅔, Vol. VII, fol. 154 ; Add. MS. 14,830, fol. 132.

NEALE, Henry, of London, 23 Dec. 1720, Vol. VII, fol. 48 ; Add. MS. 14,830, fol. 32.

„ Robert, of Yate, co. Glouc., and Corsham and Shaw House, Wilts., 1774, Vol. XII, fol. 300.

NEALE, late [? after] BURRARD [1795, Adm.], Sir Harry [Burrard-Neale], Bart., of Hampsh. and Wilts., died s.p. Escutcheon of pretence, [Neale ?] [1795] Vol. XIX, fol. 29 ; K.C.B. [1815], M.P., of Walhampton, Hampsh. Crest, [28 Oct. 1815] Vol. XXIX, fol. 140 ; G.C.B. [1822]. Supporters, [1822] Vol. XXXIII, fol. 316. Supporters [to be borne by his successors to the Baronetcy, Roy. Lic., 21 Nov. 1839], [1839] Vol. XLIV, fol. 159.

NEALE, late VANSITTART, Edward, B.C.C., of Bisham Abbey, Berks., and Taplow, Bucks. Crest, 1805, Vol. XXIII, fol. 257.

NEALE, ..., of Bisham, Berks., and Allesley Park, co. Warw., [1805] Vol. XXIII, fol. 259.

„ . . . ., of Sibston, co. Leic., and Tollerton, co. Nottingham. Crest, [1808] Vol. XXIV, fol. 430. Match with LOWE, [1809] Vol. XXV, fol. 105.

NEALE to BARRY, ..., of co. Leic. and Nottingham. Crest, [1811] Vol. XXVI, fol. 358. Match with PENDOCK, fol. 360.

NEAL, Neale, of Yeovil, co. Somerset, [1836-1837] Vol. XLII, fol. 61.

NEAME, Frederick Lutton, of Selling, co. Kent, 1885, Vol. LXIII, fol. 49.

NEATE, Richard, of the City of London, to the descendants of his father John, of Swindon, Wilts., clerk, 2 Feb. 173⅞, Vol. VIII, fol. 228ᵇ; Add. MS. 14,830, fol. 31.

NEAVE, Richard, of St. Mary-at-Hill, London, 1763,* Vol. X, fol. 467. (Berry.)

„ . . . ., of Dagnam Park, co. Essex, [1795] Vol. XIX, fol. 175.

NEDHAM, ..., of Wymondley Priory, co. Hertf. Crest for BROWNE, [1761] Vol. X, fol. 394.

NEED, Samuel, of co. Nottingham, [1779] Vol. XIV, fol. 175.

NEED to WELFITT, ..., of Langwith Lodge, Cuckney, and Blidworth, co. Nottingham; Canterbury, Hastingleigh and Glenstead, co. Kent; Ticehurst, co. Sussex; and Pelham, co. Linc., [1843] Vol. XLVII, fol. 141.

NEELD, Joseph, of Rockstone House, Shipton, Hampsh., [1828] Vol. XXXVII, fol. 62.

NEILL, Andrew Charles, of Brisbane and London, Surgeon, Madras C.S., 1876, Vol. LIX, fol. 222. (Berry's Suppl.)

NEILSON, Robert William, of Halewood, Liverpool, 1878, Vol. LX, fol. 128.

NELSON to RYCROFT, Rev. Richard, of London, [1783] Vol. XV, 223.

NELSON, Rear-Adm. Sir Horatio, K.B. [17 May 1797], son of Edmund, Rector of Burnham Thorpe, co. Norf., [1797] Vol. XX, fol. 40; Supporters, fol. 43; Augmentation, [1798] fol. 261.

„ Viscountess (WOODWARD), widow. Escutcheon of pretence, [1805] Vol. XXIII, fol. 250.

„ Earl [20 Nov. 1805] William, D.D. Augmentation and Supporters, [1807] Vol. XXIV, fol. 281; additional Augmentation, fol. 284.

„ Earl Thomas [suc. 1835]. Arms and Supporters, [1835] Vol. XL, fol. 335.

„ . . . ., of Garsdale, co. York. (See ALDERSON.) [1811] Vol. XXVI, fol. 190.

„ . . . . Match with BUCKLE. (See BUCKLE.) [1811] Vol. XXVI, fols. 346 to 348.

NELTHORPE after TUDOR, late COWNE, ..., of co. Sussex, [1806] Vol. XXIV, fol. 29.

NEPEAN, Lieut.-Col., of Chatham, co. Kent, and Saltash, co. Cornw., [1800?] Vol. XX, fol. 405.

NETTLEFOLD, ..., of Highgate, London, [1866] Vol. LVI, fol. 150.

NETTLESHIPP, ..., of Basinghall Street, London, and Cheltenham, co. Glouc., [1804] Vol. XXII, fol. 354.

NEUNBURG (VANDER), ..., of St. Martin, Stamford Baron, co. Northampton, [1807] Vol. XXIV, fol. 304.

NEVE, Richard, of London, 1763 (see Berry, under Neave).

NEVELL, Mary, relict of Vice-Adm. John, of the West Indies, to descendants of the Admiral, 15 Dec 1697, Vol. IV, fol. 239.

NEVILE, late LISTER, John, late CHARET, of co. York, and Meers Ashby, co. Northampton, [1782?] Vol. XV, fol. 109.

NEVILE to NOEL, Lieut.-Col, of Walcott, co. Northampton, and Wellingore, co. Linc., [1798] Vol. XX, fol. 152.

NEVILL, ..., of Llangennech Park, and Llanelly, co. Carmarthen, Wales, [1841] Vol. XLV, fol. 309.

NEVILLE, late ALDWORTH [Richard], Baron BRAYBROOKE, [1797] Vol. XX, fols. 47 and 50.

NEVILLE to GRIFFIN [27 July 1797], Baron BRAYBROOKE. Quarterly Arms, [1797] Vol. XX, fol. 52.

NEVILLE-GRENVILLE [1825, Rev. George, M.A, Chaplain in ordinary to the Queen, 3rd s. of the 2nd Baron Braybrooke], [1825] Vol. XXXV, fol. 246.

NEVILLE-ROLFE, ..., of Heacham Hall, co. Norfolk, [1837] Vol. XLII, fol. 91 ; [1837], fol. 110.

NEVILLE, James S., of Sloby, co. Norf., late a Judge, Calcutta, 1885, Vol. LXIII, fol. 136.

NEW to BIRCH, Samuel, of the Middle Temple, London, Bristol and Bedminster, co. Somerset. (Susannah STAGG wife of), impaled Arms, [1800] Vol. XX, fol. 421.

NEWALL, Henry, of Lane Cottage and Lower Town House, Rochdale, co. Lanc., 1843, Vol. XLVI, fol. 387.

NEWARK, Viscount [1796, Charles Pierrepont, formerly Medows], wife of [dau. of William Mills]. Mills Arms, [1796 ?] Vol. XIX, fol. 321. Supporters, fol. 322.

NEWBERRY to POWER, ..., of Charlton, co. Kent, [1778] Vol. XIV, fol. 42.

NEWBERY, ..., of Heathfield, co. Sussex, [1794] Vol. XVIII, fol. 345.

NEWBURY to KNOTT, Thomas, of co. Dorset, [1780] Vol. XIV, fol. 247.

„ to WILSON, Christopher WILSON-, of London, and Broomhead Hall, co. York. 7 May 1832, Vol. XXXIX, fol. 103. (Bishop's MS.)

NEWBURGH, Baron [5 Jan. 1822] (CHOLMONDELEY), Earl ROCKSAVAGE, &c., [1822 ?] Vol. XXXIII, fol. 110.

NEWBY to COPLEY, ..., of Netherhall, co. York, [1771] Vol. XII, fol. 111.

NEWCASTLE, Duke of, of co. Nottingham, PELHAM and CLINTON quarterly, [1807] Vol. XXIV, fol. 224.

NEWCOURT after TODD, ..., of Stamford, co. Linc., and Kirby Ireleth, co. Lanc. [1867 ?] Vol. LVI, fol. 177.

NEWDEGATE, late PARKER, Charles (Minor), of Harefield Lodge, co. Middx., and Arbury, co. Warw., [1808] Vol. XXIV, fol. 465.

NEWDIGATE, late PARKER, Francis, of Kirkhallam, co. Derby, 10 June 1773, Vol. XII, fol. 249.

NEWDIGATE before LUDFORD, formerly BRACEBRIDGE, John, D.C.L., of Harefield Lodge, co. Middx., and Arbury, co. Warw., [1808] Vol. XXIV, fol. 454 [see Burke].

NEWDIGATE-LUDFORD before CHETWODE, John, of co. Staff. and Warw. (afterwards 5th Baronet), [1826] Vol. XXXVI, fol. 73.

NEWELL, Esther, of Adwell, co. Oxf. (? remainder over), 1755, Vol. X, fol. 11. (Berry.)

NEWELL-BIRCH, ..., of Berks. and co. Oxf., [1847] Vol. XLVIII, fol. 312.

NEWLAND, William, of Newsilsbury, Barkway, co. Hertf., 1693, Vol. IV, fol. 135.

NEWLANDS, Baron (Sir William WALLACE-HOZIER, Bart.). Supporters, 1898, Vol. LXX, fol. 180.

NEWMAN, William, of Froyle, Hampsh., 2 Aug. 1727, Vol. VII, fol. 554.

NEWMAN, late TOLL, Charles, of Preston Deanery, co. Northampton, 6 Oct. 1775, Vol. XIII, fol. 127 and 129. Richard, of Thornbury Park, co. Glouc. ; Graywell, Hampsh. ; co. Northampton ; and Old Palace Yard, Westminster. Augmentation, [1802] Vol. XXI, fol. 360.

„ late TOLL-ASHBURNAM, Philip, of Fifehead Magdalen, co. Dorset [1775] Vol. XIII, fol. 130.

NEWMAN, ..., of Dartmouth, co. Devon, [1811] Vol. XXVI, fol. 248.

„ William Abiah, D.D., of ?co. Somerset, late Dean of Cape Town (died 7 Nov. 1864), grandson William Arthur Newman, [1858] Vol. LII, fol. 355.

NEWNES, Sir George, Bart., of London, 1895, Vol. LXVIII, fol. 150.

NEWNHAM. *See* KETT.

„ Lewis, of Northaw, co. Hertf., s. of John, of Maresfield, co. Sussex, gent., 6 April 1716, Vol. VI, fol. 230, to descendants of his father ; Add. MS. 14,830, fol. 117 (*see also* book marked C. T. (Townley) in Her. Coll.).

NEWNHAM-COLLINGWOOD, George Lewis, of co. Northumberland, [1819] Vol. XXXI, fol. 236.

NEWPORT, Baron TORRINGTON [20 June 1716]. Supporters, [1716] Vol. VI, fol. 243.

„ George, merchant, of St. Olave, Hart Street, London, and Camberwell, co. Surrey, 15 Mar. 172⁶⁄₇, Vol. VII, fol. 544.

NEWPORT-CHARLETT, James Wakeman, 1821 (*see* Burke).

NEWSOME to NEWSOME-KILLAM, ..., of co. York, [1871] Vol. LVIII, fol. 30.

NEWTE, late MOUNTFORD, ..., of Grove House, Brompton, and Upper Gower Street, London, [1806] Vol. XXIV, fol. 25.

NEWTON. (*See* ARCHER and HOUBLON.) [1819] Vol. XXXI, fols. 348 and 350.

HOUBLON-NEWTON (Susannah ?), dau. of John ARCHER and Lady Mary FITZ-WILLIAM [dau. of the 2nd Earl Fitzwilliam], [1818-1819] Vol. XXXI, fol. . . . .

NEWTON, ..., of Edgefield, co. Norf. (*See* COOPER.) Match, [1765] Vol. XI, fol. 81.

NEWTON, late LEAPER, John, of Derby, [1789] Vol. XVII, fol. 181.

NEWTON (Jarratt), of Trelawney, Island of Jamaica, [1793] Vol. XVIII, fol. 218.

NEWTON to FRYE, ..., of co. Surrey. Quarterly Arms, [1801] Vol. XXI, fol. 152.

NEWTON, Samuel, of Stockport and Cheadle, co. Chester, [1816] Vol. XXIX, fol. 370.

NEWTON to WATSON, William, of Wath Cottage, Pickering, and Old Malton, co. York, [1839] Vol. XLIV, fol. 180.

NEWTON, A. H., of Belsize Court, London, 1887,* Vol. LXIV, fol. 3.

„ Thomas Henry G., Bar.-at-Law, of Woolton Wawen, co. Warw., 1887,* Vol. LXIV, fol. 18.

„ Baron (LEGH), of co. Chester. Supporters ? 1892, Vol. LXVII, fol. 93.

„ Sir Alfred James, Lord Mayor of London 1899-1900, 18 . . ., Vol. LXXI, fol. . . . .

NIAS, Capt., R.N., C.B. (Adm. Sir Joseph, K.C.B. [1867]), [1843] Vol. XLVI, fol. 369.

NIBBS, James LANGFORD-, of Antigua, and co. Somerset, of St. John's Coll., Oxford, 13 Oct. 1759, Vol. X, fol. 188. (Berry.)

NIBLETT, Stephen, D.D., Warden of All Souls' Coll., Oxford, 3 June 1732, Vol. VIII, fol. 157ᵇ.

„ Daniel John ?, of Haresfield and Standish, co. Glouc., 1784, Vol. XV, fol. 247.

NICHOLAS, late HEATH, Nicholas, of co. Essex and Kent, 15 Feb. 1772, Vol. XII, fol. 127.

NICHOLAS (LITTLEGROOM-), late [after ?] FRANKLIN, of Dean's Place, Lawrence Waltham and Hall's Place, Berks. Quarterly with Franklin, [1806] Vol. XXIV, fol. 55.

NICHOLAS, John Harris, Post.-Capt., R.N., of Looe, co. Cornw. Addition to Crest. (*See* NICOLAS.) [1816] Vol. XXIX, fols. 327 and 461.

„ . . . ., of Broseley, Shropsh., [1862] Vol. LIV, fol. 262.

NICHOLL, Thomas, of Trinity Coll., Camb., s. of John, of Balham Hill, London, 22 Nov. 1817 [1818], Vol. XXX, fol. 399. (Misc. G. et H., 3rd S., III, p. 178.)

NICHOLL to CARNE, Rev. Robert, of co. Glamorgan, Wales, [1842] Vol. XLVI, fol. 218.

NICHOLL, John, F.S.A., of Theydon Garnon, co. Essex, [1844 ?] Vol. XLVII, fol. 318.

NICHOLLS, George, s. of Richard, of the City of London. Argent, a chevron sable, between three pheons, gules. [1737] Vol. VIII, fol. 211ᵇ.

NICHOLLS to BRODHURST, Maj.-Gen. Thomas (E.I.C.S.), of Shropsh., [1809] Vol. XXV, fol. 244.

NICHOLLS, Benjamin, Mayor of Manchester, [1853 ?] Vol. L, fol. 408.

NICHOLS, John Bowyer, F.S.A., of Hanger Hill, Ealing, 23 Mar. 1861, Vol. LIV, fol. 130 [see Burke].

„ H. S., of Cornwall Terrace, Regent's Park, and Piccadilly, London, Bookseller, 1896, Vol. LXIX, fol. 107.

NICHOLSON, Francis, Gov. of Maryland, 169¾. Vol. IV, fol. 153 [see Burke].

„ . . . ., of Cateaton Street, [1806] Vol. XXIII, fol. 362.

NICHOLSON before FALL, William, of co. York, [1811] Vol. XXVI, fol. 398.

NICHOLSON, Stephen, of Chapel Allerton and Roundhay Park, co. York, and Stamford Hill, London, [1817] Vol. XXX, fol. 137. (RHODES, fol. 270.)

NICHOLSON, late PHILLIPS, William Nicholson, B.A., of Roundhay and Leeds, co. York, [1827] Vol. XXXVI, fol. 365.

„ late McINNES, Alexander, of East Court, Charlton Kings, co. Glouc. (for Waterloo services), 1822, Vol. XXXIII, fol. 138. (Berry's Appx.)

NICHOLSON to SHAW, ... of Arrow Hall, co. Chester, and Liverpool, Capt. of Militia, [1837] Vol. XLII, fol. 152.

NICHOLSON, Patrick Charles, of Moresby, co. Cumberland, and Ashton-under-Lyne, co. Lanc., [1842] Vol. XLVI, fol. 26.

„ Sir Charles, Knt., of New South Wales, Speaker L. A., [25 Feb. 1852] Vol L, fol. 259.

NICKALLS, Tom, of Redhill, co. Surrey, and Sir Patteson, of Chislehurst, co. Kent, 1885, Vol. LXIII, fol. 65.

NICKELS, Walter Lanyon, 1st s. of John T. (of Birkenhead, co. Chester, and Shrewsbury, Shropsh.), 18 . . ., Vol. LXXI, fol. . . . .

NICKISSON, John Leaver (s. of John, of London), 18 . . . ., Vol. LXXI, fol. . . . .

NICKLIN, ..., of Hackney, co. Middx., [1804] Vol. XXIII, fol. 61.

NICOLAS, Sir Nicholas Harris, Kt., K.H., of East Looe, co. Cornw., and the Inner Temple, London, 1832, Vol. XXXIX, fol. 17. (See also NICHOLAS.) G.C.M.G. [1840]. Supporters, [1840] Vol. XLV, fol 23.

„ Capt. John Harris, of East Looe, co. Cornw., 1816, Vol. XXIX, fol. 327. (Burke.)

„ Capt. Toup, C.B., of East Looe, co. Cornw. Augmentation, 16 Oct. 1816, Vol. XXIX, fol. 461. (Burke.)

NICOLL, John, of Colney Hatch, co. Middx., fined for Sheriff of London, 29 April 1720, Vol. VI, fol. 408. Alteration in Arms, 7 Feb. 1722 [172¾], Vol. VII, fol. 164. (Berry.)

„ Sir Charles Gounter, K.B. [1732], of Racton, co. Sussex. Supporters, [173½] Vol. VIII, fol. 118.

„ Donald, Sheriff elect of London, of Acton, co. Middx., [1819], Vol. XLIX, fol. 171.

NICOLLS to TRAFFORD, Edward, of Swithamby Park, co. Staff, [1829] Vol. XXXVII, fol. 322.

„ to TRAFFORD, Lieut.-Col. Thomas S. (of Panthowell, co. Carmarthen), now of Hereford, [1837] Vol. XLII, fol. 217.

NIGHTINGALE, ..., of Warrington and Walton, co. Lanc., and St. Clement Danes, London, [1824] Vol. XXXV, fol. 30.

NIGHTINGALL, Lieut.-Gen. Sir Miles, K.C.B. [1815], [1819] Vol. XXXI, fol. 320.

NILSON, Lawrence, of Carlscron, Sweden [no reference], late Brig.-Gen. and Commander-in-Chief, Bombay [1784-1787].

NIXON to WILSON, Thomas, of Flatt, Bewcastle, co. Cumberland. (Wilson Arms confirmed.) 3 Nov. 1773, Vol. XII, fol. 273.

NOAKES, J. T., of Brockley Hall, Lewisham, co. Kent, 1890, Vol. LXV, fol. 342.

NOBLE, J. H., of Selby House, Ham, co. Surrey, 1891, Vol. LXVI, fol. 239.

„ Lieut.-Col. John, of Littleover, co. Derby, 1886,* Vol. LXIII, fol. 259.

NOEL, late EDWARDS [5 May 1798], Gerard Noel, of Catmose Lodge, co. Rutland, [1798] Vol. XX, fol. 150.

„ late NEVILLE, Lieut.-Col., of Wellingore, co. Linc., and Walcott, co. Northampton, [1798] Vol. XX, fol. 152.

„ late MILBANKE, Sir Ralph, Bart., M.P., of co. Durham and York, [Roy. Lic., 1815] Vol. XXIX, fol. 1.

„ late BYRON, Baron Byron, George [Gordon], of co. Durham, &c., [Roy. Lic., 27 Feb. 1822] Vol. XXXIII, fol. 150.

NOEL-HILL, ..., 2nd and 3rd sons [of Thomas Noel] Baron BERWICK, of Shropsh., [19 Mar. 1824] Vol. XXXIV, fols. 300 and 302.

NOEL, Earl of GAINSBOROUGH [16 Aug. 1841]. Supporters, [1841] Vol. XLV, fol. 291.

NOEL after KING [29 Sept. 1860], Earl of LOVELACE, [1860] Vol. LIV, fol. 58.

NOOTH to VAVASOUR, Henry, of co. York, 1791, Vol. XVII, fols. 318 and 326.

NORBURY, formerly JONES, [9 Nov.], 1840, Thomas, of Sherridge, co. Worc., [1841] Vol. XLV, fol. 297.

NORCLIFFE, late DALTON, Thomas, of Langton, co. York, 1807 [1808], Vol. XXIV, fol. 323.

„ late ROBINSON, Mrs. Rosamond, of Langton, co. York, 1862, Vol. LIV, fols. 272 and 273.

NORCOP after RADFORD, of Belton Hall, Drayton-in-Hales, Shropsh., [1862] Vol. LIV, fol. 278.

NORDEN, Solomon, of Allhallows Staining, London, and Amsterdam, 1771, Vol. XII, fol. 81. (Berry.)

NORDHEIMER, William, of Toronto, 1884, Vol. LXII, fol. 326.

NORIE to MEDOWS, ..., of Wilts., [1864] Vol. LV, fol. 246.

NORMAN to BLAKE, ..., of co. Somerset, [1833] Vol. XXXIX, fol. 210.

„ to HARE, ..., of co. Norf., reputed children of Hare, Bart., [1864] Vol. LV, fols. 200 and 201.

NORRIS, Samuel, and coz. John, Chapter Clerk of Canterbury, [1748] Vol. IX, fol. 234.

NORRIS, late HARRIS, Robt. J. J., of Davey Hulme, co. Lanc., [1808] Vol. XXV, fol. 37.

NORTH, late LONG, ..., of Dudley, co. Suff. (Match), [1797] Vol. XIX, fol. 440.

NORTH (Baroness), late DOYLE [20 Aug. 1838 and her husband], Lieut.-Col. [John Sidney Doyle], of co. Surrey, [1838] Vol. XLIII, fol. 159.

NORTH, late BURTON, North [Burton], of Thurland Castle, co. Lanc., [1867] Vol. LVI, fol. 266.

NORTH, Harry, of Eltham, co. Kent, 18 . . ., Vol. LXXI, fol. . . . .

NORTHAMPTON, [5th] Earl of ([James] COMPTON), Baroness DE FERRERS, [? 1717, Vol. VI, or 1749, Vol. IX] [1779] Vol. XIV, fol. 96.

„ Marquess of [? Charles Douglas Compton, 3rd Marquess]. Supporters, [1858], Vol. LIII, fol. 31.

NORTHBOURNE, Baron, of co. Kent and York. Supporters, 1884, Vol. LXIII, fol. 1.

NORTHBROOK, Baron [4 Jan. 1866]. Supporters, [1866] Vol. LVI, fol. 77, and [Earl of Northbrook] (1876, Vol. LIX, fol. 258).

NORTHCOTE, ..., of Somerset Court, South Brent, co. Somerset, and Bucknell, co. Devon, [1843] Vol. XLVII, fol. 32.

NORTHEY to HOPKINS, Lieut.-Col. Richard, of Bucks. and Wilts., [1799] Vol. XX, fol. 348. Crest, [1800] Vol. XXI, fol. 65.

NORTHEY, Charlotte, wife of Edward, Canon of Windsor. (Charlotte TAYLOR, see that name.) [1814] Vol. XXVIII, fol. 178.

NORTHMORE, William, of Cleve, co. Devon, 17 April 1721, Vol. VII, fol. 64.

NORTHUMBERLAND, Earl of [7 Feb. 17$\frac{49}{50}$], PERCY, late SMITHSON [12 April 1750]. Arms and Supporters, [1750] Vol. IX, fol. 377.

NORTHUMBERLAND [? Earl of, K.G., 18 Nov. 1756]. Arms and Supporters, [1757?]
Vol. X, fol. 85.
NORTHWICK, Baron [26 Oct. 1797] (RUSHOUT). Supporters, [1797] Vol. XX,
fol. 36.
„   Baron. Match with BOULES. [? the Hon. George, Rector of Burford,
Shropsh., assumed the additional Surname and Arms of Bowles, by Roy.
Lic., 20 June 1817. He was the 2nd son of the 1st Baron.] [1817] Vol.
XXX, fol. 236.
NORTON, ..., Baron GRANTLEY. (See CHAPPLE.) Supporters and Chapple
Arms, 28 May 1782, Vol. XV, fol. 51.
„   . . . ., of Southwick and Portslade, co. Sussex, [1783] Vol. XV, fol. 171.
NORTON, late BRADBURY, ..., of Rye, co. Sussex, [1797] Vol. XIX, fol. 396.
„   late HARVEY, ..., of Wonersh, co. Surrey, reputed s. of Baron GRANTLEY,
[1811] Vol. XXVII, fols. 45 and 46.
NORTON, ..., LAUNDER, wife of, of Wonersh, co. Surrey. Escutcheon of
pretence, [1815] Vol. XXIX, fol. 162.
NORTON to LOWNDES-STONE-NORTON, ..., of co. Oxf., [1872] Vol. LVIII,
fol. 177.
NORTON, Baron [1878] ([Charles] Bowyer ADDERLEY), of co. Warw. Supporters,
1885, Vol. LXIII, fol. 17.
NORWICH, Bp. of [1723-27]. (See LENG [John]) [1723], Vol. VII, fol. 220.
NOTT, Maj.-Gen. Sir William, G.C.B. [1842], Commander-in-Chief, Bengal.
Arms, [1844?] Vol. XLVII, fol. 198 ; Supporters, fol. 202.
NOTT, late HARDING, Rev. Richard, of co. Devon, [1856] Vol. LII, fol. 160.
NOTT after PYKE, John, of Parracombe, and Bydon House, Swinbridge, co. Devon,
1863, Vol. LV, fol. 106.
NOTTINGE, ..., WALL, wife of, of Bocking, co. Essex. Escutcheon of pretence,
[1784] Vol. XV, fol. 341.
NOTTINGHAM, City of. [Arms] Crest and Supporters, [10 and 11 June] 1898,
Vol. LXX, fols. 194 and 197. [Geneal. Mag., II, pp. 389 and 431.]
NOUAILLE, ..., of Great Ness and Sevenoaks and Risby, co. Kent. (See
RUDGE, Match.) [1810] Vol. XXVI, fol. 81.
NOURSE, ..., Post-Capt., R.N., of London, [1811] Vol. XXVII, fol. 11.
NOWELL, ..., of Read Hall, co. Lanc. (on Canton, see SHERSON), [1780 ?]
Vol. XIV, fol. 203.
NOWELL, late ROBINSON, Rev. Thomas William, of Netherside and Linton, co.
York, and Underley, co. Westmorland, [1843] Vol. XLVII, fol. 22.
NOWELL-USTICKE, late BEAUCHAMP, ..., of Falmouth, co. Devon, [1852]
Vol. L, fol. 131.
NOY, ..., of Cormanton, co. Cornw., [1790] Vol. XVII, fol. 232.
NUGEE, ..., of London, [1830] Vol. XXXVIII, fol. 97.
NUGENT (TEMPLE-) -GRENVILLE to TEMPLE-NUGENT-BRYDGES-CHANDOS-
GRENVILLE, [15 Nov. 1799, Richard] Earl Temple [4 Feb. 1822].
Grant of Arms of Brydges and Chandos to Earl Temple, [1800] Vol.
XXI, fol. 54.
NUGENT, Lieut.-Gen. Sir George, M.P. (nat. s. of the Hon. CRAGGS-NUGENT), of
Waddesdon, Bucks. [1807] Vol. XXIV, fol. 237.
„   [Lieut.-Gen.] Sir George, Bart. [28 Nov. 1806], M.P., of Waddesdon,
Bucks. [G.C.B., 1815]. Supporters, [1807] Vol. XXIV, fol. 239.
„   . . . ., Maria SKINNER, his wife, [1814] Vol. XXVIII, fol. 19. (Match.)
See [1807] Vol. XXIV, fol. 232.
NUGENT after HODGES, ..., Assist.-Commissary-Gen. of Forces, Ireland,
[1815] Vol. XXVIII, fol. 387.
NUGENT, Adm. Sir Charles Edmund, G.C.H. [1834], of Ireland, [1834] Vol. XL,
fol. 110.
NUGENT (GREVILLE-) [Surname and Arms of Greville, 8 Aug. 1866], Baron
GREVILLE [15 Dec. 1869], of Ireland. Supporters, [1869] Vol. LVII,
fol. 202.

NUNN, Rev. Samuel, Rector of Church Lawton, co. Chester, and Stoke-upon-Trent,
co. Staff., s. of William, of Manchester, Merchant, 7 Feb. 1885, Vol.
LXIII, fol. 15. (*See* Misc. G. et H., 2nd S., II, p. 88.)
 ,, Elias Shirley, of Bury St. Edmunds, co. Suff. [1831], Vol. XXXVIII,
fol. 222.
NUSSEY, Rev. E. R., of Longney Vicarage, co. Glouc., 1890,* Vol. LXV, fol. 305.
NUTTALL after DIXON, ..., of co. Derby, [1860] Vol. LIII, fol. 368.

O

OADES, ... (*see* HALL), of Moundesmere, Preston Candover, Hampsh., [1767]
Vol. XI, fol. 232.
OAKELEY, ..., of Shrewsbury, Shropsh., 1790, Vol. XVII, fol. 221.
OAKES, ..., of Marylebone, co. Middx., 1783, Vol. XV, fol. 132.
 ,, James, of Bury St. Edmunds, co. Suff., [1806] Vol. XXIII, fol. 365.
 ,, Lieut.-Gen. Hildebrand, Commissioner-in-Chief of Malta [1810-13]. (Allusion
in the Canton.) [1813] Vol. XXVII, fol. 386.
 ,, Lieut.-Gen. Hildebrand, Bart. [1813], G.C.B. [1820]. Supporters, [1821]
Vol. XXXII, fol. 319 or 369.
 ,, (Olivar), of London, reputed dau. of Sir H. Oakes, Bart., wife of WILDMAN,
of London, [1818] Vol. XXXI, fol. 55.
OAKES, late WOOLHOUSE, O. [? Oakes], his wife, of Edwinstowe, co. Nottingham,
[1827] Vol. XXXVI, fol. 355.
OAKLEY, Baron [10 Sept. 1831], George CADOGAN, of co. Oxf. Supporters,
[1831] Vol. XXXVIII, fol. 279.
OAKSHOTT, T. W., of Derby House, Bebington, co. Chester, 1888, Vol. LXIV,
fol. 177.
OATES, Joseph Henry, of Westwood Hall and Low Hall, co. York, [1814] Vol.
XXVIII, fol. 227. (Berry's Suppl.)
OBHARD, ..., of London, [1850 ?] Vol. XLIX, fol. 267.
O'BRIEN, ..., of Shortgrove, co. Essex. Supporters, conditionally, [1750]
Vol. IX, fol. 351.
OCHTERLONY, Maj.-Gen. Sir David, Bart., G.C.B. [1816], of Scotland. Augmenta-
tion and Supporters, [1817] Vol. XXX, fols. 87 and 92.
 ,, ..., of Scotland, and City of Delhi (nat. s. of Sir David), [1818] Vol. XXX,
fol. 420.
OCKHAM, Baron (KING), of co. Surrey, [1725] Vol. VII, fol. 420.
ODAMS, Joshua, of St. Antholin's, London, 6 Feb. 173⅞, Vol. VIII, fol. 230 ;
Add. MS. 14,831, fol. 63.
OFFLEY, ..., of Norton Hall, co. Derby, [1788] Vol. XVII, fol. 118.
 ,, ..., of co. Staff., now CREWE, Baron Crewe, of Madeley, co. Staff.,
[1806] Vol. XXIII, fol. 328.
OFFLEY after CUNLIFFE, of Madeley Manor, co. Staff., [1829 ?] Vol. XXXVIII,
fol. 35.
OGDEN, late HASSELL, Peter, of The Laurels, Iron Acton, co. Glouc., [1866] Vol.
LVI, fol. 105.
OGG, Alderm. [?] Sir [29 June 1882] W. A., [William Anderson, Sheriff of London
and Middx.], of Brentwood, co. Essex, 1881,* Vol. LXI, fol. 203. (Berry's
Suppl.)
OGILVIE, late PERRY, ... (Arms for CLARKE, his wife), of Stanwell, co. Middx. ;
Langley Park, co. Forfar, Scotland ; and St. Mary, Jamaica, 1801, Vol.
XXI, fol. 162.
OGILVIE, Hon. Edward David, 18 . . ., Vol. LXXI, fol. . . . .
OGILVY, Charles, of Gray's Inn, London, and St. Peter's, Camb., [1821] Vol.
XXXII, fol. 274.
OGLANDER, H. O. J., of Nunwell, Brading, Isle of Wight, 1895, Vol. LXVIII,
fol. 156.

OGLE, late WALLIS, ..., of Morpeth, co. Northumberland, [1786 ?] Vol. XVI, fol. 201.

O'HAGAN, Baron [11 June 1870]. Supporters, [1870], Vol. LVII, fol. 260.

O'HALLORAN, Maj.-Gen. Sir Joseph, G.C.B. [1841], Bengal Army. Supporters, [1841] Vol. XLV, fol. 123.

O'HARA, [Charles], Baron TYRAWLEY [10 Jan. 1706]. Supporters, [1707] Vol. V, fol. 268.

O'KEEFFE after DE VILLE, G. D., of Romford, co. Essex. Escutcheon of pretence to wife of N. G. FAUCHER, and Arms to the descendants of Gabriel DENIS, s. of Nicholas Gabriel, [1803] Vol. XXII, fols. 67 and 70.

O'KELLY, ... Match with TEMPLE, [1815] Vol. XXIX, fol. 59.

OLDERSHAW to LOVEBOND, ..., of London, [1861] Vol. LIV, fols. 126 and 138.

OLDES, Sir William, Knt., of London, Usher of the Black Rod, Sir William and James, his brother, of London, 25 July 1711, Vol. V, fol. 433.

OLDFIELD, ..., of Norman Cottage, co. Sussex, and Uttoxeter, co. Staff., [1814] Vol. XXVIII, fol. 80.

„ Sir R. C., of Coombe Grange, Sunninghill, Berks., 1889,* Vol. LXV, fol. 135.

OLDHAM, late LAING, ..., of Caynham Court, Shropsh., co. Somerset and Devon, [1830] Vol. XXXVIII, fol. 118.

„ [Borough of, co. Lanc., 7 Nov. 1894, Geneal. Mag., III, p. 189.]

OLDLAND, ..., of Woodford, Berkeley, Avon Grove, Stoke Bishop, co. Glouc., [1868] Vol. LVII, fol. 90.

„ Henry. (HOPPER quartering.) 1877 [1871], Vol. LVII, fol. 339.

OLDNALL-WOLLEY [Edward], of Worc. City and London, [Roy. Lic., 24 July ; Exemplification, 7 Aug. 1843] Vol. XLVI, fol. 341 or 361.

OLDNALL, Henry Cousins, of Stone House, co. Worc., [? and] Roger William, 1897, Vol. LXIX, fol. 277.

OLDYS, ..., Advocate, Court of Chivalry. (Match, see HEALY.) [1698] Vol. IV, fol. 263.

OLIPHANT-FERGUSON, ..., of co. Cumberland, [1860 ?] Vol. LIV, fol. 85.

OLIVAR, OLIVAR-OAKES, ..., of (? London), reputed dau. of Sir H. Oakes, Bart., wife of Capt. WILDMAN, [1818] Vol. XXXI, fol. 55.

OLIVE, H., of Frome, co. Somerset. [1827] Vol. XXXVI, fol. 229.

OLIVER before GASCOIGNE, Richard Philip, of co. York. Quarterly Arms, [1810] Vol. XXV, fol. 451.

OLIVER, ..., of Melton Lodge, Melton Mowbray, co. Leic., and Brill House, Bucks., [1843] Vol. XLVII, fol. 125.

OLIVER-MASSEY, Richard Mansell, of Melton Mowbray, co. Leic., and Brill House, Bucks., 1844, Vol. XLVIII [1846], fol. 217.

OLIVER to OLIVER-BELLASIS, Richard John Erskine Oliver-Bellasis, s. of Richard Aldworth Oliver ; Lieut., 20th Hussars, 1879, Vol. LX, fol. 224.

OLIVERSON, Richard, of Goosnargh, Kirkham, co. Lanc., and Middle Temple, London, [1856] Vol. LII, fol. 26.

OLLIFFE, Sir Joseph Francis, Knt. [13 June 1853], M.D., of Ireland, Phys. to Brit. Embassy at Paris, [1853 ?] Vol. L, fol. 415.

OLLIVER, ..., of Ferring-cum-Kingston, co. Sussex, [1865] Vol. LV, fol. 284.

OLMIUS, Herman, s. of Lewis, of London, s. of John, of Arton, Duchy of Luxembourg, in Flanders, father's name John Lewis Olmius, 15 Oct. 1709, Vol. V, fol. 392 ; Add. MS. 14,831, fol. 118.

OLMIUS after LUTTRELL, ..., of Philipstown, Ireland, [1787] Vol. XVI, fol. 275.

OMBERSLEY, Baroness. Supporters, [1802] Vol. XXI, fol. 410.

O'NEAL, John Carter. Patent by Ulster K. of Arms, or 18 . . ., Vol. LXXI.

O'NEILL, Baron [16 April 1868], of Ireland. Supporters, [1868] Vol. LVII, fol. 33.

ONGLEY, Sir Samuel, Knt., of London, 3 June 1720, Vol. VI, fol. 423 ; Add. MS. 14,831, fol. 123.

ONGLEY to HOPSON, ..., of co. Kent, [1825] Vol. XXXV, fol. 277.

ONLEY (SAVILLE), late HARVEY, of co. Essex and Norf., [1824] Vol. XXXIV, fol. 267 (*see* Burke).

ONSLOW, Sir Richard [Houblon ? in pencil]. (Match), [1694] Vol. IV, fol. 176.

  „ . . . ., of Evershed, co. Surrey. (Match), [1696 ?] Vol. IV, fols. 221 and 222.

  „ Adm. Sir Richard, Bart., G.C.B. [1815], Supporters, [1815 ?] Vol. XXIX, fol. 232.

  „ Baron [25 June 1716]. Quarterings and Supporters, [1716] Vol. VI, fol. 239.

  „ . . . ., Baron CRANLEY [20 May 1776]. Supporters, [1776] Vol. XIII, fol. 209.

  „ Edward, MAINWARING-ELLERKER before Onslow [27 Jan. 1843], of co. York and Surrey [Edward Mainwaring - Mainwaring - Ellerker - Onslow], [1845] Vol. XLVII, fol. 391.

  „ Edward, MAINWARING-ELLERKER before Onslow, of co. York and Surrey, [1848] Vol. XLVIII, fol. 427.

  „ Guildford James Hillier, MAINWARING-ELLERKER before Onslow, of Upton House, Abbesford, Hampsh., [19 Aug.] 1861, Vol. LIV, fol. 192.

  „ Charles Vere Townshend, [1st s. of the last] MAINWARING-ELLERKER before Onslow [1898], of Grosvenor Square, London. Supporters, [1898] Vol. LXX, fol. 155.

OPPENHEIM, Henry Maurice William, of 15, Bruton Street, London, 1897, Vol. LXX, fol. 73.

OPPENHEIMER, Sir Charles, of London, H.B.M. Consul at Frankfort-on-Main, 1882, Vol. LXI, fol. 319. (Berry's Suppl.)

ORANGE to JACKSON, ..., MALLARD, wife of, of London, [1793] Vol. XVIII, fol. 268.

ORCHARD, Paul, M.P., Sheriff of Cornwall, of Orchard, co. Somerset, 17 July 1727, Vol. VII, fol. 561.

ORD to WRIGHT, Richard, of Durham Sands and Sedgfield, co. Durham. Quarterly Arms, [1814 ?] Vol. XXVIII, fol. 251.

ORD after BLACKETT, ..., B.A., of Whitfield, co. Northumberland, Rector of Wolsingham, co. Durham, [1855] Vol. LI, fol. 406.

ORDE, John, of East Orde and Morpeth, co. Northumberland, and Dominica, [1791] Vol. XVII, fol. 300.

ORDE to [ORDE-]POWLETT, Right Hon. Thomas Orde, Jean Mary PAULETT, his wife, of co. York, Baron BOLTON [1797], [7 Jan. 1795] Vol. XIX, fol. 147.

  „ to [ORDE-]POWLETT, [formerly William Powlett-Orde], Lord [? 2nd Baron BOLTON], of co. York. Supporters, [1819] Vol. XXXI, fol. 342.

ORFORD, Edward, Earl of. Supporters, 1697, Vol. IV, fol. 225.

ORFORD-HOLTE, Richard, B.A., Trinity Coll., Camb., of co. Lanc., [1 Aug. 1825] Vol. XXXV, fol. 244. [Genealogist, VI, p. 33.] (Berry's Suppl.)

ORGILL to LEMAN, ..., M.A., of co. Suff., [1808] Vol. XXIV, fol. 372.

ORMATHWAITE, Baron [16 April 1868, Sir John Walsh, Bart.]. Supporters, [1868] Vol. LVI, fol. 350.

ORME, George Garnett, of Tarn House, Skipton-in-Craven, co. York (formerly ROBINSON), 1882, Vol. LXII, fol. 6. (Berry's Suppl.)

ORMEROD, George, LL.D., of Lenches, Bury, and Whalley and Chorlton-upon-Medlock, co. Lanc. Arms allowed and Crest granted, 1814, Vol. XXVIII, fol. 200. (Berry.)

  „ . . . ., of Tyldesley House, and Bury, co. Lanc. (a quartering), [1847] Vol. XLVIII, fol. 302.

ORMISTON, Thomas (C. E.), of Ormidale, Camberwell ? 1881, Vol. LXI, fol. 205.

ORMSBY before GORE [14 Oct. 1814], Major [William ?], of Shropsh., and Ireland. Quarterly Arms, [1815] Vol. XXVIII, fol. 393.

ORMSBY after WATT, ..., of Cheltenham, co. Glouc. ; Bath, co. Somerset ; and Dublin, [1832] Vol. XXXIX, fol. 40.

ORMSBY-GORE, ... [his son], Baron HARLECH [14 Jan. 1876], of Wales, [1876] Vol. LIX, fol. 196.
OSBALDESTON, late BROOKES, Humphrey, of Hunmanby, co. York, 1771, Vol. XII, fol. 46.
„ late WICKERS, George, s. of John, of co. Surrey, [1771] Vol. XII, fol. 47.
„ late MITFORD, Bertram, s. of John ?, of co. Northumberland (died s.p. 1842), [1836] Vol. XLI, fol. 204.
OSBORN to JENKYN, ... (infants), of St. Albans, co. Hertf., 1800, Vol. XX, fol. 443.
OSBORNE or OSBORN, Sir George, Knt. and [4th] Bart., of co. Bedf. Supporters, 1770 [1772], Vol. XII, fol. 210 (see Debrett's Baronets, 1840).
OSBORNE, [Francis Godolphin, 5th M[arquess of]] CARMARTHEN, of co. York [afterwards 5th Duke of Leeds]. (GODOLPHIN Crest), [1785] Vol. XVI, fol. 71.
„ [Francis Godolphin], of co. York. Supporters for Baron GODOLPHIN [2nd s. of the 5th Duke of Leeds, 4 May 1832], [1832] Vol. XXXIX, fol. 150.
OSBORNE, DARCY-[6 Aug. 1849, Francis Godolphin D'Arcy D'Arcy-Osborne], of co. York, Duke of LEEDS. Quarterly Arms, [1849] Vol. XLIX, fol. 189.
OSBORNE, ... of Brenchley, co. Kent, [1787] Vol. XVI, fol. 235.
„ . . . ., of London and Oxford, [1787] Vol. XVI, fol. 259.
„ Rear-Adm. (Match), [1813] Vol. XXVII, fol. 347.
OSBORNE after DELANO, ..., of Enfield and Edmonton, co. Middx., [1833] Vol. XXXIX, fol. 296.
OSBORNE, late BERNAL, Ralph, of co. Middx., and Ireland, 1844, Vol. XLVII, fol. 206.
OSMAND, William Henry S. [see OSMOND], of The Sycamores, Stawell, Victoria, 1881, Vol. LXI, fol. 100. (Berry's Suppl.)
OSMASTON, John (s. of Francis W.), of Hawkhurst Court, co. Sussex, 18 . . ., Vol. LXXI, fol. . . . .
OSMOND, late WEBBER, ..., of Tiverton, co. Devon, nat. s. of Peard Osmond, [1807] Vol. XXIV, fol. 244.
OSMOND, ..., of Coventry, co. Warw., and Bicester, co. Oxf., [1830] Vol. XXXVIII, fol. 144.
„ [see OSMAND], Hon. William Henry Seville (s. of James), of The Sycamores, Stawel, Victoria, 1898, Vol. LXX, fol. 245.
OSSINGTON, Viscountess [Charlotte, dau. of the 4th Duke of Portland, took by Roy. Lic., 26 June 1882, the name of Scott in lien of Denison], 1882, Vol. LXI, fol. 353.
OSSULSTON, Baron [24 Nov. 1682], Sir John BENNET, Knt. Supporters, 1695, Vol. IV, fol. 183. [His only son Charles succ. 11 Feb. 169⅗, and died Earl of Tankerville in 1722.]
OSWALD, Emmett, wife of, (co. Lanc. and Hertf.), [1821] Vol. XXXIII, fol. 43.
„ Lieut.-Gen. Sir John, G.C.B. [1824]. Supporters, [1825] Vol. XXXV, fol. 205.
O'TOOLE to HALL, ..., of Holly Bush, co. Staff., [1834] Vol. XL, fol. 153.
OTTER, William Bruere, M.A., Archd. of Lewes and Vicar of Cowfield, co. Sussex, of Cuckney, co. Nottingham, and Bolsover, co. Derby, [1873] Vol. LVIII, fol. 226.
OTTER to OTTER-BARRY, R. M. B., of Clarges Street, London, [1873] Vol. LVIII, fol. 235.
OTTLEY, late HOOKER, John, of Hampsh., co. Suff., Sussex, and Oriel Coll., Oxf., [1820] Vol. XXXII, fol. 123.
OTTLEY, ..., of York Terrace, Regent's Park ; Stanwell, co. Middx. ; Delaford, co. Dublin ; and St. Vincent, [1848] Vol. XLIX, fol. 32.
OTWAY before CAVE (widow), of co. Leic., and Ireland. Arms quarterly to issue, [1818] Vol. XXX, fol. 428.
OTWAY, Adm. Sir Robert Waller, K.C.B. [1826], G.C.B. [1845]. Augmentation, 16 Feb. 1829, Vol. XXXVII, fol. 273. (Crisp, Fragm. Geneal., V, p. 53.)

OTWAY, Adm. Sir Robert Waller, G.C.B. [1845]. Supporters? [1845] Vol. XLVII, fol. 378.

„   Adm. Sir Robert Waller. Supporters, baronetcy? [Bart., 15 Sept. 1831], [1845] Vol. XLVII, fol. 440.

OTWAY, late HUGHES, William J. M., of Wales, and London, 1873, Vol. LVIII, fol. 193.

OUCHTERLONY, ..., wife of LOCKHART, of Deptford, co. Surrey, [1803] Vol. XXII, fol. 291.

OUGHTON, [Lieut.-Gen.] Sir James Adolphus, K.B. [1773], Governor of Antigua. Arms, [1773] Vol. XII, fol. 234; Supporters, 1773, Vol. XII, fol. 236.

OULD-GOODFORD, John, s. of Samuel, of Yeovil, co. Somerset. (*See* GOODFORD.) [1765] Vol. XI, fol. 73.

OULD, Rev. Fielding, M.A. (s. of Rev. Frederick), 18 . . ., Vol. LXXI, fol. . . . .

OURRY, now TREBY, ..., of Goodamore, co. Devon, [1785] Vol. XVI, fol. 95.

OUTHWAITE, Lieut.-Col. F. J., of Westfield, North Berwick, Scotland, 1891, Vol. LXVI, fol. 192.

OUTRAM, ..., of Kingston-upon-Hull, co. York. (Match with PICARD, *see* PICARD.) [1809] Vol. XXV, fol. 170.

„   [Lieut.-Gen.] Sir James, of Derby, [1858] Vol. LIII, fol. 27; G.C.B. [30 July 1857] Supporters, [1858] fol. 28. Arms to descendants with the Baronetcy, [1859] fol. 77.

OVENS to ELLIOTT, ..., of Berks., [1792 ?] Vol. XVIII, fol. 143.

OVER DARWEN, Borough of, co. Lanc., 1878.

OVERSTONE, Baron [5 Mar. 1850] (LLOYD). Supporters, [1850] Vol. XLIX, fol. 288.

OVERTOUN, Baron [23 June 1893] (J. CAMPBELL-WHITE). Supporters, 1893, Vol. LXVII, fol. 225.

OVEY, Richard, of Badgemore, Henley-on-Thames, co. Oxf., 1894, Vol. LXVIII, fol. 57.

OWDEN, Sir Thomas [Scambler], [Knt., 27 Nov. 1878], Alderman of London [1868], [1870] Vol. LVII, fol. 262.

OWEN to BIGLAND, ..., of London, nephew of Ralph Bigland, Clarenceux King of Arms, [1774] Vol. XIII, fol. 23.

OWEN, ..., of Ynysymaengwyn, Wales. Match with CORBET (*see* CORBET). [1783] Vol. XV, fol. 146.

OWEN to BARLOW, Hugh, of Wales, [1788] Vol. XVII, fol. 113; [1844] Vol. XLVII, fol. 204.

OWEN, late SMYTHE, Nicholas Owen Owen, of Condover, Shropsh., 1790, Vol. XVII, fol. 205.

„   late LEWIS, ..., of Fivefields Row, co. Middx., and Glassalt, co. Carmarthen, Wales, [1798] Vol. XX, fol. 267.

„   (late LORD), John, of Lincoln's Inn, London, and Wales. (Match), 1809, Vol. XXV, fol. 255.

OWEN, Edward William Campbell Prichard [Rich.], Capt., R.N., [1814] Vol. XXVIII, fol. 223; and his brother, William Fitzwilliam Owen, Capt., R.N. (of co. Montgomery), [1845] Vol. XLVIII, fol. 91.

„   Vice-Adm. Sir Edward W. C. R., G.C.B. [1845], G.C.H. [1832]. Supporters, 16 Jan. 1846 [1845], Vol. XLVIII, fol. 91 (*see* Powys-Land Club, X, p. 417, and XI, p. 374).

OWEN, late PEMBERTON, Edward William Smythe Owen, of Condover and Longnor, Shropsh., 1814, Vol. XXVIII, fol. 229.

OWEN, ..., Commander, R.N., of Chelsea, co. Middx., [1837] Vol. XLII, fol. 125.

OWEN to SWAFFIELD, ..., of Wyke Regis, co. Dorset, [1840] Vol. XLV, fol. 5.

„   to BARLOW, Sir William, Bart., of Lawrenny, co. Pembroke, Wales [afterwards, Aug. 1844, by Roy. Lic., Sir William Owen Barlow, 8th Bart.], 1845 [1844?], Vol. XLVII, fol. 204 (Hugh [1788] Vol. XVII, fol. 113).

Owen after Bulkeley, Thomas Bulkeley (formerly Hatchett), of Shropsh. and Wales, [1848] Vol. XLIX, fols. 47 and 84.

Owen, late Cholmondeley, Thomas, of co. Chester and Shropsh. (died s.p.), 1863, Vol. LV, fol. 66.

Owen to Kynaston, Rev. Walter Charles Edward Owen, of Shropsh. and co. York, [2 June] 1868, Vol. LVII, fol. 13 (see Powys-Land Club, X, p. 422).

Owen after Humphreys, Arthur Charles, of Lincoln's Inn, London, and co. Montgomery. Exemplification, 24 Nov. 1876, Vol. LIX, fol. 284 (Powys-Land Club, X, p. 421). (Berry's Suppl.)

Owen, Peter, of The Elms, Eastham, co. Chester, 1878, Vol. LX, fol. 109. (Berry's Suppl.)

„ Sir Richard, K.C.B., of London, died s.p.m., 1885,* Vol. LXIII, fol. 45.

„ Anne Warburton (widow of William Owen, K.C.), of Glan Severn, co. Montgomery. Grant of Owen Arms, 3 April 1838, Vol. XLII, fol. .... (Powys-Land Club, X, p. 416.)

Oxenham, ..., of co. Devon, [1695 ?] Vol. IV, fol. 181.

Oxford, Earl of, and [Earl] Mortimer [23 May 1711]. Supporters, [1711] Vol. VI, fol. 9.

Oxley, ..., of Easingwold, co. York (see Rohde). (Match), [1763 ?] Vol. X, fol. 483.

Oxley, late Brathwaite, Christopher, of York, 15 May 1775, Vol. XIII, fol. 100.

Ozanne, ..., of The Landes, St. Mary de Castro and Buquettée, Isle of Guernsey, [1858] Vol. LII, fol. 338.

P

Pack, L., [1809] Vol. XXV, fol. 144.

Packe, John, High Sheriff of Suff., 20 Jan. 169$\frac{6}{7}$, Vol. IV, fol. 218 ; Add. MS. 14,831, fol 41.

„ . . . ., of Prestwold Hall, co. Leic. Crest of Hussey, [1821] Vol. XXXII, fol. 381.

Packer, C. R., of Kilravock House, Streatham, London, and New Buckenham, co. Norf., 1888,* Vol. LXIV, fol. 209.

Page before Turner, Bart., of Ambrosden, co. Oxf. (See Gregory.) Quarterly Arms, 20 Dec. 1775, Vol. XIII, fol. 151.

Page, Joseph, of Little Bromley, co. Essex, [1856 ?] Vol. LII, fol. 188.

„ . . . ., of Cardiff, Wales, and Dulwich and Panfield, co. Essex, [1861] Vol. LIV, fol. 228.

Page, late Seymour, Robert, of Norton, Henknole and Aycliffe School, Heighington, co. Durham, [1862] Vol. LIV, fol. 290.

Page, John, M.A., Oxf., of Clifton, Bristol, and Hadley, co. Middx. (s. of Samuel), 1878, Vol. LX, fol. 113. (Berry's Suppl.)

Page to Page-Darley, John, s. of Francis, of Clifton, Bristol, and Hadley, co. Middx., 1878, Vol. LX, fol. 120.

Page, Peter, J.P., of East Sheen, co. Surrey. (Burke) [no date].

Paget, Baron, Henry Bayley [afterwards, 1770, Paget], of Anglesey, and co. Staff. Arms and Supporters, 1770, Vol. XII, fol. 16.

„ [Alfred, of Croydon, co. Surrey, Vol. LXXXIV, fol. 275.]

„ [The Hon.] Sir Arthur [K.B., 1804]. Supporters, [1804] Vol. XXIII, fol. 35.

„ [Lieut.-Gen. the Hon.] Sir Edward, [K.B., Invested 12 June 1812]. Supporters, [1811] Vol. XXVII, fol. 52.

„ . . . ., of Humberstone, Ibstock, and Loughborough, co. Leic., [1845] Vol. XLVII, fol. 368.

„ . . . ., F.R.S., of Great Yarmouth, co. Norf., [1871] Vol. LVIII, fol. 34.

„ Sir Richard, Bart., of co. Somerset, 1886,* Vol. LXIII, fol. 201.

PAGET, W. S., of Forton Lodge, Great Crosby, co. Lanc., 1890,* Vol. LXV, fol. 196; and Dr. Tomlinson, W. S., of Forton Lodge, Great Crosby, co. Lanc., fol. 215. ? remainder to father's issue.

PAGGEN, Peter, J.P., of Wandsworth, co. Surrey, 25 April 1720, Vol. VI, fol. 411.

PAKE, Samuel, Doctor in Physick, of Bury St. Edmunds, co. Suff., 21 Nov. 1723, [1725] Vol. VII, fol. 425.

PAKENHAM, [Maj.-Gen. the Hon. Sir Edward Michael, K.B., 1813, G.C.B., 1815]. Supporters, [1814] Vol. XXVIII, fol. 27.

PAKINGTON, late RUSSELL, ..., of Powick Court and Westwood Park, co. Worc., [1831] Vol. XXXVIII, fol. 205.

PAKINGTON, Sir John [Bart.], G.C.B. [1859], P.C. Supporters, [1859] Vol. LIII, fol. 183.

PALEY, John, of Ampton Hall, co. Suff., and Langcliffe, Giggleswick, co. York, 1885,* Vol. LXIII, fol. 91.

PALGRAVE, ..., of Norwich. (See LUBBOCK.) [1730] Vol. VIII, fol. 75[b].

PALGRAVE, late COHEN, Sir Francis, of the Inner Temple, London, and co. Norf., 2 July 1825, Vol. XXXV, fol. 217. (Palgrave Memorials, p. 185.)

PALGRAVE, Thomas (s. of William), of Bryan-y-Gynog, co. Denbigh, Wales, and co. Norf., 26 Oct. 1877, Vol. LX, fol. 40. (Palgrave Memorials, p. 187.) (Berry's Suppl.)

PALK, Robert, of Headborough, co. Devon, 14 Nov. 1760,* Vol. X, fol. 258. (Berry.)

 „ . . . ., of Butterford, co. Devon, [1788] Vol. XVII, fol. 53.

PALLISER, Sir Hugh, Bart., of Deptford, co. Kent, and Newby Wiske, co. York, 8 Oct. 1773, Vol. XII, fol. 267. (Berry.)

 „ . . . ., of The Vache, Bucks., and Chatham, co. Kent, 1795 [1796], Vol. XIX, fol. 227.

 „ George Thomas?, of Greenwich, co. Kent, 1795 [1796], Vol. XIX, fol. 239.

PALLISER, late WALTERS, ..., Bart., of Perry Hill, Lewisham, co. Kent, and Castletown, co. Wexford. (Match.) [1798] Vol. XX, fol. 269.

PALMER, Ann (dau. of AMROYD), of Barnsby and Thurnscott Hall, co. York, [1781] Vol. XIV, fol. 361.

 „ . . . ., of St. James, Cornw., and Island of Jamaica, [1791] Vol. XVII, fol. 408.

 „ . . . ., of Spetchley, co. Worc. (See JELF.) (Match.) [1809] Vol. XXV, fol. 180.

PALMER, late HUDSON, Sir Charles Grave Palmer, Bart., of Wanlip, co. Leic., 1813, Vol. XXVII, fol. 443.

 „ late BUDSWORTH, ..., of London, and Ireland, [1815] Vol. XXVIII, fol. 379.

PALMER before ACLAND [1818], Sir John [Bart. 9 Dec. 1818], of co. Devon and Somerset, [1818] Vol. XXXI, fol. 144.

PALMER-ACLAND, Sir Peregrine Fuller [Palmer-Acland, 2nd Bart.], of co. Devon and Somerset. [Name and Arms of Fuller quarterly, 12 Aug. 1834] [1834] Vol. XL, fol. 237.

PALMER, Walworth, of co. Surrey, [1824?] Vol. XXXV, fol. 76.

PALMER-MOREWOOD, Lieut.-Col., of Ladbroke, co. Warw., and Alfreton Hall, co. Derby, [1826] Vol. XXXV, fol. 373.

PALMER-SAMBOURNE, ..., of Timsbury House, Bath, co. Somerset, [1840] Vol. XLIV, fol. 239.

PALMER, Baron SELBORNE [23 Oct. 1872, Sir Roundell Palmer]. Supporters, [1872] Vol. LVIII, fol. 168.

 „ Sir Charles Mark [Bart., 1886], of Grinkle Park, Easington, and Seton, co. York, 1874, Vol. LIX, fol. 30.

 „ George, of Reading, Berks., 1880,* Vol. LXI, fol. 77.

 „ J. D., of Heronden Hall, Tenterden, co. Kent, and London, 1890, Vol. LXV, fol. 219.

PALMER, John Irwin, F.R.C.S., of Queen Anne Street, London, 1895,* Vol. LXVIII, fol. 166.

PANMURE, Baron [9 Sept. 1831] (MAULE). Supporters, [1831] Vol. XXXVIII, fol. 370.

PANTER-DOWNES, Edward Downes Panter-Downes, Lieut., R.N., of co. Hereford and Norf., [1856] Vol. LII, fol. 87.

PANTING to GARDNER, Laurence, M.A., of London, Shropsh. and co. Staff. (Match), [1801] Vol. XXI, fol. 164.

„ to GARDNER, Robert, of Shropsh., [1844] Vol. XLVII, fol. 208 (see Kynnersley, in Landed Gentry).

PARBURY, George, s. of Charles, s. of George, of Islington, London, 14 Aug. 1835, Vol. XLI, fol. 92.

PARISH, Sir Woodbine, K.C.H. [1837], of St. Leonard's, co. Sussex, 1875, Vol. LIX, fol. 124.

PARK-YATES, E. W., Lieut., Dragoon Guards, of Ince Hall, co. Chester, and Fairlawn, co. Kent, [1857] Vol. LII, fol. 311.

PARK, William Philip Ince, of Altadore, Fulwood, co. Lanc., 1875, Vol. LIX, fol. 102.

PARKE, James, Baron WENSLEYDALE [16 Jan. 1856], of co. York [life Peer], [1856] Vol. LI, fol. 442. Supporters, fol. 444.

PARKER, John, of Fallowes Hall, co. Chester, s. of Robert, of Astle and Prestbury, co. Chester, 11 April 1702, Vol. V, fol. 78 ; Stowe MS. 714, fol. 95[b] ; Add. MS. 14,831, fol. 194.

„ Baron [10 Mar. 1716, Thomas Parker, Lord Chancellor]. Supporters, [1716] Vol. VI, fol. 234 [afterwards Viscount Parker and Earl of Macclesfield, 15 Nov. 1721].

„ Peter (Capt., R.N., 1747), of St. Margaret's, Westminster, 1772, Vol. XII, fol. 182. (Berry.)

PARKER to NEWDIGATE, Francis, of Derby, 10 June 1773, Vol. XII, fol. 249.

PARKER, John, of Greystones and Woodthorpe, co. York, and Norton, co. Derby, 10 Nov. 1775, Vol. XIII, fol. 137.

„ John, Baron BORINGDON [1784], of co. Devon. Supporters, [1784] Vol. XV, fol. 305.

„ Isaac, late FIELD, of Moorhouse Hill, par. of Heskett, co. Cumberland, 13 Nov. 1790, Vol. XVII, fol. 266. (Genealogist, IV, pp. 288-9.) (Berry's Suppl.)

PARKER to GRIFFIN, Mary, wife of William [Parker] (late WHITWELL), D.D., of St. James', Westminster, Roy. Lic., 3 June 1797 [see next name].

„ to GRIFFIN, ..., of Oundle, co. Northampton [? Mrs. Parker, of last entry], [1797] Vol. XIX, fol. 432. Escutcheon of pretence, fol. 436. [Co-heir to moiety of the Barony of] Howard de Walden.

„ to NEWDEGATE, ... (minor), of co. Middx. and Warw., [1808] Vol. XXIV, fol. 465.

„ to MANWARING, ..., of London and co. Middx., [1809] Vol. XXV, fol. 133.

PARKER, late THORPE, ..., of Hauthorpe House, Morton, co. Linc., [1831] Vol. XXXVIII, fol. 267.

PARKER, ..., of Extwisle and Cuerdon, co. Lanc., [1835] Vol. XL, fol. 393.

PARKER to TOWNLEY-PARKER, of Extwisle and Cuerdon, co. Lanc., [1880] Vol. LX, fol. 352.

PARKER, John, Capt., R.N., of Eythorne, co. Kent, [1842] Vol. XLVI, fol. 123.

„ . . . ., of Eythorne, co. Kent. Crest (to other descendants), [1842] Vol. XLVI, fol. 124.

„ . . . ., of Lewisham, co. Kent, [1858], Vol. LII, fol. 359.

PARKER-JERVIS, ..., of co. Staff., 2ud s. of Viscount ST. VINCENT, [1861] Vol. LIV, fol. 140.

PARKER, Sir William, Bart. [? 24 June 1797], Rear-Adm. of the Red, [1797] Vol. XX, fol. 102.

PARKER, Thomas, of Warwick Hall, co. Cumberland, and Christopher, of Petterel.
Green, co. Cumberland, [1823] Vol. XXXIII, fols. 387 and 389.

PARKER (late LITTLE), Henry Clarence, of co. Lanc., Wilts., and Isle of Wight.
Quarterly Arms and two Crests, 1879, Vol. LX, fol. 216. (Berry's Suppl.)

PARKES, Sir Harry Smith, K.C.B. [1862], (of London), Consul at Shanghai,
[1863] Vol. LV, fol. 112.

  „ Sir Henry, of Sydney, N. S. Wales. Supporters, 1881, Vol. LXI, fol. 249.
[? does this refer to the G.C.M.G. of Sir Harry Smith Parkes, 30 Nov.
1881. Sir Henry, of Sydney, was K.C.M.G. 31 May 1877, and G.C.M.G.
28 Jan. 1888.]

PARKHOUSE, ..., of Bitterne, Hampsh., and Cheriton FitzPayne, and Tiverton,
co. Devon, [1838] Vol. XLIII, fol. 326.

PARKIN, J. S., of Seaton, co. Cumberland, Bar.-at-Law. (See SHERWIN.) 1890,*
Vol. LXV, fol. 192.

PARKINSON, late WILSON, Rev. John Parkinson, of East Ravendale co. Linc.,
M.A., Fellow of Magdalen Coll., Oxf., and Mary GILLIOT, widow of John
Parkinson, D.D., 1842, Vol. XLVI, fol. 47.

  „ late WILSON, (John Posthumous), M.A., Fellow of Magdalen Coll., Oxf.,
1842, Vol. XLVI, fol. 106.

PARKINSON to MILWARD, ..., of Hexgreave Park, and Thurgarton Priory,
co. Nottingham, [1844] Vol. XLVII, fol. 296.

PARKINSON before FORTESCUE [1863], Baron CARLINGFORD [28 Feb. 1874].
Supporters, [1832] Vol. XXXIX, fol. 1 ; [1874 ? Vol. LVIII].

PARKYNS, Sir Thomas, Bart., of Bunny, co. Nottingham. Crest, [1757 ?] Vol.
X, fol. 125.

  „ [Thomas Boothby], Baron RANCLIFFE [3 Oct. 1795], of Bunny, co.
Nottingham. Supporters, [1797] Vol. XIX, fol. 394.

PARLANE, J., of Rusholme, Manchester, 1891, Vol. LXVI, fol. 200.

PARNALL, Robert, of The Cottage, Llanslephan, co. Carmarthen, Wales, and
Addison Road, London, 1878, Vol. LX, fol. 78. (Burke's Suppl.)

PARNELL, [Sir] Henry Brooke [4th Bart.], Baron CONGLETON [18 Aug. 1841].
Arms and Supporters, [1842] Vol. XLVI, fols. 30 and 32.

PARNELL, late GRIFFIN (Thomas Parnell), of Clevedon, co. Somerset. [?] Supporters,
[1877] Vol. LX, fol. 70. (Burke's Suppl.)

PARR, ..., of Hatton, co. Warw., the two daus. of Saml. Parr, D.D., Preb. of
St. Paul's, [1827] Vol. XXXVI, fol. 289 (see Burke).

  „ J. Charlton, of Grappenhall, Heyes, co. Chester, and Staunton Park, co.
Hereford, 1896, Vol. LXIX, fol. 197.

PARRY, late PRITCHARD, of Wales, and co. Hereford, [1787] Vol. XVI, fol. 300.

PARRY after WEBLEY, William Henry, Post-Capt., R.N., of Noyadd, co. Cardigan,
Wales, [1815] Vol. XXIX, fol. 198.

PARRY (JONES-) to YALE, ... [1821], of Madryn, co. Carnarvon, and Llwynnon,
co. Denbigh, Wales [see Burke under Yale], [1832] Vol. XXXIX
[? XXXIII], fol. 109 ; [1868] Vol. LVI, fol. 364.

PARRY-MITCHELL, H. D., of Merevale, Atherstone, co. Warw., 1889, Vol. LXV,
fol. 106.

PARSONS, Sir John, Knt. [15 Aug. 1687], Alderman of London, mar. certif. to
Thomas WRIGHT (? not a grant), [1698] Vol. IV, fol. 245. See also
BEANE, [fol. ?] 172.

PARSONS to HOPTON, ..., of co. Hereford, [1817] Vol. XXX, fol. 262.

  „ to HIGFORD, ..., of co. Glouc. and Sussex, [1825] Vol. XXXV,
fol. 293.

PARSONS-PETERS, William, of Yeabridge, South Petherton and Charlton Hore-
thorne, co. Somerset. (Arms of Peters), [1858] Vol. LIII, fol. 42.

PARSONS, William Barclay, of Cork Street, London, 1875, Vol. LIX, fol. 96.

  „ B. W., of Horley, co. Surrey, 1895, Vol. LXVIII, fol. 200 or 206.

PARTINGTON, Edward, J.P., of High Street East, Glossop, co. Derby, 1898, Vol.
LXX, fol. 272.

PARTRIDGE, ..., of the par. of Westmorland, Jamaica. (*See* JAMES.) (Match.) [1772] Vol. XII, fol. 201.

PARTRIDGE to PERRYSTON, ..., of co. Cornw. and Oxf., and Nethwold and Cranwick, co. Norf., [1874] Vol. LVIII, fol. 351.

PARUCK, Cursetjee F., J.P., of Bombay, [1864] Vol. LV, fol. 176.

PASCOE, John, of Phillack, co. Cornw., Sheriff of Cornwall, only s. of Erasmus, late High Sheriff, 26 Feb. 172⅚, Vol. VII, fol. 451.

PASKE, ... (*see* HASLEFOOT), of (co. Surrey), [1864 ?] Vol. LV, fol. 144.

PASLEY, Rear-Adm. [Thomas, Bart., 1 Sept. 1794], of Colney Hatch, co. Middx., and Craig, co. Dumfries. Augmentation, [1794] Vol. XVIII, fol. 392.

PASLEY, late SABINE, [Sir Thomas, 2nd] Bart. (infant), of Chillard Cottage, Hampsh., [1809] Vol. XXV, fol. 149.

PASLEY-DIROM, Thomas Alexander, of Scotland, [1864] Vol. LV, fol. 168.

PASSINGHAM [Jonathan], of Heston, co. Middx., and Hendwr, co. Merioneth, Wales, [1 Oct. 1795] [1796], Vol. XIX, fols. 225 and 226. [Genealogist, New S., XXVIII, p. 79.]

PASTON before BEDINGFELD, [11 April 1830, Richard Henry, 6th] Bart., of co. Oxf. and Norf., [1830] Vol. XXXVIII, fol. 81.

PASTON-BEDINGFIELD to PASTON BISHOPP-BEDINGFELD [26 Mar. 1841, Margaret, wife of the last], [1841] Vol. XLV, fol. 169.

PATCH, Frederick Owen Patch, of Tiverton, co. Devon, [1842] Vol. XLV, fol. 376.

PATCHETT, Major William, of Greenfields, Shrewsbury, Shropsh., 1898, Vol. LXX, fol. 141.

PATE, Robert Frances Pate, of Wisbeach (Isle of Ely), co. Camb., [1841] Vol. XLV, fol. 157.

PATER, Maj.-Gen., E.I.C.S. (of Fort St. George), [1811] Vol. XXVI, fol. 203.

PATERSON, ..., of St. Paul's Cray, co. Kent, [1860] Vol. LIII, fol. 294.

PATESHALL, late THOMAS-PATESHALL, of Allensmore House, co. Hereford, and Ifynonan, co. Brecon, Wales, [1855] Vol. LI, fol. 331.

PATOUN, William, of Richmond, co. Surrey, and Renfrew, Scotland, June 1772, Vol. XII, fol. 162.

PATTEN before BOLD [Peter], of co. Lanc., [1814] Vol. XXVIII, fol. 91.

PATTEN, WILSON, ..., Baron WINMARLEIGH [16 Mar. 1874, John Wilson-Patten]. Supporters, [1874] Vol. LVIII, fol. 327.

PATTENSON, late [after ?] TYLDEN, Richard Cooke, M.A., of Frinsted, Milsted, and Hornden, co. Kent, 1799, Vol. XX, fol. 364.

PATTERSON, ..., of Dry Grange, Roxburgh, Scotland. (*See* WILKIESON.) [1779] Vol. XIV, fol. 163.

PATTINSON, Hugh Lee Pattinson, and nephew, William Watson Pattinson, of Scotts House, West Boldon, co. Durham, [1852] Vol. L, fol. 163.

PATTISSON, ..., of Witham House, co. Essex, [1846] Vol. XLVIII, fol. 221.

PATTON, now MASTERMAN, John, of Stokesley, co. York, [1717] Vol. VI, fol. 326.

PATTON-BETHUNE, Gen. W. D. P., of Clayton Priory, co. Sussex, 1883,* Vol. LXII, fol. 60. (Berry's Suppl.)

PHILLIPS-PATTON, Gen. W. D., of Clayton Priory, co. Sussex, 1882,* Vol. LXI, fol. 366.

PAUL, Robert, of Hatton Garden, London, 1758, Vol. X, fol. 137. (Berry.)

„ Sir Onesiphorous, Knt. [1760], of Woodchester, co. Glouc., Sheriff, co. Glouc., 1761,* Vol. X, fol. 270.

PAUL, late TIPPETTS, ... [1787], of Tetbury, co. Glouc., [1787] Vol. XVI, fol. 315.

PAUL, William Bond, of Weame, Wyche, co. Glouc., and High Ham, co. Somerset, s. of Thomas, s. of Thomas, both of Langport, co. Somerset, and to the descendants of his Uncle Charles, 1878, Vol. LX, fol. 177. (Berry's Suppl.)

PAUNCEFOOT, Duncombe, of Bucks., [1859] Vol. LIII, fol. 134. Crest, fol. 233.

PAUNCEFOTE, late SMITH, Sir George [2nd Bart.], of Earl Stoke, co. Nottingham, and Foelt Alt, co. Cardigan, Wales (B.A., Worcester Coll., Oxford), 1803 [1809] Vol. XXV, fol. 110.

PAUNCEFOTE to BROMLEY [Sir George, 2nd Bart., 1778?] [see Burke].

PAVIER after RUSSELL, William Adey, of Heaton Moor, Heaton Norris, co. Lanc., and Hammerwick, co. Staff., 1874, Vol. LIX, fol. 48.

PAWLETT, John, of St. James', Westminster, 10 Oct. 1737, Vol. VIII, fol. 223. (Berry.)

PAWSON before HARGROVE, of co. Northumberland (George died s.p.), [1817] Vol. XXX, fol. 122.

PAWSON, ..., of Shawdon and Titlington, co. Northumberland, [1861] Vol. LIV, fol. 132.

PAXTON, Sir William, and brother Archibald, of Watford Place, co. Hertf., and Middleton Hall, co. Carmarthen, Wales (died 1824), 13 May 1806, Vol. XXIII, fol. 351. (Berry.)

PAYLER after MORGAN, Rev. F., of co. Kent, Surrey and Wales, [1854] Vol. LI, fol. 151.

PAYNE, Ralph, of Marylebone, co. Middx., and St. Christopher's, West Indies. Quartering CARLISLE, 1770 [1771?], Vol. XII, fol. 49 (Berry). Sir Ralph [K.B., 18 Feb. 1771]. Supporters, 1771, Vol. XII, fol. 75 [afterwards, 1795, Baron Lavington].

„   Col. William (half-brother to Baron LAVINGTON), of co. York, London, and St. Kitts, [1813] Vol. XXVII, fol. 454.

PAYNE before GALLWEY [7 Mar. 1814], Lieut.-Gen. Sir William, Bart., of co. York, London, and St. Kitts, [1814] Vol. XXVIII, fol. 61.

PAYNE-FRANKLAND, Lady [widow of Sir William PAYNE-GALLWEY, 2nd Bart.], of co. York, [2 Oct.] 1882, Vol. LXII, fol. 1.

PAYNE, late ROW, ..., of Withycombe Rawleigh, Rockbeare, and Broadelyst, co. Devon, [1796] Vol. XIX, fol. 315.

PAYNE to ELWES, ..., nat. s. of Elwes, of Stoke Coll., Stoke-next-Clare, co. Suff., [1824] Vol. XXXV, fol. 53.

PAYNE, Henry, of The Newark, Leicester, [inescutcheon of pretence for his wife, Elizabeth] TOWNDROW, to son Henry T. Payne, 4 April 1826, Vol. XXXV, fols. 363 and 364. (Berry's Appx.)

PAYNTER, Maj. George, of London, and co. Linc., 1895, Vol. LXVIII, fol. 229.

PEACH, Nathaniel, of Rooksmore, Woodchester, co. Glouc., and Stanley Borongh, co. Leic., Rector of Lavington, Wilts., 8 Nov. 1769, Vol. XI, fol. 362. (Berry.)

PEACH, late CRUGER, S. P., of Tockington, co. Glouc., 1788, Vol. XVI, fol. 411.

PEACH-ASTON to PEACH-PUDSEY, ..., of Seisdon, co. Staff., [1807] Vol. XXIV, fol. 203.

PEACH after KEIGHLEY, ..., of co. Warw., [1838] Vol. XLIII, fol. 219.

PEACH, late CLEAVER, ..., of co. Glouc., [1847] Vol. XLVIII, fol. 276.

PEACHEY [Sir James, 4th Bart.], Baron SELSEY [13 Aug. 1794] of co. Sussex. Supporters, [1794] Vol. XVIII, fol. 419.

PEACHY, William (s. of William), of Vicar's Island, co. Cumberland, and Gosport, Hampsh. (B.C.L., Oxf., 1790), [1799] Vol. XX, fol. 324.

PEACOCK, Simon, of Burnehall, co. Durham, 31 Oct. 1688, Vol. IV, fol. 27.

„   . . . ., Capt., R.N., of London, [1803] Vol. XXII, fol. 201.

„   . . . ., of London, [1816] Vol. XXIX, fol. 302.

PEACOCK to HOLMAN, ..., of London ; Enfield, co. Middx. ; and Jamaica, [1807] Vol. XXIV, fol. 215.

PEACOCK, Mark Beauchamp ?, of Doughty Street, London, [1828 ?] Vol. XXXVII, fol. 219 (see Burke).

„   Anthony, of South Raunceby, South Kyme and Potter Hanworth, co. Linc., 1839, Vol. XLIV, fol. 121.

PEACOCK-YATE, ..., of Arlingham, co. Glouc. [1848 ?] Vol. XLIX, fol. 86.

PEACOCK, Sir Barnes, Knt., Chief Justice, Bengal [Calcutta ?], [1864] Vol. LV, fol. 266.

,, [Simon, of Burnhall, co. Durham, 1688. (Berry.)]

,, John, of Willesden, co. Middx., 1881, Vol. LXI, fol. 166. (Berry's Suppl.) [?]

PEARCE, Maj.-Gen. Thomas, of Whitlingham, co. Norf., 20 Oct. 1715, Vol. VI, fol. 214. (Berry.)

,, Nathaniel Goldson, of London, 6 April 1720, Vol. VI, fol. 404 ; Add. MS. 14,830, fol. 29.

,, ..., of Westminster (MURREY, wife of), Arms. (Match), [1802] Vol. XXI, fol. 397.

,, Edward Serocold, of co. Cornw., M.A., Jesus Coll., Oxf., [1824] Vol. XXXIV, fol. 356.

PEARCE-SEROCOLD, Edward Seracold, M.A., of Cherry Hinton, co. Cumberland, [1842] Vol. XLVI, fol. 128.

PEARCE, Lieut.-Col. [William ?], K.H. [1835], of Staverton House, Staverton, co. Glouc., [1843] Vol. XLVI, fol. 347.

PEARCE-CHURCH, ..., of Staverton House, Staverton, co. Glouc., and of Frwdgrech, Brecon, Wales, [1845 ?] Vol. XLVIII, fol. 47 ; [1846], fol. 178.

PEARCE, ..., of London, and Sydney, New South Wales, [1865] Vol. LV, fol. 316.

,, Sir William, Bart., of London and co. Renfrew, 1887, Vol. LXIV, fol. 42.

,, Dame Dinah (SOWTER Seal), 1892, Vol. LXVI, fol. 275.

PEARCE-EDGCUMBE, Sir Edward Robert [Knt., 27 Feb. 1895], of Somerleigh Court, Dorchester, co. Dorset, 1896 [1896], Vol. LXIX, fol. 67. (Crisp, V, p. 14.)

PEARS-ARCHBOLD, James A., of Carlisle, co. Cumberland, and Fenham Hall and Gallowgate, co. Northumberland, 1870, Vol. LVII, fols. 230 and 238.

PEARSALL, Robert L., of Willoughby, Bitton, co. Glouc., and Lincoln's Inn, London, [1834] Vol. XL, fol. 219.

PEARSE, Thomas, of Little Ealing, co. Middx., 3 May 1728 [? 3 Mar. 172⅞], Vol. VII, fol. 570 ; Add. MS. 14,830, fol. 30.

,, ..., of Chilton Lodge, Berks., and Heddington, Wilts., Dir. Bank of England, [1803] Vol. XXII, fol. 127.

,, ..., of Durham, and New South Wales, [1860] Vol. LIII, fol. 308.

PEARSON, ..., of Sleaford, co. Linc. (See TUNNARD.) (Match), [1810] Vol. XXVI, fol. 68.

,, ..., of Norton, co. York, and London, [1837] Vol. XLII, fol. 108.

,, ..., of South Wingfield and Bradbourne Hall, co. Derby, [1845] Vol. XLVII, fol. 431.

,, ..., of Rochetts, co. Essex, and Bailbrooke Lodge, Bath Easton, co. Somerset, [1865] Vol. LV, fol. 330.

PEARSON to JERVIS, ..., of co. Essex, [1865] Vol. LV, fol. 338.

PEARSON, Henry Robert, Chief Clerk, Treasury, London, and to the descendants of his father John, M.R.C.S., of London, and late uncle Thomas, of Manchester, gentleman, 30 Dec. 1865, Vol. LVI, fol. 59. (See Genealogist, VII, p. 231.)

,, George, Sol[icitor ?], of Clifton, Bristol, co. Glouc., 1889, Vol. LXV, fol. 80.

,, George, of Bradford, co. York, 1892, Vol. LXVII, fol. 82.

,, Thomas S., of The Manor House, Harlaxton, co. Linc., 1892,* Vol. LXVII, fol. 53.

PEARSON-GREGORY, T. S., of The Manor House, Harlaxton, co. Linc., 1893, Vol. LXVII, fol. 132.

PEARSON, Thomas H., of Radcliffe, Newton-le-Willows, co. Lanc., 1891,* Vol. LXVI, fol. 35.

PEARSON-GEE, A. B., Bar.-at-Law, of London and Sussex, 1888, Vol. LXIV, fol. 136.

PEARSON, Hugh, s. of Matthew, s. of Daniel, 1714 (*see* Burke).
„   Lieut.-Col. John, 1698 (*see* Burke).
„   Philip P. (*See* PENNANT.) 1860.
PEART to SCROPE (VIVIAN, wife of), of Long Sutton and Cockerington, co. Linc.
       Escutcheon of pretence, [1792] Vol. XVIII, fol. 41.
PEASE, Robert, of All Hallows Lane, London, and Leeds ; Elizabeth, his cozen,
       wife of Daniel TAYLOR, 1763, Vol. X, fol. 478. (Berry.)
PEASE after ROBINSON [1778 ?], Joseph, of Kingston-upon-Hull, co. York, and
       Manchester, co. Lanc., [1783] Vol. XV, fol. 179.
PEASE, Robert Copeland, of Kirk Ella, &c., and Kingston-upon-Hull, co. York,
       Banker, [1799] Vol. XX, fol. 298.
„   Henry, of Pierremont, Darlington, co. Durham, s. of Edward and [to the
       issue ?] of his uncle Joseph, 1879, Vol. LX, fol. 245.
PEAT, ..., of Sevenoaks, co. Kent, [1838] Vol. XLIII, fol. 289.
„   Litt, of Liverpool, co. Lanc., [1806] Vol. XXIII, fol. 291
PECHELL, ..., of Pagglesham, co. Essex, and Owenstown, co. Kildare, Ireland,
       [1797] Vol. XIX, fol. 357.
PECK to BUCKLEY, ..., of co. Merioneth, Wales, nat. s. of Buckley, [1864]
       Vol. LV, fol. 164.
PECKHAM, late SMITH, Charles Peckham (minor), of Ashling Lodge, and Nyton,
       co. Sussex, 1820, Vol. XXXII, fol. 32.
PECKHAM-PHIPPS, late KELSALL, ... (Spr.), of Littlegreen, Compton, co. Sussex,
       [1837] Vol. XLII, fol. 215.
PECKHAM-MICKLETHWAITE, [1824] Sir Sotherton Branthwaite Peckham, Bart.
       [27 July 1838], of Iridge Place, Salehurst, co. Sussex, and Weston and
       Beeston, co. Norf., [1838] Vol. XLIII, fol. 95.
PECKOVER, Algernon, of Sibbalds Holme, Wisbech, co. Camb., 1880, Vol. LXI,
       fol. 94. (Berry's Suppl.)
PEDDER, Edward, of Preston and Garstang, co. Lanc. (for those in remainder, *see*
       Berry's Appx.), 26 Mar. 1814, Vol. XXVIII, fol. 53.
PEDLER, Lieut.-Col. E. H. S., of Hoo Mavey and Oakhampton, co. Devon [1836]
       Vol. XLII, fol. 32.
PEEK, John Philip Warren, of Halsenwood, Lottiswell, co. Devon, 1832, Vol.
       XXXIX, fol. 126.
„   Henry William, of London, [1868] Vol. LVII, fol. 43 (*cr.* a Baronet in
       1874).
PEEL, Robert, of Oswaldwistle, Manchester, [1792] Vol. XVIII, fol. 11.
PEEL, late ETHELSTIN, Edmund, of co. Chester and Norf., and Bryn-y-Pys, Ruabon,
       co. Flint, Wales, [1851] Vol. XLIX, fol. 418 or 468.
PEEL, Sir Robert [Bart.], G.C.B. [1866]. Supporters, [1866] Vol. LVI, fol. 87.
„   Viscount. Supporters, 1895, Vol. LXVIII, fol. 224.
„   William, of Ackworth Park, co. York, [1854] Vol. LI, fol. 143.
PEGGE-BURNELL, ..., of co. Derby and Nottingham, [1836] Vol. XLI,
       fol. 254.
PEGGE-BURNELL-SMITH-MILNES, E., of Dunston Hall, Chesterfield, co. Derby.
       (*See also* MILNES and SMITH.) 1896, Vol. LXIX, fol. 77.
PEGLER, William, of Pontypool, Trevethin, co. Monmouth, Wales. (*See* PAYLER.)
       1887, Vol. LXIII, fol. 342.
PEIRSE after BERESFORD, Henry William de la Poer, of co. York, [1851] Vol. L,
       fol. 60.
PEIRSON, [Lieut.-Gen.] Sir Richard, K.B. [1780]. Crest and Supporters, [1780]
       Vol. XIV, fol. 277.
PELHAM, Baron [of Laughton, 16 Dec. 1706, Sir Thomas Pelham, 4th Bart.].
       Pelham quarterings [mar. Grace, sister of John] (Duke of NEWCASTLE).
       Supporters, [1706] Vol. V, fol. 197.
„   [Baron, of Stanmer [17 Nov. 1768], Thomas Pelham, 6th Bart.] [afterwards
       23 June 1801] (Earl of CHICHESTER). Supporters, [1768] Vol. XI,
       fol. 346.

PELHAM after CRESSETT, Henry, of Crowhurst, co. Sussex. Quarterly Arms, [1792] Vol. XVIII, fol. 129.

„ after ANDERSON [1763], Baron YARBOROUGH [13 Aug. 1794]. Supporters, Vol. XVIII, fol. 400. Quarterly Arms, [1794] Vol. XVIII, fol. 402.

PELHAM-CLINTON, Duke of NEWCASTLE. Quarterly Arms, [1807] Vol. XXIV, fol. 224.

PELHAM after THISTLETHWAYTE, late MILBOURNE, Katherine, widow of Thomas Milbourne, of Hampsh. and Wilts. Quarterly Arms, [1811] Vol. XXVI, fol. 340.

„ after THURSBY, Henry, M.A., Rector and Patron of Cound, Shropsh. (? Sussex), [1852] Vol. L, fol. 184.

PELHAM-CLINTON-HOPE [1887], Lord Henry Francis Hope [brother of the 7th Duke of Newcastle] (of ? Ireland), 1888, Vol. LXIV, fol. 169.

PELLEW [Edward], Knt. [28 June 1793, Capt., R.N.] (impaling FROWDE, his wife), of Trevery and Flushing, co. Cornw., [1796 ?] Vol. XIX, fol. 325 [see next entry].

„ Vice-Adm. [Edward], cr. Baron EXMOUTH [1 June 1814] and Bart., of co. Devon. Supporters, [1814] Vol. XXVIII, fol. 196.

PELLING, ..., of Madras, [1788] Vol. XVII, fol. 53.

PELLY, ..., of Upton, co. Essex, Gov. Hudson's Bay Co., and Dep.-Gov. Bank of England, [1840] Vol. XLIV, fol. 306.

PEMBERTON, late COOKES, Elizabeth and Sally (Sprs.), of Middleton Hall, co. Durham, [1802] Vol. XXI, fol. 399.

PEMBERTON to OWEN, ..., of Longuor, and Condover, Shropsh. (Match), [1814] Vol. XXVIII, fol. 229.

PEMBERTON, late BUTCHER, Edward Robert, of co. Northampton, [1842] Vol. XLVI, fol. 141.

PEMBERTON-LEIGH, Thomas, Attorney-Gen. to Prince of Wales, of co. Lanc., and London. [Roy. Lic., 7 Mar. 1843], [1843] Vol. XLVI, fol. 274.

„ -LEIGH, Thomas, P.C. [1843], of co. Lanc. and Kent, [1843] Vol. XLVI, fol. 276.

„ -LEIGH, Thomas, Baron KINGSDOWN [28 Aug. 1858], of co. Kent. Supporters, [1858] Vol. LII, fol. 389.

PEMBERTON after CHILDE, ..., of Millichope, and Church Stretton, Shropsh., [1849] Vol. XLIX, fol. 182.

PEMBERTON, Rev. Joseph Hardwicke, of Havering-atte-Bower and Beauchamp Roding, co. Essex, [1850 ?] Vol. XLIX, fol. 409.

PEMBERTON-BARNES, W. H., of Havering-atte-Bower and Beauchamp Roding, co. Essex, [1850 ?], Vol. XLIX, fol. 411.

PEMBERTON, late HODGSON, Henry Williams, of co. Camb., and Inner Temple, London, [1855] Vol. LI, fol. 364.

PEMBERTON, Charles Davis (s. of Thomas), of Hove, co. Sussex, 1897, Vol. LXIX, fol. 305.

PEMBROKE, George, of St. Albans, co. Hertf., and to descendants of his father Joshua and uncle Nathaniel, of Chertsey, co. Surrey, 7 Feb. 1771, Vol. XII, fol. 57. (Berry.)

PENDARVES, late STACKHOUSE after WYNNE, Edward William Stackhouse, of Pendarves, co. Cornw., [28 Feb.] 1815, Vol. XXVIII, fol. 282. (Berry's Suppl.)

„ late WOOD, William Cole (minor), of Pendarves, co. Cornw., [1860] Vol. LIII, fol. 296.

PENDER, Sir J., of Middleton Hall, Uphall, co. Linlithgow, Scotland, 1889, Vol. LXV, fol. 19. (Berry's Suppl.)

„ Lady, of Foots Cray Place, Foots Cray, co. Kent, 1893, Vol. LXVII, fol. 189.

„ J. D. Denison, of Sloane Street, London, and co. Kent, and Scotland, 1891, Vol. LXVI, fol. 77.

PENDOCK, ..., of Tollerton, co. Nottingham, and Gutherington, co. Glouc., [1811], Vol. XXVI, fol. 360.

PENFOLD, ..., of Arundel and Cissbury Court, co. Sussex, and Wick, co. Caithness, [1839] Vol. XLIV, fol. 174.

PENFOLD to WYATT, ..., of Arundel and Cissbury Court, co. Sussex, and Wick, co. Caithness, [1839] Vol. XLIV, fol. 184.

PENFOLD, Oliver, of Sandhurst, Va., 1890,* Vol. LXV, fol. 172.

PENKIVIL, J. S. S., of Grove House, East Peckham, co. Surrey, 1883,* Vol. LXII, fol. 85.

PENKIVIL-TOMPSETT, J. S. S., of Grove House, East Peckham, co. Surrey, 1883,* Vol. LXII, fol. 104.

PENN, ..., of Stoke Park, Bucks., and Pennsylvania, N. America. Exemplification and Augmentation, [1838] Vol. XLIII, fol. 114.

  ,,   John, M.P. (s. of John, F.R.S.), of Lee and Lewisham, co. Kent. Arms also for ENGLISH, his wife, [1856 ?] Vol. LI, fol. 438.

PENN-GASKELL, ..., of co. Somerset, and Shanagarry, co. Cork, Ireland, [1868] Vol. LVI, fol. 344.

PENNANT after DAWKINS, George Hay [Dawkins], of Wales, and co. Wilts. Quarterly Arms, 1806 [1806], Vol. XXIV, fol. 414.

  ,,   after DAWKINS, ..., of Wales, 1841, Vol. XLV, fol. 57.

  ,,   after DOUGLAS, Hon. Edward Gordon Douglas, of Wales. [Arms and Surname of Pennant], 1841, Vol. XLV, fol. 55.

  ,,   after DOUGLAS-, [Edward Gordon Douglas-Pennant] Baron PENRHYN [3 Aug. 1866]. Supporters, 1866, Vol. LVI, fol. 148.

PENNANT, formerly PEARSON, Philip Pennant, 1860 (see Burke's Landed Gentry).

PENNECK, John, Rector of St. Ewe, co. Cornw. (s. of John, of Tregimba, par. of St. Hilary, in the said county, decd.), and to his brethren, William, of Exeter; Francis, of Helstone, co. Cornw.; and Charles, of Tregimba, 2 Aug. 1712, Vol. VI, fol. 80; Add. MS. 14,831, fol. 49.

PENNY after GREENWOOD, Robert Penny, of Higher Nutwell House, co. Devon, [1841] Vol. XLV, fol. 138.

PENNY to HARWOOD, ..., of London, [1853] Vol. L, fol. 313.

PENNYMAN, late WORSLEY, James White, Capt., R.E., of Thornton Moor and Ormesby Hall, co. York, [1853] Vol. L, fol. 327.

PENOYRE (STALLARD), late LEYSON, John, of Batheaston, co. Somerset; Bassaley, co. Monmouth; and Llanvigan, co. Brecon, Wales, [1834] Vol. XL, fol. 270.

PENRICE, ..., of Great Yarmouth, co. Norf., now of Wales, [1814] Vol. XXVIII, fol. 13.

PENSARN, John, of Forthampton and Corse, co. Glouc., Bar.-at-Law, of the Inner Temple, London, [1829] Vol. XXXVIII, fol. 5.

PENTON, Henry, of Winchester and Wath, co. York, Bencher of Lincoln's Inn, London, [1698] Vol. IV, fol. 275.

PENWRY, ..., of West York, par. of Ash-next-Ridley, co. Kent, [1822] Vol. XXXIII, fol. 142.

  ,, ..., of West York, par. of Ash-next-Ridley, co. Kent, [1840 ?] Vol. XLIV, fol. 198.

PENYSTON, late PARTRIDGE, John Francis, of co. Cornw., Oxf. and Norf., [1874] Vol. LVIII, fol. 351.

PENYSTON, A. F., care of E. T. Partridge, Oxford Road, Teddington, co. Middx., 1894, Vol. LXVIII, fol. 53.

PENZANCE, Baron [1869] Sir James Plaisted Wilde, of co. Cornw. Supporters, [1854] Vol. LI, fol. 137 [? 1869, Vol. LVII, fol. 137].

PEPLOE, Ven. Samuel, B.D., Archdeacon of Richmond, Chancellor of the Diocese of Chester and Warden of Manchester Coll. (s. of Samuel, Bp. of Chester), 23 Feb. 1753, Vol. IX, fol. 440 (see Misc. G. et H., 2nd S., III, p. 145). (Berry.)

PEPLOE, late [after ?] WEBB, Daniel P[eploe] W[ebb], of Garnstone, co. Hereford, [Peploe quartering Webb]. [Roy. Lic., 17 May 1845] Vol. XLVII, fol. 389.

PEPLOE, Rev. John Birch Peploe WEBB [? John Birch Webb Peploe], of Garnstone, co. Hereford. [Roy. Lic., 26 June 1866] Vol. LVI, fol. 132.

PEPPERCORN, James (of Navy Off.), of Rochester, co. Kent, [1828 ?] Vol. XXXVII, fol. 117.
PEPPERELL, William, Bart. [15 Nov. 1746], of co. Cornw. [? Devon]; Portsmouth, New Hampshire; Kittery Point, Maine, Massachusetts Bay; and New England, America, [1746 ?] Vol. IX, fol. 161.
PEPPERELL, late SPARHAWK, William, [of Boston, Massachusetts, America, cr. a Bart., 9 Nov. 1774] 31 Mar. 1775, Vol. XIII, fol. 83.
PEPPIN, Elizabeth, and her brother John, s. of George, of Combe-in-Dulverton, co. Somerset, 1757, Vol. X, fol. 104. (Berry and Burke.)
PEPYS [Sir Charles Christopher], Baron COTTENHAM [20 Jan. 1836], of co. Camb. Supporters, [1836] Vol. XLI, fol. 202.
PERCIVAL, William, of Moorlands House, Kirby Stephen, co. Westmorland, [1863] Vol. LV, fol. 16.
  „ . . . ., of Newport Pagnell, Bucks., 1745. (Burke's Armory.)
  „ Martha, wife of Rev. John POTTER, of Newton Pagnell, Bucks., 1745, Vol. IX, fol. 155. (Edmondson's Armory and Berry.)
PERCIVALL. . . . ., of co. Cornw. Samuel Percival mar. Grace PENDARVES and died s.p.; she was the widow of COSTER. (Match), [1815] Vol. XXVIII, fol. 282.
PERCY, late SMITHSON, ... [12 April 1750], Earl of NORTHUMBERLAND [1749]. Arms and Supporters, [1750] Vol. IX, fol. 377.
PERCY [Hugh], Earl of NORTHUMBERLAND [K.G., 1756-7]. Arms and Supporters, [1757 ?] Vol. X, fol. 85.
  „ . . . . [? Duke of Northumberland, 1766]. Supporters, [1766] Vol. XI, fol. 173.
  „ Algernon, Baron PRUDHOE [27 Nov. 1816]. Supporters, [1816] Vol. XXX, fol. 44.
PERCY (GREATHEED-BERTIE), Lord Charles, of co. Warw. [s. of the 5th Duke of Northumberland]. [Surname and Arms of Greatheed-Bertie, 1 April 1826.] [1826] Vol. XXXV, fol. 392.
PERCY to HEBER-PERCY, ..., of Shropsh., [1847] Vol. XLVIII, fol. 258.
PEREVIN, Francis Evaristo, of Singapore Straits, Malacca, and Gray's Inn, London, [1865] Vol. LV, fol. 334.
PERFECT, John, of Pontefract, co. York, and to the descendants of his grandfather John, 14 June 1777, Vol. XIII, fol. 305.
  „ Thomas, of Carswell, Berks., [1822] Vol. XXXIII, fol. 301.
PERFECT (to HAYWARD-SOUTHBY), Thomas, of Carswell, Berks., and Withington, co. Glouc., [1822] Vol. XXXIII, fol. 366.
  „ to DAWSON, ..., of co. York and Devon, [1879] Vol. LX, fol. 261.
PERKINS, A. F., of Oakdene, Capel, co. Surrey, 1891, Vol. LXVI, fol. 43.
  „ James, of Water Lane, London, and Doddington Lodge, Newington, co. Surrey, 1881, Vol. LXI, fol. 209.
PERRELL, ..., of London, and Guernsey, [1809] Vol. XXV, fol. 141.
PERRING, ..., of Modbury, co. Devon, [? Sir John, 2nd] Bart., [1839] Vol. XLIV, fol. 59.
PERRINS, James Dysart, of Davenham Bank, Great Malvern, co. Worc., Fellow Society of Arts, 1883, Vol. LXII, fol. 89. (Berry's Suppl.)
PERRIS, William, senior Clerk in the Six Clerks Office, Chancery, 20 or 31 Dec. 1708, Vol. V, fol. 325; Stowe MS. 714, fol. 90.
PERRON, Felix (and HOLLAND, his wife ?), of London, [1828] Vol. XXXVII, fols. 87 and 88.
PERRY, Micajah, of the City of London, 23 July 1701, Vol. V, fol. 45 (see Harleian MS. 6834, fol. 121; and Add. MS. 14,831, fol. 46, has Micajah). (8 Mar. 1700. Berry).
  „ Timothy, of London, s. of Thomas, of Cirencester, co. Glouc., decd. (see Ped., 3 D. 14, fol. 237), 14 Sep. 1708, Vol. V, fol. 302; Add. MS. 14,830, fol. 200.

288 GRANTEES OF ARMS, 1687—1898.

PERRY, Samuel, J.P., of Goodman's Fields, co. Middx., s. of Samuel, of Rodborne, co. Glouc., decd., 24 Mar. 171⅞, Vol. VI, fol. 362 ; Add. MS. 14,830, fol. 69.
PERRY to OGILVIE, ... Arms to CLARKE, wife of, of co. Middx., and Scotland, [1801] Vol. XXI, fol. 162.
PERRY, ..., of Moor Hall, co. Essex, [1849] Vol. XLIX, fol. 139.
PERRY [to PERRY-] -WATLINGTON, ..., of Moor Hall, co. Essex ; Caldecott House, Aldenham, co. Hertf. ; and the Inner Temple, London, [1849] Vol. XLIX, fol. 141.
PERRY-HERRICK [? Herrick to], ..., of co. Hereford, Leic. and Staff., [1853] Vol. L, fol. 361.
PERRY, Thomas, of Bitham House, Avon Dassett, co. Warw., [1856] Vol. LII, fol. 49.
  „   Walter C., of Manchester Square, London, Bar.-at-Law, 1886,* Vol. LXIII, fol. 209.
PERRYMAN, Robert, of Leicester Fields, par. of St. Anne, Westminster, 25 Mar. 1710, Vol. V, fol. 399 ; Add. MS. 14,831, fol. 44. (Berry.)
  „   Charles Wilbraham, of Bifrons, Farnborough, Southampton, 1895 [1897], Vol. LXIX, fol. 285.
PERTH, Baron [Drummond of Stobhall, 26 Oct. 1797, James], of Scotland. Supporters, [1798 ?] Vol. XX, fol. 120.
PETER, Francis, of Stanmore Magna, co. Middx., 25 Nov. 1729 [1730], Vol. VIII, fol. 67ᵇ [76ᵇ ?]. [R. C. Fam., I, 58.]
PETER-HOBLYN, ..., of Colquits St. Martyn, co. Cornw., [1837] Vol. XLII, fol. 127.
  „   -HOBLYN, ..., of Colquits St. Martin, co. Cornw., [1865] Vol. LV, fol. 354.
PETERS, George, of London, 1748, Vol. IX, fol. 223.
  „   . . . ., of Newcastle-upon-Tyne, co. Northumberland, [1811] Vol. XXVI, fol. 233.
  „   William Henry, of Lympstone, co. Devon, [1846] Vol. XLVIII, fol. 167.
PETERS to TURTON, ..., of Brasted Place, co. Kent ; Larpool Hall, co. York ; and Knipton, co. Leic., [1817] Vol. XXX, fol. 198.
  „   to BURTON-PETERS, Henry, of Hotham Hall and Hull Bank, co. York, [1823 ?] Vol. XXXIII, fol. 370.
  „   to PARSONS-PETERS, William, of Ycabridge, co. Somerset, [1858] Vol. LIII, fol. 42.
PETHERICK, George, of Porthpenn House, St. Austell, co. Cornw., 1886,* Vol. LXIII, fol. 177.
PETIT, ..., of Lincoln's Inn, London, and Normandy, [1795] Vol. XIX, fol. 129.
PETIT, Sir Dinshaw Manekjee [Knt., 1887, Sheriff of Bombay] (India), 1890, Vol. LXV, fol. 301.
PETO, ..., of Somerleyton Hall, co. Suff., and Cookham, Berks., [1854] Vol. LI, fol. 128.
PETRE, late VARLO, John, of Essex New House, and Westwick House, co Norf., [18 or 30 July] 1802, Vol. XXI, fol. 401. (J. J. Howard's R. C. Fam., Part I, pp. 58 and 59.)
PETRE, Mrs., of Upper Brook Street ; 1ᵇ, Montagu Mansions, London ; and Westwick House, co. Norf., 1882, Vol. LXI, fols. 255 and 281.
PETTIT, Edmund, of Leighton Buzzard, co. Bedf., 1880,* Vol. LXI, fol. 39. (Berry's Suppl.)
PETTIWARD, late BUSSELL, ..., of co. Suff., [1855] Vol. LI, fol. 416.
PETYT, William, of the Inner Temple, London, 1690, Vol. IV, fol. 59.
  „   John, of the Inner Temple, London, Ackworth Park and Hastleford, co York, 10 Nov. 1810, Vol. XXVI, fol. 120.
PHAYRE, Sir Arthur Purves, K.C.S.I. [1867], and C.B. (see Burke [no date]).

PHELP, Dorothy, widow of John. Quartering HERBERT, of Hampton Wick, co. Middx., and Crowmarsh, co. Oxf., [1780] Vol. XIV, fol. 219.
PHELPS to MARTIN, ..., of Wales. Crest to male descendants, [1788] Vol. XVII, fol. 13.
PHELPS [? John Delafield], of Dursley, co. Glouc. (See PHILIPS.) [1768] Vol. XI, fol. 264.
„ . . . ., of Dursley, co. Glouc., and Lincoln's Inn, London. Quarterly with F[Fowler ?], F[Fisher ?] and G[Gully ?], [1791] Vol. XVII, fol. 346.
„ . . . ., of Bruton Street, London (wife of), [1817] Vol. XXX, fol. 213.
PHELPS to MACDONNELL [Edmund], husband of Countess of ANTRIM [Roy. Lic., 27 June 1817], [1817] Vol. XXX, fol. 215.
PHELPS, Salisbury, [1845] Vol. XLVIII, fol. 71.
„ William, of Chestal, Dursley, co. Glouc., 1892, Vol. LXVI, fol. 311.
PHILIP-BROADE after STANIER, Francis, of co. Staff., [1858] Vol. LII, fol. 372.
PHILIPPS to LEE, William, of co. York and Berks., [1761] Vol. X, fol. 367.
PHILIPPS, late MANSEL, Richard, of Wales, [1793] Vol. XVIII, fol. 159.
„ late GRANT [Sir Richard Bulkeley Philipps Phillips, Bart.], of Picton Castle, Wales [Roy. Lic., 10 Feb. 1824], [1824] Vol. XXXIV, fol. 260.
PHILIPPS, Sir Richard Bulkeley-Philipps, Bart., Baron MILFORD [21 Sept. 1847]. Supporters, [1847 ?] Vol. XLVIII, fol. 391.
PHILIPPS after WALTERS, ..., of Newcastle Emlyn and Aber Glasney, co. Carmarthen, and Bethgeraint, co. Cardigan, Wales, [1826] Vol. XXXVI, fol. 101.
PHILIPPS, late LLOYD, John Philipps Allen Lloyd Philipps, of Dale Castle, &c., Wales, [1833] Vol. XXXIX, fol. 224.
„ late LLOYD, Col. James, of Dale Castle, &c., Wales, [1833] Vol. XXXIX, fol. 226.
„ late GWYTHER, ..., of Picton Castle, co. Pembroke, Wales, [1856] Vol. LII, fol. 151.
„ late FISHER [1876], Charles E. Gregg, of Wales, and the Middle Temple, London (GREGG-PHILIPPS, Bart.), 1876, Vol. LIX, fol. 262.
PHILIPPS to SCOURFIELD, ..., of Wales; Williamston, The Mote, and Robeston Hall, co. Camb., [1863] Vol. LV, fol. 76.
„ to MANSELL, Maj. Courtenay, of Coedgaing, co. Carmarthen, Wales. Exemplification of MANN only. [1871] Vol. LVIII, fol. 4.
PHILIPS, ..., of Dursley, co. Glouc. (See PHELPS, or rather PURNELL.) [1768] Vol. XI, fol. 264.
PHILIPS to SCOTT, (Spr.), of nr. Moreton-in-the-Marsh, co. Glouc., reputed dau. of Scott, of Bank Fee House, [1816] Vol. XXIX, fol. 417.
PHILIPS, John, of Heath House, co. Staff. STUBBS quartering, [1822] Vol. XXXIII, fol. 265.
„ Rev. Gilbert H., M.A., of co. York. Quartering STUBBS and BURTON, [1862] Vol. LIV, fol. 265.
„ Rev. Gilbert H., M.A., of co. York. Quartering HENDERSON, [1863] Vol. LV, fol. 10.
PHILIPSON, Hilton, of Newcastle-upon-Tyne, co. Northumberland, 1883, Vol. LXII, fol. 162.
DODDS-PHILIPSON, R. H., of London, 1883, Vol. LXII, fol. 168.
PHILL, Henry, Merchant, of London, 23 Oct. 1700, Vol. V, fol. 16 (see Add. MS. 14,830, fol. 76).
PHILLIMORE, Sir R. J., Bart., of Oxford, 1881,* Vol. LXI, fol. 235.
PHILLIPPS after MARCH, ..., of co. Dorset. Quartering, [1796] Vol. XIX, fol. 311.
PHILLIPPS, late WINSLOE, Thomas, of Collipriest, co. Devon, and Newport House, Camelford, co. Cornw. (Roy. Lic., 8 Nov. 1798), [1798] Vol. XX, fol. 265. (Berry's Suppl.)

PHILLIPPS, James Orchard HALLIWELL- (s. of Thomas, of Brixton Hill, decd.), F.R.S., of Jesus Coll., Camb., and Lincoln's Inn, London, 1850, aged 30, 1872, Vol. LVIII, fols. 94 and 96 [*see* Burke].

„   . . . ., of Longworth, Lugwardine and Eaton Bishop, co. Hereford, [1834] Vol. XL, fol. 234.

PHILLIPPS-FLAMANK, Rev. William [Phillipps], B.A., of Laniret and Boscarne, co. Cornw., and Glympton, co. Oxf., [1849 ?] Vol. XLIX, fol. 90.

PHILLIPS-TREBY, Col. Paul Winslow, R.A., of Goodarnor Plympton St. Mary, co. Devon, 1877, Vol. LIX, fol. 331.   (Berry's Suppl.)

PHILLIPS, Sir Thomas, Bart., of Middle Hill, co. Worc.   First grant, [1821] Vol. XXXIII, fol. 53 ; second grant, [1857] Vol. LII, fol. 257.

PHILLIPS after SPENCER, ..., of Riffhams, Langford Parsonage and Terling, co. Essex.   Quarterly Arms, [1809] Vol. XXV, fol. 295.

PHILLIPS, Thomas, of Leeds, eo. York.   (*See also* NICHOLSON, [1827] Vol. XXXVI, fol. 365.)   Match, 1817, Vol. XXX, fol. 137.

PHILLIPS to NICHOLSON, William, B.A., of Roundhay, co. York, 1827, Vol. XXXVI, fol. 365.

PHILLIPS, John, of Hanbury Hall, co. Worc., [16 Feb.] 1825, Vol. XXXV, fol. 78.   [Misc. G. et H., 5th S., I, p. 3.]

PHILLIPS, late BROWN, ..., Gov. of Penang, nat. s. of Maj.-Gen. Phillips, Gov. of Windsor Castle, and dau., wife of BIGNELL, 1825, Vol. XXXV, fol. 295.

„   late BROWN, Maj.-Gen. Sir Charles, of Lyndhurst, Hampsh., 1825, Vol. XXXV, fol. 297.

PHILLIPS, Edward, J.P., of Coventry, co. Warw., and to the descendants of his father William, decd., 14 July 1835, Vol. XLI, fol. 81.   (Bishop's MS.)

„   Maj.-Gen. Sir Benjamin Travell, Knt. [18 Feb. 1858], of Hawldston, co. Pembroke, Wales (s. of Stephen Howell Phillips, Lieut. of Body Guard of Yeomen), 1858* [1860], Vol. LIII, fol. 288.

PHILLIPS-JODRELL, Thomas, of co. Chester and Lanc., [1868] Vol. LVII, fol. 68.

PHILLIPS to CHURCH, Samuel, of Wales (name Church only).   Church and Phillips quarterly, [1869] Vol. LVII, fol. 158.

PHILLIPS, Edward Clive Oldnall Long Phillips, Vice-Consul at Kertch and of Rotherham, s. of Richard Augustus Long Phillips, of Rotherham, co. York, 1876, Vol. LIX, fol. 240.

PHILLIPS to WOLLEY, ..., of Kertch, and Rotherham, co. York, [1876] Vol. LIX, fol. 264.

PHILLIPS, Lionel, of Hohenheim, Braamfontein, South Africa, s. of Philip Saunders [Phillips], 1897, Vol. LXIX, fol. 217.

PHILLIPSON after BURTON (late WRIGHT), Charles, M.A., of co. Essex and Northampton.   Escutcheon of pretence, Phillipson and Burton quarterly, [1792] Vol. XVIII, fol. 115.

PHIPPS, Constantine, Baron MULGRAVE, of co. York, 1767, Vol. XI, fol. 240. (Berry.)

PHIPPS to WALLER, ..., of Braywrick Lodge, Berks., [1814] Vol. XXVIII, fol. 167.

PICARD, John Kirkby, of Kingston-upon-Hull, eo. York, 22 April 1809, Vol. XXV, fol. 170.

PICKARD, John, D.L., of Poxwell, Wormwell and Bloxworth, co. Dorset, [1840] Vol. XLV, fol. 9.

PICKARD to TRENCHARD, John, of Poxwell, Wormwell, and Bloxworth, co. Dorset, [1840] Vol. XLV, fol. 42.

PICKARD-CAMBRIDGE, ..., of co. Dorset and Glouc., [1848] Vol. XLIX, fol. 45.

PICKERING, Benjamin, of Bellefield House, Sutton, Hull, co. York, 1885,* Vol. LXIII, fol. 69.

PICKERSGILL, William Henry, R.A., of Stratford Place, and Barnes, co. Surrey, [1854] Vol. LI, fol. 158.

PICKERSGILL, William C., of Blendon House, Bexley, co. Kent, and Netherne House, Merstham, co. Surrey, [1867] Vol. LVI, fol. 189.

PICKERSGILL-CUNLIFFE, John Cunliffe, [1867] Vol. LVI, fol. 211.

PICKFORD, ..., of Market Street, co. Hertf., and Poynton, co. Chester, [1805] Vol. XXIII, fol. 147.

PICKFORD to RADCLIFFE, Joseph (Bart.), of Milnsbridge, co. York, and Royton [Hall, Oldham], co. Lanc., [1809] Vol. XXV, fol. 215 [Roy. Lic., 19 Dec. 1795, cr. a Bart., 2 Nov. 1813].

PICKSTOCK (Jersey), Capt. of Militia, of Colony of Honduras, [1829] Vol. XXXVII, fol. 368.

PICKUP, late BROUGHTON, William (reputed son), of Spring Hall, Accrington, co. Lanc., [1855] Vol. LI, fol. 374.

PICKWICK, Capt. William Eleazer, of Bathford, Bath, and Beckington, co. Somerset, [1838] Vol. XLIII, fol. 10.

PICTON to TURBERVILLE, Richard Turberville (s. of Thomas Picton, of Poyston), of Poyston, co. Pembroke, and Ewnney House and Sutton, co. Glamorgan, Wales, 1797, Vol. XX, fol. 61.

PICTON, Maj.-Gen. Sir Thomas, K.B. [1 Feb. 1813], of Poyston, co. Pembroke, [1812] Vol. XXVII, fol. 214 [314 ?]. Supporters, fol. 216 [316 ?].

PICTON, late WILLIAMS, John, M.D., of Poyston, co. Pembroke, Iscoed and St. Brides, co. Glamorgan, Wales, [1840] Vol. XLIV, fol. 277.

PICTON, John P., of Prince Edward's Island and Iscoed, co. Carmarthen, Wales. Supporters, 1883, Vol. LXII, fol. 149.

PIDCOCK, Henry, of Platts, co. Staff. (See HENZELL, Berry's Suppl.) [1852] Vol. L, fol. 213.

PIDDOCKE, Leonard, of Ashby de la Zouche, co. Leic., and King's Bromley, co. Staff., 7 Mar. 17$\frac{39}{40}$ [? 17$\frac{29}{30}$] Vol. VIII, fol. 73^b.

PIERCE, ..., of Bridgnorth, Shropsh. (See HAYLEY.) [1701] Vol. V, fol. 51.

PIERCE to SEAMAN, ..., M.D., L.R.C.P., of London, and Rotherly and Hoby, co. Leic., [1825] Vol. XXXV, fol. 108.

„ to SEAMAN, [1835] Vol. XLI, fol. 34.

„ to SEAMAN, [1835] Vol. XLI, fol. 51.

PIERCE, Hugh, of Wales, and Liverpool, co. Lanc., [1854] Vol. LI, fol. 51.

„ Joseph (s. of John), of Cwybyn Fawr, Rhuddlan, co. Flint, Wales, 1862 * [? 1863], Vol. LV, fol. 140.

„ . . . ., of Clevedon, co. Somerset, and Cheverell Parva, Wilts., [1868] Vol. LVII, fol. 5.

PIERREPONT, Baron [29 Mar. 1703, Gervase Pierrepont] [extinct 1715]. Supporters, [170$\frac{2}{3}$] Vol. V, fol. 116.

PIERREPONT, late MEDOWS [Charles] [afterwards Baron Pierrepont, see next name], of co. Nottingham, [17 Sept. 1788] Vol. XVII, fol. 31.

PIERREPONT, Baron [23 July 1796, Charles Pierrepont]. Arms to his wife, [Anne ORTON, yst. dau. of William] MILLS, and Supporters, [1796] Vol. XIX, fol. 321.

„ . . . ., of London, and Barbados, [1809] Vol. XXV, fol. 108.

PIERS, Walter Rumbold (s. of Henry), of South Africa, 18 . . ., Vol. LXXI, fol. . . . .

PIERSE to HUSTLER, Thomas, of Acklam House, co. York, [1784] Vol. XV, fol. 285.

PIERSON, Rev. G. J., of Norton Vicarage, co. Hertf., 1890,* Vol. LXVI, fol. 3.

PIGÉ-LEOCHALLES, H. P., of Page Green, Tottenham, co. Middx., 1883, Vol. LXII, fol. 42 (see Berry's Suppl.).

PIGGOTT, late COOKE, Simon Francis, of Fitzhall, Iping, co. Sussex, and Lincoln's Inn, London, 22 Aug. 1824, Vol. XXXV, fol. 3.

„ Jane, dau. of JAMES, wife of Simon Francis Piggott, formerly COOKE, 22 Aug. 1824, Vol. XXXV, fol. 5.

PIGOTT after SMITH, John Hugh, of Wroxall and Brockley, co. Somerset, [1825] Vol. XXXV, fols. 223 and 224. Smyth, [1824] Vol. XXXV, fol. 20.

PIGOTT (FOSTER-) after GRAHAM, Lieut.-Col. George Edward, M.P., of Berks.,
    Bucks., and co. Camb., [1827] Vol. XXXVI, fols. 299 and 303.   Foster
    after Pigott, John, [1806] Vol. XXIV, fol. 112.

 „   (FOSTER-) after GRAHAM, ..., M.P., of Bucks. and co. Camb., [1827]
    Vol. XXXVI, fol. 305.

 „   (FOSTER-), Graham, of Bucks. and co. Camb., [1829] Vol. XXXVII,
    fols. 309 and 310.   EXTON quartering, [1828] fol. 110.

PIGOTT-STAINSBY-CONANT, Paynton, of London, and Archer Lodge, Sherfield-
    upon-Lodden, Hampsh., [1835 ?] Vol. XLI, fol. 158.

PIGOTT, Francis, of Banbury, co. Oxf., and the Inner Temple, London, Bar.-at-
    Law.   Quartering PELLING and GILLERY, 16 Sept. 1775, Vol. XIII,
    fol. 121.

PIGOTT to JEAFFRESON, ... (infant), of Dullingham, co. Camb., [1838] Vol.
    XLIII, fol. 332.

PIGOTT-CORBET, ..., of Shropsh., [1865] Vol. LV, fol. 328 ; see [1890]
    Vol. LXV, fol. 309.

PIGOTT, late FOSTER, ..., D.D., of co. Camb. and Kent, Fellow Eton Coll.,
    [1806] Vol. XXIV, fol. 112.

PIJOLAS, ..., [1762] Vol. X, fol. 430 [see PUJOLAS].

PIKE, John, of co. Somerset, and Gottenburgh, 1751 [1752], Vol. IX, fol. 420 [?]
    (Berry.)

PILFOLD, John, Capt., R.N., of Horsham, co. Sussex, 29 Mar. 1808, Vol. XXIV,
    fol. 382 ; Horsham and Newtimber.   Augmentation, 14 April, fol. 384
    (1st s. of Charles) ; see Misc. G. et H., New S., IV, pp. 75-77.   (Burke's
    Armory.)

PILKINGTON to MILBORNE-SWINNERTON, ... [Act of Parliament, 1836-7],
    [-Pilkington, Roy. Lic., 15 Feb. 1856], of co. York and Staff., [1856]
    Vol. LII, fol. 78.   Mary [dau. of Thomas Swinnerton, decd., by Mary, dau.
    and h. of Charles Milborne], mother of Sir Lionel, Bart.   (Berry's Suppl.)

 „   to MILBORNE-SWINNERTON, Sir Lionel [11th Bart.], [names Milborne-
    Swinnerton by Roy. Lic., 15 Feb. 1856.   Arms, Roy. Lic., 16 Mar. 1859].
    [1859] Vol. LIII, fol. 94.

PILLING-TAYLOR, Margaret (Spr.), dau. of John Pilling, of Moreton Hall,
    Whalley, and Baxenden, co. Lanc., 1876, Vol. LIX, fol. 300.

PILTER, William Frederick, of Addlestone, co. Surrey (s. of Rev. Robert),
    18 . . ., Vol. LXXI, fol. . . . .

PINCKNEY, George Henry, of Middlesex House, Batheaston, co. Somerset, 1878,
    Vol. LX, fol. 80.   (Berry's Suppl.)

PINDAR, late LYGON, ..., of co. Linc., [1813] Vol. XXVII, fol. 439.

PINE before COFFIN, Rev. John, of Portledge, co. Devon.   Quarterly Arms,
    1797, Vol. XIX, fol. 398.

PINFOLD, Charles, Doctor of Laws, an advocate in the Arches Court of Canterbury,
    and to William (his brother), sons of Sir Thomas, Knt., D.C.L. (Advocate-
    Gen. to King William), decd., and to Charles, a Clerk in the Prerogative
    Office, London, and to Edward, of London, Goldsmith, brothers of the said
    Sir Thomas, 10 Oct. 1707, Vol. V, fol. 259 ; Add. MS. 14,830, fol. 65 ;
    Stowe MS. 716, fol. 68.

PINGO, Benjamin, Rouge Dragon Pursuivant of Arms, afterwards York Herald,
    London, [22 Feb.] 1782, Vol. XV, fol. 22.   (Crisp, Fragm. Geneal., V,
    p. 67.)

PINHORN, Sir John, Knt., of Ringwood House, Hampsh., and Newport, Isle of
    Wight, [1802] Vol. XXI, fol. 419.

PINNEY, late PRETOR, John, of Bettiscombe, co. Dorset, and Nevis, N. America,
    18 April, 1776, Vol. XIII, fol. 181.   [Burke's Suppl.]

PINNEY, now PRETOR, John Pinney ; 2. Rev. John Charles, of Somerton Erley,
    The Grange, Somerton, Carey Rivel, Burton Pinsent, [all ?] co. Somerset.
    1877, Vol. LX, fol. 56.   1. Frederick Wake, &c., of co. Somerset, 1877,
    Vol. LX, fol. 58.   [See Burke's Suppl.]

PINNIGER to COPE, ..., of Ireland, [1867] Vol. LVI, fol. 283.

PINNOCK, ..., of London, and Jamaica, [1799] Vol. XX, fol. 385.

PIOZZI after SALUSBURY, ..., of Brynbella and Bachegraig, co. Flint, Wales, [1813] Vol. XXVII, fol. 441.

PIPE before WOLFERSTAN, Samuel, of Statfold, co. Staff., 15 June 1776, Vol. XIII, fol. 191.

PIPER, John, of Ashen, co. Essex, s. of John, of Conrad Magna, co. Suff., s. of John, of the same, to descendants of grandfather, 23 or 28 July 1723, Vol. VII, fol. 208.

  ,, ..., Capt., R.E., of Colyton Manor, North Devon, and Amsterdam, [1833] Vol. XXXIX, fol. 260.

PIPPARD to BLUNDELL, Nicholas, of Little Crosby, co. Lanc., 1772, Vol. XII, fol. 141.

PIRBRIGHT, Baron [15 Nov. 1895], ([Henry] DE WORMS), 1895, Vol. LXIX, fol. 1.

PIRIE, Sir John [Bart., April 1842], Lord Mayor of London, of Dunse, Scotland, [1842] Vol. XLVI, fol. 37.

PISTOR to WORTHINGTON, ..., of Bath, co. Somerset, [1826], Vol. XXXVI, fol. 59.

PITCHER, John Southerby, of Northfleet, co. Kent, [1816] Vol. XXIX, fol. 402.

PITT, Samuel, of Blandford, co. Dorset ; Cricket and Ilminster, co. Somerset, High Sheriff (s. of William), and to John, of London, Merchant, grandson and heir to Humphrey, elder brother of the said William, and to the descendants of the said Humphrey, 26 Feb. 170¾, Vol. V, fol. 141 ; Add. MS. 14,830, fol. 64. (Pedigree D. 14 [Her. Coll.])

  ,, Humphrey, of Shifnal and Priors Lee, Shropsh., 1758, Vol. X, fol. 149. (Berry.)

  ,, Rt. Hon. William. Change of Crest (see also [170¾] Vol. V, fol. 141), 1761, Vol. X, fol. 405. (Berry.)

  ,, Baroness CHATHAM [4 Dec. 1761, Hester, wife of the Rt. Hon. William Pitt]. Supporters, [1761] Vol. X, fol. 405.

  ,, Earl of CHATHAM [4 Aug. 1766, Rt. Hon. William Pitt]. Supporters, [1766] Vol. XI, fol. 178.

  ,, Baron RIVERS [20 May 1776, George Pitt]. Supporters, [1776] Vol. XIII, fol. 217.

  ,, Lord CAMELFORD [Baron of Bonnoc, 5 Jan. 1784, Thomas Pitt]. Supporters, [1784] Vol. XV, fol. 259.

  ,, Lieut.-Gen. Sir William Augustus, K.B. [1792], bro. to Baron RIVERS. Supporters, [1792] Vol. XVIII, fol. 101.

  ,, Baron AMHERST [Aug. 1797, William Pitt Amherst]. Supporters, [1797] Vol. XX, fol. 88.

PITT after DEAN, Major (nat. s. of Baron RIVERS), [1818] Vol. XXXI, fol. 150.

PITT-RIVERS, late BECKFORD [26 Nov. 1828, William Horace, 3rd Baron] RIVERS, of co. Dorset, Glouc., and Hampsh., [1828] Vol. XXXVII, fol. 229.

PITTER, ..., of Coulsdon, co. Surrey, [1823] Vol. XXXIV, fol. 138.

PITTOCK, ..., of Eastry, co. Kent, [1810] Vol. XXV, fol. 334.

PIXLEY, S., of Leinster Gardens, London, 1890,* Vol. LXV, fol. 289.

PIZZEY to BOYMAN, ..., of Hastings, co. Sussex, and London, [1819] Vol. XXXI, fol. 214.

PLAMPIN, Thomas, of Shawell, co. Leic., 24 July 1729, Vol. VIII, fol. 37.

  ,, Rear-Adm., of Hartest, Chadacre Hall, Shrimpling, co. Suff., [1824] Vol. XXXIV, fol. 283.

PLANCHÉ, James Robinson, Rouge Croix Pursuivant of Arms, of London, [1856] Vol. LII, fol. 145.

PLASKET, ..., of Wigton, and London, [1794] Vol. XVIII, fol. 408.

PLATT, Robert Charles (of Stalybridge, co. Chester), s. of George, of Dean Water, Prestbury, co. Chester, [1853] Vol. L, fol. 288.

  ,, Frederick, of Barnley Manor, Newark, co. Nottingham, 1883,* Vol. LXII, fol. 126. (Berry's Suppl.)

PLATT, John, of Clifton Lodge, Llandudno, N. Wales, 1890, Vol. LXV, fol. 207.
PLATT-HIGGINS, Edward, of Rathcoole, Fitzwilliam Park, Shankhill, co. Antrim,
    Ireland, 1889, Vol. LXV, fol. 95. (Crisp, Notes, II, p. 106.)
  „ -HIGGINS, Frederick, M.P., of Holmleigh, Bowdon, co. Chester ; Charles, of
    Naples ; Henry, of Mount House, Cheetham Hill, co. Lanc. ; Alfred,
    Bar.-at-Law, of the Inner Temple, London ; Arthur, of High Mount,
    Didsbury, Manchester ; Walter, of Holmwood, Kersal, Manchester ;
    [Margaret, of Holmwood Turvey, co. Bedf. (Spr.)   Platt before Higgins.
    Arms of Platt quarterly with Higgins.]   [16 Aug.] 1889, Vol. LXV,
    fols. 97 and 100 (see Crisp [Notes], II, p. 106).
PLAYFAIR, Baron [The Rt. Hon. Sir Lyon Playfair, G.C.B., &c.], of London,
    1892, Vol. LXVII, fol. 103.
PLENDERLEATH to CHRISTIE, ..., of London, [1836] Vol. XLI, fol. 295.
PLOMER, ..., of Helston, co. Cornw., [1818] Vol. XXXI, fol. 138.
PLOWES, John, ex-Mayor of Leeds, co. York, and of Spain (Malaga), [1792]
    Vol. XVIII, fol. 127.
PLUCKNETT, George, of Finchley, London, [1866] Vol. LVI, fol. 123.
PLUES, Samuel Swire, of Ripon, co. York, Attorney-Gen. Brit. Honduras, [1871]
    Vol. LVIII, fol. 6.
PLUMBE-TEMPEST, Col. John, of Tonge Hall, co. York, and Aughton, co. Linc.,
    1835, Vol. XL, fol. 340.   (Crisp, II, p. 11.)
PLUM(M)ER, John Bagwill, and others, of Allerton, Dartington, co. Devon, 1892,*
    Vol. LXVI, fol. 302.   (Crisp, I, p. 218.)
  „ . . . ., of Frome, co. Somerset, and Jamaica, [1805] Vol. XXIII, fol. 209.
PLUMMER-WARD, Robert, Under-Sec. Foreign Office, of Chesham, Woburn Hall,
    Bucks. ; Crilston Park, Blakesmere, co. Hertf. ; and Cheston Hall, co.
    Suff., [1828] Vol. XXXVII, fol. 183.
PLUMRIDGE, Vice-Adm. Sir James Hanway, of Hopton Hall, co. Suff., [1859]
    Vol. LIII, fol. 108.
PLUNKET, Baron [1827], of Ireland.   Supporters, [1833] Vol. XXXIX, fol. 281.
PLYMLEY to CORBETT, ..., M.A., of Shropsh., [1804] Vol. XXIII, fol. 75.
POCKLINGTON, William, of Newark, co. Nottingham, 22 June 1761, Vol. X,
    fol. 370.   (Berry.)
POCKLINGTON-SENHOUSE, of Barrow House and Nether Hall, co. Cumberland,
    [1842] Vol. XLVI, fol. 189.
POCOCK, Adm. George, of St. Margaret's, Westminster, and Cheveley, Berks.,
    1761, Vol. X, fol. 274.   (Berry.)
  „ Adm. Sir George, K.B. [23 Mar. 1761], of St. Margaret's, Westminster,
    and Cheveley, Berks.   Supporters, [1761] Vol. X, fol. 321.   (Berry.)
  „ George, his s., of St. Margaret's, Westminster, and Cheveley, Berks.
    Augmentation, [1794] Vol. XVIII, fol. 319.
  „ . . . ., of Westminster and Bristol, [1811] Vol. XXVI, fol. 199.
  „ Sir George, Bart., of Durham.   Augmentation of HART, [1822] Vol.
    XXXIII, fol. 124.   Supporters, Hart, fol. 126.
PODE, ..., of Slade, co. Devon, [1794] Vol. XVIII, fol. 349.
POINTER before STANDLEY, ..., of Paxton Place, co. Huntingdon, [1782]
    Vol. XV, fol. 100.
POLAND, ..., of Islington, co. Middx., [1806] Vol. XXIV, fol. 91.
POLE, late VAN NOTTEN [7 Mar. 1787], Charles, of Holcroft, co. Lanc., and
    Wolverton, Hampsh., [1787] Vol. XVI, fol. 261.   [Bart., 28 July 1791.]
    Supporters, 1794, Vol. XVIII, fol. 365, to descend with his title, an
    Hessian honour (see next entry).
POLE, Elizabeth [? Anne], (daughter of [John] Johnson), wife of Charles Pole [of
    Holcroft, co. Lanc.], M.P., of Liverpool, 1741-2, Vol. IX, fols. 43 and 45.
  „ Vice-Adm. Sir Charles Morice, Bart. [12 Sept. 1801].   Supporters, [1801]
    Vol. XXI, fol. 231.   K.C.B. [1815], [1811] Vol. XXVI [XXVIII ?],
    fol. 351.   Match with GODDARD [mar., 8 June 1792, Henrietta, dau. of
    John Goddard, of Woodford Hall, co. Essex].

POLE after CHANDOS, Sacheverell, of Radborne, co. Derby. Quarterly Arms, 1807, Vol. XXIV, fol. 146.

POLE before TYLNEY-LONG-WELLESLEY, William, of Ireland, afterwards (1845) Earl of MORNINGTON (nephew of Baron WELLESLEY). Quarterly Arms, 1812, Vol. XXVII, fol. 178.

POLE, William, Baron MARYBOROUGH, of Ireland (afterwards Earl of MORNINGTON, 1842). Supporters, 1821, Vol. XXXIII, fol. 15.

POLE after VAN NOTTEN, [Sir Peter, 3rd Bart., Van Notten before Pole], Bart. [11 June 1853], of Todenham, co. Glouc., and Wolverton, Hampsh., [1853] Vol. L, fol. 345.

„   after VAN NOTTEN [? 19 July 1853], Charles, of Todenham, co. Glouc., and Wolverton, Hampsh., [1853] Vol. L, fol. 397.

POLE (CHANDOS) GELL, Henry, of Barton Fields, Barton Blount, and Hopton, co. Derby, 1863, Vol. LV, fol. 28.

POLHILL-TURNER, ..., of Howbury Hall, Renhold, Ambrosden, co. Oxford, [1853] Vol. L, fol. 315.

POLLARD, Capt. Edward John, R.N., of Wrotham House, Wrotham, and Hempstead, co. Glouc., [1868 ?] Vol. LVII, fol. 113.

POLLEN, ..., of Redenham, Hampsh., [1795] Vol. XVIII, fol. 429.

POLLEN after BOILEAU, Rev. George, of Little Bookham, co. Surrey, [1820] Vol. XXXII, fol. 183.

POLLEXFEN, John James, Capt., Bombay S.C., [1856 ?] Vol. LII, fol. 183.

POLLOCK, Maj.-Gen. Sir George, G.C.B. [1842]. Supporters, Arms ?, [1848] Vol. XLVIII, fol. 438 ; Bart., Field-Marshal [1870]. Supporters, [1872] Vol. LVIII, fol. 101.

„   Sir Frederick, Bart. [2 Aug. 1866], Lord Chief Baron of the Exchequer. Supporters, [1866] Vol. LVI, fol. 144.

POLLOCK to MONTAGU-POLLOCK [9 Aug. 1873], Sir Frederick, [2nd] Bart., of Westleton Grange, co. Suff., [1873] Vol. LVIII, fol. 248.

POLLOCK, William, of Westminster, and his wife Hannah, dau. of Rev. John COWCHER, and descendants, 1783, Vol. XV, fol. 233.

POLTIMORE, Baron [1831] (BAMPFYLDE, [6th] Bart.). Supporters, [1831] Vol. XXXVIII, fol. 275.

POLWORTH, Lord (CAMPBELL) [Alexander Hume-Campbell, cr. 20 May 1776 Baron Hume of Berwick]. Supporters, [1777] Vol. XIII, fol. 273.

POMEROY, late MASON, ..., of Holborn, London, [1893] Vol. LXVII, fol. 185.

„   late WAKEFIELD, James Pomeroy, and Emily Pomeroy Pomeroy (minors), of Epping, co. Essex, and Clapton, co. Middx., 14 Oct. 1841, Vol. XLV, fol. 305 (see Burke).

POMFRET to ALLEN, Ralph (reputed s. of Allen), of co. Essex and Hertf., [1823] Vol. XXXIV, fol. 206.

POMFRET, William Pomfret, of Ashford, co. Kent, 1884, Vol. LXII, fol. 190.

PONSFORD, William, of Exeter, co. Devon, Merchant, 20 May 1710, Vol. V, fol. 405 ; Add. MS. 14,831, fol. 68. (Berry.)

PONSONBY, Baron [13 Mar. 1806], of Imokilly, Ireland. Supporters, [1806] Vol. XXIII, fol. 354.

PONSONBY, late FISHER, ..., of Hale Hall, co. Cumberland, [1816] Vol. XXIX, fol. 362.

PONSONBY, Baron DE MAULEY [10 July 1838], of co. Dorset. Supporters, [1838] Vol. XLIII, fol. 127.

PONSONBY-FANE, [The Hon.] Spencer Cecil [Brabazon, 4th s. of the 4th] Earl of BESSBOROUGH, of co. Somerset, [5 Feb.] 1875, Vol. LIX, fol. 86.

PONTIFEX, William, of Cheshunt, co. Hertf., and London ; Edmund, of Bath, co. Somerset, [1855] Vol. LI, fol. 350. (Berry's Suppl.)

POOLE, ... (of Grissons, Switzerland). (See BARATTY.) [1753] Vol. IX, fol. 448.

POOLE, late HALSTED, ..., of Lymm, co. Chester, [1782] Vol. XV, fol. 115.

POOLE to LYDE, ..., of Shirehampton, co. Glouc., and Ayot St. Laurence, co. Hertf., [1792] Vol. XVIII, fol. 91.

„ to THEOBALD, ..., of Kingsgate Street, near Winchester, Hampsh., and Grays, co. Essex, [1816] Vol. XXIX, fol. 459.

POOLL, HEMY-BATTEN-POOLL (late LANGFORD), Robert Pooll, of Frome, Timsbury, and Road, co. Somerset, 1871, Vol. LVIII, fol. 12. (Berry's Suppl.)

POORE, ..., of Rushall and Enford, Wilts., [1795] Vol. XIX, fol. 107.

„ (DYKE) Edward, of Syrencot, Wilts., [1804] Vol. XXII, fol. 397. Quarterly Arms, fol. 401.

„ . . . ., of Grove, Isle of Wight, and Portsmouth, Hampsh., [1817] Vol. XXX, fol. 173.

POORE after COLLINS, George. Quarterly Arms, [1818] Vol. XXX, fol. 391.

POPE, Edward, D.D., of London, Archdeacon of Jamaica, [1842] Vol. XLVI, fol. 222.

„ J. B., Bar.-at-Law, of the Middle Temple, London, 1895,* Vol. LXVIII, fol. 255.

POPHAM after LEYBORNE (Brig.-Gen. Edward William, Isle of Grenada), of Littlecot, Wilts., [1804] Vol. XXIII, fol. 107 ; Quarterly Arms, fol. 109.

„ after WHITE, ..., of Shanklin, Isle of Wight, Wootton and Kitehill, Hampsh., [1852 ?] Vol. L, fol. 271.

POPPLE, John, of Laneham, co. Nottingham, 11 July 1775, Vol. XIII, fol. 103.

PORCELLI-CUST, A. R. C., of London, and the Isle of Wight (died 1897), 1894, Vol. LXVII, fol. 296.

PORCH, late REEVES, ..., of Edgarley, Glastonbury, co. Somerset, [1830] Vol. XXXVIII, fol. 148.

PORCHER, Josias du Pré, of Winslade House, co. Devon, [1818] Vol. XXXI, fol. 105.

PORCHESTER, Baron [17 Oct. 1780] (HERBERT) [Earl of Carnarvon, 3 July 1793]. ? Supporters, E. of CARNARVON, [1780] Vol. XIV, fol. 267.

PORRITT, William Henry, of Armley, Leeds, co. York [1853] Vol. L, fol. 300.

PORTAL, John, s. of Joseph, of Freefolk House, Hampsh., [1822] Vol. XXXIII, fol. 292.

„ R. B., of York Road, West Norwood, co. Surrey, 1891, Vol. LXVI, fol. 159.

PORTER, late WALSH, ..., of London, and Ireland. (Match), [1783] Vol. XV, fol. 235.

PORTER, ..., of Stansted Bury, co. Hertf., [1796] Vol. XIX, fol. 334.

PORTER, late MACNISH, ..., of Scotland, [1804] Vol. XXIII, fol. 70.

„ late CARSAN, ..., of South Carolina, America, [1808] Vol. XXIV, fol. 349.

PORTER to DE HOCHEFRIED, Lieut.-Gen. George, M.P., of Hampsh., and co. Sussex, [1819] Vol. XXXI, fol. 334.

PORTER after WARD, ..., B.A., of Henley-in-Arden, Bearley and Barford, co. Warw., [1825] Vol. XXXV, fol. 162. (Berry's Suppl.)

PORTER, late TAYLOR, Henry, Capt., 60th Foot, of Burlingham, co. Worc., 1878, Vol. LX, fol. 88.

PORTLAND, Earl of (William BENTINCK). Supporters, 3 July 1689, Vol. IV, fol. 49.

„ Duke of, K.G., BENTINCK after CAVENDISH, [5 Oct. 1801] Vol. XXI, fol. 237.

PORTMAN-SEYMOUR, ..., of co. Dorset and Somerset, [1727] Vol. VII, fol. 561.

PORTMAN, William, late BERKELEY [9 Geo. II (1735-1736)], of Orchard Portman, co. Somerset. Grant and Exemplification ; and HENRY, late SEYMOUR, a recital, 27 Aug. 1728, Vol. VIII, fol. 12.

„ Baron [27 Jan. 1837, Edward Berkeley Portman, of Orchard Portman, co. Somerset]. Supporters, [1837 ?] Vol. XLII, fol. 50.

PORTMAN [to Portman-] DALTON [1887], S[eymour] B[erkeley], of Sleningford
Park, Ripon, co. York, 1888 [1887], Vol. LXIV, fol. 132.
[PORTO RICO, Island of. Seal and Arms. William H. HUNT, Governor, 23 Dec.
1901. Geneal. Mag., V, p. 537.]
POTENGER, Richard, of Reading, Berks., 27 Aug. 1722, Vol. VII, fol. 88.
POTTER to EATON, ..., of Pole, co. Chester, [1789] Vol. XVII, fol. 147.
POTTER, William, of Liverpool, co. Lanc., [1833] Vol. XXXIX, fol. 197.
POTTER to HUGGETT, ..., of co. Kent, [1847 ?] Vol. XLVIII, fol. 240.
POTTER, Sir John, Knt. [10 Oct. 1851], Mayor of Manchester, of Buile Hill,
Eccles, co. Lanc., [1851] Vol. L, fol. 64.
POTTINGER, Maj.-Gen. Sir Henry, Bart. [27 April 1840], G.C.B. [2 Dec. 1842].
Supporters, [1845] Vol. XLVIII, fol. 10 [?].
POTTS, ..., of Broseley, Shropsh., 1864 [1862], Vol. LIV, fol. 260.
   „ William John, of Torquay, co. Devon ; Lincoln's Inn, London ; and Main-
house, co. Roxburgh, Scotland, [1864] Vol. LV, fol. 198.
POTTS-CHATTO, William John, of Torquay, co. Devon ; Lincoln's Inn, London ;
and Mainhouse, co. Roxburgh, Scotland, [1864] Vol. LV, fol. 216.
POULETT (BUNCOMBE-) before THOMSON [?], of Roehampton and Waverley Abbey,
co. Surrey, and Goathurst, co. Somerset, [1814] Vol. XXVIII, fol. 149.
POUNTAIN, ..., of Cowsleyfield House, St. Alkmund's, co. Derby, [1865] Vol.
LV, fol. 294.
POVAH, Rev. Alfred, of Church Street, Chelsea, co. Middx., 1885, Vol. LXIII,
fol. 43.
POWELL, late KYNASTON, ..., of Shrewsbury and Wortham, Shropsh., [1797]
Vol. XIX, fol. 351.
   „ late FLETCHER, ..., of Sutton, Shropsh., [1806] Vol. XXIII, fol. 382.
POWELL, Lieut.-Col. George, E.I.C.S., of co. Radnor, Wales, [1812] Vol.
XXVII, fol. 161.
POWELL, late ROBERTS, ..., of Quex House, Isle of Thanet, co. Kent, [1813]
Vol. XXVII, fol. 414.
   „ late GRANT, Capt., wife of. Arms impaled, [1815] Vol. XXVIII,
fol. 402.
POWELL, quartering [allowed] to [Thomas Baskerville ?] MYNORS-BASKERVILLE,
[1817] Vol. XXX, fol. 301.
POWELL-RODNEY, William, of Llanfihangel Court, co. Montgomery (s. of the
2nd Baron Rodney), [1841] Vol. XLV, fol. 93.
POWELL to GWYN, Thomas Gabriel Leonard Carew (minor), of Brecon and Glyn
Abbey, co. Carmarthen, Wales, [1841] Vol. XLV, fol. 95.
POWELL, ..., of Horton Hall, co. York, and Wigan, co. Lanc., [1851] Vol.
XLIX, fol. 427 ; [1852] Vol. L, fol. 237.
   „ . . . ., of Gaer Street, Woolos, and Coldra, Christchurch, co. Monmouth,
[1865 ?] Vol. LV, fol. 274.
POWELL after JEFFREYS, David, of Bryullis [Bryullis ?], co. Brecon, Wales,
[1867] Vol. LVI, fol. 250.
POWELL, Holyland, of Wath, co. York, [1870] Vol. LVII, fol. 226.
   „ Arthur, of Milton Heath, Dorking, co. Surrey, 1889,* Vol. LXV, fol. 1.
   „ George, of Tunbridge, co. Kent, 1882,* Vol. LXI, fol. 296. (Berry's Suppl.)
   „ Rev. Charles Thomas, of Worcester, s. of Edmund Henry, of Southampton,
18 . . ., Vol. LXXI, fol. . . . .
POWER, late NEWBERRY, Thomas, of Charlton, co. Kent, [1778 ?] Vol. XIV,
fol. 42.
POWER, Patrick, of Gifford's Hall, co. Suff., and Island of Teneriffe, 1819, Vol.
XXXI, fol. 313.
POWER to MANNOCKS, Patrick, of co. Suff., 1830, Vol. XXXVIII, fol. 130.
POWIS, Earl of [27 May 1748] (HERBERT). Supporters, [1748] Vol. IX,
fol. 282.
POWLES, late HARRISON, ..., of co. Durham. (Powles-Harrison-Powles.)
(Match), [1808] Vol. XXIV, fol. 340.

POWLES, John Diston Powles, of London, s. of Richard, of Lowestoft, co. Suff., and London ; (to Richard), of Stamford Hill, co. Middx., [1825] Vol. XXXV, fol. 113. (Berry's Suppl.)

POWLETT, [Maj.-Gen.] Sir Charles Armand, K.B. [1749]. Supporters, [1749] Vol. IX, fol. 322 ; [1753], fol. 472.

POWLETT, late ORDE [1795, Thomas, Baron BOLTON, 20 Oct. 1797, died 1807], Jean Mary Powlett, wife of. Impaled Arms, [1795] Vol. XIX, fol. 147.

POWLETT (ORDE-), Thomas, Baron BOLTON, [of Bolton Castle, co. York]. Supporters [William, if the reference is correct ?], [1819] Vol. XXXI, fol. 342.

POWLETT, late VANE [14 April 1813], William John Frederick, M.P., son of the Earl of DARLINGTON. (Match), [1812] Vol. XXVII, fol. 275.

POWLETT to VANE [18 Nov. 1864], William Henry, Duke of CLEVELAND [? William John Frederick, 3rd Duke, 4 Mar. 1864], [1864] Vol. LV, fol. 150.

POWLETT, late VANE, ... [18 Nov. 1864, Harry George, 4th Duke of Cleveland], [1864] Vol. LV, fol. 259.

POWLETT-WRIGHTE to BENYON DE BEAUVOIR, ... (Berks. and co. Essex), [1822] Vol. XXXIII, fol. 261.

POWLETT [WILLIAM-], late TOWNSHEND [8 Sept. 1823], Henry, 3rd Baron BAYNING, of Foxley, Berks., and Lainston House, Hampsh., 1823, Vol. XXXIV, fol. 184.

POWLETT, late WILLIAM-WALLOP, B. P. W., of Llandisil, co. Cardigan, Wales, and Lainston House, Hampsh., [1867] Vol. LVI, fol. 170.

POWNALL, John, of Saltfleetby, co. Linc., Sheriff co. Linc., 1772, Vol. XII, fol. 171.

„   . . . ., of Saltfleetby, co. Linc., and Everton House, co. Bedf., [1790] Vol. XVII, fol. 236.

„   . . . ., of Warmincham, co. Chester, [1814] Vol. XXVIII, fol. 146.

„   . . . ., of Plaistow and London, to the descendants of late Thomas Pownall, [1818] Vol. XXX, fol. 418. (Berry's Appx.)

„   William ? of Mayfield, nr. Wavertree, co. Lanc., 1833, Vol. XXXIX, fol. 312.

POWNALL after BEATY, Rev. Charles Colyton, M.A., of Clare Coll., Camb., of co. Bedf. and Sussex, [1835] Vol. XL, fol. 319.

POWNEY-PORCHER, Cecil du Pré, of Fyfield House, Hampsh., and Mildenhall, co. Suff., 1891, Vol. LXVIII, fols. 73 and 138.

POWYS, Baron LILFORD [26 Oct. 1797], of co. Northampton. Supporters, [1797] Vol. XX, fol. 64.

POWYS, late FEILDING [1832], Henry Wentworth, 2nd s. of Viscount Feilding [1st s. of Basil, 6th Earl of Denbigh], of Shropsh. (died s.p.), [1832] Vol. XXXIX, fol. 166.

POWYS-KECK, [John Henry Littelton Powys, to] 5th [the 2nd] s. of [the 2nd] Baron LILFORD, of co. Leic., [1861] Vol. LIV, fol. 102.

POYER, late GRIFFITH, ... (minor), of London, [1834] Vol. XL, fol. 193.

POYNDEN, ..., of St. Lawrence, Hampsh., and Clapham and Battersea, co. Surrey, [1827] Vol. XXXVI, fol. 206.

„   Thomas, Treasurer of Christ's Hospital, [1827] Vol. XXXVI, fol. 210.

POYNTER, John, of Lincoln's Inn, London, [1694] Vol. IV, fol. 161.

POYNTZ, Adm. [Stephen ?], of Havant and Bedhampton, Hampsh., [1842] Vol. XLVI, fol. 89.

POYSER, Charles, of St. Michael, Crooked Lane, London, and Worthenbury, co. Flint, Wales, 1772, Vol. XII, fol. 133. (Berry.)

PRAED to TYRINGHAM, ..., of Tyringham, Bucks., and Trevethre, Lelant, co. Cornw., [1859] Vol. LIII, fol. 204.

PRATT, Maj.-Gen. Sir Thomas Simson, K.C.B. [1861], [1862] Vol. LIV, fol. 326.

„   B., of Brynderwen, Meindre, co. Monmouth, [1891] Vol. LXVI, fol. 198.

„   . . . ., Baron CAMDEN [17 July 1765]. Supporters, [1765], Vol. XI, fol. 97.

„   . . . ., [2nd ?] Earl CAMDEN. Crest of JEFFREYS, [1799] Vol. XX, fol. 361.

PRATT, ..., of co. Lanc., and Delph, co. Staff. (*See* BOURNE.) [1816] Vol. XXIX, fol. 286.

PRENTICE, Thomas Angustus, of Armagh, s. of George, s. of James, Lieut., 25th Foot, by Sir J. B. BURKE, Ulster King of Arms, with remainder to the descendants of his grandfather James, 23 Aug. 1890. (Misc. G. et H., 2nd S., IV. p. 216.) (Crisp, I, p. 148.)

PRESCOTT-DECIE, Richard, Capt., R.E., of co. Essex, 1880, Vol. LX, fol. 354.

PRESCOTT, Sir . . . ., Bart., M.R.C.S., of London, 4 April 1882,* Vol. LXI, fol. 261.

PRESCOTT-WESTCAR, C. W., of Stroud Park, Herne, co. Kent, 1882, Vol. LXI, fol. 351.

PRESS, Mary (dau. of William), Lady HENNIKER. Escutcheon of pretence, 8 Jan. 1814, Vol. XXVIII, fol. 1.

PREST, William, and ELSWORTH, his wife, of co. York. Escutcheon of pretence, [1790] Vol. XVII, fol. 202.

„ Edward, of co. York, 23 July 1823, Vol. XXXIV, fol. 104. (Berry's App.)

PRESTON, ..., wife of NISBET, nat. dau. of Col., E.I.C.S., [1804] Vol. XXII, fol. 453.

PRESTON, late HULTON, Thomas, s. of Henry Hulton, of co. Norf., and Hampsh., [1805] Vol. XXIII, fol. 144.

PRESTON, Capt., R.N. (reputed s. of Sir Robert), of Valleyfield, co. Perth, Scotland, [1811] Vol. XXVII, fol. 31.

PRESTON to JERMY, ..., of co. Norf., [1838] Vol. XLIII, fol. 165.

PRETOR to PINNEY, John, of co. Dorset, and of the Isle of Nevis, 18 April 1776, Vol. XIII, fol. 181.

PRETOR-PINNEY, William, of Somerton Erleigh, co. Somerset, 1887 [1877 ?], Vol. LX, fol. 56. (Burke's Suppl.)

„ -PINNEY, Frederick Wake, of The Grange, and John Charles, of Curry Rivel, co. Somerset (cousins of William) of The Grange, &c., [1877] Vol. LX, fol. 58. (Burke's Suppl.)

PRETOR, late GILL, ..., of Sherborne, co. Dorset, [1812] Vol. XXVII, fol. 269.

PREVOST to MACKEY, ..., of London. (Match), 27 Sept. 1775, Vol. XIII, fol. 125.

PREVOST, Maj.-Gen. [George], of Greenhill Grove, co. Hertf., and Governor, Isle of Jamaica [?], [1805] Vol. XXIII, fol. 272.

„ Lieut.-Gen. [Sir George], Bart. [6 Dec. 1805] (decd. [1816]). Supporters to widow and son, [1817] Vol. XXX, fol. 124.

PRICE, Jane Turner, dau. of William Price. (*See* TURNER.) [1753] Vol. IX, fol. 434.

„ Charles, of Rose Hall, Jamaica, 13 Aug. 1766,* Vol. XI, fol. 182. (Berry.)

„ Richard, late WATKIN, 1780 [1777], Vol. XIV, fol. 10.

PRICE, late HIGGINBOTHAM, James, of Rost, nr. Radnor, Wales. (Match.) [1781] Vol. XIV, fol. 300.

PRICE, now CLARKE, ... (wife of), of Hampsh. Quarterly Arms, [1787] Vol. XVI, fol. 241.

PRICE, ..., of Shrewsbury, Shropsh., and Windsor St. Annes (? Jamaica), [1791] Vol. XVII, fol. 422.

„ Benjamin (of Windsor), late GURDON, of Bucks., [1808] Vol. XXIV, fol. 456.

PRICE to PULESTON, Lieut.-Col. . . . ., of Emrol and Bryn-y-Pys, co. Flint, Wales, [1812] Vol. XXVII, fol. 132.

PRICE, ..., of co. Glouc., [1818] Vol. XXXI, fol. 134.

„ . . . ., of co. Glouc.; Warham, nr. Hereford ; and Heywood Lodge, [Berks. ?], [1824] Vol. XXXIV, fol. 316.

„ . . . ., of Craven Street, Westminster, [1846] Vol. XLVIII, fol. 146.

„ Andrew (afterwards FOUNTAINE), for Brigge Price, s. of Capt. William Price, who mar. Elizabeth, only dau. of Col. Edward CLENT, of co. Norf. (Fountaine Coat), 1870, Vol. LVII, fol. 250.

PRICE, John or Andrew ?, of co. Norf. (Price quartering).   1874, Vol. LIX,
          fol. 38.
   „   Andrew Green Price, of Wales, [1874] Vol. LVIII, fol. 304.
PRICE to RUGGE-PRICE, ..., of Spring Grove, Richmond, co. Surrey, [1874]
          Vol. LVIII, fol. 338.
PRICE, John, of Amiens, France, 1878, Vol. LX, fol. 188.   (Berry's Suppl.)
   „   Lewis Richard, of co. Middx., and Marrington Hall, Chirbury, Shropsh.,
          s. of Stafford, of Hendon, co. Middx. (decd.), 1880, Vol. LX, fol. 334.
          (Berry's Suppl.)
PRICE to PRICE DAVIES, S. D. (minor), of co. Middx., and Marrington Hall,
          Chirbury, Shropsh. ; Stafford, Hugh Arthur L., Llewellyn A. E., and
          dau. Grace, children of Lewis, 1880, Vol. LX, fol. 350.   (Berry's
          Suppl.)
PRICE, H. J. J., of Glynllach, Ystradgynlais, co. Brecon, 1893,* Vol. LXVII,
          fol. 239.   (Crisp, II, p. 159.)
PRICE-DENT, Maj.-Gen. R. H., of The Manor House, Hallaton, co. Leic., 1885,
          Vol. LXIII, fol. 79.
PRICE-FOTHERGILL, Dame Isabella Elizabeth, 1895, Vol. LXVIII, fol. 307.
PRICHARD to CROFT, ..., of co. Somerset, [1824] Vol. XXXV, fol. 65.
PRIDEAUX-BRUNE, Rev. Charles, of co. Cornw. and Devon.   Quarterly Arms,
          1799, Vol. XX, fol. 346.   (Crisp, II, p. 98.)
PRIDHAM, ..., of St. Andrew, Plymouth, co. Devon, [1843] Vol. XLVII,
          fol. 41.
PRIESTLEY, Sir William Overend, Knt. [11 Aug. 1893], M.D., of Sherrards,
          Welwyn, co. Hertf., and London, 1895,* Vol. LXVIII, fol. 257.
PRIME, Samuel, of Whitton, Twickenham, co. Middx., [1797] Vol. XIX, fol. 408.
PRING, Dr. J. H., of Ivedon, Awliscombe, co. Devon, and Elmfield, Taunton,
          co. Somerset, 1884, Vol. LXII, fol. 228.
PRINGLE to HUGHES, ..., of Middleton Hall, Ilderton, co. Northumberland,
          [1835] Vol. XL, fol. 338.
PRINGLE, Alexander, of Whytbank, co. Selkirk, Scotland, by Tytler, Lyon King
          of Arms Depute, 18 Nov. 1828.   (Misc. G. et H., New S., IV, p. 189.)
PRINN after HUNT, ..., of co. Glouc.   Quarterly Arms, [1804] Vol. XXII,
          fol. 449 ; alteration of Hunt crest, [1804] Vol. XXII, fol. 451.
PRINN, late PROWSE, ..., of Charlton Park, co. Glouc., and Yeovil, co.
          Somerset, [1825] Vol. XXXV, fol. 313.
   „   late PROWSE, ..., of Charlton Park, co. Glouc., and Yeovil, co. Somerset,
          [1841] Vol. XLV, fol. 73 ?
PRINSEP after LEVETT, ..., of co. Staff., [1835] Vol. XLI, fol. 61.
PRIOR, Hon. Thomas H. Murray, late Postmaster-General, Queensland, M.L.C.
          (s. of Col. Thomas, M.P., served at Waterloo), 18 . . ., Vol. LXXI, fol. . . . .
PRITCHARD, now PARRY, ..., of Wales, [1787] Vol. XVI, fol. 300.
PRITCHARD, ..., of Trelech, co. Carmarthen, Wales, [1788] Vol. XVII, fol. 107.
PRITCHARD to SERGISON (S[ergison], wife of), of Cuckfield, co. Sussex, [1812]
          Vol. XXVII, fol. 171.
PRITCHARD, Sarah, 1711 (Stowe MS. 706).
   „   . . . ., of Broseley and Sutton Maddock, Shropsh., [1838] Vol. XLIII,
          fol. 38.
   „   . . . ., of Camberwell, co. Surrey, [1859] Vol. LIII, fol. 168.
PRITZLER, Maj.-Gen. Sir Theophilus, K.C.B. [3 Dec. 1822], of London, [1822]
          Vol. XXXIII, fol. 348.
PROBY to JERMY, Henry Francis, of Leghorn, Italy.   Quarterly Arms, [1784]
          Vol. XV, fol. 363.
PROBYN-NEWLAND, ..., formerly HOPKINS, of co. Glouc. (Match), [1734]
          Vol. VIII, fol. 187.   (See Misc. G. et H., 2nd S., III, p. 308, and
          Crisp.)
PROBYN, Lieut.-Col. Clifford, of 55, Grosvenor Street, London, 1898, Vol. LXX,
          fol. 225.

PROCTER to WALLER, Nicholas (minor), of Holmhead, Ingleton and Masongill, co. York, [1816] Vol. XXX, fol. 25.

PROCTER, late DEALTRY, Catherine, of co. Camb., 1847, Vol. XLVIII, fol. 283.

„ (late COLEMAN), Edward Bernard, only s. of Edward BERNARD-COLEMAN, of Wales, and Shropsh., 1879, Vol. LX, fol. 271.   (? Berry.)

PROCTOR, Sir William [Beauchamp], Bart., of co. Norf., 1761, Vol. X, fol. 304. K.B. [1761].   Supporters, fol. 313.

PRODGERS, Edwin, B.D. (Oxf.), of Ludlow, Shropsh. ; co. Hertf. ; and Wilts., [1831] Vol. XXXVIII, fol. 185.

PROSSER (-WEGG), late HAGGITT, Francis Richard, of co. Hereford ; Belmont, co. Durham ; and co. Oxf., [1849] Vol. XLIX, fol. 200.

PROTHEROE after DAVIS, ..., of co. Dorset and Glouc., [1844 ?] Vol. XLVII, fol. 301.

PROWER, John Elton (s. of John), of Purton, Wilts., 18 . . ., Vol. LXXI, fol. . . . .

PROWSE to PRINN, ..., of co. Glouc. and Somerset, [1825] Vol. XXXV, fol. 313.

PRUDHOE, Baron [27 Nov. 1816], Algernon Percy.   Supporters, [1816] Vol. XXX, fol. 44.

PRUEN, Rev. . . . ., of Cheltenham, co. Glouc. ; Dunsley, co. Staff. ; and Fladbury, co. Worc., [1820] Vol. XXXII, fols. 5 and 9.

PRUST, late HAMLYN, ..., of co. Devon, [1808] Vol. XXIV, fol. 426.

PRYCE, late BRUCE, John (now Bruce Price), of Wales, 1837, Vol. XLII, fols. 185, 187 and 188.

PRYCE-HUMPHREYS to DAVENPORT, Rear-Adm. Sir Salusbury, of co. Chester, [1838] Vol. XLIII, fol. 20.

PRYCE-JONES (see Jones), [1888] Vol. LXIV, fol. 224.

PRYER, Samuel, of Gray's Inn, London, [1809] Vol. XXV, fol. 225.

PRYOR, ... (Spr.), of Clay Hall, Walken Baldock, co. Hertf., [1872] Vol. LVIII, fol. 150.

PRYSE, late LOVEDEN, Pryse, of co. Oxf.   Quarterly Arms, [1798] Vol. XX, fol. 134.

PRYSE to LOVEDEN, Pryse, M.P., of Berks., and Wales, [1849] Vol. XLIX, fol. 184.

PRYSE, late LOVEDEN, Sir Pryse, Bart., of Wales, 1863, Vol. LV, fol. 90.

PRYSE to WEBLEY-PARRY, Edward John, [1893] Vol. LXVII, fol. 129.

PRYSE, H. L. Vanneck, of Llanbadarnffynydd, Penybont, co. Radnor, Wales, 1895, Vol. LXIX, fol. 7.

PUDSEY, late ASTON (Thomas Peach Pudsey, formerly Aston), of co. Staff. (died s.p.), [1807] Vol. XXIV, fol. 203.

„ late ASTON, John, of Seisdon, Tysall, co. Staff., died s.p., [1847] Vol. XLVIII, fol. 269.

PUDSEY after ASTON, George Pudsey, of Seisdon, Tysall, co. Staff., and Stoddesdon, Shropsh., [1861] Vol. LIV, fol. 232.

PUGET, ..., of Totteridge, co. Hertf., Director, Bank of England, [1803] Vol. XXII, fol. 130.

„ Peter, C.B., Post-Capt., R.N. (afterwards Adm.), and ELRINGTON, his wife, [1820], Vol. XXXII, fols. 151 and 152.

PUGH, Evan, Alderman of London, of Llangadran, co. Montgomery, Wales, 31 Oct. 1777, Vol. XIV, fol. 3.

PUGH, late EVANS, L. P., M.A., Oxf., of Lincoln's Inn, London, and Wales, [1868] Vol. LVII, fol. 125.

PUGH-LOVELL, Mrs., of Llanerclydd, 1882,° Vol. LXI, fol. 357 (see Berry's Suppl.).

„ -LOVELL, P. A. D. A., of Welshpool, co. Montgomery, Wales, 1882, Vol. LXI, fol. 363 (see Berry's Suppl.).

PUJOLAS, Henry, Bluemantle Pursuivant of Arms, of St. Martin's-in-the-Fields, London, 1762, Vol. X, fol. 430.   (Berry.)

PULESTON, late PRICE [8 Oct. 1812], Lieut.-Col. [Richard] (*cr.* a Bart. [2 Nov. 1813], extinct 1895) [*see* next name], [1812] Vol. XXVII, fol. 132.

PULESTON, Sir Richard, Bart., of Emral, co. Flint, Wales. Crest of Augmentation for reception of Prince of Wales in Wales [9 Sept. 1806], 1806, Vol. XXIX [XXIV ?], fol. 75.

PULFORD, ..., of Thames Ditton, co. Surrey, [1865] Vol. LVI, fol. 15.

PULLEINE (*see* COLLINGWOOD), ..., of Carleton Hall. Match, [1816] Vol. XXX, fol. 59.

PULLER (GILES), ..., of Youngsbury, co. Hertf., [1872] Vol. LVIII, fol. 128.

„ (GILES), ..., of Youngsbury, co. Hertf. Quarterly, Giles and Puller, [1872] Vol. LVIII, fol. 130.

PULLEY, ..., of Hackney and Shoreditch, co. Middx., [1818] Vol. XXX, fol. 396.

PULMAN, ..., of Parliament Street, Westminster, [1822] Vol. XXXIII, fol. 157.

PULSE, James, of Westminster (only s. of Daniel, late of St. Anne's, Westminster, decd.), 30 May 1720, Vol. VI, fol. 414 ; Add. MS. 14,830, fol. 111.

PULTENEY, Earl of BATH [14 July 1742]. Supporters, [1742] Vol. IX, fol. 67.

„ Baroness [Bath, 26 July 1792]. Supporters, [1793] Vol. XVIII, fol. 203.

PULTENEY, late MURRAY, Baroness, wife of, [1794] Vol. XVIII, fol. 373. [Sir James Murray, Bart., husband of the Baroness Bath, assumed the surname of Pulteney (Murray-Pulteney), 1794.]

„ late FAWCETT, ..., of co. Middx. Impaled Arms, [1813] Vol. XXVII, fol. 351.

PUNCHARD, Elgood George, D.D., Vicar of Christ Church, Luton, co. Bedf., s. of John Elgood [Punchard], of Framlingham, co. Suff., 1897, Vol. LXX, fol. 18.

PUNCHON, late BUCKLE, ..., of Killingworth Cottage, co. Northumberland, 1823, Vol. XXXIV, fol. 124.

PURCELL to FITZGERALD, of co. Lanc., Suff., Northampton, and Ireland, [1818] Vol. XXXI, fol. 69.

PURCHON, Thomas, of Leeds, co. York, [1845] Vol. XLVII, fol. 387. (Her. Reg., p. 3.)

PUREFOY before JERVOISE, ..., of Hampsh., Bucks. and Wilts., [1792] Vol. XVIII, fol. 67 ; [1793] fol. 212 ; [1795] fol. 435.

PUREFOY-PUREFOY, Richard (formerly FITZGERALD), of Shalston Manor, Bucks., 18 . . ., Vol. LXXI, fol. . . . .

PURLING, John, of Hatton Garden, London, and East Indies, 1759, Vol. X, fol. 172. (Berry.)

PURNELL, John, of Stancombe, Wickselm and Dursley, co. Glouc., 1768, Vol. XI, fol. 264. (Berry.)

„ . . . ., of Stancombe, Wickselm and Dursley, co. Glouc., [1790] Vol. XVII, fol. 246.

PURNELL, late COOPER, Purnell Bransby Cooper-Purnell (minor), of Stancombe Park, co. Glouc., 1805, Vol. XXIII, fol. 125.

„ late HOOPER, Robert John, of co. Glouc. and Dorset, [1826] Vol. XXXVI, fol. 119.

PURRIER, ..., of Kingston and Croydon, co. Surrey, [1801] Vol. XXI, fol. 160.

PURVIS, Charles, of Darsham, co. Suff., May 1779, Vol. XIV, fol. 137. (Berry.)

PURVIS to EYRE, ... (Eyre, wife of), of Wilts., [1795] Vol. XIX, fol. 99.

„ to ATKINSON, ..., of co. Northumberland, [1828] Vol. XXXVII, fol. 146.

PUTNAM, ..., of Massachusets Bay, New England ; Halifax, Nova Scotia ; and New Brunswick, [1804] Vol. XXII, fol. 351.

PYBUS, John, of Thirsk, co. York, and Coromandel Coast (afterwards of Greenhill, co. Glouc., and Barnet, co. Hertf.), 1768, Vol. XI, fol. 292. (Berry.)

„ John, s. of John, of Thirsk, co. York. Escutcheon of pretence, bearing SMALL quartering NEWMAN, 1794 [1795], Vol. XIX, fol. 158.

PYCROFT, ..., of Burton-on-Trent and Rolleston, co. Staff., [1797] Vol. XIX, fol. 412.

PYDDOKE, late WHATELEY, ... M.A., of Badgworth, co. Glouc., and Handsworth, co. Staff., [1847] Vol. XLVIII, fol. 375.

PYE before BENNET, William Bathurst, of Wilts., LEGH, wife of. Quarterly Arms, [1802] Vol. XXI, fol. 427.

PYE, late ALLINGTON, ..., of co. Linc., [1828] Vol. XXXVII, fol. 203.

   ,, late WOOLCOCK, ... (reputed son), of Boconnoc and Blisland, co. Cornw. ([of] Stoke Damerell, co. Devon), [1846] Vol. XLVIII, fol. 173.

PYKE, Rev. . . . ., of Parracombe and Swimbridge, co. Devon, [1860] Vol. LIII, fol. 342.

PYKE-NOTT, ..., of Parracombe and Swimbridge, co. Devon, [1863] Vol. LV, fol. 106.

PYKE, Joseph, of Devonshire Place House, Portland Place, London, 1891, Vol. LXVI, fol. 59.

   ,, Joseph, of Winckley Square, Preston, 1884, Vol. LXII, fol. 245. (Berry's Suppl.)

PYM to READING, ..., of Hasells, Sandy, co. Bedf., and Harpenden, co. Hertf., [1870] Vol. LVII, fol. 270.

PYMAN, ..., of Raithwaite Hall, and Whitby, co. York, [1872] Vol. LVIII, fol. 166.

PYMAR, ..., of Ensbury, co. Dorset, [1832] Vol. XXXIX, fol. 130.

PYNDAR to LYGON [William], Baron BEAUCHAMP [26 Feb. 1806], of co. Worc. Arms and Supporters, [1806] Vol. XXIII, fol. 332.

PYOTT, ..., of Streethay, Lichfield, co. Staff., [1815] Vol. XXVIII, fol. 414.

PYTCHES to REVETT, ..., (minor), of Groton House, and Brandeston Hall, co. Suff., [1837] Vol. XLII, fol. 177.

PYTCHES, Julia, dau. and co-h. of Sir Abraham, of Streatham, co. Surrey. Quarterly with HASSELL. Escutcheon of pretence to JOLLEFFE, 1832-3, Vol. XXXIX, fol. . . . .

Q

QUAIN, Sir [?] Richard, F.R.S. [afterwards Sir Richard, Bart., 1891], of the Middle Temple, London, s. of John, [1859] Vol. LIII, fol. 105. (Berry's Suppl.)

QUANTOCK, ..., of Norton-sub-Hampden and South Petherton, co. Somerset. (Match), [1810] Vol. XXV, fol. 310.

QUARRIER, ..., M.D., of Little Green, nr. Gosport, Hampsh., and Mussleburgh, Scotland, [1819] Vol. XXXI, fol. 234.

QUAYLE, John, of Crogga, Kirk Santon, Isle of Man, 1892,* Vol. LXVI, fol. 293. (Crisp, II, p. 40.)

QUEBEC, I . . . . MOUNTAIN, D.D., Bp. of, of Reedham and Thwaits Hall, co. Norf., [1793] Vol. XVIII, fol. 250.

QUEENSBERRY, Marquis of, his nephew from [William] DOUGLAS to IRVINE [Roy. Lic., 8 May 1845], [1845] Vol. XLVII, fol. 418.

QUILLER, Sir William Cuthbert, Bart., of Bawdsey Manor, Woodbridge, co. Suff., 1897, Vol. LXIX, fol. 329.

QUIN after WYNDHAM, ..., of Dunraven Castle, co. Glamorgan, Wales; Clearwell Court, co. Glouc.; and Adare, co. Limerick, Ireland, [1815] Vol. XXVIII, fol. 322.

R

RABAN, ..., Lieut.-Col., Bombay S. C., C.B., of London, [1823] Vol. XXXIV, fol. 188.

RABETT, Reginald, of Bramfield Hall (High Sheriff, 1737), co. Suff., 13 April 1737, Vol. VIII, fol. 209[b].

   ,, ..., of Bramfield Hall, co. Suff., 1810, Vol. XXVI, fol. 19.

RACKHAM, Rev. Robert Alfred, Fellow of Jesus Coll., Cambridge, Rector of Whatfield, co. Suff., [1865] Vol. LVI, fol. 55.

RADCLIFFE, ..., of St. Thomas, Exeter, co. Devon. (*See* FURSMAN and WYATT). [1742] Vol. IX, fol. 60.

RADCLIFF, Jasper, of Courthall-in-Hockworthy, co. Devon, 20 June 1693, Vol. IV, fol. 142.

„ Alexander, of Ordsall, co. Lanc. Arms, Atchievement, [1707] Vol. V, fol. 231.

RADCLIFFE, late FARNABY, ..., of Keppington, co. Kent. Quarterly Arms [1784] Vol. XV, fol. 265.

RADCLIFFE, ..., of London, and Calcutta, sons of MUNT, relict of Radcliffe, [1798] Vol. XX, fol. 245.

RADCLIFFE after DELMÉ, ..., CLARKE, wife of (of co. Hertf.). Quarterly Arms, [1803] Vol. XXII, fol. 270.

RADCLIFFE, late PICKFORD, Joseph, of Royton, co. Lanc., and Milnsbridge, co. York, [1809] Vol. XXV, fol. 215.

RADCLIFFE, Sir David, [Knt., 11 May 1886, then] Mayor of Liverpool, of Formby Hall, Walton-on-the-Hill, co. Lanc., 1884, Vol. LXII, fol. 337.

RADFORD-NORCOP, Alexander William, of Belton Hall, Market Drayton, Shropsh., [1862] Vol. LIV, fol. 278.

RADFORD, Herbert George (s. of Daniel), of East Sheen, co. Surrey, 18 . . ., Vol. LXXI, fol. . . . .

RADSTOCK, Baroness, [Cornelia Jacoba] VAN LENNEP (of Smyrna), wife of Baron Waldegrave, [the Hon. William Waldegrave, Baron Radstock ?]. Arms impaled, [1800] Vol. XXI, fol. 104.

RAE to HARVEY, ..., of the Island of Grenada. (Match), [1791] Vol. XVII, fol. 424.

„ to HARVEY, ... (reputed dau.), wife of LEE, now Harvey, of Scotland, [1820] Vol. XXXII, fol. 235.

RAFFLES, Sir Thomas Stamford, Knt. [29 May 1817], Lieut.-Gov., Island of Java, [1817] Vol. XXX, fol. 308.

„ Rev. Thomas, D.D., LL.D., of Liverpool, co. Lanc., and Hendon, Spitalfields and Highwood, co. Middx., [1841] Vol. XLV, fol. 223.

RAGLAN, Baron [20 Oct. 1852, Lieut.-Gen. Fitzroy James Henry Somerset], G.C.B. [1847]. Supporters, [1852] Vol. L, fol. 246.

RAIKES, Thomas, of St. Botolph, Bishopsgate, London, and to the descendants of his grandfather Timothy, 28 Aug. 1783,* Vol. XV, fol. 201.

RAILTON, Thomas, of Carlisle, co. Cumberland, 1 Aug. 1733, Vol. VIII, fol. 171ᵃ.

RAINE, J. T., of Wedford and Lemington, co. Glouc., and Battisford [co. Suff. ?], [1814] Vol. XXVIII, fol. 208.

RAINIER, Peter, C.B., Capt., R.N., with special remainder. (Match), 1810, Vol. XXVI, fol. 152.

„ Peter, Post-Capt., R.N., C.B., of Reading, [Berks. ?], and Sandwich, co. Kent, 1816, Vol. XXIX, fol. 431.

„ . . . . Crest to descendants of grandfather, 1816, Vol. XXIX, fol. 433.

RAINS, ..., of Tunbridge Wells, co. Kent, and London, [1834] Vol. XL, fol. 185.

RALLI, Thomas Stephen, Greek Consul-General, London (naturalized British subject), [1855] Vol. LI, fol. 335.

RAMMS, Nicholas, of St. James, co. Middx., and Switzerland, June 1772, Vol. XII, fol. 178. (Berry.)

RAMSAY before KARR, ..., late Gov. of Bombay, of Scotland, and co. Surrey, [1795] Vol. XIX, fol. 5.

RAMSAY-FAIRFAX-LUCY, H. W. (s. of Bart.), of Scotland, and co. Warw., 1892, Vol. LXVII, fol. 49.

RAMSAY, late BURNETT, Sir Alexander, Bart., of Scotland, 1806, Vol. XXIV, fol. 5.

RAMSBOTTOM, ..., of Milton, co. York, and Windsor and Clewer, Berks., [1809] Vol. XXV, fol. 206.

RAMSDEN, ..., of Osberton, co. Nottingham. (*See* John SMYTH.) (Match.) [1777] Vol. XIII, fol. 259.

RAMSDEN to FLETCHER, ... (reputed son), of co. Lanc. and Chester, [1843] Vol. XLVI, fol. 393.

RAMSDEN, ? Sir James [Knt., 25 June 1872], Mayor of Barrow, of Abbotswood, Barrow-in-Furness, co. Lanc., [1871 ?] Vol. LVII, fol. 334. (Berry's Suppl.)

„ Richard, of Chadwick Manor, Knowle, co. Warw., 28 Feb. 1899, Vol. LXX, fol. 340.

RAMSKILL, ..., of Lofthouse Hall, Wakefield, co. York, [1860] Vol. LIII, fol. 322.

RANCLIFFE, Baron [3 Oct. 1795] (PARKYNS), of co. Nottingham, [1797] Vol. XIX, fol. 394 [? 194].

RANDALL, James, of Lincoln's Inn, London, father of Bishop Randall, 1818, Vol. XXXI, fol. 147.

RANDLES, Edward, s. of John, of Worthen, Shropsh., and D'Urban, Port Natal, 1875, Vol. LIX, fol. 156.

RANELAGH, [? Charles], Earl of [? 4th Viscount, 1759] (JONES). (Match), [1717] Vol. VI, fol. 310.

RANKIN, James, M.P., of Bryngwyn, co. Hereford, 1884, Vol. LXII, fol. 297. (Berry's Suppl.)

RANKING, Surg.-Gen. J. L., of 30, Heath Terrace, Leamington, co. Warw., 1891,* Vol. LXVI, fol. 142.

RANNIE, ..., of Edinburgh. (*See* MIRTLE.) Match, [1768] Vol. XI, fol. 350.

RAPER, Richard, of Langthorne, co. York, and Henry, his brother ; Matthew, Citizen and Merchant of London, and Moses, his brother ; all grandsons of Richard, of Bordersby, co. York, 6 Feb. 170½, Vol. V, fol. 60 ; Add. MS. 14,831, fol. 165.

„ William, of Oundle, co. Northampton (s. of William, Rector of St. Margaret's, Westminster, s. of John, of Pontefract, co. York), 2 July 1720, Vol. VI, fol. 429 ; Add. MS. 14,831, fol. 150.

RAPER before HUNTON, John, B.A., of Londonderry, Burneston, co. York. Quarterly Arms, [1811] Vol. XXVI, fol. 420.

RAPER after LAMPLUGH, ..., of Lotherton, co. York, [1825] Vol. XXXV fol. 165 [*see* Burke].

„ after LAMPLUGH, J. L., of Lotherton, co. York, [1826] Vol. XXXV, fol. 337.

RAPHAEL, Alexander, of Ditton Lodge, Kingston-upon-Thames, co. Surrey, and the East Indies, [1832] Vol. XXXIX, fol. 158.

„ Henry Lewis (s. of Lewis), of 31, Portland Place, London, 1897, Vol. LXIX, fol. 211.

RATCLIFFE, ..., of Manchester, co. Lanc., [1810] Vol. XXVI, fol. 23.

„ Sir John, Knt. [15 June 1858], Mayor of Birmingham, co. Warw., of Wyddington, Birmingham, and to his youngest brother Charles, 7 Sept. 1850 [1858], Vol. LIII, fol. 6. (Crisp, III, p. 139.)

RATHBONE, William, J.P., of Green Bank, Liverpool, co. Lanc., [1841] Vol. XLV, fol. 258.

RATHMORE, Baron [1895, David Robert PLUNKET], of Ireland. Supporters, 1895, Vol. LXIX, fol. 11.

RATTON, Major J. J. L., of Cresswell Park, Blackheath, co. Kent, 1895, Vol. LXVIII, fol. 222. (Crisp, III, p. 158.)

„ Sr Jaques [of Lisbon, Portugal], exemplification from the Judge of Arms of the Nobility of France, 9 Dec. 1783. (Crisp, III, p. 160.)

RAVEN, ..., of Totnall Cottage, Leigh, co. Dorset, and Croydon, co. Surrey, [1845 ?] Vol. XLVIII, fol. 98.

RAVENSHAW, ..., of Bracknell, Richmond, co. Surrey, and Harley Street, London, [1850] Vol. XLIX, fol. 336.
RAVENSWORTH, [Baron, 29 June 1747 (extinct 1749), Sir Henry Liddell, 4th Bart.]. Supporters, [1748] Vol. IX, fol. 260.
  „ Baron [17 July 1821, Sir Thomas Henry Liddell, 6th Bart.]. Supporters, [1821] Vol. XXXII, fol. 355.
RAWDON, Baron [5 Mar. 1783, Hon Francis] Rawdon (of co. York). Crest and Supporters, [1783] Vol. XV, fol. 152.
  „ Baron [Hon Francis, assumed, by Lic., 10 Feb. 1790, the Name and Arms of] HASTINGS, [1790] Vol. XVII, fol. 198.
RAWLING to MADDISON, George, of co. Durham and Northumberland. (Match.) [1811] Vol. XXVII, fol. 37.
RAWLINSON to LINDOW, ..., of co. Lanc., [1792] Vol. XVIII, fol. 61.
RAWLINSON, Sir Henry Creswicke, Bart., of London, 1891,* Vol. LXVI, fol. 39.
  „ Rev. George, Canon of Canterbury, &c., 18 . . ., Vol. LXXI, fol. . . . .
RAWSON, Thomas, of Wardsend and West Don, Sheffield, co. York, 1817, Vol. XXX, fol. 151.
RAWSON, late ADAMS, Sir William, Knt. [11 May 1814], of London, and Ireland, [1825] Vol. XXXV, fols. 146 and 148.
RAWSON, John, of Undercliffe House, Bradford, co. York, 1875, Vol. LIX, fol. 165.
RAWSON-ACKROYD, John William, of The Grange, Dean, co. Bedf., [1875] Vol. LIX, fol. 171.
RAWSON, C., of Fern Bank, Petersfield, Hampsh., 1895,* Vol. LXVIII, fol. 210.
  „ H. Trafford, of Stowell Park, Marlborough, Wilts., and co. York, 1893, Vol. LXVI, fol. 342.
RAY, Richard, of Howleigh, co. Suff., and the Inner Temple, London. (Quarterly with WALKLATE), 8 Mar. 1770, Vol. XII, fols. 12 and 14. (Berry.) [Misc. G. et H., 3rd S., V, p. 219.]
RAY, late WHEELER, Herbert Reginald (minor), of Hyde Park Gardens, London, 1684, Vol. LV, fol. 190.
RAYDEN, John, of Oakleigh, Finsbury Park, London, 1886,* Vol. LXIII, fol. 233.
RAYLEIGH, Baroness [18 July 1821, dau. 1st Duke of Leinster], (of co. Essex). Supporters, [1821] Vol. XXXIII, fol. 7.
RAYMOND, Sir Jonathan, Knt. ? [20 Oct. 1679], Alderman of London. [Arms, 11 April 1687], Vol. III, fol. 312. [Misc. G. et H., 2nd S., II, p. 59.]
  „ [Sir Jemmet, mar. in 1687 Elizabeth, dau. and sole h. of Sir George Brown, Knt.]. Match, [1691] Vol. IV, fol. 89.
  „ Baron [15 Jan. 1731]. Supporters, [173?] Vol. VIII, fol. 102^h.
RAYMOND to BARKER, ..., of co. Glouc., [1788] Vol. XVII, fol. 99.
  „ to SYMONS, Thomas, of Moend, co. Hereford, and Boseley and Sibland, co. Glouc. (Match), [1797] Vol. XX, fol. 6.
RAYMOND, late BREACH, ..., of London. Quarterly Arms, [1808] Vol. XXV, fol. 14.
RAYNOR to BURTON, ..., of The Close, Lincoln, [1815] Vol. XXVIII, fol. 308.
RAYNOR, John, M.D., of Highbury, co. Middx., [1873] Vol. LVIII, fol. 222. (Berry's Suppl.)
RAYNSFORD to SHELDON, ..., of co. Worc., [1828] Vol. XXXVII, fol. 159.
  „ to EDWARDS, ..., of co. Bedf., and Lincoln's Inn, London, [1809] Vol. XXV, fol. 153.
READ, late RUDSTON, Thomas, M.A., of Sand Hutton and Hayton, co. York, 1803, Vol. XXII, fol. 44 ; Rudston-Read, [1806] Vol. XXIII, fol. 313.
READ to REVELL, ..., of Round Oak, Englefield Green, co. Surrey, [1821] Vol. XXXII, fol. 397.
READE, ..., of Holbrooke House, Sampford, co. Suff., and Madras. Quartering REVELL, [1835] Vol. XLI, fol. 118.
READ after CREWES, ..., of co. Chester and Staff., [1836] Vol. XLI, fol. 260.
READ, Henry, of Brooklands, co. Kent, 28 Aug. 1777, Vol. XIII, fol. . . . .

READE, late WAKEFIELD, ..., of Shipton Court, Shipton, Wychwood, co. Oxf., [1868] Vol. LVII, fol. 45.

READER, ..., of Stainforth, co. York. (*See* HOWARD.) (Match), [1773] Vol. XII, fol. 231.

READING (after PACKE), ..., of co. Leic., wife PACKE. Arms by authority of Act of Parliament, [1822] Vol. XXXIII. fol. 288.

[READING UNIVERSITY EXTENSION COLLEGE, Berks., 7 Aug. 1896. (Geneal. Mag., IV, p. 290.)]

READING, late PYM, Charles, of co. Bedf., [1870] Vol. LVII, fol. 270.

REASTON, Thomas, of Kingston-upon-Hull, co. York (s. of John, of Dringhoe, co. York), [1790] Vol. XVII, fol. 211.

REASTON-RODES, ..., M.A., of Barlborough, co. Derby, 1825, Vol. XXXV, fol. 315 (*see also* Rev. Cornelius HEATHCOTE, [1776] Vol XIII, fol. 227).

REAVELY, ..., of Aldgate, London, [1784] Vol. XV, fol. 251.

REBOW [John], of Colchester, co. Essex [10 April 1685], Vol. III, fol. 263. [Facsimile, Crisp, Notes, IX, p. 73.]

REBOW after SLATER [Francis (Major, 60th or Roy. Regt. of Foot) and Mary Hester], Rebow, his wife [late Mary Hester Rebow, eldest surviving dau. and co-heir of Isaac Martin Rebow Martin, late of] The Park, Wivenhoe, co. Essex [decd.] Quarterly, [4 May 1796] Vol. XIX, fol. 241. [Crisp, Notes, IX, pp. 73 and 74.]

„ after GURDON [John], of [Letton, co.] Norf. [mar. Dame Mary Martin Ormsby Rebow, widow of Sir Thomas Ormsby, of Cloghans, co. Mayo, Bart., decd., and only dau. and h. of Francis Slater-Rebow, of Wivenhoe, Essex, Lieut.-Gen. in the Army. Quarterly Arms, 16 Sept. 1835] Vol. XLI, fol. 113. [Crisp, Notes, IX, p. 75.]

RECKITT, Sir J., Bart., of Swanland Manor, North Ferriby, co. York, 1894, Vol. LXVIII, fol. 59.

REDE, late COOPER, Robert, of co. Norf., and Ashman's, co. Suff., [1822] Vol. XXXIII, fol. 338.

REDESDALE, Baron [15 Feb. 1802] (FREEMAN-MITFORD), of co. Glouc. and Northumberland. Supporters, [1802] Vol. XXI, fol. 297.

„ Baron, FREEMAN before MITFORD [28 Jan. 1809], of co. Glouc. Quarterly Arms and Augmentation to Supporters, [1809] Vol. XXV, fols. 112 and 115.

REDFEARN, Francis, of Lymm [? Lynn], co. Norf., and Middleton, co. York, [1796 ?] Vol. XIX, fol. 193.

REDWOOD, Theophilus, of London ; Llantwel-major, co. Glamorgan, Wales ; and Lawn Rhymmy and Bedwaltry, co. Monmouth ; to Lewis Redwood, of Orchard House, Boverton, co. Glamorgan, Wales, [1856] Vol. LII, fol. 38 [*see* Burke].

REED, William (s. of Sylvester, of York), 18 . . ., Vol. LXXI, fol. . . . .

„ . . . ., of Trevales, co. Cornw., [1787] Vol. XVI, fol. 307.

„ . . . ., AISKELL, wife of, of Cromer Hall, co. Norf. Arms to wife and descendants, [1811] Vol. XXVI, fol. 240.

„ . . . ., wife of Cresswell BAKER. Arms for Reed quarterly with Baker, [1840] Vol. XLIV, fols. 361 and 364.

REED to VERELST, Charles, of Aston, co. York, and Green Hayes, Claughton, co. Chester, [1851 ?] Vol. L, fol. 83.

REED, Sir E. J., J.P., of London ; Hextable, co. Kent ; and Wales, 1881, Vol. LXI, fol. 144. (Berry's Suppl.)

„ William, of 77, Onslow Gardens, London ; Brighton ; and The Warren, Lower Beeding, co. Sussex, 1896, Vol. LXIX, fol. 73.

REES, Evan, of Llanidloes, co. Montgomery, Wales, [1818] Vol. XXX, fol. 354.

REES-MOGG, ..., of Cholwell House, Cameley, Shropsh., and Brufton, Wick, co. Glamorgan, Wales, [1841] Vol. XLV, fol. 101. (Berry's Suppl.)

REES, D., of Llanelly, co. Carmarthen, Wales, and East London, Cape of Good Hope, 1891, Vol. LXVI, fol. 211.

REEVE, ..., of Hendens, nr. Maidenhead, Berks., [1794] Vol. XVIII, fol. 329.
  „   William, s. of William (-KEY, Jane, of Melton Mowbray, co. Leic., relict
    of William, of co. Leic.). Escutcheon of pretence over Reeve. Crest to
    descendants, [1807] Vol. XXIV, fol. 196.
REEVE-DELAPOLE [Roy. Lic., 5 Oct. 1838], Sir John George, Bart., of Berks. and
    Devon, [1838] Vol. XLIII, fol. 257.
REEVE, ..., of Wighton, co. Norf. [1840 ?], Vol. XLIV, fol. 202.
REEVE to BROOKE, of Wigton and Great Walsingham, co. Norf., [1840] Vol.
    XLIV, fol. 204.
REEVE-KING NEVILL, Henry, of The Hall, Ashby de la Launde, co. Linc., 1897,
    Vol. LXIX, fol. 297.
REEVES, John, of West Ham, co. Essex, Bencher of the Middle Temple, London,
    [1826] Vol. XXXV, fol. 347.
REEVES to PORCH, ..., of Edgarley, co. Somerset, [1830] Vol. XXXVIII,
    fol. 148.
REEVES, ..., of Glastonbury, co. Somerset, [1830] Vol. XXXVIII, fol. 146.
REID to BAILLIE, ..., of Jamaica, [1792] Vol. XVIII, fol. 85.
  „   to CALDECOT, ..., M.D., Caldecot formerly wife of, [1811] Vol. XXVI,
    fol. 211.
REID, Ewell, of Graystone Park, co. Dumfries, Scotland, [1823] Vol. XXXIV,
    fol. 166 or 161.
REID to FENWICK, ..., of co. Lanc., [1851] Vol. L, fols. 12 and 14.
REID-CUDDON, Rev. J. E., M.A., of Ashow Rectory, co. Warw., 1894, Vol.
    LXVIII, fol. 29.
RELFE, John, of Daventry, co. Northampton, Clerk Assistant, House of Lords,
    1693 [169⅔ ?], Vol. IV, fol. 127.
RELPH, ..., M.D., M.R.C.P., of London, and Wigton, co. Cumberland, [1801]
    Vol. XXI, fol. 132.
REMFRY, ..., of Truro, and Calcutta, [1841] Vol. XLV, fol. 262.
RENALS, Sir J. W., Bart., of London, 1895,* Vol. LXVIII, fol. 290.
RENDALL (late HOLDEN), Francis Shuttleworth, of co. Derby and Wilts., 1877,
    Vol. LIX, fol. 350. (Burke's Suppl.)
RENDEL, S., of Hatchlands, Guildford, co. Surrey, 1892,* Vol. LXVI, fol. 269.
    Baron Rendel, Supporters (1894), Vol. LXVIII, fol. 93.
RENEW, Peter, of London, and to the issue of his brother Hillary, decd., being an
    only daughter, 14 April 1715, Vol. VI, fol. 206 ; Stowe MS. 714, fol. 73 ;
    Add. MS. 14,830, fol. 175.
RENNIE after LUCAS, John, Capt., R.N., of co. Kent, and Scotland, [1833] Vol.
    XXXIX, fols. 271 and 273.
RENNY-TAILYOUR, ..., Capt., Bombay S.C., of Scotland, with designation of
    Borrowfield, co. Forfar, [1849] Vol. XLIX, fol. 252.
RENNY, George Henry, of co. Staff., 18 . . ., Vol. LXXI, fol. . . . .
RENTON, John T., of Bradston Brook, Shalford, co. Surrey, 1880,* Vol. LXI,
    fol. 81. (Berry's Suppl.)
RENWICK, Arthur, M.D., F.R.C.S., E., of Sydney, New South Wales, 1887, Vol.
    LXIV, fol. 86 (Knighted 25 June 1894).
REPINGTON after A'COURT, Rear-Adm. [Edward Henry], of co. Warw. [1847 ?]
    Vol. XLVIII, fol. 393. (Burke's Suppl.)
  „   after A'COURT, Lieut.-Gen. [Charles Ashe], C.B., [1855] Vol. LI, fol. 356.
    (Burke's Suppl.)
REVELL, Robert, of Carlingthwait, co. Derby, 25 Aug. 1712, Vol. VI, fol. 71.
REVELSTOKE, Baron (BARING). Supporters, 1885, Vol. LXIII, fol. 111.
REVETT, late PYTCHES, ... (minor), of co. Suff. [1837], Vol. XLII, fol. 177.
REYNAL, John James, of Lincoln's Inn, London ; Egginton, Leighton Buzzard,
    co. Bedf. ; and Montauban, High Languedoc, France, 3 Dec. 1737, Vol.
    VIII, fol. 226ᵇ. (Berry.)
REYNARD-COOKSON, ..., of Whitehill, co. Durham, [1873] Vol. LVIII,
    fol. 264.

REYNARDSON after BIRCH, Gen. Thomas, (Reynardson, wife of Lieut.-Col.), of co.
   Linc.   Quarterly Arms, 1812 [1811], Vol. XXVII, fol. 80.
REYNOLDS, Anthony, fined for Sheriff of London, 1706, and to his nephews
   Anthony and John, 22 May 1714, Vol. VI, fol. 154; Add. MS. 14,830,
   fol. 45.   (Berry.)
REYNOLDS to MORETON, Thomas, Baron DUCIE.   (Match.)   Supporters, 1771, Vol.
   XII, fol. 63.
REYNOLDS, Thomas, son of Baron DUCIE, of London, and co. Glouc., 1797, Vol. XX,
   fol. 73.
   „ . . . ., of Adisham, co. Kent.   (Match.)   [1809] Vol. XXV, fol. 276.
   „ . . . ., of Manchester, co. Lanc.   (See STUCKEY.)   [1810] Vol. XXV,
      fol. 351.
   „ . . . ., of Bank House, Wellington, Shropsh., [1815?] Vol. XXVIII,
      fol. 258.
   „ Capt., R.N., C.B., of Penair, co. Cornw., [1838] Vol. XLIII. fol. 123.
   „ Sir J. R., Bart., of Grosvenor Street, London (died s.p., 1896), 1895, Vol.
      LXVIII, fol. 170.
   „ William, of The Grove, Highgate, co. Middx., 1893,* Vol. LXVII, fol. 283.
REYNOUS, Isaac, of Westminster and Stanmore, co. Middx., and Penzenas,
   Languedoc, France, 1758. Vol. X, fol. 129.   (Berry.)
RHODES, Timothy, of Campsfield House, co. York. s. of Matthew, of Leeds,
   co. York, Merchant, 1807 [? 1817], Vol. XXX, fol. 270.
RHODES to DARWIN, Rev.? Francis, M.A., of co. Nottingham, [1850] Vol.
   XLIX, fol. 345.
RHODES, William Barnard, of Balby, co. York, and Epworth, co. Linc. [?] To
   William Barnard Rhodes, Robert Heaton Rhodes, and Joseph Rhodes,
   brothers, all of New Zealand.   [1865] Vol. LVI, fol. 19.
RHODES, late BAKER, Frederick Edward, of co. Devon, and Sussex (cr. Bart.,
   1882), 1879, Vol. LX. fol. 235.
RIBBLESDALE, Baron, [Thomas] LISTER, of co. York.   Escutcheon of pretence
   and Supporters, [1797] Vol. XX, fol. 77.   Day quartering, [1810] Vol.
   XXVI, fol. 12.
RIBTON, ..., of Cockermouth, co. Cumberland.   (See TIFFIN.)   [1770] Vol. XII,
   fol. 19.
RICARDE-SEAVER, F. J., Vice-Consul, of Gravesend, co. Kent (Rue Lafitte, Paris),
   1881, Vol. LXI, fol. 181.   (Berry's Suppl.)
RICARDO, ..., of Gatcombe Park, co. Glouc., and London, [1814] Vol. XXVIII,
   fol. 74.
RICE, Cecil, Baroness DINEVOR [1782, widow of George Rice].   Supporters,
   [1784] Vol. XV, fol. 277.
RICE to DE CARDONNEL [Roy. Lic., 21 May 1787], Cecil, Baroness DYNEVOR, of
   Wales, 1787, Vol. XVIII, fol. 209 [is 1793] [? 1787, Vol. XVI, fol. 209].
RICE, late DE CARDONNEL [4 Feb. 1817], George [Talbot], 3rd Baron, of co.
   Carmarthen, Wales, 1817, Vol. XXX, fol. 81.
RICE-VAUGHAN-PRYSE, J. C., of Llwyn-y-Brain, co. Carmarthen, Wales, [1887]
   Vol. LXIV, fol. 88; 1887-1888, fol. 134.
RICE-TREVOR, ..., 1st s. of Baron DYNEVOR, of Wales, [1825] Vol. XXXV,
   fol. 136.
RICE to WATKINS, ..., of Llwyn-y-Brain, co. Carmarthen, Wales, late Capt.,
   Welsh Fusiliers, [1866] Vol. LVI, fol. 89.
RICH, late WILLIAMS, ..., of co. Camb., [1786] Vol. XVI, fol. 107.
   „ late BOSTOCK, Rev. Charles, LL.D. (Rich, wife of Bostock), of co. Surrey,
      [1791] Vol. XVII, fol. 382.
   „ late MILNES, James, of co. York, BUSK, wife of.   Escutcheon of pretence,
      1802, Vol. XXI, fol. 456.
RICH, ..., of Dock Head, London.   (See ANNAND.)   [1813] Vol. XXVII,
   fol. 426.
   „ . . . ., of Sonning, co. Berks, [1862] Vol. LIV, fol. 348.

RICHARDS, (1) Henry, of Hammersmith, co. Middx., s. of John, decd., Earl
　　Marshall's Warrant, 27 Aug. 1703, for Arms to him and the descendants
　　of his father; (2) John, of Warmwell and Lewell, co. Dorset; (3) George,
　　of Litton and Long Bredy, co. Dorset; (4) James, of Kingtons, co. Dorset,
　　8 Sept. 1703, Vol. V, fol. 129; Stowe MS. 714, fols. 139ᵇ, 141 and 141ᵇ.
RICHARDS to CLAVELL, William, of Wormwell, Longbredy and Smedmore, co.
　　Dorset, [1797] Vol. XIX, fol. 359.
　„　to CLAVELL, John, M.A., of Wormwell, Longbredy and Smedmore, co.
　　Dorset. (Match), [1817] Vol. XXX, fol. 299.
　„　to EDWARDS, ..., of co. Glamorgan, Wales, [1823] Vol. XXXIV,
　　fol. 208.
　„　to YEATS, ..., of Kirkland, Kendal, co. Westmorland, [1837] Vol. XLII,
　　fol. 129.
RICHARDS, Maj.-Gen. Sir William, [1842] Vol. XLVI, fol. 41.
RICHARDS to BENNET, ..., Major in the Army, K.L.H., of co. Glamorgan,
　　Wales, [1867] Vol. LVI, fol. 298.
RICHARDS, Rev. W. J. Bruce, D.D., R. C. Church, St. Mary of the Angels,
　　Westmorland Road, Bayswater, London, 1881,* Vol. LXI, fol. 211.
　„　S. M., of Sutton, co. Surrey, 1892, Vol. LXVI, fol. 245.
RICHARDSON, Rev. Michael, M.A., of Queen's Coll., Oxf., and London, s. of
　　William, 17 June 1749, Vol. IX, fol. 316.
　„　Richard, of Brierley and Tonge, co. York, [1754] Vol. IX, fol. 511.
　„　William (s. of John), of Rotherhithe, co. Kent, and Newdigate, co. Surrey,
　　27 Nov. 1765, Vol. XI. fol. 118. (Berry.)
　„　. . . ., of Wigton, co. Cumberland. (See BLACKBURN.) [1784] Vol. XV,
　　fol. 361.
　„　Charles, Post-Capt., R.N., C.B., of Painsthorpe, co. York, 18 Sept. 1816,
　　Vol. XXX, fol. 15.
　„　Samuel, Capt., Marine, Bombay S.C., and 2nd s. William, of Hackney, sons
　　of John, of London, 11 June 1830, Vol. XXXVIII, fol. 101.
RICHARDSON-BUNBURY [Roy. Lic., 20 April 1822], Sir John [Richardson, 2nd]
　　Bart. [30 Aug. 1787], of Castle Hill, co. Tyrone, Ireland, [1832] Vol.
　　XXXIX, fol. 113 [? 1822, Vol. XXXIII, fol. 113].
RICHARDSON to SAUNDERS, ..., of Nunwick Hall, Great Salkeld, co. Cumber-
　　land, and Ardwick Place, Manchester, co. Lanc., [1837] Vol. XLII,
　　fol. 213.
RICHARDSON, Alexander Haywood, of Old Broad Street, London, [1848] Vol.
　　XLVIII, fol. 403.
　„　Charles Thomas, of Albion Street, Hyde Park, London, 1st s. of John
　　George, of New South Wales, Merchant, [1685] Vol. LVI, fol. 46.
　„　[late Massy, Mrs., widow of Hugh Massy, and only child of Maj. Richardson
　　Brady. Surname and Arms of Richardson, 1685. (Geneal. Mag., IV,
　　p. 244.)]
　„　Rev. Henry Kemp, Rector of Leire and Guthlaxton, co. Leic., [1871]
　　Vol. LVIII, fol. 18.
　„　Thomas Shepperd, of Hilden Court, Cheddingley, co. Sussex, [1874]
　　Vol. LVIII, fol. 321.
　„　Adolphus J., B. Med., London Hospital, 1885,* Vol. LXIII, fol. 163.
　„　Joseph, of Potts Hall, Whorlton, co. York, with remainder to his brothers
　　and to William Henry, 1885,* Vol. LXIII, fol. 107.
　„　W. R., of Shortlands, Beckenham, co. Kent, 1891,* Vol. LXVI, fol. 78.
　　(Crisp, V, p. 104.)
　„　Sir Thomas, M.P., of Hartlepool, co. Durham (s. of Thomas), 18 . . .,
　　Vol. LXXI, fol. . . . .
　„　John Maunsell, M.P. of Brigg Div., co. Linc., 1894-5, 18 . . ., Vol. LXXI,
　　fol. . . . .
RICHMOND, George, R.A., of Potterne, Wilts., [1874] Vol. LVIII, fol. 344.
　　(Berry's Suppl.)

RICHMOND and GORDON, Charles Henry, Duke of. Gordon and Lenox quarterly, 1876, Vol. LIX, fol. 244 [cr. Duke of Gordon, 13 Jan. 1876].

RICHMUND-GALE-BRADDYLL, Thomas, of co. Chester, Lanc. and Cumberland, [1819] Vol. XXXI, fol. 352.

RICHTER, *alias* RIDER, Jacob, of St. Bennet's, London, and Wittenburg, &c., 1 Aug. 1759, Vol. X, fol. 180. (Berry.)

RICKARDS, now MYNORS, Thomas, of co. Hereford, [1787] Vol. XVI, fol. 305.
  „   now MYNORS, ... (*see* MYNORS), [1817] Vol. XXX, fol. 301.

RICKARDS, Samuel, of St. James', Westminster, and co. Leic., [1834] Vol. XL, fol. 161.

RICKARDS-PHILLIPS, ..., Sir John, Knt., of Whitston Court, Newport, co. Monmouth, and Clifton, Bristol, 1888, Vol. LXIV, fol. 263.

RICKETTS, William Henry, of Ridgland, co. Westmorland; Longwood, Hampsh.; Jamaica; and the Jerseys, N. America, 3 Nov. 1773,* Vol. XII, fol. 271.

RICKETTS to JERVIS (Earl ST. VINCENT), co. Staff. (Match), [1801] Vol. XXI, fol. 188.
  „   to JERVIS, Viscount ST. VINCENT, of co. Staff. [1823], Vol. XXXIV, fol. 62.

RICKETTS, Robert Tristram, Post-Capt., R.N., of co. Glouc. [1827], Vol. XXXVI, fols. 404 and 406. (Crisp, I, 273.)

RICKETTS to WILKINSON, ..., of Tapton House, nr. Chesterfield, co. Derby, [1832] Vol. XXXIX, fol. 89.

RICKETTS, Jacob Wilcox, of Redlands Hill, Westbury-on-Trym, co. Glouc., [1836] Vol. XLI, fol. 335.
  „   Charles, of Dorton House, Dorton, Bucks. (Ricketts only by R. L.), 1874, Vol. LVIII, fol. 329.

RICKETTS-AUBREY, Charles, of Dorton House, Dorton, Bucks. (Ricketts only by R. L.), [1874] Vol. LIX, fol. 32.

RICKMAN, late LEVI (and HOBSON, his intended wife), of co. Sussex, [1823 ?] Vol. XXXIV, fol. 226.

RIDDELL-CARRE, Capt., R.N., of Scotland, [1828] Vol. XXXVII, fol. 47, [1829] ? 308.

RIDDLE, ..., of Bristol, co. Glouc., [1795] Vol. XIX, fol. 46.

RIDER, Richard, of Brompton, Shropsh., and The Close, Lichfield, co. Staff., 15 Dec. 1722, Vol. VII, fol. 132.

RIDER, *alias* RICHTER, Jacob. *See* RICHTER.

RIDGARD, wife of BAGSHAWE, impaled Arms. Crest to the descendants of father, of co. Linc., [1815] Vol. XXIX, fols. 79 and 80.

RIDGWAY, Joseph, of Brandfold, Gouldhurst, co. Kent, and Wallouches, Horwich, co. Lanc., 1879, Vol. LX, fol. 220. (Berry's Suppl.)

RIDLEY before COLBORNE, N. W., of co. Northumberland. Quarterly Arms, [1803], Vol. XXII, fol. 308.

RIDLEY, Thomas, Bar.-at-Law, of Newcastle-upon-Tyne, co. Northumberland, 1897, Vol. LXX, fol. 34.

RIDOUT, ..., of Eltham and Deptford, co. Kent, [1783] Vol. XV, fol. 193.

RIDSDALE, ..., of Wakefield, co. York, [1791] Vol. XVII, fol. 418.

RIGBY, late HALE, of co. Essex, [1788], Vol. XVII, fol. 29.
  „   late BALDWIN, ..., of co. Lanc., [1787] Vol. XVI, fol. 297.
  „   late BALDWIN, ..., of co. Lanc., [1796] Vol. XIX, fol. 264.

RIGBY [Sir John, Knt., Lord] Justice [of Appeal], of Chelsea Embankment, London, 1895,* Vol. LXVIII, fol. 148.

RIGG, G. S., of Motley Bank, Bowdon, co. Chester, 1892, Vol. LXVI, fol. 309.

RIGGE, now ROOKE (widow), of Arklid-in-Furness-Fells, co. Lanc., and Clifton, Bristol, [1840] Vol. XLIV, fol. 380.

RIGGS-MILLER, late MANVERS, ..., of co. Oxf., and Ireland, [1826] Vol. XXXVI, fol. 71.

RIGLEY, Joseph James Ward, of Nottingham, [1830] Vol. XXXVIII, fol. 128.

RILEY, John, of Brearley House, Halifax, and Inner Temple London, [1857] Vol. LII, fol. 236.

312   GRANTEES OF ARMS, 1687—1898.

RILEY-SMITH, H. N., of Toulston Lodge, Newton Kyme, co. York, 1895, Vol. LXVIII, fol. 276.

" -SMITH, T. R., of Inholmes, Tadcaster, co. York, 1895, Vol. LXVIII, fol. 278.

RIMINGTON-WILSON, James Wilson (minor), of Broomhead Hall, Bradford, co. York, [1840] Vol. XLIV, fol. 325.

RINGER, Thomas, of Forncet St. Peter, co. Norf., 16 April 1700, Vol. V, fol. 5.

RIPLEY, Thomas, of Westminster, and Ripley, co. York, 26 Mar. 1742, Vol. IX, fol. 54. (Berry.)

" Sir H. W., of Shropsh., 1880, Vol. LXI, fol. 3.

RISEBROW, Francis, of Norwich, co. Norf., 17 July 1725, Vol. VII, fol. 469.

RISSOWE to SHARPE, ..., of Melton and Woodbridge, co. Suff., [1800] Vol. XXI, fol. 114.

RITHERDON, ..., Maj., Hon. Artillery Company, of St. Botolph, Aldgate, London, [1801] Vol. XXI, fol. 171.

RITSON, Ulrick Alexander (s. of William), of Calf Hill, Muggleswick, co. Durham, 1898, Vol. LXX, fol. 306.

RIVERS, Baron, [20 May 1776, George] PITT. Supporters, with the consent of his brother, [1776] Vol. XIII, fol. 217.

" [? George (PITT), 2nd] Baron, [1792] Vol. XVIII, fol. 100.

" [Rev. Sir Henry, 9th] Bart., (EALES, intended wife) [mar. 2 May 1812], of Chafford, co. Kent, [1811] Vol. XXVI, fol. 384.

RIVERS, DEAN-PITT, ..., of co. Glouc. and Hampsh., [1818] Vol. XXXI, fol. 150.

RIVERS, [3rd] Baron [assumed the surname of] PITT-RIVERS, 26 Nov. 1828, of co. Dorset, late BECKFORD (of co. Dorset), of co. Glouc. and Hampsh., [1828] Vol. XXXVII, fol. 227.

RIVETT to CARNAC, James, of Bombay, and Derby, [1801] Vol. XXI, fol. 219.

RIVINGTON, C. R., of Castle Bank, Appleby, co. Westmorland, 1892,* Vol. LXVII, fol. 61.

RIVINGTON-HARMER, H. J., of Russell Square, London, 1892, Vol. LXVII, fol. 63. (Crisp, III, 23.)

RIX, George R., Bar.-at-Law, of Thorpe Hamlet, Norwich, co. Norf., 1890,* Vol. LXV, fol. 211.

ROBARTES after AGAR [30 Mar. 1822, Thomas John Agar, afterwards 1st Baron Robartes] (infant [?]), of co. Cornw., [1822] Vol. XXXIII, fol. 192.

ROBARTES, Baron [13 Dec. 1869], of co. Cornw. Supporters, [1869] Vol. LVII, fol. 206.

ROBARTS, ..., of Upper Thornbury Street, St. Pancras, London, [1815] Vol. XXVIII, fol. 384.

" . . . . (minor), reputed son, of London, [1815] Vol. XXVIII, fol. 385.

" [James Thomas, of Wimpole Street, par. of St. Mary le bone, co. Middx.], and [Charlotte] (LLOYD, his wife), [12 June 1821] Vol. XXXIII [? XXXII], fol. 309. [Misc. G. et H., 4th S., V, pp. 46 and 47.]

ROBARTS after LLOYD, Thomas, of Corfton Manor, Shropsh. (illegit.), [1854] Vol. LI, fol. 45.

ROBERTS, John, of Stepney, co. Middx., and co. Radnor, Wales, s. of Edmund, of co. Radnor, s. of John, of the same, 25 July 1720, Vol. VI, fol. 439; Add. MS. 14,830, fol. 48.

" Wilson Aylesbury, [of Bewdley, co. Worc., nephew and heir of Wilson Aylesbury], of Packwood, co. Warw., [Mr. Roberts was grandson of Henry Roberts, of] Droitwich, co. Worc. Quarterly Arms, [confirmed 1 June] 1774, Vol. XII, fol. 297. [Heraldry of Worcestershire, II, pp. 463 and 464.]

ROBERTS, late CRAMER, Martha Roberts, wife of the Rev. John, of co. Kent, and Ireland, [1801] Vol. XXI, fol. 280.

ROBERTS, ..., FENTON, wife of, of London. Escutcheon of pretence, [1802 ?] Vol. XXII, fol. 30.

ROBERTS, ... of Glassenbury, co. Kent, Brightfield Town and co. Cork, Ireland, [1809] Vol. XXV, fol. 258.

ROBERTS to POWELL, ... of co. Kent., [1813] Vol. XXVII, fol. 414.

ROBERTS, ... F.S.A., of Abberley and Ombersley, co. Worc., and Seedley, co. Lanc., [1852 ?] Vol. L, fol. 269.

„ Thomas, of Milford Haven and Trione, co. Pembroke, Wales, [1854] Vol. LI, fol. 136 [see Burke].

„ Maj.-Gen. Sir Henry Gee, K.C.B., of Hazeldine, Redmarley d'Abitot, co. Worc., and City of Glouc., [1862] Vol. LIV, fol. 423.

„ William, of Field House, Clent, co. Worc., and Drybridge, co. Monmouth, [10 Mar. 1864] Vol. LV, fol. 148.

ROBERTS-CROMPTON, Charles Henry, of London [The Field House, Clent, co. Worc.], and co. Lanc., [1864] Vol. LV, fols. 159 and 160.

ROBERTS-GAWEN, Rear-Adm. John Charles [Gawen-Roberts] (retired), [1857] of Salisbury, Wilts., and his grandson, [1851] Vol. XLIX, fol. 435.

„ -GAWEN (late BOROUGH), Charles, of Chetwynd, Shropsh., 1875, Vol. LIX, fol. 108.

ROBERTS [Major-Gen.], Sir Frederick Sleigh, G.C.B. [21 Sept. 1880]. Supporters, 1881, Vol. LXI, fol. 199, and 1883, Vol. LXII, fol. 33.

ROBERTS-AUSTEN, W. C., F.R.S., of The Royal Mint, Tower Hill, London, and co. Surrey, 1886, Vol. LXIII, fol. 207.

ROBERTS, George, of Tulsedale Villa, Lower Norwood, co. Surrey, 1885,[9] Vol. LXIII, fol. 165.

„ Sir Owen, of 48, Westbourne Terrace, London, and Dinas, co. Carnarvon, Wales, 1891, Vol. LXVI, fol. 108.

„ Dr. W. Griffith, of co. Denbigh, Wales, 1894, Vol. LXVIII, fol. 106.

ROBERTS-ATKIN. See ATKIN-ROBERTS.

ROBERTS, Ellis (portrait painter), s. of Thomas, of Burslem, co. Staff., 18 . . . .. Vol. LXXI, fol. . . . . .

„ W. R., of 51, Cambridge Street, Hyde Park, London, 18 . . . .. Vol. LXXI, fol. . . . . .

ROBERTSON, late MARJORIBANKS, Mariana S., of Scotland, [1834] Vol. XL, fol. 264, [1873] Vol. LVIII, fol. 230.

ROBERTSON-ROSS, Lieut.-Col. . . . .. K.L.H., of Glenmoidart and Kilmonivaig, co. Inverness, Scotland, [1865] Vol. LVI, fol. 25.

ROBERTSON, Rev. Robert J., of Bradford Rectory, co. York ; and William, of New Burlington Street, London, 1886, Vol. LXIII, fol. 307.

„ John Forbes, of 22, Bedford Square, London, [1886], Lyon Office.

ROBINSON, George, M.P., of Carlisle, co. Cumberland, and Moor Place, Bucks., 25 Oct. 1731, Vol. VIII, fol. 115[b]. (Berry.)

„ Samuel, Chamberlain of the City of London, 2 June 1728, Vol. VIII, fol. 124[b] [? wrong fol.] : Add. MS. 14,830, fol. 48 (2 Geo. II).

„ Sir Thomas [Bart.], K.B. [1742]. Supporters, [1742] Vol. IX, fol. 79.

„ [Sir Thomas Robinson, Bart.], Baron GRANTHAM [7 April 1761]. Supporters, [1761] Vol. X, fol. 292.

ROBINSON to WEDDELL, [7 May 1803, 2nd] Baron GRANTHAM. Quarterly Arms, [1803] Vol. XXII, fol. 234.

ROBINSON, ..., of Gosport, Hampsh. (See MAIDMAN.) (Match), [1765] Vol. XI, fol. 93.

„ William, of Bath, co. Somerset, late a Colonel, 1772, Vol. XII, fol. 147. (Berry.)

ROBINSON to HEWETT, (Dame Dorothea, wife of Sir George, Bart.), of co. Leic. and Northampton, 1773, Vol. XII, fol. 246.

„ to MONTAGU [3 June 1776]. Matthew [4th] Baron ROKEBY, of co. Northumberland and Kent, 1 July 1776, Vol. XIII, fol. 197 ; 13 Feb. 1777, quartering [Roy. Lic., 21 Dec. 1776, to quarter the Arms of Monthermer], [1777] fol. 265.

ROBINSON, Morris, Baron ROKEBY [of Armagh, by Ulster King of Arms]. [Supporters] 9 June 1801. (Genealogist, I, p. 22.)

ROBINSON before PEASE, Joseph. (Match), [1783] Vol. XV, fol. 179.

ROBINSON, Thomas, of Kingston-upon-Hull, co. York, and Newark-upon-Trent, co Nottingham. (*See* PEASE.) [1794] Vol. XVIII, fol. 316.

ROBINSON, late FREIND, Ven. John [Freind, Archd. of Armagh], of co. York (afterwards Bart. [14 Dec. 1819]), 1793, Vol. XVIII, fol. 281.

ROBINSON, ..., late wife of BOULTON, of co. Staff.   Arms to descendants, [1794] Vol. XVIII, fol. 297.

„ . . . ., of Whitbarrow, Greystoke, co. Cumberland, [1795] Vol. XIX, fol. 89.

„ . . . ., of Streatham, co. Surrey, and Nottingham Place [London ?], [1807] Vol. XXIV, fol. 155.

„ Margaret (SOUTHWELL, wife of), Capt. (Sir George A[bercrombie] Robinson, Bart [11 Nov. 1823]), of London, [1807] Vol. XXIV, fol. 158.

ROBINSON after VYVYAN, of Nansloe, Tresmarrow, Trelowarren, co. Cornw., and Lamerton, co. Devon [1818] Vol. XXXI, fol. 127.

ROBINSON, Major C. B., of Birmingham, co. Warw., [1823] Vol. XXXIV, fol. 152.

„ . . . ., Viscount GODERICH [28 April 1827, Frederick John Robinson], (Marq. [Earl of] RIPON).   Supporters, [1827] Vol. XXXVI, fol. 222.

„ James Sunderland, of Ormesby, co. York, [1828] Vol. XXXVII, fol. 153.

ROBINSON to BURTON, David, of Cherry Burton, co. York, and the Inner Temple, London, [1828] Vol. XXXVII, fol. 193.

„ to LOWTEN, ..., of co. Lanc., [1830] Vol. XXXVIII, fol. 120.

ROBINSON, ..., of Kirby Frith, co. Leic., [1837] Vol. XLII, fol. 193.

„ . . . ., of Tottenham (D.L.), co. Middx., [1838] Vol. XLIII, fol. 154.

ROBINSON, late GREY, William Robinson, of Sunderland, Silksworth and Norton, all co. Durham, 1838, Vol. XLIII, fol. 310.

„ William, of Liverpool and Seedly, co. Lanc., [1839] Vol. XLIV, fol. 28.

ROBINSON to NOWELL, ..., of co. York, and Westmorland, [1843] Vol. XLVII, fol. 22.

ROBINSON, ..., of Chesham Street [London ?], [1845] Vol. XLVII, fol. 404.

„ [John Beverley ?], C. J., C.B., Bart. [21 Sept. 1854], of Beverley House, Toronto, Upper Canada, [1854] Vol. LI, fol. 140.

„ . . . ., M.D., of Newcastle-upon-Tyne, co. Northumberland, Assist. Army Surgeon, [1856] Vol. LII, fol. 116.

ROBINSON, late JEAFFERSON, Christopher William Pigott, of co. Camb. and Suff., 1857, Vol. LII, fol. 279.

ROBINSON to NORCLIFFE, ..., of co. York, [1862] Vol. LIV, fols. 272 and 273.

ROBINSON, ..., of Heathbank, Kersal, co. Lanc., [1863] Vol. LV, fol. 118.

„ Joseph Beryn, of (Robinson Estate) Griqualand, South Africa, [1873] Vol. LVIII, fol. 282.

„ John Charles, of Newton, and Eight-holds, Swanage, co. Dorset, 1876, Vol. LIX, fol. 210. (Berry's Suppl.)

„ F. E., of Stanmore, co. Middx., 1894, Vol. LXVIII, fol. 26.

„ Rev. Thomas, Vicar of Ewshot Hurst, Farnham, Hampsh., 1898, Vol. LXX, fol. 90.

ROBISON to BROWN, ..., of co. Lanc., [1810] Vol. XXV, fol. 449.

ROBSON, (BATEMAN) late HOLLAND, (Robson, wife of) Richard, of London, and Hartford, Hampsh., [1792] Vol. XVIII, fol. 13.

„ Robert, of Bellevue House, St. Nicholas, co. Durham, 1884, Vol. LXII, fol. 172.

ROCK, Thomas, of the Middle Temple, London ; Lacock, Wilts. ; Butleigh, co. Somerset ; Over Eggleton and Bishop's Frome, co. Heref., 20 June 1707, Vol. V, fol. 217 ; Add. MS. 14,830, fol. 162.

ROCKLIFFE to WAYNE, ..., of Copt Hewick, Asenby, and Richmond, co. York, [1808] Vol. XXIV, fol. 370.

ROCKLIFFE-LUBÉ, William. [Exemplified to William Rockliff, of Liverpool, on his assuming, by Roy. Lic., 1862, the additional Surname and Arms of Lubé.] (*See* Burke.)

ROCKLIFFE, late LUNN (LUBÉ), William, of Copt Hewick, co. York, [1870] Vol. LVII, fol. 256.

RODBARD, late ELLIS, Elizabeth and Sarah, of London, 16 Jan. 1782, Vol. XV, fol. 1.

    „   late BUCHER (nat. s. of Rodbard), of co. Somerset, [1793] Vol. XVIII, fol. 207.

RODBARD, ..., of Evercreech and Shepton Mallet, co. Somerset, [1803] Vol. XXII, fol. 301.

RODBARD, late WHITLEY, ..., [1843] Vol. XLVII, fols. 162 and 163.

RODDAM, late SPENCER-STANHOPE, William, Lieut., R.N., of Cannon Hall, co. York, and Roddam, co. Northumberland, [1817] Vol. XXX, fol. 227.

    „   late FOLDER, R. J., of Roddam, co. Northumberland, [and] John Folder, of Ballincushaw, I. M. [? Isle of Man], 1865, Vol. LVI, fol. 3.

RODEN, ..., of Etruria Hall, Stoke-upon-Trent, co. Staff., [1860] Vol. LIV, fol. 74.

RODES, late HEATHCOTE, Cornelius, of co. Derby, 1776, Vol. XIII, fol. 227.

RODES after REASTON, Rev. C. H., M.A., of co. Derby, 1825, Vol. XXXV, fol. 315 ([1843] Vol. XLVII, fol. 97, Bar.-at-Law, 1846). (Berry App.)

RODGER-CUNLIFFE, W. W., of Hadlow Castle, co. Kent, 1888 [1887], Vol. LXIV, fol. 130.

RODGERS, Thomas William, of Lincoln's Inn, London, and Endcliffe Vale, Sheffield, co. York, and to the descendants of his late father, 27 Feb. 1871 [1871], Vol. LVIII, fol. 78.

RODICK, ..., of Wodlove-within-Arnside, Beetham, Westmorland ; Challen Hall, Waston, and Gatnill, co. Lanc., [1847] Vol. XLVIII, fol. 244.

RODNEY, Adm. Sir George Brydges, Bart., K.B. [1780]. Supporters, [1781], Vol XIV, fol. 350.

    „   Baron [19 June 1782, Adm. Sir George Brydges Rodney, Bart., K.B. 1780]. Supporters, [1782] Vol. XV, fol. 125.

RODNEY to HARLEY-RODNEY [4 Nov. 1805], Thomas James, 4th Baron, [1805] Vol. XXIII, fol. 243.

RODNEY after POWELL, William, of co. Monmouth, [1841] Vol. XLV, fol. 93.

ROE, Sir Frederick Adair, Knt. [5 Sept. 1832], of Brundish, co. Suff. ; Withdean, co. Sussex, and Brinwith, co. Glamorgan, [1836] Vol. XLI, fol. 236.

ROE after HENDERSON, Christopher Hope, of co. Chester, [1879] Vol. LX, fol. 307.

ROFFEY, Richard, of Adelphi Terrace, London, and Woodplace, Coulsdon, co. Surrey, 1832 or 1833, Vol. XXXIX, fol. . . . .

ROGERMAN to CHAMBERS, John, of Jamaica, [1795] Vol. XVIII, fol. 437.

ROGERS, Sir John, Bart., of Wisdome, co. Devon, Sheriff, 8 Feb. 170½, Vol. V, fol. 69.

    „   Samuel, of St. George's, Hanover Square, London, and co. Cornw. MYLOR [quarterings ?], [1772] Vol. XII, fol. 168.

    „   Samuel, s. of John, of co. Cornw. MYLOR quarterings for TRESAKER and ELLWOOD. 7 Dec. 1774, Vol. XIII, fol. 49.

    „   . . . . *See* WARDELL.

    „   . . . ., of Shifnal and Stirchley, Shropsh., [1785] Vol. XVI, fol. 37.

ROGERS-HARRISON, Valentine, of London, called (Valentine LOTT), Q.M., 11th Foot, nephew to George HARRISON, Clarenceux King of Arms, [1820] Vol. XXXII, fol. 31.

ROGERS, now ROGERS-HARRISON, ..., of London, and Hendon, co. Middx., [1839] Vol. XLIV, fol. 54.

ROGERS, Francis, (s. of John), of Yarlington Lodge, co. Somerset, and Bedford Court, co. Worc., 8 June, 1830 [1838], Vol. XLIII, fol. 28. (Bishop's MSS.)

    „   Alexander, of Brompton Park, co. Middx. [and Calcutta, East Indies (Burke)], Sheriff elect, [1841] Vol. XLV, fol. 245.

（無）

316 GRANTEES OF ARMS, 1687—1898.

ROGERS after COXWELL, Richard Rogers Coxwell-Rogers (Rev. William Rogers Coxwell in Burke), of co. Glouc., 25 April 1850, Vol. XLIX, fol. 307 (*see* Misc. G. et H., I, pp. 256-7.)

  „ after COXWELL . . . ., of co. Glouc., [1854] Vol. LI, fol. 170.

ROGERS, ..., of Liverpool, co. Lanc., [1850] Vol. XLIX, fol. 400.

ROGERS-TILLSTONE, ..., of Moulsecombe Place, Patcham, and Worthing, co. Sussex, [1868] Vol. LVII, fol. 104.

ROGERS, ..., Baron BLACHFORD [4 Nov. 1871], of co. Devon, [1871] Vol. LVIII, fol. 72.

  „ G. E., Bart., Capt., 1st Dragoon Guards, 1881,* Vol. LXI, fol. 195.

ROHDE, Castin, of London, and Meldorp, Holstein, 1765 [? 1764], Vol. X, fol. 485. (Berry.)

ROKEBY, Baron [Rt. Hon.] Morris [Robinson]. Supporters, by Sir Chichester Fortescue, Ulster King of Arms, 9 June 1801. (Genealogist, I, p. 22.)

ROKEWOOD after GAGE, ..., of co. Suff., [1838] Vol. XLIII, fol. 293.

ROKEWOOD before GAGE, ..., of co. Suff., [1843] Vol. XLVI, fol. 363.

  „ before GAGE, ..., of co. Suff., [1867] Vol. LVI, fol. 191.

ROKEWOOD after DARELL, ..., of co. Suff. and Kent, [1872] Vol. LVIII, fol. 136.

ROLFE after NEVILLE, S. E. E., of Heacham Hall, co. Norf., 1837, Vol. XLII, fol. 110.

ROLFE, Baron CRANWORTH, [20 Dec. 1850, Robert Monsey Rolfe]. Arms [1851], Vol. XLIX, fol. 418 ; Supporters, fol. 420.

ROLAND, Lady WELLESLEY [Hyacinthe Gabrielle, dau. of Pierre Roland], wife of [Richard Wellesley] Baron [Wellesley, and 2nd Earl of Mornington]. Impaled arms, [1803] Vol. XXII, fol. 140.

ROLLE, Lord [and Baron STEVENSTONE, 8 Jan. 174⅞, Henry Rolle, extinct 1750], of co. Devon. Supporters, [174⅞] Vol. IX, fol. 220.

ROLLE, late WALTER, Denys, of Hudscott, co. Devon, [1781] Vol. XIV, fol. 328.

ROLLE (CLAYFIELD), ..., of Bristol and Merton, co. Somerset. A quartering, Clayfield, of Ireland, [1801] Vol. XXI, fol. 177.

ROLLE, late TREFUSIS, ... (minor), of co. Cornw., [1851] Vol. L, fol. 74.

ROLLES, Rear-Adm. Robert, of London, [1814] Vol. XXVIII, fol. 211.

ROLLS, [? John Etherington Welch], of Camberwell, co. Surrey, and The Hendre, co. Monmouth, [1838] Vol. XLII, fols. 286 and 288.

  „ [John Allan], Baron LLANGATTOCK [30 Aug. 1892]. Supporters, 1892, Vol. LXVII, fol. 91.

ROLT, Sir John, Q.C., M.P., of Ogleworth Park, co. Glouc. [Knighted 10 Nov. 1866], [1856 ?] Vol. LII, fol. 196.

ROMAINE after LOVETT, ..., of Berks., [1826] Vol. XXXVI, fol. 125.

  „ after LOVETT, of Berks., [1827] Vol. XXXVI, fol. 266.

ROMANES, Rev. William, of Wigston Magna Vicarage, co. Leic., 1882, Vol. LXI, fol. 349. (Berry's Suppl.)

ROME, George, of Scotland, and Newport, Rhode Island, North America (ROOME, in Berry), 21 July 1772, Vol. XII, fol. 207.

ROMILLY, Baron [3 Jan. 1866, Master of the Rolls, died 1874], of London, [1866] Vol. LVI, fol. 69 ; Supporters, fol. 73.

ROMNEY, Baron of, [22 June 1716, Sir Robert] MARSHAM [4th Bart.]. Supporters, [1716] Vol. VI, fol. 263.

RONEY to RONEY-DOUGAL, Lieut.-Col., of Scotland, [1871] Vol. LVIII, fol. 20.

ROOKE, Sir William, Knt., of Leeds, co. York, Warrant, [1727] Vol. VIII, fol. 24, not a grant [Knighted 24 Mar. 172⅚].

  „ John, of the City of London, Merchant, and Carlisle, co. Cumberland, 31 Jan. 1755, Vol. X, fol. 2. (Berry.)

  „ Sir Giles [Judge of Common Pleas]. (*See* BURRARD [the same Vol. and fol.].) [Knighted 13 Nov. 1793, died 1808], [1815] Vol. XXIX, fol. 144. [He, and his brother (the next) mar. daus. of Col. William Burrard.]

  „ William. (*See* BURRARD [the same Vol. and fol.].) [1815] Vol. XXIX, fol. 144.

ROOKE, late WORRALL, ... (widow), of Frenchay, co. Glouc., and Bigswear [co. Monmouth ?], [1840] Vol. XLIV, fol. 380.

ROOKWOOD, Baron (SELWIN-IBBETSON). Supporters, 1892, Vol. LXVII, fol. 73.

ROOME. *See* ROME.

ROOPE (late HARRIS), Roope, of the City of Bristol (formerly ROOPE-HARRIS), afterwards ROOPE-ROOPE, 22 July 1771, Vol. XII, fol. 96. (Berry.)

ROOSE, Edward Charles, M.D. (3rd s. of Francis), of London, 18 . . ., Vol. LXXI, fol. . . . . .

ROPER, now CURSON, Henry, of Waterpery, co. Oxf. (afterwards 14th Baron TEYNHAM), 1788, Vol. XVI, fol. 343.

ROPER before CURZON, Henry F., of Waterpery, co. Oxf. (*See* Baron TEYNHAM), of Linstead, co. Kent. Quarterly Arms, 1813, Vol. XXVII, fol. 349.

ROPER after TREVOR, Charles Blayney (grandson Baron TEYNHAM), of Lewisham and Lee, co. Kent, and Clones, co. Monaghan, Ireland. Quarterly Arms, [1809] Vol. XXV, fol. 138.

ROPNER, Robert, of Hardwick Hall, Monk Hesleden, co. Durham, 1881, Vol. LXI, fol. 126.

ROSCOE, St. John B., of Cadogan Place, London, 1882,* Vol. LXI, fol. 303.

ROSCOW, Thomas Tattersall, B.A., M.D., Camb., of London, and Folkestone, co. Kent, [1855] Vol. LI, fol. 245.

ROSE, William, grandfather Jacob, of Carshalton, co. Surrey ; Beckenham, co. Kent ; and Hasland, co. Derby, 1781, Vol. XIV, fol. 290.

ROSE, late HOLDEN, William Lucas, of Daventry, co. Northampton, O.G., Camb. [?], and Birmingham, co. Warw., [1791] Vol. XVII, fol. 290. [1785, Rose and Holden quarterly, *see* Burke.]

ROSE, [Sir Philip], Bart. [1874], of Rayners, Penn, Amersham, and High Wycombe, Bucks., and London, [1874] Vol. LVIII, fol. 334.

  ,,   William, of Ballbrook House, Withington, 1896,* Vol. LXIX, fol. 162.

ROSHER, ..., of Crete Hall, Northfleet, co. Kent (? William Henry Burch Rosher, Bar.-at-Law), [1828] Vol. XXXVII, fols. 59 and 60.

ROSKELL, Robert, of Gateacre and Garstang, co. Lanc., [1836] Vol. XLII, fol. 15.

ROSMEAD, Baron [1896], [Rt. Hon Sir] (Hercules [George Robert] ROBINSON) [Bart. 1891, G.C.M.G. 1875]. Supporters to Baronetcy, 1895, Vol. LXVIII, fol. 164.

ROSS, Capt. Thomas, of Woolwich, co. Kent (of the Balnagowan family), to descendants of his grandfather, [1781] Vol. XIV, fols. 313 and 315.

ROSS, late GRAY, ..., of London, and Cromarty, Scotland, [1786] Vol. XVI, fol. 125.

ROSS to FARQUHARSON, ..., Capt., R.N. Escutcheon of pretence, [1806] Vol. XXIII, fol. 293.

ROSS, Maj.-Gen. [Robert], of Bladensburg [decd. Hon. Armorial Ensigns on monument to him]. Augmentation, [26 April 1816] Vol. XXIX, fol. 343. (Geneal. Mag., I, plate, p. 129.)

  ,,   Sir John, Knt., C.B., Post-Capt., R.N. (Arctic Explorer). Augmentation, [1835] Vol. XLI, fol. 73 [*see* Burke].

  ,,   Maj.-Gen. Sir Patrick, K.C.H. [1834], G.C.M.G. [1837]. Supporters, [1837] Vol. XLII, fol. 204.

  ,,   Gen. Sir Hew Dalrymple, G.C.B. [1855]. Supporters, [1855] Vol. LI, fol. 305.

  ,,   William, of Nofferton, co. York, 18 . . ., Vol. LXXI, fol. . . . .

ROSSLYN, Earl of, and Baron LOUGHBOROUGH (ST. CLAIR-ERSKINE). Quarterly Arms, [1805] Vol. XXIII, fol. 171.

  ,,   Earl of, and Baron LOUGHBOROUGH (ST. CLAIR-ERSKINE). Supporters, [1805] Vol. XXIII, fol. 174.

ROSTON-NASH, ... (Spr.), of Park Hill House, Bristol, and Newent, co. Glouc., [1831] Vol. XXXVIII, fol. 214.

ROSTRON, Simpson, of the Middle Temple, London. Match with SIMPSON, [1859] Vol. LIII, fol. 195.

ROTHERY, ..., of Greta Hall, Crosthwaite, co. Cumberland, [1850 ?] Vol. XLIX, fol. 271.

ROTHES, Countess [Henrietta Anne], wife of [George] GWYTHER, now LESLIE, [1817] Vol. XXX, fol. 206.

„　Countess, now LESLIE, [22 Jan. 1861] Vol. LIV, fol. 230.

ROTHSCHILD, ..., of London, Frankfort-on-Main, Vienna and Paris, [1818] Vol. XXXI, fol. 8.

ROTHWELL, Peter, Capt. of Yeomanry, of Sunny Hill, Bolton, co. Lanc., [1831] Vol. XXXVIII, fol. 251.

„　Rev. Richard Rainsham, of Ribbleton House, Preston, Rector of Sefton, co. Lanc., [1857] Vol. LII, fol. 246.

ROUGH, William, M.A., Camb., Sergt.-at-Law, 6 April 1817 [1816], Vol. XXIX, fol. 334.　(Bishop's MSS.)

ROUGHTON, William, of Kettering, co. Northampton, and Lisbon, Portugal, [1851] Vol. L, fol. 29.

ROUND, Joseph, of The Hauge, Rowley Regis, and Brierley, Sedgeley, co. Staff. ; and Portland House, Edgbaston, co. Warw., [1861] Vol. LIV, fol. 174.

„　James, M.P., of co. Essex, with limitation to father, James Thomas, and of uncle, Joseph Green Round, of Birch Hale and Woodham Mortimer, co. Essex, [1871] Vol. LVIII, fol. 60.

ROUND to ROUND-TURNER, Henry Lewis, Com., R.N., of co. Essex, 1872 [1871], Vol. LVIII, fol. 62.

ROUNDELL to CURRER, ..., of Gledstone House, co. York.　Quarterly Arms, [1806] Vol. XXIV, fol. 18.

ROUNDELL, Danson Richardson, M.A. [of Clifton House, co. York, assumed, Roy. Lic., 1806, the name of CURRER (see Burke)], [1806] Vol. XXIV, fol. 22.

ROUNDELL, late CURRER, D. Richardson, 1851, Vol. L, fol. 68.

ROUNSEVELL, ..., of Glen Para, Glenely, South Australia, [1871] Vol. LVIII, fol. 26.

ROUS, William, of London, s. of John, of Wotton-under-Edge, co. Glouc., 7 April 1730, Vol. VIII, fol. 65.

ROUSE, William, of St. Mary Woolnoth, London, 21 Mar. 173$\frac{2}{3}$, Vol. VIII, fol. 163.

ROUSE after BOUGHTON, of Shropsh., co. Warw. and Worc.　Quarterly Arms, [1791] Vol. XVII, fol. 352.

ROUSE, ..., of New Bridge Street, London, [1816] Vol. XXIX, fol. 408.

ROUSE-BOUGHTON-KNIGHT, ..., of co. Hereford and Shropsh., [1856 ?] Vol. LII, fol. 172.

ROW to PAYNE, ..., of co. Devon.　(Match), [1796 ?] Vol. XIX, fol. 315.

ROWCLIFFE, Charles Edward, of Halsway, Stogumber and Milverton, co. Somerset, s. of Charles, 1876, Vol. LIX, fol. 266.

ROWE, ..., of Lamerton, co. Devon, [1742] Vol. IX, fol. 60.

ROWE to HUSSEY, ..., of co. Dorset [1788] Vol. XVII, fol. 33.

ROWLAND, Jacob, Solicitor, of Birmingham, co. Warw., 1892, Vol. LXVII, fol. 29.

ROWLEY, [Adm.] Sir William, K.B. [1753].　Supporters, [1753] Vol. IX, fol. 483.

„　. . . ., of London and Deptford, co. Kent, [1823] Vol. XXXIV, fol. 90.

„　Vice-Adm. Sir Charles, Bart., G.C.B., of Hill House, Berks.　Supporters, [1841] Vol. XLV, fol. 218.　[Adm. Sir Josias, Bart. 2 Nov. 1813, G.C.B. 4 July 1840 ; Vice-Adm. Sir Charles, Bart. 21 Mar. 1836, G.C.B. 4 July 1840.]

„　Conwy C. G. H., of Bodrhyddan, Rhuddlan, co. Flint, Wales, 1896, Vol. LXIX, fol. 92.

ROWLLS to LEGH, Elizabeth, widow, of Kingston-upon-Thames, co. Surrey, [1781] Vol. XIV, fol. 352.

ROWLLS, late EASTABROOKE, ... (widow), [1808] Vol. XXIV, fol. 444.

ROWLLS, Charles, William Henry, and Elizabeth Maria (infants), nat. children of Legh Rowlls, of Kingston-upon-Thames, co. Surrey, [1808] Vol. XXIV, fols. 446, 448 and 450.

ROWLLS, ... (infant), reputed son, of Kingston-upon-Thames, co. Surrey, [1844 ?] Vol. XLVII, fol. 320.

ROWNTREE, John Russell, of Stockton-on-Tees and Elton, co. Durham, [1830] Vol. XXXVIII, fol. 58.

ROWSON, Anne, dau. and co.-h. of John, of Thelwall, co. Chester, great-grandmother of Richard Boughey MONK-LINGARD. (*See under* MONK and LINGARD.) Quartering for Rowson, 12 Jan. 1871, Vol. LVII, fol. 306. (Genealogist, V, p. 144.)

ROWTON, Baron [Lowry Corry], of Shropsh. Supporters, 1880, Vol. LXI, fol. 55.

ROXBURGH, Bruce, late Capt. Bombay C. S., of Calcutta, [1853] Vol. L, fol. 403.

ROXBURGHE, Duchess of (BETCHENOE). Escutcheon of pretence, [1804] Vol. XXIII, fol. 99.

ROXBY, ..., of Eske Hall, nr. Beverley, co. York, [1803] Vol. XXII, fol. 133.

ROXBY, late MAUDE, Rev. Henry Roxby, Vicar and Rector of . . . ., co. Surrey, [1836 ?] Vol. XLII, fols. 103 and 105.

ROYDHOUSE, John, J.P., of Westminster, 9 Feb. 171$\frac{4}{5}$, Vol. VI, fol. 186 ; Add. MS. 14,830, fol. 157.

ROYDS, James, of Mount Falinge, Rochdale, co. Lanc., 2nd s. of John Royds, of the same, Merchant, decd., 6 Oct. 1820, Vol. XXXII, fol. 155. (Misc. G. et H., 2nd S., III, p. 293.) (Crisp, III, p. 12, and Berry's Suppl.)

ROYER, James, of London, and St. James', Westminster. Certified, May 1779, Vol. XIV, fol. 141. (Berry.)

RUBIE, John, Mayor of Bath, co. Somerset, 1895-6 (s. of George, of Bursleden, Hampsh.), [1899 ?] Vol. LXXI, fol. . . . . .

RUDGE, Edward, of Wimpole Street, London. Match with NOUAILLE, [1810] Vol. XXVI, fol. 81.

RUDSTON to READ, Rev. Thomas Cutler, M.A., of co. York, [1803] Vol. XXII, fol. 44.

RUDSTON, Rudston Calvarly, of co. York, [1805] Vol. XXIII, fol. 213.

RUDYARD, Lieut.-Col. Match with PRYOR, [1809] Vol. XXV, fol. 225.

RUGGE to RUGGE-PRICE, [Sir Arthur James], Bart., of co. Surrey, [1874] Vol. LVIII, fol. 338.

RUGGLES-BRISE, John, of Spains Hall, co. Essex, and Clare, co. Suff., by Roy. Lic., 1827 (*see* Burke, ? name only), [1827] Vol. XXXVI, fol. . . . . .

RULE, John, Clerk of the Survey, of Deptford, co. Kent, [1748] Vol. IX, fol. 263.

RUMBOLD, [George Berriman, s. of 1st] Bart. Quartering BERRIMAN, [1779] Vol. XIV, fol. 145.

RUNDELL, ..., of Ludgate [London], [1788] Vol. XVII, fol. 7.

RUNDLE, Joseph Sparkhall, of East Park, Newton Bushel, co. Devon, 1877, Vol. LX, fol. 50.

RUNKEL, ..., of London, and Westphalia, [1802] Vol. XXI, fol. 335.

RUPPEL, ..., of Hornsey Lane, co. Middx., [1811] Vol. XXVI, fol. 338.

RUSH, ..., of London ; Bishop's Stortford, co. Hertf. ; and Farthingoe, co. Northampton, [1811] Vol. XXVI, fol. 200.

„ Sir William Beaumaris, Knt., of Bishop's Stortford, co. Hertf., and Wimbledon, co. Surrey. Alteration of Crest, 1827, Vol. XXXVI, fol. 180 ; Extension of limitations, fol. 203.

RUSHOUT, [Sir John, Bart.], Baron NORTHWICK [26 Oct. 1797], Supporters, [1797] Vol. XX, fol. 36.

RUSHOUT before BOWLES, [George, only brother of the 2nd Baron Northwick], of co. Worc. Quarterly Arms, [1817] Vol. XXX, fol. 236.

RUSHOUT, late COCKERELL, [Sir Charles, 2nd] Bart., of co. Worc., Essex, and Glouc., [1849] Vol. XLIX, fol. 162.

RUSKIN, John James, of London, and Herne Hill, co. Surrey, [1834] Vol. XL, fol. 297.

RUSPINI, ..., ORD, wife of, of London, [1791] Vol. XVII, fol. 324.

RUSSELL, Samuel, of Stoke Newington, co. Middx., s. of Henry, of Ashby-de-la-
Zouch, co. Leic., and Sheriff of Middx., 10 Aug. 1731, Vol. VIII,
fol. 114^b.

„   Jesse, of Walthamstow, co. Essex, 1 Oct. 1792, Vol. XVIII, fol. 113.

RUSSELL after WATTS, Jesse, of Ham Hall, (Watts, wife of).   Quarterly Arms,
1817, Vol. XXX, fol. 143.   (Berry's Appx.)

RUSSELL, ..., of Force Forge, co. Lanc. (See FERRIS.)   [1812] Vol. XXVII,
fol. 149.

„   Sir Henry Russell, Knt., Chief Justice of Bengal [1807], Bart. [1812], of
Dover, co. Kent, [1812] Vol. XXVII, fol. 157.

„   James, of Clifton, co. Glouc., 3rd s. of James Russell, of Charlestown,
America, 18 Aug. 1820, Vol. XXXII, fol. 113 (see Misc. G. et H., II,
p. 168).

RUSSELL to PAKINGTON, John Somerset, of co. Worc., [1831] Vol. XXXVIII,
fol. 205.

RUSSELL after GREENHILL, Robert, of Lincoln's Inn, London, and Checquers
Court, Bucks. (afterwards [1831] a Baronet), 1815, Vol. XXVIII, fol. 261.

„   after FRANKLAND [Feb. 1837], Sir Thomas [Robert, 7th] Bart., of Checquers
Court, Bucks., and Thirkleby, co. York, [1837] Vol. XLII, fol. 88 [?].

RUSSELL, Rev. William, B.A., Rector of Shepperton, co. Middx., [1834] Vol.
XL, fol. 284.

RUSSELL after HAMILTON, Gustavus Frederick.   (See BOYNE.)   [1850] Vol.
XLIX, fol. 352.

RUSSELL, ..., of the Middle Temple, and Registrar in Chancery, Jamaica,
[1855] Vol. LI, fol. 242.

„   (Earl) [The Rt. Hon. John Russell], of Kingston Russell, co. Dorset, and
Amberley, co. Sussex.   Supporters, [1861] Vol. LIV, fol. 156.

„   Lieut.-Col., of Manga Kuri, Prov. of Hawkesbury, New Zealand, [1864]
Vol. LV, fol. 218.

RUSSELL-PAVIER, William Adey, of Heaton Norris, co. Lanc., and Hammerwick,
co. Staff., 1874, Vol. LIX, fol. 48.

RUSSELL.   Sarah, dau. and co.-h. of Rev. John BEST, Preb. of Wolverhampton and
Vicar of Sedgley, co. Staff., wife of James Russell, on an escutcheon of
pretence, 1835.

„   James (and Sarah BEST, his wife), of Handsworth, co. Staff., 29 May 1835,
Vol. XLI, fol. 21 (see Misc. G. et H., New S., IV, p. 18).

„   Baron [The Rt. Hon. Sir Charles Russell], 31 July 1894, of Killowen, Ireland.
Arms by Ulster King of Arms.   Supporters, 1895, Vol. LXVIII, fol. 202.

RUST, Rev. Edgar, M.A., of Abbot's Hall and Drinkston, co. Suff., [1840] Vol.
XLIV, fol. 252.

RUSTON, J., of Monk's Manor, Linc., 1891,* Vol. LXVI, fol. 69.

RUTHERFORD to ATKINSON, ... (Spr.), of co. Northumberland, [1827] Vol.
XXXVI, fol. 367.

RUTHYN, (Baroness) GREY DE [Barbara ?, 1849], Vol. XLIX, fols. 92 and 93.

RUTLAND, Frederick William, of Richmond, co. Surrey, and St. Petersburg,
Russia, [1857] Vol. LII, fol. 241.

RUTSON, William, of Newby Wiske, co. York, and co. Lanc., [1850] Vol. XLIX,
fol. 332.

RUTTER, Thomas Joshua, Storekeeper, H.M.'s Ordnance, Malta [1845 ?] Vol.
XLVII, fol. 341.

RYCROFT, late NELSON, Rev. Richard, of London.   Quarterly Arms, 1758 [1783 ?],
Vol. XV, fol. 239.

RYDER [Nathaniel], Baron HARROWBY [1776], of co. Glouc. and Staff. (See
RIDER.)   Arms and Supporters, [1776] Vol. XIII, fol. 195.

RYDON, ..., of Highbury, co. Middx., [1852 ?] Vol. L, fol. 262.

RYE to BROGRAVE, ..., of St. Alban's Hall, co. Norf., [1831] Vol. XXXVIII,
fol. 271.

RYE, Walter, of Frognal House, Hampstead, co. Middx., 1898, Vol. LXX, fol. 318.

RYGATE, J. J., B.Med., of St. Leonard's-on-Sea, co. Sussex, 1885*, Vol. LXIII, fol. 142.

RYLAND, Samuel, of Sherbourne, Smallheath [co. Warw.]; s. of John, of Easy Hall, co. Warw.; Prestfields, Cannon Hill, Selby; and The Pigeons' House, co. Worc.; s. of William [of Birmingham, co. Warw.], [1836] Vol. XLI, fol. 331 [*see* Burke's Commoners, IV, fol. 406].

RYLAND, Thomas, of Erdington, Aston, co. Warw., 1890, Vol. LXV, fol. 182. (Crisp, I, p. 245.)

RYLANDS, Thomas Glazebrook, of Highfields, Thelwall, co. Chester, 7 Nov. 1877, Vol. LX, fol. 48 (*see* Genealogist, IV, p. 287, and Crisp, I, p. 16).

  „   William John, of Longford Hall, Manchester, co. Lanc., 1893, Vol. LXVII, fol. 181.

RYLE, John, of Park House, nr. Macclesfield, co. Chester, 14 Nov. 1809, Vol. XXV, fol. 288.

RYMER, Thomas, of Calder Abbey, Beckermet, co. Cumberland, s. of William, of Manchester, co. Lanc., 1897, Vol. LXX, fol. 20.

S

SABINE to [SABINE-] PASLEY, [20 Mar. 1809, 2nd] Bart., [Thomas] (infant), of Hampsh. (Match), [1809] Vol. XXV, fol. 149.

SACKVILLE, Viscount (GERMAINE), Diana, wife of, and dau. and co-h. of John SAMBROOKE. Escutcheon of pretence. Supporters, [1782] Vol. XV, fol. 30.

  „   Major, ..., E.I.C.S., nat. s. of the Duke of DORSET, [1822] Vol. XXXIII, fol. 339.

SACKVILLE-WEST, [30 Nov. 1843, George John West, 5th Earl, and Reginald Windsor West, 7th] Earl DE LA WARR, Lord Chamberlain, of co. Sussex, [1843] Vol. XLVI, fol. 403.

  „   -WEST to SACKVILLE only [24 April 1871, Reginald Windsor], Baron BUCKHURST, of co. Sussex, [1871] Vol. LVII, fol. 330. Supporters, 1876, Vol. LIX, fol. 288.

SACKVILLE after STOPFORD (GERMAINE, formerly Sackville), of Drayton House, Lowick, co. Northampton, 1870, Vol. LVII, fol. 244.

  „   after STOPFORD, William Bruce, of Drayton House, Lowick, co. Northampton, 1870, Vol. LVII, fol. 330 [230 ?].

SAGAR-MUSGRAVE, John Musgrave, of co. York, [1863] Vol. LV, fol. 30.

  „   -MUSGRAVE, ..., [1875] Vol. LIX, fol. 167.

SAINSBURY, late LANGFORD, Sainsbury, of London, and Caius Coll., Camb., [1800] Vol. XXI, fol. 16.

ST. ALBANS, See of, co. Hertf., 1877, Vol. LX, fol. 1.

ST. ALBYN, late GRAVENOR, of Alfoxton and Nether Stowey, co. Somerset, [1806] Vol. XXIII, fol. 432.

ST. AUBYN after MOLESWORTH, Rev. John, of co. Cornw., 1839, Vol. XLIV, fol. 182.

  „   after MOLESWORTH, Rev. Hender, 1844 [1843], Vol. XLVII, fol. 82.

ST. AUBYN, James and Edward, of St. Michael Mount and Clowanel, co. Cornw., nat. sons, [1861] Vol. LIV, fol. 158; [1862] Vol. LIV, fol. 310.

ST. CLAIR-ERSKINE, [James, 4th] Bart., now Earl of ROSSLYN [3 Jan. 1805]. Supporters, [1805] Vol. XXIII, fol. 174.

ST. GEORGE, [Gen.] Sir John [R.A.], G.C.B. [25 May 1889]. Supporters, 1889, Vol. LXV, fol. 93.

ST. HELENS, Borough of, co. Lanc., 1876, Vol. LIX, fol. 175.

ST. JOHN, [Henry], Viscount BOLINGBROKE [7 July 1712]. Supporters, [1712] Vol. VI, fol. 64.

ST. JOHN to MILDMAY, ..., M[ildmay] wife of, of co. Essex and Hampsh., [1790] Vol. XVII, fol. 274.

St. John-Griffiths, Col. E., of Upton House, Nursling, Hampsh., 1891, Vol. LXVI, fol. 215.

St. Leger, The Hon. and Rev., Archdeacon of Cloyne, Ireland, 1816, Vol. XXIX, fol. 276.

St. Leger, late Chester, John, of co. York, Leic., and Surrey, [1863] Vol. LV, fol. 38.

St. Levan, Baron [4 July 1887, Sir John St. Aubyn, Bart.], of co. Cornw. Supporters, [1888] Vol. LXIV, fol. 167.

St. Oswald, Baron [6 July 1885, Rowland Winn], of co. York. Supporters, 1885, Vol. LXIII, fol. 126.

St. Quintin, late Darby, William T., of Scampton, co. York, and Sunbury, co. Middx. (Match), [1795] Vol. XIX, fol. 145.

St. Vincent, [Earl 1797, Viscount 1801] Adm. [Sir John Jervis], K.B. [1782]. Supporters, [1797] Vol. XIX, fol. 455.

„ Viscount, Jervis, of co. Staff. Arms, [1823] Vol. XXXIV, fol. 62. [Edward Jervis Ricketts, 2nd Viscount, assumed, Roy. Lic. in 1823, the Surname of Jervis only.]

St. Vincent to Parker before Jervis, ..., of co. Staff., [1861] Vol. LIV, fol. 140 ; 2. S[urviving] s[on].

Sale, Col. Sir Robert Henry, G.C.B. [1842]. Arms, [1843] Vol. XLVII, fol. 188 ; Supporters, fol. 192.

Salisbury, late Markham, Richard Anthony, of Chapel Allerton Hall, co. York, and Exeter, co. Devon, [1785 ?] Vol. XVI, fol. 89.

„ Bishop of [1807], [John] Fisher, [1811] Vol. XXVII, fol. 56.

„ Marquess of, Gascoigne-Cecil quartering, [1842] Vol. XLVI, fol. 52.

Salmon, ..., of Devizes, Wilts., [1805] Vol. XXIII, fol. 150.

„ . . . ., of London, [1856] Vol. LII, fol. 42.

Salomons, (Sir) David (Bart. [26 Oct. 1869]), of London, 1825, Vol. XXXV, fol. 167.

Salt, Henry, of Lichfield, co. Staff., Consul-General in Egypt, 2 May 1816 [1819], Vol. XXXI, fol. 175.

„ [Titus ?], of Crow Nest, Alderman of Bradford, co. York, [1839] Vol. XLIII, fol. 378.

„ Thomas (Banker), of Weeping Cross, co. Staff., 12 April 1849, Vol. XLIX, fol. 124.

Salte, late Geary, William, of London, 1798, Vol. XX, fol. 145.

Saltren, late Willett to Cleveland, ..., of co. Devon, [1847] Vol. XLVIII, fol. 352.

Salusbury, late Trelawny, ..., of co. Cornw., and Wales, [1802] Vol. XXII, fol. 11.

Salusbury before Trelawny, ..., Capt. of Militia, [1809] Vol. XXV, fol. 151.

Salusbury to Burroughs, Rev. Lynch, M.A., Vicar of Offley and Graveley, co. Hertf., died 1837 s. p. m. s. (Match), 1804, Vol. XXIII, fol. 30.

Salusbury after Piozzi, John Salusbury, of Wales (John Salusbury Piozzi Salusbury), 17 Dec. 1813, Vol. XXVII, fol. 441. (Misc. G. et H., New S., IV, p. 185.)

Salvador, Francis, of London, Merchant, s. of Joseph, of Amsterdam, to the descendants of his father, 1 June 1745 [1746], Vol. IX, fol. 194; Add. MS. 14,830, fol. 78.

Samborne, late Hopewell, Mary (Spr.), of co. Hertf. and Nottingham, [1777] Vol. XIV, fol. 9.

Samborne after Palmer, Sambourne S., of co. Somerset, [1840] Vol. XLIV, fol. 239.

Sambrooke, Diana, descendants of John, the father of Viscountess Sackville. Escutcheon of pretence, [1782] Vol. XV, fol. 30.

Sampson before Tilden, of Battle and Ninfield, co. Sussex, [1795] Vol. XIX, fol. 157.

SAMPSON after HAMMOND, ..., of co. Sussex, [1811] Vol. XXVI, fol. 292.

„ after KING, ..., of co. Sussex. Quarterly Arms, [1815] Vol. XXIX, fol. 101.

SAMPSON, late GALPINE, ... (Spr.), of co. Somerset. Match with WILMONT, [1804 ?] Vol. XXII, fol. 318.

SAMPSON to CROFT, ..., of co. Sussex and Staff., [1823] Vol. XXXIV, fol. 118.

SAMPSON, ..., of Henbury, co. Glouc., [1849] Vol. XLIX, fol. 204.

SAMSON, L., of Scotchwell, Prendergast, co. Pembroke, Wales, 1893,* Vol. LXVII, fol. 165.

SAMUEL and [to SAMUEL-] GIBBON, ..., of Wales, [1864] Vol. LV, fol. 212.

SAMUEL, Sir Saul, K.C.M.G., [1882, Agent-General in London for New South Wales], of Courtfield Gardens, London, 1891, Vol. LXVI, fol. 166.

„ Alderman M[arcus], of Portland Place, London, 1893 [1893], Vol. LXVI, fol. 330.

„ Stuart M., of Old Broad Street, London, 1894, Vol. LXVIII, fol. 87.

DE VAHL-SAMUEL, Denis, of London, and Rio Janeiro, granted by Ulster King of Arms (see Burke), to the descendants of his grandfather, Moses, and great uncle, David. 1854.

SAMUELLS, ..., C.B., of Rutland Street, Edinburgh, Judge at Calcutta, B.C.S., [1860] Vol. LIV, fol. 54.

SAMUELSON, Bernard, Bart., of London, and co. Oxf., 1884,* Vol. LXII, fol. 264.

SAMWELL after WATSON, Thomas Samuel Watson Samuel, of Upton, co. Northampton, [1831] Vol. XXXVIII, fol. 284.

SAMWELL, late DROUGHT, Thomas Fuller, 1843, Vol. XLVI, fol. 287.

SANCTUARY, ..., of Weasenham and Castleacre, co. Norf., [1821 ?] Vol. XXXII, fol. 251.

SANDBACH, Samuel, of Woodlands, co. Lanc., and Tarporley, co. Chester, [1836] Vol. XLI, fol. 283.

SANDERS before BRADFIELD, ..., of co. Norf. (Match), [1815] Vol. XXVIII, fol. 416.

SANDERS, ..., of co. Surrey, and Liege, [1848] Vol. XLVIII, fol. 410.

SANDERS, late ARUNDELL, Frederick, of Cheriton Fitzpaine and Lifton co. Devon, 1873, Vol. LVIII, fol. 260. (Dr. J. J. Howard's R. C. Fam., III, p. 167.)

SANDERSON, Sir James, Knt., late Lord Mayor of London (1793). Augmentation, [1795] Vol. XVIII, fol. 433.

SANDERSON, late BURDON, Richard Sanderson, decd. [?], of Lincoln's Inn, London, [1815] Vol. XXVIII, fol. 427.

SANDERSON, Richard Withington Bromley, of Cheetham and York Street, Manchester, co. Lanc., and to the other descendants of his late father, Thomas Withington Bromley Sanderson, 27 April 1869, Vol. LVII, fol. 127. (Genealogist, IV, p. 287.) (Berry's Suppl.)

„ . . . ., of The Manor House, Clapham, co. Surrey, [1870] Vol. LVII, fol. 252.

„ Rev. Edward, M.A., of High Hurst Wood, co. Sussex, s. of Lancelot, 1879, Vol. LX, fol. 289. (Berry's Suppl.)

„ Rev. Alfred P., of Aspenden Rectory, co. Hertf., 1896,* Vol. LXIX, fol. 176.

SANDIFORD, ..., of Shropsh. Match, BROMLEY, [1768] Vol. XI, fol. 276.

SANDILAND, ..., of Speight's Town, Island of Barbados, [1798] Vol. XX, fol. 225.

SANDYS, Lord [Baron of Ombersley, 20 Dec. 1743]. Supporters, [1743] Vol. IX, fol. 93.

„ Baroness of OMBERSLEY [19 June 1802, remainder to 2nd s. of Arthur], Marquess of DOWNSHIRE. Supporters, [1802] Vol. XXI, fol. 410.

„ Baron [of Ombersley], HILL to SANDYS [11 Feb. 1861], of co. Worc., and Ireland, [1861] Vol. LIV, fol. 112.

SANDYS after BAYNTUN, ... ([? co.] Devon), of co. Gloue., Oxf., and Ireland.
Quarterly Arms, [1809] Vol. XXV, fol. 252.

SANDYS, ..., of Lanarth and Helstone, co. Cornw., [1817] Vol. XXX, fol. 202.

SANDYS, late WARREN, ..., of Helstone and St. Minver, Truro, co. Cornw.
(Match), [1817] Vol. XXX, fol. 204.

SANDYS to SPEER, ..., of Fulham and Thames Ditton, co. Surrey, [1871]
Vol. LVIII, fol. 66.

SANFORD, Joseph, of Minehead, co. Somerset (two coats). Quarterly Arms,
? certified, May 1779, Vol. XIV, fol. 149. (Berry.)

SANSOM, ..., BLOMFIELD, wife of, of London, [1799] Vol. XX, fol. 287.

SANT, James, R.A., of Lancaster Gate, London, 1881, Vol. LXI, fol. 233.

SAPWELL, Benjamin Beetham, of Sankenel House, Aylsham, co. Norf., [1873]
Vol. LVIII, fol. 216. (Berry's Suppl.)

SAREL, ..., of London, and Houghton-on-the-Hill, co. Leic., [1819] Vol.
XXXI, fol. 248.

SARGENT to ARNOLD, George, of co. Kent, [1777] Vol. XIII, fol. 287.

SARGENT, now TRENCHARD, ... (Spr.), of Lytchet Matravers, co. Dorset,
[1830] Vol. XXXVIII, fol. 116.

SARSINGHJI, ..., of Bombay, 18 . . ., Vol. LXXI, fol. . . . .

SASSOON, ..., of Cumberland Terrace, London, and Bombay, [1862] Vol. LIV,
fol. 344.

SAUMAREZ, Rear-Adm. Sir James [Bart.], K.B. [1801], of Guernsey. Supporters, [1801] Vol. XXI, fol. 250.

SAUNDERS, [Vice-Adm.] Sir Charles, K.B. [1761]. Supporters, 3 May 1761,
Vol. X, fols. 339 and 376 (see Berry's Suppl. [Arms 3 May 1761.]).

„	. . . ., of Purley and Chaddleworth, Berks. (See WILDER.)	[1766] Vol.
XI, fol. 142.

SAUNDERS, late HUCK, Richard, M.D., [1777] Vol. XIII, fol. 293.

SAUNDERS, ..., BIGLAND, wife of, of co. Gloue., [1796] Vol. XIX, fol. 215.

SAUNDERS to WEBB, James, John and Frederick, of Kensington Gravel Pitts,
co. Middx., and Great Canford, co. Dorset, [1797] Vol. XIX, fols. 414,
416 and 418.

SAUNDERS, ..., of Teale, co. Devon. (See WARREN.) [1824] Vol. XXXIV,
fol. 306.

SAUNDERS, late RICHARDSON, ..., of Manchester, co. Lanc., and Nunwick
Hall, Great Salkeld, co. Cumberland, [1837] Vol. XLII, fol. 213.

SAUNDERS after ARUNDELL, Frederick William. (See SANDERS.) 1873. (Burke's
Suppl.).

SAUNDERS, William Henry Radcliffe, of Lullote, co. Glamorgan, Wales, s. of John
Brewer Saunders, 1897, Vol. LXIX, fol. 325.

SAUNDERSON, [The Hon.] Sir Thomas Lumley, K.B. [1725] [Saunderson after
Lumley, 1723], 3rd Earl of SCARBOROUGH [1739-40]. Quartering and
Supporters, [1724⁄6] Vol. VII, fol. 453.

SAVAGE, Bessy, nat. dau. of Earl RIVERS, 3 July 1714, Vol. VI, fol. 159.

„	Charles, of St. Olave's, Hart Street, London, and Tachbroke, co. Warw.,
18 Dec. 1730, Vol. VIII, fol. 100.

SAVAGE, late CLAVERING, ..., of co. Worc., [1797] Vol. XX, fol. 12.

SAVAGE, ..., of Midsomer Norton, co. Somerset, [1815] Vol. XXVIII, fol. 420.

„	C. F. HEYWORTH-, of Elstowe, Ash, co. Surrey, 1895, Vol. LXVIII, fol. 196.

SAVARY, William James, of Greenwich, co. Kent, and Perigord, France, May 1779,
Vol. XIV, fol. 119. (Berry.)

SAVILE, Sir John, K.B. [1749], of Methby Hall, co. York. Supporters, [1749]
Vol. IX, fol. 327.

„	Christopher (late ATKINSON), Jane SLATE, wife of, of London and M[iddx.],
1789 [1798], Vol. XX, fol. 241.

SAVILE, late LUMLEY [28 Sept. 1807], the Hon. and Rev. John, of co. Nottingham
(afterwards 7th Earl [of Scarborough]). Quarterly Arms, 1807, Vol.
XXIV, fol. 273.

SAVILE after LUMLEY [14 Oct. 1836], John, 8th Earl of SCARBROUGH [21 Feb. 1835], 1836, Vol. XLII, fol. 17.

SAVILE, late LUMLEY, Henry, of Rufford Abbey, co. Nottingham, Capt., 2nd Life Guards (illegit., died s.p. 28 Aug. 1881), [1856] Vol. LII, fol. 137.

SAVILE, Augustus William, of Rufford Abbey, co. Nottingham (died unmar. 13 April 1887), 1881, Vol. LXI, fol. 237. (Berry's Suppl.)

SAVILE (LUMLEY-), 2nd Baron [Savile, 1896] (John Savile Lumley-Savile). Savile Arms exemplified, 1898, Vol. LXX, fol. 131.

„ -ONLEY, late HARVEY, Charles, M.P., of co. Essex and Norf., [1824] Vol. XXXIV, fol. 267.

SAVILL-ONLEY, C. A. O., of Boxfield, Galleywood, co. Essex, 1891, Vol. LXVI, fol. 124.

SAVORY, Sir Joseph, Bart., of Sunningdale, Berks., and brothers, 1891,* Vol. LXVI, fol. 174.

„ Sir W. S., Bart., of London, 1890, Vol. LXV, fol. 180.

SAWBRIDGE, Jacob, Merchant, of London, 26 or 28 July 1714, Vol. VI, fol. 175 ; Add. MS. 14,830, fol. 102.

„ Elizabeth FISHER, wife of Jacob, [1717] Vol. VI, fol. 299 ; Add. MS. 14,830, fol. 103.

„ William, of East Haddon, co. Northampton, [1791] Vol. XVII, fol. 332.

„ . . . ., of Charborough Park, co. Dorset, and Olantegh, co. Kent, [1829] Vol. XXXVII, fol. 362.

SAWBRIDGE-ERLE-DRAX, John Samuel W. [Sawbridge to], of Charborough Park, co. Dorset, and Olantegh, co. Kent, [1829] Vol. XXXVII, fol. 344.

„ -ERLE-DRAX, Wanley E. [Sawbridge to], of Holnest Place, co. Dorset, and Olantegh Towers, co. Kent, 1887, Vol. LXIV, fol. 102.

SAWLE, late GRAVES, ..., of co. Cornw. and Devon. (Match), [1815] Vol. XXVIII, fol. 304.

SAWLE after GRAVES, ..., of co. Cornw. and Devon, [1827] Vol. XXXVI, fol. 375.

SAWREY, ..., of Broughton Tower, co. Lanc., [1842] Vol. XLVI, fol. 86.

SAWYER, Sir James, M.D., of Green Oaks, Edgbaston, Birmingham, 1888, Vol. LXIV, fol. 305.

SAXBY, William, s. of Richard, of Chafford, Penshurst, co. Kent, 1751, Vol. IX, fol. 390. (Berry.)

SAXTON, Charles Ferdinand, of Circourt [in Denchworth] and Goosey, Berks., [1794] Vol. XVIII, fol. 377 [Bart., 26 July 1794].

SAY after HALL, Richard, of co. Lanc., [1855] Vol. LI, fol. 274.

SAYE AND SELE, Baron [Gregory William], FIENNES after TWISLETON [14 Feb. 1825] ; EARDLEY-TWISLETON-FIENNES [16 Mar. 1825], of co. Oxf., [1825] Vol. XXXV, fols. 114 and 116.

„ AND SELE [Baron, Frederick Benjamin], WYKEHAM-FIENNES after TWISLETON [14 Feb. 1849], [1849] Vol. XLIX, fol. 118.

SAYER, ..., Post-Capt., R.N., C.B., of Sandwich, co. Kent, [1821] Vol. XXXIII, fol. 73.

SAYER to MILWARD, Edward Henry, of Cambridge Terrace, Hyde Park, London, and co. Sussex, 1834 [1836], Vol. XLI, fol. 266.

SAYER-MILWARD, ..., of East Horndon, co. Essex, 1856, Vol. LII, fols. 94 and 96.

SAYER to SAYER-MILWARD, Rev. William Carlisle, of Pulloxhill, co. Bedf., Rector of Church of St. Leonard, Wallingford, Berks., 1872 [1874], Vol. LVIII, fol. 319.

SAYER, late BRADLEY, ..., [1853] Vol. L, fol. 386.

SAYLE, Robert, of Leighton House, Trumpington, co. Camb., and Southery, co. Norf., [1873 ?] Vol. LVIII, fol. 290.

SCANTLEBURY, ..., of Porchester Terrace, London, [1873] Vol. LVIII, fol. 218.

SCARBROW, ..., of London, [1837] Vol. XLII, fol. 157.

SCARBROW-WHITE, Cornelius S. (B.A., Camb.), of London, [1837] Vol. XLII, fol. 163.

SCARISBRICK, late ECCLESTON, Thomas, of co. Lanc. Quarterly Arms, 1810, Vol. XXV, fols. 426 and 428.

SCARISBRICK, Charles, late DICCONSON, Charles (heretofore ECCLESTON), of co. Lanc., 1833, Vol. XXXIX, fol. 372.

SCARISBRICK, late ECCLESTON, ..., of co. Lanc., 1834, Vol. XL, fol. 107.

  „   late HUNLOKE, Anne, Lady Hunloke, of co. Lanc. and Derby, 1860,* Vol. LIV, fol. 81.

SCARISBRICK after DE BIANDOS, Leon Remy, Marques DE CASTEJO, of Scarisbrick, co. Lanc., 31 Oct. 1873, Vol. LVIII, fol. 264. (Howard's R. C. Fam., II, p. 106 ; Berry's Suppl.).

SCARISBRICK, Charles, of Scarisbrick Lodge, Southport, co. Lanc., 1897, Vol. LXIX, fol. 315.

SCARLETT, [Sir] James [Knt. 1827], Baron ABINGER [12 Jan. 1835], of co. Surrey. Supporters, [1835] Vol. XL, fols. 334 and 336.

  „   [Lieut.-Gen.] Sir James Yorke, G.C.B. [2 June 1869], of co. Surrey. Supporters, [1870] Vol. LVII, fol. 276.

SCARSDALE, Baron [9 April 1761], ([Sir Nathaniel] CURZON [5th] Bart.). Supporters, [1761] Vol. X, fol. 298.

SCHANK [Alexander, of Castle-rigg, 23 June 1732, by Dundas, Lyon Depute. (Misc. G. et H., 2nd S., I, p. 259.)].

  „   John Mackellar Skeene-Grieve [Wight], of Teignmouth, co. Devon, 2nd s. of Rear-Adm. John WIGHT, by Margaret, only child of Adm. John Schank. [Surname and] Arms of Schank [instead of Wight] and Crest, 17 June 1843, Vol. XLVI, fol. 343 (see Misc. G. et H., 2nd S., I, p. 260).

SCHILLIZZI, John, of London, s. of Math. ZANNI, of Leghorn, 1875,* Vol. LIX, fol. 122.

SCHILLIZZI [to] VAFIADACCHI-SCHILIZZI, John, and his brothers, Lucas and Matthew, of London and Leghorn, 1875,* Vol. LIX, fol. 134 [see Burke].

SCHMILDERN, Baroness DE, of Upper Saxony. Arms for EDMUNDS, [1855] Vol. LI, fol. 267.

SCHŒDDE, Col. and Maj.-Gen. Sir James Holmes, K.C.B. [24 Dec. 1842], of China, 1844 [1843], Vol. XLVII, fol. 155.

SCHOLEY, George, of Sandal Magna, co. York, and London, [1804] Vol. XXIII, fol. 39.

SCHOLFIELD, ..., of Manchester, co. Lanc., [1853] Vol. L, fol. 303.

SCHOMBERG, ..., C.B., Post-Capt., of Kilmore, Ireland, grandfather from Germany, [1816] Vol. XXX, fol. 7.

SCHUSTER, ..., of Roehampton, co. Surrey, [1865], Vol. LV, fol. 296.

SCHUYLER, ... (see SHIELLS), of Flushing, co. Cornw., [1815] Vol. XXIX, fol. 17.

SCIEHUNA [?], Emil ?, V.P., Chamber of Commerce, Malta, 1885,* Vol. LXIII, fol. 35.

SCORER, ..., of Forest House, St. Mary, Nottingham, [1824 ?] Vol. XXXIV, fol. 245.

SCOTT, ..., wife of William JAMESON, of Cork, Ireland. (See JAMESON.) [1779] Vol. XIV, fol. 84.

SCOTT after FENTON, William, of co. York. Quarterly Arms, [1785] Vol. XVI, fol. 5.

SCOTT, Sir Samuel, Bart., and EYRE, wife of, of London. Escutcheon of pretence, [1795] Vol. XIX, fol. 169.

  „   Claude, OMMANEY, wife of, of London. Escutcheon of pretence, ? [1795 ?] Vol. XIX, fol. 182.

SCOTT to WARING, ..., of Bromley, co. Kent, and Shrewsbury and Hayes, Shropsh., 1797 [1798], Vol. XX, fol. 247.

SCOTT, ..., of Bromley, co. Kent, [1817] Vol. XXX, fol. 229.

SCOTT, Sir John, Knt., Baron ELDON [18 July 1799], Chief Justice of Com. Pleas, of co. Northumberland and Dorset. Arms and Supporters, [1799] Vol. XX, fol. 376.

„ . . . ., of Lambs Conduit Street, London, [1806] Vol. XXIII, fol. 368.

„ . . . . [Sir Joseph], Bart., of Great Barr Hall, co. Staff., [1811] Vol. XXVI, fol. 263.

SCOTT before STONEHEWER, ... (Match), [1811] Vol. XXVI, fol. 333.

SCOTT-STONEHEWER, ..., of Austin Friars and Cannon Street, London, and Abington Hall, co. Camb., [1825] Vol. XXXV, fol. 242.

SCOTT, late PHILLIPS, ... (Spr.), reputed dau. of Scott, of Bank Fee House, co. Glouc., [1816] Vol. XXIX, fol. 417.

SCOTT, ..., Baron STOWELL [17 July 1821], of co. Glouc. Supporters, [1821] Vol. XXXIII, fol. 86.

SCOTT before DOUGLAS, [Sir John James, 4th] Bart. [10 July 1822], of Scotland, [1822] Vol. XXXIII, fol. 278.

SCOTT, late SKUES, ..., of Saltash, co. Cornw., and Devonport, co. Devon, His Majesty's Coinager of Devon and Cornwall, [1827] Vol. XXXVI, fol. 182.

SCOTT, ..., of Red House, Great Barr, co. Staff., and Stourbridge, co. Worc., [1829] Vol. XXXVIII, fol. 26.

SCOTT, late WELLBELOVED, Robert, of Stourbridge, co. Worc., and the Middle Temple, London (and SCOTT, his wife), [1830] Vol. XXXVIII, fol. 98.

SCOTT, Maj.-Gen. Sir Hopton S., K.C.B., of Madras, 7 May 1835, Vol. XL, fol. 385.

SCOTT, late Moss, ... (widow and son), of co. Glouc., [1838?] Vol. XLIII, fol. 335.

SCOTT, ..., of Colney Hall, co. Norf., [1855] Vol. LI, fol. 386.

SCOTT-CHAD, ..., of Colney Hall and Thurford, Pinkney, co. Norf., [1855] Vol. LI, fol. 388.

SCOTT, Maj.-Gen., C.B., [1860] Vol. LIII, fol. 329.

SCOTT after JOHNSTONE, ..., of co. York (Baron DERWENT's family), [1860] Vol. LIII, fol. 333.

SCOTT, ..., of Oakbank, Wethered, co. Camb., [1870] Vol. LVII, fol. 240.

„ D. A., of Hougham, co. Norf., 1890,* Vol. LXV, fol. 265.

„ Mrs., of Belton Strange House, Chad, Shropsh., 1892, Vol. LXVII, fol. 1.

„ Rev. Thomas Seard, Vicar, Holy Trinity Church, Penge, co. Kent, 1882,* Vol. LXI, fol. 294. (Berry's Suppl.)

SCOTT-GATTY, Alfred SCOTT-, York Herald of Arms, of London, 1893,* Vol. LXVII, fol. 153.

SCOURFIELD, late PHILIPPS, ..., of Wales, [1863] Vol. LV, fol. 76.

SCOVELL, Lieut.-Col. Sir George, K.C.B. [1815], of London, [1815] Vol. XXIX, fol. 150.

SCRATTON, ..., and ANSELL, [his] wife, of Pennenden, near Maidstone, co. Kent, and Broomfield, nr. Chelmsford, co. Essex, [1837] Vol. XLII, fol. 150.

SCROPE, Annabella, [nat.] dau. of the Earl of SUNDERLAND. Match with HOWE, [1779] Vol. XIV, fol. 100. (See SCROPE, in Foster's Yorkshire Pedigrees.)

SCROPE, late PEART, Joshua, and Mary VIVIAN, wife of, of co. Linc. Escutcheon of pretence, [1792] Vol. XVIII, fol. 41.

„ late THOMSON, George D. P., of Waverley Abbey, co. Surrey, and Castle Comb, Wilts., [1821] Vol. XXXII, fol. 283.

SCUDAMORE-STANHOPE, ..., Bart., of Stanwell House, co. Middx., and Holme Lacy, co. Hereford, [1826] Vol. XXXVI, fol. 151.

SCULTHORPE, ..., of Holywell, co. Rutland, [1809] Vol. XXV, fol. 98.

SCURFIELD, late GREY, ... of co. Durham, [1831] Vol. XXXVIII, fol. 355.

SCUTT to SERGISON, ..., S[ergison], wife of, of Cuckfield Place, co. Sussex, [1805] Vol. XXIII, fol. 169.

SEAFORD, Baron [15 July 1826], [Charles Augustus] Ellis [Baron Howard de Walden], of co. Sussex, [1826] Vol. XXXVI, fol. 27.

SEAFORTH, Lord, Baron MACKENZIE [26 Oct. 1797], of Scotland. Supporters, [1797 ?] Vol. XX, fol. 115.

SEALE, ..., M.P., Lieut.-Col. of Mil., of Mount Boone, co. Devon, [1838] Vol. XLIII, fol. 119.

SEALY to VIDAL, ..., of Cornborough, Abbotsham, co. Devon, and the Middle Temple, London, [1842] Vol. XLVI, fol. 10.

SEAMAN, late PIERCE, ..., of Rothery and Hoby, co. Leic., [1825] Vol. XXXV, fol. 108. (Berry.)

    „   late PIERCE, ..., of Rothery and Hoby, co. Leic., [1835] Vol. XLI, fol. 51.

SEARANCKE (SEAMARKE ?), ..., of London, [1814] Vol. XXVIII, fol. 174.

SEARE, late GOUGH, ..., of Hampsh. and co. Hertf., [1800 ?] Vol. XXI, fol. 118.

SEARLE, Sir Francis, Knt. [30 Mar. 1803], of co. Surrey, KENT, wife of. Impaled Arms, [1803] Vol. XXII, fol. 190.

    „   . . . ., of Oporto, and London. (Match), [1808] Vol. XXIV, fol. 412.

SEARLE to VAN DAM, ..., of London, and Madeira, [1828] Vol. XXXVII, fol. 161.

SEATON, Baron [14 Dec. 1839, Sir John] COLBORNE, [G.C.B., G.C.H.]. Supporters, [1840 ?] Vol. XLIV, fol. 188.

SEAVER, ... See RICARDE (and Berry's Suppl.).

SEBAG-MONTEFIORE, J., of East Cliff House, St. Lawrence, Ramsgate, and London, 1885, Vol. LXIII, fol. 155.

SEBASTIAN, L. B., of New Square, Lincoln's Inn, London, 1894, Vol. LXVIII, fol. 22.

SECCOMBE, Sir Thomas L[awrence], of Yelverton, co. Devon, [K.C.S.I., 2 June 1877 ; G.C.I.E., 2 Aug. 1892], 1893, Vol. LXVII, fol. 143.

SECRETAN, James Woodhouse Samuel Secretan, S[ecretan ?], wife of, of co. Mon[tgomery ?], Wales, [1813] Vol. XXVII, fol. 378. Quartering, fol. 382.

SEDDON, George, of London, and Blakelee and Eccles, co. Lanc., [1777] Vol. XIV, fol. 7.

SEDGWICK, ..., of co. York. Match with CROFT. (See CROFT.) [1772] Vol. XII, fol. 175.

SEDLEY, ..., of Preddy's Hard, nr. Gosport, Hampsh., and Morley Hall, co. Norf. (brother of the next), [1843] Vol. XLVI, fol. 302.

SEDLEY-TILLSTONE, ..., of Preddy's Hard, nr. Gosport, Hampsh. ; Morley Hall, co. Norf. ; and Moulescomb Place, Patcham, co. Sussex (brother of the last), [1843] Vol. XLVI, fols. 304 and 306.

SEEL-(MOLYNEUX-), late UNSWORTH, ..., of co. Lanc., [1815] Vol. XXVIII, fol. 429 ; [1816] Vol. XXIX, fol. 315.

    „   (MOLYNEUX-), late UNSWORTH, ..., of co. Lanc., [1845] Vol. XLVIII, fol. 15.

SEELY, Charles, Bart., of Arnold, co. Nottingham, and Brooke, Isle of Wight, 1896,* Vol. LXIX, fol. 22.

SELBORNE, Baron [23 Oct. 1872], ([The Rt. Hon. Sir Roundell] PALMER), of Hampsh. Supporters, [1872] Vol. LVIII, fol. 168.

SELBY to EATON, Richard, of Great Budworth, co. Chester, [1781] Vol. XIV, fol. 308.

SELBY before HELE, of Colmworth, co. Bedf. Quarterly Arms, [1791] Vol. XVII, fol. 342.

    „   before LOWNDES, William, s. of Richard, of Whaddon Hall and Wavendon, Bucks. Quarterly Arms, [1813] Vol. XXVII, fol. 438.

SELBY after DONALDSON, ..., of co. Northumberland, [1839] Vol. XLIII, fol. 375.

SELLICK to GIST, ..., of London, and Bristol, [1817] Vol. XXX, fol. 184.

SELLICK, now GIST, ..., of Bristol. PLAISEWAY, his wife. Quarterly Arms, [1824] Vol. XXXV, fol. 59.

SELLON, late SMITH, ..., of The Chapter House, St. Paul's, London, and co. Mon[mouth ?], [1847] Vol. XLVIII, fol. 260.

SELMAN, Helena, dau. and co-h. of Leicester [? Lister Selman, and] wife of John LE FEVRE, of Old Ford, co. Middx., 7 July 1789. (Berry, Add.)

SELSEY, Baron [13 Aug. 1794], ([Sir James] PEACHEY [Bart.]), of co. Sussex. Supporters, [1794] Vol. XVIII, fol. 419.

SELWIN, late IBBETSON [18 Feb. 1817], Sir Charles [4th Bart., 5 May 1825], of co. Essex. Quarterly Arms, 1817, Vol. XXX, fol. 103.

„ late IBBETSON, Sir John Thomas, Bart., of co. Essex, 1825, Vol. XXXV, fol. 291.

SELWIN-IBBETSON, [Sir Henry John, 7th Bart.], Baron ROOKWOOD [18 June 1892].

SELWYN (late CLIFT), Congreve, of Cheltenham, co. Glouc., and Exeter Coll., Oxf., (reputed son), [1860] Vol. LIV, fol. 44.

SEMPILL, late CANDLER, [? Edward Candler, husband of the] Baroness Sempill, of co. Northampton, and Scotland, [23 Aug. 1853] Vol. L, fol. 392.

SENHOUSE, Joseph Tiffin, (grandfather Joseph), of Calder Abbey and Wigton, co. Cumberland. Quartering, [1781] Vol. XIV, fol. 356.

SENHOUSE after POCKLINGTON, Joseph, of co. Cumberland, 1842, Vol. XLVI, fol. 189.

SENIOR, Ascanius William, of Tewin, co. Hertf., 26 Mar. 1767, Vol. XI, fol. 204. ([26 May.] Berry.)

„ . . . ., of Musquite Cove and Shafton, co. Cornw., Jamaica, [1792] Vol. XVIII, fol. 89.

SENIOR to HUSEY-HUNT-, ..., of co. Somerset, [1833] Vol. XXXIX, fol. 337.

SEPPINGS, [Robert ?], Knt. [17 Aug. 1819], of London, and Fakenham, co. Norf., [1825] Vol. XXXV, fol. 82.

SERGISON, late WARDEN, Thomas, of Cuckfield, co. Sussex, 13 June 1733, Vol. VIII, fol. 167.

„ late JEFFERSON, ..., 1782 [? 1784], Vol. XV, fol. 383.

„ late JEFFERSON. [Sergison] late PRITCHARD, William. Match with Pritchard, S[ergison] wife of, 1812, Vol. XXVII, fol. 171. [See PRITCHARD.]

„ late SCOTT, ..., Sergison, wife of, [1805] Vol. XXIII, fol. 169.

SEROCOLD after PEARCE, ..., M.A., Camb., [1842] Vol. XLVI, fol. 128.

SETON before KARR, ..., of London, and Scotland. Quarterly Arms, [1799] Vol. XX, fol. 340.

„ before KARR, ..., B.C.S., of London, and Scotland. Quarterly Arms, [1815] Vol. XXVIII, fol. 372.

SETON, late ANDERSON, ..., of Essex, and Scotland. (Match), [1811] Vol. XXVI, fol. 381.

SEVERN, ..., of Sudbury, co. Derby, [1788] Vol. XVII, fol. 97.

SEVERNE, Samuel Amy, of Wallop Hall, Shropsh.; Thenford, co. Northampton; and Rhos Goch, co. Montgomery, Wales, [1843] Vol. XLVII, fol. 93.

SEWELL, John Henry (s. of John Goulding Sewell), of Scopwick and Kirkby, co. Linc., 1843, Vol. XLVI, fol. 322.

„ Col. Thomas Davies, of 28, Grosvenor Road, London, s. of Henry William, of Mortimer Road, Willesden, co. Middx., 1897, Vol. LXX, fol. 28. ·

„ Hon. Col. Frederick Robertson, of Brandlingill, Cockermouth, co. Cumberland, 18 . . ., Vol. LXXI, fol. . . . .

CLAY-KER-SEYMER, Harry E., of co. Dorset, Sec. to the Embassy, Ker Seymer after Clay, 1865, Vol. LV, fol. 276.

SEYMOUR-CONWAY, ..., Baron Conway [17 Mar. 170$\frac{2}{3}$]. Supporters, [1703] Vol. V, fol. 119.

„ -CONWAY, [5th] Marquess of HERTFORD, to INGRAM-SEYMOUR-CONWAY [18 Dec. 1807]. Quarterly Arms and Crest, [1808] Vol. XXIV, fols. 352 and 354.

SEYMOUR to PORTMAN, Henry, [1727] Vol. VII, fol. 561; [1728] Vol. VIII, fol. 12.

SEYMOUR, ..., Post-Capt., R.N., of High Mount, co. Cork, and Ulloa, co. Tipperary, Ireland, [1809] Vol. XXV, fol. 231.

SEYMOUR, Adm. Sir Michael, Bart. Match with HAWKER, [1813] Vol. XXVII,
    fol. 347.
  „ Rear-Adm. Sir Michael, G.C.B. [1859]. Supporters, [1859] Vol. LIII,
    fol. 258.
  „ Sir Edward (see BECKFORD). Match, [1810] Vol. XXV, fol. 388.
  „ H. A., reputed son of the Marquess of HERTFORD, of Lisnabreen, co. Down,
    Ireland, [1842] Vol. XLVI, fol. 112.
  „ Sir George Hamilton, G.C.B. [1847], Envoy to Portugal. Supporters,
    [1847] Vol. XLVIII, fol. 310.
  „ . . . . (see SOWERBY), of Norton and Henkerowle, St. Andrews, Auckland,
    co. Durham, [1862] Vol. LIV, fol. 274.
SEYMOUR (PAGE-), Robert, of Auckland, and Aycliffe School, co. Durham, 1862,
    Vol. LIV, fol. 290.
SHACKERLEY to JACKSON, ..., of co. Chester, reputed son of Jackson, [1806]
    Vol. XXIV, fol. 105.
SHADBOLD, ..., of London, and Baldock, co. Hertf., [1823] Vol. XXXIV,
    fol. 82.
SHADFORTH, ..., of Red Barns and Darras Hall, co. Northumberland, [1826]
    Vol. XXXV, fol. 325.
SHADWELL (LUCAS-), late STENT, William Drew, of co. Sussex, [1844] Vol.
    XLVII, fol. 283.
SHAFTO after DUNCOMBE, and before, Robert Eden, of co. Durham, Wilts., and
    York. (Match), 1804 [1805], Vol. XXIII, fol. 217 ; Quarterly Arms,
    fol. 226.
SHAKERLEY, formerly BUCKWORTH, ..., of co. Chester, [1838] Vol. XLIII,
    fol. 112.
SHAKESPEARE, late BOWLES, ..., of co. Leic., [1858] Vol. LIII, fol. 40.
SHANN, Rev. Thomas, M.A., Vicar of Hampsthwaite, co. York. George, M.D.,
    of Tadcaster, co. York, and Charles Shann, great grandchildren of William,
    [1850] Vol. XLIX, fol. 382. (Crisp, I, p. 168.)
SHAPLAND, Joseph, M.A., Oxf., of Marshfield, co. Glouc., and co. Worc. (Match),
    [1808] Vol. XXIV, fol. 422.
  „ William Jackson, of Hill House, Cradley, Great Malvern, co. Worc., 1892,
    Vol. LXVII, fol. 99.
SHAPTER, ..., M.D., of Topsham, co. Devon, Inspector of Military Hospitals,
    [1818] Vol. XXXI, fol. 91.
SHARD, Sir Isaac, Knt., 18 Mar. 170$\frac{7}{8}$, of Horsley Down, co. Surrey, Sheriff,
    [1713] Vol. VI, fol. 100.
SHARDON, ... (a Match only), [1823] Vol. XXXIII, fol. 355.
SHARLAND-CRUWYS, ..., of co. Devon, [1831] Vol. XXXVIII, fol. 341.
SHARP, John, D.D., Dean of Canterbury, [1689-1691], afterwards Archbishop of
    York, [1691] Vol. IV, fol. 79.
  „ George, of Hexham, co. Northumberland, and London, [1800] Vol. XXI,
    fol. 77.
SHARP before HANDASYDE, ..., of co. Northumberland. Quarterly Coat, [1808]
   · Vol. XXIV, fol. 368.
SHARP, late BOWLT, ..., M.H.O., of co. Middx., [1818] Vol. XXX, fol. 339.
SHARP, Sir Cuthbert, of Black Hall, Hartlepool, co. Durham. (See also
    BRABAZON.) [1822] Vol. XXXIII, fol. 120.
SHARP after JELF, ..., of co. Glouc., and Scotland, [1831] Vol. XXXVIII,
    fol. 216.
SHARP, William, of Claybury, Brewsters, Maxwells, and Haynesfield, Barbados [?],
    [1842] Vol. XLVI, fol. 174.
  „ . . . ., of Little Horton, co. York, [1852] Vol. L, fol. 237.
  „ Herbert (s. of Alfred), of Myrtle Grove, Bingley, co. York, 1897, Vol.
    LXX, fol. 22.
SHARPE, late JOHNSON, ..., of co. Nottingham, [1798] Vol. XX, fol. 172.
  „ late RISSOWE, ..., of co. Suff., [1800 ?] Vol. XXI, fol. 114.

SHARPE, William (? Thomas), of St. Benet, Paul's Wharf, London, [1801] Vol. XXI, fol. 142.

SHARPE to BETHUNE, Lieut.-Col., of Scotland, [1815] Vol. XXIX, fol. 196.

" to BRABAZON, William John, of Trinity Coll., Camb.; Lincoln's Inn, London; co. Sussex; and Ireland, [1841] Vol. XLV, fol. 167; [1847] Vol. XLVIII, fol. 367.

SHARPE, John, D.D., Preb. York, Vicar of Doncaster, co. York, of Brodsworth, co. York, Sidney Sussex Coll., Camb., 1854, Vol. LI, fol. 8.

SHARPE to BANKES, James F., B.A., of co. York, 1854, Vol. LI, fols. 25 and 27.

SHARPE, Mrs., of Glentarf, Camberley, co. Surrey, 1890,* Vol. LXV, fol. 297.

SHAW, Edward, Proctor, Court of Arches, 21 June, 1698, Vol. IV, fol. 265; Add. MS. 14,831, fol. 100.

" Robert, of Ardesley, co. York, (1st s. of Robert, of East Ardesley aforesaid, deed.), and to his two brothers, Henry and Thomas, belonging to the Duke of Northumberland's Royal Regiment of Horse, 4 Dec. 1707, Vol. V, fol. 328 [?]; Add. MS. 14,831, fol. 231. (Berry.)

" Thomas, s. of Thomas, of Coventry and Coundon, co. Warw., [1781] Vol. XIV, fol. 322.

SHAW, late NICHOLSON, John Ralph, of Arrow Hall, co. Chester, 1837, Vol. XLII, fol. 152.

SHAW, ..., of Winterdyne, Ribbesford, co. Worc., [1867] Vol. LVI, fol. 207.

" Bentley, of co. York, and Woodfield House, Scotswood [co. Northumberland ?], 1874, Vol. LIX, fol. 21. (Berry's Suppl.) Arms for wife, Jane Elizabeth, only dau. of John LANCASTER, 1874, Vol. LIX, fol. 23. (Berry's Suppl.)

SHAW-YATES, Ernest Bentley, of Oakwood House, co. York, [1865] Vol. LVI, fol. 17. (? Berry's Suppl.)

SHAW, George, 2nd s. of Seth, of Stamfordham, co. Northumberland, and Fairleigh, Thames Ditton, co. Surrey (? Sheriff of London, 1874-5, see Burke), 1879 [1880], Vol. LX, fol. 332.

SHAW, now HELLIER, Rev. Thomas, of Woodhouse, co. Staff. Quarterly Arms, [13 July] 1786, Vol. XVI, fol. 195.

SHAW, ..., of Coseby, co. Staff. Quarterly Arms, [1786] Vol. XVI, fol. 196.

SHAW before LEFEVRE, [Charles], of Lincoln's Inn, London, [1789] Vol. XVII, fol. 153.

SHAW LEFEVRE, [Charles], Viscount EVERSLEY [11 April 1857]. Supporters, [1857] Vol. LII, fol. 176.

SHAW, ..., of Gower Street, London, [1794] Vol. XVIII, fol. 333.

" Sir James, M.P., and ex-Lord Mayor of London (afterwards a Bart.), 1806 [1807], Vol. XXIV, fol. 277.

SHAW, late MACFIE, John, nephew of the Lord Mayor of London (minor), [1807] Vol. XXIV, fol. 279.

SHAWE before BROOKE, Rev. John K., of co. Kent. Quarterly Arms. Match with KENNARD, [1797 ?] Vol. XIX, fol. 349.

SHAWE to SHAWE-STOREY, Laurence P., of Arcot, Cramlington, co. Northumberland, Capt., Bengal Marines, [1873] Vol. LVIII, fol. 232. (Burke's Suppl.)

SHEAFFE, Maj.-Gen., of Mallow, Ireland, [1815] Vol. XXIX, fol. 165.

SHEARS, ..., of Wimbledon and Kennington, co. Surrey, [1823-1824] Vol. XXXIV, fol. . . . .

[SHEDDEN, Robert, of Paulerspury Park, co. Northampton, eldest s. of William, 3rd s. of Robert, of Beith, co. Ayr, Scotland, eldest s. of Robert Shedden, Merchant, sometime in Holland, afterwards in Beith. Confirmation of Arms, 23 Aug. 1824 (Crisp, Notes, IX, p. 154).]

SHEEPSHANKS to YORK, ..., of Leeds and Linton-in-Craven, co. York, [1796] Vol. XIX, fol. 209 or 299.

SHEEPSHANKS, (William ?), M.A., of Winpole, co. Camb.; Leeds and Linton-in-Craven, co. York; Ovington, co. Norf.; and Wymondeswould, co. Leic., 1804 [1806], Vol. XXIII, fol. 302.

SHEFFIELD, Borough of, co. York, 1875, Vol. LIX, fol. 131.

SHEFFIELD, Joseph James, of Limehouse, co. Middx., [1831] Vol. XXXVIII, fol. 246.

SHEILD, late GILSON, ..., of co. Rutland, [1851] Vol. XLIX, fol. 481.

SHEILDS, John Gore, and Francis Webb Sheilds, of Grolle Park, Blackheath, co. Kent, sons of Wentworth [Sheilds], Rector of Newtown, co. Meath, Ireland, assumed the additional prefix Surname of WENTWORTH by Roy. Lic., 27 Jan. 1877. [Arms confirmed] 1876, Vol. LIX, fol. 63 [?] [see Burke].

SHELDON to CONSTABLE, Edward and Francis, of Burton Constable, co. York, [1791] Vol. XVII, fol. 392 ; [1803] Vol. XXII, fol. 262.

SHELDON, late LESINGHAM, [Samuel, and Lucy, his wife], of co. Worc., [Feb. 1828] Vol. XXXVII, fol. 119.

   ,, late VINCENT, ... (Spr.), of Powick and Abberton, co. Worc., and Waddington Hall, co. Warw., [1828] Vol. XXXVII, fol. 157.

   ,, late RAYNSFORD, [Anne] (widow), of co. Worc., [Feb. 1828], Vol. XXXVII, fol. 159.

SHELLARD, Rev. Thomas, Vicar of Tytherington, co. Glouc., 1740 [1746], Vol. IX, fol. 179.

SHELLEY before SIDNEY, ..., of co. Sussex, Cornet, 17th Light Dragoons, [1793] Vol. XVIII, fol. 197.

SHELLEY to SIDNEY, ..., of Castle Goring, co. Sussex, [1799] Vol. XX, fol. 302.

SHELLEY, [Sir Bysshe], Bart. [3 Mar. 1806], of co. Sussex. Escutcheon of pretence, Arms of SYDNEY, decd. wife, [1806] Vol. XXIV, fol. 16.

SHELLEY and SIDNEY, ..., of co. Derby. Quarterly with HUNLOKE impaled, [1864 ?] Vol. LV, fol. 142.

SHELMERDINE, Nathaniel, J.P., s. of Nathaniel, of Eccles, co. Lanc., and Beechfield, Weasles [? Eccles, co. Lanc.], 1875, Vol. LIX, fol. 98.

SHELTON, Theophilus, of Wakefield, co. York ; Farley, co. Staff. ; and Mansfield, co. Nottingham, 11 Sept. 1690, Vol. IV, fol. 65.

[SHENSTONE (formerly SMITH), Frederick Smith Shenstone, of Sutton Hall, Barcombe, Lewes, co. Sussex, 2nd s. of Richard Smith, of The Priory, co. Worc., and Berry Hill, co. Staff. Add. MS. 37,149 has, at fol. 133, a printed Coat of Arms, and Crest, SMITH impaling KNAPP, quartering FRENCH (?) with an escutcheon of pretence WYATVILLE. It has the initials, F.S.S., Sutton Hall (see Burke's Landed Gentry, 1894).]

SHEPHERD, Francis, of Knaresborough, co. York, [1757] Vol. X, fol. 112.

   ,, ..., of Nun Green, co. Surrey, and Aberdeen, Scotland, [1830] Vol. XXXVIII, fol. 103.

   ,, ..., M.A., Camb., of Yalding, Luddesdown and Trottescliffe, co. Kent, [1855] Vol. LI, fol. 404.

SHEPLEY to HEATHCOTE, ..., of co. Derby, [1821] Vol. XXXII, fol. 393.

SHEPPARD, ..., of Balby, Doncaster, co. York, and Liverpool, co. Lanc., [1865] Vol. LV, fol. 300.

SHEPPARD to Hall, William, of Shropshire, co. Kent, and Rutland, nephew of William Hall, [1725] Vol. VII, fol. 448.

   ,, to COTTON, William T., of Bucks. and co. Staff. (Match.) 1800, Vol. XX, fol. 440.

SHEPPARD after COTTON, Sir Thomas, Bart., of Bucks and co. Staff. Quarterly Arms [1806], Vol. XXIII, fol. 370.

SHEPSTONE, Sir Theophilus, K.C.M.G. [14 Aug. 1876], s. of William, 1879, Vol. LX, fol. 318. (Berry's Suppl.)

SHERBORNE, Baron [20 May 1784, James] (DUTTON), [formerly NAPER]. Supporters, [1784] Vol. XV, fol. 313.

SHERBROOKE after COAPE, Maj.-Gen. Sir John, K.B. [16 Sept. 1809], of co. Nottingham. Match. Quarterly Arms. Supporters, [1810] Vol. XXV, fols. 414, 416 and 419.

SHERBROOKE, Viscount [25 May 1880] (Robert LOWE). Arms, 1880, Vol. LXI, fol. 25 ; Supporters, fol. 31.

SHERBURNE, late TENCH, John, of The Wilderness, Hampton Wick, and Finchley, co. Middx., 1853, Vol. L, fol. 322.

SHEREBURNE [or SHERBOURNE, Nicholas], Bart. [4 Feb. 168⅜, died 14 Dec. 1717, s.p.m.s.], of [Stonyhurst], co. Lanc. Arms and Supporters [1708] Vol. V, fol. 322 [his dau. and h. mar., 1709, the 8th Duke of Norfolk].

SHERIDAN after GRANT-BROWNE, Marcia M., of co. Dorset. Grant and Browne quarterings on escutcheon of pretence, [1836] Vol. XLI, fol. 226.

SHERIFF, Thomas (1758-63), Rouge Dragon Pursuivant of Arms, 24 April 1761, Vol. X, fol. 348. (Berry.)

SHERINGHAM, Ven. J. W., of Standish Vicarage, co. Glouc., 1888, Vol. LXIV, fol. 159.

SHERSON, Robert, Constable of Lanc. Castle. With Canton of NOWELL. Addition to Crest of Sherson, [1780 ?] Vol. XIV, fols. 203 and 204.

  „ . . . ., of Blackfriars, London, [1789 ?] Vol. XVII, fol. 139.

SHERSTON, Peter, of Wells, co. Somerset. Arms of DAVIS, 16 Aug. [May ?] 1793, Vol. XVIII, fol. 215. (Jewers, Wells Cathedral, p. 179.)

SHERWIN, late PARKIN, ... (Spr.), of Bernard Street, Russell Square, London, [1820] Vol. XXXII, fol. 159.

SHERWIN before GREGORY (formerly LONGDEN), of co. Linc. and Nottingham, [1860] Vol. LIV, fol. 56.

SHERWOOD, Oliver Caton (s. of Thomas Caton), Capt., West Indian Regt., 1897, Vol. LXX, fol. 46.

SHEWEN to MANSELL, ..., of Wales. Mansell, wife of Shewen, [1802] Vol. XXI, fol. 291.

SHICKLE, ..., of Clarendon, Island of Jamaica, [1793] Vol. XVIII, fol. 181.

SHIELD to SPENCER, Henry, of Helvington Hall, co. Durham, [1842] Vol. XLVI, fol. 143.

SHIELLS, Thomas Clinton, of East Stonehouse, co. Devon. Match with SCHUYLER, [1815] Vol. XXIX, fol. 17.

SHIFFNER, ..., M.P., of Coomble Place, co. Sussex, and Pontrylar, co. Hereford, [1811] Vol. XXVII, fol. 41.

SHIMELL, William, of Belsars Hatch, co. Essex, 9 Oct. 1727, Vol. VII, fol. 550.

SHIPPERDSON, late HOPPER, E. H., of Pittington Hall, Garth, co. Durham, [1856] Vol. LI, fol. 459.

SHIPPERY, ..., of Childrey, Berks., [1824 ?] Vol. XXXIV, fol. 238.

SHIPPHARD, ..., of Natland, co. Westmorland, by Heard, Garter, and Harrison, Norroy, Kings of Arms. Coat only. Escutcheon of pretence on WILSON, 16 Aug. 1794, Vol. XVIII, fol. . . . . . (Berry.)

SHIPSTER, ..., of London, [1867] Vol. LVI, fol. 271.

SHIPWAY, ... (see BANCE), of Beverston, co. Glouc. (Match), [1721] Vol. VII, fol. 73.

SHIRLEY, ..., Lord FERRERS. [Sir Robert Shirley, 7th Bart., cr. Baron Ferrers, 1677, mar. Elizabeth, only dau. and h. of Laurence Washington.] Supporters and quarterings. Escutcheon of pretence, WASHINGTON, [1677 ?] Vol. III, fol. 70.

  „ Earl [? Robert Shirley, 6th Earl], [1779] Vol. XIV, fol. 96.

  „ Baroness. Match [3 Mar. 171⅚] with [James Compton, afterwards 5th] Earl of NORTHAMPTON, [171⅘ ? Vol. VI].

SHIRT to HIRST, Henry John, of co. York, and London, 1820, Vol. XXXII, fol. 183.

SHITTLEWOOD, ..., widow of JACKSON, of co. Nottingham, [1819] Vol. XXXI, fol. 324.

SHORE, Offley, of Norton Hall, co. Derby, and Castle Hill, Buckland Hill, Newton, co. Dorset. To the descendants of his grandfather Samuel, 1839,* Vol. XLIV, fol. 77.

SHORROCK, Eccles, of Law Hill House, Blackburn, co. Lanc., [1863] Vol. LV,
    fol. 104. (Burke's Suppl.)
SHORT, late HASSARD, Lieut.-Col. Henry, of co. Linc., [1793 ?] Vol. XVIII,
    fol. 283.
    „   late HASSARD, Richard Samuel, of Great Bealings, co. Suff., and co. Linc.,
    [1807] Vol. XXIV, fol. 259.
SHOTTER, late TRIMMER, James, of Farnham, co. Surrey, 1795, Vol. XIX, fol. 171
    (see Berry's Suppl.).
SHOVELL, Sir Cloudesley, Knt., 6 Jan. 169½, Vol. IV, fol. 103.
SHREWSBURY, Countess of [Elizabeth, dau. of James Hoey].   Arms for HOEY
    and DENN, [1827] Vol. XXXVI, fol. 371.
[SHROPSHIRE COUNTY COUNCIL, 18 June 1896.   (Geneal. Mag. II, frontisp.)]
SHRUBB, John, of the Inner Temple, London ; Wokingham, co. Berks. ; and
    Hascombe and Godalming, co. Surrey, 25 Nov. 1729, Vol. VIII, fol. 28ᵇ.
    „   . . . ., of Stokely, Guildford, co. Surrey (hitherto borne arms of SHRUBB,
    Grants in 1729), 1840, Vol. XLIV, fol. 230.
SHUCKBURGH after BLENCOWE, Rev. Charles, of co. Warw. (Vicar), [1848] Vol.
    XLIX, fol. 69.
SHUCKBURGH (late WOOD), Richard Henry, of Bourton Hall, Bourton-on-Duns-
    more and Rugby, co. Warw., 1876, Vol. LIX, fol. 226.   (Berry's Suppl.)
SHUM, ..., of Bury Hill, Dorking, co. Surrey, [1801] Vol. XXI, fol. 278.
SHUM-STOREY, George, of Ham, co. Surrey, and Arcot, Cramlington, co.
    Northumberland, 1823, Vol. XXXIII, fol. 383.   (Berry's App.)
    „   -STOREY, ... (Spr.), of co. Northumberland, [1870 ?] Vol. LVII, fols. 292
    and [1868 ?] 58 ?
SHUTE, Henry, M.A., of Frampton Cotterell, Stapleton, and Stoke Gifford, co.
    Glouc. ; and Brancaster, co. Norf., [1805] Vol. XXIII, fol. 184.
    „   Alice Elizabeth (3rd dau. of Richmund), wife of Rev. Maurice TOWNSEND,
    Vicar of Thornbury, co. Glouc.   STEPHENS quartering, [1828] Vol.
    XXXVII, fol. 137.
SHUTTLEWORTH to HOLDEN, ..., LL.B., of Aston, co. Derby, and Forcett, co.
    York. (Match), [1791] Vol. XVII, fol. 336.
SHUTTLEWORTH after KAY, James Philips, of co. Lanc., [1842] Vol. XLV,
    fol. 393.
SHUTTLEWORTH, Joseph, of Old Warden, co. Bedf., 1881, Vol. LXI, fol. 132.
SIBBALD, [Sir James], Bart. [13 Dec. 1806], of Berks. [Eliza.] DELAGARD, wife of.
    Escutcheon of pretence, [1806 ?] Vol. XXIV, fol. 121.
SIBTHORP to WALDO-SIBTHORP, Humphrey, M.P., of Canwick, co. Linc.   Quarterly
    Arms, [1804] Vol. XXIII, fol. 11.
SIDDONS, George John, B.C.S., of Sumatra, 1819, Vol. XXXI, fol. 286.
SIDEBOTHAM, ..., of Manchester, co. Lanc., 1867 [1871], Vol. LVII, fol. 318.
SIDEBOTTOM, ..., of Harewood Lodge, co. Chester, [1839] Vol. XLIV, fol. 46 ;
    of Etheron House, Mottram-in-Longendale, co. Chester, [1870] Vol. LVII,
    fol. 218.
SIDMOUTH, Viscount [12 Jan. 1805] (ADDINGTON).   Arms and Supporters, [1804]
    Vol. XXIII, fol. 94.
SIDNEY, [Sydney], Viscount [9 Sept. 1689], Henry, of Sheppey, co. Kent.
    Supporters, 1692, Vol. IV, fol. 106.
    „   Anne, of Penshurst, co. Kent, [1752] Vol. IX, fol. 417.
SIDNEY after SHELLEY, [6 Mar. 1793, Sir] John, Bart.   Match with PENNY,
    [1793] Vol. XVIII, fol. 197.
SIDNEY, late SHELLEY [10 April 1799], Philip.   Match with PENNY, [1799]
    Vol. XX, fol. 302.
SIDNEY, [Philip Charles], Baron DE L'ISLE and DUDLEY, [13 Jan. 1835].
    Supporters, [1835] Vol. XL, fol. 313.
    „   Thomas, of Leyton House, co. Essex, Sheriff of L[ondon] and M[iddlesex],
    and of Chapel Ash, near Wolverhampton, co. Staff., [1843] Vol. XLVII,
    fol. 178.

SIDNEY-FOULIS, Philip, only s. of Baron DE L'ISLE and DUDLEY, of co. York (afterwards 2nd Baron), [1850] Vol. XLIX, fol. 350.

SIDNEY (formerly TOMSON), Frederick Edward, of Morton, Frognal, Hampstead, London, 1897, Vol. LXIX, fol. 295.

SIER, (Rev.) Thomas, of Cheltenham, co. Glouc. ; Queen's Coll., Oxf. ; and Gray's Inn, London, [1843] Vol. XLVII, fol. 5.

SIEVIER, R. S., of Conduit Street, London, 1887,* Vol. LXIV, fol. 92.

SIKES, late BAINES [14 Dec. 1857]. Francis, of co. Nottingham. [Arms granted] 7 Jan. 1858 [1857], Vol. LII, fol. 304 (see Her. and Geneal., Vol. VI, pp. 207 and 208).

SILK, ..., of the Court of Arches and St. Andrew's, Holborn, London, [1802] Vol. XXII, fol. 17.

SILLIFANT, John, of Combe, co. Devon, [1818] Vol. XXX, fol. 424.

SILLIFANT-HAMLYN, Fanny Gertrude (widow of Francis Synge Sillifant), of Leawood, Budeston, co. Devon. Arms of Hamlyn, 1898, Vol. LXX, fol. 184.

SILLITOE, ..., of London, [1811 ?] Vol. XXVII, fol. 95.

SILTZER, ... (naturalized British subject), of Cheetham, Manchester, co. Lanc., [1865] Vol. LVI, fol. 38.

SILVERTOP, George, of Minster Acres, co. Northumberland, 12 May 1758, Vol. X, fol. 141. (Berry.)

SILVERTOP to WITHAM, T. M., of Hardwick and Headlam, co. Durham, and Cliffe, co. York (impalement Witham, wife of Silvertop), [1802 ?] Vol. XXII, fol. 36.

SILVERTOP, late ENGLEFIELD, Henry C., of co. Northumberland and York, [1849] Vol. XLIX, fol. 126.

SILVESTER, (Sir) John [Bart.], of Yardley, co. Essex, Recorder of London, [1815] Vol. XXIX, fol. 83.

SILVESTER after CARTERET, (Sir Philip [Bart., 1822]), C.B., of co. Essex, [1822] Vol. XXXIII, fol. 136.

SIMCOCKS, ..., of Whitechurch. (See DAVIDSON.) (Match), [1737] Vol. VIII, fol. 218.

SIMCOE, John, of Chelsea, co. Middx., Capt., H.M.S. "Prince Edward," Aug. 22 1747, Vol. IX, fol. 202. (Crisp, Visit. of Wales, III, p. 112.) Alteration, 1747, Vol. IX, fol. 205.

„ . . . . Alteration of Crest, 4 Nov. 1879 [? 1779].

„ John Henry Walcot VOWLER-, of Penheale, co. Cornwall, s. of John N. Vowler, of Parnacott, co. Devon, 18 . . ., Vol. LXXI, fol. . . . .

SIMCOX, ..., of Harbourne, co. Staff., [1821] Vol. XXXII, fol. 304.

SIMEON, ..., M.P., of Grazeley, Berks., [1815] Vol. XXVIII, fol. 356.

„ [Sir John], Bart. Supporters, [1820] Vol. XXXII, fol. 86.

SIMKINSON to KING, ..., M.A., of co. Hereford, [1837] Vol. XLII, fol. 114.

SIMMONS, ..., of Stepney, co. Middx. (See William RICHARDSON.) (Match), [1765] Vol. XI, fol. 118.

SIMMONS to SMITH, Allyn, of Battersea, co. Surrey. Quarterly Arms, 1774, Vol. XIII, fol. 59.

SIMMONS, Gen. Sir John Lintorn Arabin, G.C.B. [1878], s. of Thomas Frederic. Arms, 1880, Vol. LX, fol. 358. Supporters, fol. 360. (Berry's Suppl.)

SIMOND, Peter, s. of Peter, of Austin Friars, London, 30 June 1760, Vol. X, fol. 250. (Berry.)

SIMONS, William, of Ullesthorp, co. Leic., [1859] Vol. LIII, fol. 63.

SIMPSON, ..., of Fairlawn, Wrotham, co. Kent ; Tileston, co. Chester ; and Bounty Hall, Trelawny, Jamaica, [1799] Vol. XX, fol. 306.

„ . . . ., of Sittingbourne, co. Kent. Impaled HOPPER, wife, [1807] Vol. XXIV, fol. 193.

„ Edward, of Lichfield, co. Staff., [1835] Vol. XLI, fol. 8.

„ Gen. Sir James, G.C.B. [16 Oct. 1855]. Supporters, [1856] Vol. LII, fol. 3.

SIMPSON, Edward Thornhill, of Walton and Sandell Magna, co. York, [1864] Vol. LV, fol. 188.

SIMS, ..., M.A., of Clifton, co. Glouc., [1814] Vol. XXVIII, fol. 99.

„ Arthur, of Grove Park, Denmark Hill, London, 1896, Vol. LXIX, fol. 101.

SINAUER, Sigismund, of Pembridge Gardens, London, 1886, Vol. LXIII, fol. 255.

SINCLAIR, F. G., of Great Shelford, co. Camb., 1890, Vol. LXVI, fol. 19.

SINGER, ..., of Chippenham, Wilts., [1804] Vol. XXII, fol. 415.

SIRR, Edward Joseph A. (s. of Richard), and others, 18 . . ., Vol. LXXI, fol. . . . .

SISSMORE, ..., B.C.L., Oxf., of Portsmouth and Wickham, Hampsh., [1796] Vol. XIX, fol. 272.

SISSON-WAYET, ..., of Gayton-le-Marsh, and Bilsby, co. Linc., [1832] Vol. XXXIX, fol. 10.

SITLINGTON, William, s. of John, of Wigton, co. Cumberland, 2 Dec. 1748, Vol. IX, fol. 271. (Berry.)

SITWELL, late HURT, Francis, of Renishaw, co. Derby, 1777, Vol. XIII, fol. 289. Hurt quartering to Sir George Sitwell, Bart., [1898] Vol. LXX, fol. 118.

WILMOT-SITWELL, Edward Sacheverell Wilmot, of Stainsby, co. Derby. (Berry Appx. and Burke.) Surname and Arms, 1772.

SKARDON, ..., Capt., B.C.S., [1823] Vol. XXXIII, fol. 355.

SKEELS, Rev. Serocold C., M.A., Camb., of St. Martin's, Stamford Baron, co. Northampton, 1868, Vol. LVII, fol. 21. (Crisp, V, p. 19).

SKEFFINGTON, late FARRELL, William Charles, of co. Leic., 13 June 1772, Vol. XII, fol. 197. (Berry.)

SKELMERSDALE, Baron, of co. Lanc.   Supporters, [1828] Vol. XXXVII, fol. 35.

SKELTON (late JONES), Arnoldus, of co. Cumberland, 19 Nov. 1774, Vol. XIII, fol. 29.

SKETCHLEY, Rev. Alexander E., D.D., of Greenwich, co. Kent, Vicar of Deptford, co. Kent, [1870 ?] Vol. LVII, fol. 294.

SKINGLEY, ..., of Great Coggeshall, co. Essex, [1828 ?] Vol. XXXVII, fol. 202.

SKINNER, Maria, 7th dau. of Cortland [Skinner], of New Jersey, North America, wife of [Sir George] NUGENT, Bart., of Berks. Impaled, [1807] Vol. XXIV, fol. 232.

„ (Cortland). Crest to Skinner, of North America. Match, [1814] Vol. XXVIII, fol. 19.

SKINNER, late LONGMORE, ..., of co. Essex and Norf., [19 Oct. 1825] Vol. XXXV, fol. 339.

SKINNER, Russell and Samuel, B.C.S., Judge of Circuit at Chittoor, Madras. Quartering WALKER, [1827] Vol. XXXVI, fol. 398 [see Burke].

SKOULDING-CANN, J. F., of co. Hereford and Norf., [1867] Vol. LVI, fol. 300.

SKRYMSHER to CLOPTON, Charles Boothby, of co. Warw., [1792] Vol. XVIII, fol. 135.

SKUES to SCOTT, ..., of co. Cornw. and Devon, [1827] Vol. XXXVI, fol. 182.

SLACK, Dr. Robert, of Leamington, co. Warw., and Newbury [Berks. ?], 1884,* Vol. LXII, fol. 226.

SLADE, Lieut.-Gen., of Burstock, co. Dorset, and Maunsell House, co. Somerset, [1831] Vol. XXXVIII, fol. 313.

SLADE-GULLY, ..., of Trevennen House, Gorran, co. Cornw., and Rector of Berry Narbor, co. Devon, [1854] Vol. LI, fol. 34.

SLADE, John, s. of George, of Yeovil and Ash Bodyn, co. Somerset, and Alexandra Road, London, 1880, Vol. LX, fol. 376. (Berry's Suppl.)

SLADEN, ..., of Lee, Swanton Court, and Ripple Court, co. Kent, [1828] Vol. XXXVII, fol. 215.

SLAGG, J., of Hertford Street, Mayfair, London, 1888,* Vol. LXIV, fol. 307.

SLANEY, Robert Aglionby ?, of Hatton Grange, Shifnal, and Wem, Shropsh. (Match), [1800] Vol. XX, fol. 415.

SLANEY after KENYON, William, of Shropsh., 1862, Vol. LIV, fol. 300.

SLATER to JOYE, Mary, of London, 1774, Vol. XII, fol. 290.

SLATER before REBOW, of The Park, Wivenhoe, co. Essex (Rebow, wife of Slater). Quarterly Arms, [1796] Vol. XIX, fol. 241.

SLATER, ..., of Margate, co. Kent, and Shelswell, co. Oxf., [1834] Vol. XL, fol. 278.

SLATER-HARRISON, ..., of co. Oxf., [1834] Vol. XL, fol. 280.

SLEIGH to LINDLEY, John, of co. Nottingham, [1773] Vol. XII, fol. 225; [1782] Vol. XV, fol. 85.

SLINGER, Matthew, B.A., Camb., of Buckden and Bickermonds-in-Langstrothdale, co. York, [1841] Vol. XLV, fol. 165.

SLINGSBY, late LESLIE, Thomas, of co. York, [1869] Vol. LVII, fol. 156 [*see* Burke].

„   late ATKINSON, Rev. Charles Slingsby (s. of Rev. Thomas), 18 . . ., Vol. LXXI, fol. . . . .

SLOANE, William, of Chelsea, co. Middx., 9 April 1726 [? 1725], Vol. VII, fol. 440.

SLOANE-STANLEY, ..., of Paultons, Hampsh., [1822 ?] Vol. XXXIII, fol. 112.

SLOANE to BIDGOOD, Henry Fisher, of co. Devon, and Tobago. Roy. Lic., 5 Nov. 1822, Vol. XXXIII, fol. 336 (*see* Burke).

SLOANE, Charles Gordon (s. of John), 18 . . ., Vol. LXXI, fol. . . . .

SLOCOCK, ..., of Newbury, Berks. (for one wife of Thomas GOODCHILD, *see* GOODCHILD). (*See* John MILLER.) Match, [1765] Vol. XI, fol. 110.

SLOGGETT, William Henry, of Tremalyn, Paignton, co. Devon, 1890,* Vol. LXV, fol. 176.

SLOPER, Robert, of West Woodhay, Berks., [1782] Vol. XV, fol. 63.

„   Lieut.-Gen. Sir Robert, K.B. [1788], of Berks.   Supporters and ? Augmentation, 1 Aug. 1788, Vol. XVII, fols. 19 and 23.

„   . . . ., of Devizes, Wilts., [1844] Vol. XLVII, fol. 240.

SMALESHAW, Dorothy, dau. of William, of Bolton, co. Lanc. (by Mary, dau. of John STARKEY, of Huntroryd, co. Lanc.), 1 June 1750, Vol. IX, fol. 357 (*see* Genealogist, IV, p. 286).

SMALL, ..., of Lewisham, co. Kent, and Ully and Minchinhampton, co. Glouc. (Quartering, escutcheon of pretence on, *see* PYBUS), [1795] Vol. XIX, fol. 161.

SMALLMAN, Alderman Henry George, of Stanstead, Sutton, co. Surrey, 1898, Vol. LXX, fol. 164.

SMALLWOOD to HERCY, ..., of Berks., [1822] Vol. XXXIII, fol. 128.

SMALLWOOD, late HEWITT, ..., of Shropsh., [1794] Vol. XVIII, fol. 355.

SMALLWOOD to FETHERSTONHAUGH, ..., of Kirkoswald, co. Cumberland. Match, [1798 ?] Vol. XX, fol. 136.

SMART, ..., Knt., of Great Portland Street, London, 1824, Vol. XXXIV, fol. 375.

SMELTER, John, of Norton, co. Derby, and Richmond and Sheffield, co. York (Anne WAINWRIGHT, wife of Smelter). Escutcheon of pretence, [1796] Vol. XIX, fol. 303.

SMETHURST, ..., of Hartwood, Chorley, co. Lanc., [1860] Vol. LIV, fol. 50.

SMITH, John, D.D., Rector of Lowther, co. Westmorland, and Preb. of Durham, 1707, Vol. V, fol. 250.

„   William, Physician to Garrison at Portsmouth, Hampsh., 17 Sept. 1711, Vol. V, fol. 447 ; Add. MS. 14,830, fol. 159.

„   Thomas, s. of Thomas, of Bristow Ox [Broxtow], co. Nottingham, and Gaddesby, co. Leic., High Sheriff, 5 Mar. 171⅞, Vol. VI, fol. 354.

„   Joshua, of Runton and Great Yarmouth, co. Norf., 3 Aug. 1722, Vol. VII, fol. 93.   (Berry.)

SMITH, late LE FEVRE, Thomas, of Hadley, co. Middx., and France, s. of Thomas, Bar.-at-Law, decd., to descendants of his father, 8 May 1728, Vol. VII, fol. 577 ; Add. MS. 14,830, fol. 48.

SMITH, [Micheal]. [CUSAC before Smith, of Newtown, King's County, Ireland. Supporters, 1799, Bart., 1799.   Grazebrook, Her. of Smith, p. 42, *see* Burke.]

SMITH, Jarrett, of Long Ashton, co. Somerset (Edmondson's Armory.) *See* SMYTH. 7 July 1767, Vol. XI, fol. 208 ; 7 April 1767, in the Heraldry of Smith.

„ James (or John), of Newland Burthwaite, co. York, 13 April 1738, Vol. VIII, fol. 238.

„ Thomas, of Eastbourne, co. Sussex, 1758, Vol. X, fol. 133. (Berry.)

„ Thomas, s. of Robert, of Bristol, Lord of the Manors of Sandford, co. Somerset, and Ircott, Alveston, co. Glouc., 4 July 1766, Vol. XI, fol. 170. (Berry.)

„ . . . . (*see* FEUILLETEAU, of the Island of Nevis). (Match), [1774] Vol. XIII, fol. 5.

SMITH, late SIMMONS, Allyn, of Battersea, co. Surrey. Quarterly Arms, 1774, Vol. XIII, fol. 59.

SMITH to BROMLEY, Sir George, Bart., of East Stoke, co. Nottingham, 1778, Vol. XIV, fol. 25.

„ to PAUNCEFOTE, ..., of co. Nottingham, B.A., Worcester College, Oxf., [1809] Vol. XXV, fol. 110.

SMITH, ..., of Lymington, Hampsh., and Woolwich, co. Kent, [1784] Vol. XV, fol. 293.

„ . . . ., of Kendal, co. Westmorland, [1784] Vol. XV, fols. 357 and 358.

SMITH to BURGES, John, of co. Essex [mar. Margaret Burges] (Bart. in 1793), [10 June] 1790, Vol. XVII, fol. 223. [Misc. G. et H., 3rd S., III, p. 237.]

SMITH, ..., of Redbourne, co. Hertf., [1790] Vol. XVII, fol. 262.

„ . . . . [of Baldahara, Scotland. (Quarterly Arms), 1765, Grazebrook, Heraldry of Smith, p. 95.]

SMITH to CHRISTMAS, John C., of Biddlesford, co. Devon, and Waterford, Ireland, [1793] Vol. XVIII, fol. 270.

SMITH, ..., of Wray, Melling, co. Lanc. Quarterly Arms, [1794] Vol. XVIII, fol. 353.

SMITH, late JONES, ..., of Castle Combe and Broad Somerford, Wilts., [1798] Vol. XX, fol. 132.

SMITH, ..., of Lee, co. Kent, and Tokenham, Wilts., Col. of Militia, 1800, Vol. XX, fol. 433.

„ Enos, P.C. and H., of Whitehall and Vauxhall, [1800] Vol. XXI, fol. 31.

SMITH to LEIGH, ..., of co. Somerset and Warw., [1802] Vol. XXI, fol. 385.

SMITH, ..., of Apsley House, co. Bedf. (*See* DOWNES.)

„ Sir William Sidney, Knt. (decd. 26 May 1840). Augmentation and Supporters, 1803, Vol. XXII, fols. 59 and 62.

SMITH, late WEBBER, Capt. James, of London, [1804] Vol. XXII, fol. 434.

SMITH, (Sir Drummond), Bart., of Tring Park, co. Hertf., 8 May 1804, Vol. XXIII, fol. 2.

„ James, of London, [1805] Vol. XXIII, fol. 223.

„ William Procter, Sec. to Adm. Young, Plymouth Dock, [1806] Vol. XXIV, fol. 82.

„ Thomas, Rec^r-General, Dean and Chapter of St. Paul's, London, [1808] Vol. XXIV, fol. 357.

„ . . . . (*see* PICARD), of Beverley, co. York, [1809] Vol. XXV, fol. 170.

„ [William, Bart. 1809], of Eardiston, co. Worc., [1809] Vol. XXV, fol. 278.

„ . . . ., Bart., of Sydling St. Nicholas, co. Dorset ; New Windsor, Berks.; and Ilminster, West Dowlish, co. Somerset, [1811] Vol. XXVI, fol. 218.

SMITH before MARRIOTT, of Horsmonden, co. Kent. Quarterly Arms, [1811] Vol. XXVI, fol. 223.

SMITH, ..., of Appleby, co. Leic., and Beewood, co. Staff. Arms to HYATT, wife of, and to descendants, [1811] Vol. XXVI, fols. 412 and 413.

SMITH, *alias* HOVELL, ..., of Ashfield, co. Suff. (*See* TORKINGTON.) [1813] Vol. XXVII, fol. 327.

SMITH, Elizabeth Mary, widow of Thomas, and dau. of Robert MOWER and Elizabeth MILNES, of Dunstan Hall, co. Derby. Arms and Crest of Smith. Impalement and Crest, [1816] Vol. XXIX, fols. 308 and 309.

„ . . . . (see RHODES), of Leeds [co. York ?]. (Match), [1817] Vol. XXX, fol. 270.

„ . . . . (of Cundal, co. York, SMITHSON), [1790] Vol. XVII, fol. 202.

SMITH to PEAKHAM, ... (minor), [1820] Vol. XXXII, fol. 22.

SMITH, David William (Bart.), J.P., of Preston, co. Northumberland, and Pickering, Upper Canada, [1821] Vol. XXXII, fol. 369.

SMITH to DODSWORTH, Sir Edward, Bart., of co. York, [1821] Vol. XXXIII, fol. 27, see [1738] Vol. VIII, fol. 238 ; Sir Charles [1846], Vol. XLVIII, fol. 103.

„ to EDWARDS, ..., of Wales, [1825] Vol. XXXV, fol. 102.

„ to ELLŒRKER, Thomas, of Durham, [1826] Vol. XXXV, fol. 394.

SMITH, ..., of St. Michael, Queenhithe, London, [1826] Vol. XXXVI, fol. 150.

SMITH and GOLDIE, ..., of North End, Little Ilford, co. Essex, [1828] Vol. XXXVII, fol. 95.

SMITH, late BRATT, ..., of Southwark and Camberwell, co. Surrey, [1828] Vol. XXXVII, fol. 211.

SMITH, Maj.-Gen. Sir Levine [Lionel ?], K.C.B., of Lys, Hampsh., [1829] Vol. XXXVII, fol. 373. Crest of Augmentation, [1838] Vol. XLIII, fol. 107.

SMITH-MILNES, ..., of Derby, [1831] Vol. XXXVIII, fol. 269 ; [1873] Vol. LVIII, fol. 271.

SMITH, late GREY, John William, of Durham (of Jesus Coll., Camb.), [1833] Vol. XXXIX, fol. 374.

SMITH, ..., F.S.A., Hanoverian Consul, Pygons Hill, Lydiate, Liverpool, [1838] Vol. XLIII, fol. 241.

SMITH to MAYDWELL, ..., of co. Camb., [1841] Vol. XLV, fol. 229.

SMITH, Mary (only dau. and h. of John, of Louth, co. Linc.), wife of Ellis WYNNE, [1836] Vol. XLI, fol. 192.

„ . . . . (? W. H. S., Baroness HAMBLEDON), of Hinton St. George, co. Somerset, and Kilburn House, Willesden, co. Middx., [1842] Vol. XLVI, fol. 72.

SMITH to HENSHAW, ..., of co. Essex, [1843] Vol. XLVI, fol. 293.

SMITH after LEADBITTER, John Leadbitter, of Durham, [1843] Vol. XLVI, fol. 295.

„ after TAYLOR, Edward Crook, of Durham, 1843, Vol. XLVI, fol. 300.

SMITH, Maj.-Gen. Sir Henry G[eorge] W[akelyn], K.C.B. [1844], of co. Camb., s. of John, of Whittlesea, co. Camb. Supporters, [1844] Vol. XLVII, fols. 237 and 238 ; [1847 ?] Vol. XLVIII, fol. 238.

„ John William, J.P. (s. of John, decd.), of Oundle, co. Northampton, and to the descendants of his father, [1844 ?] Vol. XLVII, fol. 323.

SMITH-DORRIEN, ..., of co. Hertf., [1845] Vol. XLVII, fols. 356 and 357.

SMITH after DAZLEY, ..., B.A., St. John's Coll., Camb., of co. Essex, [1845] Vol. XLVIII, fol. 49.

SMITH to SELLON, ..., of Mon. [? co. Monmouth], [1847] Vol. XLVIII, fol. 260.

SMITH, Robert Vernon, M.P., P.C., of Cheam, co. Surrey (? Baron LYVEDEN [1859]), 1846 [1847], Vol. XLVIII, fol. 306.

SMITH to VERNON, Robert Vernon, of co. Surrey ; Farning Woods, co. Northampton ; Hilton Hall, co. Staff. ; and Newmarket, co. Camb., 1846 [1847], Vol. XLVIII, fols. 324 to 326 [?].

„ to VERNON, ..., of Ardington House, co. Bedf. Quarterly Arms, [1850] Vol. XLIX, fol. 316 ; [1859] Vol. LIII, fol. 192.

„ to VERNON, ..., of co. Northampton, [1859] Vol. LIII, fol. 192.

„ to EARDLEY, Sir Culling E., Bart., of co. Hertf., [14 May 1847] Vol. XLVIII, fol. 330 ; see [1727] Vol. VII, fol. 577.

SMITH, Richard, of Berry Hill, co. Staff., and The Priory, Dudley, co. Worc. (now [of] Shenstone [co. Staff.]), [1855 ?] Vol. Ll, fol. 192.

SMITH to MARKER, Rev., of Exmouth and Aylsbeare, and Vicar of Uffculme, co. Devon, [1855] Vol. LI, fol. 272.

SMITH, ..., C.B., of Hampstead, co. Middx., [1856] Vol. LI, fol. 451.

SMITH to FOSTER, Capt. George Foster, [1856] Vol. LII, fol. 11.

SMITH, ..., of Bombay, [1859] Vol. LIII, fol. 126.

    „   [Robert Vernon], Baron LYVEDEN [1859], of co. Northampton. Supporters, [1859] Vol. LIII, fol. 190.

SMITH [to] DUFF-ASSHETON-SMITH, George William (minor), of Hampsh. and co. Carnarvon, Wales, [1861] Vol. LIV, fol. 190.

SMITH, Capt. . . . ., Bengal Army, [1862] Vol. LIV, fol. 304.

    „   Robert Claude, of Redcliffe Tower, Paignton, co. Devon. (Burke, p. 936.)

    „   John, D.D., of Durham, [1707] Vol. V, fol. 250. (Burke, p. 939.)

    „   Thomas, of Whitechapel, London. (Burke, p. 939.)

    „   Richard, of The Saltwells, Brierley Hill, co. Staff., [1855 ?] Vol. LI, fol. 192. (Burke, p. 939.)

SMITH-MASTERS, late COWBURN, Rev. Allan, of co. Kent, [1862] Vol. LIV, fol. 308.

SMITH-BOSANQUET, Horace James, J.P., of Broxbournbury, co. Hertf., [1866] Vol. LVI, fol. 154. (Crisp, I, p. 251.)

SMITH-GORDON, Sir Lionel E., Bart., of co. Devon, [1868] Vol. LVI, fol. 333.

SMITH, Benjamin, of Tan-y-Craig, Llanbeblig, Wales, 1869 [1872], Vol. LVIII, fol. 108.

SMITH-MILNES, William Broughton, of Dunston Hall, Chesterfield, co. Derby, 1873, Vol. LVIII, fol. 271 (and [1831] Vol. XXXVIII, fol. 269).

SMITH to BELL, Reginald, of co. York and Northampton, [1878] Vol. LX, fol. 76.

    „ to MILNE, Samuel, of Calverley House, nr. Leeds, and Cliffe House, nr. Halifax, co. York, [1878] Vol. LX, fol. 99.

SMITH, Sidney, of Rutland House, Hampstead, co. Middx., 1878, Vol. LX, fol. 101.

    „   Rev. Joseph Denham, of York Terrace, Regent's Park, London, and Vevey Place, Dublin, "a lay preacher," 1879, Vol. LX, fol. 232. (Berry's Suppl.)

    „   Samuel Montgomery Charles Alfred Anderson (F.R.C.S.), of Willesden, s. of Samuel Montgomery Smith, of the same, [?], co. Lanc., [12 April] 1879, Vol. LX, fol. 249 (see W. P. W. Phillimore's History of Smith, p. 31).

    „   Benjamin Brown, of Wolverhampton, co. Staff., 1879, Vol. LX, fol. 295. (Berry's Suppl.)

    „   Rev. Jeremiah Finch, of Aldridge and Brewood, co. Staff. (s. of Jeremiah), 1879, Vol. LX, fol. 316. (Berry's Suppl.)

    „   A. McK., of Bolton Hay, Roby, co. Lanc., 1890,* Vol. LXV, fol. 283.

    „   E. Octavius, of Sydney, New South Wales, 1884,* Vol. LXII, fol. 330.

    „   Sir E. F., of Margatville, South Australia, 1889, Vol. LXV, fol. 156.

    „   Ed. Fisher, of Dudley Priory, co. Worc., 1887,* Vol. LXIII, fol. 331.

    „   Rev. George, of Homersfield Rectory, Harleston, 1884,* Vol. LXII, fol. 188.

    „   Horace P., of Tong, Shropsh., 1885, Vol. LXIII, fol. 81.

    „   Joseph, of Holyrood Place, Oldham, co. Lanc., 1894, Vol. LXVIII, fol. 114.

    „   J. J., of Wells House, Ilkley, co. York, 1892,* Vol. LXVII, fol. 20.

    „   (Sir) John, of Parkfield, St. Alkmunds, co. Derby, 1886,* Vol. LXIII, fol. 257.

    „   Prince, of Hillbrook, Keighley, Southburne, and Kirkburton, co. York, 1894, Vol. LXVII, fol. 293.

    „   William, of Barnes Hall, Ecclesfield, co. York, 1887,* Vol. LXIV, fol. 98.

    „   Oswald, of Thornbury, Heston, co. Middx., and Lea Green, Cliffe, co. Kent, 1893,* Vol. LXVII, fol. 253.

SMITH-BINGHAM, O[swald], of Thornbury, Heston, co. Middx., and Lea Green, Cliffe, co. Kent, 1894, Vol. LXVIII, fol. 101.

SMITH, H. Stinton, of London. (*See* SMITH-REWSE.) 1888, Vol. LXIV, fol. 198.

SMITH-REWSE, H. S., of Edinburgh Terrace, Kensington, London ; Rev. G. F., of South Elmham Rectory, Harleston ; H. W., Maj., R.E. ; E. A., of Manley, Sydney, New South Wales, 1889, Vol. LXV, fol. 118.

SMITH-RYLAND, W. C. H. A., of Barford Hill, co. Warw., 1889, Vol. LXV, fol. 108.

SMITH, Rev. A. S. Clementi, of Chadwick St. Mary, co. Essex, [1889] Vol. LXV, fol. 43.

  ,, Edward Maule Lawson, of Togston and Amble, co. Northumberland, [1881] Vol. LXI, fol. 146.

  ,, Robert Thomas, of Burrage Road, Plumstead, co. Kent, 1897, Vol. LXIX, fol. 241.

  ,, Thomas (s. of Benjamin), of Stratford Place, London, 1897, Vol. LXIX, fol. 317.

  ,, William Macadam, of Abbotsfield, Wiveliscombe, Hampsh., 1898, Vol. LXX, fol. 139.

  ,, Richard HORTON-, K.C., 18 . . ., Vol. LXXI, fol. . . . .

  ,, Lumley, Judge of the County Court (2nd s. of Richard), 18 . . ., Vol. LXXI, fol. . . . .

  ,, Roanden A. H. BICKFORD-, (s. of William Bickford, M.P.), 18 . . ., Vol. LXXI, fol. . . . .

SMITH-GRAY, James Maclaren, of The Boltons, South Kensington, London, husband of Baroness GRAY. Gray and Smith quarterly, 1897, Vol. LXX, fol. 13.

SMITHEMAN, ..., of Buildwas and Little Wenlock, Shropsh. (*See* BROOKE.) [1788] Vol. XVI, fol. 334.

SMITHES, John Tatham, of Eveley, nr. Liphook, Hampsh., 1899, Vol. LXXVI [LXX ?], fol. 330.

SMITHSON to PERCY, ... [12 April 1750], Earl of NORTHUMBERLAND, [1750] Vol. IX, fol. 377.

SMITHSON, ..., of Cundal, co. York, [1790 ?] Vol. XVII, fol. 202.

SMITON, ..., of St. Dunstan's, London, [1792 ?] Vol. XVIII, fol. 145.

SMYTH-WINDHAM, Joseph, of Hill Hall, co. Essex ; Waghen *alias* Wawen, co. York ; and Woodmansterne, co. Surrey, [1823] Vol. XXXIV, fol. 58.

SMYTH after BOWYER, ..., of co. Essex and Norf., [1839] Vol. XLIV, fol. 40.

SMYTH, Jarritt, Bart., of Long Ashton, co. Somerset, 7 July 1767, Vol. XI, fol. 208. (Berry.)

  ,, John, of Heath, Wakefield, co. York, 29 Jan. 1777, Vol. XIII, fol. 259.

SMYTH to OWEN, ..., of Condover, Shropsh., [1790] Vol. XVII, fol. 205.

SMYTH, Commander William Henry, R.N., Knt. of St. F. and of Merit of Sicily, [1818] Vol. XXXI, fol. 84. Augmentations, [1828] Vol. XXXVII, fol. 74.

  ,, John Hugh, of Wraxall, co. Somerset, [1824] Vol. XXXV, fol. 20.

SMYTH-PIGOTT, John Hugh, of Wraxall and Brockley, co. Somerset, [1825] Vol. XXXV, fols. 223 and 224.

SMYTH to WILSON, ..., of Dalham Tower, co. Westmorland, [1825 ?] Vol. XXXV, fol. 71.

SMYTH, late UPTON, ... (minor), of Ingmire, co. York, [1852] Vol. L, fol. 195.

SMYTH, Edward, late HENLOW, of co. Bedf., 1883, Vol. LXII, fol. 100. (Berry's Suppl.)

  ,, Thomas, of the parish of St. George, Hanover Square, one of the Esquires to Charles, Earl of BELLOMONT, at his late installation, 15 June following, ? son of [? and his son Arthur] Smith, Baron of the Exchequer and [Arthur Smythe ?] Archbishop of Dublin [1776]. Certificate of Arms, 15 June 1773.

SMYTH, Gen. Sir Henry Augustus, K.C.M.G. [1890], and Augmentation, 18 . . ., Vol. LXXI, fol. . . . .

SMYTHE-GARDINER, ..., of co. Oxf., [1787] Vol. XVI, fol. 277.

„ -GARDINER, late WHALLEY, [18 Nov. 1797, Sir James, 2nd] Bart., of Clerk Hill, co. Lanc. Quarterly Arms, [1797] Vol. XX, fol. 112.

SNEAD, ..., of Calcutta, [1865] Vol. LVI, fol. 11.

SNELL before CHAUNCY, William, of Edmonton and Newington, co. Middx., [1781] Vol. XIV, fol. 306.

„ before CHAUNCY, ..., of Austin Friars, London, [1783] Vol. XV, fol. 173.

SNELL, ..., of Edmonton, co. Middx. ; Denham, Bucks. ; and Munsden Parva, co. Hertf., [1811] Vol. XXVI, fol. 182,

„ T. W. (Solicitor), of Clapham Rise, co. Surrey, 1884, Vol. LXII, fol. 335.

SNELSTON, ..., of Astle and Prestbury, co. Chester. (Match), [1702] Vol. V, fol. 76.

SNEYD, Major Edward, of Lichfield, co. Staff. Quartering for COOKE, of Sible Hedingham, co. Essex, [1805] Vol. XXIII, fol. 160.

SNEYD before KINNERSLEY, Thomas, of Sutton Hall, co. Derby, and Loxley Place, co. Staff., [1815] Vol. XXIX, fol. 3.

SNODGRASS, ..., E.I.C.S., Madras, of Blackheath, co. Kent, [1799] Vol. XX, fol. 382.

„ Lieut.-Col. . . . ., C.B., of Seedhills and Paisley, Scotland, [1829] Vol. XXXVII, fol. 406.

SNOOKE, Matthew (? formerly DILKE), of Chichester, co. Sussex, and Bedhampton, Hampsh., [1833 ?] Vol. XL, fol. 82.

SNOULTEN, ..., of Canterbury, co. Kent, [1818] Vol. XXXI, fol. 149.

SNOW, ..., of London ; St. James's, Westminster ; and Walton-on-Thames, co. Surrey, [1807 ?] Vol. XXIV, fol. 136.

„ Robert, of Savile Row, London, [1832] Vol. XXXIX, fol. 9.

SNOW to STRAHAN, ..., of The Strand, London, and Ashurst, co. Surrey, [1832] Vol. XXXIX, fol. 13.

SNOW, A. D., of Cotham, Bristol, co. Glouc., 1891, Vol. LXVI, Vol. 206.

SOAME after BUCKWORTH-HERNE, Sir Buckworth [Bart.], of co. Essex. Quarterly Arms, 1806, Vol. XXIV, fol. 99.

SODEN, ..., of Forwyn, co. Merioneth, Wales, [1865] Vol. LVI, fol. 23.

SODEN to CORBET, ..., of Ynys-y-maugwyn, co. Merioneth, [1865] Vol. LVI, fols. 27 and 29.

SOLA to IRONMONGER, ..., of co. Surrey and Sussex. IRVIN, reputed dau. of Ironmonger, [1837] Vol. XLII, fol. 154.

SOLTAU [George William], of Plymouth, co. Devon, 1841, Vol. XLV, fol. 233.

SOLTAU-SYMONS, ..., of Chaddlewood, Plympton St. Mary, co. Devon, 1845, Vol. XLVII, fol. 361.

SOMBRÉ (DYCE-), David Ochterlony Dyce Sombré, Commander of Troops of Princess SIRHAND, Province of Agra, [1838] Vol. XLIII, fol. 92.

SOMERS [or Sommers], Baron [2 Dec. 1697], John SOMMERS, Lord Chancellor [d. 1716]. Supporters, [1697 ?] Vol. IV, fol. 242.

„ Lord [and Baron of Evesham, co. Worc., 17 May 1784, Charles] (COCKS). Supporters, [1784] Vol. XV, fol. 301.

„ B. E., of Mendip Lodge, Churchill, co. Somerset, 1890,* Vol. LXVI, fol. 15. Quarterings, 1892, Vol. LXVII, fol. 106. (Crisp, II, p. 15.)

SOMERSET, John Stukeley, Capt., R.N., 1771, Vol. XII, fol. 100.

„ . . . ., Baron RAGLAN [20 Oct. 1852], Lieut.-Gen. Supporters, [1851] Vol. L, fol. 24b.

SOMERVILLE, late FOWNES, ..., of co. Devon and Somerset, [1831] Vol. XXXVIII, fol. 203.

SOMES, George, of Stratford Green [co. Essex ?], and Ratcliffe [co. Middx. ?], [1849] Vol. XLIX, fol. 101.

SONDES, Baron ([Lewis] WATSON), of co. Kent, [1760] Vol. X, fol. 242.

SOPER before DEMPSTER, William (nat. dau. of HAMILTON), Dempster, wife of William SOPER, of co. Devon, and Scotland. Quarterly Arms, 10 July 1804 [1806], Vol. XXIV, fol. 3.

SOPER, William Garland, of Caterham, co. Surrey, and Maria DAVIS, his wife, 1881,* Vol. LXI, fol. 122. (Berry's Suppl.)

SOPPER, William, of Herne Hill, co. Surrey, and Dunmaglass, co. Inverness, Scotland, 1890, Vol. LXV, fol. 259.

SOPPITT, Col., Bo. S. C. [Bombay Staff Corps], of Brighton, co. Sussex, [1850] Vol. XLIX, fol. 376.

SORELL, Major (his grandfather migrated from Normandy), [1811] Vol. XXVII, fol. 15.

SOTHEBIE, ..., of St. Edmundsbury, co. Suff. (See GRIGBY.) (Match), [1743] Vol. IX, fol. 84.

SOTHERON, Frank, Capt., R.N., of Kirklington, co. Nottingham, s. of William, of Darrington, co. York, and to his four sisters. (Match), 26 May 1810, Vol. XXVI, fol. 5. (Misc. G. et H., New S., I, p. 222.)

SOTHERON, late BUCKNALL-ESTCOURT, T. S., of co. York, [1839] Vol. XLIV, fol. 48.

SOTHERON-ESTCOURT, George Thomas John, late BUCKNALL-ESTCOURT-ESTCOURT, of Darrington Hall, co. York, 1899 [1876], Vol. LIX, fol. 198.

„ -ESTCOURT, ..., of Estcourt, co. Glouc., [1855] Vol. LI, fol. 323.

SOUPER, ..., Commissary of Musters, H.M. Forces, West Indies, [1824] Vol. XXXV, fol. 46.

SOUTH to ARCHER-BURTON, ..., of London, and co. Essex, [1835] Vol. XLI, fol. 144.

SOUTH SEA COMPANY, London, 31 Oct. 1711, Vol. VI, fol. 1.

SOUTHAMPTON, Baron [17 Oct. 1780], ([Charles] FITZROY). Supporters, [1780] Vol. XIV, fol. 263.

SOUTHBY (HAYWARD-), late PERFECT, Thomas, of Berks. and co. Glouc., [1823 ?] Vol. XXXIII, fol. 361 or 366.

SOUTHBY, late GAPPER, ..., of co. Somerset and Wilts., [1836] Vol. XLI, fol. 351.

SOUTHOUSE, Henry, Rector of Castle Combe, Wilts., [1811] Vol. XXVI, fol. 285.

[SOUTHWARK, Borough of, London, 14 June 1902. (Geneal. Mag., VI, p. 245.)]

SOUTHWELL-WANDESFORD after BUTLER-CLARKE, ... (2nd Earl of ORMOND). of Ireland, [1830] Vol. XXXVIII, fol. 111.

SOUTHWELL after TRAFFORD, Sigismund, of Wroxham, co. Norf., and Dunton. co. Linc. Arms of Trafford to Crest of T.-S. [Trafford-Southwell], [1832] Vol. XXXIX, fol. 36.

SOUTHWELL-TRAFFORD, Margaret Elizabeth (Spr.), of Wroxham Hall, co. Norf. ; Dunton Hall, co. Linc. ; and Wisbech, Isle of Ely, co. Camb., 1849, Vol. XLIX, fol. 136.

SOUTHWELL, Josiah, of Kidderminster, co. Worc., and Kingston-upon-Thames, co. Surrey, [1868] Vol. LVI, fol. 352.

„ Margaret, nat. dau. of Thomas, 14th Earl of SUFFOLK and BERKSHIRE, and wife of Sir George A. ROBINSON, 1st Bart., and her descendants (see Burke's Armory), [1807] Vol. XXIV, fol. 158.

SOWDON, late COSWAY, ... (reputed son), of co. Devon, [1855] Vol. LI, fol. 286.

SOWERBY, John PAGE-, ..., of Bishopton, co. Durham, and Stokesley, co. York, [1862] Vol. LIV, fol. 280.

SPAFFORD, George, of Eccles and Manchester, co. Lanc., 1875, Vol. LIX, fol. 76.

SPALDING, Samuel, of South Darenth, co. Kent, Stationers, of Drury Lane, London, and to the descendants of his father, the Rev. Samuel Spalding, 1878,* Vol. LX, fol. 201. (Berry's Suppl.)

SPARHAWK to PEPPERELL, Andrew (of ? U.S., America), 31 Mar. 1775, Vol. XIII, fol. 83.

SPARLING, ..., of Liverpool and Bolton-le-Sands, co. Lanc., [1785 ?] Vol. XVI, fol. 93.

SPARROW to BENCE, ..., of co. Suff., [1804] Vol. XXIII, fol. 32.

SPARROW, ..., of Blackburn, co. Lanc., [1854] Vol. LI, fol. 11.

„   William Hanbury, of Albrighton Hall, Habberley, Church Preen, and Eaton, Shropsh.; Penn, co. Staff.; and Campston, co. Monmouth, [1857 ?] Vol. LII, fol. 203. (Crisp, I, p. 227.)

„   William Arthur, of Pennfield, Penn, co. Staff., 1881, Vol. LXI, fol. 183.

SPEARMAN, ..., of Eachwich Hall and Preston, co. Northumberland, [1810] Vol. XXVI, fol. 60.

SPEARMAN, late HUNTER, John, of Eachwick Hall, co. Northumberland, 1827, Vol. XXXVI, fol. 238.

SPEARMAN, [Sir Alexander Young] (Bart. [1840]), of Thornley, co. Durham, and Hanwell, co. Middx., late Assistant Sec. to the Treasury, [1840] Vol. XLIV, fol. 218.

SPEDDING, ..., Capt., Grenadier Guards, of St. Bees and Whitehaven, co. Cumberland, [1841] Vol. XLV, fol. 210.

„   [John Carlisle Deey, Capt., 1st Batt. Border Regiment, by Capt. Nevil Rodwell Wilkinson, Ulster King of Arms, 26 Aug. 1908. (Crisp, Notes, XI, p. 38.]

SPEED to MYLLES, John, of Hampsh. Quarterly Arms, [1780] Vol. XIV, fol. 221.

SPEED, late SANDYS, Hannibal, of co. Surrey and London, 1871, Vol. LVIII, fol. 66.

SPEER, ..., of Weston Green, Thames Ditton, co. Surrey, [1803] Vol. XXII, fol. 51.

SPEKE, William, of Jordans, co. Somerset, Capt., Indian Forces, "Nile discovery." Augmentation, 26 July 1867, by Letters Patent, Vol. LVI, fol. 288. Supporters, fol. 290. (N. and Q., 3rd S., XII, p. 262.)

SPENCE, James, of Liverpool, co. Lanc., [1853] Vol. L, fol. 359.

SPENCER, Viscount. Supporters, [1761] Vol. X, fol. 286.

„   . . . ., of Newcastle-upon-Tyne, co. Northumberland, 2 Oct. 1809, Vol. XXV, fol. 291.

SPENCER before PHILLIPS, Rev. William ?, of Great Bardfield, co. Essex, [1809 ?] Vol. XXV, fol. 295.

SPENCER, Maj.-Gen. Sir Brent, K.B. [1809], [1810] Vol. XXV, fol. 337. Supporters, [1810] fol. 340.

„   (Rev.) Charles, of (London), M.A., Queen's Coll., Oxf. Match with GREENSILL, [1811] Vol. XXVII, fol. 60.

SPENCER-STANHOPE to COLLINGWOOD [Edward], of co. Northumberland and York, [1816] Vol. XXX, fol. 59.

„   -STANHOPE to RODDAM, Lieut., R.N., of Roddam, co. Northumberland, and Cannon Hall, co. York, [1818] Vol. XXX, fol. 430.

SPENCER before CHURCHILL, [26 May 1817, George, 5th] Duke of MARLBOROUGH. Quarterly Arms and Supporters, [1817] Vol. XXX, fol. 286.

SPENCER after HAMMOND, ..., of London, [1817] Vol. XXX, fol. 303.

SPENCER, Capt., R.N., C.B., of Lyme Regis, co. Dorset. Honourable distinctions, [1818] Vol. XXXI, fol. 32.

SPENCER, late SHIELD, Henry, of co. Durham, [1842] Vol. XLVI, fol. 143.

SPENCER, Frederick (s. of John P.), of Oakhill, Bath, co. Somerset, 18 . . ., Vol. LXXI, fol. . . . . .

SPENLOVE, late WAITE, ..., of Abingdon, Berks.; Merton, co. Surrey; and Gray's Inn Road, London, [1863] Vol. LV, fol. 74.

SPICER (WILLIAM-), ..., late HEAVISIDE, of co. Devon and Sussex, [1854] Vol. LI, fol. 102.

SPIEKER, now BRANDER, ..., of Hampsh., [1787] Vol. XVI, fol. 231.

SPIERS to GABBIT, ..., of Berks. and Bucks., [1795] Vol. XIX, fols. 48 and 50.

SPINCKES, Elmes, of Aldwinckle, All Saints, co. Northampton, and Nathaniel, of London, Clerk, sons of Edward, 8 Mar. 170⁹⁄₀, Vol. V, fol. 30 ; Add. MS. 14,830, fol. 68 ; 14,831, fol. 69. (Berry.)

SPLATT after COLLINS, ..., of co. Devon, [1833] Vol. XXXIX, fol. 359.

SPLIDT, ..., of Stratford Green, Lieut.-Col., Corps of St. George's in the East, [1808] Vol. XXIV, fol. 390 ; [1814] Vol. XXVIII, fol. 111.

SPODE, ..., of Fenton Hall, co. Staff., [1804] Vol. XXII, fol. 370.

SPODE to HAMMERSLEY, ..., of co. Staff. and Surrey, [1832] Vol. XXXIX, fol. 27.

SPOKES, Sir Peter, Knt., [14 Mar. 1872, Mayor] of Reading and of Wallingford, Berks., [1872] Vol. LVIII, fol. 184.

SPONG, ..., of The Manor House, Walton-on-Thames, co. Surrey, [1824] Vol. XXXIV, fol. 397.

SPOONER to LILLINGSTON, Abraham, of co. Warw. and York. Escutcheon of pretence, [1797] Vol. XX, fol. 14.

SPRATT to HUGESSON, ..., of co. Kent. (Match), [1801] Vol. XXI, fol. 267.

SPRINGMANN, E., of Drachenfels, West Derby, co. Lanc., 1894, Vol. LXVIII, fol. 91.

SPRULES, George Henry, of Reigate, co. Surrey, s. of John, of Kensington, 1899, Vol. LXXI, fol. . . . .

SPRY, John Samuel, of Place, co. Cornw., nat. s. of Samuel Spry, Knt., 1889, Vol. LXV, fol. 124.

„ Tredenham Hugh (s. of Horatio Carlyon), of Witherdon, co. Devon, 18 . . ., Vol. LXXI, fol. . . . .

SPURGEON to FARRER, ... (minor), of Farrer Grove, Bucks., [1799] Vol. XX, fol. 338.

SPURRIER, ..., of Upton House, nr. Poole, co. Dorset, [1811] Vol. XXVI, fol. 324.

STABLE, Daniel Wintringham (LL.B.) (s. of Robert Scott Stable), of Wanstead, co. Essex, and 142, Holborn Bars, London, 1898, Vol. LXX, fol. 143.

STABLES, John, of Bonegate, co. Westmorland. Quartering BAINEBRIDGE, 1767, Vol. XI, fol. 212. (Berry.)

„ John Percy Lister DURALL-, of Ebury Street, London, 1895, Vol. LXVIII, fol. 238.

STACKHOUSE, John, of Trehane, St. Erme, and Pendarves, co. Cornw., 1813 [1814], Vol. XXVIII, fol. 244.

STACKHOUSE after WYNNE, Edward William. Quartering, 1813 [1815 ?], Vol. XXVIII, fol. 246.

STACKHOUSE to PENDARVES after WYNNE, Edward. Quarterly Arms, 1813 [1815], Vol. XXVIII, fol. 282.

STAFFORD [? 2nd] Earl of [27 April 1719], ([William Stafford-] HOWARD). Supporters, quartering and badge, [1 Aug. 1720] [1721], Vol. VII, fol. 69. [Geneal. Mag., V, p. 113.]

STAFFORD-JERNINGHAM [5 Oct. 1826], Baron Stafford, [1826] Vol. XXXVI, fol. 115.

STAINBANK, John, of Witherslack, co. Westmorland, 1755, Vol. X, fol. 33. (Berry.)

STAINER, Sir John, of co. Oxf., 1891, Vol. LXVI, fol. 180.

STAINES, Sir Thomas, Knt. [1809], Post-Capt. and Commander, R.N. (K.C., St. Ferdinand of Merit, Sicily) (afterwards K.C.B.), [1810] Vol. XXV, fol. 367.

STAINIFORTH, Thomas, s. of Samuel, of Darnall, co. York, [1785] Vol. XVI, fol. 19.

STAINSBY-CONANT after PIGOTT, ..., of Hampsh. [1835 ?] Vol. XLI, fol. 158.

STALBRIDGE, Baron [21 Mar. 1886 (GROSVENOR)]. Supporters, 1886, Vol. LXIII, fol. 213.

STALLARD-PENOYRE, late LEYSON, John, of co. Somerset, and Wales, [1834] Vol. XL, fol. 270.

STALLARD, Col. Samuel, of Blandford Square, London, Col. of Artillery, s. of Samuel Frampton, 1878, Vol. LX, fol. 192.

STANCOMBE, ..., of Trowbridge, Wilts., [1842 ?] Vol. XLV, fol. 333 ; [1851] Vol. XLIX, fol. 438.

STANDISH to HOWARD. . . . ., of co. Lanc. and Westmorland.   Arms and Crest, [1730] Vol. VIII, fol. 88.

STANDISH, late STRICKLAND, ..., of Sizergh, co. Westmorland, and Standish Hall, co. Lanc.   Quarterly Arms, [1807] Vol. XXIV, fol. 211 [see Burke].

 „ late STEPHENSON, ..., of Holme Cultram Abbey, co. Cumberland, and Farley Hill, Berks., [1834] Vol. XL, fol. 187.

 „ late CARR, ..., of co. Durham and Lanc., [1841] Vol. XLV, fol. 178.

STANDLY after POINTER, ..., of co. Huntingdon, [1782] Vol. XV, fol. 100.

STANE, late BRAMSTON, Rev. John, of Skreens, &c., co. Essex.   Quarterly Arms, [1801] Vol. XXI, fol. 192.

STANFORD, ..., of Preston, Brighton, co. Sussex, [1847] Vol. XLVIII, fol. 344.

STANFORD after BENETT, ..., of Preston, Brighton, co. Sussex, and Pytt House, Wilts., [1868] Vol. LVII, fol. 74.

STANHOPE, Viscount [3 July 1717, James Stanhope].   Supporters, [1717] Vol. VI, fol. 315.

 „ Sir William, K.B. [1725].   Supporters, [172⁴⁄₆ ?] Vol. VII, fol. 494.

 „ . . . ., Baron HARRINGTON [20 Nov. 1729, William Stanhope].   Supporters, [1730] Vol. VIII, fol. 104.

STANHOPE after STOTT, Lieut.-Col., Madras S.C., retired, of Eccleshall, Bradford, co. York, and Ramsgate, co. Kent, [1856] Vol. LI, fol. 461.

STANIER, Mary (widow), of Madeley Manor, Newcastle-under-Lyne, co. Staff., [1858] Vol. LII, fol. 370.

STANIER-PHILIP-BROADE, Francis, of Madeley Manor, Newcastle-under-Lyne, co. Staff., [1858] Vol. LII, fol. 372.

STANILAND, Meaburn, of Forfarth and Eastville, co. Linc., 1895, Vol. LXVIII, fol. 180.

STANLEY, late CONSTABLE, Charles Haggerston, of co. York ; Chester ; and Scotland, [1793] Vol. XVIII, fol. 246.

STANLEY to ERRINGTON, ..., of co. Chester ; Hampsh. ; and co. Northumberland, [1820] Vol. XXXII, fol. 84.

STANLEY after SLOANE, ..., of Hampsh., [1822] Vol. XXXIII, fol. 112.

STANLEY, ..., Baron STANLEY OF ALDERLEY [9 May 1839, Sir John Thomas Stanley, 7th Bart.].   Supporters, [1839] Vol. XLIII, fol. 384.

STANLEY, late WENTWORTH, Sidney, of Longstowe Hall, co. Camb., 1836 [1856], Vol. LII, fol. 61.

STANLEY. (See ERRINGTON.) [1877] Vol. LX, fol. 22.

STANLEY, Baron Stanley, of Preston [27 Aug. 1886, The Right Hon. Frederick Arthur Stanley].   Supporters, ? (now Earl of DERBY [1893]) 1888, Vol. LXIV, fol. 217.

STANMORE, Baron, [21 Aug. 1793, The Hon. Sir Arthur Hamilton Gordon, G.C.M.G.].   Supporters, 1894, Vol. LXVIII, fol. 67.

STANSFIELD after CROMPTON, William Rookes, of co. York, [1832] Vol. XXXIX, fol. 140.

 „ after CROMPTON, William Henry, of co. York, [1872] Vol. LVIII, fol. 110.

STANSER, Robert, D.D., Bishop of Nova Scotia [1816-25], of Bulwell and Basford, co. Nottingham, [1816] Vol. XXIX, fol. 398.

STANSFIELD-TENNANT, ..., of Otley, Idle, and Chaple-House-in-Burnsal, co. York, [1833] Vol. XXXIX, fol. 294.

STANTON, ..., of Bristol and Plymouth, co. Devon, [1825] Vol. XXXV, fol. 286.

STANYFORTH, Edwin Wilfred (formerly GREENWOOD), of Kirk Hammerton, co. York, 1888, Vol. LXIV, fol. 165. (Crisp, V, p. 132.)

STAPLES, Moses William (s. of Moses William), of Norwood, co. Surrey, [1843 ?] Vol. XLVI, fol. 268.

STAPLES-BROWNE, Richard Thomas, of Launton, co. Oxf., [1843] Vol. XLVI, fol. 270.

STAPLES, Sir John, K.C.M.G., [1886, Lord Mayor of] London (died 1888), 1882,* Vol. LXI, fol. 361.

STAPLETON, formerly ERRINGTON, Thomas, of co. York, 10 June 1773, Vol. XII, fol. 247.

STAPLETON, Baron COMBERMERE [17 May 1814], Lieut.-Gen. [Sir Stapleton Cotton, Bart.], G.C.B. [1815]. Augmentation, [1815] Vol. XXVIII, fol. 347; Viscount Combermere [8 Feb. 1827], of [co. Denbigh], Wales, [1829] Vol. XXXVII, fol. 254 [? 1827, Vol. XXXVI, fol. 254].

STAPLETON-BRETHERTON, F., of Elmhurst, Fareham, Hampsh., and co. Lanc., 1884, Vol. LXII, fol. 240.

STAPYLTON after CHETWYND, [Gen. The] Hon. Granville Anson, of London. Quarterly Arms and escutcheon of pretence, [1783] Vol. XV, fol. 203.

STAPYLTON, late BREE, Martin, of Myton, co. York, and Marks Tey, co. Essex. (Match), [1818] Vol. XXX, fol. 393.

STARCY [or Starey], ..., of Milton Ernest, co. Bedf., and London, [1854] Vol. LI, fol. 165.

STARKEY, ..., of co. Lanc. (See SMALESHAW.) [1750] Vol. IX, fol. 357.
„ . . . ., of Huddersfield and Kirkheaton, co. York, 1843, Vol. XLVI, fol. 314.

STARKEY after BARBER, William Joseph, of Quorndon, co. Derby, and Kirkheaton, co. York, 1873, Vol. LVIII, fol. 204. (Berry's Suppl.)

STARKEY, late JENNINGS, ..., of co. York and Chester. (Match), 1811, Vol. XXVI, fol. 320.

STARKEY after CROSS, John. Quarterly Arms, 1813, Vol. XXVII, fols. 360 and 362.

STARR, ..., M.D., of Reading, Berks., [1838] Vol. XLII, fol. 315.

STARTIN, Rev. Henry, M.A., Oxf. of co. Devon, 1891,* Vol. LXVI, fol. 53.

STATON, ..., wife of IDLE. (See IDLE.)

STATTER, ..., of Henley-on-Thames, co. Oxf., and Beverley, co. York, Major, Russian Army, [1811] Vol. XXVI, fol. 328.

STAUNTON, late AS(H)PINSHAW, Rev. John, LL.D., of co. Nottingham. Escutcheon of pretence for BROUGH, his wife, and to descendants, 1807, Vol. XXIV, fol. 217.

STAUNTON after LYNCH, ..., of Hampsh., and Ireland, [1859] Vol. LIII, fols. 267 and 278.

STAUNTON, Sir George Thomas, Bart., 12 Sept. 1817 (see Memoirs, Sir George Leonard Staunton, Bart., p. 133).

STAVELEY, late HUTCHINSON, Thomas Kitchingman, Capt., R.E., of Hampsh., [1815] Vol. XXVIII, fol. 374. (Berry's Suppl.)

STAVELEY, ..., of Pangbourne, Berks., and Bignal, co. Oxf. (See POTENGER.) Match, [1722] Vol. VII, fol. 88.

STAWEL, Baron [15 Jan. 168⅔, Ralph Stawel]. Supporters, [1683] Vol. III, fol. 190.
„ Mary, Baroness [1760], wife of [the Right Hon.] Henry Bilson LEGGE [d. and h. of Edward, 5th Baron Stawel]. Supporters, [1760] Vol. X, fol. 246.

STEADE to PEGGE-BURNELL, Broughton Benjamin, of co. Derby and Nottingham, [1836] Vol. XLI, fol. 254.

STEBLE, ..., Lieut.-Col. of Volunteers, of West Derby, co. Lanc., [1872 ?] Vol. LVIII, fol. 86.

STEDMAN, ..., of Sudbury and Packenham, co. Suff., [1827] Vol. XXXVI, fol. 315.

STEEL, Maj.-Gen. Sir Scudamore Winde, K.C.B. [1853], Madras S.C., [1855 ?] Vol. LI, fol. 301.

STEER, ..., of Wakefield, co. York. (See LONSDALE.) [1811] Vol. XXVI, fol. 244.

STEER to JOHNSON, Robert Popplewell, of co. Linc. Johnson and Steer quarterly, both granted, [1832] Vol. XXXIX, fol. 152.

„   to HARRISON, ... (infant), of co. Surrey, [1819] Vol. XXXI, fol. 191.

STEERE, late WITTS, ..., of Jayes, co. Surrey. (Match), [1796] Vol. XIX, fol. 203 ; Quartering and escutcheon of pretence, [1797] Vol. XIX, fol. 415.

STEINMAN (formerly SMITH), ..., F.S.A., of Switzerland ; and Peckham, Kingston, and North End, Croydon, co. Surrey, [1855] Vol. LI, fol. 399.

STEINTHAL, Henry Michael, of Bradford and Manchester, co. Lanc., 1st s. of Ludwig Steinthal, of Manchester, Merchant, [1851] Vol. L, fol. 26.

STENHOUSE, Vivian Denman (s. of Edward), of Norton Fitzwarren, co. Somerset, 18 . . ., Vol. LXXI, fol. . . . .

STENT to LUCAS-SHADWELL, ..., of co. Sussex, [1844] Vol. XLVII, fol. 283.

STEPHEN, Sir J. F. [? George], Bart. [3 Mar. 1885], of London [and Canada], afterwards [23 June 1891] Baron MOUNT STEPHEN, 1891, Vol. LXVI, fol. 127.

STEPHENS, John, of St. Ives, co. Cornw., 1762, Vol. X, fol. 440. (Berry.)

„   James, s. of Philip, of Hinton, co. Glouc., and Camerton, co. Somerset. Quartering, [1781] Vol. XIV, fol. 298.

„   . . . ., of Gosport, Hampsh., and Ross, co. Hereford, [1782] Vol. XV, fol. 77.

STEPHENS to TRELAWNY, of Coldrinnick and St. Kew, co. Cornw., [1795] Vol. XIX, fol. 133.

STEPHENS, late WILLIS, Henry Hannes, of Chavanage and Iron Acton, co. Glouc., [1801] Vol. XXI, fol. 208.

„   late TOWNSEND, Col. John, of co. Glouc., [1828] Vol. XXXVII, fol. 137.

STEPHENS-TOWNSEND, Rev. Maurice F. G., Vicar of Thornbury, and of Chavanage House, Horsley, co. Glouc., 18 Aug. 1845, Vol. XLVII, fol. 433.

STEPHENS before TOWNSEND, Henry John, Lieut., Life Guards, of Thornbury, co. Glouc., and Castle Townsend, co. Cork, [1855] Vol. LI, fol. 205.

STEPHENS to KINGSMILL, ..., of Sidmanton, Hampsh., and Chewton Mendip, co. Somerset, [1806] Vol. XXIII, fol. 311.

STEPHENS [Thomasine], of Bereferris, co. Devon. [See KNIGHTON.] [2 Nov. 1812] Vol. XXVII, fol. 135.

STEPHENS, late WILKINSON, Rear-Adm. (1813), Philip, of St. Faith and Horsford, co. Norf. (died 1846), [1820] Vol. XXXII, fol. 157.

STEPHENS, ..., of Padworth and Reading, Berks., [1823] Vol. XXXIII, fol. 396.

STEPHENS after LYNE, Charles, of co. Cornw. and Dorset, [1828] Vol. XXXVII, fol. 81 [1826, Burke] ; and to his brothers, fol. 83.

STEPHENS, Edward, F.R.C.S., &c., of Manchester, co. Lanc., [1851 ?] Vol. L, fol. 96.

STEPHENSON to STANDISH, ..., of co. Cumberland and Berks., [1834] Vol. XL, fol. 187.

STEPHENSON, Sir William, Knt., Lord Mayor of London [1764-1765], and of Crosslands, Aldstone, co. Cumberland, 1764, Vol. XI, fol. 37. (Berry.)

„   [Henry Frederick, Falcon [Herald Extraordinary], of the Middle Temple, London, [1815] Vol. XXVIII, fol. 442.

„   Maj.-Gen. Sir Benjamin Charles, Knt., G.C.H. [1834], [1838] Vol. XLIII, fol. 169.

„   George ("the Engineer"), of Alton Grange, Ashby, co. Leic., and Tapton Park, Chesterfield, co. Derby, [1838] Vol. XLIII, fol. 255.

„   Sir Henry, [Knt., 5 Aug. 1887, Mayor] of Sheffield (typefounder), 1890,* Vol. LXV, fol. 174.

STEPHENSON-FETHERSTONHAUGH, S. A., of Hopton Court, Worcester, 1882, Vol. LXI, fol. 307.

STEPKIN, ..., of East Smithfield, London, 16 . . ., Vol. I, fol. 427.

STEPNEY after GULSTON, ... (Spr.), of Wales, [1855] Vol. LI, fol. 263.
 „ after COWELL, Lieut.-Col. (John Cowell), K.H., &c., of Wales, and Bucks., 1857, Vol. LII, fol. 330.
STERNDALE, William Handley, of Sheffield, co. York, and Ottar, Hindostan, [1835] Vol. XLI, fol. 164.
STERRY, Rev. F., of Eastbury Hill, Barking, co. Essex, Rector of Poltimore, Exeter, 1890,[*] Vol. LXV, fol. 303. (Crisp, I, p. 180.)
STERT, Arthur, s. of Richard, of Membland and Elburton, co. Devon, 1745, Vol. IX, fol. 153. (Berry.)
STEUART-GROSETT, ..., of Muirhead, Scotland, [1863] Vol. LV, fol. 86.
STEUART-OGILVIE, E. T., of Yulgilbar, Clarence River, New South Wales, 1892,[*] Vol. LXVII, fol. 24.
STEVENS after MOORE, Ven. John, M.A., of co. Devon, [1832] Vol. XXXIX, fol. 146.
STEVENS, Henry, of Culham, co. Oxf., 3 Dec. 1694, Vol. IV, fol. 173. (Berry.)
 „ Henry, of Culham and Henley, co. Oxf., 1762, Vol. X, fol. 436.
STEVENS, late MOORE, Thomas, of the Middle Temple, London, and co. Devon, 1817, Vol. XXX, fol. 223.
STEVENS, Sir Charles Cecil, K.C.S.I. [31 Dec. 1898] (s. of Charles), of Honiton, co. Devon, [1899] Vol. LXXI, fol. . . . .
STEVENSON, John, of Stanton and Elton-in-the-Peak, co. Derby. (See STEAVENSON, ? a fraud.) 14 June 1688, Vol. IV, fol. 11. [Guillim, p. 262.] (Berry's Suppl.)
 „ . . . . (see PERFECT), of Pontefract, co. York. Match, [1777] Vol. XIII, fol. 305.
 „ . . . ., of London and Bengal, [1785] Vol. XVI, fol. 87.
STEVENSON, now WHARTON, ..., of Skelton Castle, co. York, [1788] Vol. XVI, fol. 405.
STEVENSON, late BELLAIRS, James, of Wales, and co. Linc., [1844] Vol. XLVII, fol. 229.
STEWARD, Ambrose Harbord, of Great Yarmouth, co. Norf., and Stoke Park, co. Suff., [1834] Vol. XL, fol. 158.
 „ . . . . (see FALCON). (Berry's Suppl.)
STEWART, ..., of New York. Match with BRENTON, [1812] Vol. XXVII, fol. 113.
 „ Lieut.-Gen. [The Hon.] Sir William, K.B. [1813, G.C.B. 1815]. Supporters, with consent of his brother, the Earl of GALLOWAY. [1814] Vol. XXVIII, fol. 36.
STEWART to [?] VANE [1819 ?, Charles William], Baron Stewart [1 July 1814], [Earl Vane, 28 Mar. 1823], [1823] Vol. XXXIV, fol. 17. Supporters, fol. 21.
 „ to [?] VANE [? George Henry Robert Charles William]. Supporters, Baron Stewart, Earl Vane. (See [5th] Marquess of LONDONDERRY.) [Succeeded his father, 6 Mar. 1854, as Earl Vane and Viscount Seaham ; and on the 28 June 1854 he took, by Roy. Lic., the name of Tempest after Vane, 5th Marq. of Londonderry, 25 Nov. 1872.] [1854] Vol. LI, fol. 81.
STEWART-MURRAY, ... (minor), of Scotland, [1846] Vol. XLVIII, fol. 134.
 „ -MURRAY, now to MURRAY-STEWART, ..., of Scotland, [1855] Vol. LI, fol. 369.
STEWART, Charles Poyntz (s. of Philip), ? Lyon Reg. or Vol. LXXI.
STIBBERT, Gilbert, of London, 12 Oct. 1768, Vol. XI, fol. 317. (Berry.)
 „ Giles, of St. George's, Hanover Square, London, 25 Nov. 1774, Vol. XIII, fol. 41.
STIBBS, Edward, Chester Herald of Arms, Mayor of Bath, 4 Feb. 172$\frac{2}{3}$, Vol. VII, fol. 167.
STIFFE, Lieut. A. W., Italian [Indian in Burke] Navy, of St. George, co. Somerset, Rome, and Naples, [1861] Vol. LIV, fol. 100.

STIFFE after EVERITT, Francis William (s. of William, of Swansea), of Old
　　Square, Lincoln's Inn, London, Bar.-at-Law, [1861] Vol. LIV, fol. 118.
STILES, Joseph Haskin, of Wantage, Berks., 26 Feb. 170½, Vol. V, fol. 67.
STILWELL, John Gilliam, of Capel, Dorking, co. Surrey, and Arundel Street,
　　Strand, London, J.P. for co. Middx., [1858] Vol. LIII, fol. 18.
STIRLING, Sir James, of Ladbroke Grove, London, 1886,* Vol. LXIII, fol. 266.
STOCK, ..., of Gloucester, [1787] Vol. XVI, fol. 239.
　　„　. . . ., of Childwall and Liverpool, co. Lanc., [1846] Vol. XLVIII, fol. 212..
　　„　Rev. John R., of Langham, Oakham, co. Rutland, and Edward, Bar.-at-Law,
　　　　and Rev. John, Rector of All Hallows, London, 1880,* Vol. LXI, fol. 75.
　　　　(Berry's Suppl.)
STOCKDALE, late WALTERS, Christopher Cundall, of co. York. Quarterly Arms,
　　19 Feb. 169⅘, Vol. IV, fol. 187.
STOCKENSTRÖM, Capt., Lieut.-Gov. E. division of the Cape [Bart., 29 Mar. 1840],
　　of Maaström, Cape of Good Hope, and of Stockholm, Sweden, [1840]
　　Vol. XLIV, fol. 222.
STOCKWELL, ..., of Stratfield Mortimer, Berks., and London, [1801] Vol. XXI,
　　fol. 168.
STODDART, Sir John, Knt., D.C.L., President of the High Court of Appeal, Malta,
　　&c., 1826, Vol. XXXVI, fol. 77.
STODDART-DOUGLAS, ..., of co. Kent, and Scotland, [1833] Vol. XL, fol. 19.
STONE, James, of Badbury, Chiselden, Wilts., and New Inn, London, 2 or 22 Dec.
　　1722, Vol. VII, fol. 137. (Berry.) [22 Dec., Burke.]
　　„　Arthur, of the Inner Temple, and to the descendants of his father, John,
　　　　late of Kensington, London, and also of the Inner Temple, by his first
　　　　wife, Hephzibath, dau. and co.-h. of Arthur BANKS, late of St. Albans,
　　　　co. Hertf., gentleman, 15 Jan. 17²⁹⁄₃₀, Vol. VIII, fol. 58 ; Add. MS. 14,831,
　　　　fol. 197.
　　„　(LOWNDES-), of co. Oxf. (? A grant), 1835 [1837], Vol. XLII, fol. 86.
STONE (LOWNDES-) before NORTON, Robert, of Brightwell, co. Oxf., Capt., late
　　Gren. Guards, 1872, Vol. LVIII, fol. 177 [see Burke].
STONE, ..., of Cuddington Park and Ewell, co. Surrey, [1873] Vol. LVIII,
　　fol. 206.
STONE to ELPHINSTONE-STONE, Webb Elphinstone, Capt., R.N., of co. Devon, and
　　Scotland, [1879] Vol. LX, fol. 314. (Berry's Suppl.)
STONE, Sir J. B. [John Benjamin, Knt.], of The Grange, Erdington [and Sutton
　　Coldfield], co. Worc., 1891, Vol. LXVI, fol. 204.
　　„　Edward, of Blackheath, co. Kent, s. of Thomas, of Piddington, co. Oxf.,
　　　　18 . . ., Vol. LXXI, fol. . . . .
STONEHEWER after SCOTT, of London, and Cambridge, [1811] Vol. XXVI,
　　fol. 333 ; [1825] Vol. XXXV, fol. 242.
STONEHOUSE before VIGOR, Ven. Archdeacon Timothy Stonehouse, M.A., Vicar
　　of Sunningwell, Berks., and of Hotwells, Bristol, [1795] Vol. XIX, fol. 91
　　[see Burke].
STONES, Thomas, of Mosborough, co. Derby, [21 July] 1693, Vol. IV, fol. 147 ;
　　[Misc. G. et H., New Ser., I, p. 99].
　　„　John, of Cartmel, co. Lanc., and Westminster, 1771, Vol. XII, fol. 53.
　　　　(Berry.)
STONESTREET, ... (see KEMPE), of Lewes, co. Sussex, [1771] Vol. XII, fol. 91.
STONESTREET, late GRIFFIN, ..., of co. Bedf. (Match), [1794] Vol. XVIII,
　　fol. 292.
STONOR, Baron CAMOYS. Supporters, [1839] Vol. XLIV, fol. 155.
STOPFORD-BLAIR, Lieut.-Col., R.A., of Scotland, [1842] Vol. XLVI, fol. 59.
STOPFORD-SACKVILLE, ..., of co. Northampton, [1870] Vol. LVII, fol. 244.
STOREY, ..., of Newcastle-upon-Tyne, co. Northumberland, [1795] Vol. XIX,
　　fol. 137.
STOREY after SHUM, [George], of co. Northumberland, and [Ham] co. Surrey,
　　1823, Vol. XXXIII, fol. 383.

STOREY after SHUM, ... (Spr.), of co. Northumberland, [1870] Vol. LVII, fol. 292.

„ after SHAWE, Lawrence Paulet, Capt., R.M., of Arcot, co. Northumberland, [1873] Vol. LVIII, fol. 232. (Burke's Suppl.)

STOREY, J., of Great Waltham, co. Essex, 1888, Vol. LXIV, fol. 175.

„ Sir Thomas, [Knt., 12 Sept. 1887, Mayor] of Lancaster, 1890, Vol. LXV, fol. 234.

STORIE, Rev. John George, M.A., of co. Essex ; Thames Ditton, co. Surrey ; Stowmaries, co. Sussex ; and Paisley, Scotland, [1829] Vol. XXXVII, fol. 334.

„ Rev. John George, of Woodmausterne Manor, co. Surrey (Vicar of Camberwell). Crest, [1839] Vol. XLIV, fol. 137.

STORY, E. M. B., of Lydiard Manor, co. Somerset, 1891, Vol LXVI, fol. 88.

STOTT, Thomas, Paymaster, 29th Regiment of Foot, Quebec, [1828] Vol. XXXVII, fol. 65.

STOTT (late WILSON), ..., of Quebec, [1828] Vol. XXXVII, fol. 67.

STOTT, ..., of Brownwardle, Rochdale, co. Lanc., [1843] Vol. XLVII, fol. 47.

STOTT-MILNE, ..., of Rochdale, co. Lanc., [1843] Vol. XLVII, fol. 49.

„ MILNE, ..., of Bridge Hill, Witworth, Rochdale, co. Lanc., [1854] Vol. LI, fols. 70 and 72.

STOTT-STANHOPE, ..., Lieut.-Col., Madras S.C., of Eccleshall, Bradford, co. York, and Ramsgate, co. Kent, [1856] Vol. LI, fol. 461.

STOTT, N. Stanhope, of Chislehurst, co. Kent ; Austin Friars, London ; and Newton-in-Bolland, co. York, 1884, Vol. LXII, fol. 285.

STOURTON to LANGDALL [24 Dec. 1814], Charles, of Houghton, co. York, [1815] Vol. XXVIII, fol. 255.

„ to VAVASOUR [27 Feb. 1826], [Hon. Sir] Edward Marmaduke [Bart., 1828], of Houghton and Haselwood, co. York, [1826] Vol. XXXV, fol. 377.

STOURTON, Baron, (VAVASOUR) [?]. Supporters [altered ?], [1878] Vol. LX, fol. 181. [Geneal. Mag., III, p. 144.]

STOVELD, George John T., of Raynham, co. Norf., 1883, Vol. LXII, fol. 139.

STOVELL, Arthur, of Gloucester Crescent, Hyde Park, London, 1875, Vol. LIX, fol. 120.

STOVIN to LISTER, George, of co. Linc., [1783] Vol. XV, fol. 215.

STOVIN, Lieut.-Col. Sir Frederick, K.C.B. [1815], of Whitgift, co. York, [1816] Vol. XXIX, fol. 415.

STOWELL, Baron [17 July 1821] (SCOTT). Supporters, [1821] Vol. XXXIII, fol. 86.

STRACEY, ..., of Rockheath Hall, co. Norf., [1818] Vol. XXXI, fol. 131.

STRACEY-CLITHEROE, Lieut.-Col. Edward John, of Sprowston, co. Norf., and Boston House, Brentford, co. Middx., 1865, Vol. LV, fol. 352.

STRACHAN, Rear-Adm. Sir Richard John, Bart., K.C.B., [K.B., 1806 ; G.C.B., 1815]. Augmentation and Supporters, [1810] Vol. XXV, fols. 359 and 362.

STRAFFORD, Baron [12 May 1835] (BYNG). Supporters, [1835] Vol. XLI, fol. 59.

STRAHAN (late SNOW), ..., of The Strand, Westminster, and Ashurst, co. Surrey, 1832, Vol. XXXIX, fol. 13.

STRAKER, John C., of Stagshaw, Corbridge, and Leazes, Hexham, co. Northumberland, 1896, Vol. LXIX, fol. 71.

„ Henry Lewis, of Dipton House, Corbridge-on-Tyne, co. Northumberland (s. of John, of Murney House, co. Kildare, Ireland), 1897, Vol. LXX, fol. 75.

STRANGE, ..., of Upton, co. Essex, [1811] Vol. XXVII, fol. 78.

„ . . . ., of Enfield, co. Middx., and Swindon, Wilts., [1816] Vol. XXX, fol. 34.

STRANGE-MUIR, ..., of co. Essex, [1868] Vol. LVI, fol. 346.

STRATFORD after WINGFIELD, Lieut.-Col., of co. Kent (s. of Visc. POWERSCOURT). Quarterly Arms, [1803] Vol. XXII, fol. 72.

STRATFORD, late MORGAN, ..., of Wales, and co. Glouc. and Hereford, [1844] Vol. XLVII, fol. 211.

STRATHEDEN, Baroness [22 Jan. 1836, Dame Mary Elizabeth CAMPBELL]. Supporters, [1836] Vol. XLI, fol. 232.

STREATFIELD, ..., of Charts Edge and Hever Castle, co. Kent, and Long Ditton, and Wandsworth, co. Surrey, [1829] Vol. XXXVII, fol. 313.

STREATFIELD-MOORE, A. M. C. [and ?] E. C., of Woodcock Hill, Northchurch, and Berkhampstead, co. Hertf., 1887, Vol. LXIV, fol. 32.

STREET, Thomas George, of Kilburn, co. Middx., 1823, Vol. XXXIII, fol. 393. (Berry.)

„ James Frederick D'Arley, late Capt., R.A., of Mottram Hall, Mottram St. Andrew, co. Chester, [1865] Vol. LV, fol. 332. (Burke's Suppl.)

STREET to WRIGHT, ..., of Mottram Hall, Mottram St. Andrew, and Prestbury, co. Chester. [Match with Wright], [1865] Vol. LV, fol. 346. [Burke.]

STRETTON, ..., of Crumpsall, Manchester, [1866 ?] Vol. LVI, fol. 160.

STRICKLAND to STANDISH, ..., of co. Lanc. and Westmorland. Quarterly Arms, [1807] Vol. XXIV, fol. 211.

„ to CHOLMLEY, Sir George, of co. York, [1865] Vol. LV, fol. 341.

STRICKSON, John, of Shenstone Park, co. Staff., and to his nephew, Samuel, s. of Samuel, of the Inner Temple, Bar.-at-Law, 14 June 1707, Vol. V, fol. 212 ; Add. MS. 14,831, fol. 72 ; Harl. MS. 6834, fol. 117. (Berry.)

STRODE after CHETHAM, Thomas (brother of the next), of Southill House, West Cranmere, co. Somerset, and Mellor Hall, co. Derby, "now prisoner at Verdun, in France." Quarterly Arms, 1808 [1811], Vol. XXVI [? XXIV], fols. 317 and 335.

„ after CHETHAM, Richard (brother of the next), of Mellor Hall, co. Derby, 1827, Vol. XXXVI, fols. 345 and 349.

„ after CHETHAM, Ranoll (brother of the next), 1828, Vol. XXXVII, fol. 189.

„ after CHETHAM, Adm. Sir Edward, (K.C.B.) [1845] (brother of the last), of co. Somerset, and Forton Lodge, nr. Gosport, Hampsh., 1845, Vol. XLVII, fol. 406.

STROTHER, ..., of Woolwich, co. Kent, [1844] Vol. XLVII, fol. 227.

STRUT, Samuel, of Westminster, and co. Essex, 1772, Vol. XII, fol. 139. (Edmondson and Berry.)

STRUTT, Joseph Holden, 31 Aug. 1821, Vol. XXXIII, fol. 1.

„ [Charlotte Mary Gertrude], Baroness RAYLEIGH [18 July 1821, wife of Joseph Holden Strutt], of co. Essex, [1821] Vol. XXXIII, fol. 3. Supporters, [1877] Vol. LX, fol. 7 [1821, fols. 60 and 67 ? (she died 1836)].

„ Baron BELPER [29 Aug. 1856, the Rt. Hon. Edward Strutt], of co. Derby, [1856] Vol. LII, fol. 74. Supporters, fol. 76.

STUART, [John], Baron CARDIFF [20 May 1776], ([commonly called] Lord MOUNT-STUART). Supporters, [1776] Vol. XIII, fol. 221.

„ Lieut.-Gen. [the Hon.] Sir Charles, K.B. [1799—1800], brother to Marquess of BUTE. Supporters, [1800] Vol. XX, fol. 424.

„ Sir Charles, K.B. [26 Sept. 1812, invested 1813], Envoy Ex. to Portugal (father of Lord [? created Baron] Stuart DE ROTHESAY) [22 Jan. 1828] [son of the above Sir Charles]. Augmentation, [1812] Vol. XXVII, fol. 123.

„ Maj.-Gen. Sir John, Knt., order of the Crescent, Count of MAIDA. Crest for augmentation, [1804] Vol. XXIII, fol. 56 ; Supporters [?], G.C.B. [K.B., 13 Sept. 1806] [G.C.B., 2 Jan. 1815] (died 1 April 1815), 1804, Vol. XXIII, fol. 58 ; Augmentation, [1810] Vol. XXV, fol. 423.

STUART, now WORTLEY [Roy. Lic., 7 Jan. 1795], James Archibald, 2nd s. of the [3rd] Earl of BUTE. (Match), [1798] Vol. XX, fol. 239.

STUART-WORTLEY-MACKENZIE [Roy. Lic., 17 June 1826], James Archibald, Baron WHARNCLIFFE [12 July 1826], of co. York, and Scotland, [1826] Vol. XXXVI, fols. 37 and 41.

STUART after CRICHTON, ... [Roy. Lic., 26 Aug. 1805, John Stuart, 7th] Earl of DUMFRIES. Quarterly Arms, [1805] Vol. XXIII, fol. 196.

„ after CRIGHTON, ([21 Mar. 1817, Patrick James Herbert], 2nd s. of Baron MOUNTSTUART). Quarterly Arms, [1817] Vol. XXX, fol. 169.

STUART (CRICHTON-), [26 Aug. 1805, John, 2nd], Marquess of BUTE. HERBERT Coat [?], [1822] Vol. XXXIII, fol. 196.

STUART after FENWICK, ... (Spr.), of London. (Match), [1816] Vol. XXIX, fol. 250.

STUART-FORBES, ..., of Scotland, [1821] Vol. XXXIII, fol. 25.

STUART after VILLIERS, ..., of Bramfield, co. Hertf. ; Waldersham, co. Kent ; and Dromana, co. Waterford, Ireland, [1822] Vol. XXXIII, fols. 200 and 206.

STUART, DE DECIES, Baron Stuart [1839, Henry Villiers-Stuart]. Supporters, [1839] Vol. XLIV, fol. 34.

STUART after GORDON, ..., of London, and Scotland, [1835] Vol. XL, fol. 370.

STUART, Sir James, Bart., Chief Justice of Lower Canada, [1841] Vol. XLV, fol. 185.

STUART and DURAND, of London, and Malacca, [1847] Vol. XLVIII, fols. 256 and 257.

STUART-FORBES, (HEPBURN-), [Forbes], before TREFUSIS, [4 Sept. 1867, Hepburn-Stuart-Forbes-Trefusis, 20th] Baron CLINTON, of Scotland, [1867] Vol. LVI, fol. 303.

STUBBING, Richard, Sheriff, co. Derby, of West Broughton, co. Derby, [171½ ?] Vol. VI, fol. 22.

STUBBS, William (Bp. of Oxford), of Cholderton, Wilts., and Knaresborough and Ripon, co. York, 1877, Vol. LX, fol. 26. (Berry's Suppl.)

„ Henry, of London, and Danby, Ballyshannon and Kilbarron, co. Donegal, Ireland, s. of Thomas Troubridge, 1880, Vol. LX, fol. 372.

„ Samuel, of Hampstead Road, London, 1885, Vol. LXIII, fol. 149.

STUBS, Joseph, J.P., of Warrington, co. Lanc., and to descendants of his brother Thomas, 28 Feb. 1849, Vol. XLIX, fol. 121 (see Genealogist, IV, p. 286).

STUCKEY, Robert, of Weston, co. Devon, and Langport, co. Somerset, 1759, Vol. X, fol. 184[d] ; [1810] Vol. XXV, fol. 351. (Berry.)

STUCKEY after BARTLETT, ... (Stuckey-Bartlett ?), of Weston, co. Devon, [1810] Vol. XXV, fol. 357.

STUCKEY, late WOODS, Vincent, of Lidlington, co. Bedf., and Hill House, Langport, Eastover, co. Somerset, [1861] Vol. LIV, fol. 136. (Berry's Suppl.)

STUCLEY, late BUCK, Sir George [Stuckley Buck to George Stuckley Stuckley, of Hartland Abbey and of Afton Castle, co. Devon. Arms of Stuckley quarterly with paternal Arms, 13 Aug. 1858. (Crisp, Notes, IV, p. 130.)]. [1858] Vol. LII, fol. 381. BUCK [Arms], [1780] Vol. XIV, fol. 243.

STUDD, Lieut.-Col. Edward Mortlock, of Ipswich, co. Suff., [1834] Vol. XL, fol. 141.

STUDDY, ..., of Dartmouth, co. Devon, [1795] Vol. XIX, fol. 75.

STUPART, Robert, R.N., of Elphinstone, co. Stirling, Scotland, s. of Robert, 1762, Vol. X, fol. 450. (Berry.)

STURCH, ..., of Regent's Park, London, [1826] Vol. XXXVI, fol. 22.

STURT, Autby, of Yateley, Hampsh., Commander for victualling the Navy, 19 Oct. 1691, Vol. IV, fol. 91.

„ Henry [Gerard], Baron ALINGTON [15 Jan. 1876], of co. Dorset. Supporters, 1876, Vol. LIX, fol. 217.

STYCH, [Samuel] (see DAVISON), of Drayton, Shropsh., [1737] Vol. VIII, fol. 217[b].

STYLEMAN LE STRANGE, ..., of Hunstanton Hall and Snettisham, co. Norf., [1839] Vol. XLIV, fol. 69.

STYLES, Frederick, of Bread Street, and Westbourne Terrace, London, 1875, Vol. LIX, fol. 118.

STYMAN, ..., of Lombard Street, London, and co. York, [1807] Vol. XXIV, fol. 293.

SUCKLING, late FOX, ..., of co. Norf., [1820] Vol. XXXII, fol. 243.

SUCKLING, ...   Grant of Crest, 24 Nov. 1817. (Burke.)

SUDELEY, Baron [12 July 1838, Charles HANBURY-TRACY], of co. Glouc. Supporters, [1838] Vol. XLIII, fol. 99.

„   Baron, [eldest] son of, from LEIGH to HANBURY-TRACY. [Thomas Charles Hanbury-Tracy, 2nd Baron, Roy. Lic., 11 April 1806, assumed the Surname of Leigh. He resumed, 30 Mar. 1839, his paternal Surname.] [1839] Vol. XLIII, fol. 349.

SUFFIELD, Robert, of Wells, co. Norf. (called SUSFIELD by Berry), April 1732, Vol. VIII, fol. 143.

„   Baron [21 Aug. 1786] (HARBORD).   Supporters, [1786] Vol. XVI, fol. 185.

SUGDEN, late LONG, William James, of Bingley, co. Lanc., and Bath, co. Somerset, [1834] Vol. XL, fol. 266.

SULWAN, [Benjamin], Knt. [30 June 1801], of co. Cork, Ireland, and [Judge of the Supreme Court at] Madras, [1801] Vol. XXI, fols. 212 and 226.

SUMMERS, Lord [see SOMERS, or SOMMERS] (COCKS). Supporters, [1784] Vol. XV, fol. 301.

„   . . . ., of Pall Mall, London, [1826] Vol. XXXV, fol. 343.

SUNDERLAND, Earl of, K.G. (Match), [1813] Vol. XXVII, fol. 351.

„   . . . . (See Duke of MARLBOROUGH.)   [1817] Vol. XXX, fol. 286.

SUNKERSETT, ..., J.P., of Bombay, [1861] Vol. LIV, fol. 218.

SUPPLE to BROOKE-DE CAPELL-BROOKE, Richard, of co. Northampton, and Ireland, [1797] Vol. XX, fol. 70.

SURMAN, Robert, of London, Merchant, 5 Aug. 1720, Vol. VI, fol. 445 ; Add. MS. 14,831, fol. 111.

SURREY, Earl of, [Henry Charles] HOWARD [only s. of the 12th Duke of Norfolk] [summoned by writ as Baron MALTRAVERS, 16 Aug. 1841 ?].   Supporters, [1841] Vol. XLV, fol. 329.

SURTEES, Sir Stephenson Villiers, Knt. [25 June 1859], Chief Justice of the Island of Mauritius, of Silkmore House, Castlechurch, co. Staff., and Newcastle-upon-Tyne, co. Northumberland, to descendants of his grandfather, Aubone, [1863] Vol. LV, fol. 56.

„   Charles Freville (s. of Robert), of Mainsforth Hall, Bishop Middleham, co. Durham, 1899, Vol. LXX, fol. 322.

SUTCLIFFE, James Smith, of Beach House, Bacup, co. Lanc., [1872] Vol. LVIII, fol. 186.

SUTHERLAND, 2nd s. of the Duke of, [Francis] LEVESON-GOWER, to EGERTON [Roy. Lic., 24 Aug. 1833], [Earl of Ellesmere, 1 July 1846], [1833] Vol. XXXIX, fol. 361.

„   Duke of, K.G. [1841], [George Granville Leveson-Gower, 2nd Duke of Sutherland ?].   Supporters, [1841] Vol. XLV, fols. 176 and 180.

„   [Anne], Duchess of, [Countess of] CROMARTIE, [Viscountess of Tarbat, 21 Oct. 1861] [wife of the 4th Duke].   Supporters, [1862] Vol. LIV, fols. 240 and 241.

„   . . . ., of Crow Nest, Halifax, co. York, [1856] Vol. LII, fol. 132.

SUTHERLAND-WALKER, ..., of Crow Nest, Halifax, and Shibden Hall, co. York, [1856] Vol. LII, fol. 139.

SUTHERLAND, Sir Thomas, [M.P.], G.C.M.G. [22 June 1897].   Supporters, 1898 [1898], Vol. LXX, fol. 168.

SUTHERY, A. M., of Tolgarth Hall, Pennal, co. Merioneth, Wales, 1894,* Vol. LXVIII, fol. 136.

SUTTON, ..., B.D., Rector of St. Mary, Blandford, co. Dorset. (Match), [1699] Vol. IV, fol. 294.

„   Sir Robert, K.B. [27 May] (1725) (Bart.).   Quarterings and Supporters, [1725] Vol. VII, fol. 408.

SUTTON, Daniel, of London ; Framlingham Earl, co. Norf. ; and Kenton, co. Suff. (*see* printed Index) [? which], 23 Aug. 1767, Vol. XI, fol. 220.   (Berry.)

„   Molesey, Lieut.-Col., Militia, of co. Surrey, [1806] Vol. XXIV, fol. 110.

„   Sir Thomas [Manners-], Knt., Baron MANNERS [1807], of co. Linc.   Supporters, [1807] Vol. XXIV, fol. 183.

SUTTON-MANNERS, Sir Charles, G.C.B. [1833], Speaker of the House of Commons, [1817-1834].   Supporters, [1833] Vol. XL, fol. 9 ; 1st Viscount CANTERBURY [10 Mar. 1835], [1835] Vol. XL, fol. 378.

SUTTON, Rear-Adm. Samuel, of Screveton, co. Nottingham, [1815] Vol. XXVIII, fol. 412.

„   . . . ., of Deal, co. Kent, and Half-Moon Street, London, [1822 ?] Vol. XXXIII, fol. 345.

SUTTON, late HUTCHINSON, G. W., of Stockton, co. Durham, 1823, Vol. XXXIV, fol. 134 (*see* Berry's Suppl. and Appx.).

SUTTON after GUNNING, O. G., Com., R.N., of Hampsh. and co. Nottingham, [1850] Vol. XLIX, fol. 322.

SUTTON, Henry, of Lincoln's Inn, London, 1894,* Vol. LXVIII, fol. 75.

„   M. J., of Kidmore, co. Oxf., 1895, Vol. LXVIII, fol. 144.

SUTTON-NELTHORPE, [? Frank Hay Chapman], R.N., of Scawby Hall, co. Linc., 1884, Vol. LXII, fol. 303.

SUTTON, Martin John (s. of Martin Hope), of Henley Park, co. Oxf., 18 . . ., Vol. LXXI, fol. . . . .

SWABEY, Samuel, of Langley, Bucks., and Westminster, 1757, Vol. X, fol. 96. (Berry.)

„   . . . ., of Langley, Bucks.   New Crest, 22 Aug. 1819, Vol. XXXI, fol. 171.

„   William Procter, Bp. of British Guiana, s. of Joseph, of Tilney, co. Linc., 1897, Vol. LXX, fol. 11.

SWAFFIELD, late OWEN, ..., of Wyke Regis, co. Dorset, [1840] Vol. XLV, fol. 5.

SWAINE, ..., of Halifax and Horton, nr. Bradford, co. York, [1843] Vol. XLVII, fol. 70.

SWAINSON, Rev. Christopher, of Preston, co. Lanc. ; Mapreby, Hereford ; and Rector of Wistanstow, Shropsh., [1849] Vol. XLIX, fol. 262.

SWAN, R., of The Quarry, co. Linc., [13 May] 1891,* Vol. LXVI, fol. 96.

SWANSEA, Baron [9 June 1893], [Sir Henry Hussey] VIVIAN, Bart., 1893, Vol. LXVII, fol. 269.   Supporters, fol. 279.

SWEEDLAND, ..., of Berners Street, London, [1802] Vol. XXI, fol. 316.

„   Sir Christopher, Knt. [11 Dec. 1812], of Lambeth, co. Surrey, [1815] Vol. XXIX [? 1812, Vol. XXVII], fol. 186.

SWEETAPPLE, Sir John, Knt., Sheriff of London, 25 Aug. 1699, Vol. IV, fol. 306.

SWEETLAND, John, of co. Devon, Commissary and Receiver-Gen. at Gibraltar, 5 Aug. 1808, Vol. XXV, fol. 46.   (Berry.)

„   David, of co. Devon, an officer in Commissary Department, Gibraltar, granted in the same Patent, the Crest differenced.   They were brothers-in-law, 5 Aug. 1808, Vol. XXV, fol. 48 (*see* Berry).

SWETE, Adrian, of Train, co. Devon, and to the descendants of his father (*sic*, no name given), 13 Feb. 171⅔, Vol. VI, fol. 85 ; Add. MS. 14,830, fol. 86.

SWETTENHAM after WARREN, Robert, of Swettenham Hall, co. Chester, and Sandford Court, St. John, co. Kilkenny, Ireland, 1877 [1879], Vol. LX, fol. 273.   (Berry's Suppl.)

SWINDLEY, John Edward, Lieut.-Col., 15th Hussars, 1826, Vol. XXXVI, fols. 55 and 56.

[SWINDON, Borough of, Wilts., 23 Sept. 1901.   (Geneal. Mag., V, p. 443.).]

MILBORNE - SWINNERTON, late PILKINGTON [Sir Lionel Milborne Swinnerton Pilkington], Bart., of co. York and Staff. [? Surnames assumed by Roy. Lic., 1856], [1856] Vol. LII, fol. 78 [the Arms of Milborne and Swinnerton, by Roy. Lic., 16 Mar. 1859], [1859] Vol. LIII, fol. 94.

SWITHINBANK, H. W., of Denham Court, Bucks., 1891, Vol. LXVI, fol. 141.
SYDENHAM, Humphrey, of Coombe-in-Dulverton, co. Somerset, 1757, Vol. X, fol. 104. (Berry.)
SYDNEY, Baron [6 Mar. 1783] ([Thomas] TOWNSHEND). Supporters, [1783] Vol. XV, fol. 155.
  ,, ..., decd., wife of SHELLEY, Bart., of co. Kent. Escutcheon of pretence, [1806] Vol. XXIV, fol. 16.
SYKES, Mark (Alderman), of Hull and Leeds, co. York, [1746] Vol. IX, fol. 174.
  ,, Francis, s. of Sir Francis, Bart., of Ackworth Park, and Thornhill and Kirkheaton, co. York, 1 Mar. 1763, Vol. X, fol. 464.
SYKES to MASTERMAN, Sir Mark, 3rd Bart., [1796] Vol. XIX, fol. 287.
SYKES after MASTERMAN, Sir Mark, 3rd Bart. Quarterly Arms, [1796 ?] Vol. XIX, fol. 327.
SYKES, ..., of Wyersdale, co. Lanc., and Leatherhead, co. Surrey, [1815] Vol. XXVIII, fol. 410.
SYKES after MASTERMAN, ..., of Colthurst Hall [co. York], Bushel Eaves, and Accrington, co. Lanc., [1869] Vol. LVII, fol. 133.
SYKES, Edward H., of Edgeley Fold, Cheadle, co. Chester, 1881, Vol. LXI, fol. 239.
  ,, F. W., of Green Lea, Lindley, co. York, 1895, Vol. LXVIII, fol. 178.
  ,, Dr. John, of Doncaster, co. York, 1881, Vol. LXI, fol. 229.
  ,, J. N., of Field House, Lindley, co. York, 1896, Vol. LXIX, fol. 81.
  ,, Adriana (Lady BOYNTON), dau. of John, and sister Joanna, 21 Mar. 172¾, Vol. VII, fol. 245.
SYMES, Lieut.-Col. Richard, of Bally Arthur, co. Wicklow, Ireland (to quarter CLIFFE arms), [1788] Vol. XVI, fol. 363.
SYMES-BULLEN, ..., of Charmouth, co. Dorset, [1868] Vol. LVII, fol. 51.
SYMONDS before BREEDON, Rev. John, of co. Glouc., Fellow of St. John's Coll., Oxf., [1783] Vol. XV, fol. 127.
SYMONDS, J. F., of Hereford, took name of JEUNE, 1883,* Vol. LXII, fol. 108. (Berry's Suppl.)
  ,, Mrs. T. P., of Pengethley, Sellack, co. Hereford, 1883, Vol. LXII, fol. 44.
SYMONDS-TAYLER, R. H. T., of Okeleigh, Hereford, 1886, Vol. LXIII, fol. 179.
SYMONS, late RAYMOND, Thomas, of co. Hereford and Glouc., [1797] Vol. XX, fol. 6.
SYMONS after SOLTAU, George William, of co. Devon, [1845] Vol. XLVII, fol. 361.
SYMONS-JEUNE, John Frederic, of Axbridge, co. Somerset, 2nd s. of Francis, Bp. of Peterborough, 1879, Vol. LX, fol. 305. (Berry.)
SYMPSON after WOLCOTT, ..., of Winkton, nr. Ringwood, Hampsh.; Crorgh, co. Limerick; and Mount Eudid, co. Cork, Ireland, 1819, Vol. XXXI, fols. 302 and 304.
SYMPSON, Edward Mansel, s. of Thomas, of Deloraine Court, co. Linc., 1897, Vol LXIX, fol. 313.
SYNDERCOMBE to RAYMOND, ..., of co. Dorset, [1804] Vol. XXIII, fol. 73.

T

TABOR, ..., and MINNITT, his wife, of Lothbury, London, and Wilderwick House, Lingfield, co. Surrey, [1824] Vol. XXXIV, fol. 312; [1852 ?] Vol. L ?, fol. 265, CLIFTON, second wife.
  ,, Rev. Robert Stammers, M.A., of Pembury, co. Kent, and Cheam, co. Surrey, 1876, Vol. LIX, fol. 182.
TACON, Thomas Henry (s. of Charles), of The Red House, Eye, co. Suff., 1898, Vol. LXX, fol. 200.
TADWELL, John, of St. Marylebone, co. Middx., and co. Nottingham, 14 Sept. 1768, Vol. XI, fol. 300. (Berry.)
TAILBY, William Ward (s. of William), of Humberstone, co. Leic. (High Sheriff, 1856), [1841] Vol. XLV, fol. 272.

TAILOUR, ..., of Canada, 1781. (Burke.)

TAILYOUR after RENNY, ..., of Scotland, [1849] Vol. XLIX, fol. 252.

TALBOT, Adm. [The Hon.] Sir John, G.C.B. [1842]. Supporters, [1842] Vol. XLVI, fol. 68.

  ,, Baron, of Hensol [5 Dec. 1733, The Right Hon. Charles Talbot, Lord Chancellor]. Supporters, [1733] Vol. VIII, fol. 179b.

TALBOT, late DAVENPORT, Rev. William, of co. Worc., 9 or 19 June 1778, Vol. XIV, fol. 23.

TALBOT, CHETWYND-, Earl [Talbot]. Quarterly Arms, [1786] Vol. XVI, fol. 135.

TALBOT to DE CARDONEL, [Cecil], Baroness DINEVOR, [1787] Vol. XVI, fol. 285.

  ,, to CARPENTER [1 June 1868], the Hon. Walter Cecil, [2nd s. of the 3rd] Earl of SHREWSBURY, of co. York, [1868] Vol. LVII, fol. 27.

TALBOT, late FITZALAN-HOWARD [19 July 1876], Lord Edmund Bernard, 2nd s. of Henry GRANVILLE, 14th Duke of NORFOLK, 1876, Vol. LIX, fol. 254.

TALMASH, late MANNERS [6 April 1821], Sir William, Bart., Baron HUNTING-TOWER, [1821] Vol. XXXII, fol. 287.

TANCOCK, Osborne J., D.C.L., of Wadham College, Oxf., Incumb. of St. John, Truro, co. Cornw., [1851] Vol. L, fol. 72.

TANCRED, George (formerly CLEGHORN), of Weens, Scotland, and Arden Hall, co. York, 1888, Vol. LXIV, fol. 255.

TANKERVILLE, [Earl of], Ld. BENNETT, of co. Northumberland, [1788] Vol. XVI, fol. 379.

TANNER, ..., of Exeter, co. Devon. (See WILLIAMS.) Match, [1813] Vol. XXVII, fol. 411.

TANQUERAY, Edward, LL.B., of Tingrave, co. Bedf.; Clare Coll., Camb.; and Christ Church, Oxf., 1838, Vol. XLIII, fol. 191.

  ,, Willaume, of New Broad Street, London, and Chilton Candover, Hampsh., [1848] Vol. XLIX, fol. 11.

TAPPS, ..., of Hinton-Admiral, Hampsh., and Northchurch, co. Hertf., [1791] Vol. XVII, fol. 372.

TAPPS-GERVIS, [Sir George William Tapps, 2nd] Bart., of Hinton-Admiral, Hampsh., [1835?] Vol. XLI, fol. 174.

TAPPS-GERVIS-MEYRICK, Sir George Eliott Meyrick, Bart., of Hinton-Admiral, Hampsh., and Bodorgan, co. Anglesey, Wales, 1876, Vol. LIX, fol. 208.

TARLETON, Thomas, of Bolesworth Castle, co. Chester, and Aigburth and Liverpool, co. Lanc., 1797 [1799?], Vol. XX, fol. 310.

  ,, Lieut.-Gen. Banastre, M.P. BERTIE Arms impaled, 1804, Vol. XXIII, fol. 5 (see XL, Baronets, p. 518).

TARLETON-FOTHERGILL, Dame, of Hensol Castle, co. Glamorgan, Wales (widow of Sir Rose L. PRICE, Bart.)? this, 1888, Vol. LXIV, fol. 138.

TARN, Harry Holmes, Lyon Register [No. 5207, 1901].

TARPEY, William B. K. (s. of Hugh), Vol. I? or LXXI [granted to Alderman Hugh Tarpey, of Dublin, Lord Mayor of that city in 1877 and 1878, son of James Tarpey, of Rockfield, co. Dublin, decd. (Burke.)].

TARRATT, ..., of Downton Castle, co. Hereford, and Wolverhampton and Ford House, co. Staff., [1853?] Vol. L, fol. 291.

TARTE, John, of James' Street, Westminster, 1833, Vol. XXXIX, fol. 231 (see Berry's Suppl.).

TASBURGH, Margaret Frances (minor, aged 18), of co. Norf. and York, and Clanny, co. Glouc. (Berry.) Change of Arms, 30 April 1739, Vol. VIII, fol. 253.

TASBURGH, late ANNE, Michael, 20 June 1810, Vol. XXVI, fol. 1.

TASKER, ..., of London. Match with LANE, [1812] Vol. XXVII, fol. 145.

  ,, ... (Spr.), of Middleton Hall, Shenfield, co. Essex, [1870] Vol. LVII, fol. 274.

TASWELL, ..., of Tockington, Wotton-under-Edge and Almondsbury, co. Glouc., [1842] Vol. XLVI, fol. 100.

TATCHELL, formerly BULLEN, ..., of co. Dorset and Somerset, [1824] Vol. XXXIV, fol. 342.

TATCHELL-BULLEN, ..., of co. Dorset and Somerset [1852], Vol. L, fol. 146.

TATE, ..., of Chelsea, co. Middx., [1826] Vol. XXXVI, fol. 118.

TATE after PINFOLD, ... (Spr.), of Burleigh Hall, Loughborough, co. Leic., [1849] Vol. XLIX, fol. 180.

TATE, Henry (Bart. [27 June 1898]), of Park Hill, Streatham, co. Surrey, 1898, Vol. LXX, fol. 203.

TATEM, Samuel, Alderman of London, of Colchester, co. Essex ; All Hallows, Barking, London ; and co. York ?, 15 April 1732, Vol. VIII, fol. 135.

TATEM, late UPHAM, ..., of Stepney, co. Middx., [1807 ?] Vol. XXIV, fol. 315.

TATHAM, Rear-Adm. Edward, of Tatham and Hornby, co. Lanc. ; Hutton, co. Cumberland ; and Appleby, co. Westmorland, [1838] Vol. XLIII, fol. 56.

  ,, ... *See* WARTER.

TATHWELL, late BAKER, ..., of co. Dorset and Linc., [1804] Vol. XXIII, fol. 24.

TATLOCK, Thomas, Citizen and Grocer, of London (Stepney, [? co. Middx.]), s. of John, of Cunscough, co. Lanc., to the descendants of his father, 5 or 25 Feb. 172$\frac{5}{6}$, Vol. VII, fol. 506 ; Add. MS. 14,831, fol. 108.

TATTON to EGERTON [?], ..., of co. Chester, [1806] Vol. XXIII, fols. 415 and 417.

TAUBMAN after GOLDIE, ... (minor), of the Isle of Man, [1824] Vol. XXXV, fol. 21.

TAUNTON, Richard, s. of Richard, of Hampsh., 3 April 1735, Vol. VIII, fol. 191^{b}.

  ,,   Baron [18 Aug. 1859, Henry] (LABOUCHERE), of co. Somerset. Supporters, [1859] Vol. LIII, fols. 208 and 210.

  ,,   Rev. Frederick, of Kingswood Vicarage, Epsom, co. Surrey, 1886,* Vol. LXIII, fol. 175. (Crisp, IV, p. 167.)

TAWKE, late TUCK, ..., of Chigwell, co. Essex, and Dulwich, co. Surrey, [1818] Vol. XXX, fol. 330.

TAYLER to PORTER, Capt., 60th Regiment of Foot, of Burlingham, co. Worc., [1878] Vol. LX, fol. 88.

TAYLER, [Thomas], of London, Carlisle, and co. Glouc., [1600] Vol. II, fol. 632.

TAYLOR, Joseph, s. of James, of Sandford, co. Oxf., to the descendants of his father, 31 Mar. 1720, Vol. VI, fol. 395 ; Add. MS. 14,830, fol. 186.

  ,,   Giles, s. of Richard, of Broadclyst, co. Devon, and Lyons Inn, London, to the descendants of his father, 2 July 1734, Vol. VIII, fol. 186 ; Add. MS. 14,830, fol. 23.

  ,,   Robert, M.D., s. of John, Alderman, of Newark-upon-Trent, co. Nottingham, 5 Jan. 17$\frac{39}{40}$, Vol. VIII, fol. 263.

  ,,   John, s. of John, of Portsmouth, Hampsh., 1750, Vol. IX, fol. 372. (Berry.)

  ,,   Elizabeth Ann, widow of Daniel, of Leeds, co. York, coz. of Robert PEASE, [1763] Vol. X, fol. 479.

  ,, ..., of Moyles Court, near Ringwood, Hampsh., [1793] Vol. XVIII, fol. 235 ; *see* Christopher, [1822] Vol. XXXIII, fol. 334.

TAYLOR to WIGSELL, ... (minor), of Sanderstead, co. Surrey, [1807] Vol. XXIV, fol. 125.

TAYLOR, late CLOUGH, Edward, of Trinity Coll., Camb., and co. Hertf. and York, 1858 [1807], Vol. XXIV, fol. 267.

TAYLOR, ..., of Highfield House, in Pemberton, par. of Wigan, co. Lanc., 1865-8, Vol. LVI, fol. . . . .

  ,,   Robert, High Sheriff of co. Hertf., of Tolmers, co. Hertf. (and for wife of Taylor, reputed dau. of James, Earl of SALISBURY, and relict of John JACKSON, of Wath, co. York), [1810] Vol. XXV, fol. 439 ; Taylor impaling CECIL, fol. 443.

  ,, ..., of Uttoxeter, co. Staff., [1811] Vol. XXVI, fol. 176.

  ,,   Edward, M.P., of Bifrons, co. Kent (sister NORTHEY), and Bootle, and brothers Herbert and Brook, [1814] Vol. XXVIII, fol. 178.

  ,, ..., of Bradford House, Great Leyer, co. Lanc., 1817 ? [1815 ?], Vol. XXVIII, fol. 254.

TAYLOR after WATSON, George, of Wilts., and Jamaica. Quarterly Arms, 1815, Vol. XXIX, fol. 93.

TAYLOR, John Denham (and SHEAVILL, his wife), of Swalwell, Whickham, West Chopwell and Ryton, co. Durham, [1822] Vol. XXXIII, fol. 176.

TAYLOR to LISLE, Edward Hales, of Hampsh., [1822] Vol. XXXIII, fol. 334 ; s. of Christopher Taylor, D.D., Vicar of Selbourne, Hampsh., [1793] Vol. XVIII, 235.

TAYLOR, Capt., of Amboy, New Jersey, America, ? Taylor, of Pennington [Hampsh.], 1823, Vol. XXXIV, fol. 72.

   „ . . . ., M.D., of Wotton-under-Edge, co. Glouc., [1823] Vol. XXXIV, fol. 162.

   „ . . . ., of Hollycombe, co. Sussex, [1828] Vol. XXXVII, fol. 15.

   „ Lieut.-Gen. Sir Herbert, G.C.B. [1834]. Supporters, [1835] Vol. XL, fol. 323.

   „ . . . ., of Todmorden Hall, Rochdale, and Whitworth, co. Lanc., [1838] Vol. XLIII, fol. 231.

TAYLOR, formerly MEEKE, William, J.P. and D.L., of co. Staff., and William Bewley Taylor, of Broome Hall, co. Staff., [1840] Vol. XLIV, fol. 369.

TAYLOR-SMITH, Edward, of Crooke, co. Durham, 1843, Vol. XLVI, fol. 300.

TAYLOR, Thomas, of Dodworth, co. York, [1844] Vol. XLVII, fol. 286.

   „ . . . ., of Manchester, and Richard's Castle, co. Hereford, [1845] Vol. XLVII, fol. 413.

   „ . . . ., of Bashall Hall, co. York, Moreton Hall and Whalley Abbey, co. Lanc., [1849] Vol. XLIX, fol. 207.

TAYLOR after PILLING, ... (Spr.), Margaret, of Moreton Hall, co. Lanc., [1876] Vol. LIX, fol. 300 [see Burke, and Burke's Suppl.].

TAYLOR, Andrew, of Tunbridge Wells, co. Kent, [1855] Vol. LI, fol. 203.

   „ James Arthur, J.P. and D.L., of Strensham Court, Moseley Hall, and Moore Green, co. Worc., [1857] Vol. LII, fol. 250.

   „ ? Moore, of Harptree Court, East Harptree, co. Somerset, [1861] Vol. LIV, fol. 202.

TAYLOR-WHITEHEAD, Smith, M.A., of Bakewell, co. Derby, and the Inner Temple, London, [1873] Vol. LVIII, fol. 200. (Berry's Suppl.)

TAYLOR, Archdeacon William Francis, of St. Andrew's Vicarage, Liverpool, co. Lanc., 1892, Vol. LXVII, fol. 55. (Crisp, III, p. 95.)

   „ George, of Mark Lane, London, and West Brighton, co. Sussex, 1884, Vol. LXII, fol. 274.

   „ Capt. James Math., Vice-Consul, Stalea, Corfu, 1884,* Vol. LXII, fol. 200.

   „ J. B., of Serge Hill, King's Langley, St. Alban's, co. Hertf., 1895, Vol. LXVIII, fol. 186.

   „ Seth, of Granard, Roehampton, co. Surrey (miller), 1882, Vol. LXII, fol. 12. (Berry's Suppl.)

TAYLOUR, John, Sec. of the Treasury, of Westminster, and Oxford, 14 Feb. 171$\frac{4}{5}$, Vol. VI, fol. 189. (Berry.)

   „ [Thomas] (s. of Earl BECTIVE), Marquess of HEADFORT, of co. Westmorland, [1868] Vol. LVII, fol. 41.

TEALE, Isaac, of Hanover Square, London, and to the other issue of his father, Isaac, of Westminster, by Elizabeth, his wife, dau. of John HEARD, of co. Hertf., 26 Feb. 172$\frac{3}{4}$, Vol. VII, fol. 238 ; Add. MS. 14,830, fol. 21. (Berry.)

   „ Thomas Pidgin, F.R.C.S., of Leeds, co. York, s. of Thomas, M.R.C.S., [1855] Vol. LI, fol. 367.

TEASDALE to BURN, ..., of co. Westmorland, [1810] Vol. XXV, fol. 373.

TEED, John, M.P., of Plymouth, co. Devon, [1808] Vol. XXIV, fol. 393.

TEISSIER, ..., of Broad Street, London, [1782] Vol. XV, fol. 69.

TELEKI to HARLEY, Count of the H.R.E., [1859] Vol. LIII, fol. 264.

TEMPEST after PLUMBE, Col. John, of co. Lanc. and York, [1835] Vol. XL, fol. 340.

TEMPEST-TEMPEST, Sir Robert, of co. Lanc. and York, 1884, Vol. LXII, fol. 218.

TEMPLE, Sir Richard, Bart., K.B., [1661]. Supporters?, [1688] Vol. IV, fol. 13 ; [1661, Vol. II].

„ [Richard], Baron COBHAM [19 Oct. 1714]. Supporters, [1715] Vol. VI, fol. 201 [see COBHAM].

„ Earl [11 Sept. 1779] (GRENVILLE-N.-T.) [George Nugent-Temple-Grenville]. Quarterly Arms and Supporters, [1779 ?] Vol. XIV, fol. 195.

TEMPLE, NUGENT- [Temple] GRENVILLE to T.-N. B. CHANDOS [Temple-Nugent-Brydges-Chandos-Grenville] [15 Nov. 1799], Duke of BUCKINGHAM [1882], [1800] Vol. XXI, fol. 54.

TEMPLE after COWPER, Hon. William Francis, P.C., of Broadlands, Hampsh., 1869, Vol. LVII, fol. 210.

TEMPLE, John, of Mossley Bank, Aigburth, Liverpool, co. Lanc., 1888, Vol. LXIV, fol. 311.

„ Earl [? William Stephen GORE-LANGTON, 26 Mar. 1889]. Arms, 1892, Vol. LXVI, fol. 313. Supporters, fol. 315.

TEMPLE, late DICKIN, John, of co. Devon and Worc., [23 Sept.] 1796, Vol. XIX, fol. 313.

TEMPLEMORE, Baron [10 Sept. 1831] ([Arthur] CHICHESTER). Supporters, [1831] Vol. XXXVIII, fol. 288.

TEMPLER, James, of Stower Lodge, Exeter, co. Devon, 1765 [1763], Vol. X, fol. 475. (Berry [gives TEMPLAR].)

„ . . . ., of Salmonpool, St. James' Abbey, co. Devon ; Bridport, co. Dorset ; and of the Inner Temple, London, [1815] Vol. XXIX, fol. 59.

TENCH to SHERBURNE, ..., of co. Middx., [1853] Vol. L, fol. 322.

MacCARTHY-TENISON, C., of Brisbane, Queensland, 1891, Vol. LXVI, fol. 131.

TENNANT, William, of Little Aston Hall, co. Staff. ; Bromley St. Leonard, co. Middx. ; and Sydney Lodge, Hampsh., [1804] Vol. XXII, fol. 441.

TENNANT, late TOVEY, Lieut.-Col. Hamilton, E.I.C.S., of co. Middx. and Staff., [1832] Vol. XXXIX, fol. 65 ; [and] of Pynacles, Great Stanmore, co. Middx., a lunatic, [1867] Vol. LVI, fol. 180.

TENNANT, John (minor), (s. of STANSFIELD-TENNANT), of Otley, Idle and Chapel House, Burnsall, co. York, [1833] Vol. XXXIX, fol. 294.

„ . . . . (late VIDLER), Hamilton Dunbar, widow of John Vidler, Southsea, Hampsh. (Poole, co. Lanark, Scotland), and Overston, Shottesdon, Shropsh., 1876, Vol. LIX, fol. 224.

TENNYSON-D'EYNCOURT, ..., P.C., M.P., of Bayon's Manor and Usselby House, co. Linc., [1835] Vol. XLI, fol. 140.

TENNYSON, Baron (Alfred Tennyson), [24 Jan.] 1884.* Arms, Vol. LXII, fol. 180 ; Supporters, fol. 182.

TENTERDEN, Baron [30 April 1827, The Rt. Hon. Sir Charles Abbott, Lord Chief Justice of the King's Bench]. Supporters, [1827] Vol. XXXVI, fol. 252.

TEPPER after FERGUSON, Peter, Brit. Merchant at Warsaw. Quarterly Arms, [1779] Vol. XIV, fol. 165.

TERRY, Sir J., of Dringhouses, co. York, 1887,* Vol. LXIV, fol. 100.

„ Maj.-Gen. Astley Fellowes ([and ?] Thomas Henry F[ellowes]), Vol. LXXI, fol. . . . . [Maj.-Gen., 1 July 1887.]

TESHMAKER, of Ford's Grove, Edmonton, co. Middx., [1874] Vol. LVIII, fol. 346.

TETLEY, Rev. J. G., of Belmont, Tor Mohun, co. Devon, and Clifton, Bristol, co. Glouc., 1895, Vol. LXVIII, fol. 231.

TETLOW, Edward, s. of John, of Haughton, co. Lanc., 10 Sept. 1760, Vol. X, fol. 254. (Berry.)

THACKERAY, Thomas, D.D., Rector of Heydon and Chissul parva, co. Essex, 10 Feb. 1755, Vol. X, fol. 6 (see Her. and Geneal., II, pp. 449 and 451).

THACKWELL, Lieut.-Col. Joseph, of Norman's Land, Dymoke, co. Glouc., and Rye Court, co. Worc. Augmentation, 10 Feb. 1824, Vol. XXXIV, fol. 249 ; Crest to other descendants of his father, John, 1824, Vol. XXXIV, fol. 251.

THACKWELL, Lieut.-[? Major]Gen. Sir Joseph, G.C.B. [1849]. Supporters, [1855] Vol. LI, fol. 200.

THANET, Earl of [Sir Richard] TUFTON (reputed son of). Name and Arms [Roy. Lic., 5 May 1850]. [His son, Sir Henry James, 2nd Bart., cr.] Baron HOTHFIELD [11 Oct. 1881], [1850] Vol. XLIX, fol. 336. (Berry.)

THARP, John, of the Cape of Good Hope and Jamaica, 11 Oct. 1776, Vol. XIII, fol. 239.

THARP-GENT, Lieut., of co. Camb. and Essex, [1861] Vol. LIV, fol. 184.

THATCHER, ..., of Dover, co. Kent. Quarterly Arms, Thatcher and VICKERY, [1818] Vol. XXX, fol. 408.

THEOBALD, late POOLE, ..., of co. Essex and Hampsh., [1816] Vol. XXIX, fol. 459.

THESIGER, Sir Frederick [Knt., 23 May 1844], Solicitor-General, M.P., of London, [1844] Vol. XLVII, fols. 330 and 331; Baron CHELMSFORD [1 Mar. 1858], Lord Chancellor. Supporters, [1858] Vol. LII, fol. 334.

THEW, Major, Bo[mbay] Artillery, [1827] Vol. XXXVI, fol. 338.

THICKNESSE before WOODINGTON, Lieut.-Col., Bo. S.C., of Acton Burnell, Shropsh.; Bayton, co. Worc.; and Balterley Hall, co. Staff. Quarterly Arms, [1808] Vol. XXV, fols. 32 and 35.

THICKNESSE, late COLDWELL, Venerable Francis Henry, of co. Lanc., died Dean of Peterborough, 1859, Vol. LIII, fol. 136 [see Burke].

THISELTON-DYER, William Mathew (co. Worc.), of London, [1840] Vol. XLIV, fol. 248.

THISTLETHWAYTE-PELHAM, late MILBOURNE, Katherine, widow of Thomas Milbourne, of Berks., Hampsh., and Wilts., [1811] Vol. XXVI, fol. 340.

THOMAS, [William], of Llan Thomas, Brecon, Wales, [1552] Vol. II, fol. 442.

,, David, of Wellfield, Radnor, and to the descendants of his grandfather Edward, 1797, Vol. XX, fol. 56. (Berry's Suppl.)

,, ..., of St. Giles, Cripplegate. (See also Susannah ELYOTT, wife of . . . . THOMAS.) Arms of Thomas to self and sister Elizabeth Thomas, 1751, Vol. IX, fol. 393.

THOMAS, formerly TREHERNE, of Llatty Manor, Rees, co. Carmarthen, Wales, 8 Sept. 1768, Vol. XI, fol. 296. (Berry.)

THOMAS, late WHITE, George, of Chichester, co. Sussex, [1777-1778] Vol. XIV, fol. 12.

,, late FREEMAN, Inigo, of co. Sussex, and Antigua, 1786, Vol. XVI, fol. 161. Match, [1791] Vol. XVII, fol. 440. (Berry.)

THOMAS to PALLISER, ..., of Bucks. and co. Kent, [1796] Vol. XIX, fol. 227.

,, to BARRETT-LENNARD, ..., of co. Essex, [1801] Vol. XXI, fol. 200.

,, to GREENE, Henry, of Rolleston, co. Leic., 1815, Match, XXIX, fol. 107.

THOMAS, ..., of London, and Gilden Vane, co. Hereford, [1822] Vol. XXXIII, fol. 276.

THOMAS to PATESHULL, ..., of Wales, [1855] Vol. LI, fol. 331.

THOMAS-LE MARCHANT, ..., of the Isle of Wight, and Guernsey, [1865] Vol. LV, fol. 304.

THOMAS to KEARSEY, ..., of co. Surrey, [1867] Vol. LVI, fol. 238.

THOMAS, late HUGHES, ..., of Wales, [1853] Vol. L, fol. 428.

THOMAS, ..., of Wales, [1874 ?] Vol. LVIII, fol. 298.

,, Mrs. Samuel, of Yscyborwan, Aberdare, co. Glamorgan, Wales, 1886, Vol. LXIII, fol. 171.

,, Abraham Garrod, M.D., of Clythe Park, Newport, co. Monmouth, 1898, Vol. LXX, fol. 251.

,, William, of Tregarnedd, Llangefni, Anglesey, Wales, 1897, Vol. LXIX, fol. 293.

,, David Collet (s. of David), of 21, Second Avenue, Hove, co. Sussex, 1897, Vol. LXIX, fol. 301.

THOMAS-STANFORD, Charles Geisler, of 3, Ennismore Gardens, London. Stanford and Thomas quarterly, 1897, Vol. LXX, fol. 78.

THOMPSON [Sir John], Bart. (Baron HAVERSHAM) [4 May 1696]. Supporters, [1696] Vol. IV, fol. 215.

„ Ralph, of London, s. of Ralph, of Leicester, and to Elizabeth MILLER, dau. of Francis Thompson, of London [during her natural life], 24 Mar. 172¾, Vol. VII, fol. 259 ; Add. MS. 14,830, fol. 20.

„ Elizabeth, relict of Ralph, of London, and Rye, co. Sussex, 6 April 1734, Vol. VIII, fol. 182ᵇ.

„ Charles, Capt., R.N., [1784] Vol. XV, fol. 263.

„ Sir Benjamin, Knt. [23 Feb. 1784], of St. James', Westminster. (See BUSHMAN.) [1784] Vol. XV, fol. 373 or 393 [?].

THOMPSON, late MEYER, William, of co. York. (Match), [1794] Vol. XVIII, fol. 337.

THOMPSON, Thomas Boulden, Capt., R.N., of Hartsbourne Manor, co. Hertf. [Knt., 13 Feb. 1799], [1806] Vol. XXIV, fol. 85 ; Vice-Adm., Bart. [1797]. Augmentation, [1797] Vol. XX, fol. 98 ; G.C.B. Supporters, [14 Sept. 1822], [1822 ?] Vol. XXXIII, fol. 342.

THOMPSON to FINCH, ..., of London, [1809] Vol. XXV, fols. 208 and 210.

THOMPSON, ..., of Marston, co. York. Match with SOTHERN?, [1810] Vol. XXVI, fol. 5.

THOMPSON before CORBETT, ..., of co. Chester and Linc. Quarterly Arms, [1810] Vol. XXVI, fol. 73.

THOMPSON, ..., of Yew Tree House, Manchester, and Lancaster, [1819 ?] Vol. XXXI, fol. 155.

„ Paul B[eilby], late LAWLEY, of Shropsh., [1820] Vol. XXXII, fol. 170 ; afterwards Lawley [Thompson, 1839]. Supporters, [Baron WENLOCK, 13 May 1839], [1839] Vol. XLIV, fol. 25.

„ William, Lord Mayor of London [1828-29], [1827] Vol. XXXVI, fol. 214.

„ John, of Lansdowne Place, Bath, co. Somerset ; co. Glouc. and (Clifton) ; and Laurencetown, co. Down, Ireland, [1830] Vol. XXXVIII, fol. 161.

THOMPSON, late COATES, William, of Addingham, co. York, and Jesus College, Camb. (B.A., 1838), [1836] Vol. XLI, fol. 268.

THOMPSON, ..., of Poundsford Park, Pitminster, co. Somerset, and Vanbrugh House, Maize Hill, Greenwich, co. Kent, [1838] Vol. XLIII, fol. 297.

„ . . . ., of Gray's Inn and Upper Hamilton Terrace, London, [1847] Vol. XLVIII, fol. 350.

„ Clements, of Ilford, co. Essex, [1853] Vol. L, fol. 400.

„ Samuel Henry, of Liverpool and Thingwall Hall, Childwall, co. Lanc., [1856] Vol. LI, fol. 427.

„ H. T. ARNALL-, of Knighton, co. Leic., 1885, Vol. LXIII, fol. 146.

„ J. T., of Toronto, Canada, 1894,* Vol. LXVIII, fol. 79.

„ Sir M., Bart., of (Park Gate) Guiseley, co. York, 1890, Vol. LXV, fol. 213.

„ Sir Henry, Bart., of Wimpole Street, London, 1899, Vol. LXX, fol. 324.

THOMSON or THOMPSON, ..., of Lee, co. Kent. HUMPHRYES, widow of TUFNELL, [1708] Vol. V, fols. 287 and 292.

THOMSON-BUNCOMBE-POWLETT, Thomson to, John, of co. Somerset and Surrey. Quarterly Arms, 1814, Vol. XXVIII, fol. 149.

THOMSON to SCROPE, ..., of co. Surrey and Wilts., [1821] Vol. XXXII, fol. 283.

THOMSON, Lieut.-Col. Samuel John, C.I.E. (s. of John), 18 . . ., Vol. LXXI, fol. . . . .

THOMSON, late TOKER, Richard Edward, of Kenfield, par. of Petham, co. Kent. [Thomson quartering Toker] Exemplified, 23 Sept. 1851, Vol. L, fol. 58 (see Misc. G. et H., II, p. 177).

THORNABY-ON-TEES, Borough of, co. York, Arms, [1893] Vol. LXVII, fol. 116.

THORNBROUGH, Adm. Sir Edward, K.C.B. [of Bishopsteignton, co. Devon].
(Match), [1817] Vol. XXX, fol. 221 ; G.C.B. Supporters, [1825] Vol.
XXXV, fol. 128. Arms of wife, Elizabeth BLAXTON, and to sister,
fol. 152.

THORNBURGH-CROPPER, Edward Denman, only s. of Edward Cropper, late of
Swaylands, Penshurst, co. Kent, and San Francisco, 1876, Vol. LIX,
fol. 230.

THORNE, John, of Exeter, and Persia. (*See* HORNE, rightly so [29 Feb. 17$\frac{29}{30}$].)
1730, Vol. VIII, fol. 60b.

THORNELOE, George, D.D., Bishop of Algoma, Canada, 1897, Vol. LXX,
fol. 36.

THORNEWILL, Edward J., of Liverpool, co. Lanc., 1886, Vol. LXIII, fol. 316.

THORNEYCROFT, John, 29 Oct. 1687 [? 1693], Vol. IV, fol. 139, states that the
grant of Vol. III, fol. 327, was in reality a confirmation. [? *See*
"Grantees," Vol. I.]

„ John Isaac, LL.D., F.R.S., and William Hamo, Sculptor [R.A., 1888],
18 . . ., Vol. LXXI, fol. . . . .

THORNHILL, ..., of Fixby, co. York. (*See* HORTON.) (Match), [172$\frac{4}{?}$]
Vol. VII, fol. 533.

„ John, of Stanton, co. Derby, 9 July 1730, Vol. VIII, fol. 80.

„ John, of Stanton, co. Derby, and Fixby and Thornhill, co. York, 29 Mar.
1734, Vol. VIII, fol. 184b.

THORNHILL, late CAMM, Christopher, of Durham, [1803] Vol. XXII, fol. 156.

THORNHILL, ..., of Ollenshaw, Chapel-en-le-Frith, and Wardlaw, Hope,
co. Derby, [1841] Vol. XLV, fol. 132.

THORNHILL after CLARKE, William, of co. Middx., Norf., and York. [Match ?]
1855, Vol. LI, fol. 422 [see Burke].

THORNHILL, Henry T., per F. S. HURLOCK, of Lansdowne Place, Brighton, 1881,
Vol. LXI, fol. 219.

„ Sir Thomas, Bart., of Suffolk, 1885,* Vol. LXIII, fol. 87.

THORNTON to ASTELL, William, of co. Bedf. and Huntingdon, 1777, Vol. XIII,
fol. 285.

„ to ASTELL, William, M.P., of co. Bedf. and Huntingdon. Quarterly Arms,
1807, Vol. XXIV, fols. 288 and 290.

THORNTON, [The Right Hon.] Sir Edward, G.C.B. [8 Mar. 1822]. Supporters,
[1829] Vol. XXXVII [1822, Vol. XXXIII ?], fols. 289 and 292.

„ Diana (Spr.), (reputed dau. of Edward), of Falconer's Hall, co. York, [1838]
Vol. XLIII, fol. 233.

THORNTON before WODEHOUSE, Edward, of Boythorpe, co. Norf. (*See* the Earl
of KIMBERLEY's family.) [1838] Vol. XLIII, fol. 251.

THORNTON after WELCH, Alfred Bidwell, of Horsham and Brighton, co. Sussex,
[1861] Vol. LIV, fol. 114 (see WELCH, 1861, Vol. LIV, fol. 94).

„ after WELCH, Henry Samuel, of Brighton, co. Sussex, [1861] Vol. LIV,
fol. 116 (see WELCH, 1861, Vol. LIV, fol. 94).

THORNTON, late LEE, Richard Napoleon, of the Middle Temple, London, 1865,
Vol. LVI, fol. 1.

THORNYCROFT, [Sir John], Bart. [12 Aug. 1701], of Milcome, co. Oxf. (*See*
Elizabeth KAY [KEY ?].) [1704] Vol. V, fols. 158 and [1707 ?] 202.

THORNYCROFT, late MYTTON, Rev. Charles Mytton, of co. Chester. [Quarterly
Arms], 1831, Vol. XXXVIII, fol. 343.

THOROLD, late HART, of the Middle Temple, London, and Harmston, co. Linc.,
1820, Vol. XXXII, fol. 16.

THOROLD after GRANT, Alexander William, of Weelsby House, co. Linc., 1864,
Vol. LV, fol. 262.

THOROTON to HILDYARD, ..., of co. Nottingham and York. Quarterly Arms,
[1815] Vol. XXIX, fol. 29.

THORPE or THORP, Thomas, Citizen of London and Linendraper, and of co. York,
11 June 1709, Vol. V, fol. 362 ; Add. MS. 14,831, fol. 47.

THORP, Robert Disney, M.D., of Leeds, co. York, and Buxton, co. Derby, 183 . .,
    ? refer Grants, [1838-39] Vol. XLIII, or [1836-38] Vol. XLII.
  „ [The Ven.] Charles, D.D., of Ryton, co. Durham, and co. Northumberland
    [Archdeacon of Durham, 1831] (grandson, Charles F. Thorp), 184 . .,
    Vol. XLVI, fol. 242, [see Burke].
THORPE to PARKER, ..., of Hauthorpe House, Morton, and Edenham, co. Linc.,
    [1831] Vol. XXXVIII, fol. 267.
THORPE, ..., of The Cottage, Sonning, Berks., [1865] Vol. LVI, fol. 21.
THOYTS, William, s. of John, s. of William, of Sulhampstead, Berks., Lord of the
    Manor, with remainder to the descendants of his father, John, 30 April
    1788, Vol. XVI, fol. 337 (see Misc. G. et H., 2nd S., IV, p. 6, and
    Berry).
THRALE, [Hester Lynch], of Streatham, co. Surrey. (See SALUSBERY.) (Match),
    [1813] Vol. XXVII, fol. 441.
THRESHER, Edward, of Bradford, Wilts., 8 Dec. 1725, Vol. VII, fol. 476.
THRING, John, of Warminster, and Codford St. Peter, Wilts. (Match), [30 May
    1798] Vol. XX, fol. 166 [Jewers, Wells Cathedral, p. 82].
THROCKMORTON to COURTENAY (George, of Bucks.), and co. Devon, [1819 ?]
    Vol. XXXI, fol. 164. (Match), [1791] Vol. XVII, fol. 442.
THRUPP, John Augustus, of London, [1828] Vol. XXXVII, fol. 55.
THURLOW, Baron [3 June 1778], Lord Chancellor [died 1806].   Arms and
    Supporters, [1778] Vol. XIV, fol. 29 ; [Edward, 2nd Baron] Supporters,
    1810, Vol. XXVI, fol. 140 ; Crest, HOVELL, [1813] Vol. XXVII,
    fol. 327 ; [Thomas John, 5th Baron] CUMING-BRUCE quartering (1874),
    Vol. LIX, fol. 53.
THURSBY, formerly HARVEY, John, of Shropsh. and co. Staff., 1852, Vol. L,
    fol. 182.
THURSBY-PELHAM, Henry, of Shropsh. and Crowhurst, co. Sussex, 1852, Vol. L,
    fol. 184.
THURSTON, Sir John Bates, K.C.M.G. [24 May 1887], of co. Somerset (d. Feb.
    1897), 1895,* Vol. LXVIII, fol. 208.
THWAITES, Daniel, of Blackburn, and London, [1868] Vol. LVII, fol. 76.
    (Berry's Suppl.)
TIBBITS and HOOD, [Samuel, 3rd] Viscount Hood.   Quarterly Arms, [1841] Vol.
    XLV, fol. 97. [Roy. Lic., 6 Feb. 1851, assumed the surname Tibbits.]
TICHBORNE to DOUGHTY [29 May 1826, Sir Edward, 9th Bart.], of Hampsh.,
    [1826] Vol. XXXVI, fol. 65.
TICHBORNE, [Sir James Francis, 10th] Bart. [Roy. Lic., 6 April 1853, the
    additional Name and Arms of] (DOUGHTY), [1853] Vol. L, fol. 329.
TIDCOMBE, Col. John, of Estcott, Wilts., 169¾, Vol. IV, fol. 137.
TIDSWELL, R. J., of Haresfield, co. Glouc., 1893,* Vol. LXVII, fol. 207.
TIDY to MANDEY, ..., of co. Middx., [1821] Vol. XXXII, fol. 263.
TIERNEY [Sir Matthew John], M.D., of London, Physician-in-Ordinary to Prince
    Regent [Bart., 3 Oct. 1818], [1818] Vol. XXXI, fol. 100.
TIFFIN, Joseph, of Whitrigg, Bowness and Cockermouth, co. Cumberland, 1770,
    Vol. XII, fol. 19.
TILDEN-SAMPSON, ..., of co. Sussex, [1797] Vol. XIX, fol. 457.
TILGHMAN-HUSKISSON, of Eastham, co. Sussex, [1857] Vol. LII, fol. 267.
TILLARD, Rev. R. H., of Blakeney Rectory, East Dereham, co. Norf., 1894,*
    Vol. LXVIII, fol. 31.
TILLIE, James, J.P. 13 years past, of Pentillie Castle, co. Cornw., 21 Nov. 1733,
    Vol. VIII, fol. 173b ; Add. MS. 14,830, fol. 18.
TILLSTONE after MONKHOUSE, ..., of co. Sussex, [1830] Vol. XXXVIII,
    fol. 39.
  „ after SEDLEY, ..., of co. Huntingdon and Norf., [1843] Vol. XLVI,
    fol. 302.
TILLSTONE (SEDLEY-), ..., and MONKHOUSE, his wife, of co. Norf. and Sussex,
    [1843] Vol. XLVI, fols. 304 and 306.

TILLSTONE after **ROGERS**, Benjamin [Tillstone Rogers, of Brighton, co.] Sussex. [Quarterly Arms] 1868, Vol. LVII, fol. 104 [see Burke].

TILNEY, George Adams, of Watts House, Bishop's Lydeard, co. Somerset, 1883,* Vol. LXII, fol. 91. (Berry's Suppl.)

TILSON, Maj.-Gen. [Christopher, and to his brothers, John Henry Tilson], of Watlington Park, co. Oxf., [Esq., and James Tilson, Esq., of Hans Place, Chelsea, 20 Mar. 1812] [1811], Vol. XXVI, fol. 402. [It rehearses the early Irish Grant of 21 Dec. 1697 to Thomas Tilson, Esq., of Dublin, son of Henry Tilson, Bp. of Elphin (see Burke). This Grant superseded the Grant of 4 Sept. 1639 by Ulster King of Arms to Henry Tilson, the Bishop. (See ELPHIN.) There appears to have been no Grant of Arms to the See of Elphin, though Arms were used and recorded in the office of Ulster King of Arms in the seventeenth century.]

TILSON to **CHOWNE**, Maj.-Gen., of Watlington Parva, co. Oxf. Quarterly Arms, [1811] Vol. XXVI, fol. 404.

„ to **CHOWNE**, Maj.-Gen., [1836] Vol. XLI, fol. 238.

TILYARD, John, of Norwich, co. Norf., 9 Jan. 1772, Vol. XII, fol. 114. (Berry.)

TIMBRELL, Patience (Spr.), of Sandwell, co. Glouc., 21 Nov. 1812, Vol. XXVII, fol. 130.

„ Major Thomas, C.B., Bengal Artillery, [1840] Vol. XLIV, fol. 242.

TIMINS, ..., Com., East India Company, of London, [1802] Vol. XXI, fol. 444.

TIMMS before **HERVEY-ELWES**, John [Timms to Timms-Hervey-Elwes], of co. Suff. Quarterly Arms, [1793] Vol. XVIII, fol. 220.

TIMPERON, ..., of West Newton, Bromfield, co. Cumberland, 1803 [1801], Vol. XXI, fol. 260.

TIMPSON, Robert, of Exeter, co. Devon, and Waterford, Ireland, 1767, Vol. XI, fol. 260.

TINDAL, Acton, of The Manor House, Aylesbury, Bucks., Clerk of the Peace and Treasurer, s. of Thomas, decd., 1875, Vol. LIX, fol. 82.

TINDAL to **TINDAL-CARILL-WORSLEY**, Nicholas, B.A., of (Rusholme) co. Lanc., 1878, Vol. LX, fol. 161. (Berry's Suppl.)

TINSLEY, ... (widow), of The Limes, Sedgeley, co. Staff., [1865] Vol. LVI, fol. 53.

TIPPET to **VIVIAN**, ..., Lieut., E.I.C.S., of Falmouth and Penkallenick, co. Cornw., [1817] Vol. XXX, fol. 246 ; [1820] Vol. XXXII, fol. 55.

TIPPETTS, now **PAUL**, ..., of Tetbury, co. Glouc., [1787] Vol. XVI, fol. 315.

TISDALL, E. C. S., of Holland Park Road, London, 1890,* Vol. LXVI, fol. 21.

TIVITOL, John, of St. Bartholomew's, London, and Weymouth, co. Dorset, 13 Mar. 1761, Vol. X, fol. 282. (Berry.)

TOBIN, ..., Capt. in Army. (Match), [1810] Vol. XXV, fol. 398.

TODD, ... (and **PLOWES**, late wife), of Molesey, [1823] Vol. XXXIV, fols. 196 and 197.

TODD, Capt. George, of Belsize House, Hampstead, co. Middx., and Higingwalls, co. Durham, [1829] Vol. XXXVII, fol. 330.

TODD after **WILSON**, Capt. William Henry, of Tranby Park, co. York, and Halnaby Hall, Croft, Darlington, co. Durham, 1855, Vol. LI, fol. 358 [see Burke].

TODD-NEWCOMB, ..., of Stamford, co. Linc., and Gerards, Kirkby Ireleth, co. Lanc., [1867] Vol. LVI, fol. 177.

TODD, R. Harts, of Olveston, co. Glouc., 1896,* Vol. LXIX, fol 36.

TODHUNTER, Isaac, F.R.S., Hon. Fellow of St. John's Coll., Camb., 1881, Vol. LXI, fol. 197. (Berry's Suppl.)

[**TODMORDEN**, Borough of, co. York, 1 Dec. 1896. (Geneal. Mag., IV, p. 289.)]

TOKER, ..., of The Oaks, Ospringe, co. Kent, [1835] Vol. XLI, fol. 65.

TOKER to **THOMPSON**, ..., of Kenfield, Petham, co. Kent, [23 Sept. 1851] Vol. L, fol. 58 [see Misc. G. et H., II, p. 177].

TOLCHER, ..., of Plymouth, co. Devon, [1794] Vol. XVIII, fol. 323

TOLHURST, Alfred, of Gravesend, co. Kent, 1875, Vol. LIX, fol. 80. (Berry's Suppl.)
„ John, of Glenbrook, Beckenham, co. Kent, 1886,* Vol. LXIII, fol. 217. (Crisp, I, p. 64.)
TOLL to NEWMAN, Charles, of co. Northampton, 6 Oct. 1775, Vol. XIII, fol. 127.
„ to NEWMAN, Ashburnham Philip, of Preston Deanery, co. Northampton, [1775] Vol. XIII, fol. 129.
„ to NEWMAN, ..., of Thornbury, co. Glouc. ; Graywell, Hampsh. ; and Hamilton, Scotland. Augmentation, [1802] Vol. XXI, fol. 360.
TOLLEMACHE, late HALLIDAY, Rear-Adm. John Richard Delap, of Shropsh., and Scotland, [1821] Vol. XXXII, fol. 351.
TOLLEMACHE, Baron [17 Jan. 1876], John [formerly Halliday, of Peckforton Castle, co. Chester (see HALLIDAY), and Helmington, co. Suff.]. Supporters, 1876, Vol. LIX, fol. 192.
TOLLEMACHE, late MANNERS [30 Mar. 1821], Louisa, Countess DYSART, &c. (widow), of co. Linc., [1821] Vol. XXXII, fol. 275.
TOLLEMACHE, [Louisa, Countess Dysart], to her sons, John and Charles, and dau., Laura, [30 Mar. 1821] Vol. XXXII, fols. 277 and 279.
TOLLEMACHE, late EMBURY, of Betley Hall, co. Staff., and ? co. Chester, [1796] Vol. XIX, fol. 309.
TOLLEMACHE to WICKSTED, Charles, of Betley Hall, co. Staff., 1814, Vol. XXVIII, fol. 118.
TOLLETT, George, a Commissioner of the Navy, in default of issue to John (decd. brother), of Dublin, Ireland ; in default of issue to Thomas (decd. brother), of St. Margaret's, Westminster ; in default of issue to Charles (youngest brother), of Wandsworth, co. Surrey, 3 Dec. 1708, Vol. V, fol. 315. (Misc. G. et H., 2nd S., III, p. 72, plate.) (See WICKSTED.)
TOLLNER, ..., of Sloane Street, London, [1824] Vol. XXXIV, fol. 401.
TOLSON, Legh, of Elm Lea, Dalton, Kirkheaton, 1895,* Vol. LXVIII, fol. 172.
TOMES, Sir John, of Upwood Gorse, Caterham, co. Surrey, 1888,* Vol. LXIV, fol. 284.
TOMKINSON, M., of Franche Hall, Kidderminster, co. Worc., 1894,* Vol. LXVIII, fol. 8.
TOMKINSON to WETTENHALL, ..., of Bostock and Hankelow, co. Chester, 31 Mar. 1800, Vol. XX, fol. 445 ; [1800] Vol. XXI, fol. 3.
TOMKYNS to BERKELEY, ..., of co. Worc., [1833] Vol. XXXIX, fol. 190.
TOMKYS, Thomas, of Neachells, Wolverhampton, co. Staff., 13 Aug. 1728, Vol. VIII, fol. 9b.
TOMLINS. See COOPER.
TOMLINSON, Thomas, of Preston and Heysham, co. Lanc. (MASHITER, his wife), 1833, Vol. XL, fols. 56 and 57. (Berry's Suppl.)
„ Thomas, of co. Lanc., [1871] Vol. LVIII, fol. 72.
TOMPSON, ..., of Witchingham Hall, co. Norf., [1872] Vol. LVIII, fol. 140.
TOMPSON to KETT-TOMPSON, ..., of Witchingham Hall, Seething Hall, and Brooke Hall, co. Norf., [1872] Vol. LVIII, fol. 144.
TOMS, Peter, Portcullis Pursuivant of Arms, London, 1768, Vol. XI, fol. 268. (Berry.)
TONGE, Henry A., of Chateau du Ragotin, Avranche, Manche, France, 1889,* Vol. LXV, fol. 86.
TONKIN, ..., of Newlyn, co. Cornw. (See BOASE.) [1810] Vol. XXV, fol. 326.
TONSON, late HULL, ..., William, of Dunkettle, co. Cork, Ireland, 1773, Vol. XII, fol. 282.
TONYN, ..., of Grosvenor Square, London, and Holland. Quartering, [1788] Vol. XVI, fol. 371.
TOOKE after HALES, Rev. Tompson, of co. Norf., [1842] Vol. XLVI, fol. 134.
„ after HALES, Rev. Tompson, of Salhouse, Norwich, co. Norf., and Washbrook, co. Suff., [1876] Vol. LIX, fol. 294.

TOOKE after CHEVALL, Charles, of co. Sussex, [1859] Vol. LIII, fol. 82.

TOOKER after WHALLEY, ..., of Norton Hall, Midsomer Norton, and Winscomb Court, co. Somerset, [1836] Vol. XLII, fols. 21 and 34.

TOONE, Sweny, of London, Director, East India Company, and brother, Sir William, 4 Jan. 1828, Vol. XXXVII, fol. 3.

TOOTH, ..., of Knockholt, co. Kent, [1733] Vol. VIII, fol. 181.

„ Robert, of London, and Swifts, Cranbrook, co. Kent, 4 April 1854, Vol. LI, fol. 32 (see Misc. G. et H., 2nd S., III, p. 128).

TOPHAM, Juliet, nat. dau. of Edward Topham, of Wold Cottage and Aglethorpe, co. York, [1820] Vol. XXXII, fol. 211.

TOPLIS, ..., of Wirksworth, co. Derby, [1816] Vol. XXIX, fol. 319.

TOPP, late LLOYD, Richard, of Shrewsbury, Shropsh., 1778, Vol. XIV, fol. 44.

TORKINGTON, ..., of Brettenham, co. Suff. (See SMITH alias HOVELL.) [1813] Vol. XXVII, fol. 327.

TORR, ..., of Ribey, co. Linc., [1846] Vol. XLVIII, fol. 112.

„ Rev. T. J., of Northleigh and Honiton, co. Devon, 1889,* Vol. LXV, fol. 53.

TORRE to HOLME, Nicholas, of co. York, [1811] Vol. XXVI, fol. 373. (Rev. Henry TANNER, [1833] Vol. XL, fol. 63.)

TORRENS, Maj.-Gen. Sir Henry, K.C.B. [1815], [1829] Vol. XXXVII, fol. 384.

TORRINGTON, Earl of [29 May 1689] (HERBERT). Supporters, [1689] Vol. IV, fol. 42.

„ Baron [20 June 1716] (NEWPORT). Supporters, [1716] Vol. VI, fol. 243.

„ Viscount [21 Sept. 1721, Rear-Adm. Sir George] BYNG [Bart.], [172⅔] Vol. VII, fol. 162.

TOTTON, Stephen Dinely, M.A., of Debden, co. Essex, and Lincoln's Inn, London, 18 June 1811, Vol. XXVI, fol. 259.

TOUCHET-DAVIES, ..., of Wales, [1823] Vol. XXXIV, fol. 192.

TOULMIN, ..., wife of BAINBRIDGE, of Carleybury, co. Durham. Escutcheon of pretence, [1804] Vol. XXII, fol. 455.

TOURLE, ..., of Lewes and Landport, co. Sussex, [1801] Vol. XXI, fol. 283.

TOURLE, late COOPER, ..., of Lewes and Landport, co. Sussex, [1801] Vol. XXI, fol. 286.

TOURNAY before BARGRAVE, Robert, of Eastry, co. Kent. Quarterly Arms, 1800, Vol. XXI, fol. 74. (Berry.)

TOURNAY, late ALLEN, Henry, of Eastry, co. Kent, [1870] Vol. LVII, fol. 232.

„ late ALLEN, William, of Eastry, co. Kent, [1871] Vol. LVII, fol. 322.

TOVEY, Lieut.-Col. Hamilton, E.I.C.S., of Pynacles, Great Stanmore, co. Middx., and Erdington, co. Warw., [1832] Vol. XXXIX, fol. 44.

TOVEY to TENNANT, ..., of Pynacles, Great Stanmore, co. Middx., and Erdington, co. Warw., [1832] Vol. XXXIX, fol. 65.

„ to TENNANT, ..., of Pynacles, Great Stanmore, co. Middx., and Erdington, co. Warw., [1867] Vol. LVI, fol. 180.

TOWER, Henry, D.L., of Elimore Hall, co. Durham ; Weald Hall, co. Essex ; and Huntsmore Park, Bucks., [1843] Vol. XLVII, fol. 117. (Crisp, II, p. 33.)

TOWER to BAKER, Henry John, Lieut. of Dragoons, of Elimore Hall, co. Durham, 1844, Vol. XLVII, fol. 119 [? 219].

TOWERS to ALCOCK-BECK, William, of co. Lanc., [1856] Vol. LII, fol. 31.

TOWGOOD, Rev. MICAIAH, of Exeter and Axminster, co. Devon, 1770, Vol. XII, fol. 43. (Berry.)

TOWLE to HUGGETT, ..., of co. Kent, [1851] Vol. XLIX, fol. 475.

TOWNDROWE, Elizabeth, sole heir of Edward, of Nottingham, wife of Henry PAYNE, of Newark, co. Leic., 1826, Vol. XXXV, fol. 364 (see Berry's Appx.).

TOWNEND, George, of Grimston and Kirby-upon-Wharf, co. York, [1792] Vol. XVIII, fol. 21.

„ . . . ., of Moss Side, Manchester, and Campsall, Doncaster, co. York, [1846] Vol. XLVIII, fol. 195.

Townley, Charles, York Herald of Arms, of London. (Wilde quartering.) [1743] Vol. IX, fol. 87.

Townley-Parker, Thomas T., of co. Lanc., [1880] Vol. LX, fol. 352. (Berry's Suppl.)

Townsend, Robert [or ?] John, of Coggeshall Magna, co. Essex, 5 June 1718, Vol. VI, fol. 384 (see Berry's Suppl. [Townshend]).

Townsend to Loveden, Edward, of Berks., 1 Aug. 1772,* Vol. XII, fol. 208.

Townsend, ..., of Godmanchester, co. Huntingdon, and Poyle Park, co. Surrey, [1797] Vol. XIX, fol. 369.

Townsend after Lawrence, ... Quarterly Arms, [1806] Vol. XXIII, fol. 375.

Townsend, ..., of Newport, Rhode Island, N. America. (Match), [1812] Vol. XXVII, fol. 113.

„ . . . ., of co. Cork, Ireland. (Match), 1815, Vol. XXVIII, fol. 352.

„ Francis, Rouge Dragon Pursuivant of Arms (and Chapman, his wife), of Aisthorpe, co. Linc., and London, [1824] Vol. XXXIV, fol. 390.

Townsend to Stephens, Col. John, of co. Glouc., 1828, Vol. XXXVII, fol. 137.

Townsend after Stephens, Rev. M. F., of co. Glouc., 1845, Vol. XLVII, fol. 433.

Townsend [Rev. Maurice F., of Thornbury (co. Glouc. ?). (Burke.)].

Townsend after Stephens, Henry J., Lieut., Life Guards, of Castle Townsend, co. Cork, Ireland, 1855, Vol. LI, fol. 205.

Townsend, ..., of Honington Hall, co. Warw., [1843] Vol. XLVI, fol. 257.

Townshend, [Lady Caroline Campbell], Baroness [Townshend], of Greenwich [19 Aug. 1767, wife of Charles, 3rd Viscount Townshend]. Supporters, [1767] Vol. XI, fol. 252.

„ [Rt. Hon. Thomas], Baron Sydney [of Chislehurst, 6 Mar. 1783]. Supporters, [1783] Vol. XV, fol. 155.

Townshend to Brooke, of Haughton, Shropsh., [1797] Vol. XIX, fol. 377.

Townshend, [Charles] (Baron Bayning), [of Foxley, Berks., 20 Oct. 1797]. Supporters, [1797] Vol. XX, fol. 32.

Townshend to Poulett [8 Sept. 1823], William, [3rd] Baron Bayning, [1823] Vol. XXXIV, fol. 184.

Townshend, ..., of Sapcote, co. Leic., [1838] Vol. XLIII, fol. 314.

Townshend to Dunn-Gardner, John, of Chatteris, co. Camb., [1843] Vol. XLVI, fol. 365.

„ to Dunn-Gardner, William, of Fordham, co. Camb., [1843] Vol. XLVI, fol. 383.

„ to Dunn-Gardner, Cecil, Cornet, Light Dragoons, of co. Camb., and of Magdalen Coll., Oxford, [1847] Vol. XLVIII, fol. 290.

Tozer before (or to) Aubrey, Henry Pinson, of co. Devon and Hereford, [1813] Vol. XXVII, fol. 403.

Tozer, ..., of Alphington, co. Devon, [1824] Vol. XXXIV, fol. 262.

Tracey-Elliot, H. E. [Tracey to], of Plymouth, co. Devon, 1893 [1893], Vol. LXVI, fol. 344.

Tracy, Thomas Charles, [Viscount and] Baron Tracy, of Rathcoole, co. Dublin, Ireland, 1789, Vol. XVII, fol. 183.

Tracy to Leigh, (Henry), Viscount and Baron Tracy, of Rathcoole, co. Dublin, Ireland, [2 Feb.] 1793, Vol. XVIII, fol. 170.

Tracy after Hanbury, Charles. Escutcheon of pretence, quarterly, 10 Dec. 1798, Vol. XX, fol. 275.

Tracy to Leigh, Thomas Charles (minor), 1806, Vol. XXIII, fol. 359.

Tracy (Hanbury), late Leigh, Thomas Charles (1st Baron Sudeley), [1839] Vol. XLIII, fol. 349.

Tracy (Hanbury-), [Charles Henry], Baron Sudeley [12 July 1838], of Toddington, co. Glouc. Supporters, 1839, Vol. XLIII, fol. 99.

TRACY, late CHARTERIS, Susan, Dowager Lady ELCHO, of Stanway, co. Glouc., 1818, Vol. XXXI, fol. 125.

TRAFFORD, late LEIGH, of Trafford, co. Lanc., [1791] Vol. XVII, fol. 438.

„ late NICOLLS, Edward, of co. Carmarthen, Wales, and co. Staff. and Hereford, [1829] Vol. XXXVII, fol. 322. (Lieut.-Col. Thomas, [1837] Vol. XLII, fol. 217.

TRAFFORD, ..., to issue of Jane TRAFFORD-SOUTHWELL, of co. Norf., Linc. and Camb., [1833] Vol. XXXIX, fol. 363.

„ E[dward] W[illiam], quartering SOUTHWELL, of co. Norf., Linc. and Camb., [1836] Vol. XLI, fol. 288.

„ Edward William, of co. Norf., Linc. and Camb., quartering CROWE, [1841] Vol. XLV, fols. 71 and 100.

„ Edward William (Arms for wife, Martine LARMINACH), of co. Norf., [1841] Vol. XLV, fol. 115c.

TRAFFORD-SOUTHWELL, Margaret Elizabeth (Spr.), of co. Linc., and London [1849] Vol. XLIX, fol. 136.

TRAGETT, ..., of Awbridge Danes, Michelmarsh, Hampsh., [1863] Vol. LV, fol. 88.

TRANT after DILLON, [Trant to Dillon-Trant], Henry, of co. York, and Ireland. Quarterly Arms, [1816] Vol. XXIX, fol. 364.

TRANTMANN, ..., of Fulham, co. Middx. (naturalized Brit. subject), [1864] Vol. LV, fol. 260.

TREACHER, John, of Stamford Hill, co. Middx., 1829, Vol. XXXVIII, fol. 8.

TREACHER to BOWLES, ..., of Enfield, co. Middx., and London, [1852] Vol. L, fol. 144.

TREBY, late OURRY, ..., of co. Devon, [1785] Vol. XVI, fol. 95.

TREBY after PHILLIPPS, Paul W., Col., R.A., of co. Devon, [1877] Vol. LIX, fol. 331. (Burke's Suppl.)

TREDEGAR, Baron [16 April 1859] (MORGAN), of Wales. Supporters, [1859] Vol. LIII, fol. 130.

TREEVE, ... (wife of WILLIAMS), of Penzance, co. Cornw., [1800] Vol. XXI, fol. 12.

TREFFRY, late AUSTEN, Joseph Thomas, of co. Cornw., 1836 [1838], Vol. XLII, fol. 292. [14 Feb. 1838, Burke.]

„ late WILCOCKS, Edward John, of Place, Fowey, co. Cornw., and Lincoln Coll., Oxford, 1850, Vol. XLIX, fol. 334.

TREFUSIS, [Albertina Mariana] (GAULIS), of Lausanne, Switzerland [? wife of the 17th Baron CLINTON], [1794] Vol. XVIII, fol. 294b.

TREFUSIS to ROLLE, [Charles Henry, 1851] (minor), [afterwards 20th Baron] CLINTON, [1851] Vol. L, fol. 74.

„ to HEPBURN-STUART-FORBES [? before] TREFUSIS [4 Sept. 1867] [Charles Henry Rolle Trefusis, 20th Baron Clinton], [1867] Vol. LVI, fol. 303.

TREGONING, John Simmons, of Landuc, Lezant, co. Cornw., 1877, Vol. LX, fol. 10. (Berry's Suppl.)

TREHERNE to THOMAS, ..., of Rees, co. Cornw., and Lletley Manor, co. Carmarthen, Wales, 8 Sept. 1768, Vol. XI, fol. 296.

TRELAWNEY to BRERETON, ..., of co. Glouc., [1800] Vol. XXI, fol. 50.

TRELAWNEY after COLLINS, ..., M.A., [1838] Vol. XLIII, fol. 291.

TRELAWNY, late STEPHENS, Edward, of co. Devon [Cornw. ?], [1795] Vol. XIX, fol. 133.

TRELAWNY to SALUSBURY, William Lewis, of co. Cornw., and Cefn Coch, Wales, [1802] Vol. XXII, fol. 11.

TRELAWNY after SALUSBURY, William Lewis, of co. Cornw., and Cefn Coch, Wales, [1809] Vol. XXV, fol. 151.

TRELOAR, [William Purdie], Alderman of London, of Upper Norwood, co. Surrey (knighted 29 Mar. 1900), 1893,* Vol. LXVII, fol. 159.

TREMELLYN-HUSSEY to MORSHEAD, ..., of co. Cornw., [1830] Vol. XXXVIII, fol. 132.

TREMENHEERE, Rev. . . . ., of Penzance, co. Cornw., [1831] Vol. XXXVIII, fol. 219.

TRENCH, ..., of London, and Debden Hall, co. Essex, 10 Dec. 177⅔ [1772], Vol. XII, fol. 216 [?].

TRENCH-CHISWELL, late MUILMAN, Richard, of Debden Hall, co. Essex, 10 Dec. 177⅔ [1772]. Quarterly Arms, Vol. XII, fol. 218.

TRENCH-GASCOIGNE, F. C., of co. York, [1851] Vol. L, fol. 44.

TRENCHARD after (or late) ASHFORDBY, Rev. John, of Wilts., Berks. and co. Somerset. Quarterly Arms, 1803, Vol. XXII, fols. 55 and 57. (Berry.)

TRENCHARD, late SARGENT, ... (Spr.), of co. Dorset, [1830] Vol. XXXVIII, fol. 116.

TRENCHARD, after DILLON, Henry Luke, of co. Dorset, [1841] Vol. XLV, fol. 201 ; 1846 [Burke], Vol. XLVIII, fol. 214.

TRENCHARD, late PICKARD, John, D.C.L., of Poxwell, co. Dorset, [1840] Vol. XLV, fol. 42.

TRENDELL, ..., of The Abbey House, St. Nicholas, Abingdon, Berks., [1859] Vol. LIII, fol. 153.

TRENT-STOUGHTON, H. W. J., of Saltwood, Hythe, co. Kent, 1889, Vol. LXV, fol. 76.

TRESAHAR, quartering (see ROGERS), 7 Dec. 1774, Vol. [XIII, fol. 49].

TRESHAM, late DAVIS, ..., of co. Nottingham, [1812] Vol. XXVII, fol. 187.

TRESILIAN, ..., wife of CHINNERY, of London. Arms to self and descendants, [1800] Vol. XXI, fol. 39.

TREVANION, ... (see TREVENEN), [1775] Vol. XIII, fol. 117.

TREVANION after BETTESWORTH, John Trevanion Purnel Bettesworth Trevanion, [1802] Vol. XXI, fol. 306.

TREVENEN, John, of Camborne and Crowan, co. Cornw., 20 July 1775, Vol. XIII, fol. 117.

TREVOR, Baron [1 Jan. 171½, Sir Thomas Trevor, Chief Justice of the Common Pleas]. Supporters, [1713] Vol. VI, fol. 114.

„　. . . ., of Flitwick, co. Bedf., and Astwood, Bucks., [1797] Vol. XIX, fol. 381.

TREVOR before ROPER, ..., C.B., of co. Kent, and Ireland. Quarterly Arms, [1809] Vol. XXV, fol. 138.

TREVOR, late BRAND, Henry, of London, and co. Hertf., [1825] Vol. XXXV, fol. 100.

„　late BRAND [Roy. Lic., 12 April 1851], Thomas, [afterwards] Lord DACRE, of co. Hertf., [1851] Vol. XLIX, fol. 470.

TREVOR after RICE [28 Oct. 1824], George, M.P., of Wales, [afterwards, 1852, the 3rd] Baron DYNEVOR, [1825] Vol. XXXV, fol. 136.

TREVOR (HILL-), [Hill to Hill-Trevor, 9 Sept. 1862], Lord Arthur Edwin, 3rd s. of the 3rd Marquess of DOWNSHIRE, of co. Nottingham, and Ireland [see next name], [1862] Vol. LIV, fol. 320.

TREVOR, Baron [5 May 1880, Arthur Edwin HILL-TREVOR], of co. Denbigh, Wales. Supporters, 1885, Vol. LXIII, fol. 140.

TREVOR-BATTYE, C. E. A. F., of Tingrith, co. Bedf., 1891,* Vol. LXVI, fol. 225. (Crisp, II, p. 157.)

TRICE to WRIGHT, ... (minor), of Sevenoaks, co. Kent, and co. Surrey, [1819] Vol. XXXI, fol. 330.

TRICE, Sarah, d. of John, of Ashford, co. Kent. Escutcheon of pretence to MONINS, [1791] Vol. XVII, fol. 396.

TRICKETT to DENT, Joseph, of co. York, Linc. and Nottingham, [1834] Vol. XL, fol. 249.

TRIGGE, Lieut.-Gen. Sir Thomas, K.B. [1801]. Arms and Supporters, [1802] Vol. XXI, fol. 300.

TRIMMER to SHOTTER, ..., of Farnham, co. Surrey, [1795] Vol. XIX, fol. 171.

TRIPP, Rev. Owen Howard, of Homehurst, Beckenham, co. Kent, 1898, Vol. LXX, fol. 284.

TRISHE [TRIST ?], ..., of co. Northampton, [1709] Vol. V, fol. 340.
„ [TRIST ?], Nicholas, of Bowden, co. Devon, Sheriff, 11 April 1709, Vol. V, fol. 341 ; Add. MS. 14,830, fol. 72.
TRISHE [TRIST ?], late HAUSSONILLIER, ..., of co. Devon and Middx., [1799] Vol. XX, fol. 336.
TROLLOPE, Baron KESTEVEN [15 April 1868, The Rt. Hon. Sir John Trollope, Bart.], of co. Linc. Supporters, [1868] Vol. LVII, fol. 19.
„ Adm. Sir Henry, G.C.B. [1831]. Supporters, [29 Sept. 1831] Vol. XXXVIII, fol. 309. [Crisp, Fragm. Geneal., II, p. 48.]
TROLLOPE to FOORD-BOWES, Barnard, of co. York and Devon, [1861] Vol. LIV, fol. 210.
TROTTER, ..., of Shudy Camps, co. Camb. Crest, [1803] Vol. XXII, fol. 240.
TROTTER, late BROWN, William, of Horton Manor, co. Surrey, and co. Kent, 1868, Vol. LVII, fol. 98.
TROUBRIDGE, [? Thomas], Capt., R.N., [cr. a Bart. 23 or 30 Nov. 1799], of Plymouth, co. Devon, [1800] Vol. XX, fol. 418.
TROWER, ..., of Lincoln's Inn, London, and Jamaica, [1823 ?] Vol. XXXIII, fol. 352.
„ . . . ., of Clapton, co. Middx., [1795] Vol. XIX, fol. 125.
TROYTE, Rev. Thomas, of Chidderleigh, co. Devon, Clerk, 11 Aug. 1739, Vol. VIII, fol. 257 ; Add. MS. 14,830, fol. 26.
TROYTE, late ACLAND, Arthur Henry Dyke, of co. Devon and Somerset, 1852, Vol. L, fol. 197.
„ late BULLOCK, ..., of Christ Church, Oxford, 1852, Vol. L, fol. 256.
„ late CHAFFIN-GROVE, George, of North Coker House and Zeals House, Mere, Wilts., 1893, Vol. LXVII, fol. 138.
TRUBEY, Richard, of Breachwood Green, co. Hertf., and London, s. of John, of Oxford, to descendants of his father, 3 Mar. 1728 [172⅞], Vol. VII, fol. 573 ; Add. MS. 14,831, fol. 10.
TRUBSHAWE, Charles, of Gray's Inn, London, 1688, Vol. IV, fol. 24.
TRUEMAN, ..., of Walthamstow, co. Essex, and Hart Hill, nr. Manchester, co. Lanc., [1821] Vol. XXXIII, fol. 82.
TRUNDLE, Thomas, of Great Baddow, co. Essex, and London, 10 Sept. 1785, Vol. XVI, fol. 83. (Berry's Suppl.)
TRURO, Baron [15 July 1850] [the Rt. Hon. Sir Thomas] (WILDE), Lord Chancellor, of Bowes, co. Middx., and Saffron Walden, co. Essex. Arms, [1850] Vol. XLIX, fol. 363 ; Supporters, fol. 365.
„ See of, co. Cornw., 1877, Vol. LIX, fol. 343.
„ City of, co. Cornw., 1877, Vol. LX, fol. 45.
TRUSCOTT, Sir Francis Wyatt, Knt. [14 Mar. 1872], Alderman of London, [1872] Vol. LVIII, fol. 148.
TRUSS, Rev. William Nicholas, of Gonville and Caius Coll., Camb., and Knutsford, co. Chester, [1855] Vol. LI, fol. 372.
TRÜTER, C. J., Knt., of the Cape of Good Hope, [1837] Vol. XLII, fol. 80. [Johannes Andreas Trüter, Senior Justice at Cape of Good Hope, Knt. (Letters Patent), 11 Dec. 1823.]
TRYON, ..., [crossed out], of Colleweston, co. Northampton. (Match), [1689] Vol. IV, fol. 51.
TUCHET, Baron Audley, of Heleigh Castle, co. Staff., [1820] Vol. XXXII, fol. 32.
TUCK to TAWKE, ..., of co. Essex, [1818 ?] Vol. XXX, fol. 330.
TUCKER, William, of Coryton Hall, co. Devon, 16 Jan. 172⁰⁄₁, Vol. VII, fol. 52.
TUCKER to A'DEANE, ..., of co. Glouc., and New Zealand, [1865] Vol. LVI, fols. 35 and 36.
TUCKFIELD, late HIPPISLEY, Richard, of Fulford Park, co. Devon, and co. Glouc., 1808, Vol. XXIV, fol. 337.
TUDOR, Henry, of Sheffield, co. York, and Welchpool, co. Montgomery. Quarterly Arms, 14 Dec. 1775, Vol. XIII, fol. 149. [Misc. G. et H., 3rd S., I, p. 21.]

TUDOR, late COLE, William, of Duddington, co. Northampton, 2 Aug. 1797, Vol.
  XX, fol. 2.   Alteration, [1799] fol. 316 (see Genealogist, III, p. 151).
TUDOR-NELTHORPE, late COWNE, ..., of London, co. Sussex, and Edinburgh.
  Quartering, [1806] Vol. XXIV, fol. 29.
TUFNELL, alias TUFNAILE, Samuel, of the Middle Temple, London ; Shidlington,
  co. Bedf. ; and Monken Hadley, co. Middx.   Quarterly Arms, 23 April
  1708, Vol. V, fols. 287 and 292 ; Stowe MS. 714, fol. 76.
TUFNELL to TUFNELL-TYRELL, John Lionel, s. of William Michael, of Boreham
  House, Hatfield Place, and Hatfield Peverel, co. Essex, 1878, Vol. LX,
  fol. 84.   (Berry's Suppl.)
TUFTON, [Richard], reputed son of Tufton [11th and last], Earl of THANET (Baron
  HOTHFIELD [Henry James Tufton, Bart.]), of Hothfield Place, co. Kent,
  [? 5 May 1850] Vol. XLIX, fol. 336.
TULK to HART, ... (minors), of Hampstead, co. Middx., [1833] Vol. XXXIX,
  fol. 239.
TUNNARD, Charles Keightley (Capt. of Militia), of Frampton House, Boston,
  co. Linc., [1810] Vol. XXVI, fol. 68.
TUNNO, ..., of Llangennech Park, co. Carmarthen, Wales (and Kelson, Scotland).
  Quarterly with DICKSON, 1823-24, Vol. XXXIV, fol. . . . .
TUPPER, John Elisha (s. of Elisha), of Cotils, Island of Guernsey, 24 April 1826,
  Vol. XXXV, fol. 388.   (Misc. G. et H., New S., II, p. 1.)
  ,,   Sir Charles, G.C.M.G. [1886], of Nova Scotia, and Armdale, Halifax, co.
  York, 1886, Vol. LXIII, fol. 277 ; Supporters, fol. 279.
TURBERVILL, late PICTON, Richard Turbervill Picton, of Wales, 1797, Vol. XX,
  fol. 61.
  ,,   late WARLOW, Thomas Turbervill Warlow, of Wales, 1867, Vol. LVI,
  fol. 268.
TURBUTT, Rev. J. L., of Midgham, nr. Reading, Berks., 1896, Vol. LXIX,
  fol. 17.
TURNBULL, Walter, of Mount Henley, Sydenham Hill, London, 1891, Vol. LXVI,
  fol. 219.
TURNER, William, Governor of Christ's Hospital, London, 31 Mar. 1704, Vol. V,
  fol. 151.
  ,,   Nathaniel, of Fleet Street, London, Common Councillor, Governor of Christ's
  Hospital, 3rd s. of Francis, of Woburn, co. Bedf.   Alteration, Dec. 1710,
  Vol. V, fol. 409 (see Misc. G. et H., 2nd S., I, p. 122).
  ,,   Jane, dau. of William PRICE, [1753] Vol. IX, fol. 434.
TURNER after PAGE, Sir Gregory, Bart., of Ambrosden, co. Oxf., 20 Dec. 1775,
  Vol. XIII, fol. 151.
TURNER, Rev. Richard, M.A., Oxf., Rector of Cumberton and Vicar of Elmsley,
  co. Worc., 26 July 1785, Vol. XVI, fol. 57 (see Misc. G. et H., New S., I,
  p. 157).
TURNER to DRYDEN, ..., of co. Northampton, [1791] Vol. XVII, fol. 436.
TURNER after BECKETT, ..., of Bucks. and Wilts.   Crest, [1808] Vol. XXV,
  fol. 61 ; quarterly arms, fol. 65, and [1839] Vol. XLIV, fol. 30.
TURNER, late MERYWEATHER, ... (infants), of co. Surrey and Worc., William
  Stephens Turner (Mellish) Meryweather-Turner, of Lincoln's Inn,
  London, and Trinity Coll., Camb., [1830 ?] Vol. XXXVIII, fols. 175,
  177 and 179.
  ,,   Rev. Charles, of Park Hall, nr. Kidderminster, Rector of Eastham, co. Worc.,
  [1848] Vol. XLIX, fol. 14.
TURNER-FARLEY, ..., of Park Hall, nr. Kidderminster, and Henwick, Hallow,
  all co. Worc., [1848] Vol. XLIX, fol. 16.
  ,,   -FARLEY, Thomas M., of Park Hall and Henwick, co. Worc. ; Worthy Park,
  Hampsh. ; and Marnhull, co. Dorset, 1867, Vol. LVI, fol. 227.
TURNER after POLHILL, Capt., of co. Oxf., [1853] Vol. L, fol. 315.
TURNER to WRIGHT, ..., of Nettleton Rectory and Brattleby Hall, co. Linc.,
  [1863] Vol. LV, fol. 42.

TURNER after ROUND, ..., of co. Essex (Fleet Commander), [1871] Vol. LVIII, fol. 62.

TURNER (formerly BARNWELL), ..., of co. Norf. and Suff., [1826] Vol. XXXVI, fol. 51.

TURNER, George H., of Littleover, Mickleover, co. Derby, 1896, Vol. LXIX, fol. 15.

„ Mansfield, of Glenfield, Midsomer Norton, co. Somerset, 1882, Vol. LXI, fol. 387.

TURNOR, ..., of co. Cardigan, Wales, [1804] Vol. XXIII, fol. 103.

TURNOUR-FETHERSTONHAUGH, Hon. Keith, s. of Lord [the 4th Earl ?] WINTERTON, of co. Sussex, 1896, Vol. LXIX, fol. 47.

TURQUAND, Paul, of Stratford Green, co. Essex [and of St. Mary Matfelon, co. Middx.], [eldest] s. of Paul [Turquand by Jane MARTINEAU, his wife, and grandson of Paul Turquand], [formerly of] Châtelherault, Poiton, France, [late of Spitalfields, co. Middx.] [grant to himself, the descendants of his father and of] his uncles, René Claude and Peter Turquand, 23 June 1777], [1777] Vol. XIII, fol. 309. [Crisp, Notes, IX, p. 78.]

TURTON, late PETERS, Edmund, of co. Leic. and York, [1817] Vol. XXX, fol. 198.

TURVIN after HANKIN, ..., of co. Hertf., [1838] Vol. XLIII, fol. 316.

TWEDDALE, ..., of London, and Glenluce, co. Wigton, Scotland, [1795] Vol. XIX, fol. 103.

TWEEDMOUTH, Baron [12 Oct. 1881, Sir Dudley Coutts Marjoribanks, Bart.]. Supporters, 1881, Vol. LXI, fol. 243.

TWELLS, Rev. Henry, of Waltham Rectory, co. Leic., 1881,* Vol. LXI, fol. 107. (Berry's Suppl.)

TWEMLOW, ... (see POWNALL), of Arclid and Lawton, co. Chester ; Oldham, co. Lanc. ; and Peatswood, co. Staff., [1814] Vol. XXVIII, fol. 146.

TWIGGE, John, s. of William, of Scurffe Hall, Drax, co. York, 1878, Vol. LX, fol. 94.

TWISLETON, late COCKSHUTT, Josias, of co. Essex and Leic. (died s.p.), [1801] Vol. XXI, fol. 243.

TWISLETON-FIENNES, Gregory, 14th Baron SAYE AND SELE, [1825] Vol. XXXV, fol. 114. EARDLEY quarterly, fol. 116.

TWISTLETON before WYKEHAM-FIENNES and TWISTLETON (Frederick B., 16th Baron SAYE AND SELE). Quarterly, [1849] Vol. XLIX, fol. 118.

TWYFORD, H. R., of Cadogan Square, London, 1892, Vol. LXVII, fol. 101.

TYAS, Rev. J., of Padiham Vicarage, co. Lanc., 1892, Vol. LXVI, fol. 300.

TYLDEN to PATTENSON, Rev. Richard Cooke, M.A., of co. Kent. (See also WRIGHT.) [1799] Vol. XX, fol. 364.

TYLEE, ..., of Broadleaze, Bishops Cannings, Wilts., [1871] Vol. LVII, fol. 332.

TYLER, ... (see HEARD), of Boston, New England. Impaled Arms, [1774] Vol. XIII, fol. 33. (HEARD, match with HEARD.)

„ Vice-Adm. Sir Charles, K.C.B. [1815-16]. Trafalgar, alteration, [1816] Vol. XXIX, fol. 294. G.C.B. [1833]. Supporters, [1833] Vol. XXXIX, fol. 293.

„ Rev. James Endell, of co. Monmouth, Fellow of Oriel Coll., Oxf., and Rector of St. Giles-in-the-Fields, London, [1827] Vol. XXXVI, fol. 188.

TYLER to GRIFFIN, ..., of co. Monmouth, [1877] Vol. LIX, fol. 335.

TYLER, Sir G. R., Bart., of Pen-y-wern Road, Kensington, London, 1894, Vol. LXVIII, fol. 65.

TYLNEY after POLE before LONG-WELLESLEY, ..., of Ireland. Quarterly Arms, [1812] Vol. XXVII, fol. 178.

TYMEWELL, Benjamin, of London, a Commissary of the Navy, 27 Mar. 1703, Vol. V, fol. 103. Pedigree, see K. 9, fol. 239, Her. Coll. ; and Add. MS. 14,830, fols. 24 and 25. (Berry.)

TYNDALE before WARRE, ..., of co. Somerset. Quarterly Arms, [1817] Vol. XXX, fol. 157.

TYNDALE to BISCOE, ..., of co. Oxf., [1866] Vol. LVI, fol. 125.

TYNDALL-BRUCE, Onesiphorous, of Lincoln's Inn, London, and Scotland. Quarterly Arms, [1831] Vol. XXXVIII, fols. 233 and 238.

TYNTE, (KEMEYS-) after JOHNSON [Johnson to Kemeys-Tynte], Col. John, of Wales. Quarterly Arms, [1785 ?] Vol. XVI, fol. 97.

TYRAWLEY, Baron [10 Jan. 1706] ([Sir Charles] O'HARA), of Ireland. Supporters, [1707] Vol. V, fol. 268.

TYRELL after TUFNELL, ..., of co. Essex, [1878] Vol. LX, fol. 84.

TYRINGHAM-BERNARD, ..., of Berks. and Bucks. Quartering, [1788] Vol. XVII, fol. 118.

TYRINGHAM, late PRAED, of Bucks. and co. Cornw., [1859] Vol. LIII, fol. 204.

TYRRELL, ..., of Collier's Wood, co. Surrey. (See SKINNER.) Match, [1814] Vol. XXVIII, fol. 19.

TYRRELL after JENNER, ..., of Boreham House, and Billericay, co. Essex. (Oriel Coll., Oxf.) [1828] Vol. XXXVII, fol. 140.

TYRWHITT after DRAKE, William, of Bucks., 26 Mar. 1776, Vol. XIII, fol. 168.

TYRWHITT to DRAKE, ..., of Bucks. (Match), [1797] Vol. XIX, fol. 344.

„   to JONES [3 Mar. 1790, Sir Thomas Tyrwhitt, cr. Bart., 3 Oct. 1808], of Shropsh., [1790] Vol. XVII, fol. 213.

TYRWHITT, late JONES [25 Mar. 1841, Sir Henry Thomas, 3rd Bart.], of Stanley Hall, Shropsh., [?] widow and her son, [1841] Vol. XLV, fol. 214.

TYRWHITT to WILSON [23 Feb. 1876], Harry [eldest s. of Emma Harriet, Baroness Berners, wife of Sir Henry Thomas Tyrwhitt, 3rd Bart.], of Keythorpe, co. Leic., and Ashwellthorpe, co. Norf., 1876, Vol. LIX, fol. 190.

„   to WILSON, Hon Sir R. R. [Raymond Robert Tyrwhitt-Wilson, 4th Bart.], of Keythorpe, co. Leic., and Shropsh., 1892, Vol. LXVII, fol. 59.

TYSER, George W., of Oakfield, Mortimer, Berks., 1896,* Vol. LXIX, fol. 158.

TYSON, Samuel, of Clevedon and Birket, co. Cumberland, and Kingston Seymour, co. Somerset, Mayor of Bristol, 24 Feb. 1708, Vol. V, fol. 336 [286 ?]. (Berry.)

„   John [s. of Thomas Tyson], of Seathwaite, co. Cumberland, and London, Clerk of Survey, Woolwich Dockyard, 4 May 1803, Vol. XXII, fol. 149. (Crisp, Fragm. Geneal., I, p. 60.)

„   Edward, of Maryport, co. Cumberland, 1882, Vol. LXII, fol. 29.   (Berry's Suppl.)

TYSSEN, late DEAN, ..., of Hackney, co. Middx., [1788] Vol. XVI, fol. 391.

TYSSEN-DANIEL, Capt. William George, of co. Kent and Norf., 1814, Vol. XXVIII, fol. 66.

TYSSEN-AMHURST, ..., of Foulden Hall, co. Norf. ; Amherst, co. Kent ; Didlington, co. Norf. ; and Westbrooke, co. Dorset, [1852] Vol. L, fol. 180 ; [1867] Vol. LVI, fol. 186.

„   (DANIEL), Charles Amhurst, Capt. of Dragoons, [1867] Vol. LVI, fol. 273.

TYSSEN-AMHURST to TYSSEN-DANIEL-AMHERST, ..., [1867] Vol. LVI, fols. 278 and 280.

TYZACK, late DAVISON, ..., of co. Northumberland, and Scotland, [9 Jan. 1843] [1842 ?] Vol. XLVI, fols. 212 and 216.

U

UNDERWOOD, Cecilia Letitia (widow, late BUGGIN). [Surname and Arms of Underwood quarterly with GORE, 15 Mar. 1831.] (Crisp, Fragm. Geneal., V, p. 66.)

UNSWORTH to MOLINEUX-SEAL, ..., of co. Lanc., [1815] Vol. XXVIII, fol. 429 ; [1816] Vol. XXIX, fol. 315 ; [1845] Vol. XLVIII, fol. 15.

UNTHANK, ..., of Intwood Hall, co. Norf., [1863] Vol. LV, fol. 68.

UNWIN before HEATHCOTE, ..., of co. Hertf. and Nottingham. (Match), [1815] Vol. XXIX, fol. 105.

UNWIN, John, then Mayor of North Meols, Hampsh., 1886, Vol. LXIII, fol. 169.

UPCHER, Peter, of Colchester and Wormingfold, co. Essex, and Sudbury, co. Suff., 18 Feb. 1777, Vol. XIII, fol. 269. (Crisp, III, p. 25.)

UPHAM to TATEM, ..., of London, [1807 ?] Vol. XXIV, fol. 315.

UPPER-OSSORY (E[arl of] FITZPATRICK), reputed son of WILSON, afterwards FITZGERALD, [1842] Vol. XLV, fol. 380 [see FITZPATRICK].

UPPLEBY, George, of Barrow, co. Linc. Arms for his mother, Dorothy CROWLE, [1784] Vol. XV, fol. 269.

UPSON, John, of Vale Mascall, co. Kent, and Hollington, co. Sussex, 1892, Vol. LXVII, fol. 4.

UPTON to HOWARD, Lieut.-Col. (s. of Lord [Viscount ?] TEMPLETOWN), of co. Norf., [1807] Vol. XXIV, fol. 271.

„ to SMYTH, ... (minor), of Ingmere, co. York, [1852] Vol. L, fol. 195.

UPTON-COTTRELL-DORMER, ..., of Rousham, co. Oxf., and Ingmere, co. York, [1877] Vol. LX, fols. 15 and 17.

USBORNE, ..., of Broad Street, London, and Ware, co. Hertf., and Quebec, [1809] Vol. XXV, fol. 192.

USTICKE-NOWELL [? Nowell-Ustick (BEAUCHANT to), 23 Feb. 1852], of co. Cornw., [1852] Vol. L, fol. 131.

UTTERMARCK, ..., of Manor Place and St. Peter Port, Guernsey, Queen's Procureur-General, [1867] Vol. LVI, fol. 209.

UTTERSON, John, of Trotton, co. Sussex, and Berwick-upon-Tweed, co. Northumberland, [1785] Vol. XVI, fol. 53.

V

VADE-WALPOLE, [Walpole to], ..., of Hardingstone, co. Northampton, and Woollerton, co. Norf., [1844] Vol. XLVII, fol. 244.

VAFIADACCHI-SCHILLIZZI, John, Luke and Mathew, brothers, of London, 1875, Vol. LIX, fol. 134.

VAILE, William Phelps, M.R.C.S., of West Malling, co. Kent, 3 Mar. 1828, [1826] Vol. XXXVI [XXXVII ?], fol. 175 (see Berry's Suppl.).

VAIZEY, John Robert, of Attwoods, Halsted, co. Essex, s. of John, s. of John, 1877, Vol. LIX, fol. 326 (see BOUSFIELD, his wife, fol. 328).

VALE, Rev. Edward, M.A., Camb., [2nd s. of William Vale, late] of Montagu Place [and Hendon, co. Middx., decd.], of Chelsea, co. Middx., 12 Sept. 1826, Vol. XXXVI, fol. 69 (see Berry's Suppl.).

VALIANT, Lieut., of Whitechurch, co. Hereford, [1817] Vol. XXX, fol. 180. (Berry's Suppl.)

VALLANCE, ..., of Sittingbourne, co. Kent, [1823] Vol. XXXIV, fol. 8.

VALLENTIN, ..., of Norwood, co. Middx., and Rectory Manor, Walthamstow, co. Essex, [1866] Vol. LVI, fol. 111.

VANBRUGH, Sir John, Clarenceux King of Arms. Quarterly, from Ghent (CARLETON quartering), [30 ?] 15 April 1714, Vol. VI, fol. 148. (Berry.)

VAN DAM, late SEARLE, ..., of Madeira, and London, [1828] Vol. XXXVII, fol. 161.

VANDELEUR, Lieut.-Gen. Sir John [Ormsby], G.C.B. [1833]. Supporters, [1834] Vol. XL, fol. 262.

VANDEN-BEMPDÈ, late JOHNSTONE, Richard, of co. York. (Match), [1795] Vol. XIX, fol. 56.

„ -BEMPDÈ to JOHNSTONE, Richard, of co. York and Scotland, [1795] Vol. XIX, fol. 59.

VANDER NEUNBÜRG, George, of St. Martin, Stamford Baron, co. Northampton. (Match), [1807] Vol. XXIV, fol. 304.

VANDERPLANK, Samuel, of Tokenhouse Yard, London, 1 Aug. 1727, Vol. VIII, fol. 21b; Add. MS. 14,830, fol. 59.

VANDIEST, ..., of Stockwell, co. Surrey, [1807] Vol. XXIV, fol. 172.

VANE, [Gilbert, 2nd] Baron BARNARD. Quarterings, Supporters, [172¾] Vol. VII, fol. 261.

    ,, ..., Viscount BARNARD. Supporters and escutcheon of pretence, [172¾] Vol. VII, fol. 264. [Gilbert Vane, 2nd Baron, succ. his father, 28 Oct. 1723. His son, Henry, was cr. Viscount Barnard and Earl of Darlington, 3 April 1754.]

    ,, [Sir Frederick Fletcher, 2nd] Bart., of Hutton and Armathwaite, co. Cumberland. (BOWERBANK impaled.) [1803] Vol. XXII, fol. 230.

VANE to POWLETT, [14 April 1813], Hon. [William John Frederick], M.P. (Earl of DARLINGTON), [6th Duke of CLEVELAND, 1864], [1812] Vol. XXVII, fol. 275.

VANE, late POWLETT, [William John Frederick, 4 Mar. 1864, 6th] Duke of CLEVELAND. Vane Arms, [1864] Vol. LV, fol. 150.

VANE to POWLETT, [Sir Harry George, 18 Nov. 1864, 7th Duke of CLEVELAND ?]. Powlett Arms, [1864] Vol. LV, fol. 259.

VANE, [William Harry, 3rd] Earl of DARLINGTON, impaling RUSSELL [afterwards, 1833, Duke of CLEVELAND], [1821] Vol. XXXIII, fol. 12.

VANE, late STEWART, ..., Baron Stewart, quartering VANE-TEMPEST, [1823] Vol. XXXIV, fol. 17. Supporters, fol. 21.

    ,, ..., [2nd] Earl. Supporters, with consent of the Marquis of LONDON-DERRY, [1854] Vol. LI, fol. 81. [Tempest after Vane, Roy. Lic., 28 June 1854.]

    ,, G. M., of Ravensbourne Park, Catford, London, 1890, Vol. LXV, fol. 353.

VANN, late MARSTON, ..., of co. Leic., [1794] Vol. XVIII, fol. 381.

VANNECK, Joshua, Bart., s. of Cornelius, [1752] Vol. IX, fol. 401.

VAN NOTTEN, ..., of Wolverton, Hampsh., and Amsterdam, [1787] Vol. XVI, fol. 258.

VAN NOTTEN, now POLE, [Sir Charles, Roy. Lic., 7 Mar. 1787], of Hampsh., and Holcroft, co. Lanc., [1787] Vol. XVI, fol. 261.

VAN NOTTEN [before] POLE, [Roy. Lic., 19 July 1853] [Charles, 2nd s. of 1st] Bart., of co. Glouc., and Hampsh., [1853] Vol. L, fols. 345 and 397.

VAN RAALTE, C., of Kensington Palace Gardens, London, 1887,Vol. LXIV, fol. 120.

VANSITTART, Peter, of London, a naturalized German, born at Dantzig, 8 Nov. 1697, Vol. IV, fol. 231 ; Add. MS. 14,830, fol. 61. (Berry.)

VANSITTART to NEALE, [14 Nov. 1805, Rev. Edward], LL.B., of Berks. and co. Warw. Crest, [1805] Vol. XXIII, fol. 257. Quarterly Arms, fol. 259.'

VANSITTART, Nicholas, Baron BEXLEY [1 Mar. 1823]. Supporters, [1823] Vol. XXXIV, fol. 13.

VAN THUYSEN to COLE, ..., of co. Huntingdon, [1805] Vol. XXIII, fol. 134.

VARENNE, late GILL, ..., M.A., of co. Cumb. and Kent, [1816] Vol. XXIX, fol. 436.

VARLO to PETRE, ..., of co. Essex and Norf., [1802] Vol. XXI, fol. 401.

VASSALL, Lieut.-Col. [Spencer Thomas], killed at Monte Video, [7 Feb. 1807]. Arms to widow, 1808-10, Vol. XXV, fol. . . . .

VAUGHAN, [John], Viscount LISBURNE [29 June 1695]. Supporters, [1695] Vol. IV, fol. 201.

    ,, Lieut.-Gen. the Hon. Sir John, K.B. [15 Aug. 1792], brother of aforesaid [?]. Supporters, [1792] Vol. XVIII, fol. 105.

    ,, Sir Griffeth (VYCHAN), of co. Montgomery, Wales. (See HUMFREYS.) Arms, [1717] Vol. VI, fol. 290.

VAUGHAN to MARLOW, Capt., R.N., of Hampsh., [1784] Vol. XV, fol. 319.

VAUGHAN, ..., of Hengwrt and Mannau, co. Merioneth, [1791] Vol. XVII, fol. 380.

VAUGHAN to HALFORD, ..., M.D., of London. (Match), [1809] Vol. XXV, fol. 280.

VAUGHAN, Capt., E.I.C.S., of Long Hope, co. Glouc., [1812] Vol. XXVII, fol. 265.

VAUGHAN before JENKINS, ... (minor), of co. Somerset, [1814] Vol. XXVIII, fol. 185.

VAUGHAN-JENKINS, Frederick, of Combe Grove, Monkton Combe, co. Somerset, s. of William Vaughan, 1876, Vol. LIX, fol. 296.

VAUGHAN after EDWARDS, John, of Shropsh., 26 Feb. 1830, Vol. XXXIII [XXXVIII ?], fol. 45. (Crisp, Fragm. Geneal., VI, p. 13.)

VAUGHAN (BRETTELL-) after EDWARDS, ..., of Shropsh., [1850] Vol. XLIX, fol. 343.

VAUGHAN (GWYNNE-), late JONES, Henry, of Wales, 1855, Vol. LI, fol. 329.

VAUGHAN (formerly JONES), John, of Brecon, Wales, 1875, Vol. LIX, fol. 100.

VAUGHAN, Hugh Vaughan, of The Castle, Builth, Brecon, Wales, 1886, Vol. LXIII, fol. 192.

   „ James, of Llansantfraed House, Llansantfraed, co. Radnor, Wales, 1894, Vol. LXVIII, fol. 130.

VAUGHAN-PRYSE-RICE, J. C. P., of Llwyn-y-Brain, co. Carmarthen, Wales, 1887-8 [1887], Vol. LXIV, fol. 134.

VAUGHAN-LEE, Capt. Arthur Vaughan Hanning, of Dillington Park, Ilminster, co. Somerset. Lee and Vaughan quarterly, 1897 [1898], Vol. LXX, fol. 110.

VAUSE-WALKER, ... (Spr.), of Littlemoor-in-Mirfield, co. York (illeg.). Arms for Walker, [1870] Vol. LVII, fol. 224.

VAUX to LERNOULT, ..., of co. Hertf. (Match), [1795] Vol. XIX, fol. 93.

VAVASOUR, late NOOTH, [Roy. Lic., 21 Mar. 1791, Henry], of co. Linc., Bart. [1801], [1791] Vol. XVII, fol. 326.

   „ late STOURTON, Charles, of co. York, [1826] Vol. XXXV, fol. 377.

VAVASSEUR, Josiah, C.B. (s. of George, of Bocking, co. Essex), 18 . . ., Vol. LXXI, fol. . . . .

VAVAZON, Sir Philip, Knt., Sheriff [? co. Camb.], of Wisbech, Isle of Ely, co. Camb. and York, 1763, Vol. X, fol. 471. (Berry.)

VEEL, late JONES, David (? Edward, in Alum, Oxf.), of co. Glouc., and Brasenose Coll., Oxf., [1849 ?] Vol. XLIX, fol. 88.

VEEL after COLBORNE, Joseph V. C., of co. Glouc., and Magdalen Hall, Oxf., [1853] Vol. L, fol. 388.

VELUZ, ... (See DUVELUZ.) Impaling LEES, 1775.

VENABLES-VERNON, George, s. of Henry, of co. Warw. ?, 3 Sept. 1728, Vol. VIII, fols. 15^b and 16.

   „ -VERNON, George, s. of Henry Vernon, of Sudbury, co. Derby, allowed to quarter the Arms and use the Crest of Peter, late Baron of KINDERTON, 3 Sept. 1728. [No reference. See VERNON.]

VENABLES-VERNON to HARCOURT, [Rt. Hon. Edward], Archbp. of York, of co. Warw. [Arms quarterly] [2 Feb. 1831], Vol. XXXVIII, fols. 181 and 182. [Crisp, Fragm. Geneal., V, p. 65.]

VENABLES-VERNON to VERNON [to WARREN ?, Roy. Lic., 14 Oct. 1837, George John, 5th] Baron Vernon, of co. Warw., [1837] Vol. XLII, fol. 247.

VENABLES-VERNON after [to] BORLASE-WARREN- [-Venables-Vernon], of Stapleford Hall, co. Warw., s. of [5th] Baron Vernon, [1856] Vol. LI, fol. 414.

VENABLES-LLEWELYN, Charles DILLWYN-, of Llysdinan Hall, Brecon, Wales, 1893, Vol. LXVII, fol. 195.

VENN, ..., of Ipswich, co. Suff., and Clapham, co. Surrey, [1814] Vol. XXVIII, fol. 9.

VENNING, ..., of Copthall Court, London, and Upper Clapton, co. Middx., [1867] Vol. LVI, fol. 244.

VERDIN, Robert, of Brockhurst, Leftwich, co. Chester, 1884,* Vol. LXII, fol. 238.

VERE, Baron [28 Mar. 1750] (Vere BEAUCLERK), [1750] Vol. IX, fol. 353.

   „ . . . ., of Hints, co. Staff., and Custer Over House, co. Warw., [1806] Vol. XXIV, fol. 102.

VERE after BROKE [1822], Lieut.-Col. Sir Charles, K.C.B. [1815], [1822] Vol.
XXXIII, fol. 272.

VERELST, late REED, Charles, of co. Chester and York, [1851] Vol. L, fol. 83
(see [Foster's] Yorks. Collection, Vol. 3, under Mason).

VERITY, John (s. of John), of Sandridge Bury, Sandridge, co. Hertf., 1898,
Vol. LXX, fol. 288.

VERNELL, James, of Tavistock Square, London [1838] Vol. XLIII, fol. 52.

VERNEY [Richard], Lord WILLOUGHBY DE BROKE [13 Feb. 169⅚].   Supporters,
[1696] Vol. IV, fol. 319 [? 219].

„   . . . ., of Compton Murdach, co. Warw.   (Match), [1699] Vol. IV, fol. 317.

VERNEY (formerly WRIGHT), Catherine, wife of Robert, Clerk, and dau. of
. . . . CALVERT, 1811, Vol. XXVI, fol. 165.

VERNEY, late CALVERT, Sir Henry, Bart., of Bucks., Army Capt., 1827, Vol.
XXXVI, fol. 184.

„   late BARNARD, [17 May 1853], [Robert John, 9th] Baron WILLOUGHBY
DE BROKE, [1853] Vol. L, fol. 334.

VERNEY-CAVE (late WYATT-EDGELL) [Roy. Lic., 5 Feb. 1880], Alfred Thomas
Townshend, Lord BRAYE, of co. Staff., 1880, Vol. LX, fol. 346.

VERNON (formerly) GLADELL, ..., [1784] Vol. XV, fol. 321.

VERNON (VENABLES-), ..., Baron [?] of KINDERTON, [1728] Vol. VIII, fol. 15b.

VERNON, Baron [12 May 1762] ([George] VENABLES-VERNON).   Supporters,
[1762] Vol. X, fol. 418.   [Baron of Kinderton.]

„   [Hon. W. J. B.-W.-VENABLES.   Exemplification, 17 Jan. 1856.   (Frontispiece,
Genealogist, New S., Vol. IV.)].

VERNON to GRAHAM, ..., of Hilton Park, co. Staff., [1800] Vol. XXI, fol. 61.

VERNON-GRAHAM, now VERNON only, Col., of co. Staff., [1838] Vol. XLIII,
fol. 48.

VERNON before WENTWORTH, ..., of Hilton Park, co. Staff., [1804] Vol. XXIII,
fol. 77.

VERNON, late SMITH, Robert, of Berks., 1846 [1847], Vol. XLVIII, fols. 324
and 326 ; [1850] Vol. XLIX, fol. 316.   Baron LYVEDEN [1859], of
Berks., co. Northampton, Surrey and London, [1859] Vol. LIII, fol. 192.

„   late JENKINS, Rev. Charles ?, D.D., of co. Linc., [1860] Vol. LIII,
fol. 331.

VERNON-GORE, Georgina K. (dau. of EVANS), widow of Charles, of Clifton, Bristol,
and of Verville, Dublin, 1876, Vol. LIX, fol. 220.

VERRAL, ..., of Lewes, co. Sussex, [1835] Vol. XLI, fol. 85.

VERRAL to GREEN, of Lewes, co. Sussex, and Chiddingley, St. Michael, Ringmer,
co. Sussex, [1835] Vol. XLI, fol. 87.

VIALL quartering to Edward BELLASIS, 1879, Vol. LX, fol. 326.

VICKERS, Charles William, Bar.-at-Law, Lieut.-Col., Volunteers, [and ?] Cuthbert B.,
sons of James, 18 . . ., Vol. LXXI, fol. . . . .

„   Edward, of Millsands, Sheffield, co. York, 4th s. of John, 1878, Vol. LX,
fol. 169.   (Berry's Suppl.)

VIDAL, late SEALY, ..., of the Middle Temple, London, and Cornborough,
Abbotsham, co. Devon, [1842] Vol. XLVI, fol. 10.

VIGOR after STONEHOUSE, [Venerable Archdeacon Timothy], M.A., of co. Glouc.
[Berks. ?].   Quarterly Arms, [1795] Vol. XIX, fol. 91.

VILLETTES, Arthur, of Bath, co. Somerset, and Languedoc, France, 31 Dec. 1766,
Vol. XI, fol. 186.   (Berry.)

VILLIERS, [Baron of Hoo, and] Viscount [Villiers of Dartford, 20 Mar. 169⁰⁄₇],
Edward [Earl of Jersey, 13 Oct. 1697].   Supporters, 1691, Vol. IV,
fol. 100.

„   Baron HYDE [of Hindon, Wilts., 3 June 1756, Thomas] [Earl of Clarendon,
14 June 1776].   Supporters, [1756] Vol. X, fol. 55.

VILLIERS, late MASON, George (Viscount), of Ireland, Earl of GRANDISON, 21 Oct.
1771, Vol. XII, fol. 107.   (Berry.)

„   late LEWIS, ..., of Bucks., [1791] Vol. XVII, fol. 328.

VILLIERS to MANSELL, ... [1802, s. of] (4th Earl of JERSEY) (died s.p.). (Match), [1802] Vol. XXI, fol. 372.

VILLIERS after CHILD, [Child before Villiers ?, 1 Dec. 1819], George, [5th] Earl of JERSEY, 1812 [1819], Vol. XXXI, fol. 394.

VILLIERS-STUART, [17 Nov. 1822, the Rt. Hon.] Henry [Stuart, 1822], Vol. XXXIII, fols. 200 and 206. Baron STUART DE DECIES [10 May 1839]. Supporters, [1839] Vol. XLIV, fol. 34.

VILLIERS, Sir George William Frederick, G.C.B. [19 Oct. 1837] (afterwards 4th [8th] Earl of CLARENDON). Supporters, [1838] Vol. XLII, fol. 275.

VILLIERS (late LAWRENCE), Charles, Rector of Croft, co. York, reputed son of Thomas Hyde Villiers, younger bro. of George William Frederick, [4th, 8th] Earl of CLARENDON, 1876, Vol. LIX, fol. 256.

VINCENT, ..., C.B., Post-Capt., R.N., of Berks., [1816] Vol. XXIX, fol. 392.

„ . . . ., of Berkeley Square, London, [1816] Vol. XXIX, fol. 443.

VINCENT to SHELDON, ..., of co. Warw. and Worc., [1828] Vol. XXXVII, fols. 119 and 157.

VINER after ELLIS, ..., of co. Glouc. and Worc. Quarterly Arms, [1811] Vol. XXVI, fol. 300.

VINEY, ..., of Hollefield and Maidstone, co. Kent, 1702. (Berry and Burke.)

VIRGIN, ..., of London, and Hope Park, Clarendon, Jamaica, [1810] Vol. XXVI, fol. 15.

VIRGINIA COLLEGE OF DIVINITY, 14 May 1694, Vol. IV, fols. 158 and [1699] 284.

VIVEASH to BASKERVILLE, ..., of Wilts., [1838] Vol. XLII, fol. 334.

VIVEASH, ..., of Colne, Wilts., and Madras, [1838] Vol. XLIII, fol. 286.

VIVIAN, ..., of the Inner Temple, London ; Penalaway, co. Cornw. ; and Redland House, co. Glouc., [1817] Vol. XXX, fol. 240.

VIVIAN, late TIPPET, ..., of co. Cornw., [1817] Vol. XXX, fol. 246 ; [1820] Vol. XXXII, fol. 55.

VIVIAN, Maj.-Gen. Sir Richard Hussey, K.C.B. [1815], [Bart., 19 Jan. 1828] Vol. XXXVII, fol. 10 ; G.C.B. [1837] Supporters, [1837] Vol. XLII, fol. 197. (1st Lord [Baron Vivian, 19 Aug. 1841].)

„ Maj.-Gen. Sir Robert John [Hussey], [K.C.B., 1857] [1856] Vol. LII, fol. 154. G.C.B. [1871] Supporters, [1871] Vol. LVIII, fol. 46.

VIZARD, ..., of Dursley, co. Glouc., [1806] Vol. XXIII, fol. 420.

VOGUEL, Henry and Frederick, of London, and Westphalia Harford, [1745] Vol. IX, fol. 140 or 146.

VOWLES, William, of Brislington, co. Somerset, 1878, Vol. LX, fol. 82. (Berry's Suppl.)

VOYCE, Benjamin, of Sudbury, co. Suff., and St. Michael, Cornhill, London, 6 Feb. 172⅜ [1729 ?], Vol. VIII, fol. 47.

VYSE after HOWARD, Col., of Bucks. and co. Northampton, [1841-1842] Vol. XLV, fol. 340.

VYVYAN-ROBINSON, ..., of co. Cornw. and Devon, [1818] Vol. XXXI, fol. 127.

W

WADDELL, ..., of Walmer, co. Kent ; Chobham Park, co. Surrey ; and Aberdeen, Scotland, [1835] Vol. XL, fol. 344.

WADDINGHAM, John, of Guiting Grange, co. Glouc., [1861] Vol. LIV, fol. 120.

WADDINGTON, now FERRAND, Thomas, s. of Rev. Joseph, of co. York and Nottingham, [1788] Vol. XVI, fol. 413 (see [Foster's] Yorkshire Pedigrees).

WADDINGTON, Sykes, of Harworth and Walkeringham, co. Nottingham, [1788] Vol. XVII, fol. 69.

WADDINGTON to DRIFFIELD, William, of Boston Spa, and Bramham, co. York, [1860] Vol. LIV, fol. 20.

WADDY, His Honour Judge, Samuel D., of Fitzjohn's Avenue, London, 1896,* Vol. LXIX, fol. 199; of Newark-on-Trent, co. Nottingham, and [Waddy] of Corby, co. Linc., [1792] Vol. XVIII, fol. 53.

WADE, Matthew, of Dublin and Quebec, Montreal, 2 Dec. 1768, Vol. XI, fol. 330. (Berry.)

WADE before GERY, ..., M.A., of Newark and Bushmead Priory, co. Nottingham, [1792] Vol. XVIII, fol. 123.

WADE, Rev. Hugh, M.A., of Newark-on-Trent, co. Nottingham, and Corby, co. Linc., [1792] Vol. XVIII, fol. 53.

WADE before GERY, Rev. Hugh, of Newark and Bushmead Priory, co. Nottingham, [1792] Vol. XVIII, fol. 123.

WADE, Rev. . . . ., Incumbent of St. Anne's, Tottington, co. Lanc., 1834 [1833], Vol. XL, fol. 25.

  „ George Osborne, of Ingelrack, Isle of Man; Branghing, co. Hertf.; and Spüng, Christianstadt, Sweden, [1842] Vol. XLVI, fol. 57.

  „ Major, C.B., &c., [1843] Vol. XLVII, fol. 53.

WADE to WADE-DALTON, Col., C.B., of Hamilton Wade, co. York, 1880, Vol. LX, fol. 356. (Berry's Suppl.)

WADE, John, of Gilston Road, South Kensington, London, [1858] Vol. LII, fol. 352.

WADE-PALMER, Fairfax Blomefield, of Holm Park, Sunning, Reading, Berks. Wade and Palmer quarterly, and wife's escutcheon, Palmer and PYM, 1898, Vol. LXX, fol. 267.

WADE (formerly BASELEY), ..., of Scott's House, Boldon, co. Durham, [1821] Vol. XXXII, fol. 281.

WAGSTAFF, ..., of Budd Lodge, Norwood, co. Middx., [1856] Vol. LII, fol. 81.

WAHL, Charles Frederick, of 119, Broadhurst Gardens, Hampstead, London, 18 . . ., Vol. LXXI, fol. . . . .

WAINWRIGHT to LOWTEN, J. T., of co. Chester, [1814] Vol. XXVIII, fol. 137; (Wainwright, see SMELTER), [1796] Vol. XIX, fol. 303.

WAITE to SPENLOWE, ..., of Berks. and co. Surrey, [1863] Vol. LV, fol. 74.

WAKE, William, of Blandford (Blandford and Wareham, co. Dorset; Pedington Grange, co. Northampton); Gray's Inn, London; and Westminster, 1694, Vol. IV, fols. 162 and 163.

  „ William, D.D., of Shapwick, co. Dorset; Rector, St. James', Westminster, 169⅘, Vol. IV, fol. 185.

  „ William, of Osgathorpe House, Sheffield, co. York, 1888,* Vol. LXIV, fol. 236.

WAKEFIELD to POMEROY, ... (minor), of co. Essex, [1841] Vol. XLV, fol. 305.

  „ to READE, ..., of Shipton Court, Shipton Wychwood, co. Oxf., [1868] Vol. LVII, fol. 45.

WAKEMAN, [? Sir Henry, Bart., 1828], of Hinton Hall, Shropsh., and Perdiswell Hall, co. Worc. [1827] Vol. XXXVI, fol. 394.

WALBANKE, William, of Eppleby, Kirkbridge, and Whitehouse, co. York, 17 April 1723, Vol. VII, fol. 186.

WALCOTT, ..., of Winkton, nr. Ringwood, Hampsh., and Croegh, co. Limerick, Ireland, [1819] Vol. XXXI, fol. 300.

WALCOTT-SIMPSON, ..., of Winkton, nr. Ringwood, Hampsh., and Croegh, co. Limerick, [1819] Vol. XXXI, fols. 302 and 304.

WALDEGRAVE-LESLIE, [Henrietta Anderson Morshead], Countess of ROTHES [mar. 22 Jan. 1861]. Leslie Arms, [1861] Vol. LIV, fol. 230.

WALDO before SIBTHORP, Humphry, M.P., of co. Linc. (Match.) Quarterly Arms, [1804] Vol. XXIII, fol. 11.

WALES, H.R.H. the Princess (Charlotte Augusta of). Exemplification, 16 April 1816. (Her. and Geneal., I, p. 118.)

WALEY, late LEVI, ..., of London, [1834] Vol. XL, fol. 251.

WALFORD, ..., of Ellesmere, Shropsh., [1799] Vol. XX, fol. 391 ; *see* [1782] Vol. XV, fol. 26.

   „ . . . . (CARR, his wife), of London, [1845] Vol. XLVIII, fols. 59 and 60.

WALFORD-GOSNALL, ..., of Bentley Hall, co. Suff., now of co. Essex, [1847] Vol. XLVIII, fol. 320.

WALHOUSE to LITTLETON, ..., of co. Staff., [1811] Vol. XXVII, fol. 68.

WALKER, Sir Baldwin Wake, K.C.B. [1841], Capt., R.N., Admiral, Turkish Navy. Allusion to Turkish Order, [1842] Vol. XLVI, fol. 104.

   „ Thomas, s. of James, of Bow, co. Middx., descendants of his father, James, 28 Jan. 171¾, Vol. VI, fol. 128 (*see* Add. MS. 14,830, fol. 53).

   „ Henry, of Cotton Hall, Milwich, co. Staff., June 1726 [1727] Vol. VII, fol. 586.

   „ Hezekiah, s. of Hezekiah, of the Middle Temple, London, and Leighton Buzzard, co. Bedf., fined for Sheriff of London, 1748, Vol. IX, fol. 299.

   „ James (Sir James, Bart.), of Springhead, co. York, and Ardwick, Manchester, co. Lanc., 1772, Vol. XII, fol. 204.

   „ Samuel, of Masborough and Ecclesfield, co. York, 1778, Vol. XIV, fol. 61.

WALKER before CORNWALL, Frederick, of Shropsh., [1781] Vol. XIV, fol. 342.

WALKER, ..., of Lowestoft, co. Suff., [1786] Vol. XVI, fol. 151.

WALKER to HUNGERFORD, ..., of Wilts., [1788] Vol. XVII, fol. 121.

   „ to BLANDY, ..., of Berks., [1792] Vol. XVIII, fol. 31.

WALKER, ..., of Woodstock, co. Oxf., and East Dereham, co. Norf., [1802] Vol. XXI, fol. 363.

   „ William, M.B., of Swinnow Park, co. York (? male issue extinct, *see* ELMHIRST), 17 Feb. 1807, Vol. XXIV, fol. 169.

   „ . . . ., of Stockerston, co. Leic., [1810] Vol. XXVI, fol. 126.

   „ Maj.-Gen. Sir George Townshend, K.C.B. [1815], Lieut.-Governor of the Isle of Grenada [1815], of Bushey, co. Hertf. Allusions, [1815] Vol. XXVIII, fol. 294 ; G.C.B. Supporters, [1817] Vol. XXX, fol. 161 ; Lieut.-Gen. and Bart. [1835], [1835] Vol. XL, fol. 359.

WALKER to MUSGRAVE, ..., nat. son and dau. of Musgrave, of Borden, co. Kent, [1816] Vol. XXIX, fols. 288 and 290.

   „ to WOOD, ..., of the City of London, [1817] Vol. XXX, fol. 188.

WALKER-HENEAGE, late WYLD, ..., of Speen and Cheveley, Berks., and Compton House, Wilts., [1818] Vol. XXXI, fol. 102.

WALKER, late FLOWER, [Henry], [23 Nov. 1827] (1st s. of Viscount ASHBROOK) (Irish Peer) [afterwards 5th Viscount], [1828] Vol. XXXVII, fol. 5.

WALKER to FLOWER, [Henry], [15 July 1847] (1st s. of Viscount ASHBROOK) (Irish Peer) [5th Viscount], [1847] Vol. XLVIII, fol. 365.

WALKER, ..., of Eastwood, co. Nottingham, 1834, Vol. XL, fol. 71 [? 91] (*see* [1887] Vol. LXIV, fol. 94).

WALKER-MUNRO, Edward Lionel [Munro to], of Eastwood Hall, co. Nottingham, 1887, Vol. LXIV, fol. 94 (*see* [1833] Vol. XL, fol. 71).

WALKER, George James Alexander, of Norton Juxta, Kempsey, co. Worc., [1840] Vol. XLIV, fol. 281.

   „ Ann (Spr.), of Halifax, Cliffe Hall, and Crow Nest, co. York, [1842] Vol. XLVI, fol. 205.

WALKER after SUTHERLAND, ..., of Cliffe Hall and Crow Nest, co. York, [1856] Vol. LII, fol. 139.

WALKER, John, of Ebor House, Clifton, Bristol, [1849] Vol. XLIX, fol. 153.

   „ John Henry, of Marpool Hall, co. Devon, and Packwood, co. Warw., [1856] Vol. LII, fol. 93.

WALKER-AYLESBURY, John Henry, of Marpool Hall, co. Devon ; Packwood, co. Warw. ; Rickmansworth, co. Hertf. ; and Bromsgrove, co. Worc., [1857] Vol. LII, fol. 295.

WALKER, ..., of Hillfield House, Wootton St. Mary, co. Worc., [1870] Vol. LVII, fol. 228.

WALKER after KERRICH, Henry W., of Durham and co. Northumberland, 1877, Vol. LIX, fol. 308. (Berry's Suppl.)

WALKER, Leasowe, of Scarborough, co. York, s. of ARD, of Scarcroft, co. York, 1897, Vol. LXX, fol. 24.

„   Henry Rosenbach, B.A., Camb., 18 . . ., Vol. LXXI, fol. . . . . .

WALKEY, ..., Rector of Clyst St. Lawrence, co. Devon, [1860] Vol. LIII, fol. 314.

WALKLATE, ... *See* RAY.

WALL, ..., of Eckington, co. Worc., and Cleobury Mortimer, Shropsh., [1861] Vol. LIV, fol. 222.

„   Arthur, of Coed Maur Hall, nr. Conway, Wales (s. of Thomas, of Manchester), 18 . . ., Vol. LXXI, fol. . . . .

WALLACE, ..., E.I.C.S., of London and Madras, [1843] Vol. XLVII, fol. 101.

WALLACE after HOPE, [3 April 1844, the Hon.] James, of co. Northumberland (Baron HOPETOUN) [2nd s. of the 4th Earl], [1843] Vol. XLVII, fol. 103.

WALLER, ..., of Haverbrack, co. Westmorland, [1810] Vol. XXVI, fol. 64.

WALLER, late PHIPPS, J. W., of Berks., [1814] Vol. XXVIII, fol. 167.

WALLER, Sir Jonathan Wathen, Bart. Alteration of Arms, [1816] Vol. XXIX, fol. 395.

WALLER (formerly PROCTER), Nicholas, of co. York, [1816] Vol. XXX, fol. 25.

WALLER, William C., of Yorke Hill, Loughton, co. Essex, 1887,* Vol. LXIV, fol. 96.

WALLINGTON, Edward, of Dursley and Frampton-upon-Severn, co. Glouc. (grandson of Charles). Quarterly Arms, 3 July 1790, Vol. XVII, fol. 246.

WALLIS, now OGLE, ..., of co. Northumberland, [1786 ?] Vol. XVI, fol. 201.

WALLIS after BAYLEY, Lieut.-Col. . . . ., of London, and Plas Newydd, Anglesey, Wales. Quartering, [1800] Vol. XXI, fol. 81.

WALLIS, late LOFT, Alfred Arthur, of co. Linc., [1838] Vol. XLII, fol. 271.

WALLIS, Gilbert A. F. (s. of Gilbert), of Bathwick, Bath, co. Somerset, 18 . . ., Vol. LXXI, fol. . . . . .

WALLOP, [John], [11 June 1720, Baron Wallop and] Viscount LYMINGTON, [John] [afterwards, 1743, Earl of Portsmouth]. Supporters, [1723] Vol. VII, fol. 199.

WALLOP to FELLOWES, [Roy. Lic., 9 Aug. 1794, Newton Wallop], s. of the [2nd] [afterwards [1853] 4th] Earl of PORTSMOUTH, of Hampsh., 1794, Vol. XVIII, fol. 379.

„   to WILLIAM-POWLETT, ..., of Hampsh., and Wales, [1867] Vol. LVI, fol. 170.

WALLS, late CODD, Edward, of co. Linc., [1778] Vol. XIV, fol. 21.

WALLSEY, Sophia, wife of G. H. FLETCHER. (*See* FLETCHER.) [1868] Vol. LVII, fol. 31.

WALMESLEY, ..., Clerk of the House of Lords, [1833] Vol. XXXIX, fol. 194.

„   Elizabeth (widow). Quartering for ARCHER and of SELBY ?, [1847] Vol. XLVIII, fol. 294.

WALMSLEY, Sir Joshua, Knt. [1840], of Wavertree Hall, Liverpool, and Mayor of Liverpool, co. Lanc., [1840] Vol. XLIV, fol. 302.

WALPOLE, Lord Walpole [Baron Walpole, 10 June 1723, Sir Robert Walpole] [afterwards 2nd Earl of Orford]. Supporters and quarterings, [1723] Vol. VII, fol. 217 ; K.B. [1725]. Supporters, [1725] Vol. VII, fol. 406.

„   Sir Edward, K.B. [1753], [2nd s. of Robert, 1st Earl of Orford]. Supporters, [1753] Vol. IX, fol. 477.

„   Laura, Maria and Charlotte, her children, 8 April 1775, Vol. XIII, fol. 92.

„   Baron [of Walterton, 7 June 1756, Horatio Walpole]. Supporters, [1756] Vol. X, fol. 49.

WALPOLE after VADE, ..., of co. Norf. and Northampton, [1844] Vol. XLVII, fol. 244.

[WALRAVEN, Sir John, Envoy to Amsterdam, in 1718. (Collect. Topog. et Her., VII, 223n.).]

WALROND, late DICKINSON, ..., Bart., of co. Devon, [1845] Vol. XLVII, fol. 363.

WALSH to PORTER, ..., of London, and Ireland. (Match), [1783] Vol. XV, fol. 235.

„ to BENN, of Berks. [? Walsh after Benn, Roy. Lic., 4 April 1795, John], [1795] Vol. XIX, fol. 81.

WALSH (BENN), Baron ORMATHWAITE [16 April 1868, Sir John Walsh, 2nd Bart.]. Supporters, [1868] Vol. LVI, fol. 350.

WALSH-FREEMAN, ..., of Abbots Langley, co. Hertf., [1823] Vol. XXXIV, fol. 5.

WALSHAM before GARBETT, Lieut.-Col., Militia, of Knill Court, co. Heref. Quarterly Arms, 1800, Vol. XXI, fol. 22. Another Roy. Lic., 10 May 1837, to descendant, Garbett.

WALSINGHAM, Baron, [17 Oct. 1780, Sir William] DE GREY [Chief Justice of Common Pleas]. Supporters, [1780] Vol. XIV, fol. 255.

WALTER to ROLLE, Denys, of Hudscott, co. Devon, [1781] Vol. XIV, fol. 328.

WALTERS to STOCKDALE, Christopher, of co. York, 1695 [169⁴⁄₅], Vol. IV, fol. 187.

WALTERS, Sir Hugh, Bart., of Greenwich, co. Kent. Quartering, [1796] Vol. XIX, fol. 239.

WALTERS to PALLISER, Sir Hugh, of Perry Hill, co. Kent, and Castletown, co. Wexford, Ireland, [1798] Vol. XX, fol. 269.

WALTERS, ... of St. Athan, co. Glamorgan, Wales, and Guernsey, [1803] Vol. XXII, fol. 265.

WALTERS-PHILLIPPS, ..., of Wales, [1826] Vol. XXXVI, fol. 101.

WALTHALL, late MILNES, Henry W., of Alton Manor, co. Derby, and Trinity Coll., Oxf., [1853] Vol. L, fol. 340.

WALTON, Capt., [1811] Vol. XXVI, fol. 416.

„ Thomas Todd, of Sunnyside, Lanchester, co. Durham, [1850] Vol. XLIX, fol. 310.

„ William H. Crane, of Preston, co. Lanc., 1883,* Vol. LXII, fol. 39. (Berry's Suppl.)

WALTON-WILSON, John William, of Shotley Hall, Shotley, co. Northumberland, 1880, Vol. LXI, fols. 57 and 61.

WANDESFORD (-SOUTHWELL-) after BUTLER-CLARKE, [Charles Harward, 4th son of John] Earl of ORMONDE (2nd s. s.), of Ireland, [1830] Vol. XXXVIII fol. 111.

WANDSWORTH, Baron [19 July 1895] (STERN), of London, 1895. Arms, Vol. LXVIII, fol. 295 ; Supporters, fol. 297.

WANTAGE, Baron [23 July 1885, Sir Robert James Lloyd-Lindsay], of Berks. Supporters, [1885] Vol. LXIII, fol. 130.

WARBURTON after EGERTON, ..., B.A., of co. Chester. Quarterly Arms, [1815] Vol. XXIX, fol. 178.

WARD, William, of Houghton Parva, co. Northampton, 31 May 1695, Vol. IV, fol. 206. [Guillim, p. 229.]

„ John, of Hackney, co. Middx., 8 Sept. 1722, Vol. VII, fol. 100.

„ Richard, of Salhouse and Walcot, co. Norf., 30 Mar. 1775, Vol. XIII, fol. 81.

„ Hannah, widow of John, of Stramshall, co. Staff., dau. and co.-h. of Samuel HAWKES, of Ogbourne St. Andrew, Wilts., s. of William Hawkes and Hannah, sister and co.-h. of Sir Michael FOSTER, Kt., of Draycot Foliat, Wilts., 1833-35, Vol. XL, fol. . . . .

WARD, late COLLINS, ..., of Sandhurst, co. Kent, [1783] Vol. XV, fol. 175.

WARD before ERRINGTON, ..., of Preston, co. Northumberland, and Nether Stowey, co. Somerset. Quarterly Arms, [1791] Vol. XVII, fol. 310.

WARD to HAMILTON, ..., of co. Suff., [1818] Vol. XXXI, fols. 93, 95 and 97.

WARD-PORTER, ..., B.A., of Henley-in-Arden, co. Warw., [1825] Vol. XXXV, fol. 162.

WARD to ESSINGTON, [William Webb], of co. Warw. [and Worc., 4 Jan. 1828]
    Vol. XXXVII, fol. 16.
WARD, Robert, M.P., Under-Sec. Foreign Office, of co. Hertf.; Chesham, Bucks.;
    and Woburn Hall, [1828] Vol. XXXVII, fol. 165 (see Berry's Suppl.).
WARD after "PLUMBER," Robert, Under-Sec. Foreign Office, of co. Hertf., [1828]
    Vol. XXXVII, fol. 183.
WARD-BOUGHTON-LEIGH, ..., of co. Northampton and Warw., [1832] Vol.
    XXXIX, fols. 63 and 67.
WARD, ..., of Head House, Stepney, co. Middx., and Brighton, co. Sussex,
    [1851 ?] Vol. L, fol. 89.
    „   William, of Oaklands, Wolverhampton, co. Staff., [1855] Vol. LI, fol. 284.
WARDE, Gen. Sir Henry, G.C.B. [1831].   Supporters, [1831] Vol. XXXVIII,
    fol. 350 ; Impaled Arms, [1832] Vol. XXXIX, fol. 27.
WARDE-ALDAM, William W., of Frickley Hall, Clayton-cum-Frickley, and Hooton
    Pagnell, co. York, 1878, Vol. LX, fol. 165.   (Berry's Suppl.)
WARDELL, James, of Finchley, co. Middx., and St. Martin's, Vintry, London,
    26 June 1773, Vol. XII, fol. 259 (see Berry's Suppl.).
WARDEN to SERGISON, Thomas, of co. Sussex, 1733, Vol. VIII, fol. 167.
WARE, ..., of Hampstead, co. Middx., [1816] Vol. XXIX, fol. 422 (see
    BARNS) [same Vol. and fol.].
WARE, late CUMBERLEGE, ..., of co. Middx., [1862] Vol. LIV, fol. 330.
WARE, Samuel, M.D.   Name and Arms of Ware in lieu of HIBBERT.   1837.   (Burke.)
    „   Henry, Suff. Bishop of Barrow-in-Furness, s. of Martin Ware, of Titford,
    co. Surrey, 1897, Vol. LXX, fol. 63.
WARING, late SCOTT, ..., of Shropsh. and co. Kent.   (Match), [1798] Vol.
    XX, fol. 247.
WARING, John (s. of Joseph), of Haworth Hall, Rotherham, co. York, [1863]
    Vol. LV, fol. 46.
    „   Walter (Surgeon), of Tombland, Norwich, co. Norf., 1896, Vol. LXIX,
    fol. 124.
WARLOW to TURBERVILL, Capt., R.A., of Wales (Lieut.-Col. Thomas Picton
    Warlow), [1867] Vol. LVI, fol. 268.
WARNER (LEE-), late WOODWARD, Daniel Henry, of co. Norf., 5 Mar. 1806, Vol.
    XXIII, fols. 274 and 278.   (Berry's Appx.)
    „   (LEE-), late BAGGE, William W., 2. Edward, 3. Arthur, 4. Thomas, sons of
    Charles Elsden Bagge, M.D., Roy. Lic., 21 May 1814.   Quarterly Arms,
    [1814] Vol. XXVIII, fol. 124.
WARNER, Edward Highams, M.P., of Walthamstow, co. Essex, [1859] Vol.
    LIII, fol. 60.
WARNES, ..., of Bolwick Hall, Aylsham, co. Norf., [1851] Vol. XLIX,
    fol. 433.
WARRE, late BUTTER, Capt., of Berks., [1813] Vol. XXVII, fol. 401.
WARRE after TYNDALL, John, of co. Somerset.   Quarterly Arms, [1817] Vol.
    XXX, fol. 157.
WARREN, [Rear-Adm.] Sir Peter, K.B. [1747].   Arms by Ulster King of Arms.
    Supporters, [1747] Vol. IX, fol. 209.   Certificate, [1748] Vol. IX,
    fol. 250.
    „   Sir George, K.B. [1761].   Supporters, [1761] Vol. X, fol. 336.
    „   Susanna, dau. and h. of William, of Stallingthorne, par. of Huntsham,
    20 May 1700, Vol. IV, fol. 340.
    „   Richard, of Shepperton, co. Middx., and Forest of Dean, co. Glouc., 28 Sept.
    or 31 Oct. 1776, Vol. XIII, fol. 235.   (31 Oct , Berry.)
WARREN to HORNE, Edmund Thomas, of co. Derby, [1784] Vol. XV, fol. 323.
WARREN, Rear-Adm. Sir John BORLASE, of Stapleford, co. Nottingham.   Arms
    and supplement, [7 May 1802] Vol. XXI, fol. 370 ; Crest, fol. 413.
WARREN before BULKELEY [20 Sept. 1802], Thomas [James], Lord [Bulkeley],
    of co. Chester, and Wales.   Quarterly Arms, 1802, Vol. XXI, fol. 441.
WARREN to SANDYS, of co. Cornw.   (Match), [1817] Vol. XXX, fol. 204.

WARREN, ..., of Ottery St. Mary, eo. Devon. Escutcheon of pretence for
   HICKS, 1823-24, Vol. XXXIV, fol. . . . .
WARREN, late LEICESTER [18 Feb. 1832], George [Fleming], 2nd Baron DE TABLEY,
   1832, Vol. XXXIX, fol. 82. Supporters, fol. 87.
   „ late VENABLES-VERNON [14 Oct. 1837], George John, 5th Baron Vernon,
      of eo. Chester, 1837, Vol. XLII, fol. 247.
WARREN after CORBOULD, [William ?], of eo. Norf., [1853] Vol. L, fol. 375.
WARREN (BORLASE) before VENABLES, ..., of eo. Warw. (W. J. V. BORLASE-
   WARREN-VENABLES-VERNON), [1856] Vol. LI, fol. 414.
WARREN, Rev. Samuel, LL.D., Rector of All Souls', Amcoats, Manchester, 1859,
   Vol. LIII, fol. 97.
WARREN to WARREN-SWETTENHAM, Robert, of eo. Chester, 1879, Vol. LX,
   fol. 273. (Berry's Suppl.)
WARRINER, ..., of Conock, Wilts. Match, [1816] Vol. XXX, fol. 72.
WARRINGTON to CAREW, ..., of Shropsh., Wales, and eo. Somerset. Arms to
   wife, &c., [1811] Vol. XXVI, fol. 311.
WARRINGTON, Thomas, of Phillimore Gardens, Kensington, 1882, Vol. LXI,
   fol. 257. (Berry's Suppl.)
   „ Corporation of, eo. Lanc., [18 May] 1897, Vol. LXIX, fol. 281. [Geneal.
      Mag., I, p. 261.]
WARRY, Major Thomas, of Wimborne Minster, eo. Dorset, 1891,* Vol. LXVI,
   fol. 41.
WARTER, John, of the Inner Temple, London, Bar.-at-Law, Assist.-Counsel to the
   Admiralty and Navy of Great Britain, of Bridgnorth, Shropsh., 1 Sept.
   1714, Vol. VI, fol. 166 ; Add. MS. 14,830, fol. 131 (see MEREDYTH in the
   Landed Gentry).
WARTNABY, ..., of Market Harborough and Waltham-on-the-Wolds, eo. Leic.,
   [1870] Vol. LVII, fol. 290.
WARWICK AND BROOKE, Earl of (GREVILLE). Ancient Crest granted 2 April
   1760, Vol. X, fol. 223 (see An Historical and Genealogical Account of the
   Family of Greville, p. 98).
WARWICK, late BONNER, of eo. Cumberland and Northumberland, [1791] Vol.
   XVII, fol. 434.
WASDALE, ..., of Wasdale Head, eo. Cumberland, [1803] Vol. XXII, fol. 277.
WASEY, William, D.phys., of Westminster, and North Walsham, eo. Norf., 12 Aug.
   172⅝ [1729], Vol. VIII, fol. 41 ; Add. MS. 14,830, fol. 134. (Berry.)
WASHBOURNE, ..., of Pytchley, eo. Northampton. Quartering to MONEY-
   KYRLE ?, [1809] Vol. XXV, fol. 197.
WASKETT, Sir Francis, K.C.B., of London, and Penlow Hall, eo. Essex, to the
   descendants of his father, John, 1818, Vol. XXX, fol. 363.
WASKETT before MYERS, Sir F., of London, Monkstown and Marlesfield, eo. Dublin,
   Ireland. Quarterly Arms, 1818, Vol. XXX, fol. 365.
[WASTDALE, John, of St. Martin-in-the-Fields, eo. Middx., and City of Carlisle,
   Dr. of Physick, only issue of James, late of Kirk Oswald, eo. Cumberland,
   3rd s. of Nicholas, and to the descendants of his grandfather, Nicholas
   Wastdale, 27 June 1803.]
WATERFALL, Rev. George H., of Totley, Dore, eo. Derby, Rector of Tollard Royal,
   Salisbury, Wilts., 1882,* Vol. LXI, fol. 313. (Berry's Suppl.)
WATERFIELD, Thomas, D.Med., F.R.C.P., of Daventry, eo. Northampton, (Ch. Coll.,
   Camb.), [1839] Vol. XLIV, fol. 92.
WATERHOUSE, John, F.R.S., of Well Head, Halifax, eo. York, 1872, Vol. LVIII,
   fol. 119.
WATERHOUSE after DOHERTY, Capt. Daniel Henry, of Well Head and Hope Hall,
   eo. York, 1872, Vol. LVIII, fol. 125.
WATERLOW, [Sir Sidney Hedley, Knt., 3 Aug. 1867], Bart. [? 1873], of
   Huntingdon Lodge, Camberwell, eo. Surrey, [1866] Vol. LVI, fol. 136.
   „ Alfred James, of Great Boods, Reigate, eo. Surrey, 1881, Vol. LXI, fol. 124.
      (Berry's Suppl.)

WATERS, ..., of Brook House, Holy Cross, and St. Giles, Shrewsbury, Shropsh., [1873] Vol. LVIII, fol. 220.
WATHEN, Samuel, Knt. [1803], of co. Glouc., High Sheriff, co. Glouc., [1804 ?] Vol. XXII, fol. 311.
WATHEN to BAGHOTT, ...   Quarterly Arms, [1815] Vol. XXVIII, fol. 381.
WATKIN to PRICE, ..., of Wales, [1777] Vol. XIV, fol. 10.
WATKIN, Sir Edward, Bart. [12 May 1880], of co. Chester, 1880,* Vol. LXI, fol. 1.
     „   Thomas Morgan JOSEPH, Portcullis Pursuivant of Arms. [No reference, 1894 resumed by Roy. Lic. paternal surname of Watkin.]
WATKINS, [John Gregory ?], of Ombersley, co. Worc., [1841] Vol. XLV, fol. 154.
WATKINS to GRIFFITH, ... (minors), of Shropsh., and Wales, [1842 ?] Vol. XLV, fol. 343.
WATKINS before RICE, George, of Llwyn-y-brain, co. Carmarthen, Wales, 1865 [1866], Vol. LVI, fol. 89.
WATKINSON, Christopher, Mayor of Leeds, co. York, and of Hamburg, 8 July 1725, Vol. VII, fol. 289.
WATLINGTON after PERRY, ..., of co. Essex and Hertf., [1849] Vol. XLIX, fol. 141.
     „   after HOOPER, John, of Reading [? Berks.], [1852] Vol. L, fol. 223.
WATNEY, Daniel, of Wandsworth, Clapham and Mitcham, co. Surrey. Quartering GALPIN, 1832 [1833], Vol. XXXIX, fol. 290 ; [1870] Vol. LVII, fol. 216. (Crisp, I, p. 109.)
WATSON, Jonathan, of St. James', Westminster, J.P., of Hampsh. (s. of John, of Stone Raze, nr. Carlisle, co. Cumberland), 16 Dec. 1720, Vol. VII, fol. 41 ; Add. MS. 14,830, fol. 135.
WATSON-WENTWORTH, [Sir Thomas, K.B.], Baron MALTON [28 May 1728]. Supporters, 1728, Vol. VIII, fol. 7b.
WATSON, [Lewis Monson], Baron SONDES [2nd son of the 1st Baron] [assumed the name of Watson]. Supporters, 1760, Vol. X, fol. 242.
     „   John, s. of James, of Brookhill, co. Antrim, Ireland, 1767, Vol. XI, fol. 199. (Berry.)
WATSON, late WOOD, William, Henry (and Uncle George), of Holerood and Old Malton Abbey, co. York. (Match), [1803] Vol. XXII, fol. 273.
     „   late BAKER, Richard, of Malton Abbey, co. York, [1818 ?] Vol. XXX, fol. 310.
     „   late WOOD, John Webster, of Guillard's Oak, Midhurst, co. Sussex, and Holly Hall, Old Malton Abbey, co. York, [1839] Vol. XLIV, fol. 157.
     „   late NEWTON, William, of co. York, [1839] Vol. XLIV, fol. 180.
WATSON, Brook, of Kingston-upon-Hull, co. York, and East Sheen, co. Surrey (Barts.), [1804] Vol. XXII, fol. 363.
WATSON to BULLOCK, ..., Major of Militia, of co. Essex, [1810] Vol. XXV, fol. 328.
WATSON before TAYLOR, ..., of Wilts. Quarterly Arms, [1815] Vol. XXIX, fol. 93.
WATSON to MILLES, George John, 2nd s. of Baron SONDES (became 4th Baron), of co. Kent and Norf., 1820, Vol. XXXII, fol. 257.
     „   to FARSYDE, George James, of the Middle Temple, London, and co. York, [1826] Vol. XXXVI, fol. 105.
WATSON-SAMWELL, ..., of Upton, co. Northampton, [1831] Vol. XXXVIII, fol. 284.
WATSON, Lieut.-Gen. Sir James, K.C.B. [1839], of Windover, Bucks., [1840] Vol. XLIV, fol. 285.
     „   . . . ., of Beeston, co. Nottingham, [1852] Vol. L, fol. 173.
WATSON, late BROUGH, Robert, of co. York, [1854] Vol. LI, fol. 40.
WATSON, Thomas, M.D., of Thorpe, co. Essex, President of the Coll. of Physicians, Bart. [27 June 1866], [1866] Vol. LVI, fols. 121 and 126 * [?].

WATSON, John, of Bowdon, co. Chester, and Kidderminster, co. Worc. [? and] (Thomas Clemans Watson, of Holland Park, London), s. of John, s. of Joseph, s. of John, and to descendants of his uncle Richard, decd. 1876, Vol. LIX, fol. 292. (Berry's Suppl.)

„ William, Lord of Appeal. Arms, Lyon Register. [Baron Watson, of Thankerton, co. Lanark, and Edinburgh, Scotland, 28 April 1880, Life Peer, extinct 1899.] Supporters, 1880, Vol. LXI, fol. 49.

„ John William, of Eccleston Square, London (father of the next), 1889,* Vol. LXV, fol. 51.

WATSON-ARMSTRONG, W. H. A. F., of Craigside, Rothbury, co. Northumberland (son of John William), 1889, Vol. LXV, fol. 123.

WATSON, Sir H. E., of Shirecliffe Hall, Sheffield, co. York, 1882,* Vol. LXI, fol. 253. (Berry's Suppl.)

WATSON-COPLEY, Sir Charles, Bart. (died s.p.m. 6 April 1888), [12 Mar.] 188⅞, [1888] Vol. LXIV, fol. 163.

WATSON, James, of 2, Whitehall Court, London, and Rouen, France, 1893, Vol. LXVII, fol. 119.

WATT, ..., F.R.S., of Heathfield, Handsworth, co. Staff., and Aston Hall, co. Warw., [1826] Vol. XXXVI, fol. 113.

WATT after GIBSON, James, of Doldanlod, Llanyre, co. Radnor, Wales, [1856] Vol. LII, fol. 129. (Berry's Suppl.)

WATT-ORMSBY, ..., of Cheltenham, co. Glouc.; Bath, co. Somerset; and Dublin, [1832] Vol. XXXIX, fol. 40.

WATT, Richard, Capt., Dragoon Guards, of Bishop Burton, co. York, and Speke Hall and Childwall, co. Lanc., [1856] Vol. LII, fol. 109.

WATTS, ..., of Gower Street, London, and MORISON, his wife, of Newcastle-upon-Tyne, co. Northumberland, 1800-1802, Vol. XXI, fol. . . . . .

WATTS before RUSSELL, ..., of co. Staff. Quarterly Arms, [1817] Vol. XXX, fol. 143.

WATTS-RUSSELL (formerly BIRCH), Arthur Egerton, of Biggin Hall, Oundle, co. Northampton. Exemplification, Watts and Birch, 1898, Vol. LXX, fol. 190.

WATTS, ..., F.S.A., a Gent.-at-Arms, of London (? Francis, of Vincent Square, Westminster), [1843] Vol. XLVII, fol. 44.

„ Sir James, Knt. [30 June 1857, Mayor of Manchester], of Abney Hall, Cheadle, co. Chester, [1853 ?] Vol. L, fol. 302.

„ W. H., of Elm Hall, Wavertree, Liverpool, co. Lanc., 1894, Vol. LXVII, fol. 302.

WAUDBY, William, Lieut., Leinster Regt., s. of Major Sidney James Waudby, Bombay Native Infantry, 1898, Vol. LXX, fol. 221.

WAVENEY, Baron [10 April 1873, Sir Robert Alexando Shafto] (ADAIR), [2nd Bart.], of co. Suff. Supporters, [1873] Vol. LVIII, fol. 242.

WAY, ..., of Thame, co. Oxf., [1804 ?] Vol. XXII, fol. 326.

WAYET after SISSON, ..., of co. Linc., [1832] Vol. XXXIX, fol. 10.

WAYMOUTH, Henry, of Parker's Well, St. Leonard, co. Devon, 2 July 1799, Vol. XX, fol. 330 (see Berry's Suppl.).

WAYNE, William, of Duffield, co. Derby, and Warslow, co. Staff., 1782, Vol. XV, fol. 81.

WAYNE, late ROCKLIFFE, ..., of co. York, 1808, Vol. XXIV, fol. 370.

„ late HARRISON, ..., of co. York, 1808, Vol. XXV, fol. 49.

WEARING, J. W., of Lancaster, 1895,* Vol. LXVIII, fol. 292.

WEAVER, James, of Worcester, [1857] Vol. LII, fol. 261.

WEBB, Benjamin, of Bucklebury, Berks., 1766, Vol. XI, fol. 190. (Berry.)

WEBB, late SAUNDERS, James, of co. Dorset, and London, [1797] Vol. XIX, fol. 414.

WEBB, John, of co. Dorset, and London, [1797] Vol. XIX, fol. 416.

„ Frederick, of co. Dorset, and London, [1797] Vol. XIX, fol. 418.

„ . . . ., of Bath, co. Somerset, [1803] Vol. XXII, fol. 143.

WEBB before EDGE, ..., of co. Nottingham, [1803] Vol. XXII, fols. 258 and 260.

WEBB to CRANMER, Ann, of co. Essex. (Match), [1812] Vol. XXVII, fol. 287.

WEBB, Daniel, of Garnstone, co. Heref., [1845 ?] Vol. XLVII, fol. 354.

WEBB-PEPLOE, Daniel, [1845] Vol. XLVII, fol. 389.

,, -PEPLOE, John Birch, Vicar of Weobley, co. Hereford, [1866] Vol. LVI, fol. 132.

WEBB, ..., late Capt., J.P., D.L., of The Berrow, co. Worc., and Ledbury, co. Hereford, [1861 ?] Vol. LIV, fol. 90.

,, ..., of The Hough, Castle Church and Haselour, co. Staff., and for HORTON, his wife, [1861] Vol. LIV, fols. 162 and 163.

,, Capt. Charles Boyer (s. of Col. Charles John), of Elford House, Tamworth, co. Staff., 18 . . ., Vol. LXXI, fol. . . . .

WEBBE before WESTON, ..., of Sarnsfield Court, co. Heref. Quarterly Arms, [1782] Vol. XV, fol. 60.

WEBBE, late FRANCKLYN, ..., of co. Kent and Oxf., [1852] Vol. L, fol. 106.

WEBBER to SMITH, Capt., of London, [1804] Vol. XXII, fol. 434.

,, to OSMOND, ... (minor), natural s. of Peard Osmond, of co. Devon [1807] Vol. XXIV, fol. 244.

WEBBER, Georgiana, of Weston-super-Mare, co. Somerset, dau. of Edward [A. Webber], Rector of Bathialton, co. Somerset, to his two sons and others, 1877, Vol. LX, fol. 28.

WEBBER-GARDINER, Lieut.-Col. John, of Dinant, Brittany (Capt., 5th Dragoon Guards, 1880), 1880, Vol. LXI, fol. 14.

WEBLEY, [William Henry], Capt., R.N., of The Mead, Tyddenham, co. Glouc. Quarterly Arms, 1808-10] Vol. XXV, fol. . . . .

WEBLEY before PARRY, William Henry, C.B., Post-Capt., R.N., of Noyadd, co. Cardigan, Wales. Quarterly Arms, [1815] Vol. XXIX, fol. 198.

WEBLEY-PARRY-PRYSE, E. J., of Noyadd, Trefawr, co. Cardigan, Wales, 1893, Vol. LXVII, fol. 129.

WEBSTER, Sir Thomas, Bart., 10 Nov. 1720, Vol. VII, fol. 30.

WEBSTER, late WEDDERBURN, ..., of Scotland, [1790] Vol. XVII, fol. 196.

,, late GRAHAM, ..., of Meathie and Balmure, co. Forfar, Scotland, [1816] Vol. XXX, fol. 65.

WEDDELL, late ROBINSON, [Thomas Philip, 3rd] Baron GRANTHAM, of co. York, [7 May 1803], Vol. XXII, fol. 234.

WEDDERBURN, [Alexander], Baron LOUGHBOROUGH [14 June 1780], [Lord Chief Justice Common Pleas]. Supporters, [1780] Vol. XIV, fol. 225.

WEDDERBURN to WEBSTER, ..., of Scotland, [1790] Vol. XVII, fol. 196.

,, to COLVILE, Alex, ? Andrew, of Scotland, [1814] Vol. XXVIII, fol. 151.

WEDDERBURN, heretofore GRAHAM, ..., of Scotland, [1829] Vol. XXXVII, fol. 348.

WEEKES, ... (see TIMPSON), of Kilkenny, Ireland, [1767] Vol. XI, fol. 260.

WEELEY, late MARCH, ..., of co. Essex, [1796] Vol. XIX, fol. 317.

WEGG-PROSSER, late HAGGETT, Francis Richard, of co. Oxf., and Wales, 1849, Vol. XLIX, fol. 200.

WEIR, John, [of St. Anne's, Soho], London, [a Lieut., 43rd Regt. of Foot], s. of Alexander, of Monaghan, Devenish, co. Fermanagh, Ireland, [24 April] May, 1779, (certified), Vol. XIV, fol. 133 [see Grazebrook, Her. of Worc., p. 615].

WEISS, Henry Ravensbury, of Edgbaston, Birmingham, co. Warw., 1888, Vol. LXIV, fol. 280.

WELBANK, ..., of Cowton, co. York, and London, [1808] Vol. XXIV, fol. 396.

WELBY-GREGORY, [Sir Glynne Earle, 3rd] Bart., of co. Linc. [Roy. Lic, 5 July 1861.] Quarterly Arms, [1861] Vol. LIV, fol. 178.

WELBY after GREGORY, ..., of co. Linc., [1875] Vol. LIX, fol. 163.

WELBY before GREGORY, ..., of co. Linc., [1876] Vol. LIX, fol. 178.

WELBY, Baron [Sir Reginald Earle Welby, G.C.B., &c.]. Supporters, 1894, Vol. LXVIII, fol. 85.

WELCH, ..., of Brunswick Square, Brighton, co. Sussex, 1861, Vol. LIV, fol. 94.

WELCH-THORNTON, 1. Alfred Bedwell; 2. Henry Samuel; of Springfield, co. Sussex, 1861, Vol. XIV [LIV], fol. 116.

WELCHMAN, John, C.B., Col., Bengal S.C., 13 Aug. 1858, Vol. LIII, fol. 2.

„ George (s. of William), of Cullompton, co. Devon, 1898, Vol. LXX, fol. 227.

„ William (s. of William Longman Welchman), of Upwell, Wisbech, co. Camb., 1898, Vol. LXX, fol. 170.

WELD before FORRESTER, ..., M.P., of Shropsh. Quarterly Arms, [1811] Vol. XXVI, fol. 375.

WELD, Samuel (s. of William), of Twickenham, co. Middx., and Kinnerton-in-Hawarden, co. Flint, Wales, [1842] Vol. XLVI, fol. 116.

WELD-BLUNDELL, ..., of Lulworth, co. Dorset, and Ince Blundell, co. Lanc., [1843] Vol. XLVI, fol. 278.

WELD, Sir F. A., G.C.B. [G.C.M.G., 6 June 1885], of Lulworth, co. Dorset (died 1891). Supporters, [1885] Vol. LXIII. fol. 95.

WELDON, William Henry, Norroy King of Arms, 1891, Vol. LXVI, fol. 241. (Crisp, III, p. 40.) [See Crisp, XVI, Additions and Corrections, p. xlviii.]

WELFIT, ..., of Manby, co. Line., [1808] Vol. XXIV, fol. 318.

WELFITT, late NEED, ... of co. Nottingham, [1843] Vol. XLVII, fol. 141.

WELLBELOVED to SCOTT, Robert, of co. Staff. and Stourbridge, co. Worc., [1830] Vol. XXXVIII, fol. 98.

WELLDALE to KNOLLYS, ..., of Berks., [1794] Vol. XVIII, fol. 335.

WELLER, Jane, dau. [and sole h.] of John Badger Weller, and wife of Sir Thomas Spencer WILSON, [6th] Bart., 1785-8 [1788], Vol. XVI, fol. 333.

„ Rev. James, D.D., of East Clandon and Guildford (St. Mary), co. Surrey, 29 April 1803, Vol. XXII, fol. 140.

WELLESLEY, Marquis, 1790 [2 Dec. 1799, Richard Cowley-Wellesley]. Alterations, Supporters, Augmentation, [1804 ?] Vol. XXII, fols. 333 and 335 ; [1815] Vol. XXIX, fol. 30.

„ Marquis, K.G. [Richard]. Additional Crest, [1840] Vol. XLIV, fols. 382 and 384.

„ Maj.-Gen. Sir Arthur, K.B. [1804-5]. Supporters, [1806] Vol. XXIII, fol. 337. [Afterwards Duke of Wellington, see.]

„ [The Rt. Hon.] Sir Henry, K.B. [10 Mar. 1912], Amb. in Spain. Supporters, 15 May 1812 [1811], Vol. XXVII, fol. 3 [?].

„ Sir Henry, now Baron COWLEY [Baron, 1828]. Supporters, [1830] Vol. XXXVIII, fol. 157.

WELLESLEY after LONG, POLE and TYLNEY [14 Jan. 1812, William, 4th Earl of Mornington]. Quarterly Arms, [1812] Vol. XXVII, fol. 178.

WELLESLEY, ..., wife of LITTLETON, reputed dau. of Marquis of Wellesley, [1812] Vol. XXVII, fol. 261.

WELLINGTON, Marquis of, Lieut.-Gen. Arthur, K.B. Augmentation, [1812] Vol. XXVII, fol. 207 ; [1814] Vol. XXVIII, fol. 112 ; K.G. [1813] and Duke [1814] ; Supporters, [1855] Vol. LI, fol. 290 [? wrong reference, he died 14 Sept. 1852].

WELLS, ..., of Bickley and Redleaf, co. Kent, [1811] Vol. XXVII, fol. 48.

„ Adm. Sir John, G.C.B. [1834], of Butler's Green, co. Sussex, [1821] Vol. XXXII, fol. 291. ? Supporters, [1834] Vol. XL, fol. 274.

„ Rev. Samuel, Rector of Portlemouth, co. Devon, of East Lillington, co. Devon, [1838] Vol. XLIII, fol. 249 (see Fortescue, of Winston, in Landed Gentry).

„ Warwick [? Warrick Walter], M.R.C.S., Assistant Surgeon B.C.S., of Minehead, co. Somerset, [1852] Vol. L, fol. 221 [see Burke].

„ . . . ., of Kupon Hall, [1853] Vol. L, fol. 418.

WELLS-DYMOKE, ..., of Berks., [1867 ?] Vol. LVI, fol. 184.

WELLS, Edward, of Wallingford, Berks., 1890,* Vol. LXV, fol. 269.

WELLS, Sir Spencer, Bart., of London, 1883,* Vol. LXII, fol. 79.

WELMAN, ..., of Poundisford, co. Somerset. (*See* HAWKER.) [1836], Vol. XLI, fol. 275. (Crisp, III, p. 33.)

WELSH, late WILLIAMS, ..., Sea Captain, [1812] Vol. XXVII, fol. 176.

WENDY, ... (*see* WHISH), of co. Camb. Match, [1776] Vol. XIII, fol. 243.

WENLEY, James Adams, of Glasgow, and Java, and his brother Robert Mark, of Chelmsford, co. Essex, 1874, Vol. LIX, fol. 42.

WENLOCK, Baron [13 May 1839] (THOMPSON), of Shropsh. Supporters, [1839] Vol. XLIV, fol. 19.

   „   Baron (LAWLEY before THOMPSON) [1 June 1839], of Shropsh., [1839] Vol. XLIV, fol. 25.

WENLOCK to MYTTON (Spr.), illeg., of Cleobury, North Mortimer, Shropsh., [1865] Vol. LVI, fol. 44.

WENMAN, Baroness [3 June 1834] ([Sophia Elizabeth] WYKEHAM), of co. Oxf., [1834] Vol. XL, fol. 177.

WENSLEYDALE, Baron [23 July 1856] (PARKE), of co. Westmorland, [1856] Vol. LI, fol. 442. Supporters, fol. 444.

WENTWORTH, Sir Thomas WATSON-, K.B. [1725] [afterwards 1st Marquess of Rockingham]. Supporters, [1725] Vol. VII, fol. 496.

   „   WATSON-, Thomas, Lord WENTWORTH [?]. Supporters, 1728 [1741], Vol. IX, fol. 38. [Baron Malton, 28 May 1728, Vol. VIII, fol. 7ᵇ. (*See* MALTON.).]

   „   . . . ., of Woolley, co. York. (*See* HINCKLIFFE.) [1741 ?] Vol. IX, fol. 38.

WENTWORTH, late ARMYTAGE, Godfrey Wentworth, of Woolley, co. York, [1788] Vol. XVII, fol. 111.

WENTWORTH, John, Lieut.-Gov. of Nova Scotia [1792, afterwards Bart., 16 May 1795], [1795] Vol. XIX, fol. 115; (*see* 16 . . ., Vol. II, fol. 328.

WENTWORTH after VERNON, Frederick William Thomas (minor), of co. Staff. Quarterly Arms, [1804] Vol. XXIII, fol. 77.

WENTWORTH to BLACKETT, Sir Thomas, of co. York, [1810] Vol. XXV, fol. 392. [? Reference to Sir Thomas Wentworth, afterwards, 1777, Blackett, Bart., d. unmar. 10 July 1792. G.E.C. Complete Baronetage.]

WENTWORTH, Diana, nat. dau. of Sir Thomas, and wife of BEAUMONT, of co. York, [1810] Vol. XXV, fol. 392 [*see* BEAUMONT].

   „   William, Earl FITZWILLIAM, of co. York, 1807 [Wentworth before Fitzwilliam, Roy. Lic., 7 Dec. 1807, this would be Vol. XXIV, fol. 297 ?], Vol. XXVI, fol. 296 [would be 1811].

WENTWORTH-FITZWILLIAM, Charles William, Earl Fitzwilliam, of co. York. [Roy. Lic., 20 Aug. 1856, confirmation of the name of Wentworth before Fitzwilliam.] 1856, Vol. LII, fol. 70.

WENTWORTH, Viscount, of Wellisborough, co. Leic., and Nettlestead, co. Suff., [1815] Vol. XXIX, fol. 1.

WENTWORTH to STANLEY, Sidney, of co. Camb., [1856] Vol. LII, fol. 66.

WEST, Charles, Dr. Phys., of Iver, Bucks., and St. Margaret's, Westminster, 15 April 1732, Vol. VIII, fol. 130; Add. MS. 14,830, fol. 63.

   „   James, of Alscot, co. Warw. [co. Glouc. ?], 12 Dec. 1768, Vol. XI, fol. 334. (Crisp, VI, p. 54, and Berry.)

WEST after SACKVILLE, [George John], [Roy. Lic., 30 Nov. 1843; 5th] Earl DE LA WARR, of co. Sussex. [Arms, quarterly West and Sackville.] [1843] Vol. XLVI, fol. 403.

WEST, [Elizabeth], Baroness BUCKHURST [27 April 1864] [widow of the last-named]. Supporters, [1864] Vol. LV, fol. 184.

   „   (SACKVILLE-) to SACKVILLE only, [Reginald Windsor], [2nd] Baron BUCK-HURST, [1871] Vol. LVII, fol. 330. Supporters, [1876] Vol. LIX, fol. 288.

WESTBURY, Baron [1861] (BETHELL), of Wilts. [Lord Chancellor], [1861] Vol. LIV, fol. 170. Supporters, fol. 172.

WESTERMAN, ..., of Castle Grove, Sandall Magna, co. York, [1849] Vol. XLIX, fol. 168.

WESTERN, Baron [1833, Charles Callis Western], of Rivenhall, co. Essex, [1833] Vol. XXXIX, fol. 264.

WESTHEAD, Joshua Proctor (and CHAPPEL, his wife), of York House, Manchester, and Ulverston, co. Lanc., [1844 or 1845] Vol. XLVII, fols. 338 and 339.

WESTHEAD after BROWN [31 Jan. 1850], Joshua Proctor, M.P., of Manchester ; London ; and Lea Castle, Wolverley, co. Worc., [1850] Vol. XLIX, fol. 281.

WESTMACOTT, Sir Richard, R.A., of South Audley Street, London, [1829] Vol. XXXVII, fol. 370.

WESTMINSTER, Marquis of. Augmentation, Westminster Arms, 27 Jan. 1832, Vol. XXXIX, fol. 1.

„ [City of, Roy. Lic., 6 Nov. 1901 ; Re-grant, 6 Feb. 1902 ; Crest, 24 Oct. 1902 ; Supporters, 27 Oct. 1902. (Geneal. Mag., VIII, pp. 30 and 31.)].

WESTON, Stephen, Bp. of Exeter, 14 May 1725, Vol. VII, fol. 298.

WESTON after WEBBE, John, of co. Hereford, [1782] Vol. XV, fol. 60.

WESTON (-WEST), ..., of Countesbury, co. Devon, [1817] Vol. XXX, fol. 273.

WESTON, Sir Joseph D., Mayor of Bristol, of Dorset House, Clifton, Bristol, 1883,² Vol. LXII, fol. 147. (Berry's Suppl.)

WETENHALL to MAINWARING, ..., of co. Chester, [1797] Vol. XIX, fol. 404.

WETENHALL, late TOMKINSON, Edward, of co. Chester, 31 Mar. 1800, Vol. XX, fol. 445 ; 1800, Vol. XXI, fol. 3.

WETHERED, Thomas (and Sarah BADGER), of Marlow, Bucks., [1834] Vol. XL, fol. 247.

WETHERELL to FAWSITT, ..., of Drewton, Hunsley, par. of Rowley, co. York, [1831] Vol. XXXVIII, fol. 242.

WETHERILL, ..., of Peckham, co. Surrey, [1821] Vol. XXXII, fol. 337.

WETHEY, ..., of Honiton, co. Devon, [1867] Vol. LVI, fol. 252.

WHADCOCK, Humphrey, of Buckley Place, co. Warw., 1699, Vol. IV, fol. 291 (of Curley-Piddocke), [1730 ?] Vol. VIII, fol. 73ᵇ.

WHALE, Maj. John, Knt. [4 Jan. 1829, of North Down House, co. Kent], of Margate, co. Kent, [1829] Vol. XXXVII, fol. 245.

WHALLEY before GARDINER [Roy. Lic., 11 Nov. 1779], John [Whalley], of co. Lanc., [1779] Vol. XIV, fol. 181.

WHALLEY to SMYTHE-GARDINER, [18 Nov. 1797, James Whalley, 2nd] Bart. Quarterly Arms, [1797] Vol. XX, fol. 112.

WHALLEY-TOOKER, Hyde S., of Norton Hall and Hinton House, co. Somerset, 1836, Vol. XLII, fols. 21 and 34.

WHARNCLIFFE, Baron [12 July 1826], MACKENZIE after STUART-WORTLEY-[17 June 1826]. Quarterly and Supporters, [1826] Vol. XXXVI, fols. 37 and 41. Mackenzie quartering, 1880, Vol. LXI, fol. 87. [Edward, 3rd Baron and then Earl of Wharncliffe, took, by Roy. Lic., 18 Oct. 1880, the name of Montague in addition to and before Stuart-Wortley-Mackenzie.]

WHARTON, late STEVENSON, John Hall, of co. York, 1788, Vol. XVI, fol. 405.

„ late HALL, William, of co. York, [1808] Vol. XXIV, fol. 342.

„ late HALL, Maj.-Gen. James, [1808] Vol. XXIV, fol. 344 (died s.p.).

WHATELY to HALSEY, ..., of co. Hertf., [1805] Vol XXIII, fol. 190.

„ to PYDDOKE, ..., M.A., of co. Glouc. and Staff., [1847] Vol. XLVIII, fol. 375.

WHEATLEY, Maj.-Gen. Sir Henry, G.C.H. [1834], Keeper of the Privy Purse, of Erith, co. Kent, [1847 ?] Vol. XLVIII, fol. 248.

WHEBLE, ..., of Winchester, Hampsh., and Kensington, co. Middx., [1790] Vol. XVII, fol. 278.

WHEELER, ..., of Piggotts, co. Hertf., and Gloucester Place, London, [1820] Vol. XXXII, fol. 225.

WHEELER to RAY, Herbert Reginald (minor), of Hyde Park Gardens, London, 4 June 1864, Vol. LV, fol. 190.

WHEELER, Rev. W. C., of Ridgeway Gardens, Wimbledon, co. Surrey, and Southborough, Tunbridge Wells, co. Kent, 1895, Vol. LXVIII, fol. 316.

WHEELTON, John, of Myddleton Square, London, and Manchester, [1839] Vol. XLIV, fol. 81 (see Burke).

WHEELWRIGHT, ..., son of HOYLE, of Heathfield, Halifax, co. York, [1860] Vol. LIII, fol. 354.

„ Joseph, of Nevill Park, Tunbridge Wells, co. Kent, 1891, Vol. LXVI, fol. 82.

WHELAN, ... (and NEEP, his wife), of Harendon House, Tenterden, co. Kent, [1840] Vol. XLIV, fols. 264 and 265.

WHELER, late MEDHURST, ..., of co. Kent and York, [1843] Vol. XLVII, fol. 14.

WHEWELL, William, B.D., of Lancaster and Master, Trinity Coll., Camb., [1842 ?] Vol. XLV, fol. 351.

„ Thomas, of Wyvillstead, Langho, Billington, co. Lanc. (and Sussex ?), 1896, Vol. LXIX, fol. 156.

WHIELDON, ..., of Coton Hall and Fenton Hall, co. Staff., and Springfield House, Bedworth, co. Warw., [1829] Vol. XXXVIII, fol. 29.

WHINNERAY, Edward (4th s. of James), of Hoylake, co. Chester, 18 . . ., Vol. LXXI, fol. . . . .

WHINYATES, Maj.-Gen. F. William, of Cheltenham, co. Glouc., [1873] Vol. LVIII, fol. 250.

WHISH, Martin, of Westminster, and co. Camb., 25 Nov. 1776, Vol. XIII, fol. 243.

WHISTON, Sarah, dau of John. See CONANT.

WHITAKER, Joseph, of Hedley Hall, Harworth, co. Nottingham ; West Ardsley, co. York ; and Palermo, Italy, [1865] Vol. LV, fol. 350.

„ . . . ., of Royle Sands, Rochdale, co. Lanc., [1871] Vol. LVII, fol. 304.

WHITBURN, C. J. Soper, of Shirley Lodge, Clapham, co. Surrey, and Addington Park, West Malling, co. Kent, 1884,* Vol. LXII, fol. 208. (Berry's Suppl.)

WHITE John, s. of John, of Romsey and Hursley, Hampsh., 1750, Vol. IX, fol. 360. (Berry.)

WHITE to THOMAS (formerly Thomas ?), ..., of Chichester, co. Sussex, [1777 ?] Vol. XIV, fol. 12.

WHITE, ... (MARSH, wife of), of Brasted, co. Kent, and Brightwell, co. Oxf. Quartering with DYMOCK, and escutcheon of pretence, [1786] Vol. XVI, fol. 119.

WHITE before JERVIS, ..., of co. Staff., and Ireland. Quarterly Arms, [1793] Vol. XVIII, fol. 279.

WHITE, Thomas Woolaston, Bart., of Tuxford, co. Nottingham, and Wallingwells, co. York. Quartering, and BLAGG impalement, [1804] Vol. XXII, fol. 380.

„ Richard Samuel, of Lincoln's Inn, London, s. of Richard, decd., and to HAGGIS, &c., [1796 ?] Vol. XIX, fol. 342.

„ . . . ., of London, and Duckworth Plantations, co. Surrey, in Jamaica, [1809 ?] Vol. XXV, fol. 69.

WHITE before WILLIAMS, ..., of Duckworth Plantations, co. Surrey, in Jamaica, [1809 ?] Vol. XXV, fol. 72.

WHITE, ..., of Sutton Hall, co. Chester, [1810] Vol. XXVI, fol. 84.

„ Maj.-Gen. Sir Henry, K.C.B. [7 April, 1815], E.I.C.S., [1815] Vol. XXVIII, fol. 391.

„ Vice-Adm. Sir John Chambers, K.C.B. [29 June 1841], [1841] Vol. XLV, fol. 227.

„ John, of Lime Street, London, and Leighton Buzzard, co. Bedf., [1839] Vol. XLIV, fol. 152.

„ Charles Scarborow, of Montagu Place, London, [1821] Vol. XXXII, fol. 271.

WHITE after SCARBOROW, C. S., of Montagu Place, London, [1837] Vol. XLII, fol. 163.

WHITE, late DRIVER, Samuel White ?, of Godalming, co. Surrey, 1835, Vol. XL, fol. 389.

WHITE, John Ludford, F.R.C.S., of Wales, [1857] Vol. LII, fol. 298.

WHITE-POPHAM, Francis, of Hampsh., [1853 ?] Vol. L, fol. 271.

WHITE, [Henry], Baron ANNALY [19 Aug. 1863], of Ireland. Supporters, [1863] Vol. LV, fol. 128.

„ . . . ., of Swanscombe and Blackhall, co. Kent, [1865] Vol. LV, fol. 280.

WHITE-THOMSON, Col. R. T., of Broomford Manor, Exbourne, co. Devon, 1894, Vol. LXVIII, fol. 5.

WHITEFORD, Joseph, J.P., of Plymouth, co. Devon, grandson of Joseph, confirmed 31 Mar. 1840, Vol. XLIV, fol. . . . . (see Misc. G. et H., 2nd S., II, p. 265).

WHITEHEAD, Maj.-Gen. Sir Thomas, K.C.B. [20 July 1838, E.I.C.S.], of Uplands, co. Lanc., [1838] Vol. XLIII, fol. 245.

„ (TAYLOR-), Smith, of co. Derby, [1873] Vol. LVIII, fol. 200. (Berry's Suppl.)

„ Sir James, Bart. [1889], of co. Kent, 1888, Vol. LXIV, fol. 242.

WHITEHURST, Rev. Thomas, of Icklefield, co. Hertf., [1778] Vol. XIV, fol. 37.

WHITELOCK to HUGHES, ..., of co. Hertf. Match, [1795] Vol. XIX, fol. 95.

WHITFELD, late CLARKE, Lancelot Clarke ?, of Emanuel Coll., Camb., and co. Hertford and Wilts., [1814] Vol. XXVIII, fol. 105.

WHITGREAVE, George Thomas, of Moseley Court, co. Staff. Augmentation, 1838, Vol. XLII, fol. 312.

WHITLE, Lieut.-Col. Robert, of Whalley Abbey, co. Lanc., [1850] Vol. XLIX, fol. 397.

WHITLEY-DUNDAS, late DEANS, ..., Capt., R.N., of Berks., Wales, and Scotland. Quarterly Arms, [1808] Vol. XXIV, fol. 438.

WHITLEY to RODBARD, ..., [1843] Vol. XLVII, fols. 162 and 163.

WHITLOCK, Maj.-Gen. Sir George Cornish, K.C.B. [1859], [1863] Vol. LV, fol. 110.

WHITLOW, ... (see GREAVES-BANNING), [1865] Vol. LVI, fol. 48.

WHITMARSH, ..., of Trull, co. Somerset, [1788] Vol. XVI, fol. 403.

WHITMORE, Sir Thomas, K.B. [28 May 1744], of Apley, Shropsh., [1744 ?] Vol. IX, fol. 116.

„ William and Martin, of Epsom, co. Surrey. (Match), [1816] Vol. XXIX, fol. 276. (Match, TOOTING, [1817] Vol. XXX, fol. 111.)

WHITMORE-JONES, ..., of Chastleton, co. Oxf., [1829] Vol. XXXVII, fol. 346.

WHITMORE (WOLRYCHE-), late LAING, Rev. Francis Henry, M.A., of Shropsh. and co. Glouc., 1864, Vol. LV, fol. 270.

WHITSHED, Adm. Sir James Hawkins [K.C.B. 1815, G.C.B. 1830], Bart. [1834], of co. Wicklow and Dublin, Ireland. Supporters, [1834] Vol. XL, fol. 197, and to descend with the Baronetcy, [1834] Vol. XL, fol. 208.

WHITTAKER, Robert, of Prospect Hill, Walton-le-Dale, co. Lanc., 1890, Vol. LXV, fol. 299.

„ John, of Leyland, Preston, co. Lanc., and wife Margaret, dau. of John ASH-WORTH, of Rosehill, Bolton-le-Moors, co. Lanc., 1897, Vol. LXX, fol. 32.

WHITTAL, Charlton, of Smyrna and Constantinople, [1855] Vol. LI, fol. 377.

WHITTING, ..., of Manea and Thorney, Isle of Ely, co. Camb., [1843] Vol. XLVII, fol. 149.

„ . . . ., of Sandcroft and Uphill, co. Somerset, [1858] Vol. LIII, fol. 38.

WHITTINGHAM, Col. Samuel Ford, Knt. [1815], of Wales, [1815] Vol. XXVIII, fol. 433. (Berry.)

„ Rev. Samuel, D.D., of Polton, co. Bedf., Fellow of Clare Coll., Oxf., [1833] Vol. XL, fol. 37.

WHITTINGSTALL after FEARNLEY, ..., of Watford, co. Hertf., [1825] Vol. XXXV, fol. 168.

WHITTLE, Elizabeth, Lady Fox, of co. Lanc., 13 Sept. 1688, Vol. IV, fol. 15.
  ,, Elizabeth, Lady Fox, of co. Lanc., (altered) [? confirmed] 24 May 1694, Vol.
      IV, fol. 164. Match, fol. 165. (Berry.)
WHITWORTH, Sir Charles, K.B. [1793] (Ambassador to Russia) [afterwards
      Earl Whitworth, died s.p.]. Supporters, [1795] Vol. XVIII, fol. 440;
      [fol. 240 is 1793].
WHITWORTH after HURST, ..., of co. Linc., [1822] Vol. XXXIII, fol. 270.
WHITWORTH before AYLMER, Lieut.-Gen. Matthew, [5th] Lord Aylmer [and
      Baron of Balrath], [1825] Vol. XXXV, fol. 307.
WHITWORTH, Sir Joseph, D.C.L. [Bart., Oct. 1869], of Rusholme, co. Lanc., and
      Stancliffe, Darley, co. Derby, [1869] Vol. LVII, fol. 167.
WHORWOOD, James, Windsor Herald of Arms, 4th s. of William, late of Holton,
      co. Oxf., Sheriff of co. Oxf., confirmed 14 Feb. 17$\frac{99}{30}$, Vol. VIII, fol. 63
      (see Misc. G. et H., N. S., IV, p. 49).
WHYTE to MOYSER, ..., of co. Devon, [1815] Vol. XXIX, fol. 27.
WICKES, E. C., of Effra Road, Brixton, co. Surrey, 1890,* Vol. LXV, fol. 293.
WICKEY, ..., of Barnstaple, co. Devon. (Match), [1783] Vol. XV, fol. 213.
WICKHAM, ..., of Charlton House, co. Somerset. (See TOTTON.) [1811]
      Vol. XXVI, fol. 259.
WICKINS to OSBALDESTON, George, s. of John, of co. York and Sussex, 1771,
      Vol. XII, fol. 47.
WICKSTED, late TOLLET, Charles [Thomas ?], of co. Chester and Staff. (Match),
      [25 Mar.] 1814, Vol. XXVIII, fol. 118.
WIDDOWSON to CHESHIRE, John, of co. Chester, [1818] Vol. XXX, fol. 341.
WIDDRINGTON, late JACSON, S. H., of co. Chester, [1856] Vol. LI, fol. 446.
WIGAN, Frederick, s. John and cousins Henry and Alfred, of Clare Lawn,
      Mortlake, co. Surrey, and Clare House, East Malling, co. Kent. (See
      also GRAHAM.) 1874, Vol. LIX, fol. 34. (Berry's Suppl.)
WIGGETT, William, of Gestwick, co. Norf., 1755, Vol. X, fol. 25. (Berry.)
  ,, Rev. James, M.A., of co. Norf., Vicar of Crudwell and Rector of Hankerton,
      Wilts., 1827, Vol. XXXVI, fol. 199.
WIGGETT-CHUTE, William Lyde, of the Middle Temple, London; Pickenham,
      co. Norf.; and Crudwell and Hankerton, Wilts., 1827, Vol. XXXVI,
      fol. 201.
WIGGIN, ..., of Bromfield, co. Warw., [1797] Vol. XX, fol. 105.
  ,, Sir W. H., Bart., of co. Warw., and Wales, 1892,* Vol. LXVI, fol. 326.
WIGGINS, Capt. Arthur, of Christchurch, Hampsh., 1896, Vol. LXIX, fol. 160.
WIGHT to SCHANK, ..., of co. Devon, [1843] Vol. XLVI, fol 343.
WIGHT-BOYCOTT, ..., C.B., of Rudge Hall, Shropsh., 1886, Vol. LXIII,
      fol. 311.
WIGLEY, Sir Edward, Knt., of Scraptoft, co. Leic. Match, 1689, Vol. IV, fol. 55.
  ,, [Surname and Arms of] GRESWOLDE, Capt. Edmund MEYSEY, of Malvern
      Hall, Solihull, co. Warw., and Shakenhurst, co. Worc. (died [1833] s.p.),
      [1829] Vol. XXXVIII, fol. 13.
WIGLEY to GRESWOLDE, Henry, 1833, Vol. XXXIX, fol. 245.
WIGRAM, Robert, M.P., of Walthamstow, co. Essex, [1805] Vol. XXIII, fol. 268.
WIGSELL, late TAYLOR, ... (minor), of co. Surrey, [1807] Vol. XXIV,
      fol. 125.
WILBRAHAM after BOOTLE, ..., of co. Chester and Lanc. Quarterly Arms,
      [1814] Vol. XXVIII, fol. 215.
WILBRAHAM (BOOTLE-), ..., Baron SKELMERSDALE [30 Jan. 1828]. Sup-
      porters, [1828] Vol. XXXVII, fol. 35.
WILBRAHAM, George Barrington Baker, 3rd. s. of Sir George Baker, of Loventor,
      co. Devon, 3rd Bart., 18 . . ., Vol. LXXI, fol. . . . .
WILBY, Col. . . . ., [1865] Vol. LV, fol. 320.
WILCOCKS, late LODGE, of Berks., [1798] Vol. XX, fol. 187.
WILCOCKS to TREFFRY, ..., of co. Cornw. (M.A., Lincoln Coll., Oxf.), [1850]
      Vol. XLIX, fol. 334.

WILCOX, ..., of Pembury, co. Kent, [1838] Vol. XLIII, fol. 330.
WILCOXON, ..., of Peckham Rye, co. Surrey, and London, [1839] Vol. XLIV, fol. 166.
WILD, ..., of London, [1803] Vol. XXII, fol. 232.
„ . . . ., of Strellet House, East Peckham, co. Kent, [1859?] Vol. LIII, fol. 270.
WILD (BAGNALL-), late KIRBY, Ralph (B.A., Camb.), of Costock, co. Nottingham, and Inner Temple, London, [1868] Vol. LVII, fol. 88.
WILDE, Baron TRURO [1850, Charles Robert Claude Wilde], of Saffron Walden, co. Essex, and Bowes, co. Middx. Arms, [1850] Vol. XLIX, fol. 363. Supporters, fol. 365.
„ Baron PENZANCE [6 April 1869, James Plaisted Wilde], of co. Cornw. Supporters, [1869] Vol. LVII, fol. 137.
„ . . . ., of Long Whatton, co. Leic. (Edmondson's Armory and Berry), quartering to Charles TOWNLEY, York Herald, and to Rev. James Townley, 4 July 1743, Vol. IX, fol. 87.
WILDER, John, of Nunhide, Sulham, Berks., [25 Feb. 1766] Vol. XI, fol. 141. (Berry, and Crisp, II, p. 127.) [Crisp, Notes, IV, p. 111.]
WILDMAN, Thomas and James, of Hornby, co. Lanc.; Jamaica; and Lincoln's Inn, London, 9 Dec. 1776, Vol. XIII, fol. 247.
„ Capt., of co. (Kent?), and Arms of OLIVER (his wife) impaled, [1818] Vol. XXXI, fol. 55.
„ Lieut.-Col. . . . ., of co. Kent?, and Arms of PREISIG (his wife) impaled, [1824] Vol. XXXIV, fol. 321.
WILDMAN-LUSHINGTON, ..., of co. Kent, [1870] Vol. LVII, fol. 234.
WILES, Charles B., of Attleborough, co. Norf., 1881,* Vol. LXI, fol. 120. (Berry's Suppl.)
WILFORD, ..., of Boston, co. Linc., [1813] Vol. XXVII, fol. 450.
„ Capt., Roy. Artillery, [1818?] Vol. XXX, fol. 314.
WILKES, late FISKE, Rev. Robert, M.A., Rector of Wendon Lofts and Vicar of Elendon, co. Essex, [1858] Vol. LII, fol. 346 [see Burke].
WILKES, ..., of co. Worc., and Hall Green, Yardley, [co. Warw.?], [1866] Vol. LVI, fol. 156.
WILKIE, Patrick, of St. Vincent, West Indies, 15 Sept. 1770, Vol. XII, fol. 30. (Berry.)
„ . . . ., of Edinburgh, [1811] Vol. XXVI, fol. 169.
WILKIE after ALLEN, of co. Northumberland. Quarterly Arms, [1812] Vol. XXVII, fol. 220.
WILKIE to CROSBY, ..., of Newcastle-upon-Tyne, co. Northumberland; London; and Chester Place, St. Mary, Lambeth, Surrey, [1821] Vol. XXXII, fol. 339.
WILKIE, Sir David (portrait painter), of London, and Cults, co. Fife, Scotland. Arms and Augmentation, [1837] Vol. XLII, fol. 121.
WILKIESON, Thomas, s. of Charles, of Boroughbridge, co. York; Melrose, co. Roxburgh, Scotland; Amsterdam; and London, [1779] Vol. XIV, fol. 163.
WILKINS. Augmentation to Augusta Catherine Margaret, widow of Joseph ARNO. Match with HAYWARD, of Maeslough, co. Radnor, Wales. Name and Arms of Hayward for herself and issue, [1811] Vol. XXVI, fol. 294.
„ Walter, of co. Radnor, Wales. HAYWARD Crest for maternal grandmother; Crest of Wilkins separately (see Notes) [there are no Notes], [1821] Vol. XXXII, fols. 387 and 391.
„ (HAYWARD), Walter (a minor), of Castle Hay and Llanigan, Brecon, Wales, s. of Rev. Walter Wilkins next named, [1835] Vol. XL, fol. 362.
„ Rev. Walter, s. of Jeffreys, Vicar of Llanegan [co. Carnarvon], Prebend. of Brecon, 1835, Vol. XL, fol. 350.
„ . . . ., of Frocester, co. Glouc. (Edmondson's Armory and Berry), and quartering to BIGLAND, 1759.

WILKINS-LEIR, Rev. E. P., of Weston, co. Somerset, 1881, Vol. LXI, fol. 247.
WILKINSON to LINDLEY, ..., of Blackwall, co. Derby, and Skegley, co. Nottingham, [1782 ?] Vol. XV, fol. 121.
„ to DENISON, John, of Lothbury, London, [1785] Vol. XVI, fol. 25.
„ to MONTAGU (widow Montagu), [1798] Vol. XX, fol. 202.
WILKINSON, ..., of London, and Crosby Ravensworth, co. Westmorland, [1800 ?] Vol. XXI, fol. 110.
WILKINSON, late GREEN, ... (minor), of London. Quarterly Arms, [1805] Vol. XXIII, fol. 265.
„ late LEWIS, nat. children of John Wilkinson, of Castlehead, co. Lanc.; Mary Anne, [1808] Vol. XXV, fol. 18; Johanna, [1808] Vol. XXV, fol. 20; John, [1808] Vol. XXV, fol. 22; [1809] fol. 195.
WILKINSON, William (s. of James), of Norton, co. Durham, and Stainton-in-Cleveland, co. York, [1818] Vol. XXX, fol. 414.
WILKINSON to STEPHENS, ..., Rear-Adm., of co. Norf., [1820] Vol. XXXII, fol. 157.
WILKINSON, ..., of Elmwood House, Leeds, co. York, [1822] Vol XXXIII, fol. 135.
WILKINSON, late RICKETTS, George Yeldham, of co. Derby. (See RICKETTS, in Foster's Baronets.) [1 Sept. 1831] [1832] Vol. XXXIX, fol. 89.
WILKINSON, ... (widow), of Ward Green, Worsbrough, Darfield, Skellow, Owston, co. York, [1861] Vol. LIV, fol. 152.
WILKINSON to ATKINSON, ... (minor), [1861] Vol. LIV, fol. 176.
WILKINSON, ..., of Huyton, [co. Lanc. ?], and Stalybridge, co. Chester, [1868] Vol. LVI, fol. 335.
WILKS to DARLEY, ..., nat. s. of Brewster Darley, of co. York. Quarterly Arms, [1808] Vol. XXIV, fol. 409; Quarterly Arms, [1809] Vol. XXV, fol. 264.
WILKS, (Sir) Samuel (Bart.), of 72, Grosvenor Street, London, 1897, Vol. LXX, fol. 69.
WILL, John Shiress, Q.C., of 13, West Cromwell Road, London, 1898, Vol. LXX, fol. 108.
WILLAN after DOUGLAS, ..., of Twyford Abbey, co. Middx., [1829] Vol. XXXVII, fol. 286.
WILLANS, Benjamin, of Blaina, co. Monmouth, 1895,* Vol. LXVIII, fol. 261.
WILLAUME, Edward, of Tingrave, co. Bedf., 1767, Vol. XI, fol. 194. (Berry.)
WILLAUME after TANQUERAY, ..., of Candover, Hampsh., [1848] Vol. XLIX, fol. 11.
WILLDING-JONES, W., of Hampton Hall, Malpas, co. Chester, 1895, Vol. LXVIII, fol. 174.
WILLES, ..., and WRIGHT, his wife, of Dulwich and Chelsham Court, co. Surrey, [1819] Vol. XXXI, fols. 328 and 329.
WILLETT, late ADYE, John Willett, of Merley Place, co. Dorset. (Match), 11 Mar. 1795, Vol. XIX, fol. 19.
WILLETT (Saltren) to CLEVLAND, ..., of co. Devon, [1847] Vol. XLVIII, fol. 352.
WILLETT, late CATT, Henry, of co. Surrey, [1863] Vol. LV, fol. 78; (2) William, fol. 80; (3) John, fol. 96; (4) Edward, fol. 122.
WILLETT, W., of The Drive, Hove, Brighton, co. Sussex, 1892, Vol. LXVII, fol. 22.
WILLEY, Henry Alfred, of Exeter, co. Devon, 18 . . ., Vol. LXXI, fol. . . . .
WILLIAM-POWLETT, ..., late WALLOP, of Hampsh., and Wales, [1867] Vol. LVI, fol. 170.
WILLIAM-SPICER, late HEAVISIDE, ..., of co. Devon, [1854] Vol. LI, fol. 102.
WILLIAM-EDWARDS, ..., M.A., of Wales, [1819] Vol. XXXI, fol. 359.
WILLIAMS, Rev. John, D.D., Chaplain-in-Ordinary, Prebendary of Canterbury, 1699, Vol. IV, fol. 233 [?].
„ Sir Charles Hanbury, K.B. [1744], of Coldbrook, co. Monmouth. Supporters, [1744] Vol. IX, fol. 122.

WILLIAMS, John, of Boston, *alias* Salem, New Zealand, 1767, Vol. XI, fol. 224. (Berry.)

WILLIAMS before HOPE, John, of co. Cornw. Quarterly Arms, [1782] Vol. XV, fol. 43.

WILLIAMS to HOPE, ..., of Harley Street, London, [1811] Vol. XXVI, fol. 195.

„ to RICH, ..., of co. Camb., [1786] Vol. XVI, fol. 107.

WILLIAMS, ..., of Waterbeach, co. Camb., and Cumbrane, co. Carmarthen, Wales, [1795] Vol. XIX, fol. 79.

WILLIAMS, late HAMLYN, [2 Mar. 1798], James, of co. Devon, and Wales [s. of the 1st] Bart. [afterwards 2nd Bart.]. (Match), [1798] Vol. XX, fol. 117.

WILLIAMS, ..., TREEVES, wife of, of co. Cornw. and Wilts. Arms to her and her descendants, [1800] Vol. XXI, fol. 12.

„ . . . ., of co. Worc., and Westminster, [1800] Vol. XXI, fol. 101.

„ . . . ., wife of NAYLER, York Herald of Arms, [1808] Vol. XXV, fol. 56.

WILLIAMS after WHITE, ..., of Duckworth Plantation, Surrey, Island of Jamaica. Quartering, [1809] Vol. XXV, fol. 72.

WILLIAMS, ..., M.D., of Ewick, co. Devon. A quartering to HAMILTON, [1809] Vol. XXV, fol. 222.

WILLIAMS to WELSH, ..., Sea Captain, [1812] Vol. XXVII, fol. 176.

WILLIAMS, ..., of Hackney, co. Middx., and Epsom, co. Surrey, [1813] Vol. XXVII, fol. 340.

„ John William, of Exeter, co. Devon. (Match), [1813] Vol. XXVII, fol. 411.

„ . . . ., of Trehane, co. Cornw. Match with STACKHOUSE, [1814] Vol. XXVIII, fol. 244 and [1815] fol. 282.

WILLIAMS after GRIFFIES, ..., of Wales. Quarterly Arms, [1815] Vol. XXVIII, fol. 330.

WILLIAMS, Vice-Adm. Sir Thomas, K.C.B. [1815]. Allusion to Services, [1815] Vol. XXIX, fols. 173 and 175 ; G.C.B. [1831] Supporters, [1832] Vol. XXXIX, fol. 71.

„ Rev. . . . ., Vicar of Undy, co. Monmouth, Wales, [1816] Vol. XXIX, fol. 264.

„ Lieut.-Gen. Sir Richard, K.C.B. [1815], [1816] Vol. XXIX, fol. 268.

„ Lieut.-Col. Sir William, K.C.B. [1815], of Epsom, co. Surrey, and Lincoln's Inn Fields, London, and to brothers Thomas and Bigoe Charles, [1816] Vol. XXIX, fol. 276.

„ Martin and Pyrie, of co. Worc., [1817 ?] Vol. XXX, fol. 79.

WILLIAMS-MACKRETH, ..., of Ewhurst, Hampsh., [1820] Vol. XXXII, fol. 1.

WILLIAMS, ..., M.R.C.S., of Southwark, co. Surrey, and Hackney, co. Middx., 1820, Vol. XXXII, fol. 37.

WILLIAMS-FREEMAN, Adm., of Bucks. and co. Hertf., [1822] Vol. XXXIII, fols. 146 to 148.

WILLIAMS-GREGORY, ..., of co. Linc. and Nottingham, [1823] Vol. XXXIV, fol. 130.

WILLIAMS after HARRIS, Orlando, of Ivy Tower, co. Pembroke, Wales, and Oaklands, co. Glouc., [1824] Vol. XXXIV, fol. 332.

WILLIAMS-HOPE, William (s. of John), of co. Cornw., [1826] Vol. XXXVI, fol. 33, and Crest, fol. 35.

WILLIAMS-BULKELEY [Roy. Lic., 3 June 1826], Sir Richard Bulkeley, [10th] Bart., of Wales, 1827 [1826], Vol. XXXVI, fol. 147.

WILLIAMS, Charles Croft, of Cardiff, Wales, s. of Charles, [1836] Vol. XLI, fol. 242.

„ . . . ., of Horsham, co. Sussex, and Waterford, Eaton, Iscy, Wilts., [1839] Vol. XLIV, fol. 85.

„ . . . ., of Oxhill, Handsworth, Wednesbury, Oak, co. Staff., [1839] Vol. XLIV, fol. 109.

WILLIAMS to PICTON, John, M.D., of Wales, [1840] Vol. XLIV, fol. 277.

WILLIAMS, ..., and SANSBURY, his wife, of Enfield, co. Middx., [1842] Vol. XLVI, fols. 18 and 19.

WILLIAMS, late HOLLEST, John Leigh, of co. Surrey, [1842] Vol. XLVI, fol. 126.

WILLIAMS, John, of Elm Grove, Mortlake, co. Surrey (s. of David, of Llangollen, co. Denbigh, Wales), [1847] Vol. XLVIII, fol. 380.

„ . . . ., of The Lodge, Hillingdon, co. Middx., [1853] Vol. L, fol. 370.

„ Capt., Dragoon Guards. Crest, [1855] Vol. LI, fol. 278.

„ John (Bart.), of Scorrier House and Carhays Castle, co. Cornw., and Guaton Hall, co. Devon, 31 Oct. 1855, Vol. LI, fol. 354. (Crisp, II, p. 40.)

„ . . . ., of co. Cornw. and Devon. HARRIS quartering, [1895 ?] Vol. LXIX, fol. 15.

„ Maj.-Gen. Sir William Fenwick, K.C.B. [1856], [Bart.], of Kars, [1856] Vol. LII, fol. 52.

„ William, M.R.C.S., of co. York, [1857] Vol. LII, fol. 314.

„ Lieut.-Gen., Indian Forces, [1866] Vol. LVI, fol. 81.

WILLIAMS after JONES, Thomas, of Grove Hill, co. Worc., 1871, Vol. LVIII, fol. 36.

WILLIAMS, ... (widow, dau. of EDGER), John Edger, of co. Devon. Arms for Williams and Edger, s. to quarter Edger, of Appledore, co. Northampton, 1875, Vol. LIX, fol. 129. (Berry's Suppl. [?])

WILLIAMS to WILLIAMS-MEYRICK, Rev. John, of Beaumaris and Cefre Coch, co. Anglesea, Wales, 1877, Vol. LX, fol. 12. (Berry's Suppl.)

WILLIAMS, Rev. Edmund George, of Glasfryn, co. Swansea, Wales, 1879, Vol. LX, fol. 247.

„ Sir George [Knt., 18 July 1894], of Russell Square, London, 1894,* Vol. LXVIII, fol. 81.

WILLIAMS, MONTAGUE- (? William Montague), of Bacchus Marshc, Colony of Victoria, 1893, Vol. LXVII, fol. 259.

WILLIAMS-JONES-PARRY, Mrs., of Madryn, co. Carnarvon, Wales, 1892, Vol. LXVII, fol. 47.

WILLIAMS, Lieut.-Col. James, of Bryn Glas, Newport, co. Monmouth, 1897, Vol. LXIX, fol. 239.

„ William Bullivant, of St. Peter Hill, Caversham, co. Oxf., 1898, Vol. LXX, fol. 213.

„ Rev. Samuel B. S., Vicar of Pittington, co. Durham, s. of John, of Manchester, 18 . . ., Vol. LXXI, fol. . . . .

WILLIAMSON, ..., of Westminster. Quartering, [1788] Vol. XVI, fol. 359.

„ [Maj.-Gen.] Sir Adam, K.B. [1794-1795], Lieut.-Gov. of Jamaica. Supporters, [1796] Vol. XIX, fol. 262.

WILLIAMSON to WINN . . . ., of co. York, [1815] Vol. XXVIII, fol. 278 ; [1818] Vol. XXX, fols. 377 and 379.

WILLIAMSON, heretofore HOPPER, Robert, Recorder of Newcastle-upon-Tyne, co. Northumberland, and Durham, [1829] Vol. XXXVIII, fol. 23.

WILLIAMSON, Joshua, of Peckham, co. Surrey ; London ; and Heaton, co. York, [1833] Vol. XXXIX, fol. 214.

„ James, of co. Lanc., [1885] Vol. LXIII, fol. 31 ; Baron ASHTON, 1895. Supporters, [1895] Vol. LXIX, fol. 9.

WILLIS, Thomas and Daniel, D.L., co. Lanc., of Whaddon Hall, Bucks., and Kinnington, nr. Oxford, 1 Feb. 172⁹⁄₁, Vol. VII, fol. 79. (Berry.)

„ John, of Chelsea, co. Middx., to the descendants of his grandfather, William Willis, of Bewdley, co. Worc., 6 Mar. 173½,* Vol. VIII, fol. 120ᵇ ; Add. MS. 14,830, fol. 6.

WILLIS to STEPHENS, Henry H., of co. Glouc., [1801] Vol. XXI, fol. 208.

WILLIS, ..., of Gretford and Hickham, co. Linc., [1818] Vol. XXXI, fol. 12.

WILLIS-BUND, ..., of co. Worc., and New South Wales. Arms for Bund, [1864] Vol. LV, fol. 226.

WILLMOTT, ..., of Sherbourne, co. Dorset, [1863] Vol. LV, fol. 52.

„ Henry, of Cheltenham, co. Glouc., [1869] Vol. LVII, fol. 192. (Berry's Suppl.).

WILLOCK to DAWES, ..., of co. Kent. and Sussex, [1870] Vol. LVII, fol. 258.

WILLOCK, Henry D. and Col. George W., of Marine Parade, Brighton, 1893,* Vol. LXVII, fol. 156.

WILLOUGHBY DE ERESBY, Baron. Seal, with Supporters, 171 . ., Vol. VI, fol. 25.

„ [Sir Thomas], Knt. and [2nd] Bart., of Wollaton, co. Nottingham. Arms and Supporters, Baron MIDDLETON, [31 Dec. 1711] [171½], Vol. VI, fol. 25 ; [1712] fol. 28.

WILLOUGHBY DE BROKE, Baron, [Feb. 169⅘]. Supporters, 169 . ., Vol. IV, fol. 319 [?].

WILLOUGHBY (DRUMMOND), late DRUMMOND BURRELL [26 June 1829, Peter Robert], Baron WILLOUGHBY DE ERESBY, [1829] Vol. XXXVII, fol. 356.

WILLOUGHBY (HEATHCOTE-DRUMMOND) [4 May 1872], [Clementina Elizabeth], Baroness WILLOUGHBY DE ERESBY [13 Nov. 1871]. Quarterly Arms, 1870 [1872], Vol. LVIII, fol. 112.

WILLOUGHBY, DRUMMOND and HEATHCOTE, quarterly to issue, 1870 [1872], Vol. LVIII, fol. 114.

WILLOUGHBY DE BROKE, [17th Baron] (BARNARD). Barnard Arms, [1853] Vol. L, fol. 332. BARNARD to VERNEY, [Roy. Lic., 17 May 1853] Vol. L, fol. 334.

WILLS, Rt. Hon. Lieut.-Gen. Sir Charles, P.C., K.B. [1725]. Alterations in Arms and Crest, 7 July 1725, Vol. VII, fol. 332 ; Add. MS. 14,830, fol. 8. Supporters, [1725] Vol. VII, fol. 334.

„ Sir William Henry, Bart., of Cowle Lodge, Blagdon, co. Somerset, and co. Kent, 1893, Vol. LXVII, fol. 203.

„ Sir Alfred, Knt. [11 Aug. 1884], of Tite Street, London, and France, Justice of H.M. High Court of Justice, 1893,* Vol. LXVII, fol. 257.

„ Frederick, of Heath Lodge, Hampstead, co. Middx., 1893,* Vol. LXVII, fol. 265.

„ W. A., of Lanor Road, West Norwood, co. Surrey, 1895,* Vol. LXVIII, fol. 253.

WILLSHER, Helen, dau. of George, and wife of George Harrison ROGERS-HARRISON (Windsor Herald), and to the descendants of her grandfather, George Willsher, Vol. XLIV [1839 ?], [1778 XIV ?], fol. 54.

WILLSHIRE, Maj.-Gen. Sir Thomas, K.C.B. [1839], Bart., [1841] Vol. XLV, fol. 67 ; G.C.B. [1861]. Supporters, [1861 ?, Vol. LIV], fol. 212.

WILLSON, ..., of Dulwich, co. Surrey, [1854] Vol. LI, fol. 95.

WILMER, late GOSSIP, ..., of co. York, [1833] Vol. XXXIX, fol. 182.

WILMOT, Sir Robert, Knt., nat. son, of co. Derby, 22 Dec. 1760, Vol. X, fol. 262. (Berry.)

WILMOT-GRIMSTON, John, of co. Derby and York, [1860] Vol. LIV, fol. 38.

WILMOT, Mary, dau. of John, of . . . ., and widow of HEYWOOD, 1775, Vol. XIII, fol. 72.

WILMOT-SITWELL, Edward Sacheverell, of Stainsby, co. Derby.   ? Name only, not Arms. 1772. (Burke.)

WILMOT-HORTON, Robert J., of co. Derby [3rd Bart.], [1823] Vol. XXXIV, fol. 60 ; Sir Robert Edward, Bart., [1871] Vol. LVIII, fol. 8.

WILSHERE, ..., of Frythe, Welwyn, Hitchin and Kimpton, co. Hertf., [1829] Vol. XXXVII, fol. 381.

WILSON, Thomas, J.P., of Stratford-le-Bow, co. Middx., 12 Sept. 1716, Vol. VI, fol. 272 ; Add. MS. 14,830, fol. 9.

„ Elizabeth, dau. and h. of Thomas, of Burlington, co. York, and widow of Benjamin HUDSON, of the same. (See HUDSON.) 10 April 1766, Vol. XI, fols. 149 to 151 [see Burke].

WILSON, late NIXON, Thomas, of Flatt, par. of Bewcastle, co. Cumberland. Wilson Arms confirmed, 3 Nov. 1773, Vol. XII, fol. 273. (Berry.)

WILSON, late MACKLIN, ..., of Derby and Bath, co. Somerset, [1784] Vol. XV, fol. 325.

„ late CARUS, ..., of co. Westmorland, [1793] Vol. XVIII, fol. 195. Quarterly Arms, [1794] Vol. XVIII, fol. 359.

WILSON, Commander . . . ., of Guildford, co. Surrey, [1800] Vol. XXI, fol. 68.

WILSON after FOUNTAYNE, ..., of Melton, co. York. Quarterly Arms, [1804] Vol. XXII, fol. 347.

WILSON (FOUNTAYNE-) to MONTAGU, ..., of co. York and Nottingham, [1826] Vol. XXXV, fol. 375.

WILSON, Capt. . . . . Match, MUNKHOUSE, [1810] Vol. XXV, fol. 402.

„ Sir Thomas [Spencer, 6th] Bart. Arms for HUTCHINSON and WELLER, his wife, 1787 [1786], Vol. XVI, fol. 133.

„ Lieut.-Col. Sir Henry, Knt., of Leeds, co. York, [1803] Vol. XXII, fol. 254.

„ Sir Henry, Knt., of Leeds, co. York ; Newcastle-upon-Tyne, co. Northumberland ; and Chelsea Park, co. Middx., ([1780] ? Vol. XIV, fol. 267), [1815] Vol. XXVIII, fol. 264.

WILSON after WRIGHT [1814], Sir Henry [Knt.]. Quarterly Arms, [1815] Vol. XXVIII, fol. 266. Spinster, [1780] Vol. XIV, fol. 262 (see WILSON-HENNIKER, of Hampsh. and co. York, and Lady Frances).

WILSON (HENNIKER-WRIGHT), Henniker, Mary, and husband John, of Hampsh. and co. York, Mary then unmar., [1839] Vol. XLIII, fol. 377 (see [1836] Vol. XLI, fol. 262).

WILSON, Lieut.-Col. Sir James, K.C.B., of Tooting, co. Surrey. Escutcheon of pretence, [1816] Vol. XXX, fol. 38.

„ . . . ., of Norbreck and Preston, co. Lanc., [1817] Vol. XXX, fol. 232.

WILSON before FRANCE, of Norbreck and Preston, co. Lanc. Quarterly Arms, [1817] Vol. XXX, fol. 234.

WILSON, ..., of Sneaton, co. York, and Cane Grove, St. Vincent, [1819] Vol. XXXI, fol. 279.

WILSON (DOBIE), ... (minor), of Scotland. Quarterly Arms, [1822] Vol. XXXIII, fols. 262 and 264.

WILSON, late SMYTH, ..., of Dallam Tower, co. Westmorland, [1825 ?] Vol. XXXV, fol. 71.

WILSON, ..., of Seacroft Hall, Whitwick, co. Leic., [1827] Vol. XXXVI, fol. 292.

WILSON to STOTT, ..., of Quebec, [1828] Vol. XXXVII, fol. 67.

WILSON, ..., M.D. (Domestic Phys. to the Duke of Kent), of London and Drumrusk, co. Armagh, Ireland, [1828] Vol. XXXVII, fol. 113. (Bishop's MS.)

WILSON, late NEWBERRY, Christian Wilson, of Furnival's Inn, London, 7 May 1832, Vol. XXXIX, fol. 103.

WILSON, Baron BERNERS [7 May 1832, Robert]. Supporters, [1834 ?] Vol. XL, fol. 91.

„ . . . ., of Barton-upon-Humber, co. Linc., [1836] Vol. XLI, fol. 303.

„ Henry, of Stowlangtoft Hall, co. Suff., and Massingham, co. Norf., [1836] Vol. XLI, fol. 341.

WILSON after RIMINGTON, James Wilson (minor), of Broomhead Hall and Bradfield, co. York, [1840] Vol. XLIV, fol. 325.

WILSON to FITZPATRICK, [Roy. Lic., 12 Feb. 1842, John], reputed son of Baron Upper Ossory, [1842] Vol. XLV, fol. 380.

WILSON-FITZPATRICK, [John], Baron CASTLETOWN [10 Dec. 1869] [of Upper Ossory]. Supporters, [1869] Vol. LVII, fol. 198.

WILSON to PARKINSON, John Parkinson, of Magdalen Coll., Oxf., and co. Linc., [1842] Vol. XLVI, fol. 106.

WILSON, Thomas, of Whalley, co. Lanc., and the Netherlands, [1852] Vol. L, fol. 129.

WILSON-TODD, Capt. William Henry, of co. York, 14 Aug. 1855, Vol. LI, fol. 358.

WILSON, ..., of Abergavenny, co. Monmouth, [1853] Vol. L, fol. 325.

WILSON after ANTHONY, ..., of Westbourne Terrace, London, [1858] Vol. LIII, fol. 23.

WILSON-ATKINSON, George Christian, of co. Northumberland, [1861 ?] Vol. LIV, fol. 92.

WILSON-HAFFENDEN, Rev. John, of co. York, [1871] Vol. LVIII, fol. 76.

WILSON-FITZGERALD, William Henry, of Cliffe, co. York, and Adelphi, Corofin, co. Clare, Ireland, 1872, Vol. LVIII, fol. 138.

WILSON, Bart. [16 Mar. 1874, Matthew], M.P., of Eshton Hall, co. York, [1874] Vol. LVIII, fol. 311.

  „ George, s. of George, of Banner Cross, co. York, and Haugh Mills, Markinch, co. Fife, Scotland, 1875, Vol. LIX, fol. 149.

WILSON (late TYRWHITT), Hon. Henry, of Shropsh., co. Leic. and Norf., 1876, Vol. LIX. fol. 190 ; see also [1892] Vol. LXVII, fol. 59.

WILSON, Robert Porter, of Cumberland Terrace, Regent's Park, London, and Greenwich, co. Kent, s. of Robert, and to uncle Richard, 1880, Vol. LX, fol. 338. (Berry's Suppl.)

  „ Edward, of Western Bank, Sheffield, co. York, 1881, Vol. LXI, fol. 142. (Berry's Suppl.)

  „ Sir Samuel, Knt., of co. Antrim, Ireland, and Victoria, 1879, Vol. LX, fol. 275 [see next name].

  „ Sir Samuel, Knt. Arms with chief and to the descendants of his father, William, without the chief, 1879 [no reference, ? last entry].

  „ Rev. J. B., of Knightwick Rectory, Worcester, 1893,* Vol. LXVI, fol. 328. (Crisp, I, p. 177.)

  „ Edward Shimells, of Kingston-upon-Hull, co. York, 1884, Vol. LXII, fol. 230.

WILSON-BARKWORTH, A. B., of Kingston-upon-Hull, and Melton-in-Welton, co. York, 1884, Vol. LXII, fol. 232.

WILSON, John Alexander, of Grafton Road, Auckland, New Zealand, 1893, Vol. LXVII, fol. 191.

  „ J. G. Hannay, of Tor Mohun, co. Devon, 1885, Vol. LXIII, fol. 103.

  „ Thomas, of Oakholme, Sheffield, co. York, 1887,* Vol. LXIV, fol. 14.

  „ Thomas Newby, of The Landing, Ulverstone, co. Lanc. (s. of Thomas), 18 . . ., Vol. LXXI, fol. . . . .

  „ W. H., of Toowong, Queensland, 1893, Vol. LXVII, fol. 243.

WILTON, Joseph, of Snaresbrooke, co. Essex, 1768, Vol. XI, fol. 284. (Berry.)

  „ . . . ., of South Stoke, co. Sussex. (Match), [1809] Vol. XXV, fol. 180.

  „ Earl of (EGERTON, late GROSVENOR) [27 Nov. 1821]. Arms, [1821] Vol. XXXIII, fol. 90 ; Supporters, fol. 94.

WIMBLE, Nehemiah, of The Friars, Lewes and Southover, co. Sussex, 1830, Vol. XXXVIII, fols. 163 and 165 (see Berry's Suppl.).

WIMBORNE, Baron. Supporters, 1880, Vol. LXI, fol. 27.

WINCH, George, Solicitor, of Chatham, co. Kent, 1896, Vol. LXIX, fol. 28.

WINCHCOMBE to CLIFFORD, ..., of co. Glouc., [1801] Vol. XXI, fol. 262.

WINCHESTER (and Elizabeth AYERSH, his wife), Henry, Sheriff of London and Middx., of Oakfield Lodge, Hawkhurst, co. Kent, s. of William, of Malden, co. Surrey, and to his other descendants, 3 Oct. 1826, Vol. XXXVI, fol. 97. (Berry's Adds.)

WINCKWORTH, ..., wife of CLARKE, of London. Arms to wife and descendants, [1788] Vol. XVII, fol. 45.

WINDER after LYON, ..., of co. Chester, [1820] Vol. XXXII, fol. 98 ; [1859] Vol. LIII, fol. 173.

  „ after CORBETT, Uvedale, of Shropsh., and LYON, his wife, 1869, Vol. LVII, fol. 147 [see Burke].

WINDHAM after SMYTH, Joseph, of co. York and Essex, [1823] Vol. XXXIV, fol. 58.

WINDHAM, late LUKIN, Rear-Adm. [William ?], of co. Essex and Norf., [1824] Vol. XXXIV, fol. 372.

WINDLE, Rev. W., of St. Stephen's, Walbrook, London, and Brockley, co. Kent, 1882,* Vol. LXI, fol. 263.

WINDSOR-CLIVE [Roy. Lic., 8 Nov. 1855, Harriet Clive], Baroness Windsor, widow of [The Hon. Robert Henry] Clive. Quarterly Arms to issue, [1855] Vol. LI, fol. 408.

WINGFIELD before STRATFORD, Lieut.-Col. [The Hon. John Wingfield assumed the additional surname and arms of Stratford by Roy. Lic., 23 Dec. 1802, 2nd s. of the 3rd Viscount]. (See Viscount POWERSCOURT.) Quarterly Arms, [1803] Vol. XXII, fol. 72.

WINGFIELD to BAKER, ..., Q.C., of co. Dorset and Essex, [1849] Vol. XLIX, fol. 264.

WINGFIELD before DIGBY, ..., of co. Dorset, 1856, Vol. LII, fol. 54.

WINGROVE, ..., of Worth, co. Sussex, and Bengal C.S., [1852] Vol. L, fol. 250.

WINLAND, Rev. George Preston K., M.A. (s. of Rev. William, B.D.), 18 . ., Vol. LXXI, fol. . . . .

WINMARLEIGH, Baron [16 Mar. 1874], [John Wilson-Patten]. Supporters, [1874] Vol. LVIII, fol. 327.

WINN to ALLANSON, ... [20 Feb. 1777], Bart., of Nostell Priory, co. York, [1777] Vol. XIII, fol. 291.

WINN, late WILLIAMSON, ..., of co. York, now Baron ST. OSWALD [cr. 6 July 1885], [1815] Vol. XXVIII, fol. 278 ; [1818] Vol. XXX, fols. 377 and 379.

WINNINGTON before INGRAM, ... (B.A.), of the Inner Temple, London, and co. Worc., [1817] Vol. XXX, fol. 254.

WINSLEY, F., of Fernleigh, Nottingham, 1889,* Vol. LXV, fol. 7.

WINSLOE to PHILLIPPS, ..., of co. Cornw. and Devon, [1798] Vol. XX, fol. 265.

WINSLOE, Mrs. Richard, of Carlsruhe, Germany, 1881, Vol. LXI, fol. 153.

WINSOR after BENYON, William Henry, of Gwersyllt, Wrexham, Wales, 1867, Vol. LVI, fol. 214.

WINSTON, late BOWEN, ..., of London, [1795] Vol. XIX, fol. 139.

WINTER, ..., of Sherborne, co. Dorset, and Watt's House, Bishop's Lydiard, co. Somerset, [1865] Vol. LV, fol. 310.

WINTER-IRVING, W. J., of Noorilim, Colony of Victoria, 1891, Vol. LXVI, fol. 98.

WINTERBOTTOM, ..., of Stockport, co. Chester, [1825] Vol. XXXV, fol. 111.

WINTERINGHAM, ..., of Bridlington, co. York. (See John STONES.) [1771] Vol. XII, fol. 53.

WINTLE, ..., Judge, E.I.C.S., of Calcutta, [1818] Vol. XXXI, fol. 61.
„ . . . ., of Bristol, [1828] Vol. XXXVII, fol. 210.

WINWOOD, Thomas Henry R., of Wellisford Manor, Langford Budville, co. Somerset, 1881, Vol. LXI, fol. 185. (Berry's Suppl.)

WIRE, David, of London, Alderman, and of Stone House, Lewisham, West Cliff, and St. Lawrence, Ramsgate, co. Kent, [1853] Vol. L, fol. 395.

WIRGMAN, Augustus, of Charlewood, co. Surrey ; Kniveton, co. Derby ; and Gottenburg, Sweden, [1841] Vol. XLV, fol. 143.

WISDEN, T. F, of Broadwater, co. Sussex, 1887, Vol. LXIV, fol. 66. (Crisp, III, p. 7.)

WISE, Henry, of Brompton Park, co. Middx., Master Gardener of all H.M.'s Gardens, 4 April 1720, Vol. VI, fol. 401 ; Add. MS. 14,830, fol. 10 (see Misc. G. et H., N. S., I, p. 201).

WISEMAN, William Thomas, of Cromwell House, Lambeth, co. Surrey, 1897, Vol. LXIX, fol. 311.

WITHAM, Henry (late SILVERTOP), of co. Durham, and Lartington Hall, co. York, [1802 ?] Vol. XXII, fol. 36.

WITHER after BIGG-LOVELACE, ..., of Hampsh. and Wilts. Quarterly Arms, [1789] Vol. XVII, fol. 167.

WITHERS after MITCHELL, ..., of Sheffield, co. York, [1862] Vol. LIV, fol. 248.

WITHIM, ..., of the Middle Temple, London, 1680. (Berry and Burke.)

WITTEN, William, of Dane's Valley, &c., co. Cornw., Jamaica. [Arms] and quartering, [1777] Vol. XIII, fol. 277.

WITTS, Broome, of Chipping Norton, co. Oxf., and London, to the descendants of Edward and Richard, father and uncle of the first-named, 1 Feb. 1769, Vol. XI, fol. 358. (Bishop's MS. Berry.)

WITTS to STEERE, ..., of co. Surrey. Match, [1796] Vol. XIX, fol. 203.
Escutcheon of pretence, [1797] fol. 465.
WODEHOUSE, Baron [26 Oct. 1797, Sir John Wodehouse, 7th Bart.]. Supporters,
[1797] Vol. XX, fol. 26.
   „ (THORNTON-), ..., Commander, R.N., of co. York, [1838] Vol. XLIII,
fol. 251.
WOGDON, ..., of Grantham, co. Linc., [1802] Vol. XXI, fol. 352.
WOLCOTT, ..., of Sydbury, co. Devon, [1783] Vol. XV, fol. 239.
WOLFE (BIRCH-), Rev. Richard ?, of Woodhall and Widdington, co. Essex.
Quarterly Arms, 1827, Vol. XXXVI, fol. 311.
WOLFE, Rev. Richard (Rev. William ?), M.A., Camb., of Widdington, co. Essex,
Rector of Hardwicke. Quarterly Arms, 1859, Vol. LIII, fol. 202.
   „ Rev. William (Thomas ?), of Woodhall, co. Essex, 1864, Vol. LV, fol. 250
[see Burke].
WOLFERSTAN after PIPE, Rev. Samuel, of co. Staff., 15 June 1776, Vol. XIII,
fol. 191.
WOLFF, Rt. Hon. Sir Henry Drumond, of London, 1881, Vol. LXI, fol. 213.
(Supporters, G.C.B. [2 Jan. 1889]), [1890, Vol. LXV] fol. 215.
WOLLEY, Thomas, of Woodhall, Shropsh., 1772, Vol. XII, fol. 152. (Berry.)
WOLLEY, late HURT, Charles, of co. Derby and Nottingham, 1827, Vol. XXXVI,
fol. 351.
WOLLEY after Oldnall, Edward, of the City of Worc. [Wolley and Oldnall
quarterly] [7 Aug. 1843] Vol. XLVI, fol. 361.
WOLLEY-DOD, Rev. Charles, M.A. (and PARKER, his wife), of Edge Hall, Malpas,
co. Chester, [1868] Vol. LVII, fol. 6.
WOLLEY (late PHILLIPS), Edward Clive Oldnall Long, s. of Richard Augustus
Long Phillips, of Rotherham, co. York, 1876, Vol. LIX, fol. 264.
WOLLSTONECRAFTE (see WOOLLSTONECRAFT), Edward John, of Marks Gate, co.
Essex, and London, 1765, Vol. XI, fol. 114. (Edmondson and Berry.)
WOLRYCHE-WHITMORE, late LAING, Rev. F. H., M.A., of Shropsh. and co. Glouc.,
[1864] Vol. LV, fol. 270.
WOLSELEY, Baron [25 Nov. 1882, Sir Garnet Joseph Wolseley]. Supporters,
1882, Vol. LXII, fol. 27.
WOLSELEY-JENKINS, Major C. B. H., of Ireland, 1895, Vol. LXVIII, fol. 190.
WOLSTENHOLME, late BRETON, ..., of co. Middx. and Sussex. (Match), [1807]
Vol. XXIV, fol. 166.
WOLTON, ..., of Woodlands, Camberwell, co. Surrey, [1872] Vol. LVIII,
fol. 132.
WOLVERHAMPTON, Borough of, co. Staff., [31 Dec.] 1898, Vol. LXX, fol. 310.
[Geneal. Mag., III, p. 102.]
WOLVERTON, Baron [14 Dec. 1869] (GLYN), of Bucks. and co. Middx., [1869]
Vol. LVII, fol. 200.
WOMACK, ..., Sheriff, of Norwich, co. Norf., [1853 ?] Vol. L, fol. 272.
WOOD, ..., of Leonard Stanley, co. Glouc., 1759. (Edmondson and Berry.)
   „ . . . . (see CUSSANS), of Shrewsbury, Clarendon, Jamaica, [1767] Vol. XI,
fol. 228 ; ? Add. MS. 14,830, fol. 11.
   „ Francis, Bart. [1784] of Barnsley, co. York, [1784] Vol. XV, fol. 345.
   „ Sir Charles, Bart. Supporters, G.C.B., [1856] Vol. LII, fol. 144 ; Viscount
HALIFAX, [1866] Vol. LVI, fol. 87.
WOOD to WATSON, William, of co. York (maternal uncle, George Watson), [1803]
Vol. XXII, fol. 273.
WOOD, ..., of Broomfield, nr. Manchester, co. Lanc., and Macclesfield, co.
Chester. (See RYLE.) [1809] Vol. XXV, fol. 288.
   „ . . . ., of Bath, co. Somerset, [1810] Vol. XXVI, fol. 77.
   „ Lieut.-Col. [? George, K.C.B., 1815], Knt., [1815] Vol. XXVIII, fol. 396.
   „ Lieut.-Col. Samuel, C.B., [1815] Vol. XXIX, fol. 166.
WOOD, late WALKER, ..., of London, [1817] Vol. XXX, fol. 188.
WOOD-DAVISON, Thomas, of co. York, [1818] Vol. XXXI, fol. 56.

WOOD, ..., of Singleton Lodge, Prestwich, co. Lanc., and Leeds, co. York, [1833] Vol. XXXIX, fol. 335.

  ,, John, of Brownhills, Burslem, co. Staff., 1833, Vol. XL, fol. 46.

  ,, Edward, J.P., of Burslem and Port Hill, Wolstanton, co. Staff., [1861] Vol. LIV, fol. 206.

  ,, [Sir Mathew, Bart., 6 Dec. 1837], of Hatherley, co. Glouc. (and Exeter and Tiverton, co. Devon), [1837] Vol. XLII, fols. 256 and 258. (Baron HATHERLEY [his 2nd son]. Supporters, [1868] Vol. LVII, fol. 106.)

WOOD, late LOCKWOOD, ..., of co. Essex, Camb. and Surrey, [1838] Vol. XLIII, fol. 34.

WOOD, ..., of co. Northumberland, [1838] Vol. XLIII, fol. 43.

WOOD-CRASTER, ..., of co. Northumberland, [1838] Vol. XLIII, fol. 46.

WOOD, ..., of Thedden, Hampsh., and Horton, Bradford, co. York, [1839 ?] Vol. XLIII, fol. 344.

WOOD to WATSON, John Webster, of co. Sussex and York, [1839] Vol. XLIV, fol. 157.

WOOD, Richard, Consul at Damascus, [1847] Vol. XLVIII, fol. 328.

WOOD after EDWARDS, ..., of co. Warw., [1851] Vol. L, fol. 66.

WOOD to PENDARVES, ... (minor), of co. Cornw., [1860] Vol. LIII, fol. 296.

  ,, to STUCKEY, Vincent, of co. Bedf. and Somerset, [1861] Vol. LIV, fol. 136.

WOOD, Richard Henry, F.S.A., of Crumpsall, Manchester, co. Lanc., and Northen, co. Chester, [1871] Vol. LVII, fol. 316.

WOOD-ACTON, Augustus, of Shropsh., 1874, Vol. LIX, fol. 26. (Berry's Suppl.)

WOOD to SHUCKBURGH, Richard Henry, of co. Warwick, 1876, Vol. LIX, fol. 226.

WOOD, Samuel, of Talbot House, Whitfield, co. Derby, s. of John, 1878, Vol. LX, fol. 105. (Berry's Suppl.)

  ,, Albert, J.P., of Bodlondel, co. Carnarvon, Wales, and to the other descendants of his late father, Henry Wood, late of the City of Chester, 25 Feb. 1880, Vol. LX, fol. 348. (Genealogist, V, p. 184 ; Berry's Suppl.)

WOOD-BESLY, E. H., of Kensington Square, London, 1890, Vol. LXV, fol. 315.

WOOD, Joseph Snell, of 29 Kensington Court, London, 1898, Vol. LXX, fol. 223.

WOODCOCK to CROFT, ..., of Berks. and co. Hertford, [1793 ?] Vol. XVIII, fol. 147.

WOODCOCK, John, of Coventry, co. Warw., and Tamworth, co. Staff., 1828, Vol. XXXVII, fol. 192 (see Berry's Suppl.)

WOODCOCK to LITTLE, of Coventry and Newbold Pacey, co. Warw., [1834] Vol. XL, fol. 96.

WOODCOCK, ..., Mayor of Norwich, of Hellesdon Lodge, North Creake, co. Norf., [1850] Vol. XLIX, fol. 373.

WOODHAM, ..., of Lincoln's Inn, London, and Winchester, Treasurer of Hampsh., [1824] Vol. XXXIV, fol. 319.

WOODHAM-KINGSMILL, ..., of Winchester and Sidmanton House, Hampsh., [1824] Vol. XXXIV, fol. 394.

WOODHAM to KINGSMILL only, ..., of Winchester, Hampsh., [1826] Vol. XXXV, fol. 335.

WOODHAM (NASH-) to BELDAM-JOHNS-, ..., (see NASH), of co. Hertf. and Camb., [1867] Vol. LVI, fol. 232.

WOODHEAD, Henry (s. of Sir John), of The Gardens, Cape Town, 1898, Vol. LXX, fol. 215.

WOODHOUSE (JAMES-) after SECRETAN, F. S., of Wales, [1813] Vol. XXVII, fol. 378. Quarterly Arms, fol. 382.

WOODHOUSE, ..., of Liverpool, co. Lanc. ; Norley Hall, co. Chester ; and Marsala, in Sicily, [1850] Vol. XLIX, fol. 326.

WOODIFIELD, Matthew, of Horden Hall, co. Durham, [1840] Vol. XLIV, fol. 383.

WOODINGTON after THICKNESSE, Lieut.-Col. . . . ., of Shropsh. and co. Staff. Quarterly Arms, [1808] Vol. XXV, fol. 32 and 35.

WOODMASON, [James], of London, and South Carolina, [30 April 1790] Vol. XVII, fol. 217. [Misc. G. et H., 4th S., 1, p. 137.]

WOODMASS, Montagu, of Compstall, Stockport, co. Chester, and Alveston, co. Warw., [1870 ?] Vol. LVII, fol. 282.

WOODROFFE, John, M.A., of Bury St. Edmunds, co. Suff., 19 Feb. 171⅓, Vol. VI, fol. 193.

WOODROFFE, late BILLINGHURST, William, of co. Surrey, [1790] Vol. XVII, fol. 268. (George, [1824] Vol. XXXV, fol. 35 ?.)

WOODROW, now CREMER, ..., of co. Norf., [1786] Vol. XVI, fol. 105.

WOODS, Henry, of Wigan, co. Lanc., [1848] Vol. XLIX, fol. 42.

„ Sir Albert William, Garter King of Arms [1869], K.C.M.G. [21 May 1890], C.B. [1887], 1892, Vol. LXVI, fol. 273.

„ Lieut.-Col. Thomas, of Blundeston Hall, nr. Lowestoft, co. Suff., 1898, Vol. LXX, fol. 102.

WOODSTOCK, Thomas, s. of the Duke of GLOUCESTER. Arms to be quartered by the Earl of STAFFORD, [172? ?] Vol. VII, fol. 69.

WOODWARD, late ANDREWS, Richard, of co. Warw., Worc., and Northampton, [1796] Vol. XIX, fol. 289.

WOODWARD to LEE-WARNER, Daniel Henry, of co. Norf. and Somerset, 5 Mar. 1806, Vol. XXIII, fol. 274. (Berry's Appx.)

WOODWARD, ..., and Margaret, dau. of Nathaniel HOWORTH, his wife, of co. Somerset, and Little Walsingham, co. Norf., 5 Mar. 1806, Vol. XXIII, fol. 278.

WOODWARD (Amy), late ANDREWS, widow of Thomas Andrews, of co. Warw.; London; and Hoxton and Islington, co. Middx., [1820] Vol. XXXII, fol. 176.

„ late ANDREWS, Anne Catherine (Spr.), of Hoxton and Islington, co. Middx., and Butler's Marston, co. Warw., [1853] Vol. L, fol. 278.

„ late ATKINS, ... (widow), of London; St. Lawrence, Jersey; and Butler's Marston, co. Warw., [1853] Vol. L, fol. 276.

WOODWARD, Julia Lucy (dau. of Richard), of The Knoll, Clevedon, co. Somerset, 1897, Vol. LXIX, fol. 249.

„ Laurence, ..., 18 . ., Vol. LXXI, fol. . . . .

WOODYEARE (formerly ELWIN), Founteyn T., B.A., of co. York [1812, see Burke], [1845] Vol. XLVIII, fol. 75.

WOOLBALL, William, of London, Merchant, and sisters Mary and Sarah, daus. of Henry, of London, Grocer, decd., 26 June 1721, Vol. VII, fol. 128 [?]; Add. MS. 14,831, fol. 61.

WOOLCOCK to PYE (reputed son), of co. Cornw. and Devon, [1846] Vol. XLVIII, fol. 173.

WOOLDREDGE. See BLACKMAN.

WOOLHOUSE to OAKES, of Edwinstowe, co. Nottingham, [1827] Vol. XXXVI, fol. 355.

WOOLLAN, B. M., of Fairfield Lodge, Addison Road, London, 1896, Vol. LXIX, fol. 99.

WOOLLCOMB, E., of Anstey Hall, co. Warw., [1894] Vol. LXVIII, fol. 18.

WOOLLSTONECRAFT, Edward John, of Markgate, co. Essex [Markyate, co. Hertf.?] and London, 1765, Vol. XI, fol. 114.

WOOSMAN, ..., of Wales, [1854] Vol. LI, fol. 124.

WORKMAN before MACNAGHTEN, Knt. [1809 ?], of Ireland. Quarterly Arms, [1810] Vol. XXV, fol. 308.

WORMALD, late ARMITAGE, ..., of co. York, [1871] Vol. LVIII, fol. 53.

WORRALL to ROOKE, ..., of co. Glouc., [1840] Vol. XLIV, fol. 380.

WORRALL, J., of Whalley Range, Manchester, co. Lanc., 1890, Vol. LXV, fol. 242.

WORSLEY after CARILL, late LEES, ..., of co. Lanc., [1775] Vol. XIII, fol. 61.

WORSLEY (TINDALL-CARILL-), TINDAL [to ?], [1878] Vol. LX, fol. 161.

WORSLEY to FLEMING, [widow of], Bart., of co. Devon and Hampsh., [1809] Vol. XXV, fol. 235 [see Fleming].

WORSLEY, Maj.-Gen. Sir Henry, G.C.B. [1838]. Supporters, [1838] Vol. XLIII, fol. 76.

WORSLEY to PENNYMAN, ..., Capt., R.E., of co. York, [1853] Vol. L, fol. 327.

WORSLEY-TAYLOR, Henry Wilson, of Morton Hall, Whalley, co. Lanc., and St. Laund, Chislehurst, co. Kent, 1881,* Vol. LXI, fol. 217.

WORSOP, Richard Howden, of co. York, [1755] Vol. X, fol. 41.

WORTHINGTON, late PISTOR, ..., of Bath, co. Somerset, [1826] Vol. XXXVI, fol. 59.

WORTHINGTON-WRIGHT, ..., of Flixton House, Flixton, co. Lanc., [1848] Vol. XLVIII, fol. 412.

WORTHINGTON, Rev. William, of Sale Hall, Ashton-upon-Mersey, co. Chester, and Ardwick, Manchester, co. Lanc., [1863] Vol. LV, fol. 26.

WORTHINGTON after BAYLEY, Rev. W., of co. Chester, [1864] Vol. LV, fol. 154.

WORTHINGTON, Albert Octavius, s. of William, of Burton-on-Trent, and East Lodge, Needwood, Rolleston, co. Staff., 1879, Vol. LX, fol. 209. (Crisp, I, p. 221, and Berry's Suppl.)

WORTHINGTON-COOKSON, Thomas, of Pirtland House, Sefton, co. Lanc., 1884, Vol. LXII, fols. 287 and 290.

WORTLEY, late STUART, ..., 2nd s. of John, Earl of BUTE, of co. York, [1798] Vol. XX, fol. 239.

WORTLEY (STUART-), Mackenzie, Baron WHARNCLIFFE [12 July 1826], of co. York, and Scotland. [1826] Vol. XXXVI, fols. 37 and 41.

WOSTENHOLM, ..., of Kenwood Park, Sheffield, co. York, [1868] Vol. LVII, fol. 15.

WOWEN, John, of London, Merchant, s. of John, M.A. (decd.), 20 or 26 Dec. 1715, Vol. VI, fol. 218 ; Add. MS. 14,830, fol. 12.

WRAGGE, ..., of Oakamoor Lodge, Cheadle, co. Staff. ; Mansfield, co. Nottingham ; and Stourbridge, co. Worc., [1820] Vol. XXXII, fol. 102.

WRAXALL, ..., of Maxall, co. Somerset, [1815] Vol. XXVIII, fol. 318.

WREN, ..., of Binchester, co. Durham, 25 May 1723. (Burke.)

WREN-HOSKYNS, ..., of co. Warw. and Hereford, [1837] Vol. XLII, fol. 212.

WRIGHT, Thomas, of Mile End, London, 1698, Vol. IV, fol. 247.

„ John, of St. Nicholas Acons, London, and to the descendants of his father Joseph, late of St. Botolph's, Aldersgate, London, Merchant (decd.), 8 June 1709, Vol. V, fol. 359 ; Stowe MS. 714, fol. 75 ; Add. MS. 14,830, fol. 14 ; and Berry's Suppl.

„ Robert, of Ballenden, co. Essex, Rector of Otten Belchamp, co. Essex, 1767, Vol. XI, fol. 244. (Berry.)

WRIGHT to BURTON-PHILIPPSON, ..., M.A., of co. Essex and Northampton. Quarterly Arms, [1792] Vol. XVIII, fol. 115.

WRIGHT, ..., of Low Marple and Poynton, co. Chester, [1811] Vol. XXVI, fol. 193.

„ Anne, wife of Robert ANDERSON, of co. Chester, nat. dau. of Major Wright ? (See also Robert ANDERSON.) [1812] Vol. XXVII, fol. 224.

WRIGHT, late ORD, Richard, of co. Durham. Quarterly Arms, [1814 ?] Vol. XXVIII, fol. 251.

WRIGHT before WILSON, Sir Henry, Knt., of co. York, and the Inner Temple, London, [1815] Vol. XXVIII, fol. 264 ; Quarterly Arms, fol. 266 (and ? [1803] Vol. XXII, fol. 254, Wilson), of Hampsh. and co. Middx., and wife, Lady Frances, [1780] Vol. XIV, fol. 267.

WRIGHT, ... (see ELLIS to LLOYD), of Knutsford, co. Chester, [1815] Vol. XXVIII, fol. 326.

WRIGHT, late TRICE, ... (minor), of Sevenoaks, co. Kent, and Dulwich and Camberwell, co. Surrey, [1819] Vol. XXXI, fol. 330.

WRIGHT, Peter (formerly LUARD). Name and Arms ? by Roy. Lic., 1796, [1796] Vol. XIX, fol. . . . . ?

WRIGHT to VERNEY, Catherine, (dau. of CALVERT and) wife of Rev. Robert, 1811, Vol. XXVI, fol. 165.

WRIGHT, ..., of Bilham House, nr. Doncaster, and Kimberworth, co. York, [1830] Vol. XXXVIII, fol. 170.

WRIGHT, Edward, of Trinity Hall, Camb.; Brattleby and Owmby, co. Linc.; and Longstowe, co. Camb., 9 Oct. 1826, Vol. XXXVI, fol. 91. (Berry's Appx.)

WRIGHT, late TURNER, Rev. Samuel Wright, Rector of Nettleton, and of Brattleby House, co. Linc., [1863] Vol. LV, fol. 42.

WRIGHT, Edmund, of Manchester, co. Lanc., [1828] Vol. XXXVII, fol. 78.

„ . . . ., Bart., of Cawlside, co. Berwick, Scotland; Charlestown, South Carolina; and Palmedo, Jamaica, [1828] Vol. XXXVII, fol. 109.

WRIGHT after LEE, ..., of Flixton, co. Lanc., [1833] Vol. XXXIX, fol. 233.

WRIGHT to LAWSON, William, of Brough Hall, Cattwick, co. York, [1834] Vol. XL, fol. 145.

WRIGHT-BIDDULPH, ..., of co. Camb. and Sussex, [1836] Vol. XLI, fol. 194.

WRIGHT-WILSON, ... (Spr.), of Hampsh. and co. York, [1836] Vol. XLI, fol. 262; widow, [1868] Vol. LVI, fol. 340.

WRIGHT-HENNIKER-WILSON, ..., of co. York. (See WILSON.) [1839] Vol. XLIII, fol. 377.

WRIGHT-BRUCE, Hon. Sir Frederick William Adolphus, G.C.B. [1865], [1867] Vol. LVI, fol. 258 [see Burke].

WRIGHT-ARMSTRONG, William Jones, of co. Armagh, Ireland, [1868] Vol. LVI, fol. 339 [see Burke].

WRIGHT, ..., of Gunthorpe, and Nottingham, [1825] Vol. XXXV, fol. 229.

„ Francis, of Osmaston Manor, co. Derby, and Lenton Hall, Langan and Gunthorpe, co. Nottingham. (Alteration of Crest), [1845?] Vol. XLVII, fol. 345.

„ Marcus, Consul at Wiborg (died s.p., 1882), [1845] Vol. XLVII, fol. 345.

WRIGHT after WORTHINGTON, ... (see WORTHINGTON), of co. Lanc., [1848] Vol. XLVIII, fol. 412.

WRIGHT, Captain Edward William E. Tylden (s. of Charles), of Manor Croft, Worksop, co. Nottingham, 18 . . ., Vol. LXXI, fol. . . . . .

WRIGHT, late STREET, James F., Capt., R.A., of co. Chester, 1865, Vol. LV, fol. 346.

WRIGHT, ..., Auditor-General, Ceylon, [1865?] Vol. LVI, fol. 61.

„ Sir William, Knt. [7 Aug. 1869], J.P., of Liverpool, co. Lanc., and Sigglesthorne Hall, co. York, [1869] Vol. LVII, fol. 175.

„ Col. . . . ., C.B., of London, [1871] Vol. LVIII, fol. 28.

„ Caleb, of Lower Oak, Tyldesley, co. Lanc., 1876, Vol. LIX, fol. 236. (Berry's Suppl.)

„ Edward A., of Castle Park, Frodsham, co. Chester, 1884, Vol. LXII, fol. 309.

„ Sir Thomas [Knt., 11 Aug. 1893], of Knighton, co. Leic., 1894, Vol. LXVII, fol. 304.

WRIGHTE [-BENYON] (POWLETT-) to BENYON-DE BEAUVOIR, [Richard], of co. Essex and Berks., [1822] Vol. XXXIII, fol. 261.

WRIGHTE-WYNDHAM, ... (minor), of Bucks. and co. Norf., [1831] Vol. XXXVIII, fol. 250.

WRIGHTSON, Michael, of Osbaston, co. Leic., 1695. Vol. IV, fol. 192.

„ Rev. William G., of Neasham, Hurworth-on-Tees, co. Durham, 1887,* Vol. LXIII, fol. 329.

WRIGLEY, Edward Grundy, of Greenways, Lillingstone, co. Warw., and Timberhurst, Bury, co. Lanc., 1880,* Vol. LXI, fol. 98. (Berry's Suppl.) [?]

„ E. W., of Thornycroft, Prestwich, co. Lanc., 1886, Vol. LXIII, fol. 247.

WROTTESLEY, Baron [1838] (Wrottesley). Supporters, [1839] Vol. XLIII, fol. 392.

WROUGHTON, Sir Thomas, K.B. [1780], of Wilts. Supporters, [1780] Vol. XIV, fol. 280.

WROUGHTON, late MONTAGU, Lieut.-Col., of Wilts., [1826] Vol. XXXV, fol. 369.

WYAT, Thomas, s. of Thomas Wyat and Agnes FURSMAN (see FURSMAN), of (Plymouth Dock and Tavistock), co. Devon. Conditionally, [31 May 1742] Vol. IX, fol. 60. (Genealogist, II, p. 65.) (Berry.)

WYAT or WYATT, Richard, of Minehead, co. Somerset, 26 Feb. 173½, Vol. VIII, fol. 161, and Alteration of Crest and Motto, fol. 162.
WYATT, John and James, of Weeford, co. Staff., and London, and to grandfather, John, [1780] Vol. XIV, fol. 207.   (Berry.)
WYATT, late GOODE, ..., of Coventry, co. Warw., and London, [1814] Vol. XXVIII, fol. 155.
WYATT, ..., of Stroud, co. Glouc., [1822] Vol. XXXIII, fol. 211.
WYATT, late PENFOLD, . . ., of co. Sussex, 28 Dec. 1839, Vol. XLIV, fol. 184.
WYATT-EDGELL to VERNEY-CAVE, ..., of co. Staff., [1880] Vol. LX, fol. 346.
WYATT to WYATVILLE, Sir Jeffrey, Knt., R.A., of Windsor, Berks.   (See SHENSTONE.)   Augmentation, [1830] Vol. XXXVIII, fol. 93.
WYBERGH to LAWSON, William (minor), of co. Cumberland and York, 1821 [?] [1806] Vol. XXIII, fol. 428 ; [1815] Vol. XXVIII, fol. 376.
WYKEHAM-MARTIN, ..., of Leeds Castle, co. Kent, and Chalcombe Priory, co Northampton, [1821] Vol. XXXIII, fol. 65.   (Berry.)
   „   -MARTIN to CORNWALLIS-FIENNES, ..., of co. Northampton, and Leeds Castle, Nizell's Heath and Lidwells, all co. Kent, [1859] Vol. LIII, fol. 255.
WYKEHAM-FIENNES after TWISLETON, [Roy. Lic., 21 Feb. 1849], [Frederick Benjamin], Baron SAYE AND SELE, [1849] Vol. XLIX, fol. 118.
WYKEHAM-MUSGRAVE, Aubrey, of Wenham, co. Glouc., 1876, Vol. LIX, fol. 268.
WYKEHAM, Baroness WENMAN [3 June 1834, Sophia Elizabeth Wykeham, of Thame Park], co. Oxf.   Supporters, [1834] Vol. XL, fol. 177.
WYKEHAM-MANN, F. S., of Leeds Castle, co. Kent, and Chacombe Priory, co. Northampton, 1884, Vol. LXII, fol. 276.
WYLD, now WALKER-HENEAGE, ... (minor), of Berks. and Wilts., [1818] Vol. XXXI, fol. 102.
WYLDE after BROWNE [Ralph Browne Wylde-Browne], of Bath, co. Somerset, and Caughley Hall, par. of Barrow, Shropsh.   (Match) [? Surname of Browne after Wylde and to bear the Arms of Browne, 26 Mar. 1788. (Misc. G. et H., 2nd S., IV, p. 180)], [1788] Vol. XVI, fol. 319.
   „   after FEWTRELL, ..., of Shropsh. and co. Warw., [1852] Vol. L, fol. 193.
WYLIE, John, M.D., C.B., [1851] Vol. L, fol. 23.
WYMER, Gen. Sir George Petre, K.C.B., [1857] [1867] Vol. LVI, fol. 246.
WYNDHAM, Richard King, ? not Roy. Lic.
   „   2nd Earl of EGREMONT [1750, Sir Charles Wyndham, 4th Bart.].   Supporters, [1750] Vol. IX, fol. 351.
   „   Baron GRENVILLE [25 Nov. 1790] [William Wyndham Grenville].   Supporters, [1790] Vol. XVII, fol. 282.
   „   . . . . (widow), dau. of LEANDER, of London.   Escutcheon of pretence, [1812] Vol. XXVII, fol. 242.
WYNDHAM before QUIN, Wyndham Henry ([2nd] Earl of DUNRAVEN), of Wales, and Ireland.   Quarterly Arms, 1815, Vol. XXVIII, fol. 322.
WYNDHAM, ... (see WRIGHTE), [1831] Vol. XXXVIII, fol. 253.
WYNDHAM after CAMPBELL, John Henry, of Wilts., [1843] Vol. XLVII, fol. 95.
WYNDHAM, Col. George, of Petworth, co. Sussex ; Gen. Henry, of Cockermouth Castle, co. Cumberland ; Col. Charles, of Rogate, co. Sussex, nat. sons, [1856] Vol. LII, fol. 28.
WYNDHAM after CROLE, ..., of London, and Brighton, co. Sussex, [1865] Vol. LVI, fol. 9.
WYNFORD, Baron [1829] (BEST), Chief Justice of Com. Pleas, of London, [1829] Vol. XXXVII, fol. 388 ; Supporters, fol. 389.
WYNN, now BELASYSE, Lady, of co. York.   Quarterly Arms, [1803] Vol. XXII, fol. 74.
   „   now BELASYSE-COTYMORE, ..., of co. York, and Wales, [1833] Vol. XXXIX, fol. 319.
WYNN, late FLETCHER, ..., of Nerquis Hall, Wales, &c., [1836] Vol. XLI, fol. 264 ; [1864] Vol. LV, fol. 222.

WYNN, late CUMMING, ..., of Wales, [1843 ?] Vol. XLVI, fol. 253.
WYNNE after GRIFFITH, late FINCH, ..., of Wales. Quarterly Arms and Crest, [1808] Vol. XXIV, fol. 402.
WYNNE before STACKHOUSE, Edward William, of co. Cornw. and Somerset. (*See* ACTON.) Quarterly Arms, 1813 [1814], Vol. XXVIII, fol. 246 [? 24ᵇ].
WYNNE, late FINCH, ..., of co. Sussex, and Wales, [1828] Vol. XXXVII, fol. 142.
WYNNE-FINCH, late GRIFFITH-WYNNE, Charles, of co. Sussex, and Wales, [1863] Vol. LV, fol. 82.
WYNTER, late MAMMATT, ... (Spr.), of London, [1803] Vol. XXII, fol. 78.
WYNYARD, Col. and Dep.-Adj.-Gen., of London, [1803] Vol. XXII, fol. 205.
[WYRLEY, late LANE, ..., Lane, mar. the heiress of Wyrley in 1702 and quartered the Arms, and adopted the Crest of Wyrley. They had no Crest before. (Geneal. Mag., I, p. 278n.)]

X

XIMENES, Sir Morris, Knt., of Bearplace, Berks., and the other descendants of his father, David, 1807,* Vol. XXIV, fol. 263.

Y

YALE, late JONES-PARRY, William, of Wales, William Corbet Yale (1832), Vol. XXXIX, fol. 109 (1867, Vol. LVI, fol. 264).
YAPP, late CHAPMAN, Sarah Ann (Spr.), [1838] Vol. XLIII, fol. 183.
YAPP after CHAPMAN, Sarah Ann (Spr.), [1839] Vol. XLIII, fol. 351 ; [1842] Vol. XLVI, fols. 195 and 197.
YARBOROUGH, Baron [1794] (PELHAM), of co. Linc. Supporters, [1794] Vol. XVIII, fol. 400.
  „ Baron, PELHAM after ANDERSON. Quarterly Arms, [1794] Vol. XVIII, fol. 402.
YARBOROUGH after COOKE, ..., of co. York. Quarterly Arms, [1802] Vol. XXI, fol. 403.
YARBURGH, late GRAEME, ..., of co. Linc. and York, [1852] Vol. L, fols. 215 and [1853] 307.
  „ late LLOYD, ..., of co. York, [1857] Vol. LII, fol. 185.
YARBURGH after BATESON, ..., of co. York, [1876] Vol. LIX, fol. 204.
YARD, ..., of the par. of St. George, Barbados, [1810] Vol. XXVI, fol. 112.
YARDE-BULLER (BULLER-), [John], Baron CHURSTON [2 Aug. 1858], of co. Devon, [1860] Vol. LIII, fol. 302.
YARKER, John, of Leyburn, co. York, to grandfather, Luke, 9 May 1758, Vol. X, fol. 145.
YARMOUTH, Countess of [24 Mar. 1740] (DE WALMODEN). Supporters, [17$\frac{39}{40}$] Vol. VIII, fol. 266.
YATE after PEACOCK, ..., of co. Glouc., [1848 ?] Vol. XLIX, fol. 86.
YATES, Capt. (Yeomanry), and DRAKE, his wife, of Gospel Oak, co. Middx.; Tipton, co. Staff. ; and Masborough, co. York, [1827] Vol. XXXVI, fol. 248.
  „ . . . ., F.S.A., of Beddington, co. Surrey, and Albrighton, Shropsh., [1850 ?] Vol. XLIX, fol. 284.
YATES to LEIGH, ... (minor). Arms of Leigh, of co. Lanc., [1850] Vol. XLIX, fol. 387.
  „ to LEIGH, ... Arms of Leigh, co. Lanc., of Hindley Hall, co. Lanc., [1869] Vol. LVII, fol. 162.

YATES, ..., of Holme Cottage, Holme, co. Devon, and Barlaston Hall, co. Staff., [1855] Vol. LI, fol. 236.

  „   John Ashton, M.P., co. Lanc., of Dinglehead in Toxteth Park, co. Lanc., [1855 ?] Vol. LI, fol. 412.

YATES after PARK, ..., of co. Chester and Kent, [1857] Vol. LII, fol. 311.

YATES, James SHAW-YATES, s. of Jonathan, of Oakwood House, Whiston, co. York, [1866] Vol. LVI, fol. 117.   (Berry's Suppl.)

YATMAN, William H., of the Inner Temple, Bar.-at-Law ; Reigate, co. Surrey ; and Wellesbourne Mountford, co. Warw., [1859] Vol. LIII, fol. 123.

YEATES, late RICHARDS, ..., of co. Westmorland, [1837] Vol. XLII, fol. 129.

  „   late MICHAELSON, ..., of co. Westmorland, [1837] Vol. XLII, fol. 131.

YEATMAN, ..., of Stock House and Hinton St. Mary, co. Dorset, and East Brent and Kilve, co. Somerset.   Quartering FARR, [1808] Vol. XXIV, fol. 404.

YEATMAN-BIGGS, A. G., of Stockton House, Wilts., 1886 [is LXIII], [1883] Vol. LXII, fol. 159.   (Berry's Suppl.)

YELDHAM, John, of Great Saling, co. Essex, 1754, Vol. IX, fol. 489.   (Berry.)

YELLOBY, ..., of Finsbury Square, London, [1806] Vol. XXIV, fol. 76.

YELVERTON, [Sir Charles, 3rd Bart ?], Baron GREY [28 Jan. 1676 ?].   Supporters and quarterings, 16 . ., Vol. III, fol. 117.

YELVERTON, late GOULD, [Henry Edward] [1800], Baron GREY DE RUTHYN. Arms of Yelverton, [1800] Vol. XXI, fol. 48.

  „   late HENRY [1849, Hastings Reginald, 2nd husband of Barbara,] Baroness GREY DE RUTHYN, [1849] Vol. XLIX, fol. 92 ; [1848] fol. 34.

YELVERTON, Adm. Sir Hastings Reginald, G.C.B. [1875].   Supporters, 1876, Vol. LIX, fol. 218.

YEO, Sir James Lucas, Post-Capt., R.N.   Alterations, [1810] Vol. XXVI, fol. 70.

YEWDALL, ..., of Rawdon, Leeds, co. York, [1851 ?] Vol. L, fol. 86.

YOCKNEY, Sidney William, C.E., of Queen Anne's Gate, London, and his brother, Algernon, 1898, Vol. LXX, fol. 300.

YONGE, James and William, of Plymouth, co. Devon, 20 July 1725, Vol. VII, fol. 404.

  „   Sir William, K.B. [1725].   Quartering and Supporters, [1725] Vol. VII, fol. 430 [afterwards a Bart.].

  „   [The Rt. Hon.] Sir George [Bart.], K.B. [1788].   Supporters, [1788] Vol. XVI, fol. 395.

YORK, late SHEEPSHANKS, ..., of Whitwell, co. York.   (See YORK of Hutton.) [1796] Vol. XIX, fol. 299.

YORK, [Sir] Philip, Baron HARDWICK [1733, Chief Justice of the King's Bench]. Supporters and Crest, 29 Dec. 1733, Vol. VIII, fol. 178.

YORKE, [Lieut.-Gen. The Hon.] Sir Joseph, K.B. [1761] [afterwards Baron Dover]. Supporters, [1761] Vol. X, fol. 310.

  „   Baron DOVER [1788], [Joseph].   Supporters, [1788] Vol. XVII, fol. 37.

YORKE after DALLAS, James W., of co. Linc., Capt. of Dragoons, 1856, Vol. LI, fol. 424.

YORKE, Lieut.-Gen. Sir Charles, G.C.B. [1860].   Arms, [1860] Vol. LIV, fol. 29 ; Supporters, fol. 32.

YOUNG, ..., nat. s. of Lord ELIBANK.   (See MURRAY.)   [1787 ?] Vol. XVI, fol. 207.

  „   . . . ., of London, Rec.-Gen. Arch. Canterbury, [1810] Vol. XXV, fol. 355.

  „   [Sir Samuel] (Bart.) [24 Nov. 1813], of Formosa Place, Berks. [1813] Vol. XXVII, fol. 374.

  „   Adm. Sir William [K.B., 1814].   Supporters, [1815] Vol. XXVIII, fol. 269.

  „   [William] Capt., R.N.   (See JEYNES [Anne], Lady [wife of Adm. Sir William] Hotham, K.C.B. [1815] and her sisters).   (Match), [1815] Vol. XXVIII, fol. 352.

  „   . . . ., of London, [1817] Vol. XXX, fol. 167.

Young, [Jonathan], M.R.S., of Lambeth, co. Surrey, Apothecary [Surgeon?], father to Charles George Young, [1804] Vol. XXII, fol. 418. Alteration of Arms, [1822] Vol. XXXIII, fol. 253.

,, Charles George, Rouge Dragon Pursuivant of Arms. Crest, [1818] Vol. XXX, fol. 333. Arms for wife [?] and [a new?] Crest for Young, [1826] Vol. XXXV, fols. 329 and 330.

Young-Jamieson, ..., of co. Northumberland, [1848] Vol. XLIX, fol. 18.

Young, [Sir John, 2nd Bart.], Baron Lisgar [1870], Irish peer, [1871] Vol. LVIII, fol. 56.

,, Mrs. Eylesden, of Chart, nr. Sutton Valence, co. Kent, 1894, Vol. LXVIII, fol. 89.

Younghusband, Isaac, of Crossthwaite, co. Lanc.; Victoria Colony; and Brighton, co. Sussex, [1863] Vol. LV, fol. 114.

Yvonnet, John Paul, of Isleworth, co. Middx., and Rochelle, France, a Commissioner of Excise Appeals. Impaling the Arms of wife, David, 9 Feb. 173½, Vol. VIII, fol. 117ᵇ; Add. MS. 14,830, fol. 17.

Z

Zachary, John Lower, of Areley, co. Worc. Sacheverell quartering, [3 Aug.] 1780, Vol. XIV, fol. 239.

Zephani, John, of Walton-on-Thames, co. Surrey, late Governor of Fort William, Bengal, 1762 (see Edmondson's Armory).

Zetland, Earl of ([Baron] Dundas). Supporters, [1872] Vol. LVIII, fol. 172.

Ziegenbein to Liebenrood, ..., of Berks., [1795] Vol. XIX, fol. 13.

Zincke, ..., of London, and of the par. of St. Dorothy, Jamaica, [1812] Vol. XXVII, fol. 119.

Zwilchenbart-Erskine, ..., Mrs., of Deanwood, Speen, Newbury, Berks., 1885, Vol. LXIII, fol. 73.

Report for the Year 1916.

THE Council have to report that at and since the Annual General Meeting, held on the 5th day of February, 1916, nine new Subscribers have joined the Society, of whom five are Subscribers to the Register Section (one having joined the Register Section only).

The number on the Roll on the 31st of December is two hundred and sixty-two, of whom one hundred and seventy-one are Subscribers to the Register Section.

A second Volume of "Grantees of Arms," Part I, A to J, between the years 1687 and 1898, compiled by JOSEPH FOSTER, Hon. M.A., Oxon, Brit. Mus. Add. MS. 37,149, edited by W. H. RYLANDS, Esq., F.S.A., Vice-Chairman of the Council, forming the sixty-seventh volume of the Ordinary Publications, will be issued to the Subscribers for 1916, and will be followed by the Second Part, K to Z for 1917.

The Registers of St. Olave, Hart Street, containing the Baptisms, Marriages and Burials, from 1563 to 1700 (printed from a transcript presented to the Society by the Executors of the late BRYAN CORCORAN, Esq., C.C., a past churchwarden), edited by the SECRETARY, forming the forty-sixth volume of the Register Section, has been issued for the year 1916.

Part I of the Marriage Registers of St. Mary le Bone, Middlesex, 1668—1754, and Oxford Chapel, Vere Street, Marylebone, 1736—1754, to be edited by the SECRETARY, forming the forty-seventh volume of the Register Section, will be issued to the Subscribers for 1917.

In the early part of the year the Society's late printers, Messrs. Mitchell, Hughes & Clarke, intimated their inability to continue their printing contract with the Society, which, after invitation of tenders from other printers, has now been placed with Messrs. Roworth & Co. Limited, of 19, Newton Street, High Holborn, W.C., which is also the address of the Registered Offices of the Society.

The Balance Sheet for the year, duly audited, is appended to the Report.

W. BRUCE BANNERMAN,
Secretary.

The Harleian Society.

FOUNDED 1869. INCORPORATED 1902.

ACCOUNTS FOR THE YEAR ENDING 31ST DECEMBER, 1916.

ORDINARY ACCOUNT.

Dr.		£	s.	d.
Balance to 31st December, 1915	... ...	5	14	2
Subscriptions	... ...	331	16	0
Books purchased by Subscribers	... ...	11	16	6
Dividend, 3 per cent. Stock, Lancashire and Yorkshire Railway (£500)	... ...	12	5	7
		£361	**12**	**3**

Cr.		£	s.	d.
Messrs. Mitchell, Hughes & Clarke—Final Account on their ceasing to be Printers and Publishers to the Society	... ...	8	1	6
Expenses of Removal of Fixtures and Stock from 140, Wardour Street, to 19, Newton Street, W.C., and fitting up same	...	4	8	0
Paid for sorting and arranging Stock	...	1	10	0
Printing Paper bought in advance	...	39	16	7
Messrs. Roworth & Co. Limited, 19, Newton Street, W.C., the new Printers and Publishers to the Society:—				
General Account	... ...	30	3	6
Paid for Transcript—Grantees of Arms, Part II		43	16	9
Fire Insurance	... ...	6	5	0
Commission on Cheques	... ...	2	0	
Auditor's Fee	... ...	1	1	0
Secretary	... ...	15	0	0
Balance	... ...	211	7	11
		£361	**12**	**3**

REGISTER SECTION.

Dr.	£	s.	d.
Balance to 31st December, 1915	36	4	1
Subscriptions	221	11	0
Books purchased by Subscribers	9	15	0
	£267	10	1

Cr.	£	s.	d.
Messrs. Roworth & Co. Limited:—			
For printing St. Olave, Hart Street, Registers, less proportionate cost of Printing Paper	138	7	4
Paid for Transcript—St. Maryle Bone Registers, Part I	17	12	0
Treasurer	15	0	0
Balance	96	10	9
	£267	10	1

GENERAL BALANCE.

1916.	£	s.	d.
To Balance, Ordinary Section	211	7	11
Register Section	96	10	9
	£307	18	8

1916.	£	s.	d.
Dec. 31. By Balance in the Bank	307	18	8
	£307	18	8

Examined and approved,

M. W. KER, *Auditor.*

5th February, 1917.

W. BRUCE BANNERMAN, *Treasurer.*

The Harleian Society.

LIST OF PUBLICATIONS.

Visitations.

VOL.

1.—THE VISITATION OF LONDON IN 1568, BY R. COOKE. Edited by J. J. HOWARD, Esq., LL.D., F.S.A., and G. J. ARMYTAGE, Esq., F.S.A.   1869

2.—THE VISITATION OF LEICESTERSHIRE IN 1619, BY CAMDEN. Edited by J. FETHERSTON, Esq., F.S.A.   1870

3.—THE VISITATION OF RUTLAND IN 1618-19, BY CAMDEN; and other Descents of Families not in the Visitation. Edited by G. J. ARMYTAGE, Esq., F.S.A.   1870

4.—THE VISITATIONS OF NOTTINGHAMSHIRE IN 1569 AND 1614, WITH MANY OTHER DESCENTS OF THE COUNTY. Edited by GEORGE W. MARSHALL, Esq., LL.D., F.S.A.   1871

5.—THE VISITATIONS OF OXFORDSHIRE IN 1566 BY W. HARVEY, 1574 BY R. LEE, AND 1634 BY J. PHILPOTT AND W. RYLEY; WITH THE GATHERINGS OF OXFORDSHIRE, COLLECTED BY R. LEE IN 1574. Edited and Annotated by W. H. TURNER, Esq.   1871

6.—THE VISITATION OF DEVONSHIRE IN 1620. Edited by the Rev. F. T. COLBY, D.D., F.R.S.   1872

7.—THE VISITATION OF CUMBERLAND IN 1615, BY R. ST. GEORGE. Edited by J. FETHERSTON, Esq., F.S.A.   1872

8.—LE NEVE'S PEDIGREES OF THE KNIGHTS MADE BY KING CHARLES II, KING JAMES II, KING WILLIAM III, AND QUEEN MARY, WILLIAM ALONE, AND QUEEN ANNE. Edited by GEORGE W. MARSHALL, Esq., LL.D., F.S.A.   1873

9.—THE VISITATION OF CORNWALL, 1620. Edited by Colonel VIVIAN and Dr. H. H. DRAKE.   1874

10.—THE REGISTERS OF WESTMINSTER ABBEY, 1655—1875. Edited by Colonel CHESTER, D.C.L., LL.D.   1875

11.—THE VISITATION OF SOMERSETSHIRE IN 1623. Edited by the Rev. F. T. COLBY, D.D., F.S.A.   1876

12.—THE VISITATION OF WARWICKSHIRE IN 1619. Edited by JOHN FETHERSTON, Esq., F.S.A.   1877

13.—THE VISITATIONS OF ESSEX IN 1552, 1558, 1612, AND 1634. Part I. Edited by WALTER C. METCALFE, Esq., F.S.A.   1878

14.—THE VISITATIONS OF ESSEX, consisting of Miscellaneous Pedigrees, and Berry's Pedigrees. Part II. With General Index. Edited by WALTER C. METCALFE, Esq., F.S.A.   1879

15.—THE VISITATION OF LONDON, 1633-4. Part I. Edited by J. J. HOWARD, Esq., LL.D., F.S.A., and Colonel CHESTER, D.C.L., LL.D.   1880

16.—THE VISITATION OF YORKSHIRE IN 1564. Edited by the Rev. C. B. NORCLIFFE, M.A.   1881

17.—THE VISITATION OF LONDON, 1633-4. Part II. Edited by J. J. HOWARD, Esq., LL.D., F.S.A.   1883

18.—THE VISITATION OF CHESHIRE IN 1580. Edited by J. PAUL RYLANDS, Esq., F.S.A.   1882

19.—THE VISITATIONS OF BEDFORDSHIRE IN 1566, 1582, AND 1634. Edited by F. A. BLAYDES, Esq.   1884

20.—THE VISITATION OF DORSETSHIRE IN 1623, BY ST. GEORGE AND LENNARD AS DEPUTIES TO CAMDEN. Edited by J. PAUL RYLANDS, Esq., F.S.A.   1885

21.—THE VISITATION OF GLOUCESTERSHIRE IN 1623, BY CHITTING AND PHILLIPOT AS DEPUTIES TO CAMDEN. Edited by Sir JOHN MACLEAN, F.S.A., and W. C. HEANE, Esq., M.R.C.S.   1885

22.—THE VISITATIONS OF HERTFORDSHIRE IN 1572 AND 1634. Edited by WALTER C. METCALFE, Esq., F.S.A.   1886

23.—MARRIAGE LICENCES: Dean and Chapter of Westminster, 1558 to 1699; Vicar-General of the Archbishop of Canterbury, 1660 to 1679. Extracted by the late Colonel CHESTER, D.C.L. Edited by GEORGE J. ARMYTAGE, Esq., F.S.A.   1886

24.—MARRIAGE LICENCES: Faculty Office of the Archbishop of Canterbury, 1543 to 1869.   1886

25.—MARRIAGE LICENCES: Bishop of London, Part I, 1520 to 1610.   1887

26.—MARRIAGE LICENCES: Bishop of London, Part II, 1611 to 1828.   1887

27.—THE VISITATION OF WORCESTERSHIRE IN 1569. Edited by WILLIAM P. W. PHILLIMORE, Esq., M.A., B.C.L.   1888

28.—THE VISITATION OF SHROPSHIRE, 1623; with Additions. Part I. Edited by GEORGE GRAZEBROOK, Esq., F.S.A., and J. PAUL RYLANDS, Esq., F.S.A.   1889

29.—THE VISITATION OF SHROPSHIRE, 1623; with Additions. Part II. Edited by GEORGE GRAZEBROOK, Esq., F.S.A., and J. PAUL RYLANDS, Esq., F.S.A.   1889

30.—MARRIAGE LICENCES: Vicar-General of Archbishop of Canterbury, 1679 to 1687. Edited by GEORGE J. ARMYTAGE, Esq., F.S.A.   1890

31.—MARRIAGE LICENCES: Vicar-General of Archbishop of Canterbury, 1687 to 1694.   1890

VISITATIONS—*continued.*

[*Vols. 1—9, 11—13, and 37—39 are out of print. All other Volumes 21s. each.*]

W. BRUCE BANNERMAN,
Secretary.

4, THE WALDRONS,
CROYDON.